SCOTT FORESMAN - ADDISON WESLEY

ENVIRONMENTAL SCIENCE

DuBay ◆ Lapinski ◆ Schoch ◆ Tweed

Scott Foresman
Addison Wesley

Editorial Offices: Menlo Park, California • Glenview, Illinois • New York, New York
Sales Offices: Reading, Massachusetts • Atlanta, Georgia • Glenview, Illinois
Carrollton, Texas • Menlo Park, California

http://www.sf.aw.com
http://www.planetdiary.com

Authors

Denis DuBay, Ph.D.
Office of Environmental
    Education
North Carolina Department of
    Environment, Health, and
    Natural Resources
Raleigh, NC

Anne Tweed
Environmental Science
    Teacher
Eaglecrest High School
Aurora, CO

Robert M. Schoch, Ph.D.
Associate Professor of Science
    and Mathematics
Boston University
Boston, MA

Andrew H. Lapinski
Professor, Science and Math
    Division
Reading Area Community
    College
Reading, PA

Contributing Writer

David A. Krauss, Ph.D.
Boston College
Chestnut Hill, MA

Reviewers

David F. Anderson
Miami Northwestern Senior
    High School
Miami, FL

David M. Armstrong, Ph.D.
University of Colorado
Boulder, CO

Ray E. and Patricia S. Ashton
Ashton, Ashton & Associates,
    Inc.
Gainesville, FL

Heather Brasell
Coffee High School
Douglas, GA

Virginia Burkett, D.F.
National Wetlands Research
    Center
Lafayette, LA

John R. Faust, Ph.D.
Eastern Illinois University
Charleston, IL

Elizabeth Grumbach
Biology/Chemistry Instructor
East Greenwich, RI

Irma Jarvis
Environmental Science
    Teacher, Retired
Palm Beach Gardens, FL

Michael Lopatka
Edgewater High School
Orlando, FL

Harold J. McKenna, Ph.D.
City College School of
    Education
New York, NY

Garry McKenzie, Ph.D.
Ohio State University
Columbus, OH

Nancy Ostiguy, Ph.D.
California State University,
    Sacramento
Sacramento, CA

Michael Priano
Westchester Community
    College
Valhalla, NY

Beverly H. St. John
Milton High School
Milton, FL

Lynn Sweetay
J. P. Taravella High School
Coral Springs, FL

 **Text printed on recycled paper containing
no less than 10% post-consumer content.**

Front Cover Photographs: John Foster/Masterfile (sky/clouds), O. MacKay/Natural Selection (lightning), Andre
Gallant/The Image Bank (sunrise), A. Rohmer/Nawrocki Stock Photo, Inc. (bicyclists), M. Botzek/Natural
Selection (leaves), Steve Bloom-TCL/Masterfile (elephants), Larry Williams/Masterfile (sea turtle)

GeoSystems Global Corporation and Addison Wesley Longman are the publishers of the maps included in this
textbook. The information contained in these maps is derived from a variety of sources, the publishers assume no
responsibility for inconsistencies or inaccuracies in the data nor liability for any damages of any type arising from
errors or omissions.

BRIEF TABLE OF CONTENTS

CONTENTS

PART I PRINCIPLES OF ECOLOGY

UNIT 3

BIOMES   108

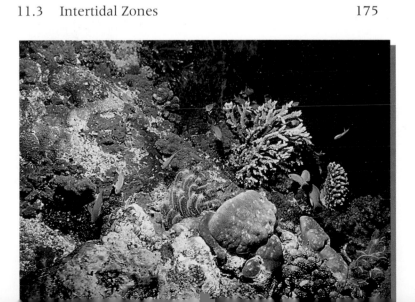

PART II PEOPLE AND THE ENVIRONMENT

UNIT 4 PEOPLE IN THE GLOBAL ECOSYSTEM 184

UNIT 5 ENERGY RESOURCES 232

Electron   Proton   Neutron

Nucleus

Helium

UNIT 6 RESOURCES IN THE BIOSPHERE   284

MANAGING HUMAN IMPACT 378

ACTIVITIES

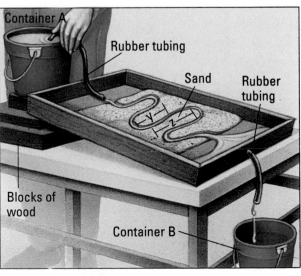

ECOLOGY IN ACTION

SUCCESS STORIES

CAREERS

ENRICHMENT FEATURES

UNIT

1

STUDYING EARTH

Have you ever observed the behavior of insects after turning over an object they were hiding under? If so, you may have questioned the insects' behavior. Scientists who study Earth and its organisms formulate many questions concerning their observations. They observe nature in an attempt to better understand the relationships and interactions between organisms and their environment. In this photograph, researchers in Yellowstone National Park patiently wait for sightings of wolf populations. From their research they hope to better understand how the wolves interact with their environment, and how changes to the environment can impact the wolves.

Discover It!

Observing Your Environment

The environment consists of both organisms and nonliving elements. These organisms and elements interact in dynamic ways. Scientists study these interactions to better understand them.

1. List two organisms that you often see around your school or home.

2. Observe each organism and how it interacts with nonliving elements. Record your observations.

PLANETDIARY.COM

You can find out more about the study of Earth by exploring the following Internet address:
http://www.planetdiary.com

CHAPTER

1

PLANET EARTH

Earth is a small island of life in the vast emptiness of space. So far, no living matter has been found anywhere else in the universe. What conditions give Earth the ability to support life? Which parts of Earth are important to the living things that make this planet their home? Understanding how this planet supports its living beings is the primary goal of scientists who study the environment. Without this understanding, Earth's inhabitants could damage, or even destroy, their only home.

1.1 PLANET OF LIFE

OBJECTIVES • *Locate* Earth in a diagram of the solar system.
• *Identify* and *describe* the regions of Earth in which living things are found.

Earth is one of the nine planets in the solar system. As you can see in Figure 1.1, Earth is the third planet from the sun. Each planet's characteristics are determined mostly by the planet's density, composition, and distance from the sun. Mercury, Venus, Earth, and Mars are known as the inner planets. These planets are made mostly of rock. The other five planets are known as the outer planets. The outer planets are made mostly of gases, with the exception of Pluto, which is rocky like the inner planets. Earth is the only planet known to support life. It is home to millions of different kinds of living things. *Living things are called* **organisms.**

Organisms can be found on the land, in the water, and in the air. *The* **lithosphere** (LITH-oh-SFEER) *is the layer of land that forms Earth's surface.* The lithosphere includes the rocks, soil, and sand that make up land. *The* **hydrosphere** (HY-dro-SFEER) *includes all the parts of Earth that are made up of water.* The hydrosphere includes oceans, lakes, and rivers, as well as underground water and clouds in the air. *The* **atmosphere** (AT-muh-SFEER) *is the layer of air that surrounds Earth.*

What characteristics make it possible for life to exist in so many parts of Earth? One of the most important reasons Earth can support life is the presence of liquid water. Although water exists elsewhere in the solar system, it is usually in the form of ice or vapor. On Earth, liquid water in the hydrosphere stores heat.

Dateline 1972

The United States launched Pioneer 10, the first human-made object to leave the solar system. The probe, launched to study Jupiter, contained a recorded greeting in many languages of Earth. The probe continues to travel through space, carrying its message to any intelligent life it may encounter in the universe.

Figure 1.1 The solar system consists of the sun and all the bodies that orbit the sun, including the nine planets, their moons, and a belt of asteroids.

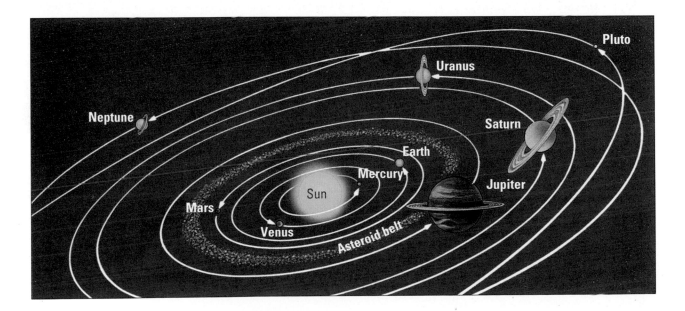

Figure 1.2 Visible light makes up only a small portion of the energy given off by the sun. Each type of wave has a specific range of wavelengths.

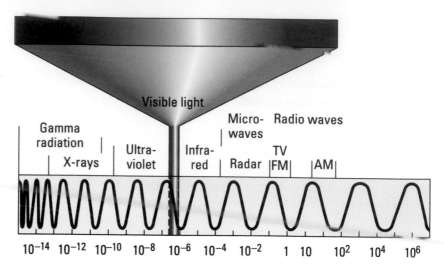

Visible light

Gamma radiation | X-rays | Ultra-violet | Infra-red | Radar | Micro-waves | TV FM | AM | Radio waves

Wavelength (m) 10^{-14} 10^{-12} 10^{-10} 10^{-8} 10^{-6} 10^{-4} 10^{-2} 1 10 10^2 10^4 10^6

Physics

The microwaves in a microwave oven are radio waves with a wavelength of about 12 cm. The energy in the waves penetrates the food and causes water, fats, and sugars in the food to absorb the energy and generate heat.

Water absorbs heat during warm periods and releases it during cold periods. Thus, water on Earth helps maintain a steadier surface temperature than other planets.

Water is also found in the bodies of organisms. Many of the substances that all living things need dissolve in water. Chemical reactions that take place within organisms occur in water.

Another reason Earth is able to support life is its atmosphere. Air is a mixture of gases, including nitrogen, oxygen, carbon dioxide, and water vapor. This layer of gases helps to keep Earth's surface temperature steady. The gases are also used by organisms. Most kinds of organisms require oxygen to use energy. Plants require carbon dioxide to help capture and store energy from sunlight. In addition to water and air, organisms also need a source of energy. Almost all the energy used by organisms originally comes from the sun. This energy travels in the form of waves. Each type of wave has a different range of wavelengths. Most waves are invisible. Waves in a narrow range of wavelengths, called the visible spectrum, can be seen by the human eye.

Scientists spend much time trying to understand how the different parts of Earth interact with each other and with the planet's living organisms. *These interactions among nonliving and living parts of the Earth are the subject of* **ecology**. The word *ecology* comes from the Greek word *oikos*, meaning home. Ecology is the study of Earth, the home of living organisms.

SECTION REVIEW

1. What parts of Earth make up the hydrosphere?
2. What characteristics of Earth enable it to support life?
3. **Infer** The temperature of a planet is determined, in part, by its distance from the sun. Which planets would you expect to be warmer than Earth? Which ones would be colder?

1.2 EARTH'S LAND AND WATER

OBJECTIVES • **Describe** the three main types of rocks that make up the lithosphere. • **Explain** why fresh water is a valuable resource for organisms.

The hydrosphere flows to almost every part of the planet. The shores and riverbanks where the lithosphere and the hydrosphere meet are some of Earth's most heavily populated parts.

The Lithosphere

The lithosphere varies in thickness from about 10 to 200 kilometers (km). Three main types of rocks make up the lithosphere: igneous rock, sedimentary rock, and metamorphic rock. The rocks are classified on the basis of how they were formed.

Igneous Rock Below the hard, solid lithosphere, Earth's interior contains hot, melted rocks in liquid form. *When liquid rock cools, it solidifies to become* **igneous** (IG-nee-us) **rock.** The lava that flows from a volcano can cool to form the igneous rock basalt. Liquid rock that cools deep within Earth can form the igneous rock granite.

Sedimentary Rock Rocks break down slowly over time. The tiny pieces of rock that wear off become sediments that are carried away by wind and water. These sediments eventually settle down into layers. *As layers of sediments accumulate, they become compressed and cemented into* **sedimentary** (SED-ih-MENT-uh-ree) **rock.** Fossils are almost always found in sedimentary rock. Limestone and sandstone are examples of sedimentary rock.

Metamorphic Rock Pressure and heat can cause igneous, sedimentary, and metamorphic rocks to undergo changes. *Rock that has been transformed by heat and pressure is called* **metamorphic** (MET-uh-MORF-ik) **rock.** Marble and slate are familiar examples of metamorphic rock.

Figure 1.3 When a volcano erupts, liquid rock called lava flows from the surface. The lava will cool to form igneous rock.

Figure 1.4 Granite is a common type of igneous rock (left). Sandstone (center) is a sedimentary rock. Gneiss (right) is an example of metamorphic rock.

The Hydrosphere

When viewed from space, Earth appears mostly blue. This blue appearance is due to the fact that more than 70 percent of Earth's surface is covered by water. Because of its large proportion of water, Earth is sometimes called the water planet.

More than 97 percent of the hydrosphere is salt water. Most salt water is located in the oceans, but there are also some salt lakes, such as the Great Salt Lake in Utah. As the name suggests, salt water is water that contains dissolved salts. About 35 grams (g) of salt are dissolved in each liter (L) of ocean water. The amounts of various types of salt in ocean water are shown in Figure 1.5. Sodium chloride (NaCl) is the salt you are familiar with as table salt.

Fresh water contains less dissolved salt than salt water does. The water in most lakes, ponds, and streams, as well as underground water, is fresh water. Fresh water makes up less than 3 percent of the hydrosphere. More than two-thirds of this fresh water exists in frozen glaciers and ice caps. Although fresh water makes up a very small portion of the hydrosphere, it is this fresh water that supports most life on Earth. Because there is so little fresh water, it is a very valuable substance. The availability of fresh water often determines the types and numbers of organisms that an area can support.

Fresh water can be divided into two types: surface water and groundwater. Surface water includes the water in lakes, streams, and rain runoff. Groundwater is found beneath the surface of Earth and moves very slowly through small spaces in and between rocks. Groundwater moves more easily through rock layers that are porous. *An underground layer of porous rock that contains water is called an* **aquifer** (AHK-wih-fer). An aquifer may reach the surface of the ground, resulting in a natural spring.

Sometimes aquifers flow between two layers of rock that water cannot seep through. Pressure in the aquifer builds up from water pressure and the weight of the rock layer above the water. If a well

Figure 1.5 More than 75 percent of the salt in ocean water is NaCl, or table salt.

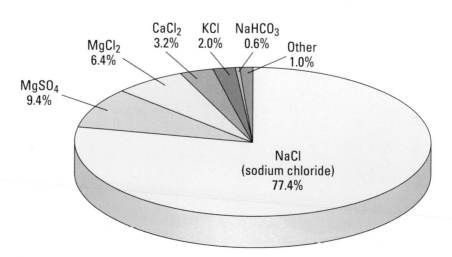

MgSO₄
9.4%

MgCl₂
6.4%

CaCl₂
3.2%

KCl
2.0%

NaHCO₃
0.6%

Other
1.0%

NaCl
(sodium chloride)
77.4%

Figure 1.6 Natural springs occur where groundwater flows to the surface.

Think About It!

Water, like all liquids, expands when it is heated.

1. If the temperature of Earth's oceans were to rise, what would happen to the size of the oceans?

2. What might happen to the land along the coasts of the continents?

is drilled into such an aquifer, water will flow freely to the surface. *Wells in which water flows to the surface due to high pressure underground are called* **artesian** (ar-TEE-zhun) **wells.** The name comes from an area in France where such wells are common.

Much of the fresh water used by people is pumped to the surface from wells drilled in aquifers. However, the water contained in aquifers is replenished very slowly. It takes many years for rainwater to seep through the soil and rocks of the surface to reach an aquifer. Because the water is pumped out faster than it is replaced, many aquifers in the United States are beginning to dry up. Many communities that currently depend on the water in aquifers will have to look elsewhere for their supply of fresh water in the future.

SECTION REVIEW

1. In which type of rock are fossils usually found?
2. Why is the presence of fresh water important to living things?
3. **Analyze** The amount of salt dissolved in the water of saltwater lakes is often greater than the amount of salt in ocean water. Why do you think this is true?

Stream Discharge

PROBLEM

A stream-gauging station measures the volume of water flowing past a certain location each second. A rain gauge provides data on the number of centimeters of rain falling per hour. Data for a sample 12-hour period are shown in the table. What is the relationship between amount of rainfall and stream discharge?

MATERIALS

- graph paper
- 2 pencils of different colors

HYPOTHESIS

Write a hypothesis that pertains to the problem.

PROCEDURE

1. On a sheet of graph paper, construct a line graph that compares the rainfall and stream-discharge data. The graph you construct should have two vertical axes and one horizontal axis, as shown in the figure. Show rainfall in cm/h on the left vertical axis and stream discharge in m³/s on the right vertical axis. The horizontal axis shows the time.
2. Plot the data points for rainfall. Connect the points to produce a curve showing the amount of rainfall over time.
3. Use the other pencil to plot the data points for stream discharge. Connect the points to produce a second curve showing stream discharge over time.

ANALYSIS

1. How much time passed between the heaviest rainfall and the greatest stream discharge? How do you explain this time difference?
2. How do the two curves compare in height? Give reasons for the difference.
3. How do the curves compare in shape and steepness? Give reasons for the differences.
4. Predict what the volume of stream discharge will be at 1:00 A.M. the following morning. Explain your prediction.

CONCLUSION

What is the relationship between rainfall and stream discharge?

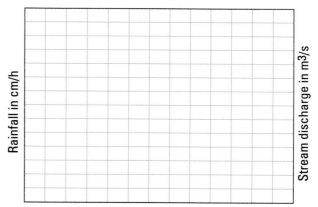

Time	Rainfall (cm/h)	Stream Discharge (m³/s)	Time	Rainfall (cm/h)	Stream Discharge (m³/s)
12:00 noon	0	220	6:00 P.M.	0.3	3400
1:00 P.M.	2.0	290	7:00 P.M.	0	2285
2:00 P.M.	5.9	440	8:00 P.M.	0	1420
3:00 P.M.	6.2	830	9:00 P.M.	0	1000
4:00 P.M.	3.2	1400	10:00 P.M.	0	950
5:00 P.M.	1.0	2000	11:00 P.M.	4.0	950

1.3 THE ATMOSPHERE

OBJECTIVES • *Diagram* the layers of the atmosphere.
• *Describe* the characteristics of each layer.

The atmosphere is an envelope of gases that surrounds Earth and includes the air you breathe. Scientists divide the atmosphere into four layers, as shown in Figure 1.7. Starting from the Earth's surface, these layers are the troposphere, stratosphere, mesosphere, and thermosphere. Gases become less dense the farther they are from Earth's surface.

The atmosphere is made up of about 78 percent nitrogen and 21 percent oxygen. Water vapor, dust particles, and small amounts of other gases make up the remaining 1 percent of the air. Only about 0.04 percent of the air is made up of carbon dioxide. Carbon dioxide is a gas that is very important to life on Earth. Carbon dioxide is one of the ingredients used by plants to make food. In this process, plants add oxygen to the atmosphere.

LINK
Biology

In the process of photosynthesis, plants, algae, and certain bacteria make sugars by combining carbon dioxide (CO_2), water, and energy from the sun. Animals and other organisms, including plants, break down these sugars, releasing CO_2, water, and energy. In humans, much of the energy is used to maintain body heat.

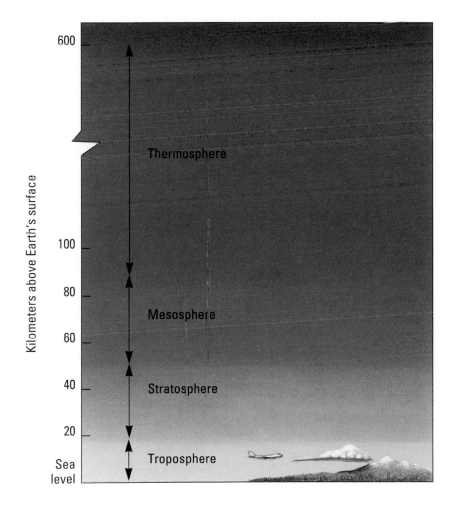

Figure 1.7 No one can say exactly where Earth's atmosphere ends. The gases simply get less dense as they get farther from the surface.

To obtain energy from food, most organisms use oxygen and give off carbon dioxide. Carbon dioxide is also released into the atmosphere by volcanic eruptions and whenever fuels such as wood, coal, and gasoline are burned. Carbon dioxide in the atmosphere lets sunlight in and traps the resulting heat. This is called the "greenhouse effect." Scientists are concerned that increasing amounts of carbon dioxide in the atmosphere are causing Earth to become warmer and changing climate patterns.

Troposphere

The layer of the atmosphere that touches the surface of Earth is called the **troposphere** (TROHP-uh-SFEER). The troposphere extends to a height of about 8 to 18 km above Earth's surface. Most of the gas molecules in the atmosphere are in the troposphere.

The troposphere contains most of the water vapor in the atmosphere and is the layer in which most weather occurs. The winds that carry weather across Earth are an important factor in the climate of an area. Figure 1.8 shows the major patterns of air currents that flow across Earth's surface.

Stratosphere

Beyond the troposphere, reaching a height of 50 km above Earth, is the **stratosphere** (STRAT-uh-SFEER). Weather disturbances that are common in the troposphere do not occur in the stratosphere.

The upper stratosphere contains a layer of gas called ozone. **Ozone** (OH-ZOHN) *is a form of oxygen gas containing three oxygen atoms per molecule.* The oxygen you breathe in the troposphere contains

Figure 1.8 Prevailing winds are caused by the rotation of Earth and by temperature differences. In which direction do winds usually blow where you live?

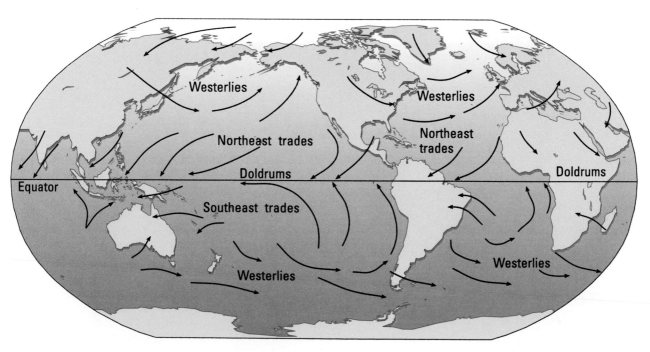

only two oxygen atoms in each molecule. The ozone layer is very important to living things because it filters out most of the ultraviolet, or UV, radiation given off by the sun. Ultraviolet radiation is one of many types of electromagnetic waves produced by the sun. Without the filtering action of the ozone layer, the sun's UV radiation would destroy much of the life on Earth.

Mesosphere and Thermosphere

Beyond the stratosphere is the *mesosphere* (MEZ-oh-SFEER), which extends up to 85 km above Earth's surface. The mesosphere is the coldest layer of the atmosphere, with temperatures as low as –100 °C.

The *thermosphere* (THERM-oh-SFEER) is the outermost layer of the atmosphere. Unlike the mesosphere, the thermosphere experiences temperatures as high as 2000 °C, though air pressure is less than one ten-thousandth of that at Earth's surface.

Gas molecules in one layer of the thermosphere are bombarded with rays from the sun. These rays cause the gas molecules to lose electrons, and they become ions. Because of these ions, this layer of the thermosphere is called the *ionosphere* (y-ON-oh-SFEER). When gas molecules interact with free electrons, light is given off. This process occurs most often near Earth's poles, resulting in a display of lights called an aurora (uh-ROR-uh).

SECTION REVIEW

1. Which layer of the atmosphere contains the ionosphere? Why does this layer have this name?
2. Why is the ozone layer important to living things?
3. **Apply** People who live at sea level often have trouble breathing at the tops of high mountains. Why do you think this is true?

1.4 THE BIOSPHERE

OBJECTIVES • **Describe** *the regions of the biosphere.*
• **Explain** *how organisms interact with the biosphere.*

Earth is home to trillions of organisms. Together, the parts of the lithosphere, hydrosphere, and atmosphere where life exists make up the biosphere. *The* **biosphere** (BY-oh-SFEER) *is all the parts of Earth that support and contain life.* The biosphere reaches from the floor of the ocean to the tops of the highest mountains. All together, the biosphere is a layer blanketing the Earth about 20 km (12.4 mi) thick. If Earth were the size of an apple, the layer that supports life would be only about as thick as the apple's skin.

Although the biosphere is 20 km thick, most organisms live in a narrower range. Deep below the surface of the ocean, life is rare because the pressure is so high and very little food is available. Few organisms live atop the tallest mountains because the air pressure is too low and the temperatures are too cold. Most life on Earth exists between 500 m below the surface of the ocean and about 6 km above sea level.

All organisms obtain the materials they need to live from the biosphere. While each individual organism may live mostly on land, water, or in the air, all organisms depend on materials from each of these three areas of Earth. For example, you live on the lithosphere, but breathe the air of the atmosphere, and drink the water of the hydrosphere. Although a bird may live in the air, it eats food that grew on the ground, which is part of the lithosphere.

Figure 1.10 Spider monkeys (left), white crabs (center), and tundra brush (right) live in very different environments.

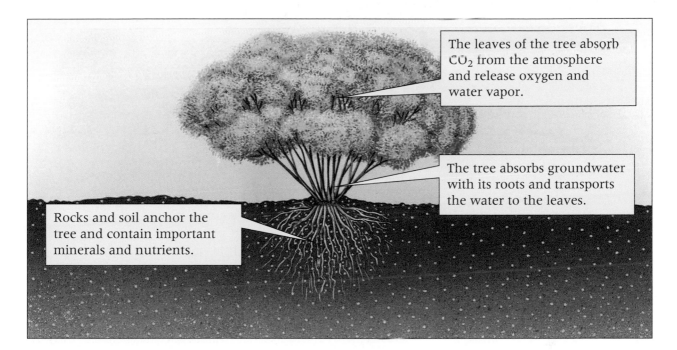

The leaves of the tree absorb CO_2 from the atmosphere and release oxygen and water vapor.

The tree absorbs groundwater with its roots and transports the water to the leaves.

Rocks and soil anchor the tree and contain important minerals and nutrients.

Organisms find the energy they need in many different parts of the biosphere. Most energy originates from sunlight, which plants use. Animals, however, obtain most of their energy by eating plants and other animals. Energy constantly flows into the biosphere as sunlight, flows through organisms and the environment, and eventually flows out of the biosphere as heat and is lost to space.

Because all organisms depend on the biosphere to meet their needs, they are affected by changes in the biosphere. For example, a change in the composition of seawater can affect the organisms in the ocean. The eruption of a volcano can affect organisms that live on the surrounding land.

While changes in the environment can affect organisms, organisms can also cause changes to occur in their environments. The damming of a river by beavers affects the flow of water. The release of gases and dust particles by a factory affects the atmosphere. Because organisms affect their environments and changes in the environment affect organisms, the biosphere is a very complex network of interactions.

Figure 1.11 Organisms interact with each part of the biosphere.

Dateline 1991

A group of adventurers entered a large domed structure called Biosphere II in Arizona to try to demonstrate living in a completely closed environment. Important lessons were learned, though the most important may have been that the "experiment" was far too complex to succeed. The original Biospherians had too many uncontrolled variables in their very large enclosure. More realistic experiments are now underway and should help us learn more about Biosphere I, Earth.

SECTION REVIEW

1. What parts of Earth make up the biosphere?
2. List two ways in which you interact with each of the three parts of the biosphere every day.
3. **Analyze** In what ways does each part of the biosphere contribute to the production of the food you eat?

Mission to Planet Earth

Scientists cannot always find answers to their questions about Earth by exploring the planet themselves. For example, if scientists are studying the extent of deforestation in a tropical rain forest, a survey would be very costly, would limit the results, and would take too much time.

For many years, researchers at NASA have explored ways to efficiently obtain information about Earth. In 1972, NASA launched the first satellite designed to relay images of Earth from space. This satellite, called Landsat, helped researchers make detailed maps of the planet. Similar satellites have been equipped to measure amounts and different types of vegetation growing in different areas of the world. Satellites help predict weather patterns, measure ozone levels in the atmosphere, and monitor agriculture.

Today, NASA is working on a project called "Mission to Planet Earth." The goal is to understand how Earth's systems—air, land, water, and life—interact with each other. A major component of the project is the Earth

This color composite photograph taken by Landsat shows coral reef formations near the Bahama Islands. Coral formations are dark blue.

Observation System, or EOS. EOS is a system of satellites and monitors, including Landsat 7, the seventh Landsat satellite to be launched. NASA estimates that by the year 2000, EOS will have cost $6.7 billion.

An important goal of the EOS is to generate a database compiled over a 15-year period to examine climate change on Earth. Studying climate change will help scientists determine if pollutants from industry and automobiles are causing an increase in Earth's temperature. Scientists will also use EOS to study ozone depletion in the atmosphere and

the amount of UV radiation Earth receives.

Scientists hope that viewing Earth from space will help them understand the effect humans have on the planet's natural resources. This knowledge has many potential benefits, including more sustainable farming practices and improved accuracy of climate forecasts.

Checkpoint

1. Why is some data about Earth easier to obtain from space than from the planet's surface?
2. How might information collected by Landsat or other Earth satellites help your community?

CHAPTER 1 REVIEW

KEY TERMS

organism 1.1	ecology 1.1	aquifer 1.2	ozone 1.3
lithosphere 1.1	igneous rock 1.2	artesian well 1.2	biosphere 1.4
hydrosphere 1.1	sedimentary rock 1.2	troposphere 1.3	
atmosphere 1.1	metamorphic rock 1.2	stratosphere 1.3	

CHAPTER SUMMARY

1.1 Earth is the third planet from the sun in the solar system. The presence of liquid water and an oxygen-containing atmosphere make life on Earth possible. Earth consists of the lithosphere, the hydrosphere, and the atmosphere.

1.2 The lithosphere is made up of three types of rocks: igneous, sedimentary, and metamorphic. The hydrosphere is made up mostly of salt water. Less than 3 percent of the water on Earth is fresh water. Much of the fresh water is contained in snow and ice.

1.3 The atmosphere is made up of several layers of decreasing density. The troposphere contains water vapor, and most weather occurs there. The stratosphere contains the ozone layer, which absorbs harmful ultraviolet (UV) radiation.

1.4 The biosphere is the part of Earth occupied by organisms. The biosphere and the organisms interact with one another. Living things get all the materials necessary for life from the biosphere.

MULTIPLE CHOICE

Choose the letter of the word or phrase that best completes each statement.

1. The five distant planets are made mostly of (a) gas; (b) water; (c) rock; (d) radiation.
2. Earth can support life because of the presence of (a) heat; (b) ice; (c) liquid water; (d) rocks.
3. Compared to visible light, the wavelength of ultraviolet light is (a) longer; (b) shorter; (c) the same; (d) brighter.
4. Earth's fairly steady surface temperature is due to the presence of (a) oxygen; (b) water; (c) rocks; (d) wind.
5. Fossils are usually found in (a) igneous rock; (b) sedimentary rock; (c) metamorphic rock; (d) lava.
6. More than 97 percent of the hydrosphere is (a) salt water; (b) fresh water; (c) underground water; (d) ice caps and glaciers.
7. Aquifers transport (a) water from reservoirs; (b) surface runoff; (c) ocean water; (d) groundwater.
8. The most abundant gas in Earth's atmosphere is (a) nitrogen; (b) oxygen; (c) carbon dioxide; (d) water vapor.
9. The ozone layer is part of the (a) troposphere; (b) stratosphere; (c) mesosphere; (d) thermosphere.
10. A bird interacts primarily with the (a) hydrosphere (b) atmosphere (c) lithosphere (d) biosphere.
11. The layer of the atmosphere in which rainstorms occur is the (a) hydrosphere; (b) stratosphere; (c) troposphere; (d) thermosphere.
12. Rocks formed from the cooling lava of volcanic eruptions are (a) igneous rocks; (b) limestone rocks; (c) sedimentary rocks; (d) metamorphic rocks.
13. Temperatures in the thermosphere can reach (a) −100 °C; (b) 200 °C; (c) 1000 °C; (d) 2000 °C.

CHAPTER 1 REVIEW

WORD COMPARISONS

Write the letter of the second word pair that best matches the first pair.

1. Atmosphere: air as (a) land: water; (b) lithosphere: hydrosphere; (c) hydrosphere: water; (d) land: lithosphere.
2. Aquifer: groundwater as (a) artesian well: spring; (b) ocean: current; (c) rain: ocean; (d) river: surface water.
3. granite: igneous as (a) fossil: metamorphic; (b) sandstone: sedimentary; (c) metamorphic: granite; (d) sandstone: marble.
4. Nitrogen: atmosphere as (a) salt water: hydrosphere; (b) glaciers: hydrosphere; (c) ozone: troposphere.
5. Weather: troposphere as (a) ozone: ionosphere; (b) water vapor: troposphere; (c) aurora: ionosphere; (d) heat: mesosphere.

CONCEPT REVIEW

Write a complete response to each of the following.

1. Which layer of the atmosphere is included in the biosphere?
2. Which of the nine planets are called the inner planets? In what way do the inner planets differ from the outer planets?
3. Why is liquid water important to living things?
4. How does the presence of plants on Earth affect the content of the atmosphere?
5. Why are organisms not equally distributed throughout the biosphere?

THINK CRITICALLY

1. Planet Mars has polar ice caps consisting mostly of frozen water. Mars also has an atmosphere containing carbon dioxide. Do you think any form of life could live on Mars? Why or why not?
2. Why are fossils not found in igneous rock?
3. Some animals live high in the tops of trees in rain forests and never touch the ground. In what ways do such animals depend on the lithosphere?
4. All commercial airplanes are equipped with oxygen masks for every passenger. Why do you suppose this is a necessary precaution?
5. Approximately what percentage of the water on Earth is liquid fresh water?

WRITE FOR UNDERSTANDING

Identify the topic of each paragraph in Section 1.2. Write a complete sentence that reflects the topic. Organize the topics into a summary of the section's contents.

PORTFOLIO

1. Research the environmental conditions on each of the planets in the solar system other than Earth. Evaluate each planet as a potential place for human colonization. Identify what challenges would be faced, and how they could be met.
2. Has the climate where you live changed during the past 100 years? Research weather history as far back as records are available. Make a graph or other visual representation of the information, and determine whether there has been a significant change.

GRAPHIC ANALYSIS

Use Figure 1.8 on page 10 to answer the following.

1. If you lived on the west coast of South America, from which direction would the wind usually blow?
2. Are winds named for the direction they flow to, or the direction they flow from? Support your answer with an example.
3. Do you think the governments of the Scandinavian countries should be concerned about air pollution in England? Explain your answer.
4. The northeastern United States tends to have colder winters than the northwestern United States. Which winds contribute to this difference?
5. From which direction does the wind usually blow at the equator? Is this the same direction or the opposite direction from the rotation of Earth?

ACTIVITY 1.2

PROBLEM
What is the percentage of oxygen in the air?

MATERIALS
- pencil
- steel wool, small amount
- test tube
- ring stand
- clamp
- metric ruler
- beaker

HYPOTHESIS
After reading the entire activity, write a hypothesis that pertains to the problem.

PROCEDURE
1. Use the eraser end of a pencil to wedge a small amount of fine, moist steel wool into the bottom of a test tube.
2. Pour water into a beaker so it is approximately half-full.
3. Invert the test tube. Use the clamp and ring stand to hold the test tube upside-down and lower it to a position just above the surface of the water. Lower the test tube straight down into the water. *Note: Because the test tube is full of air, no water will enter it.* Label your setup with your name and store it where it will be undisturbed.
4. Observe the setup closely for several consecutive days. Record your observations. During this time, oxygen will be removed from the air in the test tube as it reacts with iron in the steel wool. Water will be drawn up into the test tube to replace the oxygen.
5. After two days, use a metric ruler to measure how far the water has been drawn up into the test tube.
6. To determine the percentage of oxygen in the original air inside the test tube, divide the length measured in step 5 by the total length of the test tube. Multiply the quotient by 100.

ANALYSIS
1. Did you notice any changes in the steel wool after two days? Explain.
2. Was oxygen removed from the air in the test tube? Explain.
3. What are the possible sources of error in this method of determining the percentage of oxygen in air?

CONCLUSION
What is the percentage of oxygen in air? Show the calculations you performed to obtain your answer.

CHAPTER

2

METHODS OF SCIENCE

New information is published in the various areas of science every day. You may have heard about new discoveries that contradict what scientists published years ago or even last year. Because of these contradictions, some people distrust what scientists say. What many people do not understand is that change is a basic part of science. Each new discovery leads to a new question that requires further study. Continuing research corrects errors, refines theories, and points out new directions to explore.

2.1 THE NATURE OF SCIENCE

OBJECTIVES • *Explain* why there is always uncertainty in science.
• *Distinguish* between a hypothesis and a guess.

What is science? What do scientists do? You can probably name different kinds of scientists, such as biologists, chemists, or physicists. Each of these scientists uses different tools and instruments to measure different things, but all scientists have something in common. They all use the scientific method to gather information.

Science is a way of learning about the world. Books contain ideas and information about science. They may also tell how scientists gathered that information. The information itself, however, is not science. Science is the process by which the information was gathered and interpreted.

Uncertainty in Science

In some ways, the work of a scientist is similar to the work of a detective. The detective cannot go back in time to watch a crime being committed. Instead, the detective must solve a mystery by putting together pieces of evidence. The detective first gathers as much evidence as possible about the crime. Then, based on the evidence, the detective forms a likely explanation. If new evidence is brought to light that disproves the explanation, the detective will have to come up with a new explanation.

In a similar way, a scientist tries to find answers to the mysteries of nature. Just as the detective cannot watch the crime, the scientist often cannot see natural processes at work. Instead, the scientist must make as many observations as possible about the results of those processes. The scientist then forms an explanation for what was observed. *A* **hypothesis** (hy-POTH-eh-sis) (plural, hypotheses) *is a possible explanation for a set of observations.* A hypothesis is not just a wild guess. It must be based on observations and it must be testable.

If later observations do not fit the hypothesis, the hypothesis can be changed. For example, you may observe that after a hard rain, the gutters on your street fill up with water. You form a hypothesis that all the water in the gutter comes from rain. The next sunny day, a neighbor up the street washes her car, and the gutter fills with water even though there has been no rain. You need to revise your hypothesis. How could you restate your hypothesis about where the water in the gutter comes from?

Scientists can never be certain that they have observed everything about a particular subject. A new tool may be invented that allows additional observations. A scientist must always be ready to modify or give up an old hypothesis in favor of a better one. Because new information often causes a scientist to change a hypothesis, change is basic to science.

Figure 2.1 The transmission electron microscope (TEM) is a tool that enables scientists to see structures within a cell. Scientists had to change their ideas about some cellular structures when they saw images like this one produced by the TEM.

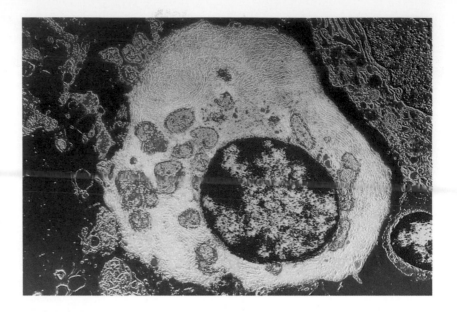

Think About It!

Housing starts, or the construction of new homes, are an important indicator of a strong economy. But building homes may also be harmful to the environment. People must make choices when the needs of the economy and the needs of the environment conflict.

1. How can science help people understand the effects of construction on the environment and the economy?

2. How can science help people decide if houses should be built in a particular area?

Science and Society

The progress of science is often driven by the needs and challenges of society. Feeding a hungry world, curing and preventing the spread of AIDS, and developing new energy sources are just some of the challenges of today's scientists.

Science cannot answer questions of ethics or personal values. Science can find out how well a new AIDS drug will work or how much electricity a new energy source will provide. But it cannot tell which research is more important.

The products of science can be of great benefit to the world. Unfortunately, the products of science also have the potential to do harm. Everyone, not just scientists, must work to make sure that scientific findings are put to good use. As a voter and a consumer of the products of science, you will be involved in making decisions about the impact of science on society. The more you know about the issues, the better prepared you will be to make these decisions.

SECTION REVIEW

1. Explain why a hypothesis is not just a wild guess.
2. Why are scientific ideas uncertain by nature?
3. **Apply** The United States government has established recommended daily allowances for many nutrients. The amounts recommended for some nutrients have changed over the years. Why do you think this has happened?

Searching the Depths

To collect data, scientists often do field research. But in some "fields," conditions make it impossible for humans to visit without special equipment. For instance, as divers go deeper into the ocean, they must deal with decreasing temperatures, diminishing light, and increasing pressure. At depths where pressure is more than the human body can stand, research must be done from within a small submarine, called a submersible.

One such submersible is *Alvin*, operated by Woods Hole Oceanographic Institution. Built in 1964 to reach depths of more than 5000 feet, *Alvin* is carried on a larger research vessel. The submersible is equipped with lights, video cameras, and robot arms. There are instruments to monitor water temperature and depth, plus a communication system for keeping in touch with the research vessel at the surface.

Alvin became internationally famous after being used in the expedition that located and photographed the remains of the RMS Titanic in 1986. However, *Alvin's* main purpose is to conduct scientific research.

The years from 1971 to 1976 were spent surveying the bottom of the Atlantic Ocean, doing both geological and biological surveys. As part of the French-American Mid-Ocean Undersea Study, *Alvin* and two French submersibles carried scientists to the Mid-Atlantic Ridge. This was the first time humans saw this geologically active area up close.

In 1988, *Alvin* enabled biologists and oceanographers to conduct detailed studies of several "hot smokers" along the Juan de Fuca Ridge in the Pacific Ocean. These are vents where an active volcano spews lava directly into the ocean at depths of several thousand feet. These vents support surprisingly diverse communities of organisms at depths that are usually lifeless. Using *Alvin's* remote-controlled temperature probe, scientists learned that the temperature inside a vent is greater than 275 °C.

Used for scientific research, *Alvin* can study the ocean at depths of more than 5000 feet.

After more than 3000 dives, *Alvin* has been used for further study of undersea vents and to perform tests on specialized underwater research equipment. *Alvin* has even run errands, making a special dive just to recover a rock drill that was lost by another expedition.

Checkpoint

1. What problems of deep-sea research does *Alvin* help scientists overcome?
2. Why is it important that *Alvin* have equipment to measure depth?

2.2 SKILLS AND METHODS

OBJECTIVE • **Describe** the steps involved in conducting a scientific experiment.

There is no single process or set of steps that all scientists use. The scientist must always be prepared to go backward, change direction, and be flexible. The scientist must be prepared for surprising results or unexpected information. One investigation may lead to another, and yet another. The result for the scientist may be a lifetime of investigation and learning. Although the exact steps may vary, good scientific investigations have certain common features. Every investigation begins with an observation.

Observing and Questioning

Observations can be made directly with the senses, such as sight or touch. But many observations are made with the help of tools. Some tools are instruments that help extend the senses, allowing more detailed observations and measurements to be made. A balance, for example, enables a scientist to measure the mass of a rock more accurately than by simply holding it. A microscope enables a scientist to view things too small for the unaided eye to see. Other tools enable scientists to measure things that could not otherwise be observed at all. For example, a Geiger counter lets scientists measure radiation that the senses cannot detect.

Observations are followed by a question. The question is based on something that was observed. For example, a scientist may observe that grass does not grow in a certain area, and ask why. A scientist may observe that people who work in a particular building often become sick, and ask why.

Researching

How would you feel if you spent years trying to solve a mystery, only to find that someone else had already solved it? An important step in solving a scientific mystery, or conducting an investigation, is to find out what others have already learned about the topic. Perhaps the earlier work can save you some steps. Perhaps your hypothesis has already been supported or disproven. A trip to the library will help a scientist learn what work has been done on the subject. Scientists also attend meetings to share information about their research.

Sometimes scientists deliberately repeat work that was done by others. Repeating an experiment is an important part of science. If someone repeats your experiment and does not get the same results, there may be a problem with your hypothesis. Experimental results that cannot be repeated are not considered valid.

Hypothesizing

Once the scientist has found out about the work others have done, it is time to determine what direction the investigation will take. This next step is developing a hypothesis. Recall that a hypothesis is a possible explanation for an observation. The scientist should try to think of several hypotheses. From all the possible hypotheses, the scientist then chooses the most likely one. The ability to develop hypotheses and then choose among them is one of the most creative, important parts of a scientist's work.

Suppose a scientist observes that grass does not grow in a certain part of a lawn. The observation may raise a question: Why does grass not grow in this area? The scientist can offer several hypotheses. For example, one hypothesis may be that the area does not receive enough water. Another hypothesis may be that the area is too shady. The presence of a grass disease could be yet another hypothesis to explain the observation. However, only one hypothesis can be investigated in one experiment.

Once a hypothesis has been chosen, the scientist makes a prediction. The prediction states what the results of the experiment will be if the hypothesis is accurate. In the grass example, the scientist may predict that if the area is given more water, grass will grow. Which hypothesis would this prediction support? Suppose the scientist's hypothesis is that a fungus is killing the grass. What prediction could be made to support this hypothesis?

Sometimes a scientist may conduct an experiment without a clear hypothesis. Such an experiment could answer a question that begins with "What would happen if...?" This type of experiment is used to produce further observations that could be used as the basis for a hypothesis later. For such an experiment to be valid, it must be considered part of a larger experiment. For example, you might conduct an experiment to see what would happen if you added bleach to your laundry. You might observe that some clothes

Literature

The mythology of many ancient cultures, such as the Greeks and Romans, was an attempt to explain observations of nature. Unlike modern science, the ideas put forth in mythology were not tested or testable.

are cleaner, some are faded, and others are not affected at all. From these observations you could develop a hypothesis such as "bleach causes colors to fade on cotton fabric." You could then predict that if you wash a bright-colored cotton tee shirt with bleach, it will fade. At this point, you would be ready to design an experiment.

Designing an Experiment

Scientists use experiments to test their hypotheses. If the results of an experiment disprove a hypothesis, the scientist may develop a new hypothesis and design a new experiment. If the results support the hypothesis, the scientist does not say that the hypothesis has been "proven." Although it is tempting to say so, scientists must be careful not to jump to conclusions. After many experiments have supported the hypothesis, the explanation is said to be valid. This means that the explanation is good. However, there is always a chance that it may be disproven by a better explanation in the future. Designing a good experiment to test a hypothesis is a very important part of scientific studies.

Variables *A* **variable** *is any factor that affects the outcome of an experiment.* An experiment usually tests one, and only one, variable at a time. Consider once again the problem of grass growth. Variables that could affect the growth of grass include water, sunlight, and diseases. Suppose the scientist exposed the grassless area to more sunlight and gave the area more water. In a few days, new grass grew. The scientist cannot know which variable—the water, the sunlight, or the combination of the two—made the grass grow.

Figure 2.3 If the data do not support the hypothesis, the scientist may make new observations, ask new questions, or choose a new hypothesis and start the process again.

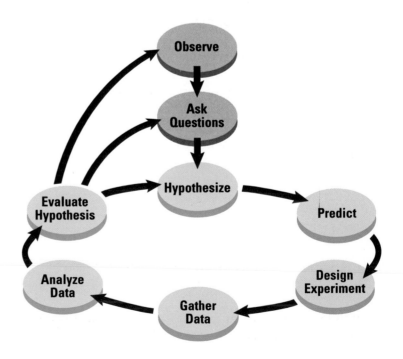

Experimental and Control Groups In designing an experiment, a scientist sets up two groups: an experimental group and a control group. The only difference between the two groups is the variable. In the problem of grass growth, the hypothesis is that the grass died because there was no water. The variable to be tested would be the presence of water. *The **control** group would have all of the factors that were there when the original observations were made,* including the lack of water. The experimental group would be the same, except for the addition of water.

After setting up the experimental and control groups, the scientist predicts how the two groups will compare. The scientist might predict that the grass in the group with water will live and the control grass without water will die. The outcome of an experiment depends on the variable being tested, called the *independent variable*. The outcome is called the *dependent variable* because it depends on the variable being tested. The water given to the experimental group would be the independent variable. The grass growth would be the dependent variable.

Collecting, Organizing, and Analyzing Data

Scientists carefully record not only the results of the experiment but also the steps they took to conduct the experiment. Once the data are collected, the scientist must decide what the results mean.

To analyze and interpret data, the scientist chooses a way to display the data. Sometimes the data are organized into a table. A graph is often used to show patterns or trends in the data more clearly. Some types of graphs are shown in Figure 2.4. In bar graphs and line graphs, the independent variable is usually shown on the x-axis. The dependent variable is shown on the y-axis.

Once the data have been collected and analyzed, the scientist communicates the work to others. Sometimes scientists share their work informally through conversations. Scientists publish reports of their experiments in scientific journals and give presentations at meetings. All reports must clearly show how the experiment was conducted, what the results were, and how the results can be interpreted.

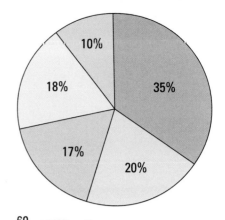

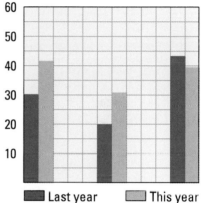

■ Last year ■ This year

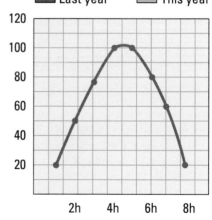

2h   4h   6h   8h

Figure 2.4 Circle graphs, or pie charts (top), show portions of a whole value. Bar graphs (center) are used to compare quantities. Line graphs (bottom) are used to show how one variable responds to change in another.

SECTION REVIEW

1. How does an experimental group differ from a control group?
2. Why should a scientist conduct library research before beginning an experiment?
3. **Infer** One of the most important skills a scientist can have is the ability to write well. Why do you think this is so?

2.3 ENVIRONMENTAL SCIENCE

OBJECTIVES • *Give* examples of how parts of the environment interact. • *Explain* how science influences decision-making processes.

LINK
Chemistry

Matter is defined as anything that takes up space and has mass. Most matter is made up of elements and combinations of elements. All the known elements are listed in the periodic table on page 429.

How would you describe your surroundings? If you are in a classroom, you might describe the tables and chairs, the posters on the wall, and the other students. You might also describe the lighting, the temperature, and a breeze from the window. If you were at home, at the mall, or camping in the woods, the descriptions of your surroundings would be different. *Everything that surrounds an organism is its* **environment**. Environmental science is the study of the environments in which organisms live and how they interact. As you learned in Chapter 1, all the environments in which organisms live make up the biosphere.

Why are people interested in studying the environment? An organism's environment provides everything the organism needs in order to live. The environment provides food, water, shelter, air, and other resources. If conditions in the environment change, the organism may not be able to survive. Keeping the environment healthy is the first step in making sure that the biosphere can continue to support life in the future.

Environmental science is an integrated science. An integrated science is one that draws from many different fields of science. Because the environment includes organisms, environmental science includes some biology. Because energy and motion are part of the environment, environmental science involves physics. Chemistry is part of environmental science as well because all parts of the biosphere are made up of matter.

Figure 2.5 Every environment has its own set of characteristics. What are the living and nonliving parts of each of the environments shown here?

Table 2.1 Areas of Study in Environmental Science

Area	Scientist	Subject
Water	Hydrologist	Flow of Earth's waters
	Oceanographer	Ocean environments
Air	Meteorologist	Weather and the atmosphere
	Climatologist	Global weather patterns
Land	Geologist	Structure and history of Earth
	Seismologist	Movements of Earth's surface
Organisms	Biologist	Structure and behavior of organisms
	Ecologist	Interactions of organisms and their environments
	Paleontologist	Prehistoric life and fossils
	Anthropologist	Structure of human societies

Table 2.1 shows some of the types of scientists that are involved in studying the environment. As you can see from the table, ecologists are scientists that study the interactions between organisms and their environments. What then is the difference between ecology and environmental science? Often the two terms are used to refer to the same thing. Indeed, you cannot study the environment without understanding the principles of ecology. The difference between the two fields of study is the role of human societies.

The principles of ecology do not change simply by including humans in the picture. After all, humans are organisms and are part of the natural world. Unlike other organisms, however, humans have the ability to create and enforce policy, and to affect the environment on a global scale. Environmental science incorporates the impact of human activities, both planned and unplanned, on the environment.

Parts of the Environment

All the factors that make up the environment can be divided into two categories: living and nonliving. *All the living parts of the environment are called* **biotic** (by-OT-ik) **factors.** Biotic factors in your classroom may include only humans and microbes too small to see. If you were camping, the list of biotic factors in your environment would be longer. The list might include plants, birds, mushrooms, insects, and so on.

All the nonliving parts of the environment are called **abiotic** (AY-by-OT-ik) **factors.** Abiotic factors include water, soil, and air, as well as temperature, wind, and sunlight. Some of the abiotic factors in an environment may once have been alive, such as your classroom's wooden chairs, which came from trees. Because the wood is no longer alive, it is therefore not a biotic factor.

LINK
Fine Arts

One way to record observations about your environment is through art. French painter Paul Gauguin (1848–1903) was fascinated with the plants, animals, and people of Tahiti. He made several trips to the islands and painted his impressions of the environment.

Environmental Interactions

Much of the research that is done in the area of environmental science involves interactions. Organisms interact with the biotic and abiotic factors in the environment. An organism may be affected by changes in the environment, and the environment can be affected by the organism. The change that occurred in the environment may, in turn, have an effect on another organism.

Sometimes it seems easy to predict how a change in the environment will affect other factors. For example, a particular species of butterfly can lay eggs on only one type of lupine flower. It is not difficult to predict what will happen to the butterflies if all the lupine flowers are destroyed. However, it is usually more difficult to predict how a change in one part of the environment will affect other parts. For example, there were once thriving populations of coyotes, deer, wolves, and mountain lions on the north rim of the Grand Canyon. In the early 1900s, the state of Arizona began rewarding hunters for killing the coyotes, mountain lions, and wolves because they were believed to be a danger to settlers and livestock. After 15 years, the hunted animals were almost completely wiped out. But these animals were the natural enemy of the deer, which were not being hunted.

Without wolves, coyotes, and mountain lions, the deer population soon grew to 25 times the size it had been before the hunting began. The deer ate all the available plants in the area. Eventually, the environment could no longer support so many deer, and approximately 60 000 deer died of starvation the following winters. Seventy years later, the plant growth in the area had not yet fully recovered. No one had predicted that the hunting would have such a destructive effect on the environment.

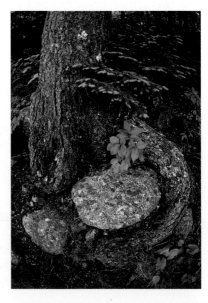

Figure 2.6 The environment can be changed by organisms, such as the change in the river caused by the beaver's dam (right). The tree responded to its environment by adjusting the direction of its growth (far right).

The Capture-Recapture Method

PROBLEM

Every year, a team of biologists estimates the population size of a rare species of trout that live in Grass Lake. Grass Lake is polluted, but efforts are being made to clean it up. The biologists make their estimation using the capture-recapture method. The biologists float on rafts and capture fish on baited hooks. The fish are marked, tallied, and thrown back into the water. The biologists repeat the procedure a week later. Imagine you are a biologist on the team trying to answer this question: What is the size of the trout population in Grass Lake?

MATERIALS (per class)

- 100 to 200 toothpicks
- Watch or small clock

PREDICTION

The capture-recapture method will produce an accurate estimate of a population size.

PROCEDURE

1. For the first sampling, go with your class to the designated grass area. The borders of this area represent the shores of Grass Lake.
2. Previously, toothpicks were spread out over Grass Lake. Toothpicks have been cut in half. Each half toothpick represents a trout. Spend 2 minutes capturing toothpicks. Keep the toothpicks you capture in your hand, and return to class with them.
3. Mark the toothpicks in an agreed-upon manner without damaging them. Tally and record the number caught by the entire class. These are the marked trout in the total population.
4. Give your half toothpicks to a designated member of your class. The designated person will throw the marked toothpicks back in Grass Lake. They should be randomly scattered across Grass Lake.

5. Return to Grass Lake with the rest of the class. Again, spend 2 minutes capturing toothpicks, and return to class with them.
6. Some of the toothpicks you've captured will probably be marked, indicating they had been previously captured. Separate these from the unmarked toothpicks.
7. Tally and record the number of toothpicks recaptured by the entire class. These are the marked trout recaptured.
8. Tally and record the total number of toothpicks, marked and unmarked, captured by the class during the second sampling. These are the total trout captured.
9. Return all toothpicks to your teacher.
10. Multiply the number of total trout captured (step 8) by marked trout in total population (step 3). Divide this product by the marked trout recaptured (step 7). The result is an estimate of the trout population in Grass Lake.

$$\frac{\text{Marked trout recaptured}}{\text{Total trout captured}} = \frac{\text{Marked trout in total population}}{X}$$

X = The size of the trout population in Grass Lake

ANALYSIS

1. To get an accurate estimate, why is it important that trout caught during the first sampling are returned to the lake unharmed?
2. What are possible sources of error with the capture-recapture method? How can these errors be minimized?
3. Could the capture-recapture method be used to accurately estimate the size of any population? Explain.

CONCLUSION

What is your estimate of the trout population in Grass Lake? Show the calculations you performed to obtain your estimate.

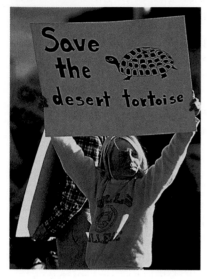

Figure 2.7 Citizens can voice their opinions by voting. Sometimes people express themselves by joining together in interest groups or by attending demonstrations to make their voices heard.

Making Decisions

Many changes taking place in the biosphere are the result of human activities. Some of these changes could cause environmental damage if they are allowed to continue. It may seem obvious that people should stop doing things that damage the environment. Unfortunately, deciding what needs to be done, and how to do it, are not such easy tasks.

The interactions that take place in the biosphere are very complex. As you have learned, it is not always possible to predict how one change will affect other parts of the environment. An organism may interact with its environment in ways scientists are not aware of. Whenever a public policy regarding the environment is put into effect, the government must try to predict what the impact of the policy will be. To do this, the government usually employs a team of researchers to study the interactions that will be affected.

In addition to a policy's impact on the environment, the government must also consider the economic effect the policy may have on society. Regulations that protect the environment may cost people their jobs. For example, efforts in the northwestern United States to protect old-growth forests and the organisms that live there have conflicted with the local economic concerns. The economy in the area depends heavily on the lumber industry, which would suffer from protection of the forest. In developing nations where food and fuel are scarce, the conflict between environmental issues and the needs of people are even more difficult to resolve.

Who should decide how, where, and when the environment is to be protected? Who will determine the steps that are to be taken in the future? One essential key to making good decisions is an understanding of the environment and its interactions. This includes thorough scientific research and well-informed citizens. The more people know about how their activities affect the environment, the better prepared they will be to protect the biosphere.

SECTION REVIEW

1. Why do governments need to study the environment?
2. Which parts of the environment respond to the activities of organisms, the biotic factors or the abiotic factors?
3. **Infer** Mosquito fish feed on young mosquitoes that can carry malaria. The young mosquitoes feed on tiny floating plants in ponds. Turtles feed on plants at the bottom of the ponds. These plants need sunlight from the surface. What might happen to the turtles if mosquito fish are brought into a pond?

KEY TERMS

hypothesis 2.1	control 2.2	biotic factor 2.3
variable 2.2	environment 2.3	abiotic factor 2.3

CHAPTER SUMMARY

2.1 Science is a way of learning about the natural world. Science is uncertain and changeable. Science is responsive to the needs of society, and voters are involved in making decisions about the impact of science on society.

2.2 A scientific investigation follows a series of steps that result in the support or rejection of a hypothesis. An experiment has a control group and an experimental group. In the control, the variable being tested is absent.

2.3 Environmental science is an integrated science, one that draws from many fields of science. The environment includes biotic and abiotic factors. Biotic and abiotic factors interact with one another, but it can be difficult to predict what the results of such interactions will be.

MULTIPLE CHOICE

Choose the letter of the word or phrase that best completes each statement.

1. Science is (a) a collection of information; (b) based on facts; (c) random; (d) uncertain.
2. Science cannot answer questions that are (a) testable; (b) observable; (c) based on ethics; (d) based on observations.
3. Observations should be made (a) before an experiment is designed; (b) while an experiment is being conducted; (c) before and during an experiment; (d) after the experiment is completed.
4. A prediction is usually made (a) before making observations; (b) before developing a hypothesis; (c) after developing a hypothesis; (d) after the experiment is conducted.
5. The part of an experiment in which the variable being tested is not present is called the (a) experimental group; (b) variable group; (c) dependent group; (d) control group.
6. If you wanted to compare the rainfall this month with the rainfall last month in various locations, you could best represent the data in a (a) circle graph; (b) bar graph; (c) line graph; (d) pie chart.
7. The abiotic factors in an environment include (a) plants; (b) animals; (c) water; (d) microbes.
8. Interactions in the environment are usually (a) complex; (b) predictable; (c) easily observed; (d) well understood.

TRUE/FALSE

Write true *if the statement is true. If the statement is false, change the underlined word to make it true.*

1. A scientist who studies movements of land is a paleontologist.
2. A prediction is a statement of what will happen during an experiment if the hypothesis is valid.
3. All the environments in which organisms live make up the biosphere.
4. A wooden chair may be one of the biotic factors in your environment.
5. It is difficult to predict the results of changes in the biosphere because interactions are simple.
6. Environmental protection policies often have economic impact.

CHAPTER 2 REVIEW

CONCEPT REVIEW

Write a complete response to each of the following.

1. How are graphs useful in a scientific investigation?
2. Why is it important that scientists communicate the results of their experimentation to other scientists?
3. How has the invention of new tools, such as the electron microscope, influenced the progress of science?
4. A hypothesis can be considered an educated guess. Explain how this is different from a wild guess.
5. Why is it necessary for people who do not plan to have careers in science to be informed about the environment?

THINK CRITICALLY

1. Suppose there is a tree growing in your backyard, and the roots of the tree have damaged the pipes that bring water into the house. To restore the water, the tree must be removed. But the tree is home to a rare bird. Would you cut down the tree? Why or why not?
2. Suppose the tree in the above example is growing in someone else's yard, and recent studies have shown that the rare bird produces a chemical that may cure cancer. Would your opinion change? Explain your answer.
3. A friend is upset because the fish in his aquarium have been dying. He raises the temperature of the water and increases the amount of available food. The fish continue to die, so your friend decides that neither temperature nor food is responsible. What is wrong with your friend's approach to solving the problem? Is the conclusion valid?
4. Suppose you had lived near the Grand Canyon in the early 1900s. Do you think you would have supported the policy of rewarding hunters for killing wolves, coyotes, and mountain lions? Explain.

Computer Activity In 1980, the flowers in a particular field were made up of 40 percent daisies, 30 percent lupines, 15 percent daffodils, and 15 percent buttercups. In 1990, the combination of flowers in the same field was 35 percent daisies, 25 percent lupines, 25 percent daffodils, and 15 percent buttercups. Use a graphing program to represent the change of flowers as a circle graph and as a bar graph.

WRITE CREATIVELY

What do you think your neighborhood looked like 200 years ago? Write a story about an animal that fell asleep 200 years ago and just woke up. In your story, describe the changes that have taken place in the animal's environment.

PORTFOLIO

1. People used to believe that life could arise from nonliving things. Research the experiments of Francisco Redi and Louis Pasteur that disproved this idea. What were the variables and controls in each experiment? Prepare a presentation describing how each scientist followed the steps of a scientific experiment.
2. Each area of specialization in science uses specific types of tools to gather data. Choose one of the areas in Table 2.1. Find out what tools are used, and the type of data that each tool provides.

GRAPHIC ANALYSIS

Use the figure to answer the following.

1. The graph represents the amount of grain consumed per person per year in various parts of the world. The graph shows consumption in 1975 and expected consumption in the year 2000. Which type of graph is shown?
2. In what part of the world is consumption not expected to rise?
3. In what part of the world was grain consumption greatest in 1975? What part of the world is expected to be the greatest grain consumer in 2000?
4. Could this information be presented in a different form? Explain your answer.

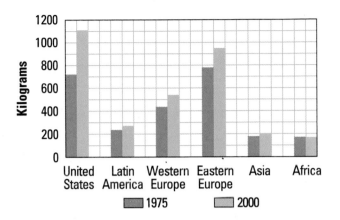

ACTIVITY 2.2

PROBLEM
How is a hypothesis tested and evaluated?

MATERIALS
- 6 radish seeds
- 6 lima bean seeds
- 2 sponges
- 2 Petri dishes
- wax marking pencil

HYPOTHESIS
Water is needed for seeds to germinate.

PROCEDURE

1. To test the hypothesis, place a wet sponge in one Petri dish. Pour a small amount of water in the dish. The top of the sponge should be moist but not submerged. Label this dish *experimental*.
2. Place a dry sponge in the other dish. Do not allow this sponge to get wet. Label this dish *control*.
3. Place 3 radish seeds and 3 lima bean seeds on top of each sponge. **Caution:** *Wash your hands after handling the seeds because they are often coated with chemicals.*
4. Keep the two dishes close together at all times. Keep all conditions, except moisture, the same for each setup. Be sure to keep the wet sponge moist.
5. Examine the seeds over the next few days.
6. Record the number of seeds that germinated from each setup in a data table.

ANALYSIS

1. Describe an observation of nature that might lead someone to develop the original hypothesis.
2. What factors did you control in this experiment?
3. What was the tested variable? Why is it important to test only one variable in an experiment? Do your observations support or reject the previously stated hypothesis? If necessary, restate your hypothesis.

CONCLUSION
Why is evaluating your hypothesis an important part of a good scientific experiment?

CHAPTER

3

CHANGE IN THE BIOSPHERE

You might think as you look around that the world has always been the way it is now, but this is not so. Ocean waves have been crashing on the shore for so long that giant rocks have been worn to sand. Rivers have flowed through the countryside for so long they have carved deep canyons along their paths. Rain forests have been growing long enough to develop life forms that exist nowhere else. Although it may seem that the world is a very stable, unchangeable place, the truth is just the opposite. All the parts of the biosphere are constantly moving, changing, and interacting—and they have been for billions of years.

3.1 THE CHANGING ENVIRONMENT

OBJECTIVE • *Describe* *ways in which the three layers of the biosphere change over time.*

Earth is approximately 4 billion years old, but humans have existed for fewer than 500 000 years. Change has been a part of Earth's nature since it first formed. Many rapid changes have taken place as a result of human activity.

Changes in the Lithosphere

The lithosphere is made up of several large, movable plates called **tectonic** (tek-TON-ik) **plates.** Figure 3.1 shows the major tectonic plates of Earth's surface. Liquid rock below the surface rises through cracks between the plates deep in the ocean floor. As the hot, liquid rock meets the cool ocean water, the rock cools and hardens. New rock pushes the tectonic plates apart, causing them to shift position. When the plates shift, earthquakes can occur along the edges of the plates. Mountain chains rise when the movements of the plates cause parts of Earth's surface to buckle.

Besides the movement of tectonic plates, weather and flowing water also affect the shape of the land. *The breaking down of rocks by weather and water is called* **weathering.** *The broken-down material is then carried off in the process of* **erosion** (eh-ROH-zhun). Together, the effects of tectonic plate movements, followed by weathering and erosion, have produced Earth's present land formations.

Figure 3.1 The surface of Earth is made up of several tectonic plates. Arrows show the direction in which the plates move.

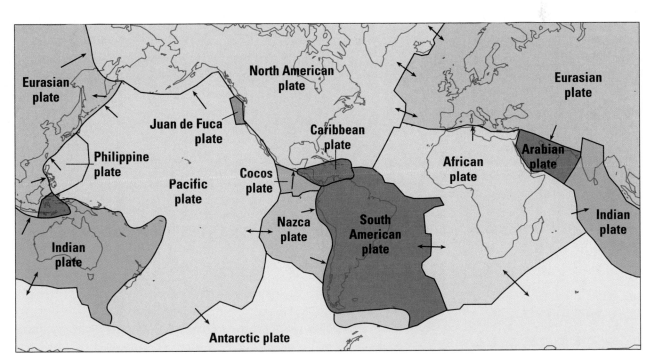

Changes in the Hydrosphere

Just as the shape and location of the continents have changed over time, so have the shapes and locations of Earth's oceans. Some of the changes that have taken place in the hydrosphere have progressed slowly and steadily. Other changes occur in repeating cycles. Ice ages are part of cycles that take place over millions of years. El Niño is a change that occurs on a cycle of 4 to 7 years.

Ice Ages   An *ice age* is a long period of cooling during which huge ice masses, called glaciers, grow and extend from Earth's polar regions, covering much of the planet's surface. After an ice age, the glaciers melt, shrinking back toward the poles. During an ice age, sea levels are lower. As glaciers melt, sea levels rise. Scientists have found evidence of at least five major ice ages in Earth's history. The most recent ice age ended between 10 000 and 12 000 years ago.

The movement of glaciers causes significant changes in the shape of the land. The scraping of the ice across the land and the displacement of rocks result in large-scale weathering and erosion in some areas and the deposit of materials in other areas. Many of the geological features of the northern United States, including the Great Lakes and the peninsula of Cape Cod, are the result of the last ice age.

No one knows what causes glaciers to grow and then retreat, although there are many testable hypotheses. Scientists know that ice ages are associated with periods of global cooling. Some scientists think that a wobbling of Earth on its axis is responsible for the ice ages.

El Niño   Every year near the end of December, a current of warm, nutrient-poor water flows southward along the coast of South America. Normally, the flow of warm water lasts only a few weeks. But sometimes the warm water current lasts for several months, a condition called El Niño (NEEN-yoh).

El Niño is one of many recurring patterns of change in ocean currents. Its conditions can have a far-reaching effect on climate and economics. The change in water temperature and nutrient content can affect the survival of fish. A drop in the number of fish means a loss of income for fishing industries. The reduced supply of fish also means increased costs for other industries that depend on fish meal, such as poultry and egg farming. The climatic changes associated with El Niño can also damage crops. As is true for ice ages, no one knows exactly what causes El Niño conditions to occur.

Changes in the Atmosphere

Sunlight and Earth's rotation about its axis drive many of the daily as well as seasonal changes in the atmosphere. However, organisms have also been affecting the content of Earth's atmosphere since life began. Before there was life, the atmosphere consisted

Dateline 1982

The El Niño that occurred in the winter of 1982–1983 was one of the most disruptive weather events of the century. Waters warmed up to 8 °C above normal. Effects of El Niño included severe drought in Australia and India, flooding in South America, and the crash of the anchovy fishing industry in Peru.

Figure 3.2 Glaciers contain bubbles of air that were trapped when the glacier formed thousands of years ago. By analyzing the gas contained in the bubbles, scientists can compare the modern atmosphere to the atmosphere at the time the glacier formed.

of many gases, among them water vapor, carbon dioxide, and sulfur gases. These are gases released from erupting volcanoes—the source of Earth's early atmosphere. Eventually, organisms evolved that could combine water, carbon dioxide, and the energy in sunlight to produce food. This process, called photosynthesis, released the first oxygen into the atmosphere.

For approximately 3.5 billion years, oxygen, carbon dioxide, water vapor, and nitrogen have been cycling from the atmosphere, through the bodies of organisms, and back into the atmosphere. You will learn more about these cycles in Chapter 4. Although some of Earth's carbon is continually being cycled, much is stored in the bodies of organisms, both alive and dead. Coal and other fossil fuels contain stored carbon from long-dead organisms. Burning organic matter releases stored carbon into the atmosphere and may influence the temperature of Earth through a process called the *greenhouse effect*.

The greenhouse effect is one way in which humans may be changing Earth's atmosphere. Loss of ozone from the stratosphere and increased pollution in the troposphere are other examples of atmospheric changes caused by humans. Natural causes, such as volcanic eruptions, continue to send gases into the atmosphere that are transported by winds around the world. These eruptions also affect global climate, as they've done since before humans existed.

Figure 3.3 When Mount Pinatubo in the Philippines erupted in 1991, it sent gases and particles high into the atmosphere. Scientists estimate that the eruption caused temperatures around the world to be 0.20 °C cooler than normal the following year.

SECTION REVIEW

1. Through what process does weather affect the shape of land?
2. In what ways does El Niño affect the economy?
3. **Integrate** Describe how ice ages are related to changes in the lithosphere, hydrosphere, and atmosphere.

3.2 NEEDS OF ORGANISMS

OBJECTIVES • **List** *factors that affect an area's ability to support life.*
• **Predict** *how changes in the environment might affect organisms.*

Organisms depend on their environment for everything they need in order to live. Every kind of organism has a different set of specific needs. For example, your needs are clearly different from those of a goldfish or a tree. Despite these differences, all organisms have certain needs in common, including water, energy, living space, and a suitable climate. The specific needs of an organism define the environment in which it must live and its role in the ecosystem.

Water

The presence of fresh water is one of the most important factors in the ability of land to support life. Water is needed for plants to grow, and plants and water are both necessary for an animal population to survive. The amount of rainfall on an area of land directly affects the characteristics and abundance of life in that area.

Organisms that live in the oceans are not usually affected by local rainfall, but fish and other aquatic organisms are affected by water quality. Temperature, nutrients, dissolved oxygen, other chemicals, and the kinds and numbers of organisms present affect water quality. These factors may interact with one another in many ways. For example, water that becomes warmer cannot contain as much oxygen as cooler water. As a result, some organisms will not be able to survive in warmer water.

Food and Energy

Almost all the energy used by living things comes from the sun. Through photosynthesis, plants and algae make food by capturing energy from sunlight. Animals and other organisms get their energy by eating plants, or by eating other animals.

Food contains not only energy, but also minerals, vitamins, and other chemicals. These materials are used by organisms to build tissues and carry out biochemical reactions. *Together, all the substances that an organism requires from food are called* **nutrients**. Like most animals, you obtain nutrients by eating, or ingesting food through your mouth. Fungi, protists, plants, and some animals, such as some worms, absorb nutrients directly into the cells of their bodies.

Some substances are stored and can build up in the cells of the body's tissues. If a stored substance is harmful, the tissues can become poisonous if eaten by other organisms. The buildup of poisonous materials in an organism's tissues allows poisons in the environment to pass from one organism to another.

Health

The average human body needs to take in about 2 L of water every day to remain healthy. In the United States, the average person uses an additional 240 L each day for bathing, washing clothes and dishes, and flushing the toilet.

Field Activity

Different organisms consume different foods. What foods do you think ants prefer?

1. Choose an area around your school where ants are likely to live.

2. Place several different types of foods in small bottle caps.

3. Return the following day and record your observations about the presence of ants.

4. Which foods attracted the most ants?

Living Space

All organisms need space to live. Living space enables organisms to obtain the materials they need from the environment. For example, plants need space so they can get enough sunlight. They also need space for their roots to grow so they can obtain water and minerals from the soil. If trees grow too closely together, some will die.

Animals need space in which to seek food, water, shelter, and mates. Many animals claim specific areas as their own. *An area that is claimed as a living space by an individual animal or group of animals is called a* **territory**. Animals that maintain territories are called *territorial animals.*

Many territorial animals mark their territory with scents to let intruders know that the area is off limits. Domestic house cats are a familiar example of a territorial animal. Cats have glands on their faces that produce scents with which they mark their territory. People often mistake the rubbing of a cat's face against a person's hand or leg as a sign of affection. Actually, the cat is marking the person as part of its territory. Some animals defend their territories with sounds or gestures.

The size of an animal's territory is determined by the needs of that animal. If there is not enough space for all the members of a population, they will compete for a territory, often to the death. Competition for space and the resources within the space is an important factor in the process of evolution. You will read more about evolution in Chapter 5.

Figure 3.4 To keep animals as healthy as possible, many zoos try to reproduce the natural environments in which the animals live.

Figure 3.5 Different types of animals require different climates. The polar bear and the camel could not survive in each other's environment.

Climate

The body temperature of most organisms is determined by the temperature of the environment. When the environment becomes cooler, so does the organism's body. Most organisms can survive only within a certain range of temperatures. The temperature tolerance for a particular organism is a factor in its global distribution.

Many organisms, especially plants that live in colder areas, survive the cold by becoming dormant. *When an organism becomes* **dormant** (DOR-munt), *the life processes within the body slow down.* Most dormant plants lose their leaves and stop growing. The growth of bacteria and other microorganisms can also be slowed by reducing the temperature of the surrounding environment. Why do you think refrigerators are used to keep foods fresh?

Birds and mammals, including humans, maintain a high body temperature regardless of the temperature of the environment. Because birds and mammals maintain a steady, warm body temperature, they are commonly called warm-blooded animals. Warm-blooded animals have a wider range of temperature tolerance, and can remain active in more diverse climates than other animals. But maintaining a high body temperature requires a great deal of food because producing and maintaining heat uses a lot of energy. Warm-blooded animals tend to need about ten times more food than other animals of the same size.

Like plants, many types of animals become dormant during periods of cold temperatures and low food supplies. *Dormancy in some animals is called* **hibernation** (HY-ber-NAY-shun). During hibernation, heart rate and breathing slow, the body temperature drops, and the animal enters a sleeplike state. Energy requirements during hibernation are very low, enabling the animal to survive a period when there is not enough food to maintain normal activities. This lowered metabolism is especially important for warm-blooded animals.

SECTION REVIEW

1. In what ways does behavior among territorial animals differ?
2. How does hibernation help animals to survive?
3. Do you think that the amount of water used by each person in the United States has changed over time? If so, in what way? Explain your answer.
4. **Predict** Suppose a particular area was to experience a sudden change in rainfall and temperature that lasts 50 years. Do you think the area would lose its ability to support life? Explain your answer.

The Mississippi Flood

During the summer of 1993, the Mississippi River and many of its tributaries overflowed their banks. Thousands of people were evacuated and some people died. Billions of dollars worth of property and crops were destroyed by the flood.

Old rivers such as the Mississippi flood regularly. The floodwaters deposit rich sediment along the banks, in areas known as floodplains. The rich soil makes floodplains ideal for growing crops.

The federal government has spent a great deal of money building flood-control projects along the Mississippi River.

Who should pay for property damage on a floodplain?

The Government Should Pay

Some people believe more money should be spent on flood control and relief. They argue that people have lived along the river for a long time. Flood-control projects help mitigate damage from floods and stimulate growth of agriculture and industry along floodplains.

Large floods such as that of 1993 occur infrequently. People who live in areas prone to tornadoes, hurricanes, and earthquakes receive federal money to help pay for disaster relief.

Property Owners Should Pay

More than $8 billion has already been spent on flood-control projects along the Mississippi River. Some people argue that no more should be spent and that people who choose to live in floodplains should be responsible for buying their own insurance.

Levees prevent the river from depositing nutrient-rich sediments on the floodplain and reduce the formation of marshlands, which help control flooding. In addition, many flood-control projects failed during the 1993 flood. The money might have been used for projects that would have been beneficial to more people.

When rivers overflow their banks, the resulting floods can cause billions of dollars in damage.

Consider the Issue

1. Do you think it is possible to live along a floodplain without being affected by the natural flooding of the river? How?

2. Do you think the government should pay to help areas built along a floodplain? Why or why not?

Environmental Needs of Land Isopods

PROBLEM

What environmental conditions do land isopods need?

MATERIALS (per group)

- shoebox with lid
- 2 paper towels
- aluminum foil
- water (Part A)
- masking tape
- 5 land isopods
- scissors (Part B)

HYPOTHESIS

After reading the entire activity, write a hypothesis that relates to the problem.

PROCEDURE

To study the preference of land isopods for moisture or dryness, do Part A. To study their preference for lightness or darkness, do Part B.

Part A

1. Line a shoebox with aluminum foil.
2. Tape two paper towels side by side to the inside bottom of the shoebox. Place a strip of masking tape between the two paper towels.
3. Moisten one of the paper towels with water.
4. Place five isopods on the masking tape between the two paper towels. Place the lid on the shoebox. **Caution:** *Handle live animals with care and respect.*
5. Leave the shoebox undisturbed for 5 minutes. Make a data table like the one shown. Substitute *Moist Paper* and *Dry Paper* for *Condition 1* and *Condition 2*.
6. After 5 minutes, remove the lid. Quickly count the number of isopods on moist paper, on tape, and on dry paper. Record your results beside *Trial 1* in the table.
7. Gently slide the isopods back onto the masking tape, and repeat steps 4–6 two more times.
8. Average the results of each column, and write the averages in the last row of the data table.

Part B

1. Follow steps 1 and 2 in Part A.
2. Cut the lid in half across the width, and cover half the shoebox with one of the pieces. **Caution:** *Handle sharp scissors with care.*
3. Place five isopods on the masking tape between the two paper towels.
4. Leave the shoebox undisturbed for 5 minutes. Make a data table like the one shown. Write *Dark* and *Light* for *Conditions 1* and *2*.
5. After 5 minutes, remove the half lid. Quickly count the number of isopods on the dark half, on the masking tape, and on the light half. Record your results beside *Trial 1* in the data table.
6. Gently slide the isopods back onto the masking tape, and repeat steps 4–6 two more times.
7. Average the results of each column, and write the averages in the last row of the data table.

ANALYSIS

1. Were you able to confirm your hypothesis? Explain why or why not.
2. Write a statement about the preference of land isopods for the factor studied.

CONCLUSION

Based on the class results, what can you infer about the environmental needs of land isopods? Describe their habitats.

Number of Isopods

Trial	(Condition 1)	Masking Tape	(Condition 2)
1			
2			
3			
Avg			

3.3 THE ECOSYSTEM

OBJECTIVES • *Describe* the structure of an ecosystem. • *Relate* the concept of habitat destruction to the loss of biodiversity.

An ecosystem is not simply a random collection of organisms and environmental factors. An ecosystem is a highly organized, structured environment in which all parts exist in a delicate balance. The structure and function of ecosystems can be studied at many levels, from individual species to the entire ecosystem.

Species

A **species** *is a group of organisms so similar to one another that they can breed and produce fertile offspring.* All members of a species have similar needs, such as the range of climate tolerance, size of territory, and types of food. Because they have the same needs, members of a species often compete with one another for resources.

The specific environment in which a particular species lives is its **habitat**. For example, the tops of the trees in a pine forest may be the habitat of a species of bird. A shallow, fast-moving, cold-water stream may be the habitat of a species of trout. A rotting log is an ideal habitat for various species of insects, fungi, and microorganisms. Within their habitats, individual organisms find the appropriate food, shelter, temperatures, and other factors needed to survive. The destruction of habitat is a serious threat to the survival of many species.

The total area in which a species can live is called its **geographical range**. The size of the geographical range depends on the availability of suitable habitat. For example, the mountain lion requires a habitat with diverse plant life, a large hunting territory, and a variety of prey animals. Because its habitat was once common,

The U.S. Congress passed the Endangered Species Act of 1973 to protect disappearing wildlife. Twenty years later, there were 278 species of animals and 298 species of plants listed as endangered in the United States. There are more than 1 million species worldwide known to be endangered. Some scientists believe that there are many more endangered species that have not been and may never be identified.

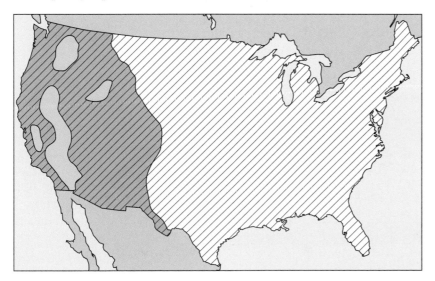

Figure 3.6 The geographical range of the mountain lion has been greatly reduced in the United States because of the destruction of its habitat. The mountain lion's range once included almost the entire country . They now live primarily in the western United States.

Figure 3.7 All the members of a species, such as giraffes, that live in an area are a population (top). All the populations of plants and animals in the area make up a community (center). The ecosystem consists of the community and the abiotic factors in the area (bottom).

mountain lions ranged throughout the continental United States. Much of the mountain lion's habitat has since been developed for farming and other uses for people. As you can see in Figure 3.6, mountain lions are now restricted to a limited range in the Rockies and other western mountains.

Populations and Communities

All the members of a species that live in the same geographic area make up a **population**. For example, all the dandelions in a field are a population. Ecologists sometimes think of a population as a single unit. The ants in an anthill, for example, can be thought of as a single unit. Although individual ants hatch and die, the anthill population remains relatively unchanged. To study the effect of a factor on ants, a researcher would probably study a population rather than an individual ant.

Populations do not live alone in their environments. In any region, many different populations share the same living space, although each one uses different aspects of the environment. Populations interact with one another in a variety of ways. *All the different populations that live and interact in the same area make up a* **community**. Communities are often referred to by their characteristic vegetation, such as the grassland community shown in Figure 3.7 (center).

Ecosystems

An **ecosystem** *includes all the communities in an area, as well as the abiotic factors in the environment.* Ecosystems therefore include the water, soil, and atmosphere in an area, as well as the energy that passes through it.

A healthy ecosystem includes a wide variety of species in its community. *The variety of species in an ecosystem is known as* **biodiversity**. If enough of a particular type of habitat is destroyed, the species that live in the habitat can die out completely, or become extinct. When species become extinct, biodiversity and stability of an ecosystem are reduced.

SECTION REVIEW

1. What factors are included in an ecosystem?
2. What do you think is the geographical range for humans?
3. **Apply** Some ancient cultures, such as the societies that live in rain forests, are shrinking as a result of the destruction of their habitats. Do you think human societies should be protected, as are endangered species of plants and animals? Explain your answer.

CHAPTER **3** REVIEW

KEY TERMS

tectonic plate 3.1   territory 3.2   habitat 3.3   ecosystem 3.3
weathering 3.1   dormant 3.2   geographical range 3.3   biodiversity 3.3
erosion 3.1   hibernation 3.2   population 3.3
nutrients 3.2   species 3.3   community 3.3

CHAPTER SUMMARY

3.1 All three layers of the biosphere have been changing since Earth formed. Erosion and the movement of tectonic plates cause changes in the lithosphere. Ice ages and El Niños are examples of cyclical changes in the hydrosphere. Changes in the atmosphere have resulted from organic and volcanic activities.

3.2 Organisms obtain what they need to live

from their environments. These needs include water, energy, living space, and a suitable climate.

3.3 Organisms of the same type make up a species. Members of a species in a given area make up a population. All the populations in an area are a community. An ecosystem includes all the communities and abiotic factors in an area.

MULTIPLE CHOICE

Choose the letter of the word or phrase that best completes each statement.

1. Glaciers, weather, and water shape Earth by (a) tectonics; (b) erosion; (c) El Niño; (d) hibernation.
2. The most recent ice age ended about (a) 10 000 years ago; (b) 100 000 years ago; (c) 1 million years ago; (d) 10 million years ago.
3. The decline in the anchovy industry of Peru is blamed on (a) pollution; (b) dormancy; (c) El Niño; (d) economics.
4. Almost all the energy used by living things comes from (a) plants; (b) animals; (c) Earth; (d) the sun.

5. Hibernation enables an animal to save (a) energy; (b) space; (c) time; (d) range.
6. The type of environment that is suitable for a certain species is its (a) geographical range; (b) habitat; (c) population; (d) community.
7. All the members of a species that live in an area make up a(n) (a) community; (b) habitat; (c) ecosystem; (d) population.
8. A stable ecosystem includes (a) one type of organism; (b) two types of organisms; (c) at least one type of plant and one type of animal; (d) a wide variety of organisms.
9. Habitat destruction can result in a loss of (a) species; (b) air; (c) energy; (d) land.

WORD COMPARISONS

Write the letter of the second word pair that best matches the first pair.

1. Territory: geographical range as (a) time: space; (b) home: job; (c) yard: neighborhood; (d) land: water.
2. Habitat: environment as (a) population: community; (b) ecosystem: community; (c) ecosystem: population.

3. Hibernation: animals as (a) erosion: land; (b) dormancy: plants; (c) volcanoes: gases; (d) habitat: geographical range.
4. Sun: plants as (a) plants: animals; (b) water: fish; (c) land: soil; (d) animals: food.
5. Ant: anthill as (a) population: species; (b) individual: population; (c) community: neighborhood; (d) population: ecosystem.

CHAPTER 3 REVIEW

CONCEPT REVIEW

Write a complete response to each of the following.

1. Describe the processes that cause change to take place in the lithosphere.
2. List four factors that currently affect Earth's atmosphere. Identify two factors that are caused by humans, and two that are not.
3. What do organisms obtain from the food they eat?
4. Distinguish between territory and geographical range.
5. Why is the geographical range of the mountain lion much smaller than it used to be?

THINK CRITICALLY

1. Explain how glaciers are involved in changes in the lithosphere, the hydrosphere, and the atmosphere.
2. Why are animals that eat other animals dependent on energy from the sun?
3. The size of an animal's territory depends more on the type of food the animal eats than on the size of the animal. Why?
4. Sometimes all the members of a species make up a single population. Sometimes a species is made up of many populations. What might be the difference between the habitats of the two species? Which species do you think is in greater danger of becoming extinct? Explain your answer.
5. The photograph on page 34 shows fossils of animals called crinoids that thrived in shallow seas 350 million years ago. These fossils were found in limestone in the central plains of North America. What changes in the biosphere can be deduced from these fossils?

Computer Activity Tropical rain forests are a type of habitat that is being destroyed in many parts of the world. The table below shows the total area of rain forest (in thousands of hectares) in selected nations, and the rate at which the rain forests are disappearing. Use a graphing program to construct bar graphs comparing the size of the forests in 1990 and the expected size in the year 2000.

Nation	Rainforest Area in 1990	Percentage Lost Each Year
Brazil	357 480	2.2
India	36 540	4.1
Ivory Coast	4458	6.5

WRITE FOR UNDERSTANDING

Use the title of each section of the chapter to create an outline of the chapter's main ideas. Under each title, write a few sentences that summarize the topic.

PORTFOLIO

1. What was your neighborhood like before it was inhabited by humans, and how has it changed? Research the types of wildlife that are native to your area, including plants and animals. Are any extinct or endangered? Prepare a presentation comparing the former habitat and that of the present.
2. How do different types of animals mark and defend their territories? Investigate the behavior of a territorial species of frog, mammal, and bird and compare their territorial activities.

GRAPHIC ANALYSIS

Use Figure 3.1 to answer the following.

1. In which direction is the North American plate moving?
2. On how many plates does the continent of South America lie?
3. Why are there more earthquakes on the west coast of the United States than anywhere else in the country?
4. In 1 million years, would you expect the continents of North America and Asia to be closer together or farther apart?

ACTIVITY 3.2

PROBLEM
What happens when a glacier moves over Earth's surface?

MATERIALS (per group)
- rocks, sand, gravel
- metal pie tin
- flat piece of wood (at least 20 cm by 40 cm)
- marker

HYPOTHESIS
Write a hypothesis that relates to the problem.

PROCEDURE
1. Use the marker to write your group's name on the bottom of a pie tin. Put rocks, sand, and gravel in the pie tin, slightly higher than the top of the sides of the tin.
2. Take the pie tin to the freezer. Pour water into the pie tin almost to the top. Some of the rocks should extend above the water level.
3. Put the pie tin in the freezer, and leave it for 24 hours.
4. The next day, examine the appearance of the piece of wood. Record your observations. Scatter small rocks and sand over the surface of the wood.
5. Remove the pie tin from the freezer. Invert the pie tin on one end of the wood. The rock-scattered wood represents Earth's surface; the ice and rock material in the pie tin represents a glacier.
6. Push the glacier in a straight line along Earth's surface to represent glacial advance. Apply moderate downward pressure to imitate the weight of a glacier. Observe what happens to the rocks and the glacier as they come in contact. Record your observations.
7. Rescatter the rocks, and repeat step 6 two more times.
8. Remove all objects from the wood, and note the appearance of the wood's surface. Record your observations and compare the wood to its original condition.

ANALYSIS
1. What happened to objects in the path of the glacier?
2. How was the glacier affected as it moved over Earth's surface? Explain.
3. What happened to the surface of the wood that the glacier passed over?

CONCLUSION
1. How do glaciers affect the surface of Earth?
2. An *erratic* is a huge boulder whose composition is inconsistent with the rocks in the surrounding area. Based on what you have observed in this activity, write a hypothesis to explain the existence of erratics.

Everglades

Protecting the Everglades

If you look at a map of Florida, you will see a region, called the Everglades, that occupies much of the southern portion of the state. The Everglades region is a wetland area that contains many endangered species of plants and animals. These species live in water that is low in nutrients such as phosphorus. When phosphorus levels rise too high, the native plants begin to die off and are replaced by algae and plants that can tolerate the high nutrient levels.

In the past few decades, more and more land around the Everglades has been given over to agriculture. Phosphorus-containing fertilizers used in these areas are carried yearly by stormwater runoff into the Everglades, threatening the entire south Florida ecosystem.

An experimental project called the Everglades Nutrient Removal (ENR) Project was put into effect to help turn the situation around.

The ENR Project uses a system of pumps, canals, and levees to divert phosphorus-rich agricultural water away from the Everglades and into constructed wetlands. The constructed wetlands contain plantings of various combinations of native plant species such as saw grass, arrowhead, and maidencane. As the diverted water flows through the constructed wetlands, the plants in the wetlands remove excess phosphorus.

Start-up operations have been successful. It is hoped that the project will serve as a model for similar systems that will help restore and protect the crucially important Everglades region as a whole.

Checkpoint

1. How does the use of constructed wetlands help protect the environment in the Everglades?

2. Why is the destruction of organisms sensitive to phosphorus a problem, even though such organisms are replaced by others that can thrive in a phosphorus-rich environment?

The Everglades National Park is a wetlands area that contains a large number of endangered plant and animal species.

Politicians

A planned project must have public support and respond to the needs of the local community. Politicians bring the voice of the people they represent into the decision-making process. Much of the job of environmental planners requires negotiating. Politicians are also professional negotiators. They must understand all aspects of a project, including its environmental impacts.

Government Planners ▶

Federal, state, and local governments employ environmental planners. Federal planners design air, water, and waste-management programs, as well as military and other federal-property development projects.

State governments employ planners to help set land-use policy and manage natural resources. Local government agencies develop zoning maps that show where and how the land may be used. They also undertake local development projects.

Companies and Consulting Firms ▲

Private companies, such as those involved with waste management, mining, timber, transportation, and construction, employ environmental planners. Planners help these companies obtain permits and comply with government policies.

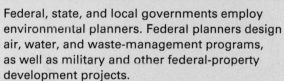

For More Information

American Planning Association (APA)
1776 Massachusetts Avenue, NW
Washington, DC 20036
(202) 872-0611
http://www.planning.org
email: APA@planning.org

Partners for Livable Places
1429 21st Street, NW
Washington, DC 20036
(202) 887-5990

UNIT 2

ECOLOGICAL INTERACTIONS

If you have ever observed a bird building a nest in a tree, or ants marching in a single-file line, then you have witnessed the interactions of organisms. It is not always obvious, but organisms have complex relationships with each other. This photograph illustrates the interaction between a sea anemone and clown fish. In this relationship, the clown fish seeks protection in the tentacles of the sea anemone and feeds on the scraps from the sea anemone's meals. In this unit, you will learn more about these types of interactions.

50

PLANET DIARY.COM

You can find out more about ecological interactions by exploring the following Internet address: http://www.planetdiary.com

Discover It!

Interacting with Your Environment

Although you may not be aware of it, you interact with organisms in your environment every day.

1. List any organisms (plants, animals, fungi, bacteria) that you come into contact with each day.

2. How do these organisms affect you? How do you affect these organisms?

CHAPTER

4

MATTER AND ENERGY IN THE ECOSYSTEM

All ecosystems do two things: they transfer energy and they cycle matter. The energy that powers most ecosystems is sunlight. A few small ecosystems are powered by inorganic molecules. In an ecosystem, energy moves in only one direction: from the sun, its source, into organisms, then into space as heat. All ecosystems require a continuous input of new energy in order to function.

Unlike energy, matter is recycled in the ecosystem. Atoms of carbon, oxygen, and other elements are used again and again by different organisms. The limits of the nutrient cycles often control the function of the ecosystem.

4.1 ROLES OF LIVING THINGS

OBJECTIVES • *Identify* the roles of producers, consumers, and decomposers. • *Explain* the concept of the trophic level.

Different living things play different roles in the flow of energy and the cycling of matter in the ecosystem. Plants get energy from sunlight, while some animals get energy by eating plants. These animals may be eaten by other animals, and some organisms may consume the wastes and dead bodies of animals and plants. The living things that play these roles vary widely among ecosystems, but they all need energy to live.

Producers, Consumers, and Decomposers

The organisms of most ecosystems gather food in three basic ways: as producers, consumers, or decomposers. Energy enters the ecosystem only at the level of the producer. All other organisms depend on the energy first captured by the producers.

Producers *Organisms that make their own food from inorganic molecules and energy are called* **producers.** Plants are the most familiar producers. Almost all producers capture energy from the sun and use it to make food through photosynthesis. The reactions of photosynthesis use the energy from sunlight to combine carbon dioxide and water to produce sugars. Nearly all the energy entering the biosphere comes from the sun through photosynthesis.

Plants are the most important producers in terrestrial ecosystems. In aquatic ecosystems, small photosynthetic protists and bacteria are the most important producers. A few nonphotosynthetic producers do not rely on sunlight for energy. These producers are bacteria that make food by using energy stored in inorganic molecules. These bacteria often live in harsh environments such as hot springs and near thermal vents on the ocean floor.

Consumers *Organisms that cannot make their own food are called* **consumers.** All animals are consumers, as are fungi and many protists and bacteria. Consumers obtain energy by eating other organisms. There are four basic kinds of consumers.

Organisms that eat only plants are called *herbivores* (ER-bih-vors). Because herbivores only eat producers, scientists call them primary consumers. Many insects and birds are herbivores, as are grazing animals such as cows, buffalo, and antelope. The bodies of herbivores are adapted to gathering, grinding, and digesting plants or other producers.

Carnivores (KAR-nih-vors) capture and eat herbivores or other carnivores. Carnivores that eat primary consumers are called secondary consumers, and those that eat other carnivores are called

Figure 4.1 Plants are the primary producers in most land ecosystems (top). Diatoms are important producers in the oceans (bottom).

tertiary consumers. Lions are carnivores, as are snakes, hawks, and spiders. The bodies of carnivores are adapted to hunting, capturing, and eating prey.

Some consumers, including human beings, are *omnivores* (OM-nih-VORS), eating both producers and consumers. Omnivores act as primary, secondary, or tertiary consumers depending on what they eat. A person who eats a potato acts as a primary consumer. If the same person eats a hamburger, however, the person acts as a secondary consumer. Animals such as bears and chimpanzees are also omnivores.

Scavengers usually do not hunt living prey, but instead feed on the bodies of dead organisms. They may eat dead plants or feed on the bodies of herbivores, carnivores, or anything else they find. Like omnivores, scavengers act as secondary, tertiary, or higher consumers depending on what they eat. Vultures and hyenas are scavengers, as are many insects. Scavengers start the process by which nutrients from dead bodies are returned to the environment.

Decomposers *Bacteria and fungi that consume the bodies of dead organisms and other organic wastes are called* **decomposers.** They consume a variety of dead organic matter, from the fallen leaves of a tree to the bodies of herbivores and carnivores. Bacteria and fungi also break down the organic matter in animal waste. Decomposers are crucial to the ecosystem because they recycle nutrients from organisms back into the environment. Without decomposers, the producers in an ecosystem would quickly run out of nutrients.

Decomposers complete the cycle of matter in the ecosystem. They do this by converting the organic matter in organisms back into a simple form. These nutrients are returned to the soil, where plants can use them as raw materials for building new organic material. As the plants use the nutrients to grow, the cycle of matter through the ecosystem begins again.

Figure 4.2 The elk (left) is an herbivore. The wolf (center) is a carnivore, and the bear (right) is an omnivore.

Field Activity

Explore the community around your school building in groups of two or three. One person should make a list of the organisms you see.

1. Return to the classroom, and classify each of the organisms on your list.

2. Make a table with these headings: Producers, Primary Consumers, Secondary Consumers, Decomposers.

3. Place each of the organisms you observed in one of these categories.

Trophic Levels

Scientists call the different feeding levels of organisms in an ecosystem trophic levels, from the root *troph,* meaning "to feed or nourish." *A* **trophic** (TROH-fik) **level** *is a layer in the structure of feeding relationships in an ecosystem.* Producers make up the first trophic level, and consumers make up several more trophic levels. The trophic level made up of producers is usually larger than the combined consumer trophic levels.

Producers make up the first and largest trophic level in all ecosystems. Because they make their own food, producers are called *autotrophs* (AHT-oh-TROHFS). Autotrophs are the sole point of entry for new energy into the ecosystem.

Consumers form the second and higher trophic levels in the ecosystem. Because they cannot produce their own food, and so must obtain nourishment by eating other organisms, consumers are called *heterotrophs.* Primary consumers that eat producers form the second trophic level, and secondary consumers form the third trophic level. Omnivores, scavengers, and decomposers feed at all trophic levels above the first level. Most ecosystems have three, four, or five trophic levels. Each trophic level depends on the levels below it.

SECTION REVIEW

1. List the different groups of organisms in an ecosystem, and explain how each type gathers food.
2. How do autotrophs and heterotrophs differ?
3. **Infer** In most ecosystems, the first trophic level contains more organisms than the second trophic level. Can you suggest a reason that explains this pattern?

4.2 ECOSYSTEM STRUCTURE

OBJECTIVES • **Describe** *food chains and food webs.* • **Examine** *how ecosystem structure is related to population changes and the transfer of pollutants.*

Producers in the first trophic level produce complex organic molecules that consumers in the second trophic level use to grow and reproduce. Consumers in the third trophic level rely on the second trophic level. The interactions between trophic levels form a chain that links the organisms in an ecosystem.

Food Chains and Food Webs

A series of different organisms that transfer food between the trophic levels of an ecosystem is called a **food chain.** All food chains begin with producers, which are usually plants in land ecosystems. The food chain continues to herbivores at the next trophic level, followed by one or more levels of carnivores. All organisms are consumed by decomposers. An example of a food chain is shown in Figure 4.4.

Few ecosystems are simple enough to portray as single food chains. Most consumers feed on more than one type of food, and some consumers feed at more than one trophic level. *A* **food web** *is a network of food chains representing the feeding relationships among the organisms in an ecosystem.* A food web includes all the food chains in an ecosystem. An example of a simple food web is shown in Figure 4.5. This web does not show decomposers, which feed at all trophic levels.

The interactions of the food web link the organisms in an ecosystem. Changes in the population of one organism can affect many other populations. This kind of interaction is often seen when an important consumer is removed from an ecosystem's food web.

Figure 4.4 This food chain is taken from the food web in Figure 4.5. The arrows show the direction in which energy is transferred through the ecosystem.

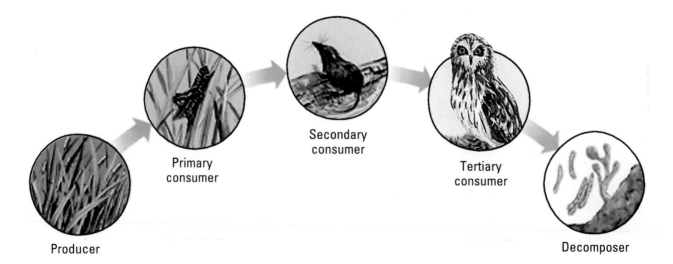

Producer

Primary consumer

Secondary consumer

Tertiary consumer

Decomposer

Figure 4.5 In this simplified food web for a tidal marsh in San Francisco Bay, which organisms are the producers? The food web does not show decomposers.

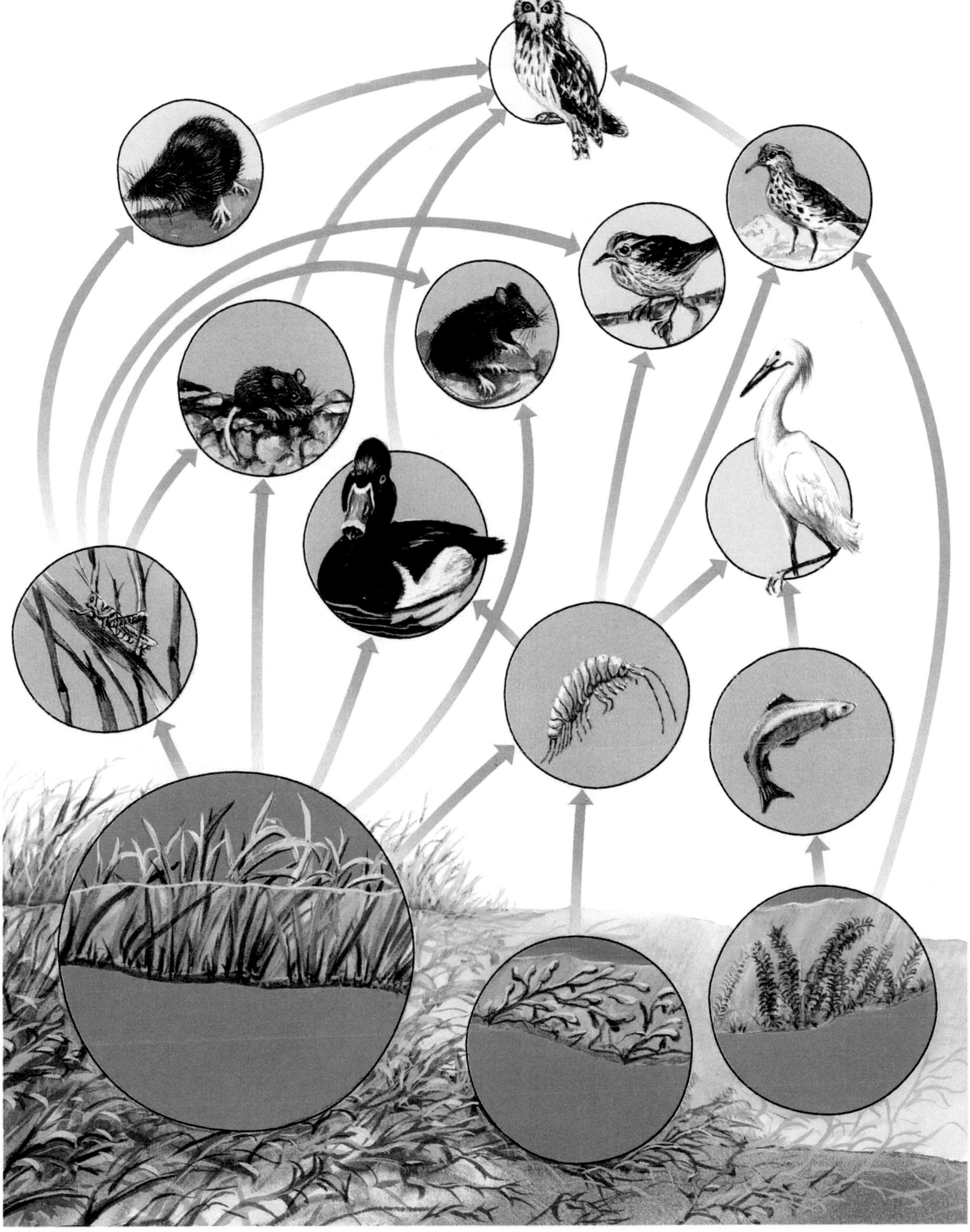

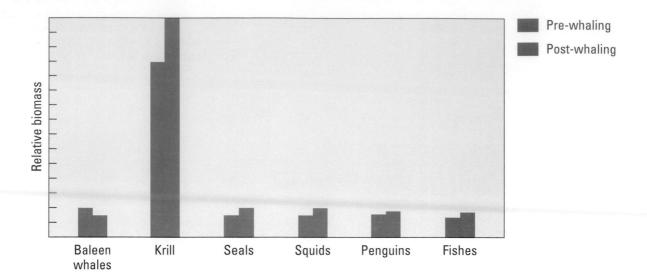

Figure 4.6 This figure compares the biomass of several marine animals before and after a period of whaling. After whaling reduced the whale population, the population of krill increased. In turn, populations of seals, squids, penguins, and fishes that fed directly or indirectly on krill also increased.

The waters around Antarctica support a productive ecosystem based on the abundance of microscopic algae, the primary producers. The primary consumers in the Antarctic food web are small, shrimplike crustaceans called krill. Krill is a food source for many higher-level consumers, including fish, penguins, seals, and large baleen whales. When commercial whaling decreased the number of baleen whales around Antarctica, the krill population grew much larger because the whales were no longer there to consume it.

The increase in the krill population sent ripples through the food web. The populations of many animals that feed on krill increased. As you can see in Figure 4.6, seals, squids, and penguins became more abundant. The example of whales and krill shows how changes in one population can have an impact on an entire food web.

Diversity and Stability

The number of links in the food web varies from one ecosystem to another. Compare the two diagrams of food webs in Figure 4.7. Notice that the one on the right has more trophic levels and more interconnections between species. Some ecologists think that a food web with more diversity is more stable than one with fewer species. A stable food web can better withstand the loss of one species than a simpler food web can. Such stability might help an ecosystem affected by natural or human-caused disasters recover faster.

A deciduous forest is an example of a stable ecosystem that has a food web with many links. A small disturbance has a small effect in a deciduous forest. The forest recovers quickly. A tundra food web, however, has fewer links. A small disturbance in the tundra can have longer-lasting effects.

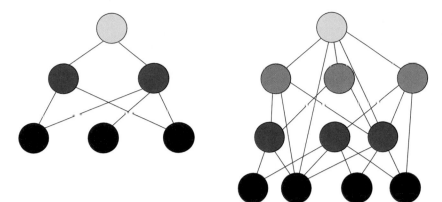

Figure 4.7 These food webs represent two ecosystems. Some ecologists think that webs with many connections are more stable than those with fewer connections.

Biological Magnification

The effects of pollution caused by humans can be magnified in a food web. Recall that a consumer such as an eagle eats organisms from lower trophic levels, such as fish. An eagle will eat many fish in its lifetime. Each fish will also eat many insects. What do you think would happen to the eagle if the insects were contaminated with a pollutant?

The pollutant DDT was actually passed through a food web in this way. DDT, a pesticide, was sprayed on crops to kill insects. Some of the DDT was washed from farmland into streams and rivers by rain. The DDT flowed into lakes and was taken in by the producers in the lake food web. These producers took in small amounts of DDT. But as the producers were eaten by primary consumers, the DDT became concentrated in the bodies of the consumers. At every level in the food web, the DDT was concentrated again because the DDT is ingested but not excreted. As the highest-level consumers, bald eagles had very high concentrations of DDT in their bodies. The DDT caused problems in reproduction, and the population of bald eagles decreased sharply.

The increasing concentration of a pollutant in organisms at higher trophic levels in a food web is called **biological magnification.** Many pollutants can be concentrated in this way, especially metals such as mercury. Biological magnification shows how pollutants taken in by a few organisms can affect the whole food web.

Dateline 1972

The United States bans the pesticide DDT. In the early 1970s, fewer than 3000 bald eagles remained in the lower 48 states. Since the banning of DDT, the bald eagle population has rebounded, growing to 12 000 in 1991. Scientists think that the DDT ban and captive breeding programs have been responsible for the bald eagle's success.

SECTION REVIEW

1. What are food chains and food webs, and how are they related?
2. Explain the process of biological magnification.
3. **Predict** Draw a diagram of a simple food chain containing grass, mice, snakes, and decomposing bacteria. What might happen to the populations of grass, mice, and snakes if a cat entered the chain? The cat feeds on mice and snakes. Redraw the food chain as a food web, and include the cat.

4.3 ENERGY IN THE ECOSYSTEM

OBJECTIVES • *Investigate* the movement of energy through an ecosystem. • *Define* ecological pyramid, and *explain* its relationship to energy in an ecosystem.

Energy from the sun enters an ecosystem when producers use the energy to make organic matter through photosynthesis. Consumers take in this energy when they eat producers or other consumers. But there is a limit to the amount of energy that producers can absorb and transfer to the food web. The limited amount of energy available affects the structure and function of the food web.

Energy and Food

Energy from the sun travels to Earth in the form of waves. Some of this energy is immediately reflected back into space and some is absorbed by Earth's surface and atmosphere. Plants receive less than one percent of the energy that reaches Earth from the sun. Of this energy, less than 30 percent is stored in the form of organic matter made during photosynthesis. Although this may sound like very little energy, it actually is not. The sun gives off so much energy that even this small percent gives plants enough energy to make about 170 billion tons of organic matter each year.

The total amount of organic matter present in a trophic level is called **biomass** (BY-oh-MASS). Biomass is potentially food for the next trophic level. Because of this, scientists follow the transfer of energy from one trophic level to the next by measuring biomass.

Energy in the form of biomass is transferred through the ecosystem as one trophic level feeds on another. However, only part of the energy transferred to one trophic level gets passed on to the next level. This is because the organisms at each level use some of the energy from the biomass they consume. This energy is used for motion, generating heat, and other life processes. Only energy that is used to make biomass is available to the next trophic level. Figure 4.8 diagrams the path of energy from the producer level to the secondary consumer level.

The loss of energy from one trophic level to the next explains why there is a limit to the number of trophic levels an ecosystem can support. Owls, for example, are not preyed upon by a still higher level of carnivores. The biomass, or available energy, of the owl population is not sufficient to support another trophic level.

LINK

Astronomy

About 33 percent of the solar energy reaching Earth is reflected back into space by clouds and by Earth's surface. Another 20 percent turns water into water vapor. This water vapor forms clouds and precipitation. The sun powers the movement of water over Earth, as well as the organisms living on its surface.

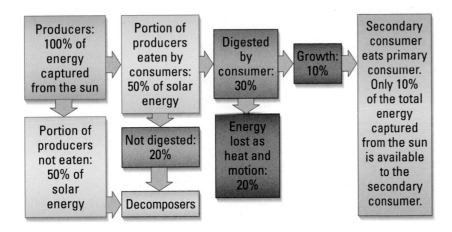

| Producers: 100% of energy captured from the sun | → | Portion of producers eaten by consumers: 50% of solar energy | → | Digested by consumer: 30% | → | Growth: 10% | → | Secondary consumer eats primary consumer. Only 10% of the total energy captured from the sun is available to the secondary consumer. |

Portion of producers not eaten: 50% of solar energy

Not digested: 20%

Energy lost as heat and motion: 20%

Decomposers

Figure 4.8 Most of the energy in one trophic level is lost before reaching the next trophic level.

Ecological Pyramids

Ecologists represent the relative amounts of energy in an ecosystem in an ecological pyramid. *An* **ecological pyramid** *is a diagram that shows the relative amounts of energy in different trophic levels in an ecosystem.* The pyramid is divided into sections, each section representing one trophic level. An ecological pyramid can show energy, biomass, or the number of organisms in a food web.

The ecological pyramid in Figure 4.9 is an energy pyramid. The base of the pyramid represents the first trophic level of the ecosystem, the producers. The second level of the pyramid represents the second trophic level, the primary consumers. Notice that, in this example, only about 10 percent of the energy in the first trophic level is present in the second level. This pattern is repeated between the second and third levels. How much of the energy present in the producers appears in the third trophic level?

Humans are omnivores and can eat both producers and consumers. Some people think that humans should eat only producers, so that the world's food supply will stretch farther.

1. What is the reasoning behind this opinion?

2. Give an example to support your answer.

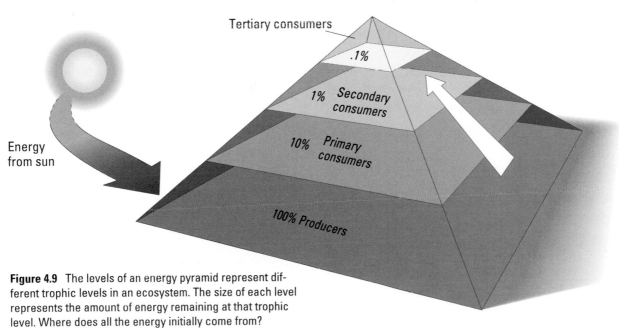

Tertiary consumers

.1%

1% Secondary consumers

10% Primary consumers

100% Producers

Energy from sun

Figure 4.9 The levels of an energy pyramid represent different trophic levels in an ecosystem. The size of each level represents the amount of energy remaining at that trophic level. Where does all the energy initially come from?

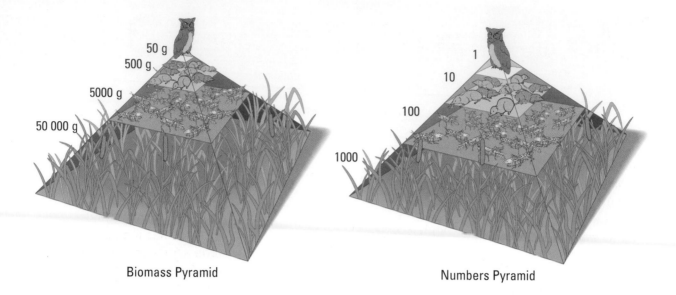

50 g
500 g
5000 g
50 000 g

Biomass Pyramid

1
10
100
1000

Numbers Pyramid

Figure 4.10 The amount of biomass decreases at higher trophic levels. The number of organisms may also decrease at higher trophic levels.

Biomass pyramids show the mass of organic matter at each trophic level. The combined mass of all producers forms the base of the pyramid, while the masses of consumers form the higher levels. Biomass pyramids often follow the same pattern as that of energy pyramids, with the biomass in one level being less than the level beneath it.

The number of organisms may be different at each trophic level. In the numbers pyramid in Figure 4.10, there are 1000 plants and one owl. This is a common pattern, but there are exceptions. For example, in a forest, there are fewer producers than consumers. One tree has a large amount of biomass and energy, but it is only one organism. The insects that live in the tree are numerous, but have less biomass and energy.

Energy moves between trophic levels in the form of food. But food also contains matter. Carbon, hydrogen, nitrogen, and oxygen are the main elements in food, although many others are present in small amounts. Molecules composed of these elements store the energy that moves from one trophic level to another. Without even one of these important elements, food cannot be produced. The growth of producers in most ecosystems is usually limited by the lack of one or more of these elements, not by the amount of energy coming from the sun.

SECTION REVIEW

1. About how much of the energy that appears in one trophic level will appear in the next?
2. What is an ecological pyramid?
3. **Infer** How is energy lost between trophic levels? Where does this energy ultimately go?

The Comeback of the Sea Otter

A food web can support a wondrous assortment of organisms. In the kelp forests along the California coast, an intricate food web includes more than 800 marine species. One of the most interesting of these species is the lively and playful sea otter. The otter rarely, if ever, comes ashore. Instead, it uses floating beds of kelp as resting places and nests on which to bear and raise its young. Otters also use the beds as hunting grounds, feeding on sea urchins, which eat the kelp.

The soft, dense fur of the sea otter has always been highly prized. The animal began to be hunted on a large scale by Russians in the 1740s. The hunting came under control in 1799, with the establishment of conservation practices. Unregulated killing began again in 1867, and the animal's population plummeted. The entire kelp food web was affected because the removal of otters caused a surge in the population of their main prey, the sea urchin. The urchins devoured large areas of the kelp forests, nearly destroying the habitats for many species.

The sea otter's increasing rarity merely served to raise the value of its fur. In

the early twentieth century, a single pelt of good quality could fetch a thousand dollars—an enormous quantity at that time—and the hunting became even more ruthless. By 1911, the sea otter had reached the very brink of extinction. In that year, a hunting ban was established by a treaty among the United States, Great Britain, Russia, and Japan.

By that point, however, only about a thousand of the animals survived, mostly in the waters off Alaska. The variety of sea otter that had lived along the California coast was thought to be extinct. Fortunately, a group of about one hundred had in fact survived near Monterey.

Numbers slowly began to rebound, in a process aided by passage of the Marine Mammal Protection Act of 1972. There are now thought to be roughly two thousand sea otters, and their range has increased to include a 300-km stretch of central California coast. Occasionally, otters are sighted as far south as northern Baja California, Mexico.

The hunting ban has not only saved the sea otter from extinction, but has also helped to restore the original balance of producers and consumers in the region. As a result, the amazing world of the kelp forest has been restored, and its rich populations of organisms have begun to flourish again.

Checkpoint

1. Why did the decline of the sea otter population affect so many other species?
2. Do you think limited hunting of sea otters should be permitted if their populations rebound to a high level? Explain.

63

4.4 CYCLES OF MATTER

OBJECTIVES • *Describe* the chemical composition of the human body.
• *Explain* the water cycle, the carbon cycle, and the nitrogen cycle.

Table 4.1
Elements of the Human Body

Element	Percent Weight of Human Body
Oxygen	65.0
Carbon	18.5
Hydrogen	9.5
Nitrogen	3.5
Calcium	1.5
Phosphorus	1.0
Potassium	0.4
Sulfur	0.3
Chlorine	0.2
Sodium	0.2
Magnesium	0.10
Trace Elements	Less than 0.01

About 96 percent of your body is made up of just four elements: oxygen, carbon, hydrogen, and nitrogen. About 78 percent of Earth's atmosphere is nitrogen, and 21 percent is oxygen. Carbon is also present in the atmosphere, as well as in rocks and in biomass. Elements in the human body are shown in Table 4.1.

Even though these elements are common on Earth, organisms cannot always use them. The elements must be in a chemical form that cells can use, and getting an element in a usable form may not be a simple process. Nitrogen is a good example. Although nitrogen makes up most of Earth's atmosphere, very little nitrogen exists in a form that plants can use. Thus, a scarcity of usable nitrogen limits plant growth in many ecosystems. The absence of an element such as potassium can also limit growth in an ecosystem.

Unlike energy, elements move within an ecosystem in cycles. The amount of matter that enters and leaves each cycle is relatively small. Matter cycles repeatedly move elements back and forth between organisms and the environment.

The Water Cycle

Water moves between the ocean, the atmosphere, and the land. Living things also take part in this cycle, which is shown in Figure 4.11. Water enters the atmosphere through the process of evaporation, as shown by the upward arrows. **Evaporation** (eh-VAP-uh-RAY-shun) *is the movement of water into the atmosphere as it changes from a liquid to a gas.* Water evaporates from bodies of water and moist areas of land.

Water can also enter the atmosphere through a process called transpiration. **Transpiration** (TRANS-peh-RAY-shun) *is the evaporation of water from the leaves of plants.* Transpiration plays an important part in plant circulation. In ecosystems such as tropical rain forests, the amount of water entering the atmosphere through plants can be large enough to affect the climate in the surrounding area.

Water that evaporates from Earth's surface rises in columns of air warmed by sunlight. The water vapor cools as it rises and condenses into tiny droplets, forming clouds. A water molecule may remain in the atmosphere for about two weeks. Water returns to Earth's surface in the form of precipitation—rain, snow, sleet, or hail. Water may return to Earth far from where it evaporated. When rain falls on the land, some of the water flows on the surface and into streams, rivers, lakes, and oceans. From there it may once again evaporate.

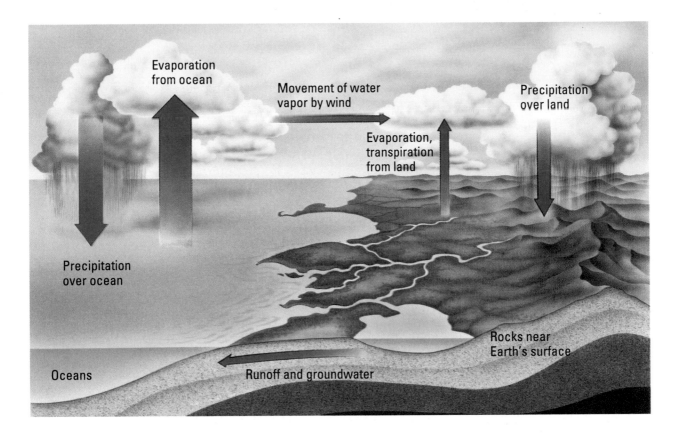

Some of the rain that falls on land soaks into the ground and becomes groundwater. Groundwater enters plants through the roots, and enters the atmosphere through the leaves. Some paths within the water cycle take longer to complete than others. Scientists estimate that it can take a water molecule that falls on land 4000 years to complete the cycle.

Figure 4.11 In this diagram of the water cycle, the amount of moving water is represented by the width of the arrows. Most of Earth's surface water is stored in the oceans.

The Carbon Cycle

Scientists think that the atmosphere of the very young Earth was much like the atmosphere of Mars and Venus today, about 95 percent carbon dioxide (CO_2). Living things have played an important role in the formation of Earth's atmosphere. The growth of photosynthetic organisms removed some CO_2 from the atmosphere and added oxygen. The amount of CO_2 in the atmosphere fell while the amount of oxygen rose. Today, the atmosphere is only 0.04 percent CO_2.

Living things are still the most important part of the carbon cycle. The reactions of photosynthesis and respiration could not occur without carbon. Look at the chemical equations below for photosynthesis and respiration. Notice that each reaction uses the products of the other:

Photosynthesis: $H_2O + CO_2 + energy \longrightarrow C_6H_{12}O_6 + O_2$

Respiration: $C_6H_{12}O_6 + O_2 \longrightarrow CO_2 + H_2O + energy$

Biology

Transpiration helps plants to move water through their tissues. Water evaporating from leaf cells pulls water from the surrounding cells, which in turn pull water from the cells close to them. This pull is relayed down to the roots of the plant. As a result, water moves up the plant stem. An average maple tree on a summer day will lose 200 L of water per hour through transpiration.

Dateline 1750

The Industrial Revolution begins. Coal and other fossil fuels are burned to power the industrial age. In the next 250 years, the amount of carbon dioxide in the atmosphere will increase by over 20 percent from the burning of fossil fuels. Other pollutants cause smog and acid rain.

Plants use CO_2 and sunlight to make sugars and starches during photosynthesis. When these nutrients are consumed by the plant or any another organism, CO_2 and energy are released. The biological reactions in organisms are the main part of the carbon cycle, which is shown in Figure 4.12. The amount of carbon tied up in organic matter at any given time is larger than the amount of carbon in Earth's atmosphere.

Two other important sources of carbon are the ocean and rocks. The ocean holds a very large amount of CO_2 because CO_2 dissolves easily in water. Carbon is also stored in rocks. Substances such as coal, oil, and limestone are formed from the bodies of dead organisms. Because the bodies of these organisms never completely decomposed, some of the carbon in them was never released. This carbon is released as CO_2 when we burn fossil fuels for energy.

The Nitrogen Cycle

The nitrogen cycle is very important to living things. Organisms require nitrogen in order to make amino acids, the building blocks of proteins. Nitrogen gas is common in the atmosphere, but most living things cannot use nitrogen gas in their cells. Organisms need nitrogen in a more chemically reactive form.

Figure 4.12 In this diagram of the carbon cycle, the amount of moving carbon is represented by the width of the arrows. Most of Earth's carbon is stored in rocks near the surface.

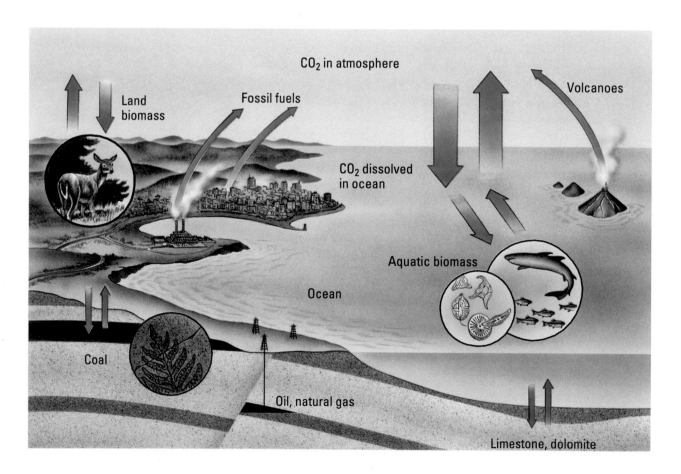

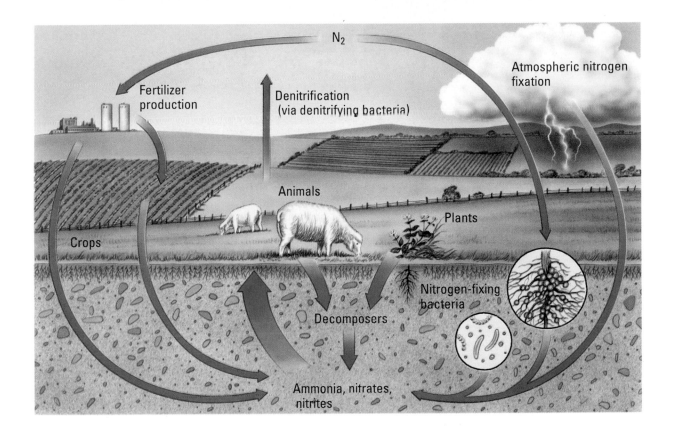

Figure 4.13 Most of the nitrogen in the nitrogen cycle is stored in organic compounds. All nitrogen originally came from the atmosphere.

Certain types of bacteria can use nitrogen from the atmosphere. Such nitrogen-fixing bacteria produce ammonia (NH_3), a form of nitrogen plants can use. Nitrogen-fixing bacteria live both in the soil and in the roots of legumes. **Legumes** (LEG-yooms) *are plants such as peanuts, beans, and clover that have colonies of nitrogen-fixing bacteria in nodules on their roots.* But most ammonia is consumed by other bacteria. These bacteria produce compounds called *nitrites* and *nitrates,* which are compounds containing nitrogen and oxygen.

Nitrate is the most common source of nitrogen for plants, and is now supplied to crop plants by using manufactured chemical fertilizers as well as through bacterial action. Animals get the nitrogen they need from proteins in the food they consume. Decomposers return nitrogen to the soil in the form of ammonia, and the cycle starts again.

SECTION REVIEW

1. What are the four most common elements in the human body?
2. How do transpiration and evaporation differ?
3. **Think Critically** Humans are releasing large amounts of carbon dioxide into the air by burning fossil fuels like coal and oil. What effect might this carbon have on the CO_2 cycle?

Plants and the Water Cycle

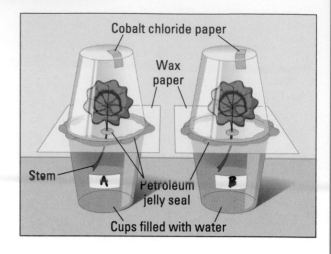

Cobalt chloride paper

Wax paper

Stem

Petroleum jelly seal

Cups filled with water

PROBLEM
What is the role of plants in the water cycle?

MATERIALS
- 4 large clear plastic or glass cups
- 2 15-cm squares of wax paper
- 2 strips of cobalt chloride paper (blue)
- paper clip
- petroleum jelly
- 2 geranium plant leaves with stems
- tape

HYPOTHESIS
Water vapor is released from the surface of leaves and enters the atmosphere.

PROCEDURE

1. Stick a small piece of tape on two of the cups. Label one of them *A* and the other *B*.
2. Fill cups *A* and *B* with water, and apply petroleum jelly to their rims.
3. Straighten the paper clip, and use one end of it to poke a hole in the center of each square of wax paper.
4. Insert a geranium leaf stem through the hole in each wax paper square. Apply petroleum jelly around each stem where it emerges from the wax paper. This makes an airtight seal.
5. Apply a coat of petroleum jelly to both surfaces of one of the leaves.
6. Position the uncoated leaf combination directly over cup *A*, and gently press down on the wax paper around the rims so the wax paper is held in place by the petroleum jelly. The stem should be in the water.
7. Position the coated plant leaf combination directly over cup *B*. As in step 6, gently press down around the rim and be sure the stem is in the water (see the figure).
8. Tape a piece of cobalt chloride paper to the inside of each of the two other cups.

9. Apply petroleum jelly around the rims of these cups.
10. Invert one of these cups over cup *A* and the other over cup *B*. Gently press them together. Do not allow the leaf to touch the cobalt chloride paper.
11. Observe both setups for 10 minutes. Record your observations each minute in a data table, paying particular attention to the color of the cobalt chloride paper.
12. Leave the setups undisturbed for 24 hours and then make your final observations.

ANALYSIS
1. What is the purpose of coating the leaf in setup *B* with petroleum jelly?
2. Which setup is the control?
3. Did the color of either piece of cobalt chloride paper change? What does this indicate?
4. What changes did you observe after 24 hours? Explain.
5. Were you able to confirm the hypothesis?

CONCLUSION
1. How are green plants involved in the water cycle?
2. What is the plant process you observed in this experiment, and how might it affect local climates?

CHAPTER 4 REVIEW

KEY TERMS

producers 4.1
consumers 4.1
decomposers 4.1
trophic level 4.1

food chain 4.2
food web 4.2
biological
   magnification 4.2

biomass 4.3
ecological
   pyramid 4.3
evaporation 4.4

transpiration 4.4
legume 4.4

CHAPTER SUMMARY

4.1 All ecosystems transfer energy and cycle matter. Organisms that make food with energy from sunlight or chemicals are called producers. Organisms that eat other organisms are called consumers. Organisms that break down dead organic matter are called decomposers. Trophic levels are layers in the structure of feeding relations in a food web.

4.2 A food chain is a series of organisms that transfers food between the trophic levels of an ecosystem. A food web includes all the food chains in an ecosystem. Population changes or pollutants that affect one population in a food web may affect other populations in the web.

4.3 The total amount of organic matter present in a trophic level is its biomass. As much as 90 percent of the energy in one trophic level is lost to the environment; about 10 percent appears in the next trophic level. Ecological pyramids represent the amount of energy, biomass, and numbers of organisms in trophic levels.

4.4 Unlike energy, matter moves through the ecosystem in cycles. Water moves between the ocean, the atmosphere, and the land. Carbon moves through the atmosphere, the ocean, rocks, and organisms. Nitrogen is common in the atmosphere but rare in usable forms. Lack of nitrogen limits growth in many ecosystems.

MULTIPLE CHOICE

Choose the letter of the word or phrase that best completes each statement.

1. Organisms that make their own food with sunlight or chemical energy are called (a) producers; (b) consumers; (c) decomposers; (d) scavengers.
2. Organisms in the lowest trophic level of an ecosystem are always (a) herbivores; (b) carnivores; (c) heterotrophs; (d) autotrophs.
3. A network of all of the feeding relationships in an ecosystem is called a(n) (a) food chain; (b) energy chain; (c) food web; (d) energy web.
4. The population that was not affected by the increase in the krill population was (a) clams; (b) seals; (c) penguins; (d) squids.
5. The pesticide that damaged the bald eagle population was (a) nitrates; (b) DDT; (c) arsenic; (d) malathion.
6. The total amount of the organic matter in a trophic level is called the (a) bioload; (b) food load; (c) biomass; (d) food mass.
7. The percentage of energy in one trophic level that appears in the next in the average ecosystem is (a) 10 percent; (b) 20 percent; (c) 30 percent; (d) 40 percent.
8. The element that is not one of the four most common in your body is (a) nitrogen; (b) hydrogen; (c) oxygen; (d) sodium.
9. Transpiration is the evaporation of water from (a) the ocean; (b) leaves; (c) lakes and ponds; (d) rivers.
10. Plants that have nitrogen-fixing bacteria in their roots are called (a) denitrifiers; (b) ammonias; (c) nitrifiers; (d) legumes.

CHAPTER 4 REVIEW

TRUE/FALSE

Write true *if the statement is true. If the statement is false, change the underlined word or phrase to make it true.*

1. <u>Herbivores</u> eat only meat.
2. Decomposers feed at <u>few</u> trophic levels.
3. Some scientists think that a food web with many connections is <u>more</u> stable than one with few connections.
4. Biological magnification <u>decreased</u> the amount of DDT in organisms higher in the food web.
5. The amount of biomass in the first trophic level is <u>larger</u> than the amount in the second trophic level.
6. In most ecosystems, there are more individuals in the trophic level <u>above</u> a given level.
7. <u>Carbon</u> is the most common element in the human body.
8. Nitrogen is returned to the atmosphere by bacteria called <u>denitrifying bacteria</u>.

CONCEPT REVIEW

Write a complete response to each of the following.

1. How do producers and consumers differ in the way they gather food?
2. Explain how the reduction in the baleen whale population affected the populations of other organisms in the Antarctic food web.
3. How much energy is lost between trophic levels in an ecosystem? How is this energy lost?
4. Would the world food supply last longer if people acted as primary consumers or secondary consumers? Explain your reasoning.
5. Explain how nitrogen can make up almost 80 percent of the atmosphere and still limit plant growth in many ecosystems.

THINK CRITICALLY

1. Many places on the ocean floor are so deep that sunlight cannot penetrate. Because there is no sunlight in these places, there can be no photosynthesis. But the deep ocean floor still supports an ecosystem. How is this possible?
2. Do you agree with scientists who think that complex food webs are more stable than simple ones? Use what you know about food webs to answer this question.
3. Some scientists think the climate of Earth is getting warmer. How would warmer temperatures affect the evaporation of water from the ocean?

Computer Activity Use a graphing program to graph the amount of energy present in the trophic levels of a food chain with four members. What percentage of the energy in the first trophic level appears in the fourth trophic level?

WRITE CREATIVELY

Suppose you are a cheetah prowling across the African savanna. What would you see? How many plants, herbivores, and other cheetahs would you see? How is your body adapted to hunting and capturing prey?

PORTFOLIO

1. Make a poster of the food web in your community. Use your list of organisms from the *Do It!* activity on page 55.
2. Many communities suffer from water shortages. Visit a local water company and collect any information they have on water conservation. Read the information, and report to the class on water-saving techniques.

GRAPHIC ANALYSIS

Use Figure 4.12 to answer the following.

1. What human activities form parts of the carbon cycle?
2. How does carbon in organisms leave the carbon cycle?

3. What is the most important source of carbon entering the atmosphere? What are the other sources?

ACTIVITY 4.2

PROBLEM

Do different kinds of decomposers grow better on different types of food?

MATERIALS

- 5 Petri dishes with lids
- blotting paper
- hand lens
- wax pencil
- scissors
- tape
- small amount of each of the following organic materials: bread (one slice), Roquefort cheese, dill pickle, orange wedge, grapes

HYPOTHESIS

Write a hypothesis that pertains to the problem.

PROCEDURE

1. Mark each Petri dish with your group name and the numbers 1 through 5.
2. Line the bottoms of the Petri dishes with moist blotting paper.
3. Moisten (don't soak) the slice of bread. Tear off some pieces of bread, and place them in Petri dish 1.
4. Place some Roquefort cheese in Petri dish 2.
5. Use the scissors to carefully cut the dill pickle to fit inside a Petri dish. Place the pieces in Petri dish 3.
6. Use the scissors to carefully cut the orange wedge to fit inside a Petri dish. Place a few pieces in Petri dish 4.
7. Cut a few grapes in half and place them in Petri dish 5.
8. Expose the uncovered Petri dishes to the air for 24 hours.

9. After 24 hours of exposure, cover the Petri dishes with the lids, tape the lids in place, and store in a cool, dark place. You may stack the dishes to save space.
10. Observe the Petri dishes each day or every other day for 1 to 2 weeks. **Caution:** *Do not remove the lids from the Petri dishes when you make your observations. The dishes may contain potentially harmful organisms.* In a data table, record the following: (a) date of observation, (b) number of Petri dish, (c) appearance of Petri dish contents to the unaided eye, (d) appearance of Petri dish contents using the hand lens.

ANALYSIS

1. How many different kinds of decomposers did you observe? What physical characteristics distinguished one kind of decomposer from another?
2. Did you find that one kind of decomposer can grow on different types of organic material? Describe your evidence.
3. What evidence did you find that organic material was being decomposed?

CONCLUSION

1. Did you find any evidence that different kinds of organisms grow better on one or another kind of food? Explain.
2. Based on your observations, what is the role of decomposers in the food web?
3. How would an ecosystem be different if no decomposers were present?

CHAPTER

5

INTERACTIONS IN THE ECOSYSTEM

An ecosystem is a network of living and nonliving things. Organisms are connected by food webs and by their common needs. All organisms need water, food, and living space. Yet each species has evolved its own way of gathering resources from the environment.

Any discussion of an organism's role in an ecosystem must center on evolution. The principle of evolution ties together biology and the physical world, just as ecology ties together the interactions between living things and their environment. Ecology is the study of how organisms and populations are adapted to their environments. Thus, the study of ecosystems is also the study of evolution.

5.1 HABITATS AND NICHES

OBJECTIVES • **Describe** *the concept of the niche.* • **Examine** *how interactions between a species and its environment define the species' niche.*

Ecosystems can be large places. They may cover many square kilometers and contain many different types of organisms. The environment in one part of an ecosystem is different from the environment in another part. The conditions near a stream may be very different from those on a dry hill above the stream.

The organisms living in each part of this ecosystem differ from each other. Each organism is adapted to the conditions in the part of the environment in which it lives. Recall from Chapter 3 that the place within an ecosystem where an organism lives is called its habitat. The habitat of a rainbow trout, for example, is a stream or river, while the habitat of a buffalo is a field in a grassland. Habitats can be small or large, depending on the size of the organism and how much the organism travels.

Niches

Every organism is adapted to life in its habitat. For example, each organism has special ways of gathering food, reproducing, and avoiding predators. The actions of an organism define its role in the ecosystem. *The role of an organism in the ecosystem is called its* **niche** (NICH). A niche is more than an organism's habitat; it is also what the organism does within its habitat.

A niche includes both biotic and abiotic factors. Some biotic factors that help define a niche are food sources and predators. Each species needs a specific type of food, such as insects or a species of plant. At the same time, most organisms are also hunted by other organisms. Temperature, amount of sunlight and water, and time of day or night are abiotic factors. All the biotic and abiotic factors taken together define the organism's niche.

All members of a species are adapted to the same niche. No two species can share the same niche in the same habitat. Two species can, however, occupy niches that are very similar. For example, the niches of different species of *Anolis* lizards in the tropics vary only in the size of the insects they eat. Lizards with large jaws eat large insects, and those with small jaws eat small insects. The different species can live side by side because they occupy different niches.

If two species try to share the same niche in the same habitat, they will compete for resources. If two lizard species eat the same size of insect, they will compete for the insects of that size in places where they live together. If one lizard species is better at catching the insects, the other species will not get enough food. The second

Figure 5.1 Different species of anoles feed on different sizes of insects.

species will have to move to another area or the population will die out. *The extinction of a population due to direct competition with another species for a resource is called* **competitive exclusion.** Competitive exclusion refers to the extinction of one population in one place, not to the extinction of the whole species.

In many ecosystems, the activity of one species can help define a species' niche. Two species of barnacles living on the coast of Scotland have very similar niches. Both species live on rocks in the surf zone of the ocean shore. One barnacle species is *Chthamalus stellatus* (species A). The other species is *Balanus balanoides* (species B). Look at Figure 5.3 as you read about the habitats and niches of these two organisms.

Species B lives on lower rocks usually covered by water, except during low tide. Species A occurs on higher rocks that are usually exposed to the air. Species B survives only in lower zones because it is vulnerable to drying out. Species A is more resistant to drying out, so it can survive higher up on the rocks.

American scientist J. H. Connell performed an experiment to study how one barnacle species affects the niche of another. He removed all of species B from a small area of the shore, and then observed the effect of the removal. He found that species A began to grow on the lower rocks. Connell hypothesized that species A could live on all parts of the rocky shore, but that species B drove out A wherever B could survive. The A population was limited to the higher rocks by B, even though A could live on all the rocks in the absence of B.

Connell realized that the niche of one species could affect the niche of another. For example, the presence of one species might limit the niche of another, as in the case of the barnacles. Connell called the theoretical niche of an organism its *fundamental niche.* The niche that the organism actually used was called its *realized niche.* Other species are one of many factors that define a species' niche.

Figure 5.2 Both of the barnacle species in J. H. Connell's experiments are shown in this photograph. *Chthamalus* (species A) are the large, ridged barnacles. *Balanus* (species B) are the smaller, smooth barnacles.

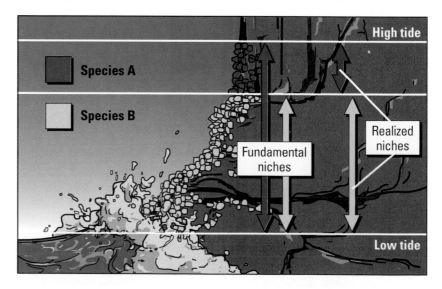

Figure 5.3 The distribution of two species of barnacles on the Scottish coast is shown here. Species A occurs on rocks usually exposed to air, and species B occurs on rocks usually covered by water. The presence of species B keeps species A from spreading downward.

Figure 5.4 This sea star is an example of a keystone predator.

Niche Diversity

Niche diversity, the number of different niches in an ecosystem, is often determined by abiotic factors in the environment. In a marsh, for example, there are many organisms. However, there are few different niches because the physical environment in a marsh is fairly constant. By contrast, in a desert ecosystem, there are fewer organisms but many different niches. Great differences in abiotic factors, such as temperature and moisture in the desert, form many niches occupied by a variety of species.

A **predator** (PRED-ut-or) *is an organism that actively hunts other organisms. The organism that is hunted is the* **prey.** Predators play an important role in increasing niche diversity by decreasing the population size of their prey species. If a predator reduces the population of one species, more resources will become available for another species. The action of the predator, therefore, can create another niche.

American ecologist Robert Paine performed an experiment that showed how predators help to form niches. Paine removed the dominant predator, the sea star, from several tidepools on the coast of Washington state. The number of mussels then increased until the mussels had "outcompeted" many of the other species in the tidepools. Without the sea stars, the number of species living in the tidepools dropped from 15 to 8. *A predator that promotes a great niche diversity in its habitat is called a* **keystone predator.**

LINK
Biology

Predators help maintain diversity in ecosystems in many ways. The Great Barrier Reef is one example. A species of sea star called the crown of thorns lives and feeds on the corals that make up the reef. In the past, the crown of thorns was rare because it was eaten by many species of predatory fish. But fishing by people has removed many of the sea star's predators. The crown of thorns' numbers increased, and they now consume large stretches of the reef every year. The destruction of the reef results in lost habitat for many species, and therefore lower diversity in the ecosystem.

SECTION REVIEW

1. How is a niche different from a habitat?
2. What is competitive exclusion? How is it related to the concept of the niche?
3. **Infer** What might happen to an ecosystem if all the carnivores were removed? Explain your answer.

5.2 EVOLUTION AND ADAPTATION

OBJECTIVES • *Explain* how a species adapts to its niche.
• *Describe* convergent evolution and coevolution, and *relate* each to the concept of niche.

Ecosystems change over time. Mountains rise and erode, rivers change course, and climate factors such as temperature and rainfall may vary dramatically. A change in the environment will affect the niches of the organisms in that environment. A species may occupy a niche successfully, but if that niche disappears the species may become extinct. Changes in the environment affect the evolution of populations.

Evolution (EV-uh-LOO-shun) *is a change in the characteristics of a population of organisms over time.* Evolution happens when some individuals have genetic variations that allow them to produce more offspring than other members of the population. Over time, these changes, or adaptations, will be passed from generation to generation. More individuals in the population will have these traits with each generation. This natural selection for advantageous traits eventually changes the whole population.

Evolving in a Niche

Evolution causes populations of organisms to be adapted to specific niches in the environment. This reduces competition with other species. Figure 5.5 shows five species of birds called warblers. The warblers live in forests of the northeastern United States. All five species

Figure 5.5 These five warbler species have different niches because they feed in different parts of the spruce tree.

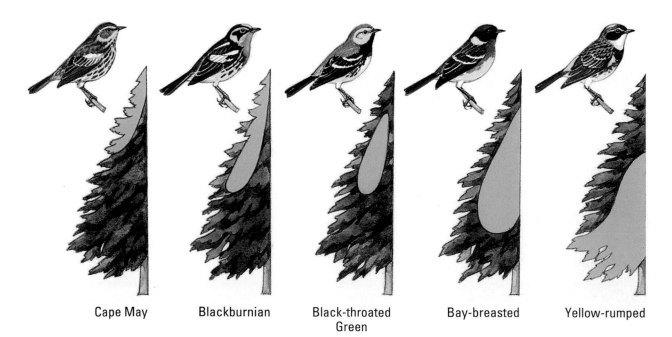

| Cape May | Blackburnian | Black-throated Green | Bay-breasted | Yellow-rumped |

feed on insects in the branches of spruce trees. Although the five species seem to compete with each other for food, each species looks for food in a slightly different part of the tree. The niches overlap a little, but are different enough to allow all five species to coexist.

Ecologists call an organism with a small niche a *specialized species*. The koala is another example of a specialized species. It feeds only on the leaves of eucalyptus trees. Specialized species are often vulnerable to extinction; a single environmental change can eliminate their niche. Koalas would quickly become extinct if eucalyptus were no longer able to grow in their habitat.

Ecologists call a species with a wide niche a *generalized species*. A generalized species has several alternate food sources and is more likely to survive in a changing environment. Generalized species such as mice and cockroaches survive well in areas altered by human activity because they can easily change their behaviors to fit new environmental conditions.

Convergent Evolution

Similar ecosystems often have similar niches, providing similar opportunities for different organisms. Environmental pressures may then select for similar adaptations in different organisms. If niches in two ecosystems are similar, the organisms that evolve there may also look alike.

The independent development of similar adaptations in two species with similar niches is called **convergent evolution.** The wings of birds and bats are an example of convergent evolution. Birds and mammals are different types of animals, and the bird and bat evolved flight independently. However, both species evolved wings as an adaptation to a niche that required flying through the air.

Another example of convergent evolution is shown in Figure 5.6. Both of these animals evolved from ancestors that lived on land. The dolphin is a mammal, while the other animal, an ichthyosaur (IK-thee-oh-SOR), is an extinct reptile from the Jurassic period. The animals share adaptations to life in water, such as fins.

Figure 5.6 The dolphin and the ichthyosaur share many adaptations to living in the water, such as a streamlined shape. What other adaptations do the two animals share?

Coevolution

Other species are an important part of an organism's environment. Recall that a keystone predator can make an ecosystem more diverse. Evolution results in species whose niches are different enough to limit competition in the ecosystem. Sometimes the interaction between species is even more complex. Organisms that live closely together and interact may have evolutionary responses to one another. *Species that interact closely may become adapted to one another through a process called* **coevolution** (KOH-EV-uh-LOO-shun).

Coevolution can occur as a result of feeding relationships. Plants and caterpillars are an example of such coevolution. Many

Figure 5.7 The acacia tree and the ants that live on it have coevolved. Neither species can survive without the other.

plants have poisonous chemicals that prevent insects from eating them. Some caterpillars have the ability to resist these poisons. They can feed on plants that other insects cannot eat. These caterpillars often become specialized and feed only on the poisonous plants. The plant and caterpillar have coevolved: As the plant adapted by producing poisonous chemicals, the caterpillar adapted by resisting them.

Species can also have adaptations that exist to their mutual benefit. Several species of acacia tree that grow in Central and South America have coevolved with insects. These trees have large, hollow thorns that provide a protected nesting site for stinging ants. The ants are totally dependent on the acacia tree. They can nest nowhere else, and the acacia is their only source of food.

The acacia tree also benefits from the ant colony it supports. The ants attack any animal landing on the tree, killing it or driving it away. The ants also clear away the vegetation surrounding the tree, which helps the tree get the sunlight it needs. Experiments have shown that the tree cannot grow properly without the ants. The acacia and the ants have coevolved to the point where one cannot survive without the other.

SECTION REVIEW

1. Why do species such as the warblers in Figure 5.5 evolve to avoid competition with other species?
2. Explain convergent evolution and give one example. Why does convergent evolution happen?
3. **Predict** What would happen to the ant colony living on an acacia tree if that tree was chopped down? What does your answer imply about the effect of destroying an organism's habitat?

Invasion of the Alien Species

It sounds like the plot of a science-fiction movie. One plant floating on the water sends out shoots, which form new plants, which in turn send out shoots, forming still more plants. A single mat, or raft, of these connected plants can cover hundreds of square meters. And when a piece of a raft breaks off, it forms a whole new raft! Soon, waterways are clogged, and boats can't get through. What is this invader, and what can stop it?

As it grows unchecked, the water hyacinth can clog waterways, making navigation difficult.

It sounds like fiction, but it isn't. The invader is the water hyacinth, a floating plant that is native to South America. These plants were given away as souvenirs at the 1884 New Orleans Cotton Exposition, and within a few decades they were spreading through the waterways of Louisiana and Florida.

Back then, people did not understand that releasing an alien species could cause problems. In South America, the water hyacinth is eaten by several species of insects. The actions of the insects balance the rapid growth of the plant. In North America, however, there are no natural controls.

In Florida, the herbicide 2,4-D has been used to kill water hyacinths. However, the plants grew back and had to be sprayed again. The repeated use of herbicides is expensive, and it adds unwanted chemicals to the water.

The State of Florida, the U.S. Army Corps of Engineers, and the U.S. Department of Agriculture decided to look to a new approach: biological control. Researchers in Florida and Argentina worked together to identify insects that would eat the water hyacinths but not native North American plants. Two insect species have been introduced, and they are controlling the plant growth. In Florida and Louisiana, many canals that once were clogged by rafts of water hyacinths are useful waterways again.

The release of the insects has been monitored by the United Nations's Food and Agriculture Organization. If the insect controls continue to work in North America, the UN may adapt this program for Asia and Africa, where hyacinths interfere with fishing and block irrigation systems.

✓ Checkpoint

1. What two factors caused the water hyacinth to become such a problem?

2. Suppose someone from Virginia visited Florida and brought home a water hyacinth. If the plant were released into Chesapeake Bay, what do you think might happen?

5.3 POPULATIONS

OBJECTIVES • *Explain* how populations of organisms grow.
• *Describe* the factors that limit the growth of a population.
• *Identify* the shapes of growth curves that represent populations of different organisms.

The biotic and abiotic factors that define a niche also limit a species' growth. For example, food may be plentiful in spring but scarce during winter. These changes affect the number of individuals the niche can support, and thus limit the size of populations of organisms.

Population Growth

In 1798, English economist Thomas Malthus made an observation about the human population. He stated that the human population can quickly grow past the environment's ability to support it. Malthus thought that humans suffered from famine and disease when the population became too large.

Malthus's observations impressed a young English naturalist named Charles Darwin, who is best known for his theory of evolution. Darwin wrote in his book *On the Origin of Species*, "There is no exception to the rule that every organic being naturally increases at so high a rate, that, if not destroyed, the Earth would soon be covered by the progeny [descendants] of a single pair." The idea that organisms produce more offspring than can survive was important to Darwin's theory of evolution. Overproduction causes competition for resources, which in turn causes the selection of the most favorable adaptations.

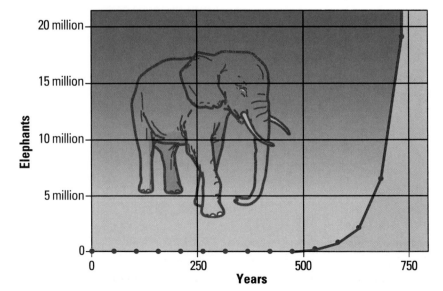

Figure 5.8 Two elephants can produce a large population if conditions are ideal. Elephants reproduce very slowly; populations of most other species would increase much faster.

Darwin illustrated overproduction with the example shown in Figure 5.8. One pair of elephants could produce more than 20 million elephants in less than 750 years if the elephants were not limited by food or other resources. And if they kept reproducing, the world would soon be covered with elephants. *Population growth in which the rate of growth in each generation is a multiple of the previous generation is called* **exponential** (EK-spoh-NEN-chul) **growth.**

Any population has the potential to increase exponentially if it has a perfect environment. In reality, however, conditions are never perfect. Resources are always limited. Although natural populations can show exponential growth, the available resources limit such growth to short periods of time and restricted geographic areas.

Carrying Capacity

As a population grows, it takes more from its habitat. Resources such as food and living space become scarce. As resources become scarce, individuals begin to compete for them because there is no longer enough to go around. The death rate in the population rises because those who cannot compete die. The birth rate decreases because producing offspring requires many hard-to-find resources. The growth of the population slows. Finally, the population will stop growing altogether because the number of births equals the number of deaths. Individuals will be born and die, but the total number of individuals will not change much.

The number of individuals of a species that can be supported by an ecosystem is called the **carrying capacity** *for that species.* The growth of a population toward its carrying capacity is shown in Figure 5.9. The **S**-shaped curve represents the change in the size of a new population of fruit flies over time. The population starts out small, and then increases rapidly. During this time, the population is growing

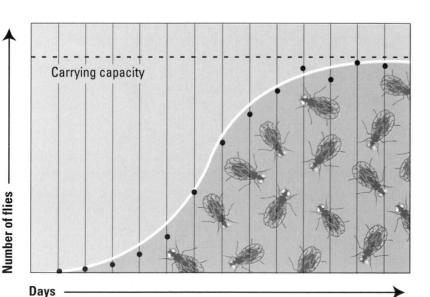

Figure 5.9 A population of fruit flies shows an S-shaped growth curve. Early population growth is exponential, but growth then slows and finally reaches zero at the carrying capacity.

Carrying capacity

Number of flies

Days

exponentially. As the size of the population approaches carrying capacity, the growth rate slows. The population stops growing when it reaches the carrying capacity.

Limiting Factors

Many populations stop growing when they reach their carrying capacity. The forces that slow the growth of a population are called *limiting factors*. Figure 5.10 shows many of the limiting factors that can affect a population.

There are two kinds of limiting factors. Some limiting factors affect a population more strongly as the population grows larger. *Limiting factors that are dependent on population size are called* **density-dependent limiting factors.** Some density-dependent factors are

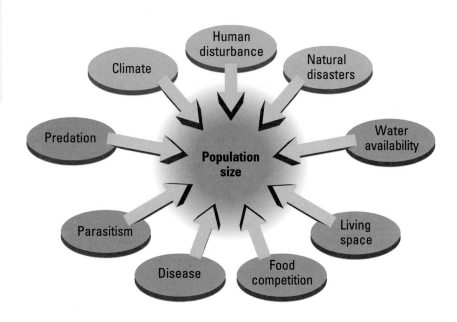

Figure 5.10 All of these factors can influence the size of a population. Factors in purple are density-dependent. Those in green are density-independent.

food supply, predation, and disease. Density-dependent factors are related to competition and other interactions between organisms. In larger populations, there are more such interactions, and limiting factors have a greater effect. As the population grows, each of these factors acts more strongly to limit growth.

Some factors limit a population's growth regardless of the population's size. A hurricane, for example, might destroy half of a population of palm trees. The size of the population does not matter because the hurricane would affect any population in the same way. *A limiting factor that affects the same percentage of a population regardless of its size is called a* **density-independent limiting factor.** Natural disasters such as hurricanes and fires limit growth independent of population density by destroying habitat.

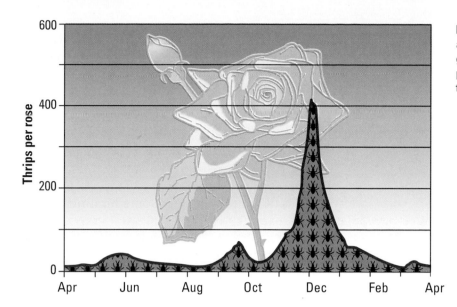

Figure 5.11 Insects called thrips show a boom-and-bust growth curve. Thrips grow on roses. The population of thrips per rose grows very quickly when conditions are favorable; then it falls quickly.

Populations controlled by density-dependent factors show an S-shaped growth curve. Populations controlled by density-independent factors show a boom-and-bust curve. A boom-and-bust curve represents a population whose size grows exponentially during favorable conditions and then collapses when conditions change. Such populations take advantage of density-independent factors that occur regularly, such as warm temperatures or rainfall. Many insect populations follow this pattern, as shown in Figure 5.11.

The Human Population

The growth curve of the human population has long been an exponential one. This continuing exponential growth has been possible because of many factors, including advances in agriculture, technology, energy development, transportation, and medicine. However, no population of organisms can grow exponentially forever. The growth of the human population on Earth must level off as the planet's resources become fully utilized. The challenges for the human species lie in minimizing our impacts on our only habitat, Earth's biosphere.

SECTION REVIEW

1. What is exponential growth? Under what conditions do populations grow exponentially?
2. **Interpret** Draw a graph of an S-shaped growth curve. Label carrying capacity on the graph, and show the region where the population shows exponential growth.
3. What is the difference between density-dependent and density-independent limiting factors?

Yeast Population Density

PROBLEM

How does the population density of a yeast cell culture change over time?

MATERIALS (per group)

- 5 empty baby food jars with lids
- 100-mL graduated cylinder
- 10% molasses solution
- yeast solution
- 2 medicine droppers
- 5 glass microscope slides
- 5 coverslips
- microscope
- pencil
- graph paper

HYPOTHESIS

After reading the entire activity, write a hypothesis that pertains to the problem.

PROCEDURE

Day 1

1. Label each baby food jar with your name. Number the jars 1 to 5. Add 10 mL of the molasses solution to each of the jars.
2. Stir the yeast solution with the medicine dropper. Transfer ten drops of the yeast solution to each jar before the solution has a chance to settle. Cover each jar and shake gently to mix the solutions.
3. Use a clean dropper to transfer one drop of the solution from jar 1 to a microscope slide. Cover the solution with a coverslip.
4. Observe the slide under the microscope at high power. Count the number of yeast individuals in five different fields of view. Buds count as individual cells.
5. Record each of the five counts in a table. Calculate an average of the five counts. Record this number in the table as well.
6. Empty and wash jar 1. Place jars 2, 3, 4, and 5 in a warm, dark place where they will not be disturbed.

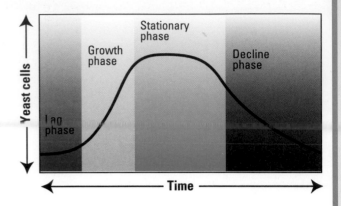

Days 3, 6, 9, and 12

7. Repeat steps 3 and 4 with jar 2 on day 3. Observe jar 3 on day 6, jar 4 on day 9, and jar 5 on day 12. Be sure to record five counts for each jar and to calculate an average. Record these numbers in your data table. Empty and rinse each jar after you count its population.
8. Use the graph paper to graph the populations of yeast in the jars. One axis should be yeast cells, the other time. Be sure to record which jar each count comes from.

ANALYSIS

1. Sketch a single yeast cell.
2. Study your graph of the yeast cell population. When did the yeast population grow fastest? Did it ever decline?
3. How did the density of the population of yeast cells change over time? Explain.

CONCLUSION

1. The figure on this page names several stages in the growth of a yeast cell population. Label these stages on your own graph if they occur. If they do not occur, suggest reasons why your curve was different.
2. Why does the number of yeast cells change over time? Write a paragraph discussing the forces that may have caused the changes in the yeast cell population.

CHAPTER 5 REVIEW

KEY TERMS

niche 5.1
competitive
exclusion 5.1
predator 5.1

prey 5.1
keystone predator 5.1
evolution 5.2
convergent
evolution 5.2

coevolution 5.2
exponential
growth 5.3
carrying capacity 5.3

density-dependent
limiting factor 5.3
density-independent
limiting factor 5.3

CHAPTER SUMMARY

5.1 The area in which a species lives is its habitat, and its role in that habitat is its niche. The niche is influenced by biotic and abiotic factors such as predators and sunlight. The niche of a species is unique to that species.

5.2 Species may evolve to avoid competition with other species for food and other resources. The niche of one organism can influence the niche of another. Convergent evolution is a change in which different species occupying similar niches evolve in similar ways. When species that interact very closely adapt to one another, the change is called coevolution.

5.3 The population growth of organisms is controlled by limiting factors. Limiting factors can be density-dependent or density-independent. Without these limiting factors, the population of a given organism would, in time, cover Earth. The carrying capacity of a species is the maximum number that an ecosystem can sustain, given the limiting factors.

MULTIPLE CHOICE

Choose the letter of the word or phrase that best completes each statement.

1. The role of an organism in an ecosystem is called its (a) habitat; (b) sleeping habits; (c) niche; (d) species.
2. Temperature, sunlight, and water are examples of (a) biotic factors; (b) abiotic factors; (c) food sources; (d) mineral sources.
3. When two species interact so closely that they are adapted to each other, the interaction is called (a) symbiotic evolution; (b) coevolution; (c) convergent evolution; (d) generalized evolution.
4. Birds and bats have similar wings as a result of a process called (a) specialization; (b) predation; (c) biodiversity; (d) convergent evolution.
5. A species fits its niche because of (a) evolution; (b) reproduction; (c) competition; (d) regression.
6. The carrying capacity for a species is the maximum number (a) born; (b) surviving; (c) eaten; (d) changing.
7. Population growth is limited by density-dependent factors such as (a) climate; (b) earthquakes and floods; (c) biotic and abiotic factors; (d) predation and disease.
8. Climate changes and earthquakes are (a) expressed by S-shaped curves; (b) density-independent limiting factors; (c) influenced by exponential growth; (d) causes of evolution.
9. Keystone predators affect a habitat's (a) boom-and-bust cycle; (b) competitive exclusion; (c) fundamental niche; (d) diversity.
10. As resources become scarce because of population growth, the growth (a) levels off; (b) is represented by a boom-and-bust curve; (c) becomes exponential; (d) increases.

CHAPTER 5 REVIEW

WORD COMPARISONS

Write the letter of the second word pair that best matches the first pair.

1. Habitat: niche as (a) address: occupation; (b) land: desert; (c) people: work; (d) house: neighborhood.
2. Keystone predator: diversity as (a) land: desert; (b) food: population growth; (c) environment: ecosystem; (d) ant: acacia tree.
3. Dolphin: ichthyosaur as (a) predator: prey; (b) convergent evolution: coevolution; (c) ant: acacia tree; (d) bird wing: bat wing.
4. S-shaped curve: food competition as (a) population: exponential growth; (b) boom-and-bust curve: environmental conditions; (c) limiting factors: population; (d) agriculture: food.
5. Agriculture: exponential growth as (a) tree: forest; (b) organism: evolution; (c) termite colony: infestation; (d) heat: expansion.

CONCEPT REVIEW

Write a complete response to each of the following.

1. Explain how the niche of one species might influence the niche of another.
2. Why are the animals in Figure 5.6 similar?
3. Describe the difference between a specialized species and a generalized species. Which species would be more tolerant to change? Why?
4. List two examples of biotic factors and two examples of abiotic factors that can limit or increase the size of a species' population.
5. What do S-shaped curves represent in graphs of population growth?

THINK CRITICALLY

1. If two different species ate exactly the same kind of food in the same location, what would you expect to happen over time?
2. Describe how predation can be an important factor in the long-term survival of a prey species' population.
3. Why would you expect evolution to take place more rapidly on land than at the bottom of the ocean?
4. Suppose a construction company was to dam a small river. Consider what changes might take place in the regions upstream and downstream from the dam. How might the population growth of species be affected? Why?

WRITE FOR UNDERSTANDING

Think of land mammals that returned to the oceans and have become what we know today as whales, dolphins, and seals. Summarize the adaptations these species have to aquatic niches. Why did these adaptations evolve? How are the challenges of living on land different than those of living in the water? How are the challenges similar?

PORTFOLIO

Construct a collage of density-dependent limiting factors on human population. Use pictures and graphs from newspapers and magazines, and also work with short articles or captions. Organize your collage so that different types of density-dependent factors occur together.

GRAPHIC ANALYSIS

Use the figure to answer the following.
1. What does this graph show?
2. When is the fruit fly population growing most quickly? What is the population size at this point compared to the carrying capacity?
3. Does the growth rate ever reach zero in the graph? If so, where does this occur?
4. Why does the growth rate of the population slow?

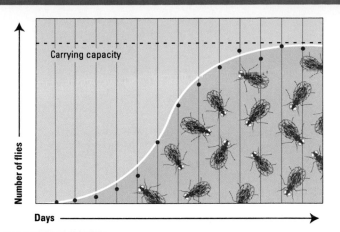

ACTIVITY 5.2

PROBLEM
How can human activities affect a deer population over time?

MATERIALS
- graph paper

INFERENCE
Write an inference that relates to the problem.

PROCEDURE
1. In 1906, the U.S. Forest Service began protecting a herd of deer on a 300 000 hectare range on Arizona's Kaibab Plateau. In previous years, the Kaibab forest area had been overgrazed by cattle, sheep, and horses. Graph the Forest Service's data. Plot the year along the *x*-axis and the population size along the *y*-axis.
2. In 1906, the Forest Service estimated the carrying capacity of the range to be about 30 000 deer. Draw a straight horizontal line across your graph beginning at the 30 000-deer level. Label this line *Carrying capacity.*

ANALYSIS
What was the relationship of the deer herd to the carrying capacity of the range in 1915? 1920? 1924?

CONCLUSION
1. Describe the effects of the following actions taken by the Forest Service:
   a. 1907: Hunting of deer was banned. Also, the Forest Service began a 32-year campaign to exterminate natural predators of the deer. Thousands of predators were killed.
   b. 1920: Seeing that the range was deteriorating rapidly, the Forest Service reduced the number of livestock grazing permits.
   c. 1924: The deer population was on the brink of starvation.
   Deer hunting was allowed again. Deer shot by hunters in autumn represented about one-tenth the number that had been born the previous spring.
2. What do you think the Forest Service learned between 1905 and 1939?

Deer Population, 1905-1939

Year	Population	Year	Population
1905	4000	1927	37 000
1910	9000	1928	35 000
1915	25 000	1929	30 000
1920	65 000	1930	25 000
1924	100 000	1931	20 000
1925	60 000	1935	18 000
1926	40 000	1939	10 000

Together the organisms in an ecosystem work like parts of a machine, capturing energy and using it to cycle matter. Each organism plays a part in keeping the whole ecosystem functioning. The interactions among species and abiotic factors maintain the ecosystem in a dynamic balance.

Yet change is inevitable in even the most stable ecosystems. Change is usually gradual, but severe disturbances, such as fires, storms, or landslides, can cause rapid changes. Scientists think that stability, or balance, in ecosystems is dynamic, or in a constant state of change. Even though change occurs continuously, the ecosystem maintains the flow of energy and nutrient cycling necessary for life.

6.1 RELATIONSHIPS IN THE ECOSYSTEM

OBJECTIVES • **Explain** the relationship between the population sizes of predator and prey. • **Define** symbiosis and **describe** several symbiotic relationships.

Complex webs of relationships exist among all the species in an ecosystem. To understand this complexity, scientists first find out all they can about how two populations interact with each other and their environment. With this knowledge base, ecologists can then expand their studies to include the more complex interactions among the many populations in an ecosystem.

Predators and Prey

All organisms need food and all consumers must eat other organisms to get it. Consumers that actively hunt other living organisms are called *predators*. The organisms a predator eats are called *prey*. A praying mantis that eats a dragonfly is a predator. The dragonfly is the prey. The praying mantis itself is prey to other organisms such as snakes and birds. These predators are, in turn, prey to larger carnivores.

Predator and prey population sizes are closely linked. A large prey population can support more predators than a small prey population. If a prey population grows or shrinks, the number of predators the community can support changes as well. An example of this linkage is shown in Figure 6.1.

The snowshoe hare is the prey the lynx eats most often. The number of hares changes greatly from year to year. The number of lynxes also changes greatly from year to year. Observe the

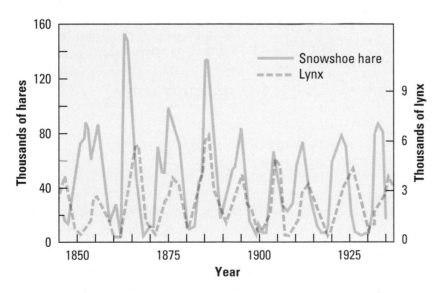

Figure 6.1 A change in the size of one population causes a change in the size of the other population.

pattern in Figure 6.1. Increases in the hare population are usually followed by increases in the lynx population one or two years later. The increasing number of prey allows the predator population to grow because there is more food. A decline in the number of hares is also followed by a decline in the number of lynxes, again after a delay of one or two years. Can you explain this pattern?

The lynx and hare populations rise and fall about once every ten years. In general, large herbivores, such as the hare, muskrat, and large birds, have peaks in their population sizes every ten years. Small herbivores, such as mice and lemmings, have population cycles similar to that of the lynx, but the populations cycle once every four years. Larger animals have longer cycles because they live longer and reproduce more slowly than smaller animals.

Many predators have population cycles that match those of their prey. Predators such as the Arctic fox that eat herbivores with four-year cycles also have four-year cycles. Predators that eat herbivores with ten-year cycles also have ten-year cycles. The population of the colored fox cycles every ten years in some places and every four years elsewhere, depending on which herbivore the fox eats. The changing population size of the prey species controls the population size of the predator species.

Figure 6.2 The lynx generally feeds on the snowshoe hare. The population sizes of these two animals are closely related.

Parasitism

Some organisms do not kill the prey they feed on. **Parasitism** (PAYR-uh-sɪт-ɪz-um) *is a relationship in which one organism feeds on the tissues or body fluids of another.* The organism on which a parasite feeds is called the *host.* A parasite is harmful to its host and may even be fatal. Most parasites, however, do not kill their hosts. Fleas are parasites, as are ticks, lice, and a variety of worms, protists, and other organisms.

Although herbivores usually do not kill the plants they consume, they are not considered parasites. A true parasite lives on or in the body of its host. A parasite depends on its host for many functions. Many parasites cannot perform functions that the host provides for them. A tapeworm, for example, has no sensory organs and cannot move by itself. Tapeworms live in the intestines of mammals. The tapeworm does not need to move or use senses because it lives inside the body of its host. It has special adaptations for living in this environment.

The population size of a parasite is closely related to the population size of its host. A large host population can support more parasites than a small host population. Parasite populations are also affected by the density of the host population. Parasites thrive in crowded host populations because the parasite can be transferred to new hosts easily. Parasites are a density-dependent limiting factor because parasites are more successful in dense host populations.

Symbiosis

Any relationship in which two species live closely together is called **symbiosis** (sim-by-OH-sis). Parasitism is one kind of symbiotic relationship. Parasitism harms one organism and benefits the other. Some symbiotic relationships do not harm either organism.

A symbiotic relationship that benefits one species and neither helps nor harms the other is called *commensalism* (ku-MEN-sul-ɪz-um). Barnacles living on the skin of a whale, such as those in Figure 6.3, are one example of commensalism. The barnacles do not harm or help the whale. But the barnacles benefit from the constant movement of food-carrying water past the swimming whale.

A symbiotic relationship in which both species benefit is called *mutualism* (MYOO-choo-ul-ɪz-um). The ants and acacia trees discussed in Chapter 5 are one example of a mutualistic relationship. Another example is the relationship between flowers and the insects that pollinate them. The flower provides the insect with food in the form of nectar, and in return, the insect pollinates the flower.

The yucca plant and yucca moth in Figure 6.4 have coevolved to the point where one cannot survive without the other. The yucca moth crawls inside the yucca flower to lay its eggs. The moth then gathers a ball of pollen, carries it to another plant, and places the pollen ball in a special part of the yucca flower to pollinate it. The yucca plant provides food for growing yucca moth caterpillars. The yucca plant and yucca moth are an example of a mutualistic relationship.

Figure 6.3 These barnacles have hitched a ride on the back of a whale. The barnacles do not help or harm the whale, but the barnacles benefit. This relationship is an example of commensalism.

Figure 6.4 The Mojave yucca plant and the yucca moth have a mutualistic relationship. Both species benefit from their interaction.

SECTION REVIEW

1. What processes link the sizes of predator and prey populations?
2. Why are herbivores not considered to be parasites?
3. **Compare and Contrast** Write definitions of the three types of symbiosis. How are the three relationships different? How are they similar?

6.2 ECOLOGICAL SUCCESSION

OBJECTIVES • *Contrast* primary and secondary succession.
• *Describe* the sequence of ecological succession in a lake and on an island.

Organisms affect the environments in which they live. For example, plants help form soil by breaking down rocks and making organic matter. The changes a species causes in its environment may not be helpful to that species. The environment may change so much that the species' niche disappears. Old niches are replaced by new niches to which different species are adapted. A species can be the cause of its own destruction.

Other forces also change the environment. A forest formed slowly over hundreds of years can be destroyed in minutes by fire. Change is a fact of life in all ecosystems, and living things have evolved in response to change. As an environment changes, the community living in that environment changes as well. In many cases, different communities follow one another in a definite pattern.

Primary Succession

Imagine you are standing on the beach during a volcanic eruption. The shore grows as a black and orange river of molten rock flows slowly into the sea. The lava hisses and gives off steam as it cools. After the eruption has ended and the steam has cleared, a new shoreline is visible, one made of bare rock. Organisms move into this lifeless habitat almost immediately. These first organisms are followed by others. *The sequence of communities forming in an originally lifeless habitat is called* **primary succession** (suk-SESH-un).

Primary succession occurs in new habitats that are without life, such as the cooled lava field in the example above, or the bare rock exposed by a retreating glacier. Primary succession is an orderly process. It follows the same general pattern in most ecosystems. The first steps in primary succession are colonization by new organisms and formation of soil from exposed rocks.

On land, exposed rocks are first colonized by organisms called lichens. *A* **lichen** (LY-kun) *is a fungus and an alga living in a mutualistic relationship.* Unlike most organisms, lichens can live on bare rock. Lichens secrete acids that break down the rock and form organic material by photosynthesis. Rocks are also broken down by weathering caused by wind, rain, and frost. The action of lichens and weathering form soil. Scientists call the lichen community a *pioneer community* because it is the first to colonize a new area.

Once soil has formed, grasses and other small plants begin to grow from seeds carried to the habitat by wind or animals. Root growth and the accumulation of dead leaves accelerate the process

Figure 6.5 A lichen is an example of a symbiotic relationship between an alga and a fungus. Lichens are often a major part of a pioneer community during primary succession.

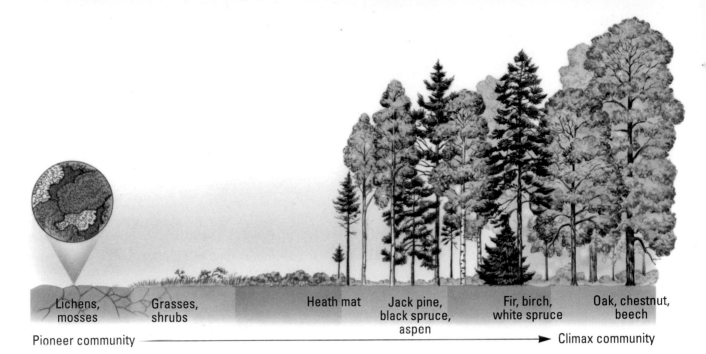

| Lichens, mosses | Grasses, shrubs | Heath mat | Jack pine, black spruce, aspen | Fir, birch, white spruce | Oak, chestnut, beech |

Pioneer community —————————————————————————————→ Climax community

of soil formation. In time, the plants grow dense enough that lichens cannot get enough light. The lichens disappear. The lichen community is replaced by the grasses.

The grass community survives for many generations and makes the soil deeper and more fertile. Eventually the soil is deep enough to allow the growth of nonwoody plants with deeper roots. These plants are taller than the grasses and shade them out in the competition for sunlight. Since both the grass and shrub communities are usually not diverse, a small disturbance may cause drastic changes in the community.

Pines or other trees with shallow roots invade when the soil is deep enough. As trees move in, the community changes again. Trees shade out the shrubs and grasses found on what is now the forest floor. The soil continues to deepen. Finally, broadleaf trees take root and hardwood trees begin to replace the pines. The hardwood forest is the final stage of succession in many areas. In the absence of external disturbances, this mature ecosystem will change very little over time. *A community that does not undergo further succession is called a* **climax community.** Climax communities are usually highly diverse and can often survive even severe local disturbances.

Secondary Succession

Primary succession occurs only on freshly exposed rock or in places where a severe disturbance has destroyed all the organisms and the soil. However, most disturbances are not this drastic. A fire may kill many plants but leave the soil in place. Living things quickly colonize clear patches created by these disturbances.

Figure 6.6 This diagram shows the process of primary succession as it occurred on Isle Royale in Lake Superior. One community gave way to the next until a climax community was established.

Field Activity

Secondary succession often occurs after human disturbance. Find an abandoned farm field or a vacant lot near your school, and arrange a field trip to study the area. When you arrive, study the plants that have colonized the disturbed area. Try to answer the following questions.

1. How tall are the plants? Are they grasses and weeds, shrubs, or trees?

2. How does this plant community differ from undisturbed communities in the surrounding area?

3. After you have completed your study, analyze your findings.

Figure 6.7 Secondary succession has begun in this area. The original community was destroyed by a forest fire, and new plants are moving in. The process of secondary succession will eventually restore the climax community.

Biology

Many communities are adapted to occasional fires. Some pine forests are subject to ground-level fires from time to time. The longleaf pine has very thick bark on the lower trunk. This adaptation helps the trees survive while the fire kills competing seedlings.

Succession that occurs where a disturbance eliminates most organisms but does not destroy the soil is called **secondary succession.** Fires, storms, and human activity are common initiators of secondary succession.

Secondary succession resembles the later stages of primary succession. Fast-growing grasses and nonwoody plants are the first plants to colonize the area, followed by larger shrubs. Fast-growing trees such as pines then crowd out the shrub community, followed finally by slow-growing hardwood trees. Eventually, a climax community forms again, and the process of succession is complete.

Results from long-term research have shown that many habitats never develop climax communities. If disturbances recur in less time than the several hundred years needed to complete the process of succession, a climax community may only rarely form. Grasslands are a good example of this type of habitat. Frequent fires continually disrupt grasslands. These fires kill the seedlings of shrubs and trees. As a result, succession in this habitat is held at the grass-community level. Periodic disruption maintains the balance in these communities.

Aquatic Succession

The process of succession also occurs in aquatic habitats. Imagine a clear mountain lake just formed by a retreating glacier. The lake is much like barren rock; the water is low in nutrients and supports few organisms. As time passes, reeds and other water plants begin to grow in the thin sediments near the shore of the lake, supporting other organisms. Organic matter begins to collect in the lake.

As the lake begins to fill with sediment, the water becomes richer in nutrients. More organisms can survive, and water plants begin to cover the surface of the lake. Eventually the lake fills with sediment and becomes a marsh. Land plants begin to colonize the marsh. Finally, the lake becomes a fertile meadow covered with land plants and may ultimately turn into a forest.

Figure 6.8 This lake is filling quickly with plant material and other sediments. When the process of aquatic succession is complete, dry land will have replaced the lake.

Island Succession

Islands undergo succession in much the same way as land on the continents. New islands can form quickly through volcanic eruptions. Living things are quick to colonize this new land. Seagulls are observed nesting on some islands before the volcanic activity stops.

Islands are isolated by the water that surrounds them. Any organism found on an island must have ancestors that were carried there by water, wind, or by other organisms. These ancestors may have arrived on the island by chance alone. Many islands therefore have large bird populations, because birds can reach islands much more easily than land animals.

The rare organism that arrives on a new island and can find a mate is often faced with an opportunity. There are many unfilled niches on the island, because the organisms that would fill the niches on the mainland have no way of getting to the island. In this situation, the offspring of a few organisms can evolve to fill several niches, because there is no competition. Populations of organisms adapt to their new niches, and several new species form. The offspring of a few ancestors can adapt to several different niches.

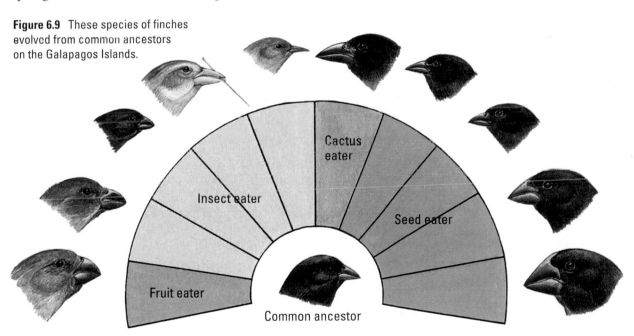

Figure 6.9 These species of finches evolved from common ancestors on the Galapagos Islands.

Cactus eater

Insect eater

Seed eater

Fruit eater

Common ancestor

SECTION REVIEW

1. How does primary succession differ from secondary succession?
2. What is a climax community?
3. **Predict** Suppose humans put out all the fires in a large area of grassland over a period of 100 years. What would happen to the grassland community?

People vs. Preservation

When Theodore Roosevelt visited the Grand Canyon in 1903, he urged Americans to protect it. "Do nothing to mar its grandeur," he said. "Keep it for your children, your children's children and all who come after you, as one great sight which every American should see."

If Theodore Roosevelt were alive today, he would probably be amazed to learn that 266 million people visited national parks in 1996. However, the parks are also habitats for many species, and increasing numbers of visitors threaten those habitats. In recent years, the National Park Service has been looking for ways to limit access to the parks in hopes of preserving these habitats.

Should access to national parks be limited?

Parks Are for Preservation

National parks are supposed to preserve some of the natural wonders of the United States. The ecosystems of many parks are too sensitive to survive the increasing pollution from cars, sewage from restrooms, and trash from picnics or snack bars.

When people visit the parks, they damage the natural areas. Many people do not realize that when they wander off designated trails and boardwalks, they trample plants and increase soil erosion.

Parks Are for People

The national parks belong to the American people. Because people pay taxes to support the parks, people should be able to go into the parks. The government should make sure that there are good roads and places to eat so that people can enjoy the parks. In parks where cars are a problem, buses can be used to transport visitors.

Allowing people access to the parks is good for the parks. By visiting national parks, more people will become aware of the importance of caring for these areas.

National parks were established to preserve natural wonders such as the Grand Canyon.

Consider the Issue

1. Many national parks have restaurants and other tourist facilities. The Park Service would like to eliminate many such facilities. Do you agree? Explain your answer.

2. Propose a solution that would help preserve the parks while satisfying park visitors.

6.3 STABILITY IN THE ECOSYSTEM

OBJECTIVES • *Explain* the concept of ecosystem stability.
• *Characterize* the effects of disturbances on ecosystems.

Stability is a measure of how easily an ecosystem is affected by a disturbance and how quickly it returns to its original condition after a disturbance. The original condition for an ecosystem includes its biotic and abiotic components as well as the patterns of energy flow and nutrient cycling. Community structure is also an important aspect of ecosystem stability. A more stable ecosystem will return to a steady pattern of energy flow and nutrient cycling with fewer evolutionary, food-web, and abiotic environmental changes. Averaged over longer periods and larger areas, even frequently disturbed ecosystems can show some degree of stability.

Ecosystem stability may be related to the complexity of the food web that manages the system's energy flow and nutrient cycles. More connections in this web may decrease the overall impact on the ecosystem if a single species is lost or one part of the system is disrupted. Such changes would be counteracted by changes in other parts of the system, such as the evolution of adaptations to cold weather. The disrupted ecosystem will return to a state of balance, called *equilibrium.*

Major disruptions can cause drastic changes as the ecosystem adjusts to the new conditions. Some disruptions can even destroy whole ecosystems. But a new ecosystem will develop to replace the one destroyed. The evolution of many kinds of mammals after the extinction of the dinosaurs is an example of a changing ecosystem. The general rule is: Species and whole ecosystems evolve and may die out, but new species and ecosystems can evolve to replace them.

LINK

Astronomy

The remains of a large crater were found in 1990 under the Yucatan Peninsula and the Gulf of Mexico. The crater is several hundred kilometers in diameter and is approximately 66 million years old. Scientists think that a large object hit Earth at the end of the dinosaur era. But the impact and the extinction may be a coincidence. Proving that there was an impact does not prove that the impact destroyed the dinosaurs' ecosystem.

Figure 6.10 A large comet or asteroid hit Earth 66 million years ago. Some scientists think this event led to the extinction of the dinosaurs, while other scientists disagree. Did a comet kill the dinosaurs, or were other factors such as a changing climate responsible? People may never know for certain.

Scientist James Lovelock first published the controversial Gaia hypothesis. Lovelock proposed that Earth acts as if it were one giant living organism. Although most scientists do not agree with Lovelock, his idea focused scientific attention on the interaction between different parts of the world's ecosystems. The concept of Earth as a single biosphere composed of integrated systems is now central to environmental science.

Scientists do not understand every detail of how even simple ecosystems function. They do understand that, like a series of falling dominoes, changes in one part of a system can trigger changes in other parts. But scientists cannot always predict how changes in one part of the system will affect another part. Recently, a few scientists have tried to apply a new kind of mathematics called *chaos* (KAY-oss) *theory* to the problem of ecosystem function. Chaos theory suggests that ecosystems may be sensitive to very small changes, and that the initial state of an ecosystem is crucial to its later development. Yet scientists are still a long way from understanding exactly how ecosystems function.

At present, species are becoming extinct at the fastest rate since the extinction of the dinosaurs. The growth of the human population may be causing more extinctions than any other factor. Habitat destruction, the introduction of foreign species to new ecosystems, and the pollution of fresh water are major impacts of the human population. It is very difficult for scientists to predict the long-term effects of these disruptions on the biosphere and its ability to support the human population.

Figure 6.11 This image is called a fractal. It is a visual representation of a mathematical formula. Complex images like this one may be a good representation of the complexity in ecosystems.

SECTION REVIEW

1. Why is the study of ecosystems so complex?
2. Why is an ecosystem stable? How does it react to a change in one of its parts?
3. **Write Creatively** Write a short essay that describes what the ecosystem in which you live will look like in 50 years.

6.4 LAND BIOMES

OBJECTIVES • *Explain* the concept of the biome, and *name* the eight major land biomes. • *Illustrate* where each of the eight major land biomes occurs.

The movement of matter and flow of energy are common to all ecosystems on Earth. Yet Earth is a very large and diverse place. Environments range from the ice of Antarctica to the heat and rain of the Amazon. Differences in temperature and rainfall create a vast array of conditions on the surface of Earth. Life has adapted to almost all of these environments.

The ecosystems of Earth can be divided into several broad categories. *A major type of ecosystem with distinctive temperature, rainfall, and organisms is called a* **biome** (BY-ohm). Biomes are either terrestrial (on land) or aquatic (in water). On land, the type of biome that occurs in a given area depends on the average temperature and amount of precipitation the area receives. The type of aquatic biome is determined by water depth, nutrients, and nearness to land.

The biome is the largest category scientists use to classify ecosystems. Because each biome is a general category instead of a specific definition, the conditions in a biome may vary from place to place. Smaller ecosystems within a biome may also have different habitats with different conditions and organisms. Every habitat on Earth is different, and any attempt to classify these habitats is an overgeneralization. But the concept of the biome is useful as a way to talk about sets of related habitats.

The terrestrial ecosystems of Earth can be divided into eight major biomes. Two of these biomes—the *desert* and the *tundra*—receive very little water and support only a small amount of biomass. Recall that biomass is the total mass of organic material in an ecosystem. Desert, for example, covers 25 percent of Earth's land surface but contains only 1 percent of Earth's biomass. The lack of water in the desert and in the tundra makes plant life scarce in these areas.

Forest biomes contain 75 percent of Earth's biomass. There are three forest biomes: the *coniferous* (ku-NIF-er-us) *forest*, the *deciduous* (dih-SIJ-oo-us) *forest*, and the *rain forest*. Forests receive abundant precipitation. Rain forest covers only 6 percent of Earth's land surface, but contains more than 50 percent of all Earth's biomass. The rainforest biome is also the most diverse biome. The destruction of the rain forests is a serious environmental problem.

The other three land biomes are grasslands. They are the *steppe*, *prairie*, and *savanna*. Grassland biomes cover about 22 percent of Earth's land surface, and contain about 8 percent of Earth's biomass. The grasslands receive less precipitation than do the forest

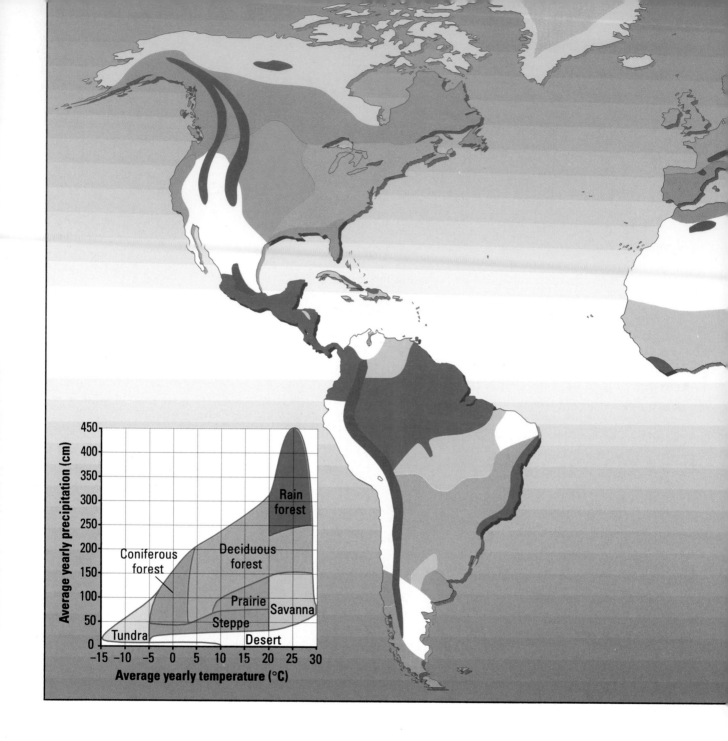

Figure 6.12 This map shows where the major biomes of the world occur. The graph shows the precipitation and temperature usual for each biome.

biomes and may have long dry seasons. Grasslands may be frequently disturbed by fire. Large herds of migrating herbivores are common grassland organisms.

Figure 6.12 shows where each biome occurs on Earth. The areas are color-coded to the key on the right. The graph on the left shows what temperature and precipitation conditions occur in each biome. The areas in the graph are color-coded to the same key as the biome map.

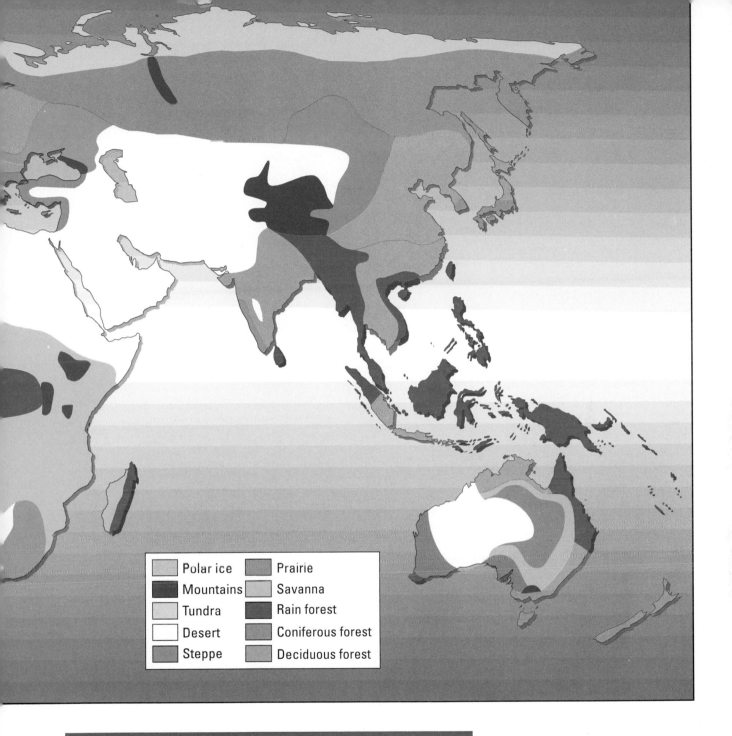

Polar ice   Prairie
Mountains   Savanna
Tundra   Rain forest
Desert   Coniferous forest
Steppe   Deciduous forest

SECTION REVIEW

1. What is a biome? Which biome covers the largest land area?
2. **Interpret** What biome would you expect to find in an area having 312 cm of rain a year and an average annual temperature of 24 °C? Use the graph in Figure 6.12 to find the answer.
3. **Relate** Locate the position of the city or town where you live on the biome map. In what biome is your city or town?

Succession in Aged Tap Water

PROBLEM
How does a microscopic community change over time?

MATERIALS (per group)
- paper
- tap water
- 500-mL beaker
- 1000-mL beaker
- soil
- grass
- dropper
- glass slide
- coverslip
- microscope
- pH paper
- leaves

PREDICTION
After reading the entire activity, write a prediction that relates to the problem.

PROCEDURE

1. Make a data table by dividing a sheet of paper into two columns. Label one column *Date* and the other column *Observations*.
2. To make aged tap water, fill a 500-mL beaker with tap water and leave it for 48 hours. This will allow gases to evaporate that might be harmful to microorganisms.
3. After 48 hours, place a 1-cm layer of soil in the bottom of a 1000-mL beaker. Loosely fill the rest of the beaker with a mixture of grasses and leaves.
4. Pour the aged tap water into the 1000-mL beaker.
5. Place the beaker in a cool place overnight.
6. The next day, examine the water in the beaker for signs of living things, such as cloudy water or a strong odor. Fuzzy growths or threads are evidence that molds are growing. A greenish tint in the water shows that algae are present.
7. Use a dropper to remove some of the water. Place a drop of it on a glass slide, and put a coverslip over it.
8. Place the slide under the microscope. Start with low power, and focus on some debris.

The debris will probably have bacteria and other microorganisms on or around it. Switch to high power.

9. Record the date in the data table, and note your observations. Count or estimate the number of organisms under one field of view. Estimate the approximate sizes of the organisms. (*Hint: The diameter of the field of view under high power of most microscopes is 0.4 mm.*) Try to identify some of the organisms you see, using reference sources. Also measure and record the pH of the water.
10. Repeat steps 6–9 each day for two weeks.

ANALYSIS
1. How did the numbers and types of organisms change over the two weeks you made observations?
2. Why might certain populations have disappeared after some time?
3. What is the relationship between pH and the number of organisms that were present in the community?

CONCLUSION
Did you see any evidence of ecological succession? If so, describe it.

CHAPTER 6 REVIEW

KEY TERMS

parasitism 6.1
symbiosis 6.1
primary succession 6.2

lichen 6.2
climax community 6.2
secondary succession 6.2

biome 6.4

CHAPTER SUMMARY

6.1 Species interact with the other species in their habitats. All consumers must eat other organisms. There are several kinds of symbiotic relationships between species: parasitism, commensalism, and mutualism.

6.2 In the process of primary succession, bare rocks are colonized by a series of communities, ending with the climax community. Secondary succession occurs when the plant community in an area is removed, but the soil remains. Island succession is affected by which plants and animals manage to travel to the island.

6.3 Ecosystems exist in a state of equilibrium. If an ecosystem goes out of balance, it will adjust to regain the balanced state. Some disturbances may destroy whole ecosystems. The activity of humans is causing disturbances in the ecosystems of Earth.

6.4 The surface of Earth is very diverse. Conditions of precipitation and temperature differ from place to place. The general categories of ecosystems are called biomes. There are eight major land biomes: desert, tundra, steppe, prairie, savanna, deciduous forest, coniferous forest, and rain forest.

MULTIPLE CHOICE

Choose the letter of the word or phrase that best completes each statement.

1. An organism that actively hunts other organisms is a(n) (a) herbivore; (b) insect; (c) predator; (d) prey.

2. A relationship between species in which one species benefits and the other is harmed is called (a) parasitism; (b) commensalism; (c) mutualism; (d) symbiosis.

3. A relationship between species in which both species benefit is called (a) parasitism; (b) commensalism; (c) mutualism; (d) symbiosis.

4. An example of an organism from a pioneer community is (a) lichen; (b) white spruce; (c) heath mat; (d) grass.

5. Secondary succession occurs in an area where the community has been destroyed and the soil has been (a) removed; (b) destroyed; (c) compressed; (d) preserved.

6. Birds are more common in island communities than are mammals because birds can (a) eat different foods; (b) fly; (c) swim and walk; (d) adapt to new conditions.

7. If an ecosystem is disturbed, goes out of balance, and cannot return to a state of equilibrium, the species living there will most likely (a) freeze; (b) find new resources; (c) move; (d) become extinct.

8. The kind of biome that will develop in an area is determined mainly by temperature and (a) pressure; (b) precipitation; (c) average wind speed; (d) types of animals present.

9. A land biome that is not a grassland is the (a) savanna; (b) prairie; (c) tundra; (d) steppe.

10. The land biome that covers the largest percentage of land is the (a) desert; (b) tundra; (c) steppe; (d) savanna.

TRUE/FALSE

Write true *if the statement is true. If the statement is false, change the underlined word or phrase to make it true.*

1. The population of the snowshoe hares in Figure 6.1 was usually <u>larger</u> than the population of lynxes.
2. In a commensal relationship, one species is <u>harmed</u> while the other benefits.
3. Parasites are usually <u>larger</u> than their host organisms.
4. A lichen is one organism usually found in a <u>climax</u> community.
5. <u>Secondary succession</u> often happens after human disturbance.
6. The finches of the Galapagos Islands adapted to fit several different <u>niches</u>.
7. <u>Grassland</u> biomes contain the largest percentage of Earth's biomass.
8. Desert and tundra biomes have different temperatures, but the amount of precipitation each receives is <u>nearly equal</u>.

CONCEPT REVIEW

Write a complete response for each of the following.

1. How are predators different from parasites? What do these two groups have in common?
2. Use the example of the yucca plant and the yucca moth to describe the concept of mutualism.
3. Explain the process of primary succession. How does one community help establish the community that follows it?
4. How does the evolution of finch species on the Galapagos Islands support the idea of competitive exclusion introduced in Chapter 5?
5. Deserts usually have mineral-rich soil and cover a large part of Earth's surface. Why do deserts support only 1 percent of Earth's biomass?

THINK CRITICALLY

1. Suppose an unusually severe winter killed most of the snowshoe hare population in an area of northern Canada. How would the lynx population be affected?
2. The yucca plant and the yucca moth cannot survive without each other. How could a relationship like this evolve? Assume that both organisms had ancestors that were not dependent on one another.
3. What might happen to the finches on the Galapagos Islands if humans introduced seed-eating mice to the islands?
4. Why are temperature and rainfall so important in determining which biome will develop in an area? What other factors might also be involved?

Computer Activity Write a computer program that performs the function of the graph in Figure 6.12. The program should ask for the average annual temperature and precipitation for an area and then output the predicted biome for that area based on these two pieces of information. Use the data in the graph in Figure 6.12 when writing your program.

WRITING CREATIVELY

Imagine you are a scientist studying a new volcanic island that has just formed far out at sea. Describe the process of primary succession on the island. Which organisms arrive first? Describe how each species travels to the new island. How do species evolve once they settle on the island?

PORTFOLIO

Make a videotape, a photographic diary, or a series of sketches showing the plants and other organisms around your school and home. Write a short essay discussing how these organisms fit into the biome in which you live.

....

GRAPHIC ANALYSIS

Use Figure 6.12 to answer the following.

1. Which biome covers most of Florida?
2. Which continent has most of the world's rain forests?
3. Where are most deserts located?
4. Where are most coniferous forests located?

ACTIVITY 6.2

PROBLEM

If a grass-and-clover lawn is not cut, which plant is likely to dominate?

MATERIALS

- 3 paper cups
- enough soil to fill the cups
- grass seeds
- clover seeds
- metric ruler
- 3 sheets of paper
- water
- graduated cylinder

PREDICTION

After reading the entire activity, write a prediction that relates to the problem.

PROCEDURE

1. Label the paper cups *A, B,* and *C.* Fill each cup a few centimeters from the top with soil.
2. Sprinkle some grass seeds on the soil in Cup *A.* Sprinkle clover seeds on the soil in Cup *B.* Sprinkle both grass and clover seeds on the soil in Cup *C.*
3. Place the cups in a well-lit area. Water the cups each day. Pour the same amount of water in each cup, and do not overwater.
4. Allow the plants to grow until one type of plant in Cup *C* crowds out and clearly dominates the other. *Note: This step will probably take 2–3 weeks.*
5. Label three separate sheets of paper *A, B,* and *C.* Pull four grass plants from Cup *A,* four clover plants from Cup *B,* and two grass and two clover plants from Cup *C.* Place the uprooted plants on the appropriate sheet of paper. Pull the plants gently from the soil by the base so that the roots do not break off.
6. Measure the number and length of the roots on each plant that was pulled. Also measure the color and number of leaves on each plant. Record the measurements in a data table.

ANALYSIS

1. How did the measurements of the grass plants grown alone compare to those of the grass plants that were grown with clover?
2. How did the measurements of the clover plants grown alone compare to those of the clover plants that were grown with grass?

CONCLUSION

How did the grass and clover plants compete? What was the outcome of their competition?

PEREGRINE FALCON

The Peregrine Falcon Returns!

Peregrine falcons once hunted in the skies over much of North America. These fierce predators, about the size of large crows, can catch prey in midair at speeds of over 200 miles per hour. They reside at the top of their food chain. But by the 1960s, their numbers were dwindling.

The culprit, according to scientists, was DDT, a pesticide that only a decade earlier had been called the "wonder pesticide." In addition to effectively killing agricultural pests, DDT played an important role in controlling insects that spread diseases such as malaria. It was used in many countries all over the world.

Unfortunately, many of the insects killed by DDT were eaten by birds. Peregrine falcons prey on other birds. As the falcons ate poisoned birds, DDT built up in their bodies.

DDT did not always kill falcons outright, but it interfered with reproduction. Falcons began to lay eggs with shells so thin that they broke when the parents tried to incubate them.

Unable to successfully reproduce, peregrine falcons became endangered. By 1970, they had vanished from the eastern United States, and fewer than 50 birds remained in western states.

In 1972, the United States banned the use of DDT. At the same time, conservation groups began breeding peregrine falcons in captivity and releasing them into the wild.

Gradually, the peregrine falcon population began to increase. By 1996, more than 2000 peregrine falcons were living in the continental United States. A surprising number have adapted to city life. In cities, they nest on the window ledges of skyscrapers and prey on pigeons and starlings. New York City alone has 15 nesting pairs of falcons. With its successful return, the peregrine falcon has now had its status upgraded from endangered to threatened.

Checkpoint

1. What actions did people take to help the peregrine falcon?
2. How might the need for pesticides be balanced with the needs of wild animals?

These peregrine falcons are part of a captive breeding program designed to increase the size of their population.

◀ Wildlife Biologist

Wildlife biologists study organisms and how they interact with each other, with other species, and with their environments. These scientists also study how human impact on the environment might affect species that live in the same area.

Park Ranger ▶

One responsibility of a park ranger includes educating the public about wildlife ecology. Teaching wildlife ecology fulfills several functions: educating students about current environmental methods and procedures, carrying out valuable field studies and research, and increasing public awareness about local and global ecological issues.

Wildlife Manager ▲

Most wildlife managers are employed by the federal government, typically in the Department of Agriculture's Forest Service or in the Department of the Interior's Fish and Wildlife Service. However, state and local governments generally provide the most challenging opportunities, including the implementation of endangered species recovery programs.

For More Information

National Wildlife Federation
8925 Leesburg Pike
Vienna, VA 22184
(703) 790-4100
http://www.nwf.org
Publications: *Conservation Directory* and *National Wildlife Magazine*

U.S. Fish and Wildlife Service
U.S. Department of the Interior
Washington, DC 20240
(202) 208-5634
http://www.fws.gov

The Wildlife Society
5410 Grosvenor Lane, Suite 200
Bethesda, MD 20814
(301) 897-9770
http://www.wildlife.org
email: tws@wildlife.org

BIOMES

D o the plants and animals in this photograph look similar to those that live near you? Probably not. This photograph is of the savanna grassland of the Masai Mara National Reserve in Kenya, Africa. The savanna grasslands are one of a number of biomes that are characterized by the climate and the organisms that live in them. The wide open grasslands enable the cheetahs to use their incredible speed to chase and capture prey. In this unit, you will learn more about the climates and organisms that make up Earth's biomes.

Discover It!

What Is Your Biome?

Land biomes are determined by the climate in that region. Study the climate and vegetation of the countries on the maps on pages 436–447.

1. What type of biome is characteristic of where you live?

2. How is the biome you live in different from the biomes in Africa?

CHAPTER

7

DESERT AND TUNDRA BIOMES

For most of the year, the desert looks practically lifeless. Nothing seems to move except for a few insects and some hardy plants blowing in the dry wind. But when the rainy season comes, the landscape explodes into life, with many plant and animal species hurrying to feed, grow, and reproduce. Then, as suddenly as it began, the rain is gone, and life seems to go into hiding until the cycle begins anew.

This brief seasonal growth period occurs each year in the two harshest terrestrial biomes: the desert and the tundra. In the desert, the growth follows brief periods of heavy rain. In the Arctic tundra, it comes with the short summer.

7.1 DESERTS

OBJECTIVES • *Describe* the characteristics of a desert. • *Explain* how desert organisms are adapted to live in their environment.

What do you think of when you hear the word *desert?* You may imagine a scene with camels trekking across hot, barren sands. Perhaps you think of a scene with tall, spiny cacti and balls of tumbleweed rolling by. From just these two scenes, you can see that not all deserts are alike. Deserts in different parts of the world have different characteristics and are home to different organisms. All deserts have one thing in common, however. They all receive very little rain during the course of a year.

Desert soils tend to be rich in minerals but poor in organic material. *Rainwater moving through soil carries minerals deeper into the soil in a process called* **leaching**. Because deserts do not receive much rainfall, there is very little leaching of the soil. As a result, the upper layers of desert soil are rich in minerals. The dryness of a desert prevents many plants from living there. The lack of rainfall also slows the decay of organic material. Because decayed organic matter is an important part of topsoil, deserts do not have much topsoil.

Loose, dry desert soil is easily blown away by wind. *If the loose soil is removed, a lower layer of soil called* **pavement** *becomes exposed.* The pavement is the desert floor. The desert floor is made mostly of hard-baked sand, bare rock particles, or both.

In the United States, deserts can be divided into two main types: cool deserts and hot deserts. Cool and hot deserts result from variations in elevation and latitude that affect their winter and summer climates. Cool deserts are located on the eastern side of the Sierra Nevada and Rocky Mountains. Hot deserts are located in the southwest, particularly Arizona, New Mexico, and western Texas.

LINK

Social Studies

Irrigation of desert soils has enabled some nations to turn deserts into croplands. In the Middle East, for example, irrigation projects have turned the Golan Heights into citrus orchards. Such projects require careful planning and management to avoid draining water resources and accumulating salts in the soil.

Figure 7.1 The cool deserts of North America are dominated by sagebrush (left). Cacti are a dominant plant of North American hot deserts.

Desert Climate

Deserts rarely get more than 25 cm of precipitation in any single year. The lack of precipitation in a desert determines the kinds of plants that can live in the region. Because plants are at the base of the food web, the types of plants determine the types of animals in the area as well. The lack of precipitation, therefore, is the limiting factor of the desert biome.

How much precipitation does a desert get? Although the exact amount varies from place to place and from year to year, most deserts receive less than 10 cm of rain each year. Most of the rain in the desert falls during a few short thunderstorms, followed by long dry periods. Because the desert pavement tends to be dry and compacted, the rain that falls on the desert usually runs off rather than being absorbed into the ground.

The lack of moisture also affects desert temperatures. Moisture in the atmosphere has a stabilizing effect on a region's temperature. It acts as a blanket over the ground, absorbing heat during the day and holding in the warmth at night. Because desert air contains so little moisture, temperatures can rise and fall dramatically, with very hot days followed by very cold nights.

Desert Organisms

Organisms that live in the desert are adapted to survive two challenges: lack of water and extreme temperatures. Some of the adaptations that enable organisms to live in the desert involve physical structures. Other adaptations involve behaviors. Although the challenge of living in the desert may seem great, deserts are actually species-rich, complex ecosystems.

Figure 7.2 Although not related to the cactus, the aloe plant (left) has similar adaptations to the desert. The mesquite tree (right) has very deep roots that draw water from underground sources.

Desert Plants   Plants that live in the desert must be able to absorb water from the ground. They must also prevent the loss of

water from their tissues. The spines of a cactus are a familiar adaptation for preventing water loss. Cactus spines are actually the leaves of the plant. The spines reduce the loss of water by reducing the surface area from which water can evaporate.

Cacti are also able to store water in their tissues. *Plants such as cacti, which have thick, water-filled tissues, are called* **succulents** (SUK-yu-luhnts). The stored water in succulents enables the plants to survive long dry periods. Because cacti contain stored water, they are an attractive source of both food and water for desert animals. The spines of the cactus help protect the plant from being eaten by most animals.

Although cacti are native only to the American continents, deserts elsewhere also have succulents. Aloe vera is a succulent native to Africa. Cacti and aloe are not related, but both types of plants have similar adaptations that include the presence of succulent tissues surrounded by protective spines.

Adaptations to the dryness of a desert can also be seen in the roots of desert plants. Some desert plants have very shallow roots that grow over a wide area. These roots maximize the amount of rain the plant can absorb during the infrequent rainstorms. Other desert plants, such as the mesquite tree in Figure 7.2, have roots that extend deep into the ground, drawing up water as far as 20 m.

Desert Animals   The desert is home to many types of animals, including insects, reptiles, birds, and mammals. Most desert animals get the water they need from their foods. Like plants, desert animals face the challenge of reducing water loss.

All insects and reptiles have an outer coating that reduces water loss. The shells of insects and the scales of reptiles evolved as these animals adapted to life on land. The protective coverings make insects and reptiles well equipped to survive the dryness of a desert.

Most desert animals also have adaptations that enable them to survive the heat. Rodents, including the kangaroo rat, are common desert mammals. Desert rodents spend their days in underground burrows where they are protected from the heat of the sun. They come out of their burrows to seek food at night. *Animals that are active at night and sleep during the day are called* **nocturnal** (nok-TERN-ul) animals. Many of the animals in the desert are nocturnal.

LINK
Health

Aloe is a commonly used plant in the traditional medicine of Egypt and other cultures. The gel-like tissue beneath the tough, spiny exterior is used to soothe mild burns and other skin irritations.

Figure 7.3 The fennec is native to North Africa and the Middle East. The mammal's long ears help release heat from its body.

SECTION REVIEW

1. What is meant by the pavement of a desert?
2. Explain why desert soil tends to be rich in minerals but poor in organic material.
3. **Infer** How would the relatively small size of desert animals be an advantage in such a warm climate?

7.2 FORMATION OF DESERTS

OBJECTIVE • ***Illustrate*** *the processes that cause deserts to form.*

Deserts cover 30 percent of Earth's surface and are found on every continent except Antarctica. Most deserts lie within two broad belts known as desert belts on either side of the equator. The deserts of the northern belt are near the Tropic of Cancer (23°N), and the southern desert belt is near the Tropic of Capricorn (23°S).

Natural Desert Formation

Air over the equator receives the most direct radiation from the sun. This direct radiation raises temperatures and causes rapid evaporation of water from the surface. The high rate of evaporation causes the air over the equator to be very moist. This moisture returns to Earth in frequent rainstorms, causing the region near the equator to be very wet. The wet region between the Tropic of Cancer and the Tropic of Capricorn is commonly called the *tropics*. Once the moisture in the air has fallen as rain, the air becomes quite dry and flows toward Earth's poles. As it does, the air becomes cooler and denser. Beyond the tropics, the cool, dry air sinks back to Earth's surface. These dry winds result in the formation of deserts.

The exact locations of deserts within the desert belts are determined, in part, by local geographic features, such as mountain ranges. The deserts of the United States are an example. In the United States, most winds move from west to east. As winds move

Figure 7.4 As warm, moist air rises over mountain ranges, the water cools and falls to the ground as precipitation. The dry air then descends, contributing to the formation of deserts.

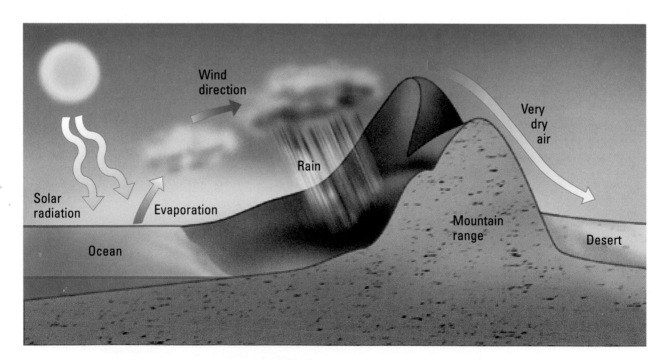

Figure 7.5 The Sahel region bordering the Sahara Desert was once a productive cropland. A natural drought and poor land management have turned the area into a desert that can no longer support agriculture. Food must now be brought in from elsewhere.

across the western part of the country, they force warm, moist air up and over the Sierra Nevada. As the air rises above the mountains, it cools and drops most of its moisture as rain or snow.

Because the air blowing across the mountains drops its moisture on the western slope, it is very dry when it reaches the eastern side. This dry air allows moisture to evaporate from the soil. The result is either a desert or a *semiarid* (SEM-ee-AYR-id) region, a region that is dry, but not as dry as a desert. The drying of the eastern side of the mountains is called the *rainshadow effect*.

Desertification

Deserts are often bordered by semiarid regions. These areas support communities of grasses and shrubs. Human activities, especially raising livestock, have caused many semiarid regions to become deserts. *The transformation of semiarid land into desert is called* **desertification** (de-ZERT-ih-fih-KAY-shun).

Desertification can begin when too many animals graze on too little land. The animals eat all the vegetation and compact the soil with their hooves. Without plants, the topsoil erodes quickly. The bare land reflects more of the sun's heat. This process can change weather patterns, reducing local rainfall. Without rain or topsoil, the area becomes a desert. Desertification has occurred on every continent except Antarctica, and is especially severe where deserts occur nearby. About 6 million hectares of land become desert each year. This is an area about the size of the state of Maine.

Field Activity

Temperature on Earth's surface depends on the angle of the sun's rays. Test this by making two solar collectors.

1. Construct the solar collectors by lining two shoeboxes with foil and taping a thermometer to the bottom of each one. Keep one held at a right angle to the sun, the other held at a wider angle.

2. Measure the rise in temperature in both boxes every 5 minutes for 30 minutes. Which one warmed up faster?

SECTION REVIEW

1. How do semiarid regions differ from deserts?
2. Explain the role of mountains in the formation of deserts.
3. **Deduce** Why do you think a farmer would try to raise more livestock than the land can support, considering the end result?

7.3 TUNDRA

OBJECTIVES • **Describe** *why the characteristics of the tundra make it a fragile ecosystem.* • **Compare** *the characteristics of tundra organisms with those of their relatives in warmer climates.*

The tundra is a cold, windy, dry region. The tundra is located in the Northern Hemisphere just south of the polar ice caps in Alaska, Canada, Greenland, Iceland, Scandinavia, and Russia. In the Southern Hemisphere, the region that would be the tundra is covered by oceans.

The tundra is one of the largest biomes, making up almost 10 percent of Earth's surface. However, fewer types of organisms live in the tundra than in any other biome. The lack of biodiversity makes tundra ecosystems very fragile and unstable if disturbed.

Tundra Climate

Like the desert, the tundra receives little precipitation. In fact, the tundra usually receives less than 25 cm of precipitation each year. The main difference between deserts and tundra is temperature. In the tundra, air temperature rarely reaches above 10 °C, even in summer. Because temperatures in the tundra are below freezing almost all year, most precipitation falls as ice and snow. Temperature, therefore, is the limiting factor in the tundra.

Summer days are long and cool in the tundra. Because of the low temperatures, only the top layer, or active zone, of soil thaws during the summer months. The active zone may be as thin as 8 cm in some areas. Beneath the active zone, the soil never thaws. *The frozen soil below the active zone is called* **permafrost**. A dense mat of mosses, grasses, and other plant life covers the active zone during summer. This mat keeps the ground insulated and prevents the permafrost from melting. Therefore, any disruption of the plants in the active zone can affect the permafrost.

Because of the short growing season and low temperatures, tundra vegetation does not recover from disruption as quickly as does vegetation in other biomes. Tracks from wagons that crossed the tundra 100 years ago are still visible in some areas.

The tundra receives a small amount of rainfall in summer. Rain that falls during the summer months cannot drain through the permafrost. Instead, the water collects at the surface, forming bogs, marshes, ponds, and small streams. These areas serve as the breeding grounds for insects such as mosquitoes and black flies. These insects are an important link in the food web of the tundra. The permafrost is therefore an important factor in the stability of a tundra ecosystem.

Dateline 1974

After several years of planning, construction began on the Alaska oil pipeline, which transports oil 1285 km south from the North Slope of Alaska. The pipeline was completed three years later. Because oil must be kept warm in order to flow, parts of the pipeline were constructed above the ground to protect the permafrost from melting. To avoid interfering with the migration of caribou and other animals, the pipeline includes 554 elevated and 23 buried sections for animal crossings.

Figure 7.6 Summers in the tundra are short and cool. Although the tundra supports a year-round community, some animals, such as the red-throated loon (inset), migrate to the tundra only during their breeding season.

Tundra Organisms

In spite of the cold climate and the lack of rainfall, some plants do grow in the tundra. The summer growing season lasts only about 60 days. The most common tundra plants are mosses, shrubs, grasses, and small, colorful wildflowers.

Tundra Plants   The ground is warmed by radiant energy from the sun. Tundra plants tend to be small and grow close to the warm ground. The roots of tundra plants grow very close to the ground's surface because they cannot penetrate the permafrost. Trees that grow in the tundra such as willow and alder are much smaller than their relatives in warmer climates. In fact, tundra trees are usually less than 1 m tall and are more like shrubs than trees. These plants are dwarfed by the short growing season, by the limited space for roots to grow, and by strong polar winds.

Tundra Animals   Many of the animals that live in the tundra are seasonal visitors. *Seasonal travel is called* **migration**. Many species of birds, for example, migrate to the tundra during their breeding season. There are fewer predators in the tundra, which makes it a safer place than most to raise young. Migratory birds of the tundra feed mostly on the abundant flies and mosquitoes that breed in the bogs and ponds during summer. The birds, in turn, serve as a food source for migratory predators such as the Arctic fox. Small herbivores are also common, but there are no reptiles or amphibians.

The caribou, a close relative of the reindeer, is a large migratory mammal of the tundra. The adaptations that enable caribou to live in their environment are common among tundra mammals. Like

Think About It!

Warm-blooded animals that live in colder climates tend to have larger bodies with relatively smaller protruding parts, such as limbs and ears, than closely related species that live in warmer climates.

1. What do you think is the advantage of a large body size?

2. What do you think is the advantage of small limbs and ears?

Figure 7.7 The Arctic hare (left) is adapted to live in the tundra. The jackrabbit (right) is a desert dweller. What differences can you see in the adaptations of these two animals to their environments?

many mammals of the tundra, caribou have a thick coat. The hairs of their coat are filled with air. The air acts as insulation, reducing the loss of body heat. Caribou also have wide hooves to help them move easily through snow or on the muddy ground in warmer months.

Huge herds of thousands of caribou thunder across the tundra every year in search of food. The caribou feed primarily on lichens that grow on rocky surfaces. As you learned in Chapter 6, *lichens* are organisms that are made up of a fungus and an alga. Lichens grow very slowly and are very sensitive to air pollution. In recent years, the sizes of the caribou herds have dropped quite a bit. This decline may be due, in part, to the loss of lichens as a result of pollution. Caribou and other migratory animals are also threatened by structures that interfere with their migratory routes. The instinctive behaviors that enable these animals to follow the correct path year after year tend to be very inflexible.

Some of the mammals in the tundra are year-round residents. The Arctic fox hunts migratory birds during summer and buries them in the permafrost, to eat during the long winter. Musk oxen, coastal polar bears, and wolverines are other permanent members of the tundra community.

SECTION REVIEW

1. What are lichens? What is their ecological role in the tundra?
2. **Infer** Many mammals of the tundra have brown coats during part of the year and white coats the rest of the year. Why is this change of color an adaptation to the environment?
3. **Analyze** You have read that permafrost is an important abiotic factor in the tundra. Describe how the melting of permafrost could affect the tundra food web.

Oil in the Tundra

In 1968, oil geologists found a large oil deposit in northern Alaska. The deposit was estimated to contain 10 to 20 billion barrels of oil, making it the largest oil field in the United States.

To transport the oil from Alaska's north coast to port cities along the south coast, oil companies built an 800-mi pipeline extending from Prudhoe Bay to the port of Valdez. Before the pipeline was built, many environmental studies were done to determine the potential impact the pipeline might have on huge herds of caribou and other species of birds and fish.

Is the pipeline worth the environmental risk?

Alaska Needs the Pipeline

The Trans-Alaska Pipeline is essential to the state's economy. Revenues from the pipeline cover 85 percent of Alaska's state budget. Some of the revenue goes into a special fund that pays all residents of Alaska a dividend of about $900 per year. Alaska's land is unsuitable for farming or ranching, so there are not many other options for generating income for the state.

Critics say that the pipeline may not be safe for animals. But the route of the pipeline was designed so that there are many places where the migrating caribou can cross.

The Pipeline Puts the Tundra at Risk

Although it is true that the pipeline was designed with many features to protect wildlife, accidents have occurred. In the first three years of operation, the pipeline cracked twice. One break caused the release of over 5000 barrels of crude oil onto the tundra and into local rivers.

The oil companies say that they have emergency plans in case of oil spills. But the tundra is a delicate biome, with a very simple food web. If an oil spill kills large numbers of trout, a major part of the grizzly bear's diet would be lost. Also, the growing season is short, so plant communities will not be reestablished quickly, even if a spill can be cleaned up.

Consider the Issue

1. Do you think the pipeline should have been built? Why or why not?
2. A road runs along the entire route of the pipeline. How do you think this affects the safety issues? Explain your answer.

The Trans-Alaska pipeline runs over 800 miles, from Prudhoe Bay in the north to the port of Valdez in the south.

Climatograms

PROBLEM

How are climatograms constructed and interpreted?

MATERIALS

- graph paper
- pencil

PREDICTION

Write a prediction about the advantage of using climatograms instead of tables to analyze data.

PROCEDURE

1. Climatograms are graphs that summarize the measurements of temperature and precipitation in an area. Study the climatogram for a deciduous forest.
2. Climatic data for four cities are given in the table. Using graph paper, construct a climatogram for each city.

ANALYSIS

1. Which cities are located in desert biomes? How can you tell?
2. Which cities are located in tundra biomes? How can you tell?

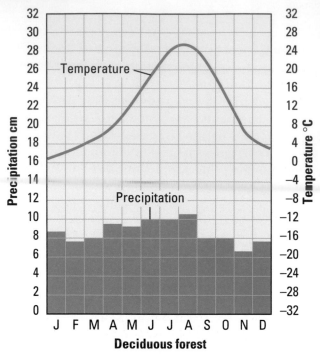

Deciduous forest

3. How are the climates of the two desert cities different?
4. How are the climates of the two tundra cities different?

CONCLUSION

What are the advantages of constructing climatograms compared to studying the same data from tables?

Climates of Four Cities

City 1	J	F	M	A	M	J	J	A	S	O	N	D
T (°C)	-26	-28	-26	-20	-8	0	4	3	-2	-10	-18	-24
P (cm)	0.5	0.5	0.5	0.5	0.5	1	2	2	1.5	1	0.5	0.5
City 2	J	F	M	A	M	J	J	A	S	O	N	D
T (°C)	-1	2	6	8	12	16	20	14	14	10	4	0
P (cm)	3	3	2	1	1	1	0.5	0.5	0.5	1	1	2
City 3	J	F	M	A	M	J	J	A	S	O	N	D
T (°C)	24	25	26	28	31	32	31	30	31	29	27	25
P (cm)	1	0.5	1	0.5	0.3	0.3	0	0.3	0.3	0.3	0.3	0.3
City 4	J	F	M	A	M	J	J	A	S	O	N	D
T (°C)	-23	-23	-21	-14	-4	2	5	5	1	-4	-10	-17
P (cm)	1	1	2	2	2	1	2	3	3	3	3	1

CHAPTER 7 REVIEW

KEY TERMS

leaching 7.1

pavement 7.1

succulent 7.1

nocturnal 7.1

desertification 7.2

permafrost 7.3

migration 7.3

CHAPTER SUMMARY

7.1 All deserts receive very little annual rainfall. Desert soils are rich in minerals but lack organic materials and topsoil. Desert climates have a wide temperature variation, due to low atmospheric moisture. The desert ecosystem is rich with plants and animals that have adapted to the lack of water and severe temperatures.

7.2 Desert formation may occur naturally or as a result of human activity. Natural causes are global air movement driven by solar heating and geo-graphic features, such as mountains. Human activities, such as raising livestock, also produce deserts by the process of desertification.

7.3 Cold temperatures distinguish the tundra from deserts. Located in the Northern Hemisphere, the tundra is large in surface area but low in biodi-versity. The tundra's permafrost layer is a key fea-ture of the tundra. Few plants have adapted to the harsh climate, and many of the tundra's animal inhabitants are migratory.

MULTIPLE CHOICE

Choose the letter of the word or phrase that best com-pletes each statement.

1. The common characteristic of all deserts is (a) hot temperatures; (b) low annual rain-fall; (c) simple ecosystems; (d) mineral-poor soil.

2. The rainshadow effect causes (a) desertifi-cation; (b) leaching; (c) natural desert for-mation; (d) increased precipitation.

3. The main difference between deserts and the tundra is (a) amount of precipitation; (b) moisture content of the air; (c) limited topsoil; (d) temperature.

4. Leaching (a) is common in desert climates; (b) increases the mineral content of the soil; (c) is unrelated to the amount of rain-fall; (d) washes minerals from the topsoil.

5. Desertification is caused by (a) human activ-ity; (b) solar heating patterns; (c) leaching of the soil; (d) temperature variations.

6. Adaptations to desert life do not include (a) long limbs and ears; (b) a waterproof covering; (c) a large, compact body; (d) an ability to store water.

7. The spines of desert plants (a) provide pro-tection; (b) increase surface area; (c) store water; (d) are unique to the cacti of the Western Hemisphere.

8. The limiting factor in the tundra is (a) rain-fall; (b) temperature; (c) sunlight; (d) soil nutrients.

9. Migratory birds in the tundra feed mostly on (a) seeds; (b) small rodents; (c) lichens; (d) flies and mosquitoes.

10. Tundra ecosystems are considered to be fragile because of (a) the low humidity; (b) low biodiversity; (c) low economic value; (d) low latitude.

11. The Trans-Alaska Pipeline was built above ground to prevent (a) the migration of cari-bou and other animals; (b) damage to the fragile tundra topsoil; (c) melting of the permafrost; (d) tourists and other travelers from crossing.

12. Compared to the desert fennec in Figure 7.3, you might expect the Arctic fox to have (a) longer legs; (b) shorter ears; (c) shorter fur; (d) larger eyes.

WORD COMPARISONS

Write the letter of the second word pair that best matches the first pair.

1. Desert: pavement as (a) tundra: cement; (b) pavement: city; (c) tundra: permafrost; (d) tundra: desert.
2. Desert belt: tropics as (a) middle latitude: equatorial; (b) hot: cool; (c) wet: dry; (d) east: west.
3. Precipitation: desert as (a) rain: tropics; (b) temperature: tundra; (c) desert: heat; (d) mountains: rain shadow.
4. Cool deserts: sagebrush as (a) lichens: tundra; (b) hot deserts: dwarf trees; (c) tundra: migration; (d) hot deserts: cacti.
5. Cactus: the Americas as (a) aloe: Africa; (b) Arctic hare: jackrabbit; (c) mesquite: dwarf birch; (d) tundra: willow.

CONCEPT REVIEW

Write a complete response to each of the following.

1. Explain why desert soils tend to be rich in minerals but poor in topsoil.
2. How does the behavior of desert rodents aid their survival?
3. How are reptiles and insects adapted to life in the desert? Why do these animals have such adaptations?
4. Desert plants may have very deep root systems or very shallow root systems. Describe the advantage of each.
5. Describe the process of desertification.

THINK CRITICALLY

1. List three potential problems that could arise from drilling for oil in the tundra.
2. Deserts tend to be hotter during the day and cooler at night than other areas with similar latitude. Explain why this is true.
3. Describe two ways in which the permafrost layer affects tundra ecosystems. How might the ecosystems be affected if the permafrost were to melt?
4. Many scientists predict that the temperature of Earth could rise as a result of the greenhouse effect. How might an increase in temperature affect the deserts and tundras of the world?

WRITE FOR UNDERSTANDING

Suppose a government leader in a small, semi-arid nation is planning to convert unused land into farmland for cattle grazing. Write a letter to this person explaining the risks of such farming in semiarid regions, and long-term factors that must be considered.

PORTFOLIO

1. In 1991, the United States and other members of the United Nations participated in Operation Desert Storm in the deserts near the Persian Gulf. Conduct library research about the problems faced by soldiers fighting in the desert environment. Make a presentation of your findings to the class.
2. There are several communities of people who live in the tundra of Alaska and Canada. Locate a high school in a tundra region, and contact the school about establishing pen pals. From your pen pal, find out how living in the tundra affects the daily lives of teenagers in their community.

GRAPHIC ANALYSIS

Use the figure to answer the following.

1. According to the map, in which parts of North America is the risk of desertification highest?
2. Why do you think the risk of desertification is lower in most of Canada and Mexico than in the United States?
3. Why do you think there are no deserts in the eastern United States, even though it is within the desert belt? Explain your answer.

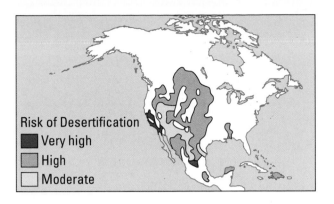

Risk of Desertification
- ■ Very high
- ■ High
- □ Moderate

ACTIVITY 7.2

PROBLEM

How can off-road vehicles affect a desert food web?

MATERIALS

- 4 sheets of white construction paper
- reference sources

PREDICTION

Predict how the use of off-road vehicles could affect the desert ecosystem.

PROCEDURE

1. The organisms shown in the table are producers, or primary or secondary consumers. They are part of a food web in a California desert. You probably know something about the niche of some of the organisms. Use reference sources to find out more about those that are unfamiliar to you.
2. On construction paper, draw a food web involving at least ten of the desert organisms.
3. The desert habitat of these organisms has become a popular site for driving off-road vehicles. Choose a species of (a) producer, (b) primary consumer, and (c) secondary consumer that you think would be directly affected by off-road vehicles. Draw three new food webs. In each new food web, show how the original food web would be

different if one of the three populations you chose was destroyed.

Organisms of a Desert Ecosystem	
Kangaroo rat	Wildflower (seeds)
Sidewinder	Raven
Pocket mouse	Sagebrush
Kit fox	Desert bighorn sheep
Coyote	Roadrunner
Antelope jackrabbit	Insects
Mule deer	Flatland desert lizard
Bobcat	Desert tortoise

ANALYSIS

Describe how two different populations would be affected when (a) one population of producer was destroyed, (b) one population of primary consumer was destroyed, and (c) one population of secondary consumer was destroyed.

CONCLUSION

1. How can off-road vehicles affect the food web in a desert ecosystem?
2. What limits, if any, should be placed on off-road vehicles in desert ecosystems?

CHAPTER

8

GRASSLAND BIOMES

Have you ever stood on a lawn, looked at the short blades of grass, and thought, "It's just grass"? It is simple and green, and sometimes it turns brown and looks dead. As simple as grass seems, this grass and grasses like it feed billions of organisms all over the world. The bread on your sandwich and the cereal in your breakfast bowl are made from grasses. All grains are domesticated grasses. Cattle and sheep eat grass. Prairie dogs and billions of insects eat grass. Grasses can survive temperatures from –25 °C to 70 °C. Grass fires can burn hundreds of thousands of acres. Still, grasses survive and are the most widely distributed flowering plant in the world. Is it really "just grass"?

8.1 GRASSLANDS

• **Describe** the characteristics of grasslands.
• **Identify** where grasslands are located.

A **grassland** *is an ecosystem in which there is more water than in a desert, but not enough water to support a forest.* Grasslands begin at the edges of the desert biome and stretch across the land to the forest biome. Grasslands exist in Africa, central Asia, North America, South America, and Australia. Scientists think that at some time in Earth's history, grasslands covered nearly half the land. In the United States, grasslands stretch from the Rocky Mountains in the west to the forests in the east, and from Canada to Mexico. The vegetation maps in the Atlas at the back of this book show the locations of Earth's grasslands.

Grassland Climate

The climate of grasslands is a little wetter than the climate of deserts. Recall from Chapter 7 that many deserts are located in the rain shadows of mountain ranges. In rain shadows, dry air blows across the land and drops very little or no rain. As the dry air blows, it absorbs the water that evaporates from the land and becomes moist again. Eventually, there is enough moisture for more rain to fall.

The **desert-grassland boundary** *is the area between deserts and grasslands where increased rainfall enables some grasses to grow.* Because rainfall is an abiotic factor affecting both deserts and grasslands, long-term changes in climate patterns can change the desert-grassland boundary. If rainfall increases, the desert can become grassland. If the climate becomes too dry in a grassland, the biome cannot support the organisms that usually live there and it will become a desert.

Grassland Organisms

The biotic and abiotic factors characteristic of a grassland ecosystem determine what types of organisms will be found there. Although many kinds of organisms live in the grasslands, grasses are the most common.

Grasslands have hot, dry summers, making rainfall a grassland's most significant limiting factor. Without enough rain, grasslands cannot develop. However, scientists have determined that natural grass fires, ignited by lightning, also play an important role in the development of grasslands.

The occasional fires common in grasslands keep the number of trees and shrubs there low. Grass fires destroy trees and saplings because most of their mass is aboveground and

Figure 8.1 Abiotic factors such as rainfall and fire are important for the formation and maintenance of grasslands. Wildfires started by lightning or controlled burns remove small trees and other woody plants. Burning helps maintain grassland areas.

Figure 8.2 The bison of the North American prairies once numbered in the millions. They continuously grazed and fertilized the prairies, maintaining the grasses and keeping other woody plants from growing.

therefore vulnerable to fire. But grasses have most of their mass belowground, which helps them survive in periods of low rainfall. One rye plant, for instance, may grow as high as 2 m but have up to 600 km of roots beneath the soil. When the grassland burns, the grasses are relatively unharmed. Fires thereby remove species that compete with grasses for resources.

Another benefit of fires is that they burn away the layer of dead grass that accumulates during the year, converting it to valuable nutrients. The nutrients act as fertilizer, giving grasslands a deep, fertile soil held in place by grass roots. Heat from fires also aids the germination of many grass seeds.

Grasses are abundant in grassland areas because of biotic factors as well as abiotic factors. Grazing animals, such as the bison in Figure 8.2, and burrowing animals help maintain grasslands with their activities above and below the ground. Grazing animals act as natural lawn mowers, keeping the vegetation of grasslands close to the ground. When kept this low, tree saplings and shrubs become too damaged to grow well. With most of their growth below ground level, the grasses remain unharmed. Animals such as earthworms, prairie dogs, and insects, which aerate the soil by making tunnels and digging, also live below ground. When the soil is aerated, grasses can grow more successfully because nutrients oxygen, and water can reach their roots more quickly.

The amount of rain a grassland area receives also affects the sizes and textures of the grasses, as shown in Figure 8.3. The tall-grass prairies and short-grass prairies of the midwestern and western United States and Canada form because of differences in rainfall and soil nutrients. Similar regions exist in the South American pampas, the South African veldt, and the steppes of central Europe and Asia. Most tall-grass prairies, where the fertile soils can support grass 2 m tall, have been cleared for crops such as corn and wheat. Short-grass prairies are now used for cattle grazing and irrigated crops.

Figure 8.3 Sizes and kinds of grasses are related to the amount of rain a grassland receives. The drier the climate, the shorter and finer the grasses. The wetter and more humid the climate, the taller the grasses will grow.

Although the *amount* of rain an area receives is important to grassland ecosystems, *when* it rains is also important. Some grasslands experience cycles of heavy rain followed by long periods of little or no rain, called *rainy seasons* and *drought seasons*. The rainy season and drought season determine, in part, the kinds of organisms that live in the grasslands. The trees and shrubs in grasslands often grow near ponds, streams, and springs. In grasslands where months may go by without rain, many plants and trees have adaptations that make them *drought-resistant*. These trees and shrubs survive in the dry grasslands, despite small amounts of rain.

All grasslands contain large grazing animals such as antelope and bison. Their ability to run quickly across the prairie is an adaptation that helps them avoid predators. Grasshoppers and other insects feed on the seeds and leaves of grasses, as do many other small herbivores including mice, gophers, prairie dogs, and birds. Some of these animals burrow underground and are only active at night, to avoid predators and intense daytime heat. Predators in the grassland are different throughout the world. In the North American prairies, coyotes, foxes, snakes, and birds of prey are the top consumers.

Grasslands around the world vary by climate and types of organisms. Although scientists do not always agree about how to classify grasslands, one method is to divide the grasslands into three different biomes. These three biomes, shown in Figure 8.4, are called the *steppe, prairie,* and *savanna.*

Figures 8.4 The steppes (left), are located at the edges of deserts. Tall-grass prairie gayfeathers (center) grow in the wetter eastern region of the U.S. prairie. Africa's savanna (right) supports scattered trees because of the local rainy seasons.

Do It!
Field Activity

Select areas around your school or home that display interactions between grass and animals. Try to relate the conditions of the grass to the conditions of the soil, or to the activities that take place on the grass.

1. List factors that appear to be beneficial to both grass and animals. Also, list factors that make the grass seem unhealthy.

2. How do your findings relate to grasses in the grasslands?

SECTION REVIEW

1. Where are grasslands located in relation to deserts and forests?
2. **Identify** some biotic and abiotic factors affecting the growth of grasslands.
3. **Think Critically** Suggest reasons for the relationship between grass size and climate.

The Spirit Animal

It is difficult today to imagine the great herds of bison (sometimes called buffalo) that once roamed the great plains. They ranged over 142 million acres of open tallgrass prairie from the Appalachian Mountains in the East to the Rocky Mountains in the West. In the early 1800s, settlers recorded an estimated 60 million bison in North America. Herds were so large that trains were sometimes forced to stop while herds crossed the tracks.

Native Americans living on the plains depended on the bison for food and used their skins for clothing, bones for tools, and sinew as binding. Among tribes in the Sioux Nation, the bison earned the name *Tatonka*, or "spirit animal."

Between 1870 and 1885, a period of just 15 years, hide hunters decimated the bison herds. By 1903, only 1644 bison existed in zoos and on private ranches. A small herd in Yellowstone National Park was the only wild herd left in the United States.

About 150 000 bison now live in the United States and the species is no longer in danger of extinction. However, most bison still live on private ranches because more than 90 percent

In the early 1900s, only about 1600 bison existed in the United States. Since then, the numbers have increased to around 150 000.

of the original tallgrass prairie has been replaced by agriculture or housing developments. The prairie is now the rarest of the North American biomes. A wild herd remains in Yellowstone, but after a devastating winter in 1996–1997, only about 1500 animals remain.

Despite these discouraging statistics, conservationists are making an effort to restore some of the tallgrass prairie and wild bison herds. The climate of the prairies, frequent fires, and grazing bison all contributed to the prairies' rich plant life. (Bison used to maintain the prairies by cropping and trampling the grasses, encouraging new plants to grow.) Now, conservationists use carefully controlled fires to mimic the natural burns that occurred in the past. Following these fires, many of the fire-adapted plants that once lived on the prairie return.

In 1993, an environmental group released 300 bison onto 37 000 acres of restored tallgrass prairie near Pawhuska, Oklahoma. By 1997, the numbers had increased to 650. The group hopes to eventually increase and maintain the numbers around 2200.

Checkpoint

1. What are some of the factors that help maintain the prairie ecosystem?
2. How do bison help maintain the prairie?

8.2 STEPPES AND PRAIRIES

OBJECTIVES • *Compare* and *contrast* a steppe and a prairie.
• *Describe* the importance of steppes and prairies in agriculture.

Steppes are similar to deserts in many ways. **Steppes** *are grasslands of short bunchgrasses that get less than 50 cm of rain a year.* Rainfall is very low and plant life is sparse. Because of such similarities, some scientists consider steppes to be semiarid deserts rather than grasslands. In the United States, steppes are located at the western and southwestern edges of the grasslands. Large areas of steppes exist within the wetter areas of the deserts of the Southwest and the Great Basin. Steppes are also located within drier areas of the prairies.

Prairies make up most of the grasslands in the United States. **Prairies** *are grasslands characterized by rolling hills, plains, and sod-forming grasses.* In the United States, the prairies are often called the Great Plains. The Russian steppes in central Eurasia and the veldt in South Africa are local names for prairies in those locations. The prairies in Argentina are known as the pampas. Whatever name they are given, the prairies of the world are large, fertile areas where the human population gets most of its food. Because breads and cereals come from grains grown on the prairies, the prairies are sometimes called "breadbaskets."

Steppe and Prairie Climates

To distinguish between a steppe and a desert, scientists define a desert as a region that gets less than 25 cm of rain a year and a steppe as receiving 25 cm or more. Most of the rain on the steppes evaporates very quickly or reaches only the upper 25 cm of soil. High winds and high temperatures across the steppes are responsible for rapid evaporation. Throughout the year, temperatures on the steppes can fall to –5 °C or rise as high as 30 °C.

The amount of rain in the prairies is about 50 to 75 cm a year. Occasionally, however, prairies get up to twice that much rain in a year, as in the midwestern United States during 1993. The rain often comes in thunderstorms during the rainy seasons.

Steppe and Prairie Organisms

Soil in the prairie can hold water very well because soil organisms create air spaces that can hold water. Most of the grasses of the prairie have roots that form a mat in the soil. The mat of soil and roots is called *sod. Grasses that form a mat of soil and roots are called* **sod-forming grasses.** Lawns are an example of sod-forming grasses. The roots of the sod-forming grasses hold the soil together. When the soil is held together, it does not dry out very quickly,

Figure 8.5 Vast fields of wheat and other cereal grains now grow in large areas of the world's grasslands. The native grasses that once thrived have been replaced because of the human need for food and space.

and it does not blow away in strong winds. *As plants and animals decompose, they form a layer of organic matter called* **humus** (HYOO-mus). The humus helps hold moisture and provides additional nutrients and food for grasses and other organisms to grow.

Steppes are sometimes referred to as short-grass prairies. The grasses of the steppes are mostly bunchgrasses. **Bunchgrasses** *are short, fine-bladed grasses that grow in a clump.* Clumping helps save water by holding the water in a small root area, under the shade of the grass. The short, fine blades of the bunchgrasses prevent them from losing moisture in the dry climate. The roots of the steppe grasses may grow only as deep as 50 cm. At that shallow depth, the roots can absorb as much of the scarce rainwater as possible before it evaporates.

Animals of the steppes and prairies have adapted to the changing conditions of these grasslands by migrating, hibernating, or burrowing underground. The grasses and small shrubs also have adaptations that use the energy of the wind, as shown in Figure 8.6. The wind carries the grasses' seeds and pollen over wide areas of land. With the aid of the wind, grasses can cover large areas rapidly. However, when one area of the prairie or steppe gets very dry or cold, the grasses cannot grow very well.

In colder areas, some of the animals of the steppe hibernate to save energy. Others migrate to other areas in search of more food and warmer temperatures. During hot periods, many small animals, like the prairie dogs in Figure 8.7, remain in their burrows to keep from overheating. A cluster of prairie dog burrows, known as towns, can be as large as several hundred square kilometers. Except during winter, the cooler nights are ideal times for burrowing animals to come aboveground to eat. Many of these animals eat at night or in the early or late parts of the day.

The steppe and prairie grasses are only slightly affected by the feeding habits of migrating grazers, because these animals move from place to place. But poor farming and ranching practices can

Figure 8.6 The dandelion, which is native to Europe, disperses its seeds with the aid of wind. Many grassland plants use this seed dispersal method to take advantage of strong winds.

Figure 8.7 Prairie dogs aerate the soil of the prairies with their underground network of tunnels, called towns. Around the turn of the century, a prairie dog town was discovered in Texas that covered an area of 64 000 km². An estimated 400 million prairie dogs were thought to live there.

Figure 8.8 As a result of overgrazing, poor farming practices, and a series of terrible droughts, one of the worst environmental disasters in U.S. history occurred. From 1934 to 1938, strong winds stripped the unprotected soil from grasslands in parts of Oklahoma, Texas, New Mexico, Kansas, and Colorado, and formed an area known as the "dust bowl."

cause extensive damage to the grasses of the steppes and prairies. One harmful practice is concentrating the feeding of sheep and cattle in small areas. When grazing animals eat too much in one place, they destroy most of the grass in a process called overgrazing. Some farmers and ranchers replace native grasses with grasses that are poorly adapted to the area. The grasses may not survive, making it harder for the land to support as many animals as it did before. The grass roots that hold the soil together die, and the loose soil is blown away. You may recognize this as the first step toward desertification. Since the time of the "dust bowl" (see Figure 8.8), American farmers have developed many grazing and growing techniques that help to assure a reduced impact on these ecosystems.

Many farmers are replacing the native species of the grasslands with species specialized for agriculture. The native grasses and animals have been replaced by huge herds of grazing cattle and sheep. Wide fields of grains such as wheat and corn have also been planted. Bison, deer, wolves, and grizzly bears were all once very common in the grasslands of the United States, but they have been partially replaced because of humans' demand for space and food. Without a better understanding of steppe and prairie ecosystems, agriculture may turn more of these grasslands into deserts or semi-arid scrubland.

Think About It!

Although agriculture in the grasslands of the world feeds billions of people, millions die annually from starvation.

1. Do you think that more land should be developed into agricultural land? Why or why not?

2. Discuss some reasons for existing problems and predict problems the world might face in the future.

SECTION REVIEW

1. Why are prairies called the breadbaskets of the world?
2. How are steppes and prairies similar? How are they different?
3. **Apply** Name some ways in which steppes and prairies are damaged, and how desertification occurs.

Dateline 1959

In 1959, Drs. Mary and Louis Leakey, a noted team of British anthropologists, reported the discovery of what was thought to be the remains of an ancient ancestor of humans. The discovery was made in the Olduvai Gorge at the eastern edge of the Serengeti Plain in East Africa. The Serengeti Plain makes up a large part of the savanna in Africa. The Leakeys named this ancient ancestor *Zinjanthropus,* which was determined to be over 1 million years old. *Zinjanthropus,* also called *Australopithicus boisei,* is now known to be a side branch in the human family tree, not a direct ancestor of modern humans.

Figures 8.9 Runners (right) keep a vital link in the food chain alive despite extreme conditions of drought, heat, and fire. Pampas grasses (left) are an example of tufts. Tufts are very durable and resistant to the grazing of large herbivores.

8.3 SAVANNAS

OBJECTIVES • *Describe* savannas, and state where they are located.
• *Explain* how organisms have adapted to survive on the savanna.

Savannas *are tropical or subtropical grasslands ranging from dry scrubland to wet, open woodland.* Savannas occur in Asia, from India to Southeast Asia, and in Africa, from the Sahara and Kalahari deserts to the southern tip of Africa. The llanos of Venezuela and the campos of Brazil are regions of savanna in South America.

Savanna Climate

Rainy seasons and long periods of drought are typical of savannas. The amount of rain in a savanna can be as high as 150 cm a year, but most of it falls heavily during thunderstorms in the short rainy season. In Africa, the rainy season usually lasts from January to April. During the rest of the year, the savanna may be very dry. The extreme climate demands a wide range of adaptations in the organisms of the savanna.

Savanna Organisms

In order to survive, the grasses, shrubs, and trees of the savanna must be resistant to drought, fires, and grazing animals. Many plants of the savanna grow runners. **Runners** *are long horizontal stems above or below the ground.* Runners are used by some plants to reproduce; they spread quickly and can extend for several meters. When a fire occurs, the underground runners are protected.

Savanna grasses grow in tufts. **Tufts** *are large clumps of tall, coarse grasses.* The savanna trees and shrubs have thorns or sharp leaves that keep them from being eaten by grazing animals, such as gazelles. Another adaptation of savanna plants is the ability to grow rapidly. This adaptation enables the plants to recover quickly from the damage caused by fire and animals. Growing quickly also gives the plants a better chance to use the water available during the rainy season.

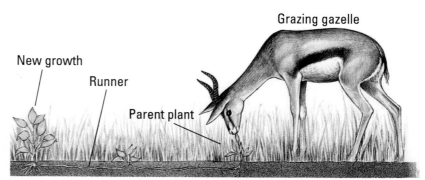

New growth
Runner
Parent plant
Grazing gazelle

Figure 8.10 Vertical feeding patterns minimize the competition for food among the herbivores of the savanna. Vertical feeding patterns occur among the open woodland and the grasses of the open plain. The dik-dik (foreground, far left) eats grasses and leaves from small shrubs. The warthog (drinking from stream) eats roots, grasses, and leaves from small shrubs. Rhinoceroses eat grasses and small shrubs. However, they also eat leaves from large shrubs and the lower branches of small trees. The elephant and giraffe are capable of reaching high into tall trees where they obtain the leaves and small branches for their diets. Elephants also uproot tough grasses and trees, which they may completely strip of bark and branches, for food.

The concentration of animal populations in smaller areas around streams and watering holes is also influenced by the rainy season of the savanna. Because of this concentration, some animals are adapted to make use of the available food in what is called a vertical feeding pattern, shown in Figure 8.10. *In a* **vertical feeding pattern**, *animals eat vegetation at different heights.* Vertical feeding patterns enable animals with different eating habits to feed in the same area without competing for food. The pattern allows more animals to live on limited resources because the animals can have smaller, more specific niches.

As in the prairie, many larger animals migrate to areas of the savanna where rain has fallen, often traveling great distances to find water. In Africa, lions, cheetahs, and other predators prey on migrating herds of wildebeest, zebras, and various species of antelope. Sometimes habitat loss due to human activities disrupts the migration patterns of these animals. Survival for many species depends on wildlife preserves and global conservation efforts.

LINK
Archaeology

Scientists think that an important step in the evolution of humans occurred when human ancestors left the trees of the forest and began to live on the grasslands. On the grasslands, a human ancestor called *Homo habilis* began to develop tools to aid in hunting and food gathering.

SECTION REVIEW

1. What are savannas? Where can they be found?
2. How have plants adapted to savanna life?
3. Make a list of ways animals have adapted to the extreme conditions of savannas for eating and reproducing.
4. **Hypothesize** What could happen to the migrating animals in a savanna if they were fenced in a large wildlife park for protection?

Seed Dispersal

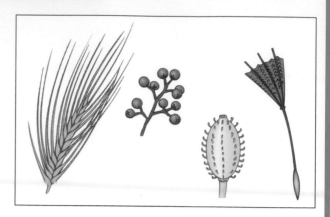

PROBLEM
How are the seeds of plants in a grassland biome adapted for dispersal?

MATERIALS (per group)
- reference sources
- medium-size paper collecting bag
- paper
- glue

INFERENCE
The seeds of grassland plants that fall beneath the parent plant probably could not compete for nutrients and water. Therefore, the seeds of successful plants usually have some adaptation that enables dispersal.

PROCEDURE

1. Use reference sources to find out how seeds from four of the following plants are adapted to be dispersed: milkweed, Russian thistle, dandelion, ragweed, cocklebur, shepherd's purse, goose grass, scarlet pimpernel, knotweed, wisteria, yellow oxalis, chickweed, annual bluegrass, and black mustard.
2. Reproduce the data table below on a separate piece of paper. Include eight rows.
3. Take the collecting bag to an area designated by your instructor.
4. Collect about 12 different types of seeds per group. Look for seeds similar to those shown in the figure or seeds that have obvious adaptations for dispersal. *Note: You may obtain seeds from live plants, but do not disturb the ecosystem any more than necessary. Do not remove seeds from trees or cultivated plants that may be in the area.*
5. In the classroom, check for seeds that may have become attached to your clothes. Add those seeds to your collection.
6. Separate 8 seeds from those collected by your group that are most clearly adapted for dispersal.
7. Glue each of the 8 seeds to the empty area in the left-hand column of the data table. In the middle column, classify each seed according to the general way it is dispersed (wind, water, animal, etc.). In the right-hand column, describe the observable adaptations of the seed that allow it to be dispersed.

ANALYSIS
1. Which four types of seeds did you choose to research in Step 1? How is each type of seed dispersed?
2. Did any seeds become attached to your clothing? Describe how the seeds were able to stay attached to you.
3. Were there any seeds that could be dispersed by more than one method? Explain.

CONCLUSION
1. Into which categories did you classify the seeds you collected? Describe how seeds in each category are dispersed.
2. What human activities help to disperse seeds?

Seed	Type of Dispersal	Adaptations

CHAPTER **8** REVIEW

KEY TERMS

grasslands 8.1
desert-grassland
boundary 8.1
prairie 8.2

steppe 8.2
sod-forming
grasses 8.2
humus 8.2

bunchgrasses 8.2
savanna 8.3
runner 8.3
tuft 8.3

vertical feeding
pattern 8.3

CHAPTER SUMMARY

8.1. Grasslands are ecosystems in which the climate is too wet to be a desert, but too dry to support a forest. Biotic and abiotic factors such as rainfall, grass fires, and grazing animals help maintain the growth of grasslands. Most of the biomass of grasses is below the ground. Many of the world's grasslands have been replaced by cultivation.

8.2. Steppes are considered by many scientists to be either a part of the desert biome or a short-grass prairie. Prairies are important agricultural regions. Most steppe grasses are short bunchgrasses. Most prairie grasses are sod-forming.

Many organisms have adapted to wide climate changes by living underground or by migrating. The diversity of organisms has been reduced because of human need for food and space.

8.3. Savannas are tropical grasslands where rain is heavy during a short part of the year. Rainy and drought seasons are major influences, demanding that organisms grow quickly or migrate. Through such adaptations as thorns and runners, many trees, shrubs, and grasses are resistant to drought, fires, and grazing animals. The concentration of many animals in small areas has resulted in vertical feeding patterns.

MULTIPLE CHOICE

Choose the letter of the word or phrase that best completes each statement.

1. Fires in grasslands prevent the growth of (a) plants; (b) scrubs; (c) migrating animals; (d) runners.
2. The main difference between deserts and steppes is the (a) grass fire frequency; (b) vegetation density; (c) annual rainfall; (d) animal population.
3. The wind is helpful to prairie grasses because it helps them (a) reproduce; (b) start grass fires; (c) keep their leaves dry; (d) carry away dead grass.
4. The major factor keeping forests from growing in grassland areas is (a) grazing; (b) rainfall; (c) grass fires; (d) soil structure.
5. One way of telling if you are in a wet grassland is by the (a) forest of trees; (b) short, fine-bladed grasses; (c) tall, coarse-bladed grasses; (d) presence of animals.
6. Soil aeration is caused by (a) grazing animals; (b) tree roots; (c) earthworms; (d) fertilizers.
7. An adaptation that helps trees survive in dry grasslands is (a) having most of their mass below the ground; (b) having shallow roots; (c) growing rapidly; (d) being drought-resistant.
8. Most grasses of the prairies (a) are bunchgrasses; (b) are sod-forming grasses; (c) grow in tufts; (d) grow in clumps.
9. Savannas do not exist in the United States because (a) they have been destroyed by overgrazing; (b) they are only in Africa; (c) they exist only in the tropics; (d) it is too dry.
10. A vertical feeding pattern is (a) a separation of animal habitats; (b) the amount of food predators eat; (c) a way for animals to avoid competition; (d) the time of day animals eat.

CHAPTER 8 REVIEW

TRUE/FALSE

Write true *if the statement is true. If the statement is false, change the underlined words to make it true.*

1. Wetter areas of the <u>desert</u> can be considered steppes.
2. The grazing habits of bison in North America were very <u>damaging</u> to prairie grasslands.
3. Soil aeration helps the soil <u>hold water</u>.
4. Steppes can also be called <u>short-grass prairies</u>.
5. Sharp leaves on the trees of the savanna protect them from <u>drought</u>.
6. Vertical feeding patterns allow animals to occupy <u>larger</u> niches.
7. Large herbivores migrate to find <u>food and water</u>.
8. Because savanna plants grow <u>quickly</u>, they can recover well from fire damage.

CONCEPT REVIEW

Write a complete response for each of the following.

1. List four factors that influence the development of grasslands. Identify two as biotic and two as abiotic.
2. Describe the importance of soil aeration to healthy plant growth.
3. Compare and contrast the effects of migrating grazers with domesticated grazers on grasslands.
4. What factors contributed to the dust bowl of the 1930s?
5. Distinguish between the characteristics of a typical grass for a steppe, prairie, and savanna.

THINK CRITICALLY

1. Besides protection from fire, why might runners be a valuable adaptation for grasses growing around a watering hole?
2. Suggest some of the risks involved in replacing native species with specialized species.
3. When soil structure collapses, the soil may be removed by high winds. Deduce how the soil may be affected by rainfall and water flow if the soil structure is no longer absorbent.
4. Grasses grow tall and fast during the rainy seasons in prairies and savannas. During the drought season, the aboveground mass of the grasses dies. Discuss a possible role of grass fires in connection with this dead layer of grass.

Computer Activity The average annual increase in the world's human population is about 1.5 percent. Currently, there are about 6 billion people on Earth. In 1991, it was estimated that there were about 1.5 billion hectares of land used for crops. The area of land on Earth is about 14.5 billion hectares. Use a graphing program to make a line graph that compares human population growth and an appropriate increase in area of land used for crops. Assume that all crops are consumed by humans and each human has an equal share of food. How long would it take before the entire Earth would need to be cultivated to feed the human population?

WRITE CREATIVELY

Apply the concept of a vertical feeding pattern to the human population, and think of some alternative eating habits people may try to ensure that everyone gets enough food to eat. Write a story about a human society that uses this vertical feeding pattern.

PORTFOLIO

1. Find two typical grassland scenes from steppes, prairies, or savannas. Choose a scene from the 1800s and a current scene. Make a poster that compares the two scenes. Try to identify the changes, if any, that have occurred, and note the changes on the poster. Draw the poster, or use illustrations or photographs from books and magazines.

2. How have human societies adapted to living in a savanna? Choose a society from Africa, India, or South America that lives in the savanna. Prepare a presentation on an average day in the life of a teenager in the society you choose.

GRAPHIC ANALYSIS

Use Figure 8.10 to answer the following.

1. Which animals would do best finding food during the first few months after a small grass fire? Why?
2. Which animals would do best after a 5-year period in which there were no large grass fires? Why?
3. For two of the animals, list adaptations that enable the animals to fit into the vertical feeding pattern.

ACTIVITY 8.2

PROBLEM
How do species interact in a grassland ecosystem?

MATERIALS (per group)
- graph paper
- large jar with a lid
- gravel, rocks, and soil
- pinch of grass seeds
- pinch of clover seeds
- 12 mung bean seeds
- 5 of each animal: cricket, mealworm, land isopod, earthworm
- water
- colored pencils

HYPOTHESIS
Write a hypothesis about the food relationships that exist in your grassland ecosystem.

PROCEDURE
1. Place rocks and gravel in the bottom of the container. Then add a few centimeters of soil, and plant the seeds. Water lightly. Put a lid on the container, and place the ecosystem in indirect sunlight for 1 week. You may wish to place the jar outside in case of accidents.
2. Place the animals in the jar, and place the lid lightly on top. Observe the ecosystem for a few minutes every day for 3 to 4 weeks.
3. In a data table, record any increase or decrease in the number of organisms. Record any other changes you observe.
4. Graph each population on a separate sheet of graph paper. Use a different color to distinguish between each population. Compare population changes by comparing the curves.

ANALYSIS
1. Describe any population changes you observed over the 3 to 4 weeks. What might have caused the changes?
2. What relationships did you observe between different species in step 4?

CONCLUSION
Do your observations support or refute your hypothesis? Explain.

CHAPTER

9

FOREST BIOMES

9.1 Coniferous Forests

9.2 Deciduous Forests

9.3 Rain Forests

Forests are more diverse than any other terrestrial ecosystem. Although forests cover only 30 percent of Earth's land surface, they contain 75 percent of its biomass. While tropical rain forest covers only 6–7 percent of Earth's land surface, it holds more than 50 percent of land biomass and may contain 70 percent of Earth's terrestrial species. The rain forests are the most complex and diverse ecosystems on the planet.

The forest biomes are crucial to humans. Wood is the most common building material on Earth. Many forests have been harvested to meet the demand for wood and farmland, resulting in widespread ecosystem destruction.

9.1 CONIFEROUS FORESTS

OBJECTIVES • **Describe** *the characteristics of the coniferous forest.*
• **Explain** *adaptations that enable organisms to survive in coniferous forests.*

The coniferous forest biome is located primarily in the subarctic regions of North America, Europe, and Asia. The summers are warm, lasting 2 to 5 months. The winters are long, cold, and dry, and there is very little sunlight. Precipitation falls as rain during summer and as snow during winter. Coniferous forests receive 40 to 200 cm of precipitation a year. In the Southern Hemisphere, coniferous forests are generally found on high mountains, where conditions are similar to high northern latitudes.

Coniferous means cone-bearing. *Coniferous trees, or* **conifers** (KOHN-ih-fers), *are trees that produce seed cones.* The cones hold the seeds of the tree. Conifers share an unusual type of leaf called a needle. These leaves are long and thin and covered in a thick, waxy substance. The needles help the trees conserve water. Most conifers are also evergreen, meaning they do not lose all their leaves at a given time each year. Conifers lose and replace their leaves slowly throughout the year. The needles of conifers help the trees shed snow during winter.

Species of pine, hemlock, fir, spruce, and cedar are common in coniferous forests. Some broad-leafed trees, such as aspen and birch, are also present. Coniferous forests are not diverse, and most contain only a few species of trees. The trees must be able to survive during winter, when the soil moisture is frozen and unavailable. The soil is poor and acidic because conifer needles are acidic and decompose slowly. Harsh winters and nutrient-poor soils are limiting factors in the coniferous forest. Ferns, lichens, and sphagnum moss are plants that can grow in the dim light of the forest floor.

Figure 9.1 Conifers produce cones (left) to hold their seeds. Conifer needles (center) have several adaptations that enable them to conserve water. The triangular shape of conifer trees (right) helps them avoid damage from heavy snowfall.

Figure 9.2 Coniferous forests cover wide belts of the northern continents. Snow is common in this biome, and the growing season is short.

Figure 9.3 The Steller's jay and the moose are animals from the coniferous forest. The jay survives the long winter by eating seeds. The moose eats bark, young tree branches, and any other plants it can find.

The heavy winter snow that falls in most coniferous forests is important to the ecosystem. The snow acts like an insulating blanket, trapping heat and preventing the ground from forming permafrost. This insulating effect protects the roots of the forest trees. Small animals such as mice that would freeze to death above the snow can also survive underneath the ground.

Many animals in the coniferous forest are adapted to the cold winters, and to life in the conifers. Most small herbivores are seed eaters, such as mice, squirrels, jays, and other rodents and birds. Insects are common during summer, when the soil is moist and poorly drained.

Larger herbivores, such as moose, elk, beaver, and snowshoe hares, feed on plants and bark. These herbivores are pursued by predators, such as grizzly bears, wolves, and lynxes. All these animals have adaptations that enable them to survive the long winters. Many species migrate, while some hibernate or live under the snow. All have thick body coverings to protect them from the cold.

Vast stretches of coniferous forest cover the northern parts of the former Soviet Union and North America. Because of the harsh climate, these have not been logged as extensively as other forest types. However, the growing need for wood has led to tree harvesting, and large areas of forest have been lost in some regions. The governments of the republics of the former Soviet Union, badly in need of money, are selling the rights to large stretches of forest to domestic and foreign companies. How much logging the coniferous forests can sustain has yet to be determined.

SECTION REVIEW

1. What characterizes a coniferous forest?
2. List several adaptations that enable organisms in coniferous forests to live through the harsh winter.
3. **Deduce** Conifer needles decompose slowly on the forest floor. Suggest two reasons explaining this slow rate of decomposition.

The Spotted Owl

The Pacific Northwest is one of the few regions of the United States that still contains undisturbed old-growth forests. These forests are home to many species found nowhere else on Earth, including the spotted owl.

The number of spotted owls has dropped sharply as the old-growth forests have been harvested. After privately held lands were fully logged, the logging companies asked the government for permission to cut forests on government lands. Under the terms of the Endangered Species Act, however, the spotted owl is considered a threatened species and must be protected.

Should old-growth forests be harvested?

Logging Must Continue

Thousands of people depend on the timber industry to make a living. If logging is not permitted, the economy of the Pacific Northwest will suffer.

There is little research to indicate that the spotted owl lives only in old-growth forests. In addition, logging companies have learned a great deal about preserving the environment. If they manage the harvest carefully, there is room for loggers and owls.

The spotted owl is a threatened species that lives in the Pacific Northwest.

The Forests Should Be Protected

The logging industry says the spotted owl is responsible for people losing their jobs. But these jobs were lost as a result of increased automation, exports, and the fact that huge log harvests could not continue forever. Once the available forests were cut, the jobs for loggers were lost. Moving onto government land only postpones the loss of jobs.

Although spotted owls have been seen in younger, second-growth forests, there is no research to show that they will stay there and reproduce in these forests. If the old-growth forests are logged, and it turns out that owls cannot survive in the second-growth forests, the owls will become extinct.

Consider the Issue

1. Why does preserving the old-growth forests protect the spotted owl?
2. List several suggestions that could help satisfy both sides in the debate over old-growth forests.

141

9.2 DECIDUOUS FORESTS

OBJECTIVES • *Identify* the characteristics of the deciduous forest.
• *Describe* the organisms that inhabit deciduous forests.

Forests also grow at lower latitudes than the coniferous forest. These latitudes are called the temperate zone. Temperate zones have climates with four well-defined seasons. The forests in the temperate zone are made up largely of deciduous trees. *A* **deciduous** (dee-SIJH-oo-us) *tree is a tree that sheds its leaves during a particular season of the year.* These trees are the basis of deciduous forest biomes.

Temperature varies greatly in deciduous forests. Temperatures in summer can be as high as 30 °C, while in the winter they can fall to −30 °C. Precipitation falls as rain or snow, depending on the temperature and season. Deciduous forests receive 50 to 300 cm of precipitation a year. Precipitation falls fairly regularly throughout the year.

Deciduous trees are adapted to the highly variable climate of the temperate zone. The growing season lasts about 6 months. During the growing season, a tree grows quickly and produces and stores large amounts of food. In autumn, the shortening daylight and cooling temperatures trigger changes in the tree. The tree sheds its leaves and becomes dormant. The loss of leaves is an adaptation that enables a tree to conserve water during the cold winter months. Photosynthesis stops, and the tree no longer makes food. The tree survives winter by consuming food stored in its trunk, branches, and roots. The tree grows new leaves in spring. Photosynthesis begins again in preparation for the next winter.

Maple, oak, beech, ash, hickory, and birch are examples of deciduous trees. The inhabitants of deciduous forests are more diverse than those in coniferous forests. The forest has three distinct vegetation layers, and each layer has its own group of plant species. Figures 9.4 and 9.5 show deciduous forests.

Biology

Chlorophyll is a green pigment that traps light in plants. Most plants also have other pigments in smaller amounts. In summer, leaves have a large amount of chlorophyll, and they appear green. But as autumn approaches, leaves stop making chlorophyll. As the remaining chlorophyll breaks down, the other pigments show through and give leaves their beautiful fall colors.

Figure 9.4 The leaves of deciduous trees often change colors before they fall. These trees will soon lose their leaves and enter a state of dormancy for the winter.

Figure 9.5 Deciduous forests were once common across Europe and North America. Humans have disturbed almost all of this biome, although many trees have been replanted.

The highest layer of a deciduous forest is called the *canopy* (KAN-uh-pee). The canopy is made up of the upper branches and leaves of tall trees. The canopy captures most of the sun's direct light, but some filters down to the forest's lower levels. Beneath the canopy is the understory. The *understory* is made up of trees that are younger and smaller than those of the canopy. A layer of shrubs also grows in the understory, while mosses, ferns, and other plants grow on the forest floor.

The leaves that fall from forest trees enrich the soil. The leaves decay quickly during the warm, humid summer months. The decaying leaves produce a deep, rich layer of soil called humus. The humus and fallen leaves are home to many insects and other invertebrates that feed on the abundant organic matter.

Because the deciduous forest produces abundant food and has many different habitats, it supports a diverse community of animals and other organisms. Fungi and other decomposers, along with insects and invertebrates, are common in the leaf litter and on fallen trees. These organisms are preyed upon by birds, mice, and small mammals. White-tailed deer are common. Reptiles and amphibians are present in warmer forests. Predators such as wolves, mountain lions, birds of prey, and foxes fill the higher trophic levels in this ecosystem. Migratory birds come to feed and breed in the summer.

The deciduous forest has been changed drastically by human activity. This biome once stretched across Europe and Asia and covered the eastern United States. Today, very little of the original deciduous forest still stands worldwide. Farms, orchards, and urban development have replaced the native deciduous forests over most of North America and Europe.

Do It!
Field Activity

In Chapter 6, you determined which biome you live in. What kinds of trees would you expect to find in your biome? Take a tree survey from around your school, or organize a field trip to a forest in your area.

1. Gather samples of dead leaves and any seeds you find. Note which tree each sample comes from, and make sketches of the trees showing the tree's shape and the texture of its bark. (Do not take living samples from the trees.)

2. Use a field guide to identify the tree species each sample comes from. Did you find the types of trees you expected? See if you can identify at least one species that has been introduced to your area by humans.

Figure 9.6 The earthworm (left) is common in the leaf litter of the deciduous forest. The fox (center) and the deer (right) are common mammals found in the deciduous forest.

Two factors have driven the human consumption of the deciduous forest. The first is rich soil. The humus in deciduous forest soil makes it deep and fertile, and the soil makes excellent farmland if the trees above it are cleared. Many forests were cleared to provide land for fruit trees and other crops. The second reason for the consumption of the deciduous forest is the trees themselves. Deciduous trees generally have harder wood than conifers, making the wood a better material for making furniture and flooring. The wood is also used as fuel.

Some of the world's deciduous forests have been replanted. But a forest ecosystem is not just a group of trees. The ecosystem does not simply reappear when new trees are planted. The forest ecosystem regenerates slowly because the many species that were dependent on the trees have also disappeared. These species must migrate back into the ecosystem or new species must adapt to empty niches. Also, the tree and plant diversity in most replanted forests is very low. Planted forests are usually monocultures of a particular species. Monocultures are often very productive but have very low biodiversity and are highly susceptible to diseases, parasites, and pollution damage.

SECTION REVIEW

1. How do deciduous trees change their biological processes during the year?
2. Why is the soil of a deciduous forest more fertile than that of a coniferous forest?
3. **Hypothesize** What factors might make it difficult for species to return to a regenerating forest?

Year of the Fires

During 1988, approximately 60 000 wildfires burned about 2.4 million hectares (6 million acres) of forest in Alaska, California, and Wyoming. A combination of factors helped cause the fires, including dry ground conditions, little summer precipitation, and the 1963 "let-it-burn" policy. The "let-it-burn" (or natural-burn) policy allows natural fires to burn unless they threaten people, property, or endangered species. But what is the cost?

Did "let-it-burn" backfire?

"Let-It-Burn" Is Hazardous

The 1988 fire in Yellowstone National Park destroyed nearly 400 000 hectares (1 million acres). The "let-it-burn" policy assumes that a fire will eventually burn out because of factors such as rain or natural barriers. When that didn't happen in Yellowstone, park officials had to call in 25 000 firefighters. Far fewer people would have had to risk their lives if the fire had been dealt with right away.

The people who believe in "let-it-burn" say that fire is part of the natural cycle of forests. However, many people live near these forests and are at risk if a forest fire is allowed to burn.

"Let-It-Burn" Works

Ecologists have learned that burning is essential for the preservation of many natural forest communities. For example, the cones of the lodgepole pine, a major species in Yellowstone, only release seeds after being exposed to the intense heat of a forest fire. Fires also help deer, elk, and other animals by opening the canopy and clearing the soil, allowing new vegetation to grow.

Many of the 1988 fires would not have been so severe if the "let-it-burn" policy had been in effect long before 1963. If earlier fires had been allowed to burn, forest fires in 1988 would have been smaller.

The "let-it-burn" policy allows natural fires to burn unless they threaten people, property, or endangered species.

Consider the Issue

1. What are the problems with the "let-it-burn" policy?

2. Some scientists say that different forest communities burn differently. Some have fairly frequent small fires. Others have widespread but infrequent fires. How do you think these differences affect forest-management policies?

145

9.3 RAIN FORESTS

OBJECTIVES • *Describe* the characteristics of the tropical zone and of the rain forest. • *Illustrate* the complexity and diversity of the rainforest ecosystem.

The *tropical zone* is located at latitudes near the equator. Because the tropical zone is near the equator, it receives direct rays from the sun during most of the year. As a result, temperatures in the tropical zone average about 25 °C all year long. The wide temperature ranges between summer and winter in the temperate latitudes are absent in the tropical zone. The growing season can last 12 months. Precipitation falls as rain except on the tops of high mountains. The amount of precipitation varies from 200 to 450 cm a year. With an almost unchanging climate, water and temperature are not limiting factors. Soil nutrients, however, may be.

Rainforest Structure

The constant warmth and abundant rain in the tropical zone have given rise to the rain forest. It is the most diverse terrestrial biome on Earth. *A* **rain forest** *is a biome with a dense canopy of evergreen, broadleaf trees supported by at least 200 cm of rain each year.* Rain forests may contain as much as 70 percent of all the terrestrial species on Earth. Though they cover only 6 percent of Earth's land surface, rain forests hold 50 percent of Earth's land biomass. The rain forest has great biodiversity and shows the vast evolutionary possibilities present here as in no other biome.

Trees are the basis of the rain forest. Thousands of species of cypress, balsa, teak, mahogany, and other trees grow in this biome. The trees in a rain forest are amazingly diverse. For example, British ecologist Peter Ashton found 700 species of trees in just 10 hectares of tropical rain forest in Borneo. Many of these trees reach heights of 50 or 60 m, where their leafy tops form a dense canopy.

Figure 9.7 The rain forest is the most productive and diverse biome on Earth. Rainforest trees can grow to be 60 m tall.

Labels in figure: Bright light, Emergent trees, Filtered light, Upper canopy, Lower canopy, Understory, Dense shade, Shallow roots

Figure 9.8 The rain forest has several different levels, and each supports its own community. The amount of sunlight available to plants decreases quickly beneath the canopy.

Think About It!

Rain forests take much longer to regenerate damaged areas than other forest biomes.

1. Briefly explain how a deciduous forest would regenerate an area from which all vegetation had been removed.

2. Why might this process not occur in the case of a rain forest? *(Hint: Think about where the biome's nutrients are stored.)*

The canopy captures almost 99 percent of the light falling on the forest. The 1 percent of sunlight that filters through supports the lover levels of vegetation, as shown in Figure 9.8. Vegetation on the forest floor is sparse because there is not enough sunlight or nutrients to support many plants.

The dead organic matter that enriches the soil in other biomes does not last in the rain forest. It is decomposed and recycled in days or weeks instead of years. The warm temperatures and constant moisture of the rain forest arc ideal conditions for decomposers such as insects, fungi, and bacteria. Nutrients that fall to the forest floor are quickly recycled and lifted back up into the trees. The rain forest as an ecosystem contains as many nutrients as other biomes, but most of these nutrients exist in living organisms.

Because most of the rain forest's matter is held in its organisms, the topsoil is thin and poor. Nearly all of the available soil nutrients are in the top 5 cm of soil. As a result, rainforest tree trunks widen at their bases, with ridges of wood called *buttresses* that support the trees. Tree roots must be shallow to take advantage of the thin topsoil. Woody vines called lianas grow up the sides of tree trunks to reach the sunlight in the canopy. Other plants called epiphytes, such as orchids and bromeliads, live entirely on the trunks or limbs of trees, absorbing airborne nutrients and moisture.

Most of the activity in the rain forest occurs in the trees. The canopy supports countless species. Each species occupies a niche in the trees. Many of these *arboreal,* or tree-dwelling, organisms live their whole lives without ever touching the ground. If you walked through a rain forest, most of the organisms around you would be over your head. Different organisms have adapted to the conditions in different levels of the forest.

Organisms and Diversity

The amazing animal diversity in the rain forest is caused by two factors. The first is the diversity of rainforest plants. Each species of tree or plant provides niches for specialized pollinators and herbivores. High plant diversity leads to high animal diversity. The second factor is the wide variety of habitats that exist in the different forest levels. Conditions high in the canopy are different than conditions lower down, and different communities evolve to occupy each habitat.

Habitats in the rain forest vary from tree to tree and from one part of a tree to another. The result is a complex, three-dimensional mosaic of habitats with a tremendous variety of organisms. The food webs that join these organisms are complex, with many specially adapted species and interrelationships.

Five rainforest organisms are shown on this page. Each organism appears in the area it would if this page were a cross section of a forest. The tapir at lower left is from the forest floor, and the organisms across the top of the page are from the canopy. Remember that these photographs show only five of the millions of species that inhabit Earth's rain forests.

Scientists are not sure how many species may live in the rain forest. American biologist E. O. Wilson found 43 species of ants on a single rainforest tree. British ecologist Terry Erwin estimates there may be over 30 million species of insects on Earth, mostly in rain forests. There are millions more species of animals, plants, bacteria, and fungi. Although scientists do not know how many species there are, the more they look, the more they find.

Figure 9.9 The tapir (bottom) lives on the rainforest floor. The margay (center left) is a cat that hunts on the forest floor and in lower branches. The beetle (top left), the toucan (top center) and the spider monkey (top right) all live in the rainforest canopy.

Deforestation

For a long time, difficult conditions kept most nonnative peoples out of the rain forest. But now, as a result of human activity, the rainforest biome is changing. In 1950, over 10 percent of Earth's land surface was covered by rain forests. Rain forests now cover

Figure 9.10 Earth's rain forests are rapidly being lost to deforestation. This new highway in Brazil will allow people access to the rain forest.

6 percent, and the area is decreasing. *The destruction of forest as a result of human activity is called* **deforestation**.

The force behind the destruction of the rain forests is the human population's need for space and wood. Most rain forests are in developing countries. Many of these countries are faced with rapid population growth. Rainforest trees are logged for export and burned to clear land for farming, grazing, mining, and living space for people. Because of the poor soil fertility, new land must be cleared every few years.

Recall that the rainforest ecosystem is a vertical one. When the trees in a rain forest are destroyed, the habitats in the canopy and in lower levels of vegetation are destroyed as well. When these habitats are gone, the animals that have evolved to live in them become extinct. Scientists do not know how many species are lost every day, but if a single tree can hold 43 species of ants, the total may be huge.

If an area of rain forest is burned, it may be able to regenerate after several hundred years if there is more rain forest around it. The diversity in the regenerated forest will still be low, however, because an ecosystem as complex as a rain forest cannot just reappear. But if the forest is destroyed in large tracts or if the fragile soil is bulldozed, the rain forest will be unable to regenerate. Loss of biodiversity in the tropical rain forests is now a global issue with no simple solution.

LINK
Biology

Rain forests fix huge amounts of carbon through photosynthesis. When these forests are destroyed, the carbon dioxide they would have removed from the atmosphere remains. Deforestation may account for as much as 25 percent of the annual rise in atmospheric carbon dioxide. Carbon dioxide is a greenhouse gas, and large increases may cause global warming. You can learn about greenhouse gases and global warming in Chapter 22.

SECTION REVIEW

1. Why do rainforest trees have buttresses?
2. What two factors make the animal community in the rain forest diverse?
3. **Hypothesize** Plants on the floor of a rain forest often have very large leaves. Propose a hypothesis explaining this observation.

The Water-Holding Capacity of Conifer Needles

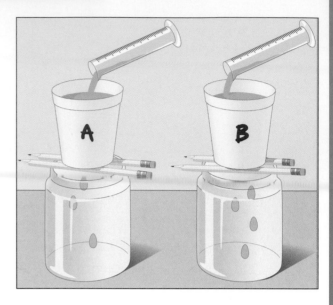

PROBLEM
How do conifer needles affect the water-holding capacity of a forest's soil?

MATERIALS (per group)
- 2 plastic foam cups
- marking pen
- garden soil (1 cup)
- soil containing dead conifer needles (1 cup)
- 4 pencils
- 2 jars (without lids)
- graduated cylinder
- paper towels
- tap water

HYPOTHESIS
Write a hypothesis that is related to the problem.

PROCEDURE
1. Use the marking pen to label one plastic foam cup A. Label the other cup B.
2. Poke four small holes in the bottom of each cup. Mark a line around each cup that is 2 cm from the top.
3. Pack cup A tightly to the line with plain garden soil. Pack cup B tightly to the line with soil containing dead conifer needles.
4. Place 2 pencils across the rim of each jar. Balance cup A and cup B on the pencils as shown in the figure.
5. Use the graduated cylinder to pour 100 mL of water into each cup. Let the water drain through the holes.
6. After the water has stopped draining, measure the amount of water in each jar by pouring the water back into the graduated cylinder. Discard this water after recording your measurements.
7. Make two stacks of paper towels with three towels in each stack. Dump the wet soil from cup A onto one stack and the wet soil from cup B onto the other stack. Move the soil around on each stack of paper towels so that they absorb as much of the moisture as possible.
8. Put the soil back into the plastic foam cups and compare the wetness of the two stacks of paper towels. Record this subjective measure of moisture.

ANALYSIS
1. In which biome will you find soil like that in cup B?
2. Did the jar under the plain soil or the one under the conifer-needle soil contain more water after water was poured through the cups?
3. Which stack of paper towels got wetter after wet soil from each cup was dumped on them?

CONCLUSION
1. How do dead conifer needles affect the water-holding capacity of soil?
2. Relate your observations of the effect of conifer needles on the soil to the conditions in the coniferous forest biome. How do the needles affect the biome?
3. Did your observations support your hypothesis? Explain.

CHAPTER 9 REVIEW

KEY TERMS

conifer 9.1   deciduous 9.2   rain forest 9.3   deforestation 9.3

CHAPTER SUMMARY

9.1 Coniferous forests are located in northern latitudes on the continents of North America, Europe, and Asia. Temperatures are warm in the short summers and very cold in the long winters. Evergreen trees called conifers are the principal components of this biome. Conifers have several adaptations that enable them to survive winter. Coniferous forest organisms are also adapted to surviving the long winter.

9.2 Deciduous forests are located in the temperate zones. Deciduous forest trees lose their leaves in fall and enter a state of dormancy that lasts through winter. The falling leaves produce a thick, fertile soil called humus. The deciduous forest has been extensively altered by human activity. Very little of this biome remains in its undisturbed state today.

9.3 Rain forests are located in the tropical zone. The rain forest is the most productive and diverse biome on Earth. The growing season lasts all year, temperatures are always warm, and rainfall is abundant. The soil in rain forests is thin and poor because most of the nutrients in the ecosystem exist in organisms at any one time. The large diversity of tree species and many levels of vegetation in the rain forest give rise to diverse communities of other organisms. Human activity is destroying the rain forests, and severely damaged rain forests may regenerate slowly or not at all.

MULTIPLE CHOICE

Choose the letter of the word or phrase that best completes each statement.

1. The forest biome receiving the most annual precipitation is the (a) deciduous forest; (b) coniferous forest; (c) rain forest; (d) steppe forest.
2. A tree that sheds its leaves at a particular time of the year is (a) deciduous; (b) evergreen; (c) coniferous; (d) tropical.
3. Conifers have needles and enclose their seeds in (a) cones; (b) pods; (c) sacks; (d) root nodules.
4. An adaptation that does not help organisms survive the long winter in the coniferous forest is (a) migration; (b) hibernation; (c) thick fur; (d) bright colors.
5. Falling leaves in the deciduous forest produce a thick, rich soil called (a) pumice; (b) humus ; (c) peat; (d) loess.
6. All of the following are uses for North American deciduous forest land except (a) farms; (b) orchards; (c) urban development; (d) grazing land.
7. The biome with the most diverse communities of organisms is the (a) deciduous forest; (b) rain forest; (c) coniferous forest; (d) prairie.
8. The layer of leaves that blocks most of the sunlight from reaching the ground in the rain forest is called the (a) shrub level; (b) understory; (c) canopy; (d) humus.
9. Most of the nutrients in the rainforest ecosystem are in the (a) organisms; (b) topsoil; (c) air; (d) groundwater.
10. A rain forest from which all trees and soil are removed will regenerate (a) in 10 years; (b) in 50 years; (c) in 100 years; (d) cannot be determined.

CHAPTER 9 REVIEW

WORD COMPARISONS

Write the letter of the second word pair that best matches the first word pair.

1. Evergreen: coniferous as (a) deciduous: humus; (b) deciduous: consumer;(c) leaf-shedding: deciduous; (d) rainfall: deciduous.
2. Coniferous forest: low diversity as (a) rain forest: high diversity; (b) rain forest: low diversity; (c) deciduous forest: high diversity; (d) deciduous forest: low diversity.
3. Plant diversity: animal diversity as (a) rain: precipitation; (b) photosynthesis: carbon dioxide; (c) sunlight: forest floor; (d) different habitats: diversity.
4. Deforestation: human population growth as (a) tree: forest; (b) deciduous tree: humus; (c) forest floor: sunlight; (d) loss of diversity: deforestation

CONCEPT REVIEW

Write a complete response to each of the following.

1. Describe some of the adaptations that enable organisms to survive winter in the coniferous forest. To what conditions are all coniferous forest organisms adapted?
2. Why do deciduous trees shed their leaves? How do these leaves affect the rest of the ecosystem?
3. Where are most of the nutrients in a rain-forest ecosystem at any one time? How does the soil in the rain forest reflect this distribution?
4. What two factors lead to high animal diversity in the rain forest?
5. How has human activity affected the three forest biomes?

THINK CRITICALLY

1. How does a conifer's shape help it survive the winter?
2. Why have deciduous forests been disturbed by human activity?
3. Illustrate the vertical structure of the rain forest by drawing a diagram. Include the canopy, the understory, forest floor plants, soil, and rainforest trees.
4. Contrast the diversity of organisms in the three forest biomes. Which biome is most diverse? Which is least diverse?

Computer Activity Rain forests covered 10 percent of Earth's land surface in 1950. That number dropped to 6 percent in 1993. Suppose the rain forests disappear completely by the year 2015. Use a graphing program to show the loss of rain forests.

WRITE FOR UNDERSTANDING

The size and shape of plant leaves are discussed several times in this chapter. Write a short essay explaining how the characteristics of coniferous, deciduous, and rainforest plant leaves are adapted to their environments. Your essay should include information on leaf shape, size, and other adaptations.

PORTFOLIO

The conflict between human needs for an old-growth forest's land and resultant products and the needs of the organisms living in the forest is a hotly debated issue. Study an example of this conflict, then write a letter to your congressional representative expressing your opinion and suggesting ways in which old-growth forests can be used by all.

GRAPHIC ANALYSIS

1. This figure shows the movement of rainwater through a rain forest and over deforested land. What percentage of rainwater is transpired from the forest and from deforested land?
2. What percentage of rainwater is absorbed by the soil in each case?
3. What percentage of rainwater leaves each area as runoff?
4. What effect do you think the increased runoff and decreased transpiration have on the soil of the deforested region?

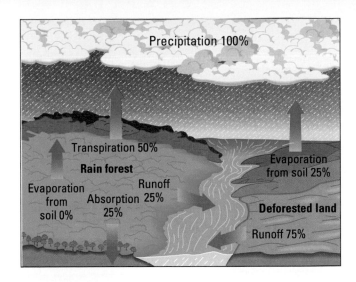

Precipitation 100%

Transpiration 50%

Rain forest

Evaporation from soil 0%

Absorption 25%

Runoff 25%

Evaporation from soil 25%

Deforested land

Runoff 75%

ACTIVITY 9.2

PROBLEM
On which side of a tree do lichens grow most abundantly?

MATERIALS (per group)
- reference sources
- construction paper
- glue or tape
- meter stick
- hand lens (tripod type)
- compass

PREDICTION
Write a prediction that is related to the problem.

PROCEDURE

1. Use reference sources to find out as much as you can about lichens. Be able to identify crustose lichens, foliose lichens, and fruticose lichens.
2. Read the procedures and make a data table to record the data you will collect. Then make a frame out of construction paper that measures 1 m by 10 cm.
3. Go to an area designated by your teacher.
4. Locate a tree that has lichens on its bark. Examine the lichens with the hand lens, and record your observations in the data table. *Note: Lichens develop slowly, so do not disturb them.*
5. Use the compass to find north. Curl the narrow sides of the paper frame around the north side of the lowest part of the tree. Only north-facing bark should be inside the frame.
6. Estimate the percentage of bark area inside the frame that is covered with lichens. Repeat for the east, south, and west sides of the tree. Record your estimates in the data table.
7. Repeat steps 4 through 6 for three other trees.

ANALYSIS
1. What types of lichens did you find attached to trees in the area?
2. Why was it important to examine areas of bark at the same height?

CONCLUSION
1. Did lichens cover more of one side of trees than others? Explain.
2. How would you improve the procedures of this activity if you were a scientist with more time and resources?

Since the dawn of civilization, people have settled and thrived by the banks of the world's freshwater supplies. Rivers, lakes, and swamps gave people water for drinking, cooking, and bathing. As societies grew, waterways were put to work transporting goods and irrigating farms. In addition to traditional uses, rivers now help supply electrical energy and cool nuclear reactors. But precious freshwater supplies are also important to the other organisms in the biosphere. Are people putting too many demands on the world's supply of fresh water? An understanding of freshwater ecosystems is crucial if these valuable habitats are to be preserved.

10.1 AQUATIC BIOMES

OBJECTIVE • *Describe* the factors that characterize the various types of aquatic biomes.

All the biomes you have read about so far have had one thing in common. They are all land, or terrestrial, biomes. But land covers less than 30 percent of Earth's surface. With water covering so much of Earth, it is not surprising that many of Earth's organisms live in aquatic habitats. An *aquatic* (uh-KWAHT-ik) *habitat* is one in which the organisms live in or on water. Aquatic biomes are not grouped geographically the way terrestrial biomes are, and it is difficult to show them on a map. Aquatic biomes and their ecosystems are scattered and are often determined by depth rather than location.

The characteristics used to describe aquatic biomes are different from those used to describe terrestrial biomes. Recall that temperature and rainfall are important factors in distinguishing one terrestrial biome from another. While these factors do have some effect, the temperature in large bodies of water is more stable than the temperature on land. Also, rainfall has less effect on many aquatic biomes than on terrestrial biomes because the organisms are already underwater. For aquatic biomes, two of the most important factors are the amount of dissolved salts in the water and the depth of the water. The rate of flow and the amount of dissolved oxygen in the water are also important factors in determining the types of organisms that live in an aquatic ecosystem.

Salinity

Aquatic biomes can be divided into two main groups, based on the amount of dissolved minerals in the water: saltwater and freshwater. Although all bodies of water contain some dissolved salts and other minerals, ocean water has a good deal more than the water in most lakes, ponds, and streams. *The amount of dissolved salts in a sample of water is called* **salinity** (suh-LIN-ih-tee).

Salinity is measured in parts per thousand, or the number of units of salt in a thousand units of water. The salinity of ocean water is about 30 parts per thousand. The salinity of fresh water is 0.5 parts per thousand or less. Water that is more saline than fresh water, but less saline than ocean water, is called brackish water. Brackish water is common in areas such as river deltas and coastal marshes, where fresh water meets the ocean.

The water in most lakes, ponds, and rivers is fresh water. There are, however, some exceptions. Some lakes, such as the Great Salt Lake in Utah and Mono Lake in California, are more saline than the ocean. Such lakes are called hypersaline lakes, and they may be as salty as 40 parts per thousand.

Field Activity

Microorganisms can be found almost any place there is water.

1. Use small jars to collect samples of water near your school or home that may contain organisms. Label the samples, so that you know where the water was collected. **Caution:** *Wash your hands after handling collected samples.*

2. Bring your samples to class, and examine them under a microscope or hand lens. Share your samples with other students.

3. What type of water contains the most microorganisms? The fewest organisms? Propose a hypothesis to explain why some water samples contain more organisms than others.

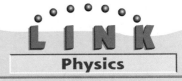

Physics

Salty water is denser than fresh water. The salinity of water can be tested using a tool called a hydrometer. A hydrometer measures the density of water by testing its buoyancy, or how much mass can float on the water. Because it is denser, objects in salt water have more buoyancy than in fresh water.

Figure 10.1 In deep bodies of water, only the photic zone is well sunlit. The water is less dense and warmer. In shallow water, sunlight reaches to the benthic zone.

Depth

The ecosystem present in a body of water, whether deep or shallow, is greatly influenced by the amount of sunlight that penetrates to the bottom. The amount of sunlight is important in determining the types and amounts of plants that can grow at various depths. As the producers in the ecosystem, plants form the base of the food web.

Bodies of water can be divided into depth zones, shown in Figure 10.1. *The top layer of water, which receives sunlight, is called the* **photic** (FOHT-ik) **zone**. The depth of the photic zone depends on how clear or cloudy the water is. In the open ocean, the photic zone is up to 200 m deep. Although sunlight reaches the bottom of the photic zone, the amount of light available decreases steadily as the depth increases. Below the photic zone is the aphotic zone. Sunlight never reaches the aphotic zone. Only the ocean and very deep lakes have aphotic zones.

The floor of a body of water is called the **benthic zone.** The benthic zone of the open ocean supports microscopic decomposers and scavengers. In shallow water, sunlight reaches the benthic zone and plants can grow. Common freshwater benthic animals include insect larvae, snails, catfish, and turtles.

SECTION REVIEW

1. What characteristic distinguishes the photic zone from the aphotic zone?
2. How is salinity determined and measured?
3. **Predict** Suppose a friend wants to set up an aquarium and discovers that saltwater fish are more attractive, but a freshwater aquarium is easier to maintain. Your friend decides to set up a freshwater aquarium but buys some saltwater fish to place in it. Predict what the result of this decision would be, and why.

10.2 STANDING-WATER ECOSYSTEMS

OBJECTIVES • **_Identify_** _the characteristics of different types of standing-water ecosystems._ • **_Explain_** _the value of wetlands and the reasons for their decline._

Freshwater biomes can be divided into two main types—standing-water ecosystems and flowing-water ecosystems. Lakes and ponds are the most common types of standing-water ecosystems. Standing-water ecosystems also include many types of wetlands, such as bogs, prairie potholes, swamps, and freshwater marshes. Table 10.1 shows some of the characteristics of different standing-water ecosystems.

Although there is little net flow of water in and out of most standing-water ecosystems, there is usually a characteristic flow of water circulating through the system. This flow helps to distribute warmth, oxygen, and nutrients throughout the system.

Table 10.1 Types of Standing-Water Ecosystems

	Abiotic Factors	Biotic Factors
Lake	Deepest type of standing water; may have an aphotic zone; may be fed by underground aquifers.	Main producers are floating algae in the photic zone and benthic plants along the shoreline; complex food webs.
Pond	Light reaches benthic zone; fed mostly by rainfall; may be seasonal.	Main producers are plants and algae that grow on the bottom; food web usually simpler than in lakes.
Marsh	Very shallow water with land occasionally exposed; soil is saturated; water often lacks oxygen; may be freshwater, saltwater, or brackish; often tidal; Florida Everglades is the largest freshwater marsh in the United States.	Plants have roots under water, but leaves are above the water (emergent); mostly grasses, cattails, and rushes; ducks, waterfowl, and benthic animals are common.
Swamp	Land is soaked with water because of poor drainage; usually along low streambeds and flat land; mangrove swamps are salty and found along coastlines.	Dominated by large trees and shrubs; plants are adapted to grow in muddy, oxygen-poor soil; cypress trees common in the south, willow and dogwood common in the northern United States.
Bog	Inland wetland with little inflow or outflow; soil is acidic; decay is slow; carbon is stored in dead plants.	Sphagnum moss is the dominant organism; partly decayed moss accumulates as peat.

Standing-Water Organisms

Many standing-water ecosystems have several levels of habitat. Organisms that live in the upper levels of water are different from those are that live in the middle and bottom levels. The upper levels of the water are warmer and better sunlit than the lower levels.

The top level of a standing-water ecosystem supports the plankton community. *Plankton* is a general term for organisms that drift in the water. Most freshwater plankton are about the size of dust particles. There are two main types of plankton: phytoplankton and zooplankton. *Plankton that carry out photosynthesis are called* **phytoplankton** (FYT-oh-PLANK-tun). Although they are usually too small to see without a microscope, phytoplankton are the main producers in most aquatic biomes. In lakes that are too deep for plants to grow on the bottom, phytoplankton are particularly important. Why do you think this is true?

Plankton that do not carry out photosynthesis are called **zooplankton** (ZOH-oh-PLANK-tun). Zooplankton include microscopic animals and protists. Because zooplankton are unable to carry out photosynthesis, they are consumers in the ecosystem. Zooplankton feed on phytoplankton. Small fish feed on plankton and insects on the surface of the water. Larger fish feed on smaller fish, and so on. As you can see, plankton are an essential part of the aquatic food web.

The benthic community of a standing-water ecosystem is quite different from the community at the surface. Many benthic organisms are scavengers, feeding on the remains of other organisms. This is particularly true of deep lakes, where sunlight does not reach the benthic zone. The benthic community depends on a steady rain of organic material that drifts down from the top. The decomposers of standing-water ecosystems are also members of the benthic community.

Wetlands

There is no single definition for wetlands that all scientists and government officials agree upon. As the name suggests, wetlands are found where water and land come together. *In general,* **wetlands** *are ecosystems in which the roots of plants are submerged under water at least part of the year.* Marshes, swamps, and bogs are just a few of the many types of wetlands. Wetland soils are soaked with water and contain very little dissolved oxygen. The water in most types of wetlands is standing water that may be fresh or brackish. However, there are also wetlands with flowing water and salt water.

Wetlands are a very important part of the biosphere that have not, until recently, been fully appreciated by most people. Wetlands act as filters, detoxifying chemicals in the water that passes through them. Wetlands are so efficient in this process that they can be used as part of treatment systems for waste water. Wetlands are also important breeding, feeding, and resting grounds for migratory waterfowl, such

Figure 10.2 Although they are rarely larger than pieces of dust, plankton form the base of the food web in freshwater and saltwater ecosystems.

Figure 10.3 Wetlands serve many purposes in the environment. They purify water, recharge aquifers, provide a breeding ground for many animals, and protect the surrounding land from floods.

as ducks and geese, and other animals. Wetlands along the banks of rivers act as flood protection regions. And the water that seeps into the ground under wetlands contributes to the refilling of aquifers.

Wetlands are being destroyed by human activity in the United States and other parts of the world at an alarming rate. There are several reasons for the disappearance of the wetlands. Many people do not find wetlands as attractive as other natural habitats. They are often breeding grounds for mosquitoes. Wetlands may give off an unpleasant odor, due to the methane, or "swamp gas," released by the organisms in the muddy, oxygen-free soil.

Because wetlands are often found in coastal areas, the land they occupy may be very valuable for other uses. People like to own property with a waterfront view. Many wetlands have also been used as landfill sites, helping solve garbage-disposal and land-shortage problems at the same time. Large areas of many coastal cities in the United States have been built on filled wetlands. The Swamp Lands Act passed by Congress in 1849 encouraged the filling and draining of wetlands. More than half the wetlands in the United States have been destroyed. The Clean Water Act has subsequently prohibited the filling of wetlands, but only 8 percent of remaining wetlands in the United States are federally protected.

Biology

Swamps and marshes in which the water contains no oxygen are often home to a type of bacteria called methanogens. These anaerobic bacteria release the gas methane, also known as swamp gas. Methanogens also live in the digestive tracts of many mammals, helping break down plant material that would otherwise be indigestible. The methane released contributes to digestive gas.

The Florida Everglades

The history of the Florida Everglades shows how difficult it is to manage a wetland area. The Everglades were once a swampy marsh that spanned 160 km from Lake Okeechobee to the southern tip of Florida. Water flowed slowly in a wide sheet across the whole region, varying in depth from a few centimeters to 2 m. There is a wet season from May through October, followed by a dry season. Many areas that are under water during the wet season are exposed during the dry season. Natural fires occur during the dry season, burning off dried plant material that grew during the wet season.

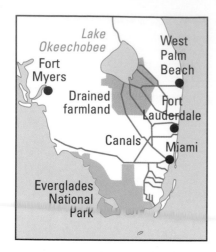

Figure 10.4 The Florida Everglades were originally formed by a slow-moving sheet of water that flowed south from Lake Okeechobee. Drainage canals converted much of the swamp to farmland and changed the flow of water through the park.

Figure 10.5 Alligators form holes in the mud by swinging their powerful tails. Fish and other organisms survive the dry season by living in the nutrient-rich gator holes.

The Everglades is home to a huge number of organisms. These organisms are adapted to the annual cycle of growth, drought, and fire. Alligators scoop out large depressions in the ground, forming pools called gator holes. During the dry season, fish, turtles, and other aquatic animals survive by living in the water that remains in the gator holes. Birds build nests on the exposed land and feed on the animals trapped in the gator holes. Without the gator hole, neither the fish nor the birds would survive.

To create farmland, water from Lake Okeechobee was channeled, and much of the wetland south of the lake was drained. To save the wetland, Everglades National Park was established in 1947. But without the water from the lake, the ecosystem was in danger. In 1967, a canal was dug to bring water from the lake to the park. Soon, flooding became a problem. The water came too fast and in too narrow a stream. The gator holes were flooded, bird and alligator nests were flooded, and birds could no longer feed on the fish in the gator holes. Eventually, the population of wading birds had dropped by 93 percent from what it had been in 1870. The alligator population declined as well.

In 1983, park officials and the state of Florida launched a "Save Our Everglades" campaign. The plan included cleaning up nutrient contamination from nearby farms and restoring a more natural flow to the Everglades' waterways. Since then, 100 000 acres of agricultural land have been returned to the wetland. There is now hope for short-term recovery and long-term survival of the Everglades wetland system.

SECTION REVIEW

1. What are the major characteristics of a marsh?
2. What is the difference between the role of phytoplankton and the role of zooplankton in an aquatic food web?
3. **Infer** The number of migratory birds in the tundra during the summer has been declining in recent years. How might changes that have taken place in wetlands have contributed to this decline?

10.3 FLOWING-WATER ECOSYSTEMS

OBJECTIVE • **_Describe_** how abiotic factors of gravity, erosion, and sedimentation affect stream ecosystems.

Flowing freshwater environments have many names: _rivers, streams, creeks,_ and _brooks_ all refer to water that flows over land. To most people, the different names suggest bodies of water of different sizes. To a scientist, however, all aboveground bodies of flowing fresh water are called streams. Recall that fresh water can also flow underground through aquifers. Even though they are under the ground, there is some life in aquifers. Some aquifers contain fish and other animals. In these cases, the aquifers are the animals' habitats.

Stream Organisms

Organisms that live in flowing-water habitats are adapted to the rate of the water's movement. Some organisms such as insect larvae have hooks that enable them to grab hold of plants. Others have suckers that anchor them to rocks. One type of animal that has adapted to life in freshwater streams is the fish of the salmon and trout families. Salmon and related fish breed and grow in freshwater streams but spend their adult lives in the oceans. When the fish mature and are ready to breed, they swim upstream and return to the very same spot in which they hatched. Research has shown that salmon find the stream and the breeding spot by "smelling" tiny amounts of chemicals in the water.

Stream Flow

Most streams begin at high altitude, often from the runoff of melting snow on the tops of mountains. Gravity causes streams to flow downhill. Because inland areas usually have higher altitudes than coastal areas, streams usually flow toward the ocean. The place where the stream begins is the source, or head, of the stream. Water near the source is called headwater. Headwaters in the mountains are often cold and contain large amounts of dissolved oxygen that can support a variety of organisms. But these headwaters tend to flow too rapidly for most organisms to live in the water.

As the slope of the land becomes more gentle, the stream slows down. As the flow of water slows, small particles of minerals, sand, and organic material that were picked up by the flowing water begin to settle. _Small particles that settle to the bottom of a body of water are called_ **sediments.** Sediments accumulate on the bottom of the streambed and provide a place for plant roots to grow. The plant growth further slows the flow of water, allowing the water to be warmed by the sun. Phytoplankton multiply in the warmer water, and soon there is enough food to support populations of consumers.

Figure 10.6 When they are ready to breed, salmon swim upstream and return to the very spot where they hatched. Research has shown that salmon use their keen sense of smell to locate the specific stream.

Chemistry

According to a law of chemistry, gases such as oxygen dissolve more readily in cold water than in warm water. This law explains why sodas lose their fizz quickly at room temperature, and why air bubbles appear in water when it is heated. Because of this law, colder water usually contains more dissolved oxygen and can support more animal life than warmer water can.

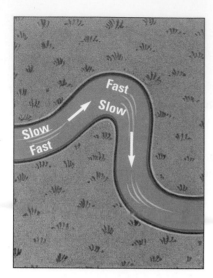 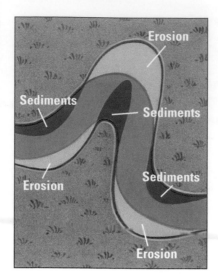 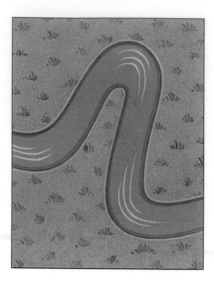

Figure 10.7 Erosion along the fast-flowing outer edge, and sedimentation along the slow-flowing inner edge, result in the winding, or meandering, of a stream.

The processes of sedimentation and erosion cause the course of a stream to change naturally over time. Use Figure 10.7 to follow the steps of this process. As a stream curves, or meanders, the water flowing along the inside of the curve slows down. At the same time, the water on the outside of the curve speeds up. Sediments accumulate along the inner edge because of the slowed flow. The increased flow on the outer edge, however, increases the rate of erosion along the banks of the stream. As a stream becomes older, it becomes more and more curved.

The flow of many streams has been changed dramatically by human activities. Some streams have been dammed to create reservoirs. These reservoirs help provide water, recreation, flood control, and hydroelectric energy for growing human needs. Dams, dikes, and irrigation canals have been used to change streams' courses, often damaging their fragile ecosystems. Many dams are intended to control flooding in river systems, but flooding is a natural and beneficial part of many ecosystems. In 1996, the Grand Canyon was artificially flooded with water released from the Glen Canyon Dam. The ecological and economic impacts of this flood are still being evaluated, but early results seem positive.

SECTION REVIEW

1. What condition encourages sediments to settle out of the flowing water in a stream?

2. Why are there fewer organisms in the headwater of a stream than further downstream?

3. **Apply** The headwaters of a stream often contain more dissolved oxygen than the water hundreds of kilometers downstream. Why is this true?

Fish Can Climb Ladders!

Dams provide hydroelectric power, create lakes for recreation, and lay the groundwork for ship canals from the ocean to inland lakes. For these reasons, dams are very beneficial to people. Dams, however, are a formidable obstacle for migrating fish, such as salmon and trout. These fish, called anadromous fish, are born in inland streams, migrate to the ocean, and then return to their birthplaces to mate and spawn. Dams block the way for adult salmon on their way to spawning grounds, and the turbines of hydroelectric dams can trap and kill young fish trying to make their way to the sea.

The dams have a negative economic impact on many commercial fishermen. If the fish do not reach the spawning grounds upstream, they cannot reproduce. The declining populations have put some commercial fishermen out of business.

Dams need to be built with modifications that allow migrating fish to pass through. As early as 1917, a dam was built in Seattle, Washington, to provide a ship corridor between Lake Washington and the ocean. Next to the dam, engineers built a "fish ladder." The ladder was a series of 10 pools that gradually elevated, much like the rapids in a stream. Fish could jump between pools to make their way past the dam.

Since 1917, fish biologists and engineers have made improvements to fish ladders so that more fish can successfully reach their destinations. The fish ladder at Lake Washington was rebuilt in 1976, at a cost of $2.3 million. The new structure has 21 weirs (enclosures) to allow the fish to move upstream on a more gentle slope.

Another improvement made was the addition of underwater openings, called orifices, that fish swim through. The orifices give the fish the option of swimming through an orifice or jumping to get to the next pool. Other improvements include special lights to attract adult fish to the entrance of the ladder, and "smolt slides" that allow young fish to migrate safely past the dam on the way to the sea.

This fish ladder at Rocky Reach Dam in Washington State allows migrating fish to pass the dam on their way to spawning grounds.

Checkpoint

1. Why are dams a problem for migrating fish?
2. What features need to be considered when designing a fish ladder?

163

Deposition of Sediments in a Meandering Stream

PROBLEM
What causes a stream's meanders to become larger over time?

Assumption 1: A fast-moving stream erodes its banks quickly.

Assumption 2: A slow-moving stream deposits sediment quickly.

MATERIALS (per group)
- stream table (see figure)
- metric ruler
- beaker
- clock with second hand
- graduated cylinder

HYPOTHESIS
Write a hypothesis that is related to the problem.

PROCEDURE
1. Set up a stream table that looks like the one in the figure. Be sure that the sand is wet, piled deeply enough, and contoured according to the sketch. The sand should be about 3 cm deep at the thickest part of the layer.
2. With your finger, cut a meandering streambed through the sand that has the shape of the one in the figure. The streambed should be cut almost to the bottom of the sand.
3. Make fine adjustments to the sand, if necessary, so that the slopes of opposite banks are about equal.
4. Determine the size of the curves by measuring distances y and z shown on the figure. Record all the measurements in a data table.
5. Set up a siphon with a long piece of rubber hose so that the water flows from container *A* into the upper river reservoir and then down the streambed. Half the groups in the class should adjust the rate of water flow to about 4 mL/s. The other groups should adjust the rate to about 8 mL/s. *Hint*:

Measure the flow rate using the clock. Intercept and measure the water draining into container B with a graduated cylinder.

6. Allow the water to flow down the streambed for 20 min. Observe and compare the flow rate of water near the outside and inside bank. You will need to continuously refill container *A* and drain container *B*. Turn off the water, but leave the sand in place.
7. Compare the slopes of the inside and outside banks at the center of each curve. Repeat step 4.

ANALYSIS
1. Was the flow rate of water fastest near the outside or the inside bank?
2. How did the slopes of the inside and the outside banks change relative to each other after water flowed down the stream?
3. How did the size of the meanders change after water flowed down the stream?
4. Compare your group's data with the data of a group that used a different water-flow rate. How do your results differ?

CONCLUSION
How do erosion and sedimentation cause the meanders of a stream to become larger?

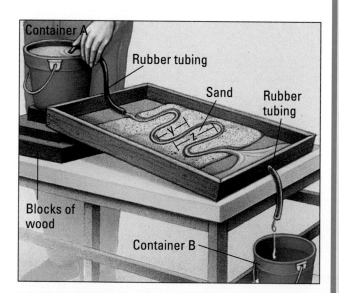

CHAPTER 10 REVIEW

KEY TERMS

salinity 10.1

photic zone 10.1

benthic zone 10.1

phytoplankton 10.2

zooplankton 10.2

wetlands 10.2

sediments 10.3

CHAPTER SUMMARY

10.1 Many of Earth's habitats are under water and are called aquatic habitats. Salinity, depth, rate of flow, and amount of dissolved oxygen are factors that determine the types of organisms that live in different aquatic biomes.

10.2 Standing-water ecosystems include lakes, ponds, marshes, swamps, and bogs. Phytoplankton are often the main producers in deep standing water. Wetlands are habitats where water and land come together. Wetlands are a very important part of the biosphere that are in particular danger from human activities.

10.3 All bodies of flowing fresh water are considered streams. Stream organisms are adapted to the rate of flow in the stream. The course of a stream changes naturally over time, but stream-diversion projects have changed or destroyed many stream habitats. Stream-diversion projects provide water and energy for growing human populations.

MULTIPLE CHOICE

Choose the letter of the word or phrase that best completes each statement.

1. To be considered fresh water, water must contain salt in a concentration (a) more than 30 parts per thousand; (b) less than 0.5 parts per million; (c) more than 40 parts per million; (d) less than 0.5 parts per thousand.

2. Brackish water is common in (a) lakes; (b) oceans; (c) coastal marshes; (d) aquifers.

3. Sunlight reaches the benthic zone in (a) ponds; (b) deep lakes; (c) oceans; (d) vents in the ocean floor.

4. Organisms that live in the benthic zone of deep lakes are often (a) producers; (b) plants; (c) scavengers; (d) plankton.

5. A type of standing-water habitat in which the soil is acidic and decay is slow is called a (a) bog; (b) swamp; (c) marsh; (d) pond.

6. Cypress trees are adapted to living in (a) stream beds; (b) swamps; (c) the northern United States; (d) bogs.

7. Phytoplankton are (a) consumers; (b) decomposers; (c) producers; (d) scavengers.

8. Wetlands (a) are easy to define; (b) have traditionally been protected by laws; (c) are nonproductive areas that could be better used for other purposes; (d) are important breeding grounds.

9. Sediments tend to accumulate (a) in slow-moving parts of a stream; (b) on the outer edge of a curve in a stream; (c) in fast-moving parts of a stream; (d) near the beginning of the stream.

10. Streams always flow (a) south; (b) toward the ocean; (c) downhill; (d) toward the poles of Earth.

11. Levees and dams are *beneficial* to farmlands because they (a) prevent stream sediments from being deposited on the fields; (b) protect the fields from floods; (c) provide a source of irrigation; (d) help refill aquifers.

12. Levees and dams are *harmful* to farm lands because they (a) prevent stream sediments from being deposited on the fields; (b) protect the fields from floods; (c) provide a source of irrigation; (d) help refill aquifers.

TRUE/FALSE

Write true *if the statement is true. If the statement is false, change the underlined word to make it true.*

1. Organisms that live on the bottom of aquatic habitats are <u>benthic</u> organisms.
2. <u>Zooplankton</u> are the main producers in <u>deep-water</u> ecosystems.
3. Salinity is measured in parts per <u>million</u>.
4. Sunlight always reaches through the <u>photic</u> zone.
5. Wetlands contribute to the <u>depletion</u> of aquifers.
6. Methane is produced in swamps by <u>benthic animals</u>.
7. The course of a stream can change over time as a result of sedimentation and <u>erosion</u>.
8. The <u>Swamp Lands Act</u> encouraged the draining and filling of wetlands.

CONCEPT REVIEW

Write a complete response to each of the following.

1. Explain how a stream's flow rate affects its benthic community.
2. List four abiotic factors that determine the types of organisms in aquatic ecosystems.
3. Compare and contrast the characteristics of a swamp and a lake.
4. How does depth affect the food web of a lake ecosystem?
5. Describe four beneficial functions of wetlands.

THINK CRITICALLY

1. Why do you think the food webs in lakes are generally more complex than the food webs in small ponds?
2. Why does the reproductive behavior of salmon make the fish vulnerable to changes in habitat?
3. Certain farming and irrigation practices increase the amount of sediments that are carried by streams. How might these practices affect the ecosystem in the stream?
4. Fish that are adapted to live in cold water may not survive in warmer water. Why does temperature affect the ability of an animal to survive in the water?
5. Suppose advances in technology made it very easy to make fresh water out of seawater. How might this affect the impact of human activity on freshwater ecosystems?

WRITE CREATIVELY

Imagine you are a drop of water that has just melted from a snowcapped mountaintop. Write a short story about the experiences you have on your journey down the stream to the ocean.

PORTFOLIO

1. Where does your tap water come from? Investigate the source of tap water in your community. Include projects such as dams and aqueducts that were built to help deliver water. What was the impact of this construction on the natural ecosystems?
2. Research the complex ecosystem of the Florida Everglades. Create visual presentations of the ecosystem dynamics and relationships among organisms in the Everglades. Include the changes that have occurred in the ecosystem during the past 50 years.

GRAPHIC ANALYSIS

Use the figure to answer the following.

1. Many rivers have been dammed to provide clean water for people. According to the graph, did the percentage of people with clean water worldwide increase or decrease between 1970 and 1980?
2. Was the change in percentage greater in rural areas or in urban areas?
3. Although the information in the graph is accurate, the worldwide supply of clean drinking water actually increased during the 1970s. Give two reasons that would explain the apparent contradiction.

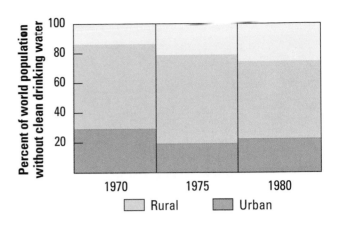

ACTIVITY 10.2

PROBLEM
To what kind of environment are tardigrades adapted?

MATERIALS (per group)
- depression slide
- spatula
- 2 cryptobiotic tardigrades
- dropper
- coverslip
- dissecting microscope
- distilled water

HYPOTHESIS
After reading the entire activity, write a hypothesis that is related to the problem.

PROCEDURE

1. Use a spatula to place two cryptobiotic tardigrades on a depression slide. View them under a dissecting microscope. Look for signs of life. Describe their appearance and sketch what you see.
2. Add three drops of distilled water to the tardigrades on the slide, and put a coverslip on the slide. **Caution:** *Handle glass slides and coverslips carefully.*

3. Observe the tardigrades in water. Note any changes you observe in the tardigrades' appearance and behavior. Sketch the appearance of the tardigrades in water.
4. Take off the coverslip. Leave the slide undisturbed overnight so that the water will evaporate.
5. The next day after all the water has evaporated, observe the tardigrades again under the microscope. Describe them, and make a sketch of what you see.

ANALYSIS
1. Describe what the tardigrades looked like when they were in the cryptobiotic state.
2. How did the tardigrades change when water was added?
3. What happened to the tardigrades when the water dried up?

CONCLUSION
1. Where did you hypothesize the tardigrades live? What evidence did you obtain in this activity to support your hypothesis?
2. Under what conditions would the changes that you observed be advantageous to the survival of the organism?

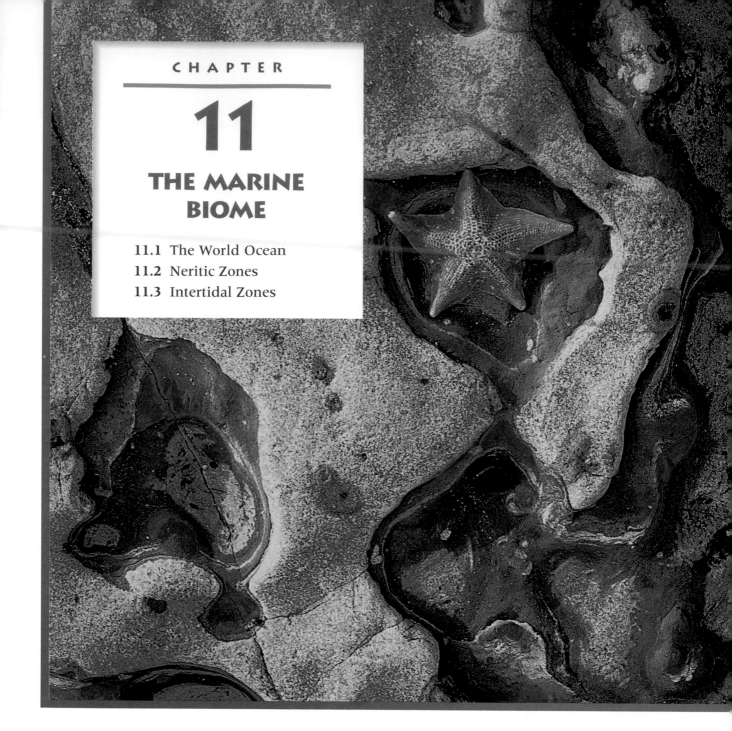

CHAPTER

11

THE MARINE BIOME

If you stand on a beach, the ocean may appear to be infinitely huge. It would seem, from its vastness, that the ocean is too big to be affected by the activities of the organisms on the relatively small patches of land. Yet the impact of human activities can be found from the open seas to the calm tide pools along the ocean's shores.

Oceans have been called the lungs of Earth, cycling carbon dioxide and oxygen constantly. The ocean also serves as a buffer that modifies temperature changes. In addition, oceans are home to many organisms. Without a healthy ocean, Earth may not have the stability to support its complex web of life.

11.1 THE WORLD OCEAN

OBJECTIVES • *Locate* the major ocean zones based on their relationship to the shore. • *Describe* the flow of water through the world ocean and the characteristics of ocean water in different parts of the world.

All the water between the continents on Earth's surface can be thought of as one big ocean. Although people have given names to separate oceans, such as the Atlantic and Pacific, all the oceans of the world are connected and therefore make up one large body of water. Because this body of water, called the world ocean, is interconnected, it can be thought of as one large biome with many ecosystems and habitats.

The world ocean can be divided into zones both horizontally and vertically. You are already familiar with the vertical zones. The photic, aphotic, and benthic zones that apply to large lakes also apply to the ocean. In addition to the depth zones, oceans can also be divided into zones based on distance from the shore. These zones, called the oceanic, neritic, and intertidal zones, are shown in Figure 11.1

The Oceanic Zone

The open ocean, or **oceanic zone,** *is by far the largest zone in the ocean.* It occupies over 90 percent of the surface area of the world ocean. The oceanic zone is very deep, ranging from about 200 m along continental slopes to as deep as 11 000 m below the surface. Sunlight does not penetrate very deeply into the oceanic zone.

Dateline 1972

Congress passed the Marine Protection, Research, and Sanctuaries Act. This act authorized the government to create national marine sanctuaries. Once established, the waters of these sanctuaries would be subject to stricter government oversight, allowing the habitats within them to be preserved for future generations. The largest of these sanctuaries is off the coast of central California, at Monterey Bay. It is over 5300 square miles in size, and contains rocky shores, thick kelp forests, and deep ocean canyons. It was designated as a sanctuary in 1992.

Figure 11.1 The oceanic zone is mostly aphotic, but the neritic zone, which lies above the continental shelf, is mostly photic.

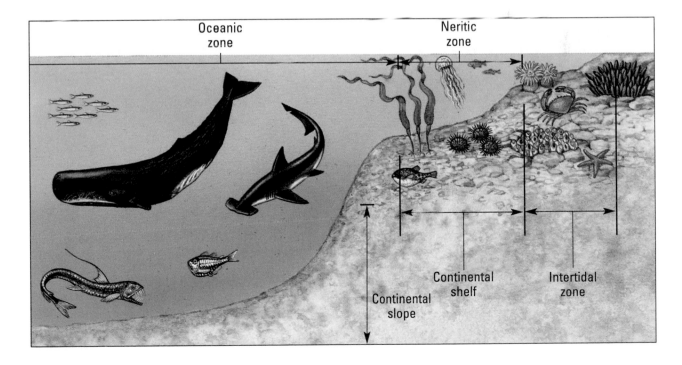

Oceanic zone — Neritic zone — Continental slope — Continental shelf — Intertidal zone

Figure 11.2 Fishes that live in deep ocean habitats (left) have many unique adaptations to their environments. The deep-sea angler fish has a glowing "lure" that attracts prey. Baleen whales, such as the humpback whale (right) feed primarily on plankton, especially a small species of crustacean called krill.

Field Activity

Most pet shops and aquariums that sell tropical fish carry saltwater varieties as well as freshwater fish.

1. Find out what factors must be considered when setting up a saltwater environment in a fish tank. What kinds of food and maintenance are required to keep a healthy saltwater aquarium?

2. Use the information you obtain to write a set of instructions for setting up and maintaining a saltwater aquarium.

The photic zone accounts for a layer at the surface of the ocean up to 200 m deep. Therefore, the only producers of the open ocean ecosystem are phytoplankton. It may seem that microscopic plankton are too small to support much life. But each year, the phytoplankton in the world ocean convert CO_2 into billions of tons of organic carbon, the basic material of living tissue that forms the base of the food web. Within the photic zone, zooplankton feed on phytoplankton, and small fishes feed on both types of plankton. Plankton are a major food source for many larger animals of the oceanic zone as well. Despite their enormous size, baleen whales, such as the humpback whale in Figure 11.2, feed primarily on plankton.

In terms of biomass, the aphotic zone of the open ocean can be thought of as the desert of the marine biome. Just as the lack of rain in the desert limits the number and types of organisms that live there, the absence of sunlight limits the diversity of the deep ocean. Deep ocean organisms have adapted to the cold, dark, deep waters. Many organisms in the deep ocean feed on pieces of dead organic material that drift down from the surface. *Tiny pieces of dead organic material that are food for organisms at the base of an aquatic food web are called* **detritus** (de-TRY-tus). Benthic organisms that feed on detritus in many types of aquatic habitats include invertebrates such as clams, worms, and sponges.

Ocean Water

Although all the oceans of the world are connected, not all ocean waters have the same characteristics. Differences in the amount of energy received from the sun cause oceans in different parts of the world to vary in temperature, salinity, and density. Water near Earth's equator receives more radiation from the sun than water elsewhere. This increased radiation causes the water to be warmer and evaporate more rapidly in the tropics. As a result of the evaporation, the

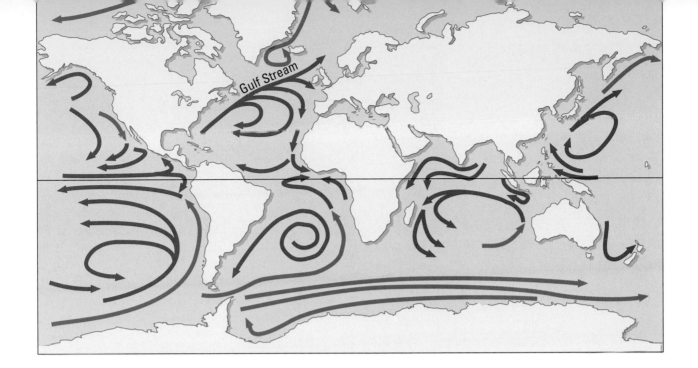

Gulf Stream

Figure 11.3 The major currents of the world are driven by energy from winds. Warm currents are shown in red. Cold currents are shown in blue. The Gulf Stream carries warm water north along the eastern coast of the United States.

water in the ocean near the equator tends to be more saline and have a higher mineral content than average. In contrast, the ocean in the polar regions is fed by melting glaciers and polar ice. Because of the influx of frozen fresh water, the ocean near the poles is less salty and colder than elsewhere. Low temperatures make the water near the poles denser than water elsewhere as well.

The water in the ocean flows in characteristic patterns called *ocean currents*. Although ocean currents vary somewhat during the year and from one year to the next, certain patterns are quite stable. Ocean currents are driven mostly by winds. Because of these currents, one mass of water can be very different from an adjacent mass. Fish and other ocean organisms often travel within specific water masses, following the pattern of currents over large distances. Because of the vastness and motion of the ocean currents, people have dumped various pollutants at sea for many years, believing that they would be diluted to safe levels. However, many pollutants can become concentrated in fish eaten by humans. The Ocean Dumping Act (1988) banned the disposal of industrial wastes at sea.

SECTION REVIEW

1. What is detritus made of, and why is it important to deep-sea organisms?
2. Why does the deep oceanic zone have no plants? What are the producers of the open ocean?
3. **Synthesize** Compare the map in Figure 11.3 to the one in Figure 1.8 on page 10. What type of winds drive the Gulf Stream current?

11.2 NERITIC ZONES

OBJECTIVES • *Describe* the factors that define a neritic zone.
• *Compare* and *contrast* two types of neritic zone ecosystems.

The edges of continents do not drop suddenly into the ocean. Instead, the major landmasses are surrounded by an area of relatively shallow water. *The shallow border that surrounds the continents is called the* **continental shelf.** The continental shelf is the area between the shore and about 200 m below the surface of the water. The width of the continental shelf varies among the different continents and coasts.

The ocean region between the edge of the continental shelf and the low tidemark is called the **neritic** (ne-RIHT-ihk) **zone.** Because the continental shelf is usually shallow enough to be within the photic zone, the waters in the neritic zone receive enough sunlight for photosynthesis to occur. Although the neritic zone accounts for only about 10 percent of the ocean, these shallow, warmer waters are the most productive part of the ocean. Two types of very productive neritic ecosystems are reefs and estuaries.

Coral Reefs

A **reef** *is a natural structure built on a continental shelf.* The structures are made from products of the reef organisms. Coral reefs are found in warm, tropical waters. Kelp reefs, also called kelp beds, are common in colder waters.

Coral reefs can be thought of as the tropical rain forests of the marine biome. Coral reefs are not only productive ecosystems, as are rain forests, but are also home to a huge variety of organisms. The coral reef ecosystem is extremely important to both the ocean organisms and the human populations living near the reef. Coral reefs are the breeding and feeding grounds for many economically important types of fish. In fact, one-third of all bony fish live on or depend on coral reefs. The reef itself protects the shoreline from erosion. Like the species of the rain forests, many coral reef organisms may have medicinal value that has not yet been identified. And like the rain forests, the delicate coral reef ecosystems of the world are vulnerable to human activities.

The ecology of the coral reef is unique and fragile. The reef itself is made of the calcium carbonate skeletons of millions of tiny corals. Only the top layer of the reef is alive. Corals depend on a symbiotic relationship with a form of alga, called **zooxanthellae** (ZOH-oh-ZAN-thel-ay), that lives inside the tissues of the coral. The algae carry out photosynthesis and provide corals with food. Like all photosynthetic organisms, the algae that live inside corals require an adequate amount of sunlight and cannot grow below a certain depth.

Figure 11.4 Coral reefs are made of the skeletons of millions of tiny corals. Corals belong in the group of animals called Cnidarians, which also includes jellyfish and sea anemones.

Figure 11.5 Coral reefs are complex communities that are home to a wide variety of organisms.

Human activities can harm coral reefs in many ways. The reef is often blasted with dynamite to make harbors and shipping channels. The coral itself is often harvested and sold for jewelry. Many of the bright, colorful fishes that inhabit coral reefs are popular for use in home aquariums. The methods used to collect the fish, however, can damage the reefs.

Water pollution is also a major cause of coral reef damage. Toxic chemicals can kill the corals and other organisms that live on the reef. Silt, sand, and topsoil that wash into the water make it cloudy and reduce the amount of light available for photosynthesis. The condition of a coral reef can be an indicator of water quality. When the corals begin to die rapidly, it is a sign that there is something wrong with the quality of the water.

Estuaries

An **estuary** (ES-tyoo-ayr-ee) *is a region where a freshwater source, usually the mouth of a river, meets the salt water of the ocean.* Estuaries are subject to the rise and fall of ocean tides that mix the nutrient-rich waters and sediments. The water in estuaries is usually brackish, but the salinity varies with depth, time of year, flow rate, and tide. Many marine organisms, including commercially important food species, use estuaries as spawning grounds. Humans use estuaries for recreational activities, such as boating, hunting, and fishing. Estuaries function as important buffer zones, filtering sediments and pollutants from the water. They also ease the effects of storms and floods by slowing the flow of water.

Neritic Zone Productivity

Many factors contribute to neritic zone productivity. The fact that sunlight can reach the benthic zone of the continental shelf is the

Health

Competition for food and space is intense on densely populated coral reefs. To protect themselves, many reef animals secrete chemicals that are toxic to other organisms. Some of these chemicals include antibiotics and hormones that may be useful to people. For example, one species of reef sponge produces a chemical that may help reduce the pain and swelling of arthritis. Medical researchers are studying many reef organisms for new sources of medicines.

Figure 11.6 Reefs are among the most
productive ecosystems on Earth.

Productivity of some ecosystems

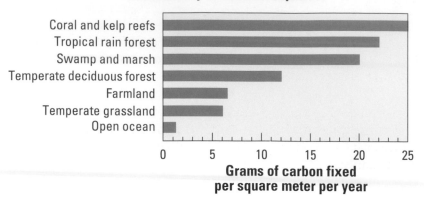

Figure 11.6 Reefs are among the most
productive ecosystems on Earth.

Think About It!

The graph in Figure 11.6 shows that the open ocean produces far less biomass than a reef.

1. Based on the information in the graph, do you think the open ocean contributes significantly to the overall productivity of the biosphere? Why or why not?

2. What sort of additional graph might help others make this judgment for themselves?

Figure 11.7 As coral reefs grow larger, less oxygen and fewer nutrients from the ocean are carried by the surf to the corals closest to land. Eventually, a channel forms between the reef and the land, creating a barrier reef.

most important factor. The availability of sunlight allows photosynthesis to take place throughout the zone. Waters in neritic zones also tend to be high in mineral nutrients. The nutrients are washed into the water from the shore, either in rain runoff or in the streams that feed into the ocean. Tides also play a role in the productivity of neritic ecosystems. The tide washes a fresh supply of nutrients and oxygen over the zone and carries away wastes. Figure 11.6 compares the productivity of neritic ecosystems with that of other aquatic and terrestrial ecosystems.

The effects of tides on coral reefs can be seen in the way the reefs develop over time. When a reef first forms, it grows just off the shore of the land. Such reefs are called fringe reefs. As the reef ages, it grows farther and farther out onto the continental shelf. As it grows, water from the ocean tides has to travel a longer distance to reach that part of the reef closest to land. Along the way, nutrients and oxygen are used up by the corals and other organisms. Eventually, the water that reaches the reef along the shore is so low in oxygen and nutrients that it cannot support the live corals. Corals nearest the shore begin to die, and a channel forms between the land and the reef. Reefs that are separated from the shore by a channel are called barrier reefs. The barrier reef surrounding the island of Bora Bora in French Polynesia can be seen in Figure 11.7. The Great Barrier Reef of Australia is the largest coral reef in the world.

SECTION REVIEW

1. Where in the ocean does the neritic zone begin and end?
2. Continental shelves have been called the breadbaskets of the ocean. Explain this statement.
3. **Infer** Some types of ecosystems recover from damage more quickly than others. Would you expect coral reefs to recover quickly from the types of damage described in this section? Why or why not?

11.3 INTERTIDAL ZONES

OBJECTIVES • *Explain* the processes that contribute to the formation of salt marshes and mangrove swamps. • *List* several human activities that damage intertidal habitats.

The intertidal zone is located along the shoreline of the world ocean. *The* **intertidal** (in-ter-TI-duhl) *zone alternates twice each day between periods of exposure at low tide and periods of submersion at high tide.* Organisms in the intertidal zone must be able to survive both exposed and submerged conditions. These organisms must also be able to withstand the constant pounding of the surf. Some organisms attach themselves to the rocks. Others burrow into the sand.

Because intertidal zones occur where the water meets the land, they are often surrounded by wetlands, such as tidal salt marshes and mangrove swamps. Like other types of wetlands, salt marshes and mangrove swamps are vulnerable to human activity.

Salt Marshes

Salt marshes are flat, muddy wetlands that often surround estuaries, bays, and lagoons. Most salt marshes are influenced by tides. The mud flats of tidal salt marshes are exposed during dry periods and low tides, but submerged during wet periods and high tides. Salt marshes are a common form of wetland along the coast of the United States, especially the east coast and the shores of the Gulf of Mexico.

Many of the environmental roles of wetlands described in Chapter 10 also apply to coastal salt marshes. One of the most important functions of salt marshes is their role in supporting migratory bird populations. Migratory birds use salt marshes for feeding and resting during their long journeys. Salt marshes are also essential in supporting the ocean ecosystem. The abundant plant life, especially grasses, of the salt marsh supports a rich community of fish and invertebrates. Many of the commercial fish and shellfish harvested in the United States spend at least part of their life cycles in the salt marsh. The plant material becomes food for the animals that breed, hatch, or grow in the water. Many of these animals then move out to sea or become food for ocean animals.

Salt marshes form when streams flow into the calm waters of an estuary or other shallow, neritic waters. The slowing of the water causes sediments, picked up by the stream, to be deposited at the mouth of the stream. The sediments build up over time, forming a delta. *The weight of the accumulated sediments causes the delta to sink under the water in a process called* **subsidence** (sub-SID-ents). To remain stable, there must be a balance between the rate

Figure 11.8 Most migratory birds that summer in the tundra and other cold regions rely on coastal salt marshes to rest and feed during their journey.

of sediment deposition and the rate of subsidence in a salt marsh. Sometimes, the course of the stream may change as a result of these two factors. The Mississippi River delta undergoes a 5000-year cycle of sediment accumulation, subsidence, and change in the river's course. With every change, the Mississippi delta changes shape. The salt marshes of the Mississippi River delta account for 40 percent of the coastal wetlands of the contiguous United States.

Mangrove Swamps

Figure 11.9 The tangled, stiltlike roots of the red mangrove trap sediments that accumulate as mud behind the trees. Other swamp plants then take root in the mud, causing the growth of mangrove forests.

Mangrove swamps are a type of coastal wetland that occurs only in warm climates. Frost kills the plants in a mangrove swamp. Therefore, mangrove swamps can exist only in areas that do not freeze for more than one or two days each year. The dominant plant life in a mangrove swamp is the mangrove, a woody plant that can be either a tree or a shrub. There are about 68 species of mangroves worldwide, of which only 10 live in the United States. The red mangrove is the most common U.S. type.

The water in mangrove swamps typically has very little dissolved oxygen. Mangroves are adapted to the low oxygen by having roots that emerge from the water. Some species have roots that grow up from the bottom of the plant, with tips that stick out above the water. Other species have roots that grow from high up on the tree's trunk. The roots make the plant appear to be up on stilts. These elaborate root structures trap sediments, causing soil to accumulate behind the plants. This soil enables other plants to grow. In some parts of the world, such as Southeast Asia, mangrove swamps can develop into extensive mangrove forests.

Mangrove swamps and forests support complex ecosystems full of organisms with unique adaptations. Like many ecosystems worldwide, some species that live in the mangrove swamps are endangered due to loss of habitat. In the Philippines, for example, the 5000 km^2 of mangrove swamps that existed in the 1920s have been reduced to less than 1400 km^2 today. The swamps are destroyed for many reasons, including the creation of aquaculture ponds used for raising commercial fish and shrimp. Other reasons for mangrove swamp destruction include coastal construction projects and waste dumping.

SECTION REVIEW

1. Why are salt marshes considered part of the intertidal zone?
2. In what parts of the United States would you expect to find mangroves?
3. **Apply** Much of the Mississippi River has been contained by levees, dikes, and other flood-control structures. How do you think this change has affected the river's delta?

Draining Salt Marshes

Salt marshes are among the most biologically productive environments on Earth. These marshes make up a complex ecosystem that includes marsh grasses, snails, bacteria, crabs, clams, worms, and birds.

Humans have also been attracted to the salt marshes. In part, this was due to easy access by water transportation and an abundant source of food. In addition, coastal land offers many recreational possibilities. To meet the human demand for more coastal land, salt marshes are often drained for development.

Should salt marshes be drained for development?

People Need the Land

Coastal land is desirable property for housing and recreation. People enjoy living and vacationing near the water. The development of marsh land helps the economy by providing employment.

Salt-marsh property is also valuable for industry. The easy access to water makes the shipping of raw materials and finished products possible. Industry helps the local economy by providing jobs and paying taxes to local municipalities.

Salt marshes provide a productive environment for a diverse number of species.

People Need the Marsh

So much salt marsh has already been developed that it is especially important to save what little remains. Salt-marsh habitats support many different species of organisms, including several endangered birds. The salt marsh is also home to many edible species, such as crab, fish, and oysters. Draining the marsh would remove a source of food and a source of local employment.

Salt marshes are also natural flood-control zones. The marsh holds much of the extra water caused by rains and high tides. If the marsh is filled in and paved over, these developed areas will flood, as the water will have nowhere to go.

Consider the Issue

1. Do you think salt marshes should be converted to real-estate property? Explain your reasoning.
2. If a hotel were built on land that was formerly a salt marsh, how might the ecology of the area change? How might the economy of the area change?

Saltwater Concentration and Brine Shrimp Survival

PROBLEM
At what concentration of salt can brine shrimp hatch and survive?

MATERIALS (per group)
- marking pen
- 5 plastic cups
- 250-mL beaker
- salt
- measuring spoons
- brine shrimp eggs
- cotton balls
- shoebox
- plastic wrap
- glass stirring rod
- dropper
- Petri dish
- hand lens or dissecting microscope
- dry yeast

PREDICTION
Write a prediction that is related to the problem.

PROCEDURE
1. Copy the data table onto a separate sheet of paper.
2. Use the marking pen to label each cup with a different letter, A through E.
3. Pour 250 mL of water into each cup.
4. Use the measuring spoons to add 1 tsp of salt to cup A, 2 tsp of salt to cup B, 5 tsp of salt to cup C, and 10 tsp of salt to cup D. Do not add any salt to cup E. Stir the water in each cup.
5. Put a dry cotton ball into the container of brine shrimp eggs so that the eggs stick to the cotton. Dip the cotton ball into cup A, and swirl the cotton around so the eggs transfer to the water.
6. Repeat step 5 for cups B through E. Use a dry cotton ball each time.
7. Cover each cup with plastic wrap, and store them in the shoebox. Put the shoebox in a safe place where the temperature will remain stable.
8. The next day, gently stir the eggs in cup A to spread them throughout the cup. Remove a dropperful, and squirt the contents into the Petri dish.
9. Observe the contents of the Petri dish with the hand lens or microscope. Count and record the number of eggs and the number of hatched shrimp.
10. Add a small amount of dry yeast to the cup if brine shrimp have hatched.
11. Repeat steps 8–10 each day for the next 3 days for cups A through E.

ANALYSIS
1. In which cups did brine shrimp eggs hatch? In which cup did the greatest number hatch?
2. Were physical differences noticeable between brine shrimp raised in different salt concentrations? Explain.
3. In which cup did brine shrimp survive the longest time?

CONCLUSION
Based on your data, make an inference about the natural habitats of brine shrimp.

Cup	Amount of Salt Added	Number of Brine Shrimp in Sample							
		First Day		Second Day		Third Day		Fourth Day	
		Eggs	Shrimp	Eggs	Shrimp	Eggs	Shrimp	Eggs	Shrimp
A	1 tsp								
B	2 tsp								
C	5 tsp								
D	10 tsp								
E	none								

KEY TERMS

oceanic zone 11.1	continental shelf 11.2	reef 11.2	intertidal zone 11.3
detritus 11.1	neritic zone 11.2	estuary 11.2	subsidence 11.3

CHAPTER SUMMARY

11.1 Scientists divide the ocean into zones horizontally and vertically. The vertical photic, aphotic, and benthic zones that apply to deep lakes also apply to oceans. The oceanic zone, or open ocean, makes up more than 90 percent of the surface of the world ocean. Water flows in large masses through the currents of the ocean, driven by energy from winds.

11.2 The neritic zone of the ocean lies between the low tidemark and the edge of the continental shelf and accounts for about 10 percent of the world ocean. Reefs and estuaries are two types of ecosystems in the neritic zone. Neritic zones are more productive per square meter than is the open ocean because of the penetration of sunlight to the benthic zone.

11.3 The intertidal zone of the ocean is located along the shoreline and alternates between periods of exposure and periods of submersion. Salt marshes are a type of coastal wetland that exists in the intertidal zone in temperate regions. Salt marshes are common along the shores of estuaries. Mangrove swamps are coastal wetlands found in the intertidal zone of tropical regions. Mangrove swamps contain woody mangrove trees and shrubs.

MULTIPLE CHOICE

Choose the letter of the word or phrase that best completes each statement.

1. The oceanic zone is (a) mostly aphotic; (b) mostly photic; (c) mostly benthic; (d) mostly photic or aphotic, depending on the distance from shore.
2. The main producers of the open ocean are (a) ocean plants; (b) symbiotic algae; (c) phytoplankton; (d) zooplankton.
3. In terms of biomass, deep ocean habitats are similar to (a) rain forests; (b) deserts; (c) grasslands; (d) coral reefs.
4. Ocean currents are driven by (a) wind energy; (b) gravity; (c) temperature differences; (d) density differences.
5. The location of the neritic zone is determined by (a) water temperature; (b) the amount of sunlight; (c) productivity of the ecosystem; (d) the location of the continental shelf.
6. Coral reefs are made of (a) sodium chloride; (b) calcium carbonate; (c) rock; (d) silica.
7. Topsoil that washes onto a coral reef (a) makes the water less fertile; (b) is used as food for reef organisms; (c) helps protect the reef from the surf; (d) makes the water cloudier.
8. The water in estuaries is usually (a) very salty; (b) as salty as the ocean; (c) brackish; (d) fresh water.
9. Compared to a temperate deciduous forest of the same size, a swamp is about (a) twice as productive; (b) half as productive; (c) one-third as productive; (d) three times as productive.
10. Sediment accumulation contributes to the formation of (a) salt marshes; (b) mangrove forests; (c) both salt marshes and mangrove forests; (d) neither salt marshes nor mangrove forests.
11. You would be most likely to find a mangrove swamp along the shores of (a) Florida; (b) southern Argentina; (c) the Great Lakes; (d) Japan.

CHAPTER **11** REVIEW

WORD COMPARISONS

Write the letter of the second word pair that best matches the first pair.

1. Mangrove swamp: tropical water as (a) kelp reef: temperate water; (b) salt marsh: temperate water; (c) estuary: fresh water; (d) rain forest: land biomes.
2. Sunlight: oceanic zone as (a) rain: desert; (b) sunlight: desert; (c) temperature: climate; (d) saltiness: estuary.
3. Salt marsh: intertidal zone as (a) mangrove: neritic zone; (b) wetland: oceanic zone; (c) reef: intertidal zone; (d) estuary: neritic zone.
4. Mangrove: swamp as (a) coral: reef; (b) sand: beach; (c) mud flat: salt marsh; (d) estuary: salt marsh.
5. Wind: ocean currents as (a) heat: growth; (b) reefs: erosion; (c) sunlight: photosynthesis; (d) energy: light.

CONCEPT REVIEW

Write a complete response for each of the following.

1. Explain how topsoil erosion from nearby farmlands could affect a coral reef.
2. What factors contribute to the high productivity of neritic ecosystems? What is the effect of each of these factors?
3. What are some human activities that result in the destruction of coral reefs? What are the benefits of these activities to humans?
4. How might building construction on temperate salt marshes affect the tundra ecosystem?

THINK CRITICALLY

1. Many scientists predict that the level of water in the world ocean will rise as a result of global warming. How do you think a rise in sea level would affect the coral reefs of the world?
2. An island in the tropics routinely dumped sewage into the ocean several hundred meters offshore. After about 10 years, the coastline began to crumble, and large buildings along the shore washed into the ocean. What might have been the connection between the sewage and the collapse of the coastline?
3. Green peas help attract the colorful fish that live on coral reefs. Many areas now prohibit tourists from feeding peas to the fish. How might feeding peas to the fish affect the ecosystem?

WRITE FOR UNDERSTANDING

Suppose you read in the newspaper that the owner of a tropical resort is planning to dynamite the coral reef surrounding the resort in order to make a port for cruise ships to dock. Write a letter to the owner of the resort expressing your opinion of the plan.

PORTFOLIO

1. Compare the coral reef communities of at least two different regions of the world. What are the roles of the various organisms that occupy the reefs? What factors, if any, threaten the survival of the reefs you chose?
2. Greenpeace is a large citizens' action group. Research the various issues that the organization has been involved in. Decide whether you agree or disagree with their actions and present a persuasive report expressing your opinion.

GRAPHIC ANALYSIS

Use the figure to answer the following.

1. Compare the graph on the right to the graph on page 174. How can you explain the difference in open ocean productivity shown on the two graphs?
2. What can you deduce from the two graphs regarding the relative amount of farmland compared to deciduous forests worldwide? How did you reach this conclusion?
3. How would you expect the quantities shown on this graph to change during the next 10 years? Explain your answer.

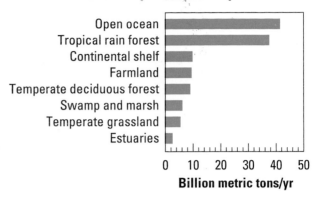

Productivity of some ecosystems

Billion metric tons/yr

ACTIVITY 11.2

PROBLEM
How is the metabolic rate of clams affected by water temperature?

MATERIALS (per group)
- biology references
- aged tap water
- salt
- balance
- 500-mL beaker
- 1-L beaker
- 2 jars
- pan of ice
- 2 thermometers
- food coloring
- 2 live clams

HYPOTHESIS
Write a hypothesis that is related to the problem.

PROCEDURE

1. Use reference sources to find out how clams obtain food.
2. To make seawater, add 35 g of salt to 1 L of aged tap water. Stir.
3. Add 500 mL of the seawater to each jar. Place a clam in each one. **Caution:** *Handle live animals with care and respect.* Place one of the jars in the pan of ice for 10 minutes.
4. After 10 minutes, measure the temperature of the water in each jar, and record the data. Remove the jar from the pan.
5. Place a drop of food coloring next to the clam, about 1 cm away from the side of the shell that is pointed. Have your partner do the same for the other clam.
6. Each partner should look for colored water being forced out from the shell of the clam. A third partner should record the time that it takes for each clam to expel the colored water.

ANALYSIS

1. What was the temperature of the uncooled water? How long did it take for the clam to take in and expel the food coloring?
2. What was the temperature of the water that was cooled? How long did it take for the clam to take in and expel the food coloring at this temperature?

CONCLUSION

1. Did the results of this experiment support or refute your hypothesis? Explain.
2. How do you think the metabolic rates of clams at the bottom of shallow water compare to those of clams at the bottom of deeper water? Explain.

KENYA

Kenyan Forests Multiply!

In 1977, a young Kenyan woman named Wangari Maathai planted seven trees in her nation's capital of Nairobi in honor of World Environment Day. By 1997, more than 15 million trees had been planted and more than 1500 nurseries were established. What started as a small-scale project has bloomed into a nationwide reforestation program called the Green Belt Movement.

The Green Belt Movement has three main goals. The first goal is to halt soil erosion and desertification caused by extensive cultivation. The second goal is to promote tree planting for firewood, because fuel shortages can lead to malnutrition in many villages. The third goal is to educate the local people about environmental conservation and sustainable development.

Villagers learn about the causes and effects of ecological destruction, deforestation, and desertification. They learn about the importance of planting multipurpose trees—those that can be used as food for people and livestock, and those that produce good firewood.

Within 10 years, the Green Belt Movement grew into a self-help community action program that involved 80 000 women and 500 000 children. The long-term goal is to plant one tree for each of Kenya's 27 million residents.

In 1991, Wangari Maathai was awarded the Africa Prize for creating a program that combined community development with environmental protection. Her efforts have encouraged thousands of people to actively protect the environment. The success of the Green Belt Movement has led to the creation of similar reforestation programs in more than 30 other African countries. A branch of the Green Belt Movement also exists in the United States.

Checkpoint

1. How does the Green Belt Movement help village residents in Kenya?

2. How does the tree-planting project help restore the environment?

During the last 20 years, Wangari Maathai has led the Green Belt Movement in planting more than 15 million trees.

◀ Urban Foresters

Urban foresty is one of the most rapidly growing fields in forestry management. Urban foresters and arborists work at the local level caring for trees and forests in their communities, adding beauty and enhancing the quality of life in that area. Because trees play such a fundamental role in an ecosystem, urban foresters also indirectly help protect the air and water quality of their communities.

Forestry Technicians ▶

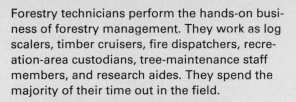

Forestry technicians perform the hands-on business of forestry management. They work as log scalers, timber cruisers, fire dispatchers, recreation-area custodians, tree-maintenance staff members, and research aides. They spend the majority of their time out in the field.

For More Information

American Forestry Association
1516 P Street, NW
Washington, DC 20005
(800) 368-5748
(202) 667-3300

Society of American Foresters
5400 Grosvenor Lane
Bethesda, MD 20814
(301) 897-8720
http://www.safnet.org

Natural Resources Defense Council
40 West 20th Street
New York, NY 10011
(212) 727-2700
http://www.igc.apc.org/nrdc/

Forestry Manager ▲

A large percentage of forestry managers are employed by the federal government, where they balance forest preservation and commercial interests. These federal employees are members of the Forest Service, the Soil Conservation Service, and the National Park Service.

PEOPLE
IN THE GLOBAL
ECOSYSTEM

· ·

CHAPTERS

Humans are skilled at adapting to their environments. This photograph of a farmer in Bali, Indonesia, is an excellent example of these skills. The farmer does not have access to flat land for planting his rice crops, so he has adapted to his environment by carving out rice fields in the side of a hill. In this unit, you will learn more about how people adapt to their environments and how the growing human population is forcing people to find effective alternative methods for utilizing Earth's precious resources.

Discover It!

Populations and Limited Resources

Suppose you have a classroom with 15 students and 15 pencils to write with. Then the population increases to 30 students and you do not have access to any other writing instruments.

1. How would you adapt to this situation?

2. How would an increase in the population size affect the demand for pencils?

CHAPTER

12

PEOPLE AND THEIR NEEDS

In the 1600s, British philosopher John Locke wrote that people must be "emancipated from the bonds of nature," and that "the negation of nature is the way toward happiness." Locke's words express the attitude held by industrial societies toward nature. In this view, the natural world is something to be conquered and consumed for the benefit of humans. People are seen as being separate from the natural world.

Most cultures do not share Locke's view of Earth. Many indigenous peoples view Earth as a living being. According to this viewpoint, people are a part of nature and just one of Earth's many interconnected communities.

12.1 A PORTRAIT OF EARTH

OBJECTIVES • **Describe** Earth as a network of systems and connections. • **Explain** how Earth is closed with respect to matter, and open with respect to energy.

The first part of this textbook discusses how Earth functions. The lithosphere, hydrosphere, and atmosphere are the abiotic parts of the planet. Parts of these three spheres come together and form the biosphere, the zone that contains living things. The science of ecology studies the interactions between nonliving and living things in the biosphere. The interactions among organisms and abiotic factors give rise to distinct ecosystems, called biomes. An understanding of these concepts, explained in Part 1, enables one to paint a portrait of Earth and how it functions.

Systems and Connections

The portrait of Earth outlined in Part 1 is one of *systems* and *connections*. There are many kinds of systems on Earth. One system is plate tectonics, the movement of the plates of Earth's crust. Another system is ocean circulation, or the movement of water from one part of the ocean to another. Climate is determined largely by the interaction between the ocean, air, and land. Ecosystems are affected by all of these systems. Each system has its own interactions and is governed by the physical laws of energy and matter.

The connection between ecosystems and abiotic systems such as climate is very close. The characteristics of living things in each biome are determined largely by the temperature and precipitation in that biome. Other systems, such as ocean circulation and plate tectonics, are also linked to the world's ecosystems. The movements of continents can change ocean basins and thus change the circulation of seawater. This change in circulation can lead to a

Think About It!

In many rain forests around the world, people are cutting down trees for lumber and to clear land for farming.

1. Do you think that cutting down trees in a rain forest could affect the rainfall in a rainforest region?

2. Explain your answer.

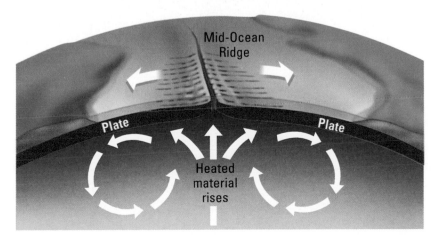

Figure 12.1 Plate tectonics is one example of Earth's many systems. The movement of Earth's crust may form geologic structures that influence the world ecosystem.

Biology

The number of amphibians is declining worldwide. In 1994, scientists presented evidence that the decline may be due to thinning of the ozone layer. The thinning layer allows more of the sun's UV light to strike Earth. The increased UV damages DNA in the amphibian's eggs, and may cause declines in species unable to repair the damage.

change in climate and, therefore, to a change in the ecosystem affected by the climate change. All the systems on Earth—from a community of insects and birds high in a rainforest tree to the movement of the continents—are connected.

Another way to think about Earth is in terms of matter and energy. Earth is a closed system with respect to matter. Only tiny amounts of matter leave or join Earth as it journeys through space. The planet is open, however, with respect to energy. Earth receives a huge amount of energy from the sun, and this energy eventually radiates back into space as heat. Some energy is reflected immediately by clouds and by the surface. The energy that is absorbed powers many of the planet's systems. The movement of ocean currents, the formation of clouds, and the growth of plants and animals are all powered by energy from the sun.

Connected systems of energy and matter form the portrait of Earth. The planet is made of various elements of matter. Energy from the sun moves this matter, organizing it and rearranging it through systems such as weather and ecosystems. Each system affects every other system because matter does not enter or leave Earth. Systems are connected through biotic and abiotic interactions. Every nonliving and living thing—including every human being—is a part of these systems.

Perceptions of Earth

As human societies have changed over thousands of years, ways of viewing Earth have changed as well. The perception of Earth as a living being, often referred to as "Mother Earth," is a view traditionally held by people in many cultures. But, in modern industrial society,

Figure 12.2 This illustration shows the portrait of Earth. Earth is an open system with respect to energy, and a closed system with respect to matter. Energy from the sun powers cycles of matter on Earth.

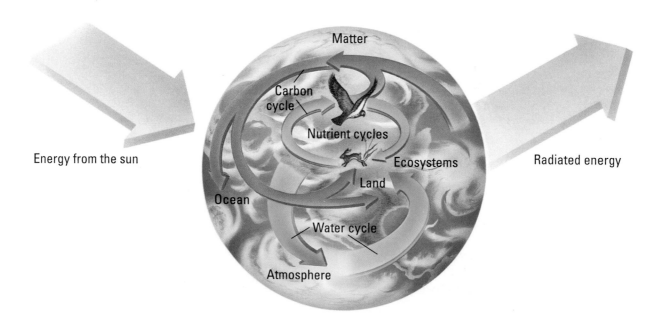

Figure 12.3 The winged figure on this totem pole is a thunderbird. Many Native Americans look at this bird as a symbol that helps explain the power of thunderstorms. In part, objects such as the thunderbird were created by humans to explain Earth's phenomena in ways that were understandable.

people see nature as something to be controlled and consumed. Many people view Earth as existing for human use. People are separate from the systems that govern the rest of the biosphere.

It is impossible, however, to completely separate ourselves from the rest of Earth's biosphere. Like any other population of organisms, humans are part of Earth's systems. The principles that govern lynx and hare populations in an ecosystem govern the human population as well. Human activities, like dumping wastes, cutting down forests, and replacing natural ecosystems with cities, can change both local and global climates. Many scientists are now studying the effects of human actions on Earth's systems.

In 1972, British scientist James Lovelock proposed the Gaia hypothesis. *The* **Gaia** (GY-uh) **hypothesis** *states that Earth functions like a single, living organism that regulates itself to maintain life.* Changes in one system cause changes in other systems. Lovelock suggested that the systems of Earth function together as an integrated whole, responding to changes in the physical environment.

Although the details and implications of Lovelock's Gaia hypothesis remain controversial, the hypothesis has influenced the way many scientists look at the world. Increasing numbers of scientists are studying large-scale connections among the various systems of the biosphere and the physical environment and Earth as a whole.

SECTION REVIEW

1. How could species in the rainforest canopy be affected by a moving continent?
2. Describe how Earth is a closed system with respect to matter, and an open system with respect to energy.
3. **Analyze** What is the Gaia hypothesis? Do you agree with it? Give reasons for your answers.

12.2 HUMAN SOCIETIES

OBJECTIVES • *Identify* hunter-gatherer, agricultural, and industrial societies. • *Describe* how the impact of humans on the environment has increased over time.

Human beings have lived on Earth for a long time. Fully modern *Homo sapiens* first evolved from ancestral humans about 35 000 years ago. Scientists know very little about these early people, called Cro-Magnons. All that remain of the Cro-Magnons are a few bones, artifacts such as tools and jewelry, and haunting cave paintings such as those at Lascaux, in France. These humans were as intelligent as modern humans. Their tools are intricate and finely made, and the cave paintings and other art show they had an artistic and spiritual sense.

Since the time of the Cro-Magnons, people have devised many different ways of solving the problems of survival. These strategies for living on Earth can be divided into three main categories: hunter-gatherer, agricultural, and industrial. These are broad categories, and no human society fits perfectly into any one of them. However, the categories do describe three general ways of dealing with the problems of survival.

Hunter-Gatherer Societies

A **hunter-gatherer society** *is a society in which people gather natural food, hunt, and are nomadic.* Nomadic people do not settle permanently in one place. Hunter-gatherers usually do not plant crops. They gather naturally occurring plants and hunt wild animals. Hunter-gatherer societies make little or no effort to control the natural resources of the area in which they live.

Hunter-gatherer cultures have a small impact on the environment because their population density is low. Hunter-gatherers take advantage of the resources they find and then move on. Their low population density allows the environment time to regenerate. A hunter-gatherer society lives within the ability of the land to sustain it. It can survive indefinitely unless it is disturbed from outside.

Agricultural Societies

Beginning about 10 000 years ago, peoples from the Middle East, Southeast Asia, and Africa began to plant crops and raise animals for food. Farming caused two changes in the way the people lived their lives. The first was that many people stopped roaming and settled permanently. The second was that people began to divide the work among members of society.

One important invention during the rise of agriculture was the plow. The plow enabled people to plant more land and grow more

Figure 12.4 This San woman is from the Kalahari Desert in South Africa. Almost all hunter-gatherer societies are threatened by the expansion of industrial societies.

food. The plow and the domestication of animals caused a large increase in the food supply. The human population began to grow.

Because farming produced a relatively large amount of food, some people did not have to farm at all. They began to form cities and to engage in crafts and manufacturing. Intricate trade networks developed to facilitate the movement of food into the city and finished goods out of the city. *A society in which crops are grown and people have specialized roles is called an* **agricultural society**. Figure 12.5 shows some places where agriculture began and the locations of some early civilizations.

If an agricultural society can live within the limits of its environment, it can sustain itself indefinitely. Practices such as rotating crops and allowing fields to lie fallow periodically can help to replenish the soil. However, early agricultural societies often harmed their environments. Increased logging, overgrazing, and poor farming practices also led to the loss of soil and vegetation. The loss of vegetation often led to changing rainfall patterns, and fertile land turned into desert.

Industrial Societies

Until the late 1700s, the production of food and goods was done entirely by human and animal labor. At that time in England, and later in the rest of Europe and the United States, the production of goods switched from skilled craftspeople to machines. Coal-fired steam engines powered factories that mass-produced clothes and other products. Machines such as tractors and irrigation pumps became common on farms as well, and more food could be produced by fewer people. *A society in which the production of food and other products is performed by machines, demanding large amounts of energy and resources, is called an* **industrial society.**

Dateline 1600 B.C.

The Babylonian Empire fell to invading armies. The empire had been weakened after overgrazing, poor farming methods, and excessive timber cutting, combined with a natural decrease in rainfall in the region, caused massive soil erosion and the formation of deserts on once-fertile land. The lack of food and wood helped weaken the empire to a point where it could be conquered by armies of the Hittites.

Figure 12.5 Agriculture first appeared about 10 000 years ago. This new strategy for meeting the needs of people arose in many different cultures and made use of many different crops.

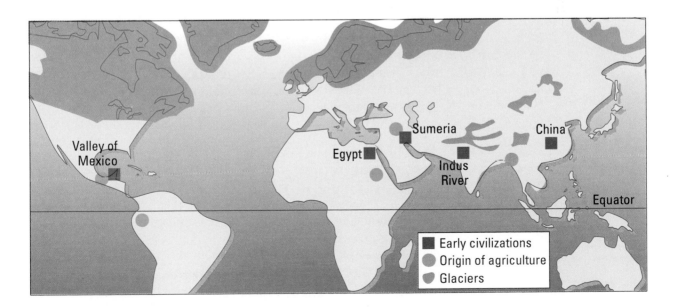

Valley of Mexico · Egypt · Sumeria · Indus River · China · Equator

■ Early civilizations
● Origin of agriculture
● Glaciers

Table 12.1 Characteristics of Human Societies

	Hunter-Gatherer	Agricultural	Industrial
Lifestyle	Mostly nomadic.	Permanently settled.	Often permanently settled.
Technology	Simple tools and weapons.	The plow and agriculture. Cities allow the advance of technology, simple machines.	Mass production based on large amounts of energy and materials. Advanced technology, biotechnology, nuclear weapons.
Resource use	Use sustained by the environment.	Some overuse of soil, forest, other resources. Sometimes sustainable.	Overuse of soil, forest, mineral resources. Not sustainable.
Environmental knowledge	Intimate knowledge of the environment.	Knowledge of the environment, farm organisms.	Generally little or no environmental knowledge.
Health	Healthy lives, well fed, low disease rates. High infant mortality, short life span.	Healthy, usually well fed, diseases common in cities.	Pollution is health threat. Stress-related illnesses are common. Medical advances increase life span.
Environmental impact	Use of fire causes some environmental damage.	Overgrazing, poor farming methods, timber cutting cause widespread damage.	Damage caused by industry, large population, high energy use. Global ecosystem threatened.
Energy use	Small energy use; fuel is wood.	Larger energy use. Fuel is wood, wind, water, animal power, some coal.	Very large energy use. Fuel is fossil fuels, hydroelectric, nuclear, and other.

The rise of industry was accompanied by advances in other areas. Scientists began to breed plant varieties to increase crop yield. Advances in medicine helped people live longer. Because of the increased food supply and better medical care, the human population began to grow very quickly.

Increases in production, energy use, and the human population can lead to environmental damage. Pollution of the air, land, and water has been a widespread problem of the twentieth century. Raw materials are running out. Technological advances have caused changes in the environment, but technology can also be used to help solve environmental problems. The interaction between the industrial society and the natural environment is a principal theme of this text.

SECTION REVIEW

1. What technological advance increased food production in agricultural societies?
2. How do an industrial society and an agricultural society differ?
3. **Infer** Give three reasons why hunter-gatherer societies generally cause less environmental damage than industrial societies.

Industry for Developing Nations

Until recently, most developing countries were agricultural. Many of the people in these countries were involved in nonmechanized farming. Typically, they grew their own food, using hand tools rather than large machinery.

In recent decades, many attempts have been made to transform these developing nations into industrial societies. In order to convert to expensive, large-scale mechanization, these nations typically have had to borrow large quantities of money.

Should develop-ing countries become industrialized?

Industrialization Can Bring Prosperity

Machines make agricultural and industrial processes easier and more efficient. Great wealth can be created, and the standard of living of the population as a whole can rise dramatically.

At present, there is much poverty, malnutrition, and unemployment in many developing nations. These problems can be addressed by converting these societies into modern industrial ones. Debts that are taken on will be paid off eventually through increased economic growth.

Industrialization Can Bring Misery

The debts owed by industrializing societies are often very large. To make payments, agricultural areas once devoted to raising food for local use are now used by governments for the production of cash crops for export. Some of these crops, including soybeans and peanuts, might have been used to feed the hungry native population. Often, the debt load forces developing countries to reduce spending on education and social services desperately needed by their populations.

This farmer in China tends to his crops, which grow near a new industrial development.

Consider the Issue

1. Describe several of the benefits of modernization and industrialization.

2. Do you think the possibility of such benefits is worth the risks and problems involved? Explain why or why not.

193

12.3 SUSTAINABLE DEVELOPMENT

OBJECTIVES • *Define* the frontier ethic and the sustainable development ethic. • *Contrast* renewable and nonrenewable resources.

The concept of a *resource* is common in industrial societies. Oil and coal are resources, as are minerals and trees. Books and people are also resources. The dictionary defines a resource as "something that lies ready for use." The assumptions behind this term help illustrate the way in which industrial societies view the world. Viewing Earth as a mass of raw materials that lie ready for use by humans has led to many of the environmental problems that challenge the world today.

The Frontier Ethic

An *ethic* is a set of standards or rules that serves as a guideline for determining right from wrong. Every society has a system of ethics; they are the rules by which the society operates. Early European-based industrial society was largely based on the frontier ethic. *The* **frontier ethic** *is founded on the assumption that human society is separate from nature.* Three basic concepts are derived from the frontier ethic:

- Resources are unlimited and meant for human consumption.
- Humans are separate from nature and not subject to natural laws.
- Human success is measured in terms of control over the natural world.

These basic concepts of the frontier ethic are no longer considered valid. As the human population has grown and consumption of resources has increased, we have become aware of the limits of many resources on a finite planet. We have also come to realize that we are a part of nature and our actions affect and are affected by changes in the rest of the natural world.

The concept that human success can be measured in terms of control over the natural world is a statement of values. Viewing human control over nature as success may be dangerous. This view ignores what scientists know about how Earth functions. An alternative way to measure success is by the degree to which humans can learn to live in harmony with the natural world. This concept forms the basis for a newly developed ethic of the environment.

The Sustainable Development Ethic

The new ethic of the environment is called sustainable development. *The* **sustainable development ethic** *is an ethic that meets current global human needs without limiting the ability of future generations to meet*

Field Activity

Form groups of two or three. Take a notebook and pencil and look for evidence of the frontier ethic around your school, outside your school, or in your home.

1. Make a list of ten observations that seem to support one of the three basic concepts of the frontier ethic.

2. When your group has finished its list, write a short essay stating what an ethic is, what the frontier ethic is, and how the frontier ethic appears in your life.

Figure 12.6 These oil wells were damaged in the Persian Gulf War. Damage like this led to massive pollution of the air, land, and sea. Conflicts over resources and the hunger of industrial societies for raw materials and energy have made scenes like this more and more common.

their own needs. It relies on reducing demand, recycling, conservation, and the wise use of resources. Like the frontier ethic, the sustainable development ethic can be summarized in three basic components:

- Resources are limited and are not all meant for human consumption.
- Humans are part of nature and are subject to natural laws.
- Human success is living in harmony with the natural world.

The concepts of the sustainable development ethic contrast with the concepts of the frontier ethic. Sustainable development is an ethic that can help ensure that the human future on this planet is a pleasant one. This ethic reflects the way Earth functions.

Some of the materials used to build societies, such as animals, wood, and other plant products, can regenerate fairly quickly. Other materials, such as minerals and oil, regenerate very slowly, if at all. *A resource that regenerates quickly is called a* **renewable resource.** *A resource that cannot regenerate quickly is called a* **nonrenewable resource.** Industrial societies have traditionally been based on the use of many nonrenewable resources. No society that depends on nonrenewable resources can last forever. Sustainable development is based on the use of renewable resources where possible, and the reuse or recycling of nonrenewable resources. Ideally, a society based on the sustainable development ethic should be able to survive indefinitely.

SECTION REVIEW

1. What is the frontier ethic?
2. How does the sustainable development ethic differ from the frontier ethic?
3. **Apply** List ten ways you can implement sustainable development in your life.

A Nonrenewable Resource

PROBLEM
Will the world's zinc reserves run out?

MATERIALS (per group)
- reference sources
- 152 paper clips
- watch or clock with a second hand

PREDICTION
Read the entire activity, then write a sentence that predicts the outcome of the experiment.

PROCEDURE
1. Use reference sources to find out about industrial uses for zinc.
2. Copy the data table on a separate sheet of paper. Add rows as needed.
3. Each person in the group will play a different role in this model.
   a. The Zinc Reserves person gets 120 of the paper clips and places them in a pile. This pile represents zinc that can be economically recovered from Earth.
   b. The Natural Processes person gets 32 paper clips. These represent metals or metal compounds in the ground that will form new ores, adding to the Zinc Reserves.
   c. The World Need person will acquire paper clips throughout the model from the Zinc Reserves person to represent ore that has been mined.
   d. The Timekeeper will announce the time every 15 seconds throughout the model.

4. When the first 15 seconds have passed, Natural Processes adds a paper clip to Zinc Reserves' pile. Natural Processes will continue to do this every 15 seconds throughout the model.
5. At the end of the first minute, World Need removes 1 paper clip from Zinc Reserves. At the end of each succeeding minute, World Need will double, so remove twice as many paper clips as were removed in the preceding minute. The model is over when Zinc Reserves can no longer meet World Need.
6. As the model proceeds, record the world status during each minute in the data table. Each minute represents five years into the future. Each paper clip represents 2 million metric tons of zinc.
7. Plot Zinc Reserves and World Need over the next 50 years on a graph.

ANALYSIS
1. What are some of the industrial uses for zinc?
2. How is the world's need for zinc increasing? How much zinc will be needed in 15 years? In 30 years?

CONCLUSION
Can the world's zinc reserves run out? If you answer no, explain why not. If you answer yes, state when, and describe the possible effects.

World Status of Zinc

Minutes Elapsed	Zinc Reserves at Start of Minute	Input from Natural Processes	World Need	Zinc Reserves at End of Minute
1	120	+4	−1	123

CHAPTER **12** REVIEW

KEY TERMS

Gaia hypothesis 12.1
hunter-gatherer
 society 12.2

agricultural
 society 12.2
industrial society 12.2

frontier ethic 12.3
sustainable develop-
 ment ethic 12.3

renewable
 resource 12.3
nonrenewable
 resource 12.3

CHAPTER SUMMARY

12.1 The portrait of Earth is one of systems and connections. All the systems on Earth are connected to all others, and almost all systems are powered by the sun. Earth is an open system with respect to energy and a closed system with respect to matter. The one-way flow of energy drives cycles of matter on Earth's surface. The Gaia hypothesis views Earth as a single living being.

12.2 Fully modern humans first evolved on Earth 35 000 years ago. Humans have developed many strategies for dealing with the challenge of survival. These strategies can be placed in three categories: hunter-gatherer, agricultural, and industrial. The environmental damage that each of these strategies causes is related directly to population density and resource use. The total amount of damage has increased over time.

12.3 Societies use ethics to determine what is right and what is wrong. Modern industrial societies have a frontier ethic. In the frontier ethic, resources are thought to be unlimited, and people are seen as being separate from nature. The frontier ethic does not reflect the way Earth functions. A new ethic called sustainable development is on the rise. This ethic reflects a society that can last indefinitely.

MULTIPLE CHOICE

Choose the letter of the word or phrase that best completes each statement.

1. Earth is an open system with respect to
   (a) matter; (b) energy; (c) information;
   (d) people.
2. Earth is a closed system with respect to
   (a) matter; (b) energy; (c) information;
   (d) people.
3. The Gaia hypothesis states that Earth is a
   (a) nonliving planet; (b) nonliving planet
   with living parts; (c) nonliving being;
   (d) living being.
4. Fully modern humans have lived on Earth
   for about (a) 1000 years; (b) 10 000 years;
   (c) 35 000 years; (d) 1 million years.
5. Hunter-gatherer societies are often (a) nomadic; (b) semipermanent; (c) permanent;
   (d) very dense.
6. An early invention that helped raise food
   production in agricultural societies was
   (a) mass production; (b) gunpowder;
   (c) sustainable development; (d) the plow.
7. Industrial societies were made possible by
   inventions such as the steam engine and
   (a) mass production; (b) gunpowder;
   (c) sustainable development; (d) the plow.
8. A renewable resource is one that regenerates (a) slowly; (b) not at all; (c) quickly;
   (d) without human action.
9. A nonrenewable resource is one that
   regenerates (a) only after human action;
   (b) slowly or not at all; (c) quickly;
   (d) without human action.
10. An ethic is a set of rules in a society that
    determines (a) right and wrong; (b) holidays;
    (c) economic function; (d) government.

CHAPTER 12 REVIEW

TRUE/FALSE

Write true *if the statement is true. If the statement is false, change the underlined word to make it true.*
1. Almost no <u>energy</u> enters or leaves Earth.
2. The Gaia hypothesis states that Earth acts as a <u>nonliving being</u>.
3. The major source of energy in hunter-gatherer societies is <u>wood</u>.
4. <u>Industrial</u> societies use more energy per person than any other society.
5. Agricultural societies often cause <u>more</u>

damage to the environment than hunter-gatherer societies.
6. People in hunter-gatherer societies are generally <u>more</u> nomadic than people in agricultural societies.
7. The <u>sustainable development</u> ethic holds that humans are separate from nature and immune to nature's laws.
8. Oil is an example of a <u>renewable</u> resource.

CONCEPT REVIEW

Write a complete response for each of the following.
1. What is the Gaia hypothesis?
2. Which factor is most important in determining the amount of environmental damage caused by a society?
3. Which inventions led to the formation of industrial societies?
4. What environmental factors contributed to the fall of the Babylonian Empire?
5. Write a short essay in which you define the following terms: ethic, frontier ethic, sustainable development ethic. Use your own words as you describe each term.

THINK CRITICALLY

1. Do you think the Gaia hypothesis is valid? Give reasons explaining your answer.
2. Write a paragraph stating the similarities and differences between renewable and nonrenewable resources.
3. The human population has grown much more quickly during the last 200 years than at any other time in human history. List some reasons for this sudden increase in the growth rate.

WRITE CREATIVELY

Reread the short essay you wrote in response to Question 5 in the Concept Review section. Then write a longer essay expressing how you feel about the concept of ethics, and how ethics relate to you personally. Do the ethics of a society always reflect the personal ethics of the people in the society? How can people work to change a prevailing view with which they disagree?

PORTFOLIO

1. Use pencils, paint, computer drawing programs, videotape, or other media to create your own portrait of Earth. Emphasize the systems and connections on Earth in your portrait. How do people fit into your portrait?
2. Take photographs, draw pictures, or write descriptions of five objects or activities that embody the ethic of sustainable development.

GRAPHIC ANALYSIS

Use the figure to answer the following.

1. In what area did most agriculture and early civilizations arise?
2. Why did no civilizations appear in the far north of Europe or North America?
3. Do the origins of agriculture and early civilizations seem to be related? How?
4. Did agriculture tend to arise near water, or in the center of continents away from water? Can you explain this pattern?
5. Humans first evolved in Africa. How do you think humans traveled to the Americas?

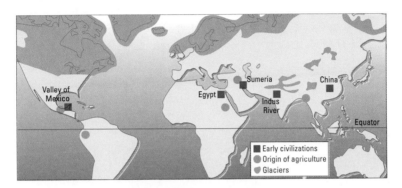

ACTIVITY 12.2

PROBLEM
How does the availability of food affect a population?

MATERIALS (per group)
- scissors
- Petri dish with lid
- paper towel
- dropper
- fresh green leaf
- cotton-tip swab
- 5 aphids

INFERENCE
Read the entire activity, then write an inference that is related to the problem.

PROCEDURE

1. Cut a piece of paper towel to fit the bottom of the Petri dish, and place it there.
2. Use the dropper to moisten the paper towel with water. Place a green leaf in the Petri dish.
3. Take the Petri dish and its lid outside to an area designated by your instructor. Find a plant that has aphids on it. Use the cotton-tip swab to transfer five aphids to the Petri dish. Cover it and return to the classroom. *Note: Aphids suck juices from plant stems and leaves. Look for aphids on both sides of the leaves.*
4. Each day for the next 2 weeks, lift the lid and count the number of living aphids. Be sure to check both sides of the leaf. Record the number of aphids each day. Make a graph to show any population changes over the 2 weeks.

ANALYSIS

1. Did the number of aphids change from day to day during the 2 weeks? What caused the changes?
2. What might the aphids and the leaf represent? How did changes in the aphid population affect the population later on?

CONCLUSION
What inference did you make at the beginning of this activity? Do your observations support it? Explain.

CHAPTER

13

HUMAN POPULATION

Much attention is currently given to the question of human population growth. In 1650, only about 500 million people inhabited Earth. Today, there are close to 6 billion people living on this planet, and that number increases by over 90 million every year. Many of the environmental problems discussed in this book can be traced indirectly to this population increase. Some scientists predict that if current trends continue, the human population could be 10 billion by 2050, and possibly 11–12 billion by 2100. How will such a large population impact Earth's ability to provide the resources necessary for the continuation of the human species?

13.1 HISTORY OF THE HUMAN POPULATION

OBJECTIVE • **Describe** *the major events that have affected the rate of human population growth throughout history.*

The issue of overpopulation has been a subject of concern for at least four centuries. In the 1500s, English statesman Thomas More portrayed the ideal state in his book *Utopia.* In More's ideal state, population is kept constant, crops are controlled, and food is distributed at public markets and in common dining halls.

Some of the best-known ideas about population growth in the past two centuries were proposed by British economist Thomas Malthus. Writing in 1798, Malthus argued that population growth was not always desirable. Malthus pointed out that populations tend to increase geometrically (1, 2, 4, 8, 16…) whereas the food supply tends to increase arithmetically (1, 2, 3, 4, 5…). The human population, therefore, has the potential to increase at a much faster rate than the food supply. Malthus believed that the tendency of the human population to outgrow its resources would lead to such conditions as famine, war, and other human suffering. To avoid such outcomes, Malthus advocated practices that would reduce the population growth rate, including late marriages and small families. These ideas have been widely discussed and debated ever since.

Increases in Growth Rate

Scientists estimate that the first modern humans evolved on Earth approximately 100 000 years ago. Scientists can only guess about population size and growth during the early stages of human history. However, there is some agreement that during this time, the population consisted of hunter-gatherers who lived in small families or tribal groups.

When humans roamed the forests and plains as hunter-gatherers, populations grew slowly. Starvation, predation, and disease prevented people from living long lives—35 may have been considered very old. These conditions kept the infant mortality rate high as well. Between 10 000 and 20 000 years ago, some people began to establish permanent settlements. Evidence suggests that these people did not cultivate food, but they did store food they gathered. Food storage reduced the threat of starvation and lowered the death rate, causing an increase in population size.

Agriculture A major period of population growth occurred around 10 000 years ago when people began to cultivate crops and domesticate animals. *This shift from harvesting wild food sources to producing food through the techniques of farming and herding is known as the* **agricultural revolution.** As agriculture spread and dominated

Biology

In 1838, the ideas of Malthus greatly impressed a young naturalist named Charles Darwin who had recently returned from a sailing trip around the world. Malthus's idea that populations tend to outgrow their resources became a major point in Darwin's theory of evolution by natural selection. According to Darwin's theory, organisms produce many more offspring than can survive. Within the population there are a variety of traits. Those individuals with the most favorable traits are the ones that survive and pass their traits to their offspring. Over many generations, favorable traits accumulate in the population, resulting in evolution.

Figure 13.1 The human population grew slowly and irregularly for thousands of years. The growth rate has increased dramatically over the last 300 years, since the beginning of the industrial revolution.

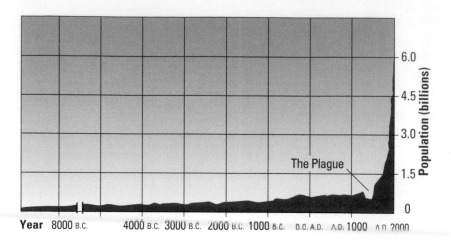

other means of obtaining food, nomadic hunter-gatherer societies were gradually replaced by small farming communities, each with its own social structure.

Farming provided an increased and steady food supply, which led to an increase of Earth's human population. In addition, social structure caused a general rise in the standard of living, which reduced mortality rates and increased life expectancy. It is estimated that 9000 years ago there may have been between 5 and 10 million people on Earth.

Industry   Another major period of population growth has occurred during the past 300 years. This period of history, marked by the industrial revolution, has included a number of events that favor population growth. Technological advancements have improved food production and distribution, reduced the length of the work day, and provided people with safer work environments. In addition to a greater availability of goods and materials, there have been major technological advances that have improved the quality of health care and medicine.

Health Care   The development of the germ theory of disease occurred at the height of the industrial revolution in the late 1800s. *The* **germ theory** *of disease identified bacteria and other microorganisms* (MY-kro-OR-guhn-izuhms) *as the agents responsible for many diseases.* Before the development of the germ theory, people did not recognize the connection between health and hygiene. The germ theory resulted in improved hygiene, sterile surgery, better methods of waste disposal, and water treatment. These developments reduced the death rate, particularly among infants and children.

The biomedical revolution of the twentieth century has also resulted in an increase in population growth. During this revolution, death rates continue to decrease as health and hygiene improve. The discovery of antibiotics and vaccines has wiped out or controlled many life-threatening diseases. In particular, infant mortality has decreased due to better prenatal care.

Declines in Growth Rate

Throughout most of human history, the human population has been increasing. However, population growth has not always been steady and uninterrupted. If you look at the growth curve in Figure 13.1, you will observe a sharp decline in population growth during the mid-fourteenth century. This decline is a result of the bubonic plague, or Black Death, that struck much of Europe and Asia. The plague may have killed more people than any other single disease. So devastating was the plague that within several years it claimed the lives of more than 25 percent of the adult population of Central Europe and Asia. The population of England was reduced by about 50 percent between 1348 and 1379. In addition to the plague, worldwide outbreaks of cholera, typhus, malaria, yellow fever, and smallpox claimed hundreds of thousands of lives. The more densely populated cities became, the more quickly diseases spread.

Figure 13.2 The death and despair brought on by the bubonic plague were common themes in the art of the Middle Ages.

Famine Famine can also devastate human populations. The Irish Potato Famine of the 1840s resulted in the death of more than one million people. At this time, the potato was a main food staple in Ireland. A disease called potato blight destroyed the potato crop, resulting in severe starvation. A famine in China during 1876–1879 was responsible for more than 9 million deaths.

War Wars have a destructive effect on human populations. Combat can claim many lives in a short time period. Other factors that reduce populations, such as disease, famine, and environmental destruction, can occur due to military activities. Cutting off food supplies is a common tactic among warring groups. Examples of wars that have taken enormous tolls on human life include the Thirty Years' War (1618–1648), when about one-third of the inhabitants of Germany and Bohemia were killed. Historically, many lives have also been lost in tribal and civil wars throughout Africa, India, China, South America, and the United States. World War I claimed an estimated 21.5 million lives, while an estimated 35–60 million people may have died as a result of World War II.

SECTION REVIEW

1. What changes in human society occurred during the agricultural revolution?
2. What are some factors that can result in a decline in human populations?
3. **Analyze** If the human population increased arithmetically instead of geometrically, would the potential for an overpopulation problem still exist? Explain your answer.

13.2 GROWTH AND CHANGING NEEDS

OBJECTIVES • *Identify* factors that affect the size of a population.
• *Compare* and *contrast* population growth trends in developing and industrialized nations.

Many environmentalists believe that overpopulation is one of the most serious problems we currently face. According to this view, many other significant environmental problems may never be resolved unless worldwide population growth is slowed and ultimately reaches a replacement rate of zero.

Measuring Growth Rate

Determining the rate of population growth is helpful for scientists, urban planners, and others who have to anticipate the needs of the population of the future. Growth rates are determined by subtracting the death rate (number of deaths per one thousand people) from the birth rate (number of births per one thousand people). For example, in recent years the birth rate in Egypt has averaged 29 births per year per 1000 people. The death rate has averaged 8 deaths per year per 1000 people. Thus, the population grew at a rate of 21 persons per year per 1000 people, or 2.1 percent (2.1 persons per 100 people).

The doubling time of a population indicates how long it will take, at the present rate of growth, before a particular population doubles its size. The populations of some cities and countries have doubled in 10 years. The population of Mexico City doubled between 1960 and 1970, and doubled again by 1980. The populations of entire countries, such as Honduras, Kenya, Syria, Iran, and Guatemala, are currently doubling in fewer than 30 years.

Doubling time can be used to illustrate the negative potential of uncontrolled population growth. For example, consider the need to double housing, food supplies, jobs, education, water, energy, and

LINK
Social Studies

Most governments conduct a survey called a census every few years to determine the size of the population. Censuses were conducted in ancient Babylonia, Palestine, and China. A census is conducted by the U.S. government every ten years to determine the age, sex, employment, and other data about the population. The information is used to determine such things as the number of representatives for each state in the House of Representatives.

Table 13.1 Doubling Time of the Human Population

Year	Approximate population size	Doubling time (in years)
8000 B.C.	5 million	1500
A.D. 1650	500 million	200
1850	1 billion	80
1930	2 billion	45
1975	4 billion	50
2030 (projected)	8 billion	

health facilities, just to maintain the present standard of living. Then consider the challenge of attempting to improve that standard of living in the same time period.

When measuring the growth rate of a specific population, births and deaths are not the only factors to be considered. Immigration and emigration can also affect the size of a population. Immigration is the movement of individuals into an area, while emigration is movement out of an area. When determining the size of the human population in a specific area such as a city or nation, the factors of immigration and emigration must be considered. When studying the size of the entire population of Earth, however, these factors do not apply. Humans cannot leave the planet, nor can newcomers arrive from elsewhere.

Demography

When scientists, planners, and policy makers study populations, they need to know not only how many people there are, but also what types of people make up the population. By including such information in their studies, scientists can determine how the population is changing. Are people becoming older, richer, or better educated? Are they having more children? Are there more women than men? These questions can be answered by demographic studies. *The science of the changing vital statistics in a human population is called* **demography** (de-MAH-gruh-fee). Figure 13.3 shows the demographic statistics of population ages in three nations: one growing quickly (Mexico), one growing slowly (United States), and one that is not growing at all (Sweden). Notice how much younger

Figure 13.3 These charts show the percentage of the population in each age group of three nations: one growing rapidly (Mexico), one growing slowly (U.S.), and one that is not growing at all (Sweden). The darkly shaded areas show people in their child-bearing years.

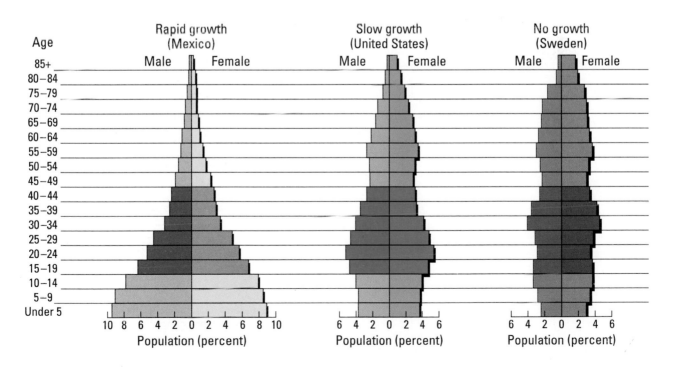

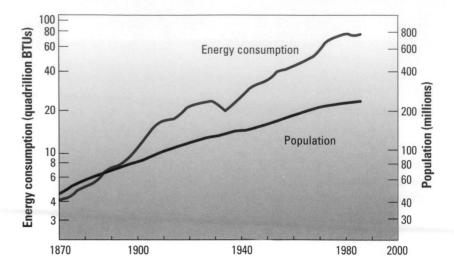

Figure 13.4 During the 1900s, the energy consumption of the United States grew faster than the population. What do you think was the reason for the drop in energy use in the 1930s?

the population of Mexico is compared to Sweden. The information in these graphs is much more useful than a simple number showing population size. With the additional information, plans can be made to accommodate the future needs of society such as child care and care for the elderly.

Changing Needs

It is not difficult to understand that a society with more people has greater needs than a society with fewer people. However, population size is not the only factor that determines the needs of a society. Changes in technology, lifestyles, and standards of living all affect the needs and consumption rates of a population. Notice the change in energy use during the period shown in Figure 13.4. The energy use far outpaced the population growth. Much of this change in usage was due to increased industrialization and modernization. Industrial societies generally use more resources than underdeveloped societies. As more nations of the world develop into industrialized nations, their needs can be expected to increase faster than the population increases. Ironically, it is the least developed nations of the world that are expected to experience the greatest increase in population during the coming decades.

SECTION REVIEW

1. List four types of information that may be included in demographic studies.
2. What factors are considered when measuring population growth?
3. **Calculate** What is the percentage of population growth in a region if the number of people per 10 000 individuals increases by 330 each year?

Mobilizing Against Meningitis

Meningitis is an infectious disease caused by bacteria. The disease is spread by airborne droplets that are released when an infected person sneezes or coughs. Symptoms of meningitis include headache, fever, vomiting, and a stiff neck. If left untreated, meningitis can be deadly. Even with treatment, 10 percent of the patients may die.

The disease is common in both temperate and tropical regions. In Africa, it is most commonly seen in a 600-km-wide band that reaches across the continent from Senegal and Gambia to Ethiopia. In the 1996 meningitis epidemic in this part of Africa, an estimated 250 000 people were infected, and more than 10 percent of them died.

In 1997, several organizations began to work together to fight the spread of meningitis in Africa. The International Coordinating Group (ICG) included representatives from the World Health Organization (WHO), UNICEF, the International Red Cross, Médecins Sans Frontières (Doctors Without Borders), and the manufacturers of meningitis vaccines. The immediate goal of the ICG was to ensure that the most needy areas got help first.

The ICG launched a two-pronged attack on meningitis epidemics. One action taken was the administration of antibiotics to people who were already infected. This helped speed recovery and reduce the period of time during which a patient can infect others. The other action taken was the vaccination of people who had not yet been infected. Both approaches required the training of many local health-care workers. A critical lesson was learning to store the vaccine correctly. The vaccine must be kept cold, between 2° and 7°C. Many of the areas to which health-care workers had to take the vaccine did not have refrigerators, so the transport and storage of the vaccine had to be carefully planned.

The program was successful. During 1997, there were fewer than 60 000 cases of meningitis. This figure represents a 75 percent reduction in the number of cases from 1996.

In Africa, an aggressive vaccination program was developed to prevent the spread of meningitis.

The long-range goal of the ICG is to improve the monitoring of populations in order to identify epidemics at the earliest possible stage. ICG is working with public health officials in several African countries to develop plans for local programs to predict and deal with meningitis epidemics in the future. If these plans work well, they may be used against other infectious diseases.

Checkpoint

1. Where in Africa is meningitis most common?

2. Why is it important to develop a way to predict epidemics of such diseases as meningitis?

Figure 13.5 The problems of over-crowding can be seen in urban centers throughout the world. In 1970, about 37 percent of the human population lived in cities. This number is expected to climb to more than 60 percent by the year 2025.

Dateline 1873

Ellen Richards became the first woman to graduate from the Massachusetts Institute of Technology, where she was awarded a degree in chemistry. She went on to establish the first modern sewage treatment testing laboratory. She analyzed water and sewage samples in Massachusetts and helped to develop the first water quality standards in the United States. Her work helped reduce the threat of diseases such as cholera, typhoid fever, and dysentery.

13.3 CHALLENGES OF OVERPOPULATION

OBJECTIVES • *Relate* overpopulation to use of natural resources, energy demands, and biodiversity. • *Hypothesize* about the effect of availability of resources on population growth.

Rapid population growth directly affects the global ecosystem. An increase in population places a greater demand on the space needed to sustain large numbers of people. Population growth also places a greater demand on resources, such as minerals, fuels, and food. As humans take up more space on the surface of Earth, there is less land available for the planet's other inhabitants. When this happens, it becomes difficult to convince people to give up the land and other resources they need to survive for the sake of saving wildlife.

As you have read throughout this text, however, all life on Earth is interconnected. Overpopulation and increased use of resources and energy in any country can affect other countries. Countries with growing populations may rely on the resources of other nations. Pollution from one country may affect a neighboring country.

Human health problems can be directly tied to overpopulation. The more crowding there is in a given area, the more contacts people make with other people. For example, people who live in crowded cities are exposed to more illnesses than are people in remote areas. Diseases related to malnutrition, poor hygiene, and a lack of medical facilities are also problems associated with over-population.

Overpopulation also causes the harmful effects of the things that people do to the environment to be magnified. For example, exhaust fumes from one car do not pose a serious threat to the environment, but those of several million cars do. Clearing a tract of land to build a house may not seem harmful in an area with several square kilometers of undisturbed grassland or forest. But building a house on the last available tract of land within an ecosystem may have a serious environmental impact, destroying the homes and breeding grounds of several species.

Controlling Population Size

It may seem obvious that controlling the birth rate is the answer to the problems of overpopulation. However, empowering people to control the number of children they have is not easy; convincing them that they *should* have fewer children is even more difficult. Forcing people to limit the size of their families is a step that most people find unethical and unacceptable.

Large-scale efforts are underway in many underdeveloped and developing countries to educate people and provide effective methods of birth control. There are many factors, however, that contribute to people's continuing desire to have children. In many religions, any effort to prevent pregnancy, other than avoiding sexual activity, is considered unacceptable. Also, many people feel that children are a source of pride and joy, and without them their lives would have little meaning. In many societies, a large number of children is considered important for helping to work the family farm or care for aging parents. Such basic cultural beliefs are very difficult to change, even if the change seems to be warranted for the common good.

In several nations, such as Bulgaria, Hungary, and Latvia, the birth rate has fallen below the death rate. Such nations face special challenges due to an aging and declining population. Decreasing numbers of soldiers and working taxpayers threaten to weaken the military and economic strength of these nations. The governments of some nations with a shrinking population offer financial support and tax advantages to encourage couples to have more children. On a global scale the human population continues to increase, but it is also aging. There will be a much higher proportion of middle-aged and elderly adults in the year 2050 than there are today.

Figure 13.6 The government of China strongly encourages couples to have only one child. Incentives to comply with this policy include better housing, longer vacations, and an extra month's pay each year to single-child families.

Is Technology the Answer?

Many of the advances of modern technology have the potential to increase the resources available to humans. New sources of renewable energy, new strains of crops developed through genetic engineering, and other scientific breakthroughs could help relieve many of the problems of overpopulation. Will these solutions be adequate to meet the challenges that lie ahead?

Some researchers believe that the increasing human population is not a problem. More people implies more brain power, and technology will continue to advance. Many environmentalists, however, feel that there is a limit to the number of people that can live comfortably on Earth. Earth's ecosystems can support only a finite number of people on the planet.

Think About It!

How do you think people in the United States would feel about the government limiting the number of children a family could have?

1. Would people feel differently if the limit was one child, two children, or ten children?

2. Explain your answer.

SECTION REVIEW

1. How can overpopulation affect human health?
2. How might overpopulation in one area affect ecosystems in other areas?
3. **Hypothesize** What effect does increasing the resources in an area have on the population in that area?

Modeling Disease Transmission

PROBLEM
How are diseases transmitted?

MATERIALS (per student)
- wax pencil
- empty baby food jar
- safety goggles
- rubber gloves
- dropper
- stock solution
- phenol red indicator
- lab apron

HYPOTHESIS
After reading through the activity, write a hypothesis that explains how disease moves through a population.

PROCEDURE

1. Write your name on the empty baby food jar with the wax pencil.
2. Transfer to your jar three droppersful of the stock solution provided by your teacher.
   Caution: *Wear goggles, gloves, and apron when handling solutions. Do not let skin or clothing come into contact with solutions.*
3. Take one dropperful of solution from the jar of a classmate, and empty it into your own jar. Gently swirl the mixture.
4. Record the other student's name. This person represents your first "contact."
5. Exchange a dropperful of solution with two other students, and record their names.
6. Add one dropperful of phenol red to your jar, and record the color of your solution.
7. You can tell by the color of your solution if you were infected or not. A red solution means you were infected; a yellow solution means you were not. Inform your teacher if you were infected, and provide the names of your contacts. Your teacher will write the names of all infected persons and their contacts on the chalkboard.
8. After the whole class has completed the experiment and collected all data, work together and deduce who was the original source of infection (there was only one infected source). Then trace the routes of the transmission of the disease.

ANALYSIS
1. Draw a diagram that traces the disease transmission in your class.
2. Were you infected? If so, who infected you? How many people did you infect?
3. What is the maximum number of infected persons after two rounds of exchanging solutions? What is the maximum after three rounds?
4. Phenol turns yellow in acidic solutions and red in basic solutions. Which represented the infectious microbe in this model, the acidic or the basic solution?

CONCLUSION
1. Using the data you gathered as a class, write a paragraph stating your conclusion including your observation.
2. Suppose you had exchanged solutions with six contacts instead of only three. What would have happened to your chances of becoming infected?

CHAPTER **13** REVIEW

KEY TERMS

agricultural
   revolution 13.1

germ theory 13.1
demography 13.3

....

CHAPTER SUMMARY

13.1 The human population has grown at various rates throughout history. The agricultural revolution, the germ theory of disease, and modern developments in medicine have contributed to a very rapid population growth. Disease, famine, and war are factors that cause the human population to decline.

13.2 As the human population increases in size, the need for resources also increases. The percent growth rate of the human population can be determined by subtracting the number of deaths per year per 100 people from the number of births

per year per 100 people. Immigration and emigration can affect the growth rate of the population. Demographic studies help planners to anticipate the future needs of a society.

13.3 Efforts to reduce the growth rate of the human population are difficult to implement. Social and religious beliefs about family size and birth control vary from culture to culture. Technological advances that increase the carrying capacity of Earth by increasing available resources are often followed by spurts in population growth.

....

MULTIPLE CHOICE

Choose the letter of the word or phrase that best completes each statement.

1. Of the following, the factor most likely to result in a decrease in the size of a specific population is (a) improved medical care; (b) increased food availability; (c) famine; (d) industrialization.

2. The agricultural revolution took place approximately (a) 100 000 years ago; (b) 10 000 years ago; (c) 300 years ago; (d) during the past 100 years.

3. The germ theory of disease established that many diseases are caused by (a) microorganisms; (b) water; (c) poor nutrition; (d) overpopulation.

4. A dramatic decline in the population of Europe in the 1300s was caused by the (a) potato famine; (b) bubonic plague; (c) Thirty Years' War; (d) outbreak of cholera.

5. A nation with a population that is not increasing is (a) Peru; (b) Guatemala; (c) Sweden; (d) Kenya.

6. When calculating global population growth, the death rate is (a) added to the birth rate; (b) subtracted from life expectancy; (c) multiplied by 100; (d) subtracted from the birth rate.

7. At present, the growth patterns of the human population are best described as (a) above carrying capacity; (b) geometric; (c) arithmetic; (d) stable.

8. The greatest growth of human populations today is occurring in (a) industrial societies; (b) tribal societies; (c) developing nations; (d) hunter–gatherer societies.

9. Problems associated with a declining population size include (a) increased famine; (b) decreased health care; (c) loss of habitat; (d) weakened economic strength.

10. The change in energy consumption in the United States during the past 100 years is due to (a) population growth; (b) modernization; (c) both population growth and modernization; (d) neither population growth nor modernization.

CHAPTER **13** REVIEW

TRUE/FALSE

Write true *if the statement is true. If the statement is false, change the underlined word to make it true.*

1. The person who compared the growth of the human population to its food resources was Thomas <u>More</u>.
2. The life <u>expectancy</u> of people in industrial societies has <u>increased</u> over time.
3. A population that shows growth of 24 persons per 1000 has a population growth of <u>24 percent</u>.
4. The population of Mexico City has doubled within <u>20</u> years.
5. The increase in modern machinery tends to <u>decrease</u> the energy needs of a society.
6. The period of the twentieth century marked by huge advances in medicine is sometimes called the <u>biomedical</u> revolution.

CONCEPT REVIEW

Write a complete response to each of the following.

1. How did the discovery of the germ theory of disease impact society?
2. Describe three factors that can cause a population size to decrease.
3. Why have infant death rates decreased in the past 50 years?
4. Explain the concept of doubling time.
5. Why does an increased number of people affect the availability of resources?

THINK CRITICALLY

1. Why is the growth rate of the human population difficult to control?
2. Describe three ways that a growing human population affects other organisms.
3. Some scientists consider the hunter-gatherer societies that exist today to be endangered species. How would people living as hunter-gatherers be similar to species of other organisms that are considered endangered?

Computer Activity (Use a spreadsheet program to solve the following problem.) Population A and Population B both start with 100 people. With each generation, Population A grows by 2 percent, while Population B grows by 5 percent. How many generations will it take for each population to double?

WRITE CREATIVELY

Write a fictional story that describes the life of a hunter-gatherer living 10 000 years ago in a society that is just beginning to establish its first permanent settlement.

PORTFOLIO

1. The People's Republic of China is one of the few nations in the world that limits family size. Research the changes that have occurred in Chinese society as a result of the one-child-per-family rule. Make a presentation of your findings, including how people in China feel about the rule.
2. There are organizations that enable people in the United States to sponsor a needy child in various parts of the world. Research one such organization and find out how much it costs to sponsor a child, and how the money is used to help the children and their communities.

Use Figure 13.3 on page 205 to answer the following.

1. Which of the three nations has the highest percentage of children under the age of 15? What does this imply about the amount of money needed for schools and children's services?
2. In which nation would you expect to find the largest population of elderly people?
3. What can you infer about the life expectancy of men compared to women in the three nations shown?
4. In which nation would you expect to find the greatest percentage of children ten years from now? Explain your answer.

ACTIVITY 13.2

PROBLEM

What happens when too many people are crowded into a living space, and what are the advantages of careful community planning?

MATERIALS

meter stick or metric tape measure

PREDICTION

After reading through the activity, predict how you will feel when restricted to a small area.

PROCEDURE

1. Measure the length and width of your classroom. Calculate the area of the room using this formula: length (m) × width (m) = area (m²)
2. Count the number of people in the class. Then calculate the population density (number of people per square meter) using this formula:

$$\frac{\text{number of people}}{\text{area (meters}^2)} = \text{population density (people/m}^2)$$

3. Your teacher will draw an imaginary line dividing the classroom in half. Then all students will move to one half of the room. Determine the new population density.
4. Observe your classmates in this restricted environment: note how people talk, sit or stand, what they say, and how the area looks.
5. Again the teacher will draw an imaginary line, this time dividing the classroom into fourths. Repeat steps 3 and 4.

ANALYSIS

1. After you finish recording your calculations and observations, comment on the behavior of the class members as the available living space got smaller and smaller.
2. Discuss how and why some individual behaviors change as the density increases.

CONCLUSION

1. What conclusions can you draw from the data you gathered? Does increased population density adversely affect a community?
2. Record how you felt as the classroom got smaller and more crowded.

Population Density Data Table

Classroom Size	Length (m)	Width (m)	Area (m²)	Population Density (people/m²)
Full				
Half				
Fourth				

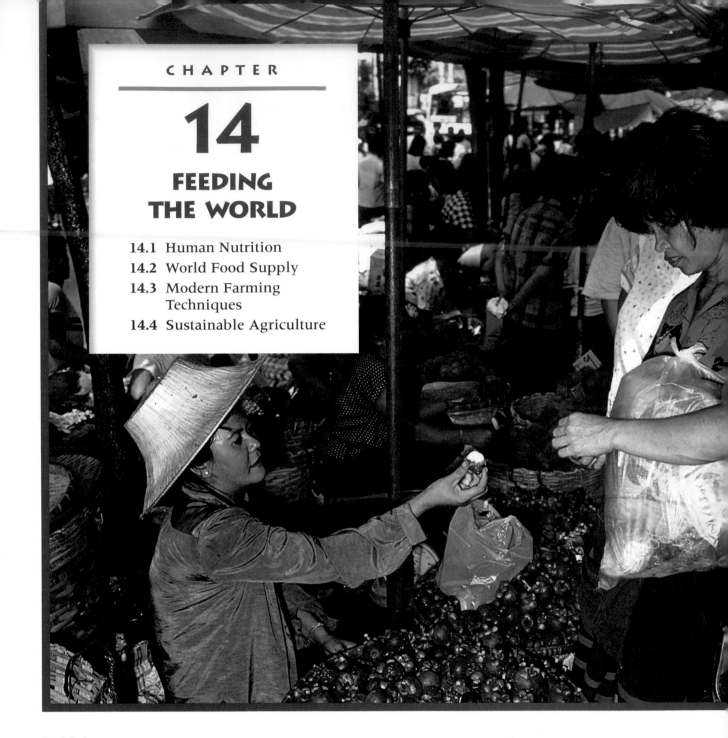

You have probably seen horrifying images on television and in news magazines of starving children in developing nations. You may have seen hungry people in the United States waiting in lines at soup kitchens and shelters for a hot meal. Perhaps you or someone you know has been in such a situation.

Yet during the past 40 years, world food production has increased faster than the rate of population growth. The real reason for hunger is often not the amount of food available. Instead, it is the unequal distribution of food around the world and within individual nations that can result in starvation and other social crises.

14.1 HUMAN NUTRITION

OBJECTIVES • *List* the major groups of nutrients and the amount of energy provided by each type.

Like all organisms on Earth, humans need energy to carry out their life processes, which include growth, movement, and tissue repair. Humans are omnivores, or animals that can consume either plants or animals for food. Dietary habits vary a great deal from one society to another. Because all humans belong to one species, all have the same basic nutritional needs. In addition to the energy required for life processes, people also need a blend of other substances, or nutrients, to maintain good health.

Nutrients

Nutrients can be divided into two main groups: macronutrients and micronutrients. *Macronutrients* (MAK-roh-NOO-tree-unts) provide the body with energy. *Micronutrients* (MYK-roh-NOO-tree-unts) provide the body with small amounts of chemicals needed in biochemical reactions.

Energy provided by macronutrients is measured in units called kilocalories (kcal). One kilocalorie provides enough energy to raise the temperature of 1 kilogram of water 1 degree Celsius. In nutritional information for consumers, kilocalories are commonly referred to simply as Calories. The number of Calories contained in a food indicates how much energy the food provides. The three types of macronutrients are carbohydrates, proteins, and fats.

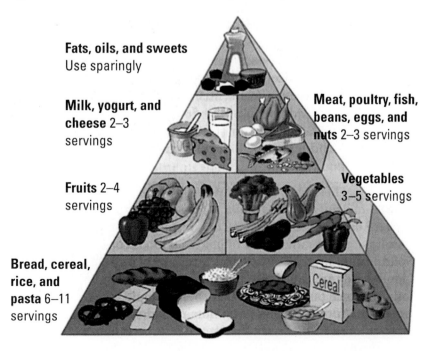

Fats, oils, and sweets
Use sparingly

Milk, yogurt, and cheese 2–3 servings

Meat, poultry, fish, beans, eggs, and nuts 2–3 servings

Fruits 2–4 servings

Vegetables 3–5 servings

Bread, cereal, rice, and pasta 6–11 servings

Figure 14.1 According to the nutritional guidelines of the U.S. Food and Drug Administration, a healthful diet contains many more servings of plant products than animal products each day.

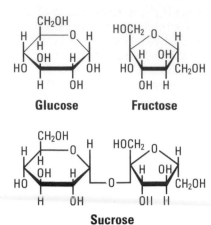

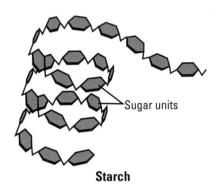

Figure 14.2 Simple sugars like glucose and fructose contain one carbon ring. Double sugars like sucrose contain two. Starches are made up of long chains of simple sugars.

Carbohydrates   *A* **carbohydrate** *is a compound made up of carbon, hydrogen, and oxygen in approximately a 1:2:1 ratio.* There are two main types of carbohydrates that can be used as an energy source by humans. Sugars are small, simple carbohydrates that can be absorbed by the body relatively quickly, providing almost immediate energy. Starches are larger, more complex carbohydrates that provide the body with steadier, longer-lasting energy. Regardless of the source, taste, or complexity, all carbohydrates provide the body with about 4 kcal per gram. Foods that are high in carbohydrates include fruits, vegetables, bread, and grains such as wheat, corn, rice, and oats.

Protein   *A* **protein** *is a large compound made of amino acids that provides the body with the construction materials for making blood, muscle, and other tissues.* Amino acids are small organic molecules that contain nitrogen. Without nitrogen, proteins cannot be made by any organism, either plant or animal. Recall from Chapter 5 that the cycling of nitrogen through an ecosystem is an essential function of the biosphere. Like carbohydrates, proteins provide about 4 kcal per gram. However, proteins are not recommended as a major source of energy. Proteins provide the building blocks that make up most body tissues, including muscles, blood, skin, and enzymes.

All the proteins in the human body are made up of 20 different amino acids arranged in an almost infinite number of ways. The ability of the body to make millions of different proteins from the same 20 amino acids is similar to the way the English language contains many words all made from the same 26 letters. Of the 20 amino acids, the human body can make 12. The remaining 8 amino acids must be obtained from foods. *The eight amino acids that must be obtained from foods are called* **essential amino acids**.

Foods that come from animals, including meats, eggs, and dairy products, are high-protein foods that generally contain all the essential amino acids. Grains, such as wheat, rice, and corn, and legumes, such as peas, beans, and peanuts, are foods from plants that are also good sources of protein. Unfortunately, most plant proteins lack one or more of the essential amino acids. To obtain all the essential amino acids, people who do not eat meat must combine proteins from different types of plants. By eating meals that include both grains and legumes, a vegetarian can get all the protein needed for good health.

Fats   Fats belong to a group of organic compounds called lipids. *A* **lipid** *contains three long chains of fatty acids attached to a molecule of glycerol.* Certain lipids, which are called phospholipids and contain a phosphate group, are the principle components of cell membranes. Solid lipids, such as butter and lard, are commonly called fats. Liquid lipids are called oils, but they are also considered to be fats for nutritional purposes. Whether solid or liquid, fats provide 9 kcal per gram. Notice that fats provide more than twice the amount of energy per gram as carbohydrates and proteins.

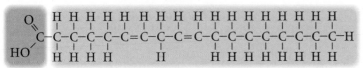

Linoleic acid (unsaturated)

Stearic acid (saturated)

Figure 14.3 Unsaturated fats contain double bonds between the carbon atoms of the fatty acid molecules, reducing the number of places for hydrogen to bond. Saturated fats contain only single bonds and have the maximum amount of hydrogen atoms.

Fats may be saturated or unsaturated. A *saturated fat* contains the maximum number of hydrogen atoms on the fatty acid chains. In an *unsaturated fat*, some hydrogen atoms are missing. A monosaturated fat contains only one double carbon bond. A polyunsaturated fat, such as the linoleic acid shown in Figure 14.3, contains more than one double carbon bond. Naturally occurring fats contain saturated, monounsaturated, and polyunsaturated fats in varying amounts. Food labels often show the amounts of each type of fat in the food.

Most animal fats are highly saturated, while most plant oils are highly unsaturated. You can tell how saturated a fat is by how firm it is at room temperature. The more saturated the fat, the more firm it is. Margarine manufacturers often *hydrogenate* liquid vegetable oils by adding more hydrogen, giving the margarine the firm texture of butter. Although a high-fat diet in general presents many health risks, nutritional research has shown that saturated fats contribute to the risk of heart disease. People with diets high in saturated fats tend to develop fatty deposits inside blood vessels, causing high blood pressure and heart attacks.

Vitamins and Minerals   Vitamins and minerals are micronutrients. Although they do not provide energy directly, vitamins and minerals play key roles in the biochemical reactions that release energy. All the micronutrients that humans need can be obtained from plants, although meats and other animal products are good sources as well. Fruits, vegetables, and breads made from whole grains are particularly good sources of vitamins and minerals.

Many of the micronutrients that occur naturally in plant-based foods are removed by improper processing, cooking, or storage. Proper handling is very important to preserve the vitamin and mineral content of most foods. Plants grown in soil that is low in certain minerals may also have reduced nutritional value.

Nutritional Deficiency

Adult humans typically require 2000 to 2800 kcal per day, depending on metabolism, activity levels, health, and many other factors.

Field Activity

How healthful is healthful? Go to the supermarket and compare the nutritional information labels on two similar products, one regular and one "healthy." For example, you can compare a regular frozen turkey dinner with one sold as a healthful dinner. You can compare cookies, ice creams, or other foods for which there is a "healthy" counterpart on the market.

1. Compare the fat content in the two products as well as sodium (salt), protein, vitamins, serving size, and cost per serving.

2. Evaluate the advantage, if any, in buying the more healthful product.

Figure 14.4 When there is not enough food to eat, it is the children (right) who suffer the most.

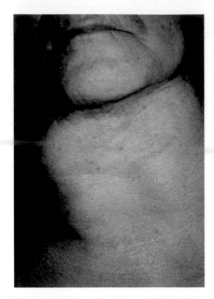

Figure 14.5 A goiter is a swelling of the thyroid gland that results from a shortage of iodine in the diet. Because iodine is common in seafoods, goiters are most common in inland areas.

Health

For many years, people in Japan considered whole-grain brown rice to be peasant food, while members of the rich upper class ate only polished white rice. People did not realize that most of the nutrients in rice are contained in the parts that are removed during polishing. As a result, nutritional deficiencies were more common among the rich than among the poor.

People who receive less than 90 percent of their energy needs are considered undernourished. Those who receive less than 80 percent are seriously undernourished. Children who are seriously undernourished often suffer from permanently stunted growth and incomplete mental development. It is estimated that 800 million people worldwide do not eat an adequate diet, and that 500 million of these are chronically hungry. Approximately 13 million people die of starvation each year. This works out to an average of someone dying of hunger every 2.5 seconds.

Although lack of energy is a serious nutritional problem, many people who receive enough energy lack one or more of the other nutrients. **Malnutrition** *is the lack of a specific type of nutrient in the diet.* Malnutrition can also result from an inability to absorb or use a particular nutrient. Vitamin deficiency is a type of malnutrition that occurs in all nations of the world, and it may even affect those who have an adequate supply of food. Scurvy, beriberi, and rickets are vitamin-deficiency diseases that result from a lack of vitamins C, B1 (thiamine), and D.

Kwashiorkor (KWAH-shee-OR-kor) is a deficiency disease caused by too little protein in an otherwise adequate diet. This condition occurs when people live on diets of starchy, low-protein foods. Children with kwashiorkor develop a characteristic "flag" of red hair, a bloated belly, become unresponsive, and catch infectious diseases easily.

SECTION REVIEW

1. Explain the difference between being undernourished and having malnutrition.
2. Which contains more calories, a food that is two-thirds protein and one-third carbohydrate, or a food that is one-third protein and two-thirds carbohydrate?
3. **Analyze** About 90 percent of the people in the United States have enough to eat. Why do you think vitamin supplements and vitamin-fortified foods are so popular?

Measuring the Energy in Food

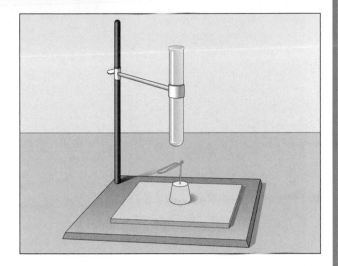

PROBLEM
How is the energy in food measured?

MATERIALS (per group)
- ring stand
- test-tube clamp
- test tube
- paper clip
- fireproof pad
- matches
- thermometer
- safety goggles
- laboratory apron
- metric ruler
- cork stopper (at least 4-cm base diameter)
- 4 food samples (such as nuts, dried beans, cereals, potato chips, and sharp cheese)
- heat-resistant gloves
- triple-beam balance
- 100-mL graduated cylinder

PREDICTION
After reading through the activity, predict which of the food samples will give off the most energy.

PROCEDURE

1. Set up the ring stand, test-tube clamp, test tube, and fireproof pad as shown.
2. Make a food platform for the calorimeter by bending the outer end of the paper clip straight down so it is at a right angle to the rest of the clip. Insert the free end of the clip into the middle of the narrow end of the cork stopper (see figure).
3. Adjust the height of the test tube so that the space between the food platform and the bottom of the test tube is 2 cm.
4. Measure exactly 15 mL of water into the test tube. Record the mass of the water in a data table. *Note: 1 mL of water has a mass of 1 g.*
5. Measure and record the temperature of the water in the test tube. Remove the thermometer from the test tube after you record the temperature.
6. Select a food sample and measure its mass. Record the mass in the data table.
7. Place the food sample on the paper clip. Quickly ignite the food sample with a match, and place the platform under the test tube. **Caution:** *Wear safety goggles. Use care when using matches.* Allow the food to burn completely.
8. Measure and record the temperature of the water in the test tube. **Caution:** *Do not touch the test tube; it may be hot.*
9. Determine the change in mass of the food sample.
10. Determine the change in temperature of the water.
11. Repeat steps 3–10 using three other food samples.

ANALYSIS
Use the formula to find the calories per food sample. *Note: The specific heat of water is 1 kcal per kilogram degree Celsius.*

Calories per food sample = Change in water temperature × Mass of water × Specific heat of water × $\frac{1 \text{ kg}}{1000 \text{ g}}$

CONCLUSION
1. Which of your food samples contained the most energy?
2. How do your results compare with your predictions? As a class, discuss what you learned about the foods you tested.

14.2 WORLD FOOD SUPPLY

OBJECTIVE • *Explain the effects of economics on the production of food.*

Food supplies worldwide have increased a great deal during the past 40 years. Not only is there more food being produced, but there is more food available per person than at any point in history. Why, then, are there so many starving people? Part of the reason is that much of the food increase has been accomplished through advances in agricultural practices and improvements in crop plants. The main reason, however, is that food is traded as a commodity whose price is driven by economic factors.

The Green Revolution

The **Green Revolution** *began in the mid-1960s with the development of new strains of wheat and rice, the two main foods of the world.* The new varieties are more responsive to the use of fertilizers and irrigation than are older plant varieties. Given adequate water and fertilization, the new crops have better resistance to disease, grow faster, and can survive in a wide variety of climates. The new "miracle" plants can increase crop yields as much as four times the normal yield. Green Revolution farming also uses modern farming methods and machinery to plant, maintain, and harvest the crops efficiently. The Green Revolution has resulted in a large increase in food production without a large increase in the amount of farmland used.

Green Revolution farming, though intended to help underfed nations feed themselves, is often not available to the people who need it the most. Many farmers in developing nations do not have the water necessary to maintain the new crops. These farmers rarely have the money to buy fertilizers, and they do not own modern machinery. Even if they did have the machines, few could afford the fuel to run them. Farmers in the developed nations can take full advantage of Green Revolution farming, producing huge crops. These large crops increase the world's supply of grains, which drives down the price of grains on the market. Poorer farmers who cannot use the new methods find that the price they receive for their crops is even lower than it used to be.

Cash Crops

In developing nations, many farmers or landowners cannot generate the income they need to maintain their farms by growing food to feed the local people. The people are often too poor to pay much for food, and the foods they eat tend to be low-priced grains. Instead, many farmers have chosen to grow crops that can be exported to other nations for higher prices. *A* **cash crop** *is a crop grown for the*

Figure 14.6 When regular wheat is given extra water and fertilizers, it grows too tall, falls over, and cannot be harvested.

purpose of sale. For example, many farmers in African nations grow cash crops that are exported to Europe to feed livestock.

In many developing nations, as much as 85 percent of the farmland is owned by less than 5 percent of the people. Often, the income from the sale of cash crops is used to buy weapons and support political leaders that help the landowners. Although much of the hunger in the world results from natural causes, especially drought and overpopulation, the role of governments and profit-driven land management cannot be ignored.

Food from the Water

Food crops grown on land provide a large portion of the world's food supply, but not all of it. Fish and other sea animals provide much of the animal protein consumed by people around the world and roughly 40 percent of the animal protein supply in developing nations. Annually, an estimated 55 billion metric tons of biomass are produced naturally by the oceans, as compared to approximately 115 billion tons of terrestrial biomass.

It has been estimated that the oceans of the world can provide up to 100 million metric tons of food per year without damaging the marine biome. The world harvest from the open ocean is now over 90 million metric tons per year. Many environmentalists believe that we have exceeded limits of a safe harvest. Quantities of some kinds of fishes are beginning to drop in many areas. Commercial fishermen are catching fewer fishes per boat, and the fishes are often small and immature. About 40 of the 280 species of fishes harvested commercially are now in danger.

An alternative to fishing in the open oceans for food is to raise fish in confined pools. *Commercial production of fish in a controlled, maintained environment is called* **aquaculture.** Fish can be raised in either fresh water or salt water, in coastal swamps or inland ponds, in small areas or on a large scale. Over 21 million metric tons of animal protein are produced by aquaculture annually. More than 80 percent of this total is produced in Asia. In China, India, Thailand, and Vietnam, fish are raised on algae grown in wastewater ponds. Most of the clams and oysters eaten in the United States are produced by aquaculture.

Figure 14.7 Aquaculture has provided food for people in many nations of Southeast Asia for centuries. This technique is now becoming an important source of food for the United States and China.

SECTION REVIEW

1. What occurred during the Green Revolution?
2. How does the growing of cash crops help individual farmers?
3. **Apply** Do you think aquaculture is damaging to the environment? Why or why not? (*Hint: Review sections of Chapters 10 and 11.*)

Feeding A Growing World

Many attempts have been made to help solve the problem of world hunger. Often those attempts have focused on increasing the size of farms to make them more productive, or on introducing crops and importing methods from the developed world.

However, most such attempts have met with only limited success. The use of non-native crops and new farming methods is generally impractical for people with limited resources. Conversion to large-scale agribusiness has often hurt small farmers, who cannot compete with large producers and have been forced to sell their produce cheaply to government-controlled food monopolies, or quit farming and migrate to cities to find work.

Because of such results, the efficiency of large, highly mechanized farms in developing nations has been called into question in recent years. Attention has been focused on countries that are attempting to return to some of the old traditions in farming. One noteworthy example is China, a country of nearly a billion people. The Chinese government is now promoting the use of small farms. Today, the typical Chinese farm is only about an acre in size. Such farms are worked by individual families, who rely upon the produce to feed themselves and as a source of cash. The quality of life for such farming families is tied directly to the time and attention that they devote to their farms. They do not use practices that involve expensive machinery, large-scale irrigation, and ecologically harmful fertilizers.

Such low-impact farms are managing to compete with large farms. The farm sector in China has grown by 6 percent per year over the past decade. This rate of growth is much greater than in developing countries that have modeled their agriculture on large-scale Western practices.

The success of Chinese low-impact farms has led to greater prosperity and stability for rural areas. As the small farmers prosper, they purchase more finished goods and services in the surrounding areas, which improves the local economy.

These Chinese women harvest their rice crop that was produced using low-impact farming methods.

The benefits extend throughout the region as a whole. In east Asia in general, where small-farm development has been encouraged, the percentage of malnourished people has decreased faster than anywhere else in the world. At least as far as farming is concerned, it seems that small can be productive as well as ecologically sound.

Checkpoint

1. How has the support for small farms been beneficial to Chinese farmers?

2. Do you think returning to the idea of small farms would work well in the United States and the rest of the developed world? Explain.

14.3 MODERN FARMING TECHNIQUES

OBJECTIVE • ***Describe*** *how farming techniques have changed during the past 50 years.*

As you learned in the last section, the Green Revolution changed the way commercial farming is conducted. In addition to the development of improved varieties of grains, the techniques and machines of modern farming have also changed. Modern farming techniques have some advantages and disadvantages in feeding the world.

Historically, agriculture was a very labor-intensive occupation. The jobs of preparing the soil, planting seed, maintaining crops, and harvesting were all done by humans and their animals. To grow more crops, the farmer needed to cultivate more land, which required more labor. Farmers grew a variety of crops, rotating the use of land. Occasionally farmers allowed the land to lie fallow, growing no crops, in order to restore the fertility of the soil.

In the middle of the twentieth century, agriculture in the United States and other developing nations began to change. Large pieces of farm equipment powered by fossil fuels replaced human-powered tools. In 1950, less than half a barrel of oil was used to produce a ton of grain. By 1985 this quantity had doubled. This modern method of farming is often called industrialized agriculture.

Industrialized agriculture is highly efficient and productive. For example, each modern U.S. farmer can feed 78 people, while in 1850 the average farmer fed only five people. However, industrialized agriculture requires large inputs of energy, pesticides, and fertilizers. Large, industrialized farms are often run by corporations called agribusinesses. Some agribusinesses control several stages of food production, packaging, and transport.

Dateline 1972

The U.S. secretary of agriculture called upon American farmers to help "feed the world," predicting an unlimited international market for U.S. grains. Farmers were encouraged to drain wetlands and plant on every available inch of land. The price of farmland went up, and farmers invested in modern machinery. The result was a huge increase in production, which was not met with the expected demand. In the late 1970s, matters became worse when the U.S. refused to sell grain to the U.S.S.R. because of its invasion of Afghanistan. Surpluses piled up, and grain prices fell. Many farmers, now heavily in debt, were forced out of business.

Figure 14.8 When grain elevators are full, the excess grain may have to be stored outside, where it can be destroyed by birds, rodents, and wet weather.

Figure 14.9 The routine, scheduled dusting of crops with pesticides, whether pests are present or not, has contributed to the development of pesticide-resistant insects.

Think About It!

Describe a mechanism by which insects can develop a resistance to pesticides. *Hint: Review the process of evolution discussed in Chapter 5.*

1. Which flies does the pesticide kill?
2. Which flies does it not kill?
3. How does this result in a resistant population?

The widespread use of pesticides has altered ecosystems in many harmful ways. One problem with the use of pesticides is an increase in resistant insects and other pests. In 1992, many of the crops in California were destroyed by an infestation of white flies. Because the white flies had evolved to be resistant to insecticides, growers were unable to protect their crops from the pest.

Many farms that used to grow a variety of crops shifted toward growing only one or two crops that commanded the highest prices. This technique, called *monoculture* farming, can cause several problems. Large numbers of genetically identical crops are grown. All the plants are vulnerable to the same diseases, which can result in a loss of most of the crop. Also, the soil becomes depleted of the mineral nutrients needed to grow the monoculture crop. Eventually, the ability of the soil to produce a healthy crop is reduced.

The Green Revolution produced new varieties of grains. However, some of the newer, higher-yielding grains were not well adapted to local conditions. Scientists are now looking at traditional grains as alternative crops in some areas. For example, the grain quinoa (KEEN-wah) was once so important to the Incas of South America that they called it the "mother grain." Quinoa is very high in protein, has a good balance of amino acids, and grows well in mountainous areas. It can be made into flour for baking, breakfast cereal, beverages, and livestock feed. Quinoa may hold promise for improving the diets of people in poor mountainous regions of Southeast Asia, Africa, and the Himalayas.

SECTION REVIEW

1. What is monoculture farming, and why can it be a problem?
2. Why have many American farmers gone out of business since the early 1980s?
3. **Infer** Many of the lesser-known plants of the world are in danger of extinction. How might this affect food supplies of the future?

14.4 SUSTAINABLE AGRICULTURE

OBJECTIVE • *Describe* the basic components of sustainable agriculture, and explain why they are desirable.

Modern agriculture is driven by economics and by international trade. The need to remain competitive in the global market has resulted in soil erosion, deforestation, desertification, hunger, war, and environmental damage on a global scale. As the population of the world continues to increase, it is becoming clear that people will have to find methods of producing foods that have a minimal impact on the environment. To do so, many people in the United States and around the world are working toward developing sustainable agriculture. *Also called regenerative farming,* **sustainable agriculture** *is based on crop rotation, reduced soil erosion, integrated pest management, and a minimal use of soil additives.*

Crop rotation means changing the type of crop grown in an area on a regular cycle. The cycle for crop rotation is usually 1 to 6 years. Crop rotation helps prevent soil from becoming depleted in mineral nutrients, especially nitrogen. As you have learned, nitrogen is necessary for plants to make proteins. Most plants extract nitrogen from the soil. The bacteria in the roots of some plants, however, especially legumes, can convert the nitrogen in the air to a usable form. Soils in which such plants grow become rich in nitrogen. By alternating legumes with other crops, farmers can avoid the use of synthetic nitrogen fertilizers. Nitrogen-fixing plants can also be used as a cover crop. Cover crops are nonfood plants that are grown between growing seasons. Cover crops not only restore nitrogen to the soil, they also help reduce one of the other major problems of modern agriculture: erosion.

Reducing Erosion

Erosion is a natural process by which soil is formed, transported, and sometimes lost to a particular ecosystem or region. Wind and flowing water are the main agents of erosion, carrying away soil that is not held in place by plants. When the soil being lost is topsoil, full of the organic and mineral nutrients needed to make farmland fertile, the processes of weathering and erosion can be disastrous for local agriculture.

Erosion can be reduced by careful irrigation and soil management. In traditional irrigation systems, water floods the fields and then drains off, carrying valuable topsoil away. Drip irrigation, which delivers small quantities of water directly to the roots of plants, reduces the erosion of soil by flowing water.

Since the 1800s, heavy tilling has been part of traditional agriculture. Tilling is the process of turning the soil so that lower

Social Studies

In 1959, Chairman Mao Tse Tung brought all farming in China under the control of the government. The government set schedules for planting, standardized crops, and ordered the planting of all land, regardless of its condition. The poorly managed plan resulted in the greatest famine in world history, which claimed about 30 million lives between 1959 and 1961. After the death of Mao Tse Tung in 1976, farms were returned to family control. The family farms now produce 50 percent more crops and require about one-fifth the amount of labor as the government-controlled farms. This dramatic change demonstrates how government policy can affect agriculture.

Figure 14.10 In an integrated pest management system, natural predators such as ladybugs are used to combat insect pests. The predators would be killed by traditional pesticide use.

layers are brought to the surface. Extensive tilling destroys weeds and other pests, brings fresh nutrients to the surface, improves drainage, and aerates the soil. Unfortunately, this process also wastes water, uses energy, and increases soil erosion. Farmers are now finding that reducing tillage sometimes increases crop yields.

Pest Management

A new approach to managing pests, called integrated pest management, or IPM, is being used successfully in many areas. IPM can reduce the use of pesticides by as much as 90 percent. Many IPM systems make use of the natural predators of pest organisms. Wasps, ladybugs, and a variety of viruses and bacteria are the natural enemies of many insect pests. Farmers in the United States have increased their use of IPM and reduced their use of pesticides over the last five years.

One of the most successful IPM systems is now in use in Indonesia. There, farmers were routinely spraying their crops with insecticides on a regular basis. An insect called the brown planthopper developed a resistance to insecticides and was destroying the nation's rice crop. In 1986, the president banned 56 of the 57 insecticides commonly used and launched a program to educate farmers about the dangers of pesticides. By reducing the use of insecticides so dramatically, the natural insect predators of the planthopper were able to combat the pest. Farmers using the IPM system are now enjoying higher crop yields.

SECTION REVIEW

1. Explain the role of tilling in soil erosion.
2. Describe how crop rotation benefits a field. What might be a disadvantage of crop rotation?
3. **Apply** Why do you think sustainable agriculture is sometimes called regenerative farming?

CHAPTER **14** REVIEW

KEY TERMS

carbohydrate 14.1

protein 14.1

essential amino acid 14.1

lipid 14.1

malnutrition 14.1

Green Revolution 14.2

cash crop 14.2

aquaculture 14.2

sustainable agriculture 14.4

CHAPTER SUMMARY

14.1 Humans need to consume enough energy, or Calories, to carry out life processes, as well as a blend of other nutrients to maintain good health. Carbohydrates, protein, and fat are macronutrients that provide energy. Vitamins and minerals are micronutrients needed for biochemical reactions. Nutritional deficiencies result from too little of a particular type of nutrient in the diet.

14.2 The world's food supply has been increasing faster than the population, but the economics and politics of food distribution often prevent food from reaching hungry people. The Green Revolution of the 1960s increased the productivity of modern farms, but did not help the poorer farmers of the world who cannot compete with the machinery

and high-yield grains used in developed nations. Cash crops are often grown for export because they command higher prices. Aquaculture of seafood can contribute to the food supply.

14.3 Modern farming is based on the use of machinery, chemical fertilizers, pesticides, and monoculture crops. Each of these practices has some problems, including environmental damage.

14.4 Sustainable agriculture, or regenerative farming, is based on practices that enable fields to produce crops without damaging the soil. Sustainable farming practices include crop rotation, reduction of erosion, and integrated pest management.

MULTIPLE CHOICE

Choose the letter of the word or phrase that best completes each statement.

1. The kilocalories in a food indicates the amount of (a) protein; (b) carbohydrates; (c) healthfulness; (d) energy.
2. Energy in foods is provided by (a) vitamins; (b) minerals; (c) macronutrients; (d) micronutrients.
3. Nitrogen is a component of all (a) proteins; (b) carbohydrates; (c) fats; (d) vitamins.
4. The nutrient that provides the greatest amount of energy per gram is (a) fat; (b) vitamins; (c) protein; (d) carbohydrate.
5. The Green Revolution occurred during the (a) Middle Ages; (b) nineteenth century; (c) the 1960s; (d) the 1980s.
6. A cash crop is a crop intended for (a) animal feed; (b) sale; (c) protecting the soil between

growing seasons; (d) local use.
7. In some developing nations, the percent of animal protein that comes from fish can be as high as (a) 10 percent; (b) 20 percent; (c) 40 percent; (d) 80 percent.
8. To help restore nitrogen to the soil, fields should occasionally be planted with (a) cash crops; (b) grains; (c) legumes; (d) weeds.
9. Quinoa is a (a) type of wheat; (b) historical food of the Incas; (c) plant native to Asia; (d) type of cover crop.
10. The effects of tilling include (a) reduced soil drainage; (b) improved crop production; (c) reduced need for energy input; (d) increased soil erosion.
11. An IPM system is used to (a) control pests; (b) aerate soil; (c) improve soil nutrients; (d) reduce erosion.

CHAPTER 14 REVIEW

TRUE/FALSE

Write true *if the statement is true. If the statement is false, change the underlined word to make it true.*

1. A saturated fat contains <u>more</u> hydrogen than an unsaturated fat.
2. The essential amino acids are those that <u>can be made by the body.</u>
3. Compared to protein, carbohydrates contain <u>fewer</u> calories per gram.
4. The use of pesticides tends to <u>decrease</u> the number of resistant pests.
5. Tilling of soil has the effect of <u>increasing</u> soil aeration.
6. A monoculture crop contains <u>a variety of species.</u>
7. Agribusiness corporations produce more than <u>two-thirds</u> of the food in the U.S.

CONCEPT REVIEW

Write a complete response to each of the following.

1. Explain how the Green Revolution caused hardship for some farmers.
2. Describe the difference in structure between a saturated and an unsaturated fat.
3. Explain the benefits and problems associated with heavy tilling of farm soil.
4. What are cover crops, and why are they grown?

THINK CRITICALLY

1. What might be the economic value of paying farmers not to grow crops? Who would benefit from such a policy?
2. If you were the owner of a small farm in a developing nation, would you grow food for people or animal feed for export? Would your answer be the same if you could receive three times the price for the animal feed? Explain your answer.
3. Describe the principle behind crop rotation and its benefit to farmers. Can you think of any drawbacks to crop rotation?
4. Abraham Lincoln once said, "You cannot escape the responsibility of tomorrow by evading it today." How can this idea be applied to the world's food situation?

WRITE CREATIVELY

In the Charles Dickens novel *The Prince and the Pauper*, two boys, one rich and one poor, trade lifestyles. Write a similar short story about a teenager from the United States who trades places with a teenager from a developing nation. Be sure to include the perspective of both characters.

PORTFOLIO

1. There have been many famines that have affected the progress of human civilization. Choose a major famine in human history and research the causes and effects of the famine. Make a poster or other visual representation showing the flow of events leading up to and following the famine.
2. There are hunger relief centers, such as soup kitchens and shelters, in the United States. Visit one of these establishments, and talk with some of the people, including workers at the facility. Determine what factors contributed to the situations the people are now facing. Write a magazine-style article about your findings.

GRAPHIC ANALYSIS

Use the figure to answer the following.

1. During which year did the greatest percentage increases in insecticide-resistant species occur?
2. Why do you think there was relatively little change between 1943 and 1957?
3. Between 1961 and 1965, the amount of DDT needed to kill a tobacco budworm increased from 0.13 mg to 16.51 mg. How does this relate to the graph?

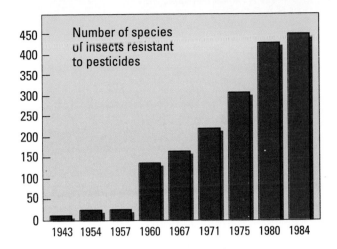

Number of species of insects resistant to pesticides

ACTIVITY 14.2

PROBLEM
Which foods contain more protein than others?

MATERIALS (per groups of 2 or 3)
- 5 test tubes
- test-tube rack
- Biuret's solution
- small amount of each of these 5 foods:
  cooked egg white
  potato
  tuna fish packed in water
  mashed lima beans
  white bread

PREDICTION
After reading through the activity, predict which food sample will contain the most and the least protein.

PROCEDURE
Biuret's solution is light blue. When combined with protein, it turns purple.
1. Label five test tubes *A* through *E*, and place them in the test tube rack.
2. Place a small sample of these foods in the test tubes: tube *A*, cooked egg white; tube *B*, potato; tube *C*, tuna fish packed in water; tube *D*, mashed lima beans; tube *E*, white bread.
3. Add 5 mL of Biuret's solution to each test tube. **Caution:** *If you get any of the Biuret's solution on your skin or clothes, immediately wash off the area with water.*
4. Wait several minutes, then observe the color of the Biuret's solution in the test tubes. Record your observations.
5. Rank the food samples with numbers from 1 (most protein) to 5 (least protein).

ANALYSIS
1. How did your results compare with your prediction?
2. Can you make a generalization about the amount of protein in animal products compared to plant products based on your results? Why or why not?
3. Why was there no control test tube in this experiment?

CONCLUSION
Based on your observations, which of the foods that you tested would you send to an area where people were starving? Discuss this issue as a class.

Hands-On

Students Learn Outdoors

In the study of environmental science, one of the biggest challenges for both teachers and students is finding time and opportunities for field studies. Field studies provide a greater depth and understanding of Earth's complex systems and interactions because they offer students firsthand observations and hands-on experiences. More and more environmental groups and foundations are recognizing the need to implement programs that greatly enhance the study of environmental science. One of the most successful programs is at the National Zoo's Conservation and Research Center (CRC) in Front Royal, Virginia.

As part of its education programs, the CRC runs a summer camp. Administered by the Friends of the National Zoo (FONZ), the camp offers students a chance to learn about the environment and interactions in the ecosystem. The FONZ camp offers many of the usual summer-camp activities, such as hiking, swimming, and sleeping under the stars. But this camp also has many special activities. When they go hiking, campers can study and compare four different environments: wetlands, forests, meadows, and streams. Campers also get a look at the endangered-species projects, with tours of the CRC's barns and veterinary hospital.

FONZ campers get a chance to see firsthand what field work is like. Working with the scientists at the CRC, campers learn field-study techniques. For example, campers have learned how to track animals using an antenna and radio-telemetry equipment. Campers have also learned how to trap, measure, and release mice without harming them. In doing this, campers learn the importance of teamwork and careful record keeping.

Although this program is fairly new, it has been extremely popular and successful in engaging students and allowing them to experience the complexity and value of our fragile ecosystems.

Field studies provide students with firsthand observations and experiences.

✓ Checkpoint

1. What kinds of environments can campers study at the FONZ camp in Front Royal, Virginia?

2. How are field studies useful for learning about environmental science?

◀ Environmental Journalists

Environmental journalists are public educators atlarge, spreading information, in print or electronically, about the latest issues in the field. They report on new techniques that are protecting the environment, which companies are taking active steps to correct past mistakes, and which companies are playing a positive role in helping preserve our fragile ecosystems. Many journalists get their start by volunteering. Volunteering opens doors and provides new journalists with valuable experience.

Interpretive Naturalists ▶

Interpretive naturalists work at the hub of public education in state and national parks, as well as in the community. These naturalists lead groups, conduct lectures, and distribute a wealth of information about their particular areas. They raise public awareness about issues that impact the environment.

Environmental Studies Educators ▲

Teachers of environmental studies are responsible for educating students about their interrelationship with the environment. These teachers provide students with some of their first experiences of how humans affect their environment, and what students can do in their communities to protect and preserve the ecosystem.

For More Information

Outdoor Writers Association of America
2017 Cato Avenue, Suite 101
State College, PA 16801
(814) 234-1011

North American Association for
Environmental Education
P.O. Box 400
Troy, OH 45373
(937) 676-2514
http://eelink.umich.edu/naaee.html

Center for Environmental Journalism
University of Colorado
Campus Box 287
Boulder, CO 80309
http://campuspress.colorado.edu/cej.html

UNIT 5

ENERGY RESOURCES

If you have ever been in an automobile that has run out of gasoline you can appreciate the importance of this form of energy. Gasoline is only one of several natural energy resources that include coal and natural gas. Although we depend heavily on these natural resources, they are limited. We must find alternative sources as we exhaust these resources. This photograph shows how one alternative source of energy, the sun, is being harnessed. These large, mirrorlike dishes are used to reflect the solar rays of the sun onto a source of water. This water is heated to its boiling point, which provides steam that is used to power a generator, producing electricity. In this unit, you will learn more about the needs and uses of energy.

Discover It!

How Do You Use Energy?

Every day you are directly or indirectly involved with the use of energy. Take two minutes and think of the daily activities in which you participate that require the use of electricity, petroleum (gasoline), or natural gas.

1. List those activities that require electricity, gasoline, or natural gas.

2. How would your life be different if these three forms of energy were not available?

CHAPTER

15

ENERGY FROM ORGANIC FUELS

What would your life be like without electricity? Of course, there would be no electric lights, televisions, stereo systems, or video games. There would also be no movie theaters or amusement parks. Most large home appliances, such as dishwashers, washing machines, and refrigerators, would also not exist. People have come to take for granted the conveniences and pleasures that electricity can provide. Where does the electricity come from? Although electricity can be generated from many types of fuels, most electricity is produced by burning organic fuels. Much of the oil pumped by off-shore drilling is used to produce electricity.

15.1 THE NEED FOR ENERGY

OBJECTIVES • *Explain* how changes in human societies have changed the demand for energy. • *Describe* the structure of organic fuels

Heat, light, and electricity are three forms of energy with which you are probably familiar. Other forms of energy include mechanical energy, chemical energy, and nuclear energy. Together, these forms of energy meet the energy needs of the people on Earth.

One of the laws of physics states that energy cannot be created or destroyed. Energy can, however, be changed from one form to another. The storage, transfer, and conversion of energy are the driving forces behind all life on Earth. For example, the energy in the food you eat once came from the sun. First, the energy is converted to chemical energy that is stored in plant material. When you eat food, the energy stored in the plant or animal tissues is converted to heat, mechanical energy, and the chemical energy used to carry out life processes. Food is a form of fuel that your body uses for energy. *A **fuel** is any substance from which energy can be obtained.*

Except for lightning, electricity is not a form of energy that is common in nature. Electricity is generated by the conversion of other forms of energy. To produce electricity, fuel is burned to boil water, producing steam. The steam exerts pressure on giant machines called *turbines,* causing them to turn. The mechanical energy of the turning turbine generates electricity. Much of the fuel consumed by today's society is used to generate electricity. But this conversion is not 100 percent efficient. During this process, some energy is converted to heat, light, or sound.

Changing Energy Needs

The energy needs of most nations of the world have changed over time. Hunter-gatherer societies had very limited energy requirements. People used energy only for light, heat, and cooking. Wood adequately met these needs. Later, as agricultural societies emerged, some energy demands changed. For example, domesticated animals such as horses, mules, and oxen became the energy sources for powering plows and other farm equipment.

Following the Industrial Revolution in the late eighteenth century, societies that had been based largely on agriculture turned to industry to meet the needs of their growing populations. Tasks that used to be done by people and animals were taken over by machines. For example, farm equipment such as the horse-drawn plow gave way to tractors and harvesters. Manufacturing these

Figure 15.1 The manufacture and operation of machinery have greatly increased the need for energy in agriculture.

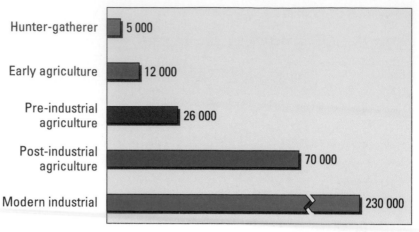

Figure 15.2 The amount of energy used has changed over time as societies changed from agricultural to industrial cultures.

Energy use per person per day (kilocalories)

Field Activity

Many households use more than one kind of fuel to meet their energy needs.

1. Conduct a survey of five families to find out what kinds of fuels they use in their homes.

2. Try to interview families that live in different areas. Include information in your survey about what energy sources are used for cooking, home heating, and for the heating of hot water.

3. Graph the results of your survey.

machines in factories required large amounts of fuel, as did using the machines themselves.

Factories that produce the clothing, furniture, and building materials needed by a growing population also increase fuel consumption. Even more fuel is required to distribute and market these products. As societies have developed, their energy demands have changed. Figure 15.2 shows how each person's share of a society's energy use has increased.

Fuels from Organisms

Organic fuels are fuels that contain carbon compounds that were once part of living organisms. In addition to carbon, organic fuels also contain hydrogen. *A compound composed only of carbon and hydrogen is called a* **hydrocarbon.** Methane is a simple hydrocarbon. As shown in Figure 15.3, the chemical formula for methane is CH_4. Ethane is a hydrocarbon with the formula C_2H_6. Octane is an eight-carbon hydrocarbon with the formula C_8H_{18}.

With the exception of single-carbon methane, all hydrocarbon molecules contain carbon atoms bound together in a chain. The chain may be straight, branched, or arranged in a ring. In nature, the activities that take place within the cells of organisms cause carbon to be arranged in such chains.

Notice in Figure 15.3 that the atoms of C_8H_{18} can have two different configurations, that of a straight chain called octane or a branched chain known as iso-octane. Both forms of octane are flammable liquids, but iso-octane is less volatile and less flammable. Iso-octane is added to gasoline in varying amounts to control the rate at which it burns in a car's engine. The octane rating of gasoline is derived from a complex formula based on the amount of energy contained in the gasoline compared to the energy of pure iso-octane.

In addition to hydrocarbons, many organic fuels contain other chemicals, such as sulfur or lead compounds. These other chemicals

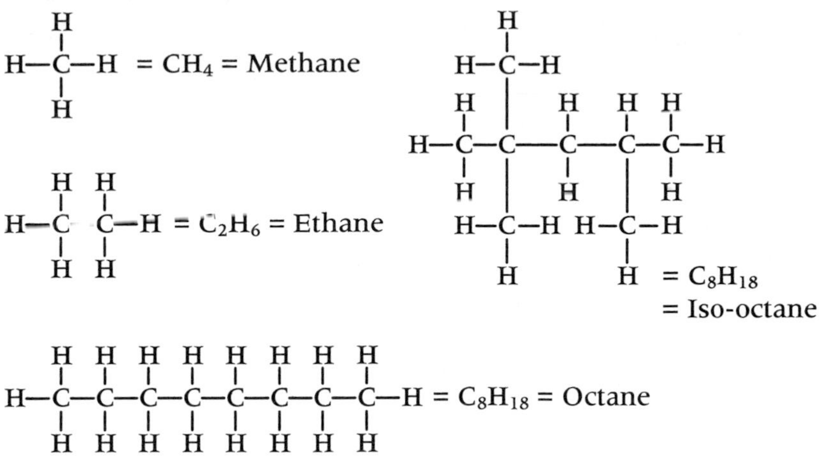

H—C—H = CH₄ = Methane (Methane structure)

H—C C—H = C₂H₆ = Ethane

H—C—C—C—C—H ... = C₈H₁₈ = Iso-octane

H—C—C—C—C—C—C—C—C—H = C₈H₁₈ = Octane

Figure 15.3 Hydrocarbons contain only carbon (C) and hydrogen (H). The carbons may be arranged in a variety of structures.

are considered to be impurities in the fuel. Some of these impurities, such as lead in gasoline, improve the ability of the fuel to provide usable energy. Unfortunately, impurities also contribute to the pollution released when the fuels are burned.

Fossil Fuels

Like the organisms of today, ancient organisms required energy to carry out their life processes. Energy provided by the sun was converted to chemical energy by plants and microorganisms. This energy was used by the organisms directly or passed on to consumers in the food chain. When these organisms died, some energy remained stored in their cells. If the organisms became buried and did not decay, this energy remained stored within Earth.

The energy stored within the cells of organisms that died millions of years ago is used today as fuel. *Fuels derived from the remains of organisms that lived long ago are called* **fossil fuels**. Fossils are the remains or traces of living things. Fossil fuels are one category of organic fuel. Examples of fossil fuels include coal, petroleum, and natural gas.

SECTION REVIEW

1. What role did machines play in the world's changing energy needs?
2. How can you recognize a hydrocarbon from its molecular structure?
3. **Apply** Make a list of four activities in your daily life that can be accomplished with or without tools that require energy. Example: you can open a can manually or you can use an electric can opener.

Figure 15.4 Peat (top) is not coal, but it is the first stage of coal formation. Lignite (center) gives off little smoke, but less heat than other forms of coal. Anthracite (bottom) is the purest and hottest-burning form of coal. It is also the least common and most expensive.

15.2 COAL

OBJECTIVES • *List* the stages of coal formation and describe the characterisitics of each stage. • *Locate* the major coal deposits on a map of the United States.

Millions of years ago, many parts of Earth that are now dry land were covered by swamps. These areas had a warm, humid climate that was ideal for plant growth. As these plants died, their remains accumulated and, in time, were covered by sediments. With time, layer upon layer of sediment covered the plant remains. The heat and pressure produced by the weight of these sediments caused chemical changes to occur within the plant matter. At the same time, water was forced out. These processes changed the plant material into a solid rock called coal.

Coal formation occurs in stages over millions of years. With each stage, the plant matter loses more hydrogen and oxygen and the remaining carbon becomes more concentrated. As a coal's carbon content increases, so does the amount of energy given off by burning it.

Peat

Plant materials become compressed, forming a compacted mass of twigs, leaves, and branches called peat. **Peat** *is a brittle, brown plant material containing a great deal of water and a low percentage of carbon.* Peat is not a form of coal, but its formation is the first stage in the formation of coal. Peat resembles decaying wood and is usually located at or near Earth's surface. Peat gives off a large amount of smoke because of its high percentage of water and impurities.

Lignite

The second stage in coal formation is lignite. Over millions of years, layers of sediment are deposited on top of beds of peat. The heat and pressure caused by the weight of these sediments compress the peat, forcing out water and changing it to lignite. **Lignite** (LIG-nyt) *is a soft, brown coal composed of about 40 percent carbon.* Lignite burns quickly and gives off very little smoke. Unlike peat, most lignite is located below Earth's surface and must be mined.

Bituminous Coal

Over time, heat and pressure change lignite into a purer form of coal called bituminous coal. **Bituminous** (by-TOO-mih-nus) **coal** *is a soft coal composed of up to 85 percent carbon.* It forms deep in Earth's crust. Bituminous coal is the most abundant type of coal mined in the United States.

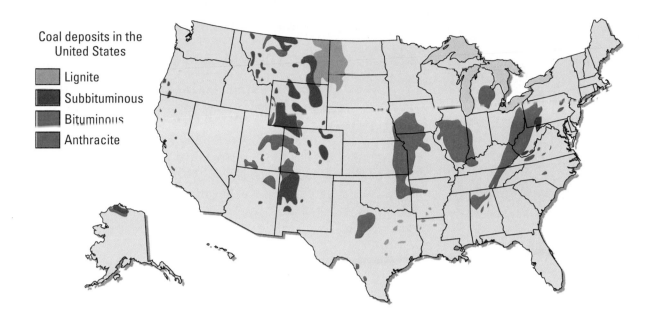

Coal deposits in the United States

■ Lignite
■ Subbituminous
■ Bituminous
■ Anthracite

Bituminous coal has less water and fewer impurities than lignite. It also has a higher carbon content and burns hotter and with less smoke than peat or lignite. Bituminous coal is widely used in industry. This coal is used by many power plants to produce the energy needed to heat water and convert the water into steam that generates electricity.

Anthracite Coal

As more sediments are added to the upper layers of rock, greater pressure and heat are exerted on the bituminous coal. Extreme pressure and heat change the sedimentary bituminous coal into a metamorphic rock. *This rock is called* **anthracite** (AN-thruh-cyt) ,*a hard coal composed of up to 95 percent carbon.* Anthracite has a shiny black color, and is often located deeper in the ground than any of the other forms of coal.

Anthracite has the least water, fewest impurities, and highest carbon content of all forms of coal. These characteristics make anthracite burn the hottest with the least amount of smoke. Because it is less abundant and often located deeper in the ground than other coals, anthracite is generally the most expensive form of coal.

Figure 15.5 Bituminous coal is the most common form of coal in the United States. Subbituminous coal is a stage of coal formation that occurs between lignite and bituminous forms.

Geology

Coal and diamonds are very different substances, but both are composed primarily of carbon. Unlike coal, which is formed from decayed plant matter in Earth's crust, diamonds are formed by extreme temperatures and pressures in Earth's mantle. Many diamond mines are located in South Africa. The hardest of the minerals, diamonds are used in cutting and drilling tools as well as for jewelry.

SECTION REVIEW

1. What is the most common type of coal in the United States?
2. How does anthracite form?
3. **Infer** Explain why peat is not considered to be a fossil fuel.

15.3 PETROLEUM AND NATURAL GAS

OBJECTIVES • *Describe* the processes of petroleum formation and extraction. • *List* several uses for petroleum and natural gas.

Each kind of fossil fuel occurs naturally in a different state of matter. Coal is a solid fossil fuel. **Petroleum** (puh-TRO-lee-um), *which is also called crude oil, is a liquid fossil fuel.* Fossil fuel in the gaseous state is called natural gas.

Petroleum

As you have read, coal is a fossil fuel formed from the remains of plants that lived in swamps. Petroleum is a liquid fossil fuel. Scientists think that petroleum formed from the remains of plankton and other microscopic protists, plants, and animals living in shallow seas millions of years ago. The remains of these organisms settled on the ocean floor and were covered by sediments. Over millions of years, the pressure and heat produced by the sediments converted the remains of these organisms into a syrupy liquid called petroleum.

Pressure of overlying rocks forced the petroleum to move upward through pores and cracks of sedimentary rocks. When the petroleum met nonporous rock such as shale, it became trapped below the surface. Other substances, such as water and natural gas, also became trapped.

A great deal of pressure can build up in an oil pool trapped deep in the ground. When a well is drilled into this pool, the pressure forces the oil to shoot upward, forming a gusher. Where there is little or no pressure, oil must be pumped to the surface.

Petroleum is one of the world's most important resources. The petroleum pumped from a well is separated, or refined, to make a variety of products. Gasoline and jet fuels come from petroleum.

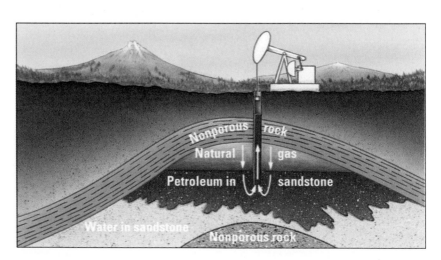

Figure 15.6 Petroleum and natural gas are trapped below the surface by a layer of nonporous rock, such as shale. The pressure exerted by the rocks above the pool of oil forces the oil to the surface once the pool has been tapped.

The diesel fuel used by trucks, ships, and trains is also a petroleum product. Fuel oil is used to heat homes and to produce electricity in generating plants. Petroleum is also used to make nonfuel products. Grease and other lubricants used to reduce friction are petroleum by-products. The asphalt used to pave roads, synthetic fabrics such as nylon and polyester, and many forms of plastics are also made from petroleum.

Because petroleum takes millions of years to form, it is not a renewable resource. As the worldwide population increases, so does the demand for petroleum. Each day, industrialized nations continue to use increasing amounts of petroleum to meet the needs of their people.

Natural Gas

Natural gas is a mixture of mostly gaseous hydrocarbons. Methane is the primary component. Other hydrocarbons such as ethane and propane may be present, along with trace amounts of gases such as hydrogen sulfide, carbon dioxide, nitrogen, and helium.

Over 2000 years ago, the Chinese used bamboo poles to pipe natural gas to areas where it was burned in order to boil seawater and recover the salt. The people of Italy made commercial use of natural gas in 1802 when they began burning it to light the streets of Genoa. Today, natural gas is widely used in industry. In many homes and businesses, natural gas is used instead of coal or oil for heating because it burns cleaner than these other fuels. Household appliances that can use natural gas for fuel include stoves, water heaters, and clothes dryers. Because the natural gas does not have to be converted to electricity first, appliances that use natural gas instead of electricity are more energy-efficient and less expensive to use.

Natural gas forms in much the same way as petroleum and is often found trapped above petroleum pools. The same well frequently produces both natural gas and oil. In fact, natural gas is sometimes viewed as a waste, or by-product, of petroleum drilling. Petroleum processing plants, such as the one in Figure 15.7, can sometimes be seen burning off the natural gas.

Figure 15.7 Natural gas is sometimes burned off as a by-product of petroleum drilling and processing.

SECTION REVIEW

1. List five different products made from petroleum. Include fuels and other products in your list.
2. Why is using natural gas as a fuel for cooking more efficient than using electricity?
3. **Compare and Contrast** Compare and contrast the formation of petroleum and the formation of coal.

Getting Around

Each year, the average American travels about 9000 mi by car. One-fourth of all the energy consumed in this country is used for transportation. In fact, the use of urban public transit has declined by more than 50 percent since the early 1970s.

Tax money pays for both the building and maintenance of roadways and mass transit. However, because this money is limited, governments and citizens must decide if the money should be spent on roadways or on mass transit systems.

Should money be spent on private or public transportation?

The Economy Is Supported by Private-Transportation Use

The use of private transportation supports jobs such as building, selling, and repairing cars. Twenty-two percent of American workers depend on the automobile industry for a living. An increase in the use of mass transit would mean fewer cars, which would cause automobile workers to lose their jobs.

Private transportation is the only way some people can get to their jobs. In addition, many people complain that mass transit is not time efficient. Buses and trains make many stops, which makes taking mass transit slower than driving a car.

The Environment Is Protected by Public-Transportation Use

If more people used public transportation, fewer cars would be on the road. This would decrease the amount of automobile exhaust, which is a major source of carbon monoxide and other pollutants. Cars also release large amounts of carbon dioxide. This gas is one of the greenhouse gases that contributes to global warming.

Fewer cars on the road would also ease traffic problems. Because it can carry more people than a car, a bus is 1.5 times more fuel efficient. The use of public transportation also saves gasoline. Petroleum must be removed from underground, refined, and shipped to wherever it is needed. Reducing the use of petroleum will reduce the chances of serious environmental damage.

In New York City, the streets are congested with automobiles used for both public and private transportation.

Consider the Issue

1. Do you think tax money should be spent to build roads for automobiles or to improve public transportation?

2. How would better public transportation affect your area?

15.4 OTHER ORGANIC FUELS

OBJECTIVES • *Describe* some of the problems associated with the use of fossil fuels. • *Compare* biomass fuels to fossil fuels, and give an example of a bioconversion technique.

There are many problems associated with the increasing use of fossil fuels. To help resolve some of the problems, scientists are looking into developing fuels from other organic sources. Alternative fuels can solve some, but not all, of the problems of using fossil fuels.

Problems with Fossil Fuels

Most of the problems associated with the use of fossil fuels fall into two general categories: availability and pollution. The availability problem stems from the fact that fossil fuels are not renewable. All the coal, oil, and natural gas that will ever be available to humans is already formed. To reach these resources, people have to keep looking deeper beneath Earth's surface and exploring farther into natural areas. The proposal to search for oil in the Alaska tundra was examined in Chapter 7. California and other coastal states are constantly addressing the question of whether or not to explore for oil offshore. Wherever exploration for fossil fuels takes place, there is a risk of environmental damage. Oil spills and other forms of widespread habitat alteration are possible results of exploring for fossil fuels.

An alternative to seeking new fossil fuel sources is to depend on the large deposits of oil that are already known to exist. Unfortunately for many nations, oil deposits are not always located in the same country that needs the fuel. In 1991, Operation Desert Storm, also known as the Persian Gulf War, reminded many Americans of the need to reduce their dependence on imported oil.

Dateline 1973

OPEC, the Organization for Petroleum Exporting Countries, put an oil embargo into effect. An embargo is a government order to stop ships from entering or leaving a port. The embargo disrupted the shipping of oil to the United States and the Netherlands, resulting in massive oil shortages and long lines at gas stations. The oil shortages led many nations to analyze their energy consumption and begin searching for alternative fuels to meet their needs.

Figure 15.8 Seeking, drilling, and transporting fossil fuels can result in accidents that damage the air, water, and land.

Pollution of various kinds, especially air pollution, is produced by the use of fossil fuels. When fossil fuels are burned, they release carbon dioxide. As a result of the increased use of fossil fuels since the Industrial Revolution, the amount of carbon dioxide in the atmosphere has increased by more than 20 percent. Many scientists, as well as other citizens, think that this increase in carbon dioxide could raise the temperature of Earth through a process called the greenhouse effect. You will read more about the greenhouse effect in Chapter 22.

Obtaining fossil fuels can also be dangerous. Because natural gas is extremely combustible, obtaining natural gas is hazardous. The danger created by natural gas combustion also exists when mining for other fossil fuels. For example, coal miners can die of suffocation by natural gas. At other times, miners have perished from explosions of natural gas and coal dust.

Biomass Fuels

Have you ever used wood to make a fire? Wood is an example of a biomass fuel. *A* **biomass fuel** *is a fuel formed from the products of living organisms.* Other biomass fuels include garbage, methane, and alcohol. Unlike fossil fuels, biomass fuels are a renewable resource. They can be produced in large quantities specifically for use as fuels.

Recall that in a food pyramid, lower-level organisms are the energy source for the next-higher-level organisms. The amount of energy available at any given level depends on the mass of the organisms. The total mass of organisms at a given trophic level is the biomass of that level. The amount of biomass at an energy level determines the amount of energy available.

Wood   Many people in the United States who once used wood for fuel now use other fuels as their energy source. However, in developing nations where other fuels are too expensive or unavailable, people still rely on wood as a fuel source. In some parts of the world, people spend a great deal of time searching for the wood necessary to meet their energy needs.

Using wood for fuel has advantages and disadvantages. Wood gives off a great deal of smoke that is high in carbon dioxide. Also, obtaining wood can be damaging to natural forests. Trees grown specifically for use as fuel could help reduce this problem.

Garbage   The materials you throw away, like those in Figure 15.9, are collectively called garbage. Much of the garbage produced in homes is composed largely of organic materials, such as paper and food scraps. About two-thirds of the material in garbage can be burned. Some cities in the United States are now burning garbage to produce electricity. In this process, heat produced from burning garbage is used to change water into steam. The steam turns the turbines that generate electricity.

Mathematics

Scientists estimate that 2 metric tons of garbage produce an amount of energy equal to that of 1 metric ton of coal. In Paris, France, about 1.7 million metric tons of garbage are burned each year for the production of heat and electricity. How much coal is conserved by this use of garbage?

Figure 15.9 Burning garbage for fuel helps provide energy and reduce the problem of solid waste disposal. Garbage dumps also produce methane, which can be used like natural gas.

Methane   People have long known that swamp gas is produced in swamps from decaying plants. Swamp gas is a naturally produced form of methane. Recall that methane is a hydrocarbon and is a main component of natural gas. Decaying garbage in dumps also produces methane. Today, methane is being removed from swamps and garbage dumps for use as a fuel. The methane is used the same way as natural gas.

Alcohol   *The conversion of organic materials into fuels is called* **bioconversion** (BY-oh-cun-ver-zhun). One example of bioconversion is the use of plants to make alcohol. Sugarcane and corn are two plants that can be used to make alcohol through bioconversion.

An alcohol is a hydrocarbon in which one of the hydrogen atoms has been replaced with a hydroxyl, or oxygen-hydrogen group, as shown below:

```
               H   H                          H   H
               |   |                          |   |
Ethane   H – C – C – H        Ethanol   H – C – C – OH
               |   |                          |   |
               H   H                          H   H
```

The alcohol called ethanol, or ethyl alcohol, is made by yeast through the process of fermentation. Ethanol is a liquid biomass fuel that burns cleanly and is a renewable resource. In Brazil, more than 2 million cars are fueled by ethanol. Other cars in that country are fueled by a gasoline-alcohol mixture called gasohol. Gasohol is a mixture of 90 percent gasoline to 10 percent ethanol. Manufacturers are now producing car engines that run on alcohol made from sunflower or peanut plants.

Think About It!

Propane is a hydrocarbon with a chain of three carbon atoms. Isopropyl alcohol has the same formula as propanol, but the hydroxyl group is attached to the middle carbon.

1. Draw the chemical structure of the alcohol propanol.
2. Draw the structure for isopropyl alcohol.

SECTION REVIEW

1. How does using fossil fuels contribute to air pollution?
2. Name three types of plants that can be used as biomass fuels.
3. **Infer** What are the two ways that using garbage as fuel helps the environment?

Supply and Demand of Crude Oil

PROBLEM

So far, about one-quarter of the world's petroleum reserves have been consumed. How long will the supply of oil continue to meet the demand?

MATERIALS (per group)

- graph paper
- pencils, 3 different colors

PREDICTION

Read the entire activity, then write a prediction that is related to the problem.

Oil Production

Year	World Oil Production (× 10⁹ barrels)	U.S. Oil Production (× 10⁹ barrels)
1900	1	0
1925	1	0.6
1950	4	2.3
1975	18	3.2
2000	37	1.6
2025	19	0.4
2050	9	0.1

PROCEDURE

1. Study the information in the data table. Some of the information is the result of analyzing trends. Trends are general movements or directions that have happened in the past. The information is also based on oil reserves known to exist and thought to exist.
2. Using the Oil Production table, make a line graph of the information showing world oil production. Use a whole sheet of graph paper. Plot time along the x-axis, and billions of barrels of crude oil on the y-axis. Connect the data points. Label this line "World Oil Supply."
3. On the same graph that you plotted world oil production, plot the information for U.S. oil production from the same table. Connect the data points using a different colored pencil. Label this line "U.S. Oil Supply."
4. Oil consumption in the United States is currently about 6 billion barrels of oil per year, and has been increasing at a rate of approximately 5 percent each year. Construct a table to show what U.S. oil consumption would be each year between now and the year 2050, based on the expected 5 percent per year increase.

5. Use your table to plot data points on the graph showing your projected consumption of oil in the United States between now and 2050. Use a third colored pencil to connect these points. Label this line "U.S. Oil Demand."

ANALYSIS

1. How do current U.S. oil production and world oil production compare in terms of volume?
2. When did U.S. oil production peak? Do you think U.S. demand for oil peaked in the same year? Explain.
3. If the U.S. demand for oil is 6 billion barrels this year, how will it be supplied?
4. If demand continues to increase at 5 percent per year, approximately how much oil will have to be imported into the United States annually in 5 years?

CONCLUSION

1. Do you think the world supply of oil will be able to meet the U.S. demand when you are 30 years old? When you are 50?
2. Two-thirds of the world's oil reserves are in the Middle East. What is your opinion regarding U.S. dependence on foreign oil? What are the alternatives?

KEY TERMS

fuel 15.1
hydrocarbon 15.1
fossil fuel 15.1

peat 15.2
lignite 15.2
bituminous coal 15.2

anthracite coal 15.2
petroleum 15.3
biomass fuel 15.4

bioconversion 15.4

CHAPTER SUMMARY

15.1 Energy can take many forms, including heat, light, electrical, mechanical, chemical, and nuclear energy. The rise of agriculture and the Industrial Revolution increased the energy needs of many human societies. Organic fuels contain hydrocarbon molecules. Fossil fuels are organic fuels formed from the remains of organisms that lived millions of years ago. Coal, petroleum, and natural gas are fossil fuels.

15.2 Coal is a solid fossil fuel made from the remains of plants that lived millions of years ago. It forms when heat and pressure force out water and chemically change the plant remains. Coal forms in several stages: peat, lignite, bituminous coal, and anthracite.

15.3 Petroleum is a liquid fossil fuel formed from the remains of plants, animals, and protists. Petroleum is used to make heating oil, gasoline, and other liquid fuels. It is also used to make plastics and synthetic fabrics. Natural gas is a fossil fuel made of a mixture of gases, including methane, ethane, and propane. Appliances that use natural gas are more energy-efficient than those that use electricity.

15.4 The use of fossil fuels is associated with many problems, including lack of availability, pollution, and habitat disruption. Biomass fuels, made from the products of organisms, can help solve some of these problems. Biomass fuels include wood, garbage, methane, and alcohol.

MULTIPLE CHOICE

Choose the letter of the word or phrase that best completes each statement.

 1. The first stage in the formation of coal is (a) lignite; (b) peat; (c) anthracite; (d) bituminous coal.
 2. Crude oil is another name for (a) alcohol; (b) methane; (c) peat; (d) petroleum.
 3. The use of corn to make alcohol is an example of (a) bioconversion; (b) fossil fuels; (c) hydrocarbon; (d) refining.
 4. Compounds that contain only carbon and hydrogen are (a) fuels; (b) fossil fuels; (c) organic fuels; (d) hydrocarbons.
 5. The type of society that has the greatest energy needs is the (a) hunting society; (b) gathering society; (c) industrial society; (d) agricultural society.
 6. The type of coal that has the highest carbon content is (a) peat; (b) lignite; (c) bituminous coal; (d) anthracite.
 7. Of the following, the only example of a biomass fuel is (a) coal; (b) petroleum; (c) wood; (d) natural gas.
 8. The process by which alcohol is made by yeast is called (a) fermentation; (b) bioconversion; (c) purification; (d) distillation.
 9. Unlike fossil fuels, biomass fuels (a) do not release carbon dioxide; (b) are renewable resources; (c) are buried beneath the surface; (d) are not products of living things.
10. The most abundant form of coal in the United States is (a) peat; (b) lignite; (c) anthracite; (d) bituminous coal.

CHAPTER 15 REVIEW

WORD COMPARISONS

Write the letter of the second word pair that best matches the first pair.

1. Coal: fossil fuel as (a) petroleum: crude oil; (b) peat: coal; (c) methane: swamp gas; (d) alcohol: biomass fuel.
2. Crude oil: petroleum as (a) brown coal: lignite; (b) corn: alcohol; (c) gasoline: alcohol; (d) alcohol: gasohol.
3. Methane: natural gas as (a) petroleum: crude oil; (b) carbon: anthracite coal; (c) petroleum: plastic; (d) yeast: corn.
4. Petroleum: plastics as (a) alcohol: gasoline; (b) coal: carbon; (c) garbage: electricity; (d) industry: fuels.
5. Mines: coal as (a) petroleum: refineries; (b) corn: alcohol; (c) land: agriculture; (d) wells: petroleum.

CONCEPT REVIEW

Write a complete response for each of the following.

1. Why are coal, oil, and natural gas referred to as fossil fuels?
2. How do biomass fuels differ from fossil fuels?
3. Explain why the making of alcohol for use as a fuel is an example of bioconversion.
4. What chemical properties are shared by coal, oil, and natural gas?
5. Why do societies based on industry have greater fuel needs than societies based on hunting and gathering or agriculture?

THINK CRITICALLY

1. How might an increase in the use of biomass fuels benefit an agricultural society?
2. If you were to search for fossil-fuel deposits, what information would you try to find out to help you decide where to look?
3. What environmental risks are associated with offshore oil exploration?
4. Explain why biomass fuels are considered renewable and fossil fuels are considered nonrenewable, when both types of fuel are formed from living things.
5. How does the use of fuels such as alcohol, gasohol, and methane help conserve fossil fuels? Why is conserving fossil fuels important?

WRITE FOR UNDERSTANDING

Identify the topic of each paragraph in Section 15.1. Write a sentence that summarizes the topic of each paragraph. Organize the topics into a summary of the section.

PORTFOLIO

1. Research the locations of petroleum and natural gas deposits in the United states. Combine this information with Figure 15.5 to identify the locations of the major deposits of all types of fossil fuels in the United States. Create a visual representation of the information you collect.
2. Conduct library research to find out what kinds of synthetic fuels are being developed in the laboratory. Determine the uses of each fuel and the benefits and drawbacks associated with the use of synthetic fuels. Present your findings in a written or an oral report.

GRAPHIC ANALYSIS

Use the figure to answer the following.
1. During which decade did the quantity of coal used as fuel surpass the quantity of wood used?
2. What event occurred in the 1970s that affected the use of petroleum? What was the effect of this event on coal consumption?
3. Why does the line representing petroleum and natural gas not appear at the far left side of the graph?

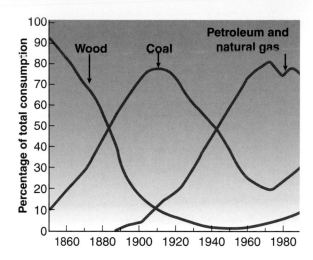

PROBLEM
What is the effect of coal mining on the environment?

MATERIALS (per group)
- 3 jars or beakers
- masking tape or labels
- cloth rag
- safety goggles
- hammer
- pyrite
- sulfur coal
- water
- blue litmus paper

PREDICTION
Read the entire activity, then write a prediction that is related to the problem.

PROCEDURE
1. Make a data table on a separate sheet of paper to record your observations.
2. Label the 3 jars *Pyrite, Coal,* and *Water.* Also label the jars with your name or your group's name.
3. Wrap some pyrite in the cloth. Crush the pyrite with a hammer. Place the crushed pyrite in its jar.
   Caution: *Wear safety goggles. Be careful when using the hammer.*
4. Repeat step 3, using coal instead of pyrite.
5. Drip tap water over the pyrite and coal until they are submerged in the jars. Pour tap water in the last jar.
6. Set the jars in the sun or a warm place for 3 days.
7. After 3 days, test the water in each jar with blue litmus paper. Record any changes in the color of the paper.

ANALYSIS
1. What source of water in a natural environment might the water in the jars represent?
2. Which jar was the control?
3. Which jar(s) contained water that changed the color of the litmus paper after 3 days?
4. What type of substance, if any, formed in the jars?

CONCLUSION
What effect did you predict mining coal might have on the environment?

Nuclear energy is derived from the splitting of atoms. Atoms of a heavy element, such as uranium, are broken apart. In this process, a small amount of matter is converted to a large amount of energy. The energy released can then be used to generate electricity.

Many places in the world depend on nuclear energy for power. France, for example, gets over 70 percent of its energy from nuclear power. Questions about the cost and safety of nuclear energy, as well as the disposal of radioactive wastes, have yet to be answered.

16.1 ATOMS AND RADIOACTIVITY

OBJECTIVES • **Describe** the structure of the atom and the atomic nucleus. • **Explain** how unstable nuclei become stable by releasing radiation.

All common forms of matter are made up of atoms. All atoms are composed of three major kinds of particles: protons, electrons, and neutrons. Figure 16.1 shows an atom of the element helium. Notice that the protons and neutrons occur together in the middle of the atom. *This cluster of protons and neutrons in the center of an atom is called the* **nucleus** (NOO-klee-us). Nearly all the mass of an atom is in its nucleus. The nucleus is orbited by the electrons of the atom. Atoms that are electrically neutral contain the same number of protons and electrons.

Atoms and Isotopes

The basic properties of an atom are determined by the number of protons in its nucleus. All atoms of the same element have the same number of protons in their nuclei. The number of protons in an atom is called the *atomic number* of the element. For example, oxygen has 8 protons, and its atomic number is 8. The atomic number of uranium is 92. Uranium has 92 protons.

The atoms of most elements, except for hydrogen, have neutrons as well as protons and electrons. The number of protons plus the number of neutrons in an atom is referred to as the *mass number* of the atom. Electrons are not counted in determining mass number. This is because electrons have so little mass as compared to protons and neutrons.

Individual atoms of the same element may have different mass numbers because the number of neutrons in the nucleus can vary. For example, all atoms of the element oxygen have 8 protons. Most atoms of oxygen have 8 neutrons and a mass number of 16. However, some oxygen atoms may have 9 or 10 neutrons. *Atoms of the same element that have different numbers of neutrons are called* **isotopes** (EYE-soh-tohps). Uranium has 92 protons, and most uranium atoms contain 146 neutrons and have a mass number of 238. This form of uranium is commonly called U-238. Another isotope of uranium, called U-235, has only 143 neutrons and has a mass number of 235.

Radioactivity

Some isotopes of atoms are unstable. Unstable atoms decay, emitting particles and energy from their nuclei. Atoms that decay in this way are called *radioactive atoms*. Marie Curie, a Nobel Prize-winning physicist and chemist, was the first person to use the word

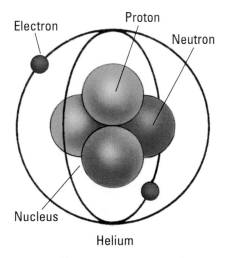

Figure 16.1 A helium atom contains two protons and two neutrons in its nucleus. The nucleus is orbited by two electrons.

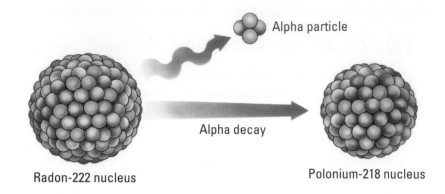

Figure 16.2 Atoms of radon decay into atoms of polonium by releasing an alpha particle. The radioactive decay of radon gas, which occurs in soil, is the largest single source of radiation in many homes in the United States.

Alpha particle

Alpha decay

Radon-222 nucleus

Polonium-218 nucleus

Figure 16.3 Radiation produced by this uranium ore has exposed the photographic film.

radioactive to describe an element. After a series of decay changes, a radioactive element becomes stable and stops decaying.

There are many radioactive elements. In most cases, only certain isotopes of an element are radioactive. For example, the most common isotope of hydrogen, H-1, is not radioactive. However, H-2 and H-3 are radioactive.

Two kinds of particles given off by the nuclei of radioactive atoms are *alpha* (AL-fuh) *particles* and *beta* (BAY-tuh) *particles*. Alpha particles are made up of two protons and two neutrons. A beta particle is a high-speed electron. Beta decay converts a neutron into a proton. Radioactive elements can also give off energy in the form of *gamma* (GA-muh) *rays*. Gamma rays are a form of electromagnetic radiation. *The alpha particles, beta particles, and gamma rays given off in the decaying of unstable nuclei are called* **radiation.**

An atom that emits alpha particles loses protons and neutrons, while an atom that emits beta particles converts neutrons to protons. These changes alter the atomic number and mass number of the atoms. Since the atomic number of an atom determines the identity of the element, the decay process changes one element into another.

Two radioactive isotopes of uranium are U-238 (over 99 percent of all uranium found in nature) and U-235. Both isotopes ultimately decay into stable forms of lead, but this process takes a long time. *The amount of time it takes for half of the atoms in a sample of a radioactive element to decay is called the isotope's* **half-life.** Half-lives for various radioactive elements range from a few seconds to billions of years. The half-life for U-238 is about 4.5 billion years, while that of U-235 is around 700 million years.

SECTION REVIEW

1. What is the difference between two isotopes of an element?
2. Name and describe the three kinds of radiation emitted by radioactive elements.
3. **Explain** What is the half-life of a radioactive sample? Explain the meaning of the term *half-life*.

16.2 REACTIONS AND REACTORS

OBJECTIVES • **Illustrate** the fission chain reactions that power nuclear reactors and breeder reactors. • **Diagram** the structure and function of a nuclear reactor.

Energy is required to hold the protons and neutrons in an atom's nucleus together. Scientists have discovered ways to release the energy inside an atom. One way to release this energy is by splitting the nucleus of the atom apart. *A reaction in which the nucleus of a large atom is split into smaller nuclei is called* **nuclear fission** (NOO-klee-er FIZH-un). When an atom is broken apart through nuclear fission, it emits large amounts of energy. This energy can be used to generate electricity.

Nuclear Fission

Uranium-235 is the atom used most commonly in fission reactions. An atom of U-235 is *fissionable,* which means it splits when its nucleus is struck by a neutron. When U-235 splits, it releases energy and forms new nuclei, called daughter nuclei. These daughter nuclei are often the elements barium or krypton, although there are several hundred possible nuclei that can form in the fission of U-235. Many of these daughter nuclei are radioactive.

The steps in the fission of a U-235 atom are shown in Figure 16.4. To begin the reaction, a neutron is fired into the nucleus of the atom. The neutron strikes the nucleus, which splits, forming two daughter nuclei. The reaction also releases energy and several more neutrons. These neutrons can strike other U-235 nuclei, causing those nuclei to split and release more energy and more neutrons. This continuous action of neutrons splitting atomic nuclei is called a chain reaction.

Figure 16.4 Atoms of uranium-235 undergo a chain reaction in a nuclear reactor. The fission of one atom of U-235 releases several neutrons. Each of these neutrons can trigger the fission of another atom of U-235.

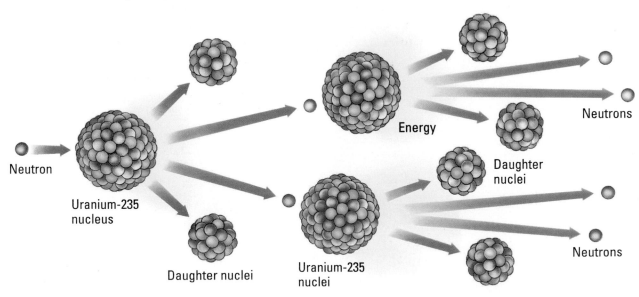

Neutron

Uranium-235 nucleus

Daughter nuclei

Uranium-235 nuclei

Energy

Daughter nuclei

Neutrons

Neutrons

When the nucleus of an atom of U-235 splits, the resulting nuclei have less mass than the original nucleus. For example, the combined mass of a barium nucleus and a krypton nucleus is less than the mass of the original U-235 nucleus. Some of the missing mass is in the neutrons emitted during the fission reaction. The rest of the mass was converted directly into energy.

Nuclear Reactors

Electricity is produced from nuclear fuel in much the same way as electricity is produced from fossil fuels. However, in the case of nuclear reactors, heat is produced through the fission of nuclear material instead of the burning of fossil fuels. Nuclear fuel is usually about 97 percent U-238 and 3 percent U-235. The U-238 is not fissionable, so it does not take part in the nuclear reaction.

In a typical American reactor, the fission of U-235 takes place inside a *nuclear reactor vessel.* This vessel can be as tall as 20 m, with steel walls at least 15 to 30 cm thick. The walls are surrounded by a large shield that keeps neutrons and other radiation from escaping from the reactor. The reactor is housed inside a thick concrete containment building. The fuel for the reactor consists of long rods filled with pellets that contain the fissionable U-235.

The fuel rods are positioned vertically in the center of the reactor so that water can circulate between them. The water performs two functions. It acts as a coolant, which absorbs heat and keeps the core from melting. It also slows the movement of the neutrons released during the chain reaction. A U-235 nucleus will split only when it captures a slow-moving neutron.

The speed of the chain reaction is regulated by *control rods.* Control rods are made of cadmium, boron, or other materials that absorb neutrons. Lowering the control rods into the reactor allows

Figure 16.5 A nuclear power plant generates heat that is used to produce electricity. Waste heat leaves the plant through the cooling tower.

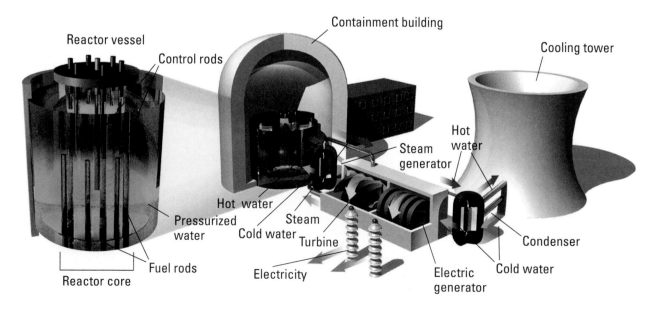

the rods to absorb more neutrons, thus slowing the chain reaction. Raising the rods results in the absorption of fewer neutrons, and the speed of the chain reaction increases.

Raising or lowering the control rods also regulates the amount of heat produced. The temperature of the coolant water circulating within the reactor may reach temperatures above 275 °C. This hot water moves inside pipes to a heat exchanger, where it heats water for steam. The steam is then used to turn turbines connected to electric generators.

Breeder Reactors

Over 99 percent of the naturally occurring uranium is the nonfissionable isotope, U-238. However, U-238 can absorb a neutron, giving rise to a fissionable atom of plutonium-239 (Pu-239). Pu-239 can be used as a fuel in a nuclear reactor. A *breeder reactor* uses this process to produce new fuel while it generates usable energy.

Figure 16.6 shows how plutonium is made in a breeder reactor. During the reaction, the U-238 captures a free neutron and changes to a very unstable atom of U-239. The U-239 changes, by radioactive decay, into a fissionable atom of Pu-239. The Pu-239 can then be used as nuclear fuel. A breeder reactor with an ample supply of U-238 can produce more fuel than it uses.

Breeder reactors are not used in the United States because of concerns about nuclear terrorism. The plutonium produced by breeder reactors can be used to make atomic bombs as well as energy. If this material fell into the wrong hands, the results could be horrific.

Use Einstein's equation to calculate the amount of energy produced by 1 kg of uranium in a fission reaction. The mass of the fission products is 0.941 kg.

1. How much energy is produced in the reaction? (Ignore the mass released as free neutrons. Energy is measured in joules. One joule is $1 \text{ kg} \times \text{m}^2/\text{sec}^2$.)

2. It takes $3.6 \times 10^5 \text{ J}$ to light a 100-watt lightbulb for 1 hour. How many bulbs could you light for 1 hour with the amount of energy produced in question 1?

Figure 16.6 A breeder reactor produces more fuel than it consumes. Neutrons from the fission in a nuclear reactor change atoms of uranium-238 into fissionable plutonium-239. Plutonium-239 can then be used as a nuclear fuel.

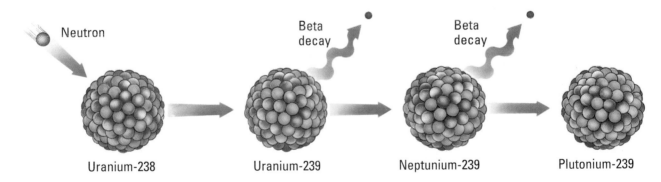

Neutron   Beta decay   Beta decay

Uranium-238   Uranium-239   Neptunium-239   Plutonium-239

SECTION REVIEW

1. Describe what happens in the fission chain reaction of U-235.
2. What function do the control rods perform in a nuclear reactor?
3. **Predict** What would happen to the nuclear fuel in a reactor if the water-cooling system and control rods stopped working?

16.3 RADIOACTIVE WASTE

OBJECTIVES • *Define* radioactive waste, and explain the dangers that arise from it. • *State* the problems involved in the safe disposal of radioactive wastes.

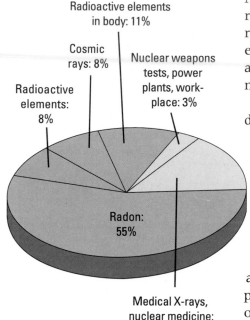

Radioactive elements in body: 11%

Cosmic rays: 8%

Nuclear weapons tests, power plants, workplace: 3%

Radioactive elements: 8%

Radon: 55%

Medical X-rays, nuclear medicine: 15%

■ Natural sources
■ Human produced

Figure 16.7 This graph shows the sources of annual radiation exposure of an average person in the United States. Over half the radiation comes from decaying radon gas. Radon gas comes from decaying uranium atoms in Earth's crust. Average exposure per person per year is about 0.2–0.5 rems, although the actual amount can vary.

Nuclear power plants produce radioactive wastes. About 32 metric tons of spent fuel is produced by a typical 1000 MW nuclear reactor each year. This waste could be reprocessed into 1.5 tons of extremely radioactive materials, but such work is a dangerous activity. Nuclear plants also produce large quantities of low-level nuclear wastes during the course of normal operation.

Radiation is unhealthy for living things. Cells that are actively dividing, such as skin cells and the blood-cell producing cells in bone marrow, are especially sensitive to radiation. The amount of exposure determines the extent of damage. Large doses of radiation can cause severe, immediate effects, including skin burns and anemia, even death. Radiation also causes changes in DNA, leading to long-term effects such as cancer and genetic mutations.

Radiation exposure is measured in rems. Most Americans receive between 0.2–0.5 rems per year from background radiation. Figure 16.7 shows the sources of radiation for an average person. Most of the background radiation comes from naturally occurring elements in our surroundings. Radiation exposure varies widely, depending on where a person lives and where he or she works.

Types of Waste

Radioactive wastes that emit large amounts of radiation are called **high-level wastes.** High-level waste materials include used uranium fuel rods, control rods, and the water used to cool and control the chain reactions. The vessel that surrounds the fuel rods is also radioactive. These wastes are very dangerous to handle and may also be poisonous.

Medium-level and low-level wastes *are not as radioactive as high-level wastes, although a much larger volume of these wastes is generated.* Medium-level and low-level wastes can be anything from the mine wastes scattered around a uranium mine to the contaminated protective clothes of a power plant worker. Low-level radioactive wastes are also produced by hospitals and laboratories. The damage to people's health that these wastes cause is not as obvious as the damage caused by high-level wastes. Because they are more common, however, medium-and low-level wastes may pose a greater risk to human health.

Waste Disposal

Radioactive wastes are very difficult to dispose of safely. The contaminants may have long half-lives, taking thousands of years to decay. Low-level wastes can be dangerous for 300 years or more. High-level wastes may be dangerous for tens of thousands of years. Plutonium-239, for example, is a high-level waste product of nuclear reactors. Pu-239 has a half-life of 24 000 years. Plutonium waste will remain dangerous for 192 000 years. Plutonium is also a deadly poison, even in minute amounts.

The long half-lives of elements in radioactive wastes pose a serious disposal problem. Wastes must be sealed in containers that will not corrode for thousands of years. The U.S. government has decided to seal the wastes in thick blocks of glass. The site where wastes are stored must be geologically stable. An earthquake or volcano could spill the stored wastes, so the chance of geologic activity must be low. The wastes must also be stored deep under the ground. The cost of this disposal method is very high.

Almost all the high-level radioactive wastes in the world have not been disposed of permanently. They sit in storage tanks outside nuclear power and weapons plants. In many cases, these tanks have begun to leak, contaminating the groundwater and releasing radioactive wastes into the environment. These wastes must be permanently removed before the contamination gets worse. The government predicts that the cleanup of 20 of the most contaminated nuclear weapons sites in the United States could cost $600 billion.

Medium-level and low-level wastes also pose disposal problems. Low-level wastes are often buried or, in the past, were enclosed in concrete and dropped into the ocean. These methods of disposal expose the environment to contamination. Most medium-level wastes have not been disposed of permanently. A permanent disposal site for medium-level wastes presents many of the same problems as does a site for high-level wastes.

Figure 16.8 This is the Hanford Reservation nuclear weapons facility in Washington state. Large amounts of radioactive wastes have been released into the environment at Hanford. The Columbia River (foreground) has been contaminated several times. The last facility at Hanford was shut down in 1987. Cleanup at the site has begun.

Figure 16.9 A meltdown destroyed the Chernobyl reactor (right). The areas surrounding the reactor were contaminated with radioactivity (far right).

Dateline 1979

On March 28, 1979, the nuclear power plant on Three Mile Island in Pennsylvania began to malfunction. A valve in the cooling system stopped working, leading to a partial core meltdown. Radioactive steam and water were released into the environment. A major disaster was narrowly avoided.

LINK
Mathematics

When the Chernobyl accident occurred, people living near the reactor received a radiation dose of between 20 and 100 rems. This exposure level is 400 to 2000 percent of the level considered safe by the U.S. government. Exposure at this level causes nausea, vomiting, and a greatly increased risk of cancer. About one out of ten of these people will probably die of cancer caused by Chernobyl radiation.

Safety and Cost

The danger that radioactive contamination creates for the environment makes safety at nuclear power plants very important. If the cooling and control systems in a reactor core fail, the chain reaction can no longer be controlled. The core will grow hotter, causing the fuel rods and even the reactor vessel to melt. *The process by which a nuclear chain reaction goes out of control and melts the reactor core is called a* **meltdown.** A full meltdown would release huge amounts of radiation into the environment.

Nuclear power plants are built to avoid meltdowns and to contain them if they occur. In April 1986, however, one core of the Chernobyl nuclear power plant in Ukraine did melt down. The plant's control rods were made of graphite. The graphite began to burn, and fire spread radioactivity over a vast area. More than 30 people were killed immediately, and 116 000 people had to permanently leave their homes. Scientists think that Chernobyl radiation may eventually cause as many as 15 000 cases of cancer.

The Chernobyl plant was old and lacked many of the safety features built into newer plants. The accident itself was caused by human error. The severity of this accident and the problems with radioactive waste disposal have led many people to question the wisdom of using nuclear power. Nuclear power plants are also very expensive because the required safety measures are very costly.

SECTION REVIEW

1. What makes radioactive waste difficult to dispose of?
2. What percentage of the average person's radiation exposure is due to radon gas?
3. **Analyze** What was the cause of the Chernobyl nuclear accident? Is there any way that this factor can be eliminated?

Disposal of Nuclear Waste

PROBLEM

What problems are encountered when storing nuclear waste?

MATERIALS (PER GROUP)

- 4 sodium hydroxide pellets
- 4 jars with lids
- phenolphthalein solution
- water
- plastic wrap
- twist-tie
- aluminum foil
- modeling clay
- tweezers
- safety goggles
- tap water
- medicine dropper

INFERENCE

Read the entire activity, then write an inference that is related to the problem.

PROCEDURE

1. You are a scientist who tests nuclear waste storage containers that will be used underground. The sodium hydroxide pellets represent solid nuclear waste that will be radioactive for thousands of years.
   Caution: *Do not touch sodium hydroxide pellets with your bare hands. Use the tweezers and wear safety goggles.*
2. Copy the data table onto a separate sheet of paper.
3. Fill each jar about three-quarters full with water. Use the medicine dropper to add four drops of phenolphthalein solution to each jar.
4. Use the tweezers to put one sodium hydroxide pellet in one of the jars. Observe any changes in the water. This jar is your control. Be sure to label all jars.

5. Handling the pellet with tweezers, wrap one of the remaining pellets tightly in the aluminum foil. Try to make it watertight. Wrap another pellet in plastic wrap, and tie it securely with the twist-tie. It should be watertight as well. Insert the last pellet into the clay. Bend the clay around the pellet to make a watertight seal.
6. Gently drop each wrapped pellet into one of the three remaining jars. This action represents soaking nuclear waste storage containers in groundwater. Screw the lids on the jars.
7. Observe the jars for 3 days. Look for signs of leaks. Record the information in the data table.

ANALYSIS

1. What happened when you put a sodium hydroxide pellet into the water of the control jar?
2. Did any of the wrapped pellets show signs of leakage? If so, which type of wrapping was used and on which day was the leak noticed?
3. Compare your data with that of other groups in your class. Which material would make the best storage container? Which, if any, material would make a storage container with an acceptable risk against leakage?

CONCLUSION

What did you infer at the beginning of this activity regarding the problems associated with storing nuclear waste? Did your observations support the inference? Explain.

Table 16.1

Storage Container	Observations		
	Day 1	Day 2	Day 3
Control			
Aluminum			
Plastic			
Clay			

Yucca Mountain

Almost one-fifth of the world depends on nuclear power for electricity. But nuclear power also generates radioactive wastes. For many years, nuclear power plants have stored their own wastes, but storage space is running out.

Several ideas for long-term storage of radioactive waste have been proposed. One idea is to build a geologic repository where waste can be buried several hundred meters deep in solid rock or salt beds.

In 1987, the U.S. Congress selected Yucca Mountain in the Nevada desert as a possible geologic repository. If the project is approved, it is estimated to cost between $30 and $50 billion and could be fully operational by 2010. The proposal of using Yucca Mountain, however, has raised many questions.

Should Yucca Mountain be used for a nuclear-waste repository?

Use Yucca Mountain As a Repository

Geological evidence indicates that the Yucca Mountain area has changed little over the last million years. Scientists predict it will remain undisturbed for up to one million years after the repository is sealed.

The repository will be 300 m deep, within hard rock deposits. At this depth, it is still 300 m above the water table. Little groundwater flows through Yucca Mountain, so the waste canisters will stay dry and remain intact.

Don't Use Yucca Mountain As a Repository

Scientists cannot predict every problem that might arise in the repository. Heavy precipitation or seismic movements could raise the water table, causing canisters to corrode and leak waste into the groundwater. Once in the groundwater, the waste could reach the area's water supply, causing serious illness to people who drink the water.

Some of these chemicals remain radioactive for thousands of years. Scientists do not know for certain how long waste can remain buried without affecting the surrounding area.

Yucca Mountain, in the Nevada desert, is a potential site for the storage of nuclear waste.

Consider the Issue

1. Should Yucca Mountain be used to store radioactive wastes? Explain your answer.
2. Would you want to live in the area around Yucca Mountain? Why or why not?

CHAPTER **16** REVIEW

KEY TERMS

nucleus 16.1
isotope 16.1
radiation 16.1

half-life 16.1
nuclear fission 16.2
high-level waste 16.3

medium-level and
  low-level wastes 16.3
meltdown 16.3

CHAPTER SUMMARY

16.1 The nucleus of an atom is made up of protons and neutrons. The number of protons in the nucleus determines the identity of an atom. Atoms of the same element with different numbers of neutrons are called *isotopes*. Unstable isotopes emit radiation when they decay to stable atoms. The half-life of a radioactive element is the amount of time it takes for half of a sample of the element to undergo radioactive decay.

16.2 The reaction used to generate energy in a nuclear power plant is called *nuclear fission*. Uranium-235 is the most common fuel in nuclear power plants. U-235 atoms are split by free neutrons. The fission of a U-235 nucleus generates more free neutrons, maintaining a fission chain reaction. Nuclear power plants use the heat generated by fission to boil water and drive steam generators. Breeder reactors make more nuclear fuel than they consume.

16.3 Nuclear power plants produce radioactive wastes. Radiation is harmful to living things. High-level wastes stay dangerous for many thousands of years. Medium-level and low-level wastes are dangerous for hundreds of years and are produced in large amounts. A safe, inexpensive, and effective way to dispose of radioactive wastes has not yet been found. The Chernobyl nuclear accident released large amounts of radiation into the environment.

MULTIPLE CHOICE

Choose the letter of the word or phrase that best completes each statement.

1. Protons and neutrons are found together in the part of the atom called the (a) alpha particle; (b) electron; (c) nucleus; (d) isotope.
2. Two atoms of the same element with different mass numbers are called (a) isotopes; (b) nuclei; (c) electrons; (d) neutrons.
3. One kind of radiation not released by radioactive decay is (a) alpha particles; (b) free protons; (c) beta particles; (d) gamma rays.
4. The fuel most commonly used in fission reactions is (a) Np-239; (b) U-238; (c) U-235; (d) Pu-239.
5. Devices that absorb neutrons and are used to control the speed of a fission reactor are called (a) reactor vessels; (b) fuel rods; (c) containment buildings; (d) control rods.
6. A breeder reactor produces (a) Np-239; (b) U-238; (c) U-235; (d) Pu-239.
7. Each year, an average person in the United States is exposed to a radiation level of (a) 2 rems; (b) 0.2 rems; (c) 20 rems; (d) 200 rems.
8. Pu-239 has a half-life of (a) 24 years; (b) 240 years; (c) 2400 years; (d) 24 000 years.
9. Losing control of the fission reaction in a reactor core may result in a (a) cooldown; (b) meltdown; (c) draindown; (d) cooling tower.
10. The number of people forced to evacuate because of the Chernobyl accident was (a) 1160; (b) 11 600; (c) 116 000; (d) 1 160 000.

CHAPTER 16 REVIEW

TRUE/FALSE

Write true *if the statement is true. If the statement is false, change the underlined word or phrase to make it true.*

1. All isotopes of an element contain the same number of <u>neutrons</u>.
2. <u>Beta particles</u> contain two protons and two neutrons.
3. A fission chain reaction begins when an atom of U-235 is struck by a <u>neutron</u>.
4. In a fission reaction, some of the mass of the original atom is converted to <u>energy</u>.
5. In a breeder reactor, neutrons change <u>U-238</u> into Pu-239.
6. Radon gas is responsible for <u>25 percent</u> of the radiation in most U.S. homes.
7. Plutonium must be stored for <u>192 000 years</u> before it is safe.
8. The cleanup of the 20 most polluted nuclear weapons facilities in the United States will cost <u>$600 billion</u>.

CONCEPT REVIEW

Write a complete response for each of the following.

1. Describe how an unstable nucleus of radon-222 decays into the element polonium-218. By what amount does the mass number change? How does this change take place?
2. Write a paragraph summarizing the events in a fission chain reaction.
3. What function do the control rods serve in a nuclear reactor?
4. Are there sources of radioactive waste other than nuclear power plants? Name some of these sources.
5. Explain how the half-life of a radioactive element determines how long it will be dangerous to living things.

THINK CRITICALLY

1. An atom of radon-222 releases an alpha particle when it decays into polonium-218. Must the radon atom also emit a beta particle? Explain your answer.
2. Fission bombs work by assembling a large mass of pure uranium-235, or another unstable isotope. This mass, called a critical mass, then undergoes a spontaneous chain reaction and explodes. Why did the reactor core of the Chernobyl nuclear plant melt down instead of exploding like a fission bomb?

Computer Activity Use a computer graphing program to graph the decay of 1 kg of Pu-239 over 200 000 years. How did you calculate the numbers for your graph?

WRITE CREATIVELY

Write an essay stating your position on the use of nuclear power. If you think using nuclear power is a good idea, suggest ways to solve the disposal and safety problems caused by radioactivity. If you think nuclear power is a bad idea, suggest other energy sources that would replace the energy now supplied by nuclear reactors. Explain how you made your decision.

PORTFOLIO

Use balls of colored clay to build a model of a uranium-235 nucleus. Use more clay to build models of daughter nuclei and the other parts of a fission reaction. Mount and label your model.

GRAPHIC ANALYSIS

Use the figure to answer the following.

1. Which state gets the largest percentage of its energy from nuclear power?
2. Do any of the states on this graph get less than half of their energy from nuclear power?
3. Where are these states located? Is there a pattern to the distribution of the states that rely heavily on nuclear energy?
4. Would you expect this graph to show the same states if it graphed the total amount of energy produced by each state instead of a percentage? Why or why not?

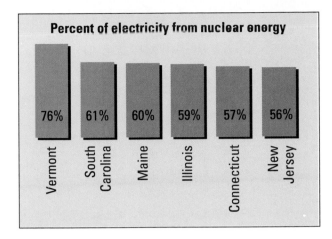

Percent of electricity from nuclear energy

Vermont 76% | South Carolina 61% | Maine 60% | Illinois 59% | Connecticut 57% | New Jersey 56%

ACTIVITY 16.2

PROBLEM
How can you model the reactions that occur in a nuclear reactor?

MATERIALS (per group)
- 15 dominoes
- stopwatch
- ruler

INFERENCE
Read the entire activity, then write an inference that is related to the problem.

PROCEDURE
1. Stand 15 dominoes in a single straight row. The distance between them should be about half their height. Knock over the first domino. Measure and record the time it takes for all the dominoes to fall.
2. Repeat step 1 two more times. Average the three times.
3. Arrange the dominoes in four rows. The distance between rows should be about half their height. Arrange them so that each domino in the first three rows will knock over two others. The row closest to you should have only one domino. The second row should have two dominoes. The third row should have four dominoes, and the fourth row should have eight dominoes. Knock over the first domino. Measure and record the time it takes for all the dominoes to fall.
4. Repeat step 3 two more times. Average the three times.
5. Set up the dominoes again, as in step 3. This time, hold a ruler on edge between the third and fourth rows. Knock over the first domino. Observe what happens.

ANALYSIS
1. How did the average falling times compare when the dominoes were arranged in single file and in four rows?
2. What type of reaction is represented by the falling dominoes arranged in single file? In four rows?
3. When the dominoes were arranged in four rows, what did your finger striking the first domino represent? What did the ruler represent?

CONCLUSION
1. Describe how dominoes can be used to model the reaction in a nuclear reactor.
2. Discuss the strengths and limitations of the model.

People have always been fascinated by the power of the sun. In ancient Greek mythology, the character Icarus perished because he ignored warnings not to fly too close to the sun. People have long been aware of the role of the sun in growing plants and providing warmth and light. In recent years, the sun has taken on a new role in human society. Using the energy produced by the sun, people are discovering a new source of clean, renewable energy that will last as long as Earth itself. Combined with other renewable energy sources such as water and wind, people are finding alternatives to the use of fossil fuels.

17.1 SOLAR ENERGY

OBJECTIVES • **Explain** the importance of the sun in supplying energy to Earth. • **Describe** how solar energy can be used to heat buildings and generate electricity.

The sun is the source of almost all the energy on Earth's surface. *Energy from the sun, or* **solar energy**, *is absorbed by plants and used as fuel by virtually all organisms.* Because fossil fuels contain energy from the remains of organisms, they also contain energy originally from the sun.

Solar energy does more than provide energy for the organisms on Earth. The source of energy that drives the water cycle is the sun. The flow of streams on Earth's surface is part of the water cycle. Fast-moving rivers are often used to generate electricity. Since the water in the rivers results from the sun-driven water cycle, the energy produced by the flow of rivers can be traced to the sun. The sun also produces uneven warming of Earth's surface. These temperature differences cause winds to blow. Therefore, wind energy is also driven by energy from the sun.

The Sun As Fuel

The sun obtains its energy through thermonuclear (THER-moh-NOO-klee-ur) fusion. In this process, high temperatures in the sun's core cause hydrogen nuclei to fuse, or join, forming helium nuclei. As each helium nucleus forms, a loss of mass occurs. This lost mass is converted to the heat and light energy of the sun.

Earth receives less than one billionth of the energy produced by the sun. Much of the solar energy that reaches Earth is in the form of visible light and infrared radiation. Recall that energy cannot be created or destroyed. It can, however, be changed in form. When light energy from the sun strikes objects, the energy in the light is absorbed by these objects. The absorbed energy is changed to heat, or thermal energy. Solar energy can be harnessed and used to generate heat and electricity. In some places, solar energy is replacing nuclear, biomass, and fossil fuels as an energy source.

The use of solar energy has many advantages. It is free, clean, and nonpolluting. Although you must buy the equipment for capturing and storing solar energy, the cost may be recovered by the savings in fuel bills over many years.

One drawback to solar energy systems is that the energy source is not constant. There is limited sunlight on cloudy or rainy days, and no sunlight at night. However, solar energy collected during the day can be stored. Another drawback to solar energy is that devices for harnessing and storing solar energy are not very

Field Activity

Take a hand lens and a thin sheet of paper to a paved area on a sunny day. Place the paper on the pavement, and hold it down with a small rock. Hold the hand lens above the paper at an angle that focuses the sun's rays as sharply as possible onto the paper. **Caution:** *Have a container of water handy in case the paper catches fire. Do not do this activity in a grassy area.*

1. Observe what happens.

2. Based on your observations, what conclusions can you make about the energy in sunlight?

efficient. The size and cost of the equipment may outweigh the benefits. But as technology progresses, the use of solar energy is becoming more cost-effective.

Passive Solar Energy

If the energy of sunlight is used directly as a source of light or heat, the energy use is described as passive. *In* **passive solar heating**, *the sun's energy is collected, stored, and distributed naturally in an enclosed dwelling.* You have experienced passive solar heating if you have ever walked through a greenhouse or sat inside an enclosed car on a sunny day. Passive solar energy is not used to produce electricity. But it can reduce the need for electricity or fuels by providing an alternative source of heat. Passive solar energy therefore helps reduce the use of fossil and nuclear fuels.

Passive solar heating of homes is mostly accomplished through well-planned building design and construction. In North America, houses that make optimum use of passive solar heating have large windows that all face south. South-facing windows can gather the greatest amount of the sun's energy for the longest number of daylight hours. In addition, these homes contain building materials and furnishings that best absorb solar energy. Examples of such materials are stone, brick, and concrete.

Buildings that make use of passive solar energy often have glass-enclosed areas. A glass-enclosed area functions much like a greenhouse. The area generally has walls and floors made from dark-colored, light-absorbing materials such as concrete and brick.

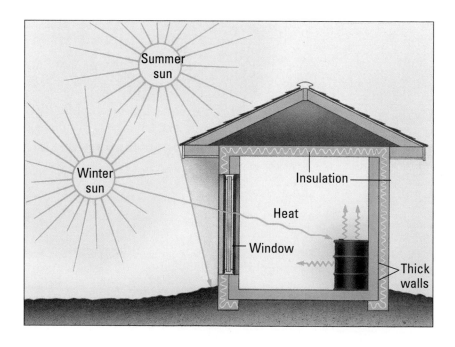

Figure 17.1 A house with passive solar heating has large windows that face south. In winter, when the sun is low in the sky, sunlight warms barrels of water. The barrels release heat after the sun goes down. In summer, the roof shades the windows.

Notice the large, dark, water-filled barrel in the glass enclosure in Figure 17.1. Such barrels are used as energy-absorbing and storage structures. During the day, the barrels absorb energy, and the water inside becomes heated. At night, when temperatures become cooler, the heat energy in the water is returned to the air in the room. To get the greatest benefit from passive solar heating, good insulation is needed to prevent the escape of the captured energy from the house. Thick, heavy curtains or shutters also help prevent heat from escaping from a room when there is no sunlight.

In existing homes, passive solar energy may not be practical as a primary energy source. Such homes may require costly renovations or major construction to obtain the greatest benefit from solar heating. However, when new homes are built, passive solar heating should be considered. The University of Saskatchewan in Canada built a house using passive solar heating. During one year, the house saved $1,350 in fuel bills compared to an average house.

Active Solar Energy

An active solar energy system has a greater capacity for storing and distributing energy than a passive system. *In* **active solar heating**, *devices are used to collect, store, and circulate heat produced from solar energy.* In a passive system, the building itself and its position act as the system. An active system, however, uses tubes, tanks, fluids, pumps, fans, and other devices to collect and distribute energy. These pieces of equipment can release the sun's energy to the system long after the sun has set.

Buildings that use active solar energy gather the sun's energy by using *solar collectors.* Most solar collectors are mounted on the roofs of houses or buildings where they can capture a maximum amount of the sun's energy. Placement of the collector on roofs also saves space on the ground.

Most solar collectors are flat-plate collectors. A flat-plate collector is a large, flat box. The base is made of a black metal plate that covers a layer of insulation. Tubes filled with fluid run across the top of the metal. The fluid inside the tube is usually water, but air or antifreeze may also be used.

Figure 17.2 The Solar One facility in the Mojave Desert of California uses more than 1800 mirrors focused on a single collector.

Figure 17.3 Flat-plate collectors began to appear on rooftops all across the United States in the early 1980s, when the federal government offered tax incentives to homeowners who installed the energy-saving devices.

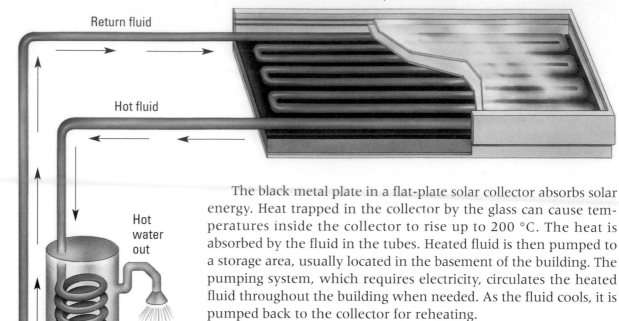

Flat–plate collector

Return fluid

Hot fluid

Hot water out

Cold water in

Pump

Figure 17.4 A house with an active solar heating system has flat-plate collectors on the roof. Heat is absorbed by fluid in tubes. The fluid is pumped into the house. The hot fluid from the collectors can be used to heat water, as shown, or to heat a room.

The black metal plate in a flat-plate solar collector absorbs solar energy. Heat trapped in the collector by the glass can cause temperatures inside the collector to rise up to 200 °C. The heat is absorbed by the fluid in the tubes. Heated fluid is then pumped to a storage area, usually located in the basement of the building. The pumping system, which requires electricity, circulates the heated fluid throughout the building when needed. As the fluid cools, it is pumped back to the collector for reheating.

Active solar energy systems are being used successfully in many parts of the world. In areas where other fuel sources are scarce or too expensive, solar energy is a cost-effective heat source. For example, many people in Israel, India, Japan, and the West Indies use active solar energy for heating hot water or their homes.

Solar energy can be used to produce the steam needed to rotate the turbines that generate electricity. Scientists and engineers working in the Mojave Desert near Barstow, California, used more than 1800 giant mirrors to concentrate the sun's rays at one position. Enough heat was obtained to make steam. This steam was used to rotate turbines that generate electricity. This project, called Solar One, can produce enough electricity for a town of 10 000 people. The Solar One Facility is shown in Figure 17.2.

Photovoltaic Cells

Of all the devices that use solar energy, the solar cell, or photovoltaic cell, is the only one that produces electricity directly. *A* **photovoltaic** (FOH-toh-vol-TAY-ik) **cell**, *or PV cell, uses thin wafers*

Figure 17.5 A PV cell is made from two thin layers of semiconductor material. When energized by the sun, electrons move from the top layer to the bottom layer, making the top layer positively charged and the bottom layer negatively charged. This difference in charges forces electrons to flow through the circuit.

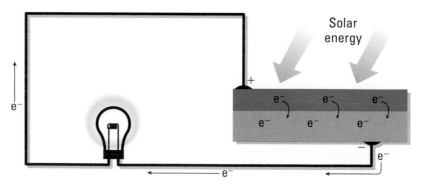

Solar energy

Figure 17.6 The GM Sunraycer is an experimental car that uses 7200 PV cells as its only energy source. This car raced more than 3000 km across Australia at an average speed of 67 km/h (about 43 mph).

of semiconductor material to produce electricity directly from solar energy. Semiconductors are made of elements such as silicon or selenium. These elements can conduct electricity very quickly when mixed with tiny amounts of other elements. A PV cell is made up of two thin slices of a semiconductor material joined together. Sunlight striking the cell causes electrons to move from one slice of the material to the other. This movement of electrons results in an electric current.

PV cells are commonly used today. For example, you may use a solar-powered calculator or wear a solar-powered watch that uses PV cells. PV cells are convenient to use because they are light-weight and produce no wastes or pollutants. They also have no moving parts, nor do they consume any materials, so they last a relatively long time. PV cells may have even more uses in the future. For example, most space satellites depend on PV cells for their power, and it is likely that they will continue to do so. PV cells can produce electricity for homes, industry, and some means of transportation. Currently, engineers are trying to develop economical solar-powered automobiles that will run as efficiently as gas-powered models.

Dateline 1958

PV cells made their debut in space aboard the *Vanguard I* space satellite, the second space satellite launched by the United States. Many satellites since the *Vanguard I* have made use of PV-cell technology.

SECTION REVIEW

1. How does active solar energy differ from passive solar energy?
2. List three electrical devices that currently make use of solar energy to operate.
3. How can solar-powered automobiles help reduce pollution?
4. **Evaluate** Suppose a classmate suggested that PV cells could be used to power street lights. Do you agree or disagree? Explain your response.

Storing Solar Energy

PROBLEM
Which materials store solar energy best?

MATERIALS (per group)
- 5 thermometers
- 5 250-mL beakers
- 3 sheets of newspaper
- large black cardboard box with lid
- stopwatch or clock
- wax marking pencil
- salt
- sand
- water at room temperature

PREDICTION
After reading the entire activity, predict which of the materials tested will store the most solar energy.

PROCEDURE
1. Using the wax marking pencil, label the five beakers *Sand, Salt, Water, Paper,* and *Air*.
2. Mark each beaker about seven-eighths of the way up from the bottom.
3. Pour sand up to the mark on the first beaker. Pour salt to the mark on the second beaker, and water to the mark on the third. In the fourth beaker, stuff crumpled newspaper up to the mark. Leave the fifth beaker empty.
4. On a separate sheet of paper, copy the data table shown.
5. Place a thermometer in each beaker, and record the starting temperature of each beaker in the data table.
6. Place all beakers inside the black box, and cover the box with the lid. Put the covered box in direct sunlight for 30 minutes. After the time has elapsed, record the temperatures from each beaker in the data table.
7. In a shaded area, remove the beakers from the box, and note the temperature changes after 5 min, 10 min, and 30 min. Record all temperatures in the data table.
8. Follow your teacher's instructions for disposal of all materials.

ANALYSIS
1. In which beaker did the temperature rise the most after being heated for 30 min? In which did it rise the least?
2. Rank the materials tested from the one that increased the most in temperature to the one that increased the least.
3. In which beaker did the temperature drop the fastest? In which did it drop the slowest?

CONCLUSION
1. From your test results, which substance has the best heat-storing capacity?
2. From the results of your investigation, explain why certain materials are used for the construction of solar panels on new homes.

	Sand	Salt	Water	Paper	Air
Room temperature					
After 30 min in sun					
5 min after removal from sun					
10 min after removal from sun					
30 min after removal from sun					

17.2 HYDROELECTRIC ENERGY

OBJECTIVES • ***Describe*** *two ways that moving water can be used to produce electricity.* • ***Discuss*** *the benefits and drawbacks of producing electricity through the use of hydroelectric power.*

The kinetic energy of flowing water can be used to produce electricity. *Electricity that is produced from the energy of moving water is called* **hydroelectric power**. Moving water is a nonpolluting energy source that is readily available in many areas. Producing electricity using hydroelectric power is less expensive than using fossil or nuclear fuels, although the initial costs of constructing plants can be high.

Energy from Flowing Streams

People have made use of the energy released by moving water for centuries. For example, waterwheels positioned on fast-moving rivers have been used for hundreds of years to grind grain. In the late 1800s, turbines were invented that could produce electricity from the energy of flowing water. Today, huge dams are built across waterways to generate electricity. Nearly 20 percent of the world's electricity is generated by flowing water.

To generate electricity, water behind a dam is directed at the blades of huge turbines. When water pushes against the turbine blades, the energy in the moving water is transferred to the turbine, causing it to turn. The motion of the spinning turbine is transferred to coils of wire located within generators. The coils spin through a magnetic field, producing electricity.

In addition to their use in producing hydroelectric energy, dams provide other benefits. Because dams control the flow of water, they are important in flood control. Dams also determine the speed at which water flows, which can help in the navigation of boats. Lakes created behind dams often serve as recreation areas for fishing, boating, and swimming. Dams also create reservoirs that store water for irrigation and for home use in towns and cities.

Figure 17.7 Dams and reservoirs provide many benefits to society, including recreation, flood control, and a reliable supply of fresh water. However, they can negatively impact existing ecosystems.

Figure 17.8 The rotation of turbines converts mechanical energy into electrical energy. In the case of a hydroelectric plant, the mechanical energy is supplied by flowing water.

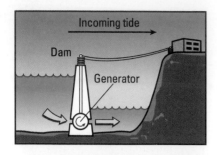

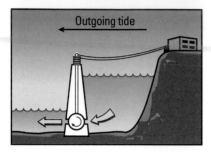

Figure 17.9 The turbines in the generator of a tidal energy system should be able to turn either way, according to the direction of the water flow. Tidal energy systems are effective only in places where the tide flows through an inlet, estuary, or other narrow opening.

Although dams have many benefits, they can also harm the environment. By altering water depth and flow, dams can alter the natural plant life of streams. Altering the plant life also alters the animal life. The rising and falling water level, both upstream and downstream from a dam, affects the food chain. There may also be flooding of the land behind the dam, leading to both shoreline erosion and a change in shoreline ecosystems.

Dams containing turbines pose a problem for fish living in the stream. Fishes may be caught in the blades of the turbine. Dams also interfere with the reproductive processes of some fish species. For example, adult salmon return to the stream where they were born to spawn. Dams create a barrier that prevents salmon from fulfilling their reproductive cycle.

Water stored behind dams often develops a cold bottom layer. When cool water from behind the dam is released through the dam, the cool water mixes with the warmer water downstream, resulting in rapid changes in temperature. Changes in temperature can upset the balance of an ecosystem by making it unsuitable for the organisms that are adapted to living in the water.

Energy from Tides

The tides of the ocean contain huge amounts of energy. Like the energy in streams, the energy in tides can be converted to electricity by rotating turbines inside dams. Figure 17.9 shows how the water moves through a tidal energy system. For maximum efficiency, the turbines in a tidal generator should be able to turn in both directions, depending on the direction of the tide.

So far, the use of tidal electrical generators is limited. A few operating tidal plants do exist, including ones in France and Nova Scotia, Canada. In most areas, the difference between high and low tide is insufficient to power a tidal generator. Also, there are serious environmental consequences associated with tidal generators. The project can damage wetlands surrounding the generator and affect the benthic community near the generator. Scientists are also studying the possibility of harnessing the energy in ocean waves to generate electricity.

SECTION REVIEW

1. What is hydroelectric power?
2. How might the formation of a reservoir behind a dam affect the environment?
3. **Justify** Do you think the benefits of generating hydroelectric power by using dams outweigh the drawbacks? Give reasons to support your response.

The Ocean Resource

What substance can be used to make electricity, air-condition buildings, raise prawns, and produce fresh water? Seawater! At Keahole Point, Hawaii, scientists use seawater to do all of these things.

The machinery at Keahole uses the temperature difference (about 20 °C in the tropics) between deep-ocean water and warm surface water to generate electricity. Pipes plunge 1000 m into cold deep water. Other pipes collect warm surface water. The water flows into a 13 m tall tower, called an ocean thermal energy conversion system, or OTEC.

The warm water enters a vacuum chamber where it becomes vapor. The vapor turns a turbine, generating about 210 kW of electricity. Compared to a nuclear reactor, which generates 1100 MW, this is not much power. But OTEC fuel is free, limitless, and non-polluting.

Pipes containing cold water make the vapor condense as fresh water. The fresh water—up to 5 L per 1000 L of seawater pumped through OTEC—can be used for drinking or irrigation.

The cool seawater continues its journey for use in air-conditioning. At the Keahole site, the 10 °C water cools several buildings, resulting in savings of $1300 each month in electrical bills.

The pipes containing cold seawater also run through a garden. The cool pipes cause water vapor in the humid air to condense and drip onto the soil as fresh water. Vegetables and fruits grow larger and sweeter than in most gardens as a result of the cooler temperatures and steady water supply. Note that it is not the seawater itself that is used for irrigation. It is the vapor in the air condensing on the cold pipes that provides fresh water.

The water has now been warmed to about 13 °C. In its final stop, the seawater is pumped to many small aquaculture businesses. The

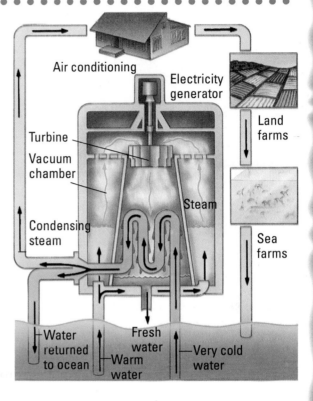

Air conditioning

Electricity generator

Turbine

Vacuum chamber

Steam

Condensing steam

Land farms

Sea farms

Water returned to ocean

Fresh water

Warm water

Very cold water

nutrient-rich ocean water nourishes seaweed, lobsters, and fish. Finally, the water is returned to the ocean.

Checkpoint

1. Do you think there are environmental problems caused by the OTEC systems described? Explain.

2. Compare the advantages and disadvantages of seawater used to generate electricity and a nuclear power plant.

17.3 WIND ENERGY

OBJECTIVES • *Explain* how the energy in wind can be used to produce electricity. • *Describe* some advantages and disadvantages of using wind energy.

In ancient times, Egyptians used wind to move their sailing ships. Babylonians used windmills to pump water to irrigate their land. Windmills are still in use today. They are used to grind grain, pump water, and generate electricity. *Windmills that are used to generate electricity are called wind turbine generators, or* **aerogenerators** (AYR-oh-GEN-er-ay-ters).

The use of wind power to generate electricity has many of the same advantages and disadvantages as the use of solar power. Like solar power, wind power is free, unlimited, and nonpolluting. Unfortunately, wind power is not constant or steady, and elaborate storage devices are needed to make wind power available during periods when there is no wind.

Today's windmills are constructed of strong, lightweight materials. Vanes of aerogenerators are connected to coils of wire. Winds blowing against the aerogenerator vanes cause the vanes to spin. As the vanes are turned by the wind, electricity is produced by a generator similar to the generator at a hydroelectric plant.

There are two different types of aerogenerators commonly in use. In traditional aerogenerators, the vanes turn on a horizontal axis. The vanes are shaped like the propeller of an airplane. This shape allows the vanes to turn at great speeds and generate large amounts of electricity. Aerogenerators with two or three very long vanes have proven to be the most efficient.

The other type of aerogenerator turns on a vertical axis and is shaped like an upside-down eggbeater. First patented in 1927 by G. J. M. Darrieus of France, the Darrieus rotor can produce electricity at a lower wind speed than is required by the traditional type.

Figure 17.10 People have been using wind power to provide energy for hundreds of years. Windmills have traditionally been used to pump water and grind grain.

Figure 17.11 Traditional aerogenerators (left) can produce large amounts of electricity, but require high wind conditions. The Darrieus rotor (right) cannot produce as much electricity, but it can operate effectively under calmer wind conditions.

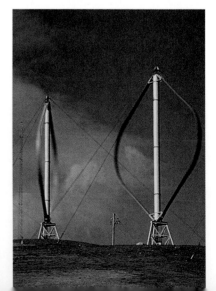

Figure 17.12 Wind farms require large amounts of land. Fortunately, the high-wind conditions that make a location attractive for a wind farm often make the area undesirable for other development.

Wind farms are sites where many aerogenerators are placed together. Wind farms are located in open areas where wind conditions are favorable. Favorable conditions include steady winds of at least 15 mph every day. One such place is Altamont Pass near San Francisco. There are more than 7000 aerogenerators in this area. There are many other wind farms in California and throughout the world. At the end of 1996, the global wind-generating capacity was equivalent to six typical modern nuclear reactors. The number of wind farms around the world continues to increase.

Wind energy is not without its problems. As you have learned, winds are not always steady or strong enough. Wind farms take up a lot of land, which means that they must be located far from heavily populated areas where the price of land is high. They may also interfere with radio and television reception. Birds may be severely injured when they fly into the spinning vanes of the aerogenerators. This is a particular concern in California, where the wind farms are located near sensitive habitats of the endangered California condor. Some people consider aerogenerators to be ugly, disturbing the look of the otherwise natural landscape. In addition, the current cost of constructing towers and generators is fairly high.

LINK

Literature

Cervantes' epic tale *Don Quixote* makes extensive use of windmills as part of its story line. Read the story of Don Quixote, and write a report that explains the importance of windmills to the plot.

SECTION REVIEW

1. What is an aerogenerator?
2. List several benefits and drawbacks to using wind as a source for producing electricity.
3. **Analyze** Do you think it is likely that aerogenerators could be used to produce electricity in the region where you live? Explain your response.

17.4 GEOTHERMAL ENERGY AND NUCLEAR FUSION

OBJECTIVES • *Describe* how geothermal energy is used.
• *Explain* how nuclear fusion could be a valuable source of energy in the future.

The most important source of Earth's energy is the sun, but it is not the only source. Earth itself generates heat energy deep below its surface by the decay of radioactive elements. Imagine the energy that could be made available if people could use the energy of the planet itself. Perhaps even more attractive would be the possibility of reproducing the reactions that release energy in the sun. Geothermal energy makes use of the energy inside Earth. Nuclear fusion, the process that produces the sun's energy, may be the answer to the energy needs of the future.

Geothermal Energy

The heat energy generated within Earth is called **geothermal energy**. Geothermal energy is generated by the decay of radioactive elements deep beneath the ground. As these elements decay, they give off energy in the form of heat. Depending on the location, temperatures can rise between 30 °C and 45 °C with every kilometer of depth.

Enough heat is present deep within Earth to melt rock. This molten rock is called *magma*. The lava that flows from volcanoes is magma that has reached the surface. Rocks closer to the surface are also heated by geothermal energy. Water that collects near the heated rocks is heated and may be changed to steam. Cracks in the rocks allow steam, hot water, and heat to escape to the surface. Geysers, steam vents, hot springs, and bubbling mud are heated by geothermal energy.

Geothermal energy is used in some regions where the source of the energy is near the surface. In both ancient and modern times, steam baths have been common in areas where steam and hot water come to the surface naturally. In 1904 in Larderello, Italy, an engine driven by natural steam was connected to an electric generator. This was the first attempt to produce electricity from Earth's heat. Today, there are about 250 geothermal electrical plants operating around the world.

Worldwide, at least 20 nations are using geothermal energy to heat homes. Most of Iceland obtains its energy from geothermal energy. About 65 percent of the homes in Iceland are heated using geothermal energy. Fresh vegetables are grown in heated greenhouses during the long winter. In addition to using geothermal

Figure 17.13 Energy from radioactive decay inside Earth heats the water that flows underground in certain areas, resulting in hot springs and geysers.

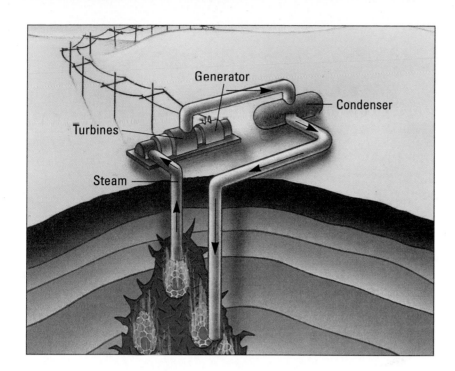

Figure 17.14 Hot rocks below the surface heat water pumped into the ground in pipes. The heat turns the water to steam, which turns the turbines.

energy for home heating, some areas in New Zealand, Japan, and China are producing electricity from geothermal energy. In the United States, some parts of California and Hawaii also use geothermal energy to generate electricity.

There are several methods used to extract usable energy from geothermal sources. One method that is commonly used involves hot-rock zones. Hot-rock zones are areas where the bedrock is heated by magma below the surface. A simplified diagram of a hot-rock extraction system is shown in Figure 17.14. Explosives are used to break up a portion of the bedrock. Cool water is pumped into the area of hot, broken rocks. The water turns to steam, forming a steam reservoir underground. The steam is then extracted through additional pipes and used to rotate turbines that produce electricity.

Using geothermal energy to produce electricity has both advantages and disadvantages. Most areas do not have enough concentrated geothermal heat to be worth the cost of extraction. Suitable geothermal areas are not always easy to locate. In some areas that have adequate geothermal energy sources, the air is naturally polluted by toxic hydrogen sulfide gas that is given off along with the heat. Mineral wastes, salts, and toxic metals are also abundant in geothermal areas. These waste products tend to corrode the pipes and boilers that carry the steam and water heated by geothermal energy. Another problem with geothermal energy is the lack of an adequate water supply for the production of steam. It is often too expensive to pipe water over long distances for use in the production of electricity.

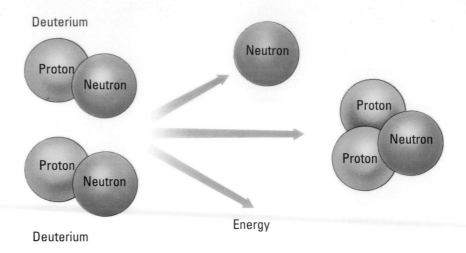

Figure 17.15 In nuclear fusion, two deuterium nuclei fuse to become a helium-3 nucleus. Extra mass is converted to energy.

Social Studies

Some energy analysts have estimated that, at the present rate of consumption, fusion of the deuterium in seawater could meet the world's energy needs for tens of millions of years.

Nuclear Fusion

Perhaps one of the most promising potential sources of energy for the future is nuclear fusion. **Nuclear fusion** (NOO-klee-er FYOO-zhun) *occurs when two atomic nuclei fuse to become one larger nucleus.* Do not confuse nuclear fusion with nuclear fission, in which nuclei are split. Nuclear fusion is the source of the energy given off by the sun. Although nuclear fusion reactions can produce enormous amounts of energy, scientists have not yet learned to control and harness this energy and use it efficiently.

The fuel for nuclear fusion reactions is usually deuterium, the H-2 isotope of hydrogen. Deuterium is fairly common in seawater, and is therefore abundant in nature. In nuclear fusion, the deuterium nuclei are subjected to enormous pressure and temperature, supplied either by a magnetic field or by laser beams, until the nuclei collapse into a single nucleus. So far, controlled and sustained fusion reactions are still in the developmental stage and are not yet a commercially available energy source.

In theory, nuclear fusion has many advantages over most other energy sources. Much less radioactive waste is produced by fusion than by traditional nuclear fission energy. Also, the fuel is more easily obtained. Unfortunately, technology will have to overcome many roadblocks before nuclear fusion can become a source of usable energy.

SECTION REVIEW

1. Describe what occurs during the process of nuclear fusion.
2. How can geothermal energy be used to provide usable energy for people?
3. **Analyze** Could geothermal energy be used as a source of energy in the region where you live? Explain.

CHAPTER 17 REVIEW

KEY TERMS

solar energy 17.1
passive solar heating 17.1
active solar heating 17.1

photovoltaic (PV) cell 17.1
hydroelectric power 17.2
aerogenerator 17.3

geothermal energy 17.4
nuclear fusion 17.4

CHAPTER SUMMARY

17.1 Solar energy, the energy of the sun, is the main source of energy on Earth. Solar energy can be used to heat homes either passively or actively. Photovoltaic (PV) cells convert the sun's energy to electricity. In the future, solar energy may provide the best alternative to the use of fossil, biomass, and nuclear fuels.

17.2 Electricity produced from the energy of flowing water is called hydroelectric power. Hydroelectric power makes use of dams containing turbines to generate electricity. Hydroelectric power is renewable and nonpolluting, but does threaten some parts of the environment.

17.3 Aerogenerators are devices that use the energy of wind to produce electricity. Aerogenerators may be clustered in areas called wind farms. Wind is a renewable, nonpolluting energy source, but it is not a practical source of energy in all parts of the world.

17.4 Geothermal energy is the energy produced by heat deep below Earth's surface. Geothermal energy has limited use because it is not available in many places. Nuclear fusion is a potential source of huge amounts of energy, but scientists have not yet learned to control and efficiently use this energy.

MULTIPLE CHOICE

Choose the letter of the word or phrase that best completes each statement.

1. Of the following, the energy source that can be used in the greatest number of areas is (a) geothermal energy; (b) wind energy; (c) hydroelectric power; (d) solar energy.
2. Aerogenerators are used to produce electricity from (a) wind; (b) moving water; (c) the sun; (d) heat inside Earth.
3. Photovoltaic cells convert the energy of the sun to (a) heat; (b) light; (c) electricity; (d) fuel.
4. The production of electricity from moving water is called (a) solar energy; (b) wind energy; (c) hydroelectric power; (d) geothermal energy.
5. Iceland is a country that makes extensive use of (a) solar energy; (b) nuclear energy; (c) fossil fuels; (d) geothermal energy.

6. A characteristic common to all the alternative energy sources discussed in this chapter is that they (a) can be produced anywhere; (b) do not use fossil fuels; (c) are nonrenewable; (d) must be used along with fossil fuels.
7. The sun is not involved in providing the energy in (a) wind energy; (b) hydroelectric energy; (c) solar energy; (d) geothermal energy.
8. Photovoltaic cells are used to provide the energy for all of the following except (a) passive solar heating systems; (b) space satellites; (c) calculators; (d) wristwatches.
9. Nuclear fusion (a) produces no wastes; (b) uses fuels that are difficult to obtain; (c) is not yet available; (d) is an inexpensive energy source.
10. The tubes in a solar collector are filled with (a) metal; (b) solid; (c) fluid; (d) insulation.

WORD COMPARISONS

Write the letter of the second word pair that best matches the first pair.

1. Hydroelectric power: moving water as
   (a) solar energy: light; (b) wind energy: moving air; (c) heat: geothermal energy; (d) solar cells: electricity.
2. Windows: passive solar heating as (a) PV cells: active solar heating; (b) PV cells: flat-plate collectors; (c) flat-plate collector: active solar heating; (d) solar energy: sun.
3. Nuclear fusion: nuclear fission as

(a) addition: division; (b) subtraction: multiplication; (c) division: multiplication; (d) subtraction: addition.

4. Dams: hydroelectric power as (a) solar collectors: passive solar heating; (b) solar collectors: electricity; (c) solar collectors: active solar energy; (d) aerogenerators: geothermal energy.
5. Magma: geothermal energy as (a) PV cells: active solar energy; (b) wind: air; (c) fusion: solar energy; (d) water: dams.

CONCEPT REVIEW

Write a complete response for each of the following.

1. What are some advantages of using solar energy instead of fossil fuels?
2. Discuss how geothermal energy, solar energy, wind energy, and hydroelectric power conserve fossil fuels and reduce pollution.
3. What are the ways wind energy is used today?
4. Why is the sun considered a renewable resource?
5. What factors limit the use of geothermal energy?

THINK CRITICALLY

1. If you were going to use one of the alternative energy sources mentioned in this chapter to heat your home, which would you use? Explain your choice.
2. Explain how the sun is involved in the availability of solar energy, wind energy, and hydroelectric power.
3. Deep ocean vents give off heat produced by geothermal energy. Do you think it is possible and practical to harness the energy given off by these vents for use in home heating systems? Why or why not?
4. Explain the benefits and drawbacks of hydroelectric power to people, other organisms, and the environment.
5. Explain how generators are used to produce electricity from moving water and wind.

WRITE FOR UNDERSTANDING

Suppose your utility company is planning to build a wind farm on the outskirts of town. Write a letter to your local newspaper supporting or opposing the construction. Defend your point of view.

PORTFOLIO

1. Find out what types of energy sources are used in your community. If possible, make a videotape of sites using alternative energy sources.
2. Conduct library research to find information on other methods people of the past or present have used to meet their energy needs. Make a poster that summarizes your findings.

GRAPHIC ANALYSIS

Use Figure 17.4 to answer the following.
1. Look at the diagram of active solar heating. Does the liquid that flows through the collector need to be replaced when the shower is used? Why or why not?
2. If the house using this system was in Argentina, which direction should the collectors face?
3. If this active solar heating system was to be used to heat a room, how would this diagram be different? On a separate piece of paper, sketch a diagram of the system.

ACTIVITY 17.2

PROBLEM
How does the design of a windmill affect its ability to harness wind?

MATERIALS (per group)
- hand drill
- hammer
- scrap wood
- bolts
- washers
- 3 nuts
- 3 or 4 foil pie tins
- crayon
- thread spool
- scissors
- protractor
- clock or watch with second hand
- electric fan (1 per class)

HYPOTHESIS
After reading the entire activity, write a hypothesis that explains how the design of a windmill affects its ability to use wind power to do work.

PROCEDURE
1. Break up into groups of three or four students. One person per group makes the handle of the windmill by drilling a small hole through a piece of scrap wood.
2. Each group makes windmill blades of its own design. Use the pie tins for the blades, and experiment with different shapes, lengths, and number of blades. *Note: When constructing the blades, think about the best lengths combined with the best angles.* Measure and record the angle of the blades with a protractor.
3. Fasten the windmill blades to a thread spool with the long bolt. Secure the blades, spool, and handle with the washers, nuts, and bolts as shown in the figure. Fasten the bolts lightly so that the blades can rotate freely.
4. With a crayon, make a mark at the edge of one of the blades. This mark will help you count the number of times the windmill turns per minute.
5. While holding the windmill 1 m away from an electric fan, count the number of revolutions the windmill makes in 1 min.
6. One person from each group makes a table with these headings: *Number of Blades, Diameter of Windmill (cm), Angle of Blades,* and *Turns in 1 min.*

ANALYSIS
1. What factors have the greatest effect on the speed of the windmill?
2. Why do you think many new windmills have only two blades?

CONCLUSION
Based on the findings of your group, what windmill design is the most effective at harnessing wind power?

LOTS $ FOR SALE!

From Brownfields to Buildings

Abandoned factories and warehouses are common sights in cities. In the past, developers did not want to buy such properties because of the possibility they were contaminated with heavy metals or other pollutants. The purchaser of such a property became responsible for cleaning up the pollution, even if the pollution was caused by a previous owner. Abandoned properties that may have environmental contaminants on the site are called *brownfields.*

Now, in many cities, developers are buying brownfield sites as more and more states enact brownfield legislation. The new laws provide for tax incentives and loans for developers who buy, clean up, and redevelop brownfield sites. These projects are being started and managed by the private sector. The state and local governments assist, as does the Environmental Protection Agency, but they do not control the projects.

One such success story is in Dallas, Texas, where brownfield laws have streamlined the testing and paperwork by combining the regulations of several agencies into one set of rules. After developers removed all contaminated soil from an 22-acre site, they were able to pass their inspections and construct an apartment complex. The first units were ready in 1997.

Although brownfield development costs more than development of clean land, there are few clean undeveloped lots in downtown areas. Therefore, if developers want to build an apartment or office building downtown, a brownfield lot can be a promising opportunity. If the brownfield movement is successful, more and more cities will see crumbling, dangerous eyesores transformed into clean places to live, work, or shop.

✔ Checkpoint

1. Why can buying a brownfield be a risk for a developer?

2. One developer said that you can't put a price tag on some aspects of these developments. What do you think this statement means?

New legislation provides tax incentives for developers to transform contaminated and abandoned factories into places to live and work.

Hazardous-Wastes Lawyers ▶

These lawyers, working together with other specialists in the hazardous-wastes field, determine the financial costs of damages due to hazardous-wastes contamination. They prepare court cases and may represent the companies responsible for dumping the hazardous materials. They may also represent the people and communities that are directly affected by a hazardous spill or accident.

◀ Hazardous-Materials Specialists

These professionals are experts in identifying hazardous wastes at an affected site. They are responsible for handling, transporting, and disposing of toxic substances. Hazardous-materials specialists are called upon to assess damage at large hazardous-wastes sites, such as Love Canal. Others may evaluate the impact of chemicals used by local unregulated businesses on the environment.

Household Hazardous-Wastes Coordinators ▲

Hazardous-wastes coordinators work in local governments to educate the public about common household hazardous wastes. They inform the community about the best methods of disposal and offer suggestions as to what nontoxic substitutes can be safely used in the home. They also coordinate grassroots efforts to collect and dispose of household toxic pollutants in their communities.

For More Information

American Chemical Society
1155 16th Street NW
Washington, DC 20039
(202) 872-4600
http://www.acs.org/

Citizens' Clearinghouse for Hazardous Wastes (CCHW)
Center for Health, Environment, and Justice
150 S. Washington, Suite 300
P.O. Box 6806
Falls Church, VA 22040
(703) 237-2249
http://www.essential.org/cchw/

Center for Hazardous Materials Research
320 William Pitt Way
Pittsburgh, PA 15238
http://www.chmr.org/

UNIT 6

RESOURCES

IN THE BIOSPHERE

CHAPTERS

I f you have ever seen a previously vacant lot or field transformed into a new development of buildings, then you have witnessed the need for resources such as land. Land is a valuable resource that is able to provide living space, important minerals, and a place for growing crops. Because a given area of land is limited in its uses, humans must decide how the land will be used. Choosing one particular use of the land often prevents it from being used in other ways. This photograph shows a newly built housing development among the fields in Napa Valley, California. In this unit, you will learn more about the value of natural resources such as land, water, and air.

Discover It!

You and Your Resources

Every day you are required to make decisions about how you will use a particular resource, such as food, money, or the television. By choosing one use, you give up other alternative uses.

1. Make a list of your daily activities that require the use of water.

2. If you had enough water to do only three of these activities, which three would you choose? Explain.

PLANETDIARY.COM

You can find out more about resources in the biosphere by exploring the following Internet address: http://www.planetdiary.com

CHAPTER

18

MINERALS AND SOILS

Stone Age, *Bronze Age*, and *Iron Age* refer to time periods in many human cultures when technological breakthroughs influenced the course of human history. Stone, bronze, and iron are all made of minerals. The Iron Age began about 3000 years ago in some cultures. Today's technology is still deeply rooted in the use of minerals.

R. Neil Sampson, an expert in agriculture, once wrote, "We stand only six inches away from desolation, for that is the thickness of the topsoil layer upon which the entire life of the planet depends." The food that every land organism needs comes from the soil. However, soil mismanagement threatens this 6-in. lifeline.

18.1 MINERALS AND THEIR USES

OBJECTIVES • **_Describe_** minerals and identify some of their characteristics. • **_List_** several ways that minerals are used.

Humans and other organisms use nutrients contained in food to carry out their life processes. For example, human bodies use iron, a nutrient found in meat and grains, to help blood carry oxygen from the lungs to every cell of the body. Many of the nutrients needed for daily life are made of substances that are also important for science and industry. Those substances are called _minerals_.

Characteristics of Minerals

To be defined as a mineral, a substance must possess specific characteristics. _A_ **mineral** _is an inorganic, naturally occurring, solid material with a definite chemical composition, and with its atoms arranged in a specific pattern._ Do you think coal can be considered a mineral?

Minerals may be either elements or compounds. Elements are substances that are made up of one kind of atom. For example, gold (Au) is a mineral that is made up of one kind of atom. Quartz (SiO_2) is an example of a mineral made of a compound of the elements silicon (Si) and oxygen (O). Elements and minerals may be metals, such as gold, or nonmetals, such as quartz.

Rocks are composed of one or more minerals. For example, the granite shown in Figure 18.2 is a rock composed mostly of the minerals quartz, feldspar, and biotite.

Some metals, like gold and copper (Cu), can be found in Earth's crust as pure elements. However, most metals and nonmetals occur as part of compounds. _Rocks or minerals that contain economically desirable metals or nonmetals are called_ **ores**. For example, the mineral hematite shown in Figure 18.2 is an ore from which the valuable metal iron (Fe) can be obtained.

Figure 18.1 This family in Japan is enjoying a healthy meal of rice and fish. The nutrients in the rice come from the minerals in soil. The fish also provides valuable nutrients.

Figure 18.2 Granite (left) is a rock made mostly of the minerals quartz (clear), feldspar (pink), and biotite (black). The mineral hematite (right) is an ore that can be processed to obtain iron.

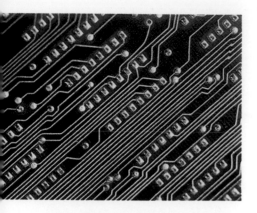

Figure 18.3 The sand that is found on beaches or in streams is made up of quartz. This mineral contains silicon, which is used to make the microprocessors that go into powerful computers.

Table 18.1 Some Minerals and Their Common Uses

Mineral	Uses
Copper	Electrical wiring, water pipes
Aluminum	Packaging for foods and beverages, airplanes
Lead	Car batteries, paint
Gypsum	Concrete, wallboard
Iron	Automobiles, construction
Quartz	Glass, microprocessors
Gold	Electronics, aerospace, jewelry
Silver	Photography, jewelry
Sulfur	Batteries

Uses of Metals and Nonmetals

Most metals, including iron, lead, and aluminum, occur naturally in ores. These ores must be refined and heated in order to extract the desired metal. The process of heating and refining an ore to separate the valuable material is called *smelting.*

Metals have several properties that make them important in technology and industry. Metals are *ductile* (DUK-til), or able to be pulled and stretched into wires. They are also *malleable* (MAL-ee-uh-bul), or able to be hammered and shaped without breaking. These two properties make metals ideal for construction and other industries. Another property of metals is that they are good *conductors,* materials that allow electricity and heat to flow through them. This additional property makes metals such as copper and gold especially important for use in electronic devices.

Ores containing nonmetals are also useful. Nonmetallic minerals such as sulfur, gypsum, and halite (common table salt) are valuable resources. Sulfur is used to make sulfuric acid, the acid in car batteries. Gypsum may be used in concrete for construction. Table 18.1 shows several minerals and their common uses.

Every mineral has distinct properties. These properties are like fingerprints that can be used to identify the mineral. Some mineral properties are color, hardness, cleavage, and fracture. Cleavage and fracture refer to the way a mineral breaks apart. Other mineral properties are luster, crystal shape, and streak. *Luster* refers to the way a mineral reflects light from its surface. *Streak* is the color of the mineral's powder.

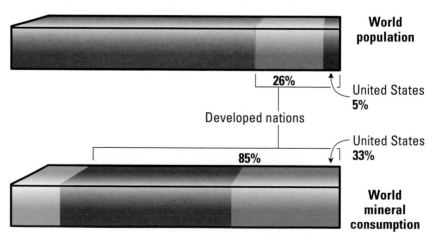

World population

26%
Developed nations
United States 5%

United States 33%

85%

World mineral consumption

Figure 18.4 The use of minerals in the United States is enormous compared to that of other nations with larger populations. Because the United States is an industrial nation, the need for mineral resources is great.

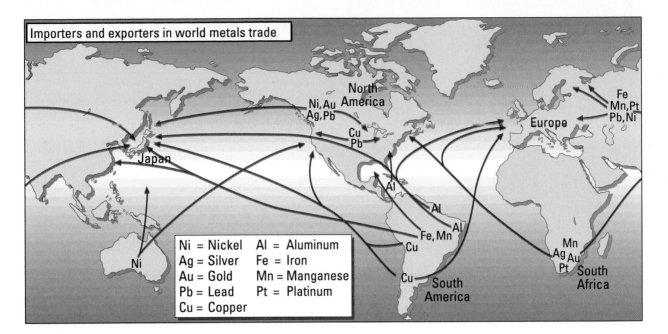

Importers and exporters in world metals trade

North America — Ni, Au, Ag, Pb — Cu, Pb

Europe

Fe
Mn, Pt
Pb, Ni

Japan

Al

Al

Fe, Mn

Cu

Cu

Cu
South America

Mn
Ag Au
Pt South Africa

Ni

Ni = Nickel   Al = Aluminum
Ag = Silver   Fe = Iron
Au = Gold   Mn = Manganese
Pb = Lead   Pt = Platinum
Cu = Copper

Figure 18.5 The human dependence on metals derived from minerals connects the nations of the world in a global import and export system.

Metals in International Trade

Metals derived from minerals are crucial to economic and technological development. Industry and agriculture rely heavily on metals for machinery and building materials. If key metals such as iron or aluminum were unavailable, the industries that form the basis of industrial societies would be crippled. To prevent this, some nations store 3- to 5-year reserves of scarce metals.

The unequal natural distribution of metals, such as those shown in Figure 18.5, adds to an interdependence among the global community. Some metals occur only in specific areas of the world. The political, environmental, and economic stability of nations in these areas is vital on a local level and on an international level. Nations that depend on resources from unstable regions are vulnerable to the changes in those regions.

In 1971, poor management and sabotage of copper mines in Chile resulted in decreased production of copper. Copper mines were deliberately destroyed because of land use disputes and disagreements over wages for miners. The decreased production of copper forced the government of Chile to decrease payments of debts owed to the United States.

SECTION REVIEW

1. What is a mineral?
2. **Identify** five minerals or metals and list the ways they may be used.
3. **Compare** How does the amount of mineral resources used by the United States compare with that of all other nations?

18.2 OBTAINING MINERALS

OBJECTIVES • *Describe* methods for extracting minerals.
• *Identify* and *explain* ways in which extraction methods may affect the environment.

People who study Earth and earth processes, such as earthquakes and volcanoes, are called earth scientists. These scientists use their knowledge of minerals and earth processes to determine where minerals of economic or scientific value are located. Drill core samples, satellite imagery, and aerial photography are useful aids for locating minerals.

Mining and the Environment

Different methods are used to extract minerals depending on where they are located. Those minerals at or near the surface are often removed by surface mining. Minerals located deep below the surface are extracted by subsurface mining. Minerals may also be removed by a method called *dredging.*

Surface Mining   In surface mining, layers of rock, soil, and vegetation are removed to uncover mineral deposits. A common method of surface mining, shown in Figure 18.8, is called *open-pit mining.* In open-pit mining, large machines are used to dig ore from huge holes in the ground. Bulldozers and power shovels gather the ore for processing. Large deposits of discarded materials, called *tailings,* are left near the mines in heaps known as *spoil piles.* Tailings often contain toxic substances in the form of heavy metals such as lead and copper. Heavy metals are poisonous to living things.

Figure 18.6 Studies of core samples give earth scientists an idea of where to look for minerals. By tracing sediments back to their source, scientists can determine where the minerals in the sediments originated.

Figure 18.7 A pick and shovel are no longer enough to extract the minerals needed by technology and industry today. Giant power shovels are used to dig out the mineral deposits held in Earth's crust.

Figure 18.8 Open-pit mines are dug in order to extract mineral ores. Open-pit mining can form deep depressions where hills once stood.

Tailings in spoil piles can be eroded by wind and running water. Winds may carry dust and harmful particles, such as lead, arsenic, and sulfur. Rainwater may leach through spoil piles and pollute groundwater, or carry toxic materials into fields or streams. Open-pit mines often fill with water that becomes polluted. In time, this process affects the groundwater in the area.

Subsurface Mining   In subsurface mining, shown in Figure 18.9, a shaft is dug into the crust. When the mineral deposit is reached, explosives are used to expose the minerals. Machinery is then lowered into the shaft to loosen the mineral deposits and bring them to the surface.

Subsurface mining creates less environmental damage than surface mining, but it is more dangerous to the workers. Walls, ceilings, and underground chambers and tunnels may collapse, trapping miners. Miners are also in danger of explosions of natural gas and dust in the mines. In addition, dust inhaled over long periods of time can cause life-threatening lung diseases.

Figure 18.9 Subsurface mining requires a complex network of tunnels and shafts to remove the minerals from deep deposits.

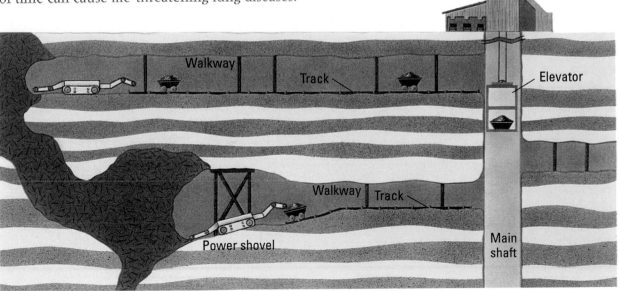

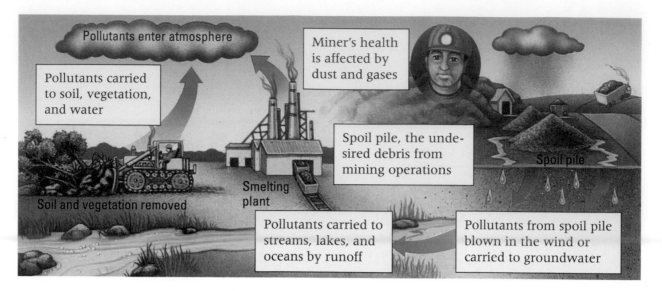

Inside figure labels:
- Pollutants enter atmosphere
- Pollutants carried to soil, vegetation, and water
- Miner's health is affected by dust and gases
- Spoil pile, the undesired debris from mining operations
- Spoil pile
- Soil and vegetation removed
- Smelting plant
- Pollutants carried to streams, lakes, and oceans by runoff
- Pollutants from spoil pile blown in the wind or carried to groundwater

Figure 18.10 The extraction and processing of minerals for use in industry and agriculture can have harmful effects on the environment.

Dredging Dredging involves scraping or vacuuming desirable minerals from ocean floors, lake bottoms, and streambeds. Dredging is used to obtain sand and gravel for construction. Dredging is also used to clear away the sand and silt that accumulate at harbor mouths or behind dams.

Many people are concerned about the dredging of the ocean floor. They feel that removing organisms and nutrients may alter complex aquatic food webs. They also question the effects dredging may have on currents, coral reefs, and beaches.

Other environmental damage caused by mineral extraction is caused by smelting and heap leaching processes. Recall that smelting is the removal of desirable materials from ores. Smelting generates about 8 percent of the worldwide sulfur dioxide emissions. Sulfur dioxide is one of the chemicals that causes acid precipitation, which is discussed in Chapter 22. Smelting also emits large volumes of arsenic and lead into the atmosphere. These toxic metals contribute

Figure 18.11 Dredging may disturb the food chains in certain ecosystems. Dredgers scrape sediments from streambeds and ocean floors, possibly removing nutrients needed by organisms.

Figure 18.12 A pile of used cars is far from worthless. The energy it takes to recycle the metal in dumps and junkyards is far less than the amount of energy it takes to process new metal materials. Recycling this metal reduces the demand for new material.

to the formation of large areas where plant and animal life cannot live. For example, one smelting plant in Canada is surrounded by about 10 000 hectares of dead landscape.

Heap leaching, a process used to extract gold, involves the use of cyanide, a poisonous chemical sprayed over piles of ore. The cyanide dissolves gold and leaches it from the crushed ore. The gold is then collected from the cyanide liquid. Cyanide collection ponds can contaminate groundwater and are responsible for the deaths of thousands of birds every year.

Mineral Conservation

Some experts warn that the major ore deposits of over a dozen important minerals and metals may be depleted in only a few decades. These materials include gold, silver, mercury, and sulfur. Effective resource management is needed to prevent this depletion.

Plans for mineral resource management and conservation have been suggested and implemented by concerned groups in government, industry, and in communities. These plans include recycling, substitution, and reuse. In *recycling*, waste materials are treated and used to make more products. *Substitution* uses an abundant material, instead of a less plentiful one, to make products. *Reuse* is using the same product over and over again.

SECTION REVIEW

1. What is substitution?
2. List three methods that are used to extract minerals. Describe how each method is carried out.
3. **Infer** How can recycling and reuse reduce pollution?

Coming Apart at the Seam

The mountains of eastern Pennsylvania contain deposits of anthracite coal. In some places, these deposits, called coal seams, are near the surface of the ground. Mines were opened at these points, and the tunnels followed the coal seams deep into the mountains.

With the growth of the mining industry came the development of many towns. One such town is Centralia, which is literally sitting on top of a maze of old tunnels.

In 1962, a waste dump that was on top of the coal seam caught fire. The fire spread to the coal seam and has been burning ever since. Because of the limited availability of oxygen, this fire is not blazing. It is slowly smoldering beneath Earth's surface, and it won't go out.

As the coal seam burned away, the land that it had been supporting collapsed. In 1981, a huge hole opened, and the fire could be seen along the side of a cliff. After a few months, a rock slide covered the hole, but the fire continued to burn. Around this time, the residents in Centralia began to discover other evidence of the fire that burned beneath them. One resident couldn't keep the furnace in the basement burning because

This coal seam has been burning in Centralia, Pennsylvania, since 1962.

there was so little oxygen. Another resident nearly died because of the level of carbon monoxide in his home.

Residents had much to worry about. There was the possibility of further sinking of the ground and new surface fires. There was also the possibility of carbon monoxide poisoning inside their homes. Carbon monoxide monitors were installed in homes, and attempts were made to put out the fire. With many small cracks in the land above the coal seam acting as vents, attempts to smother the fire failed.

When it became clear that there was no way to stop the fire, the state and federal government offered to buy the homes in the

affected part of town. This provided homeowners with the opportunity to relocate somewhere away from the fire. At first, many residents refused to go. But eventually, most agreed to the buyout and moved away. Now, only a few families remain in the otherwise deserted town. And the fire continues to burn beneath them.

Checkpoint

1. What were the dangers to people living in Centralia in the 1980s?
2. What would you have done if you had lived in Centralia in 1981? Explain your answer.

18.3 SOIL AND ITS FORMATION

OBJECTIVES • *Identify* different soil types and how they influence soil characteristics. • *Describe* the relationship between climate and soil formation.

Soil is home for many organisms. Some of these organisms, such as earthworms, aerate the soil and contribute to its formation. All organisms that live in the soil are vital to the energy and nutrient cycles of Earth.

Soil Formation

Wherever rock is exposed to changing conditions, either at or near Earth's surface, it will break down, or weather, into smaller and smaller fragments. The weathering of exposed rock may occur mechanically or chemically. An example of mechanical weathering is the pounding of waves on a sea cliff. An example of chemical weathering is the oxidation, or rusting, of iron-containing minerals, such as biotite, in granite.

The igneous, metamorphic, and sedimentary rock of the lithosphere that may exist as mountains, cliffs, or low-lying plains is called **bedrock**. As the solid bedrock weathers, it supplies the material needed to build soil. *An area of bedrock that is the source of an area of soil is called the soil's* **parent rock**.

The exposed outer layers of a rock are the most unprotected and easily weathered layers. It is the outer layer that begins to change in structure, with cracks and holes beginning to develop, as in Figure 18.13. With time and further weathering, cracks and holes reach deeper and deeper into the bedrock, and the outer layer becomes broken into smaller mineral particles. **Soil** *is a mixture of mineral particles, air, water, and living and decaying organisms.* Hundreds to thousands of years may be required to form just 10 cm of soil.

The organic activity of plants and animals can also influence the weathering and structure of soil and bedrock. Burrowing animals and plant roots mechanically break down bedrock and aerate the soil. Many organisms aerate the soil enough for water and air to

Figure 18.13 Not all soils form at the same rate, but all are formed from parent rock. The hard bedrock begins to weather because of temperature changes and moisture (left). Holes and cracks develop deeper in the rock as the layer above weathers into smaller and smaller pieces (center). Layers of small particles sit on top of larger particles, which in turn sit on the original bedrock (right).

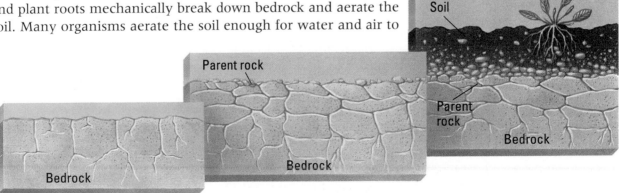

Soil

Parent rock

Parent rock

Bedrock

Bedrock

Bedrock

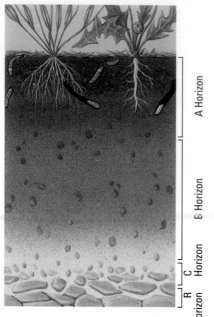

Figure 18.14 A mature soil profile contains layers, or horizons, commonly known as topsoil, subsoil, and parent rock. However, soil scientists often divide these layers further into many horizons to describe them in greater detail.

Figure 18.15 Particle size and mixture determine, in part, whether or not plants will grow in an area of soil. The sand particles (left) enable soil to drain well but dry out quickly. Clay particles (center) are flat and trap water, preventing water drainage. Loam soil (right) contains a mixture of particle sizes that provides good drainage and moisture for plant roots.

reach deeper into it. Water and air carry with them agents of chemical weathering, such as carbon dioxide and oxygen. When soil organisms die, they again contribute to the soil by becoming the organic material of humus.

As weathering progresses, distinct layers of weathered bedrock become apparent. These layers, shown in Figure 18.14, form what are known as the A, B, C, and R horizons in a mature soil profile. A **soil profile** *is a vertical cross section of soil from the ground surface down to the bedrock.* The A horizon in a soil profile is commonly known as the topsoil. The B horizon is often called the subsoil. However, the C horizon is a layer of partially weathered parent rock. The R horizon is the bedrock.

Composition and Characteristics of Soil

Although there are thousands of different types of soil, the simplest separation of soils is into three major soil textures, based on the sizes of the particles within them. It should be noted, however, that the mixture of the particles is equally important to the classification of soil. The three major soil textures, shown in Figure 18.15, are sandy, clay, and loam.

In *sandy soils*, most of the mineral grains vary in size from 0.05 to 2.0 mm in diameter. Soil that contains a high number of clay-sized grains (smaller than 0.002 mm in diameter each) are called *clay soils*. Mineral grains from 0.002 to 0.05 mm in diameter are called *silt*. Soils containing roughly equal amounts of sand, clay, and silt particles are called loam soils.

The sizes and amounts of mineral particles, or grains, in the soil determine some characteristics of the soil. Sandy soil has good drainage and good aeration, but it does not store water very well. This characteristic makes sandy soil unsuitable for many plants. Clay soils, however, hold water very well, but they do not drain well and do not contain much space for air. Clay soils are also unlikely to sustain many plants. Loam soils, on the other hand, with their even mixture of different particle sizes, are ideal for many plants. The even mixture enables loam soils to hold water and air.

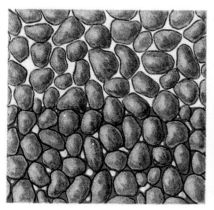
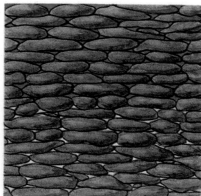

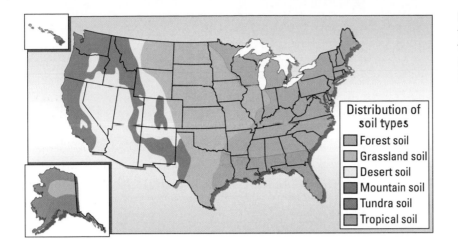

Figure 18.16 This map shows a simplified distribution of different soil types throughout the United States. There are over 20 000 different types of soil in the United States alone.

Distribution of soil types

- Forest soil
- Grassland soil
- Desert soil
- Mountain soil
- Tundra soil
- Tropical soil

The Interaction Between Soil and Climate

Because climate affects the rate of weathering, climate is one of the most important factors in the formation of soil. In the desert and tundra, for example, the soil profile may be only a few millimeters or centimeters thick because there is less water to break down the bedrock. Soil particles in these biomes are generally larger in size because strong winds and infrequent rainfall only remove the smaller, lighter particles from the thin layer of soil.

Grasslands may have a thicker soil profile because of greater precipitation. Also, the weathering of the bedrock underlying grasslands may occur at a faster rate because of the activity of more plants and burrowing animals. The soils of the midwestern United States began forming long ago as rock fragments deposited by glaciers that covered the area.

The high amount of rainfall on tropical soils results in thick soil profiles. However, the structure of these soils is very fragile because the high rainfall quickly leaches nutrients and small clay particles into the subsoil. An accumulation of nutrients and clay particles occurs in the subsoil. But because of the large amounts of clay in the subsoil, the subsoil does not drain well and is not well aerated. For these reasons, accumulated nutrients in tropical soils are usually unavailable for plant roots. The fertility of tropical soils is maintained by the rapid decay of a constant fall of organic matter from trees and native vegetation.

Figure 18.17 The fertile soils along a floodplain are often used for agriculture. These soils may form without the influence of local climate.

SECTION REVIEW

1. What is a soil profile?
2. How are climate and soil thickness related?
3. **Think Critically** How is the fertility of a tropical rain forest influenced by the removal of native vegetation for space to grow grain crops?

Looking for Life in Soil

PROBLEM
Are there living microorganisms in soil?

MATERIALS (per group)
- safety goggles
- ring stand
- Bunsen burner
- tongs
- sugar
- methylene blue solution
- graduated cylinder
- 3 test tubes with stoppers and a rack
- wax pencil
- balance
- garden soil
- wire gauze
- crucible

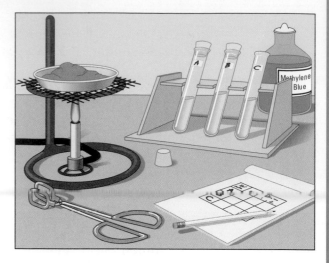

INFERENCE
Read the entire activity, then write an inference about what gases would be given off by living organisms in a stoppered test tube.

PROCEDURE

Test Tube	Contents	Observations	
		Day 1	Day 2
A			
B			
C			

1. Copy the data table onto a separate sheet of paper. Label three test tubes A, B, and C.
2. Transfer 1 g of the soil to a crucible. Set the wire gauze and crucible on the ring stand, and heat the soil in the crucible over a Bunsen burner for 10 minutes.
   Caution: *Be careful around the Bunsen burner. Tie back long hair and wear safety goggles. Use tongs to move the hot crucible.*
3. Transfer 1 g of unheated soil to test tube A. Add 1 g of sugar and 10 mL of methylene blue solution. *Note: Methylene blue solution is an indicator of carbon dioxide (CO_2).*
   Caution: *Methylene blue may stain.*
4. To test tube B, transfer the heated soil from the crucible, 1 g of sugar, and 10 mL of methylene blue solution.
5. To test tube C, transfer 1 g of sugar and 10 mL of methylene blue solution.
6. Observe the liquid in each test tube. In the *Day 1* column of the data table, describe the colors using the terms *blue*, *light blue*, and *colorless*.
7. Put a stopper in each test tube and shake them well. Return them to the test-tube rack and leave them overnight.
8. The next day, observe the test tubes again. Do not shake them. Record your observations in the *Day 2* column using the same terms as before.

ANALYSIS
1. What was the purpose of heating the soil that was placed into test tube B?
2. Carbon dioxide causes methylene blue solution to change to light blue or colorless. What color changes did you observe in each test tube on Day 1? Day 2? What do these color changes indicate?
3. Was your inference accurate? Support your answer with data.

CONCLUSION
Does soil contain any living microorganisms? What evidence do you have to support your answer? Explain your conclusions.

18.4 SOIL MISMANAGEMENT

OBJECTIVES • *Identify* causes of soil mismanagement.
• *Predict* possible outcomes from such mismanagement.

Fragile soil structures may be abused by the simple act of planting something other than what is naturally suited for the region. Care must be taken to maintain the connection between soil and life. The human population is straining the connection through lack of information and careful planning.

Symptoms of Soil Mismanagement

You may have seen news stories about famines, a symptom of poor land management and planning. In 1992 and 1993, the United Nations sent men and women into Somalia to help get food to starving people. Many in the United Nations and International Red Cross claimed that long-term drought was responsible for the famine. However, studies show that the major cause is most likely soil erosion. In the mid-1980s, the head of Kenya's agricultural ministry stated that the widespread famine in areas such as Ethiopia, Chad, and Somalia was closely related to the absence of soil conservation programs.

Another symptom of soil mismanagement is the fact that nearly one billion dollars a year are spent on clearing sediment from streams and lakes in the United States. The sediment comes from hills and mountains where protective vegetation has been removed, allowing wind and water to carry away exposed soil. Fortunately, goals are being redirected from plans to clean up damage to methods for preventing damage. Some methods for controlling soil erosion are discussed in Chapter 19.

Figure 18.18 Here are a few examples of how soil is poisoned, compacted, and stripped of its protective vegetation.

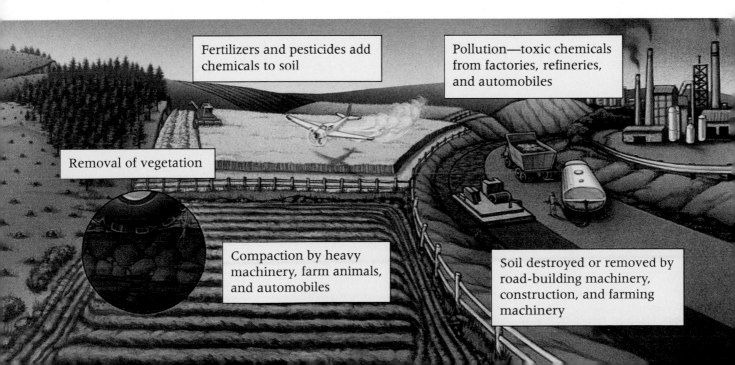

Fertilizers and pesticides add chemicals to soil

Pollution—toxic chemicals from factories, refineries, and automobiles

Removal of vegetation

Compaction by heavy machinery, farm animals, and automobiles

Soil destroyed or removed by road-building machinery, construction, and farming machinery

Figure 18.19 Vegetation protects soil from erosion. Here, soil erosion has removed all but what was held by the roots of a few scattered trees and shrubs.

Dateline 1991

In 1991, the National Resources Defense Council presented a report on the use of insecticides. The report stated that farmers could reduce their use of insecticides by 80 percent. This reduction could be accomplished by using already existing methods of insect control. Methods include rotating crops, or planting different crops during different seasons, and planting insect-resistant crops. Another method is using predator insects that kill insect pests but do not feed on food crops.

Causes of Soil Mismanagement

The removal of vegetation is widespread due to mining, construction, and agriculture. These industries remove vegetation to make access to minerals easier, to clear space for housing and buildings, and to plant crops that have immediate economic value. Human needs drive these industries.

Political needs also contribute to soil mismanagement. In the case of Ethiopia and Somalia, government officials wanted to have mostly nomadic peoples settle down permanently. Nutrient-poor soils in Ethiopia and Somalia are naturally unable to sustain millions of people over long periods of time. The previously nomadic people had rarely worked the same area of soil for more than a year. Keeping these nomads in one area depleted the soils within two or three years.

Overgrazing and deforestation are results of poor agricultural practices that lead to soil mismanagement. Pesticides, fertilizers, and irrigation also contribute to soil deterioration. Poisons may be added to the soil when gardeners and farmers use chemical fertilizers and pesticides to increase productivity. These chemicals can accumulate to dangerously high levels in the soil. Irrigation can recirculate salts to topsoils, poisoning soil organisms and vegetation.

SECTION REVIEW

1. What is compaction?
2. Identify three major causes of soil abuse and describe how each results in soil loss.
3. **Think Critically** Compare the energy and mineral resource requirements for raising farm animals, such as cattle and pigs, and those for growing only crops. Which do you think uses the most resources? Which has less environmental impact?

KEY TERMS

mineral 18.1	bedrock 18.3	soil 18.3
ore 18.1	parent rock 18.3	soil profile 18.3

CHAPTER SUMMARY

18.1 A mineral is a solid, inorganic, naturally occurring material with a definite chemical composition and a specifically arranged pattern of atoms. Minerals are used in a wide variety of ways, depending on the properties of the mineral. The availability of metals derived from minerals influences technology and economics.

18.2 The processes that form Earth's crust determine the location of minerals. Methods such as satellite imagery, drill core samples, and aerial photography are used to find minerals. Methods such as open-pit mining, subsurface mining, and dredging are used to extract minerals from the crust. Methods for extracting and processing can have serious environmental impacts.

18.3 Soil is formed by the weathering of rock. The soil profile from surface to bedrock consists of horizons. Topsoil and subsoil are common names for these horizons. Soil is composed of mineral fragments, air, water, and organic matter. The size and amount of grains determine some soil characteristics. Three major soil types are clay, sandy, and loam. Soil organisms and vegetation are vital to healthy soil.

18.4 Removal of vegetation leaves the soil unprotected. Chemicals and pollution can poison the organisms that help support soil structure. Topsoil may be removed for mining, construction, or agriculture. Political needs can also contribute to soil mismanagement.

MULTIPLE CHOICE

Choose the letter of the word or phrase that best completes each statement.

1. Minerals are solid, inorganic substances that (a) are made by machines; (b) are found only on Earth; (c) exist naturally; (d) are made of iron.
2. Some metals are very important in electronics because they are (a) conductors; (b) inexpensive; (c) magnetic; (d) strong.
3. The United States is a major producer of (a) copper; (b) diamonds; (c) aluminum; (d) mercury.
4. Mineral deposits in streams may be extracted by (a) open-pit mining; (b) satellite imagery; (c) dredging; (d) leaching.
5. The environmental impact of mineral extraction can be reduced by (a) 15 percent; (b) using clean minerals; (c) recycling; (d) getting minerals from the ocean floor.
6. The fertile layer of a soil profile is the (a) subsoil; (b) topsoil; (c) bedrock; (d) rooting layer.
7. Soils with a high percentage of clay are (a) ideal for growing all crops; (b) able to drain rapidly; (c) full of large grains of sand; (d) able to hold water for too long a time.
8. The bedrock from which an area of soil may have formed is called the soil's (a) B horizon; (b) mineral deposit; (c) parent rock; (d) A horizon.
9. Fertilizers and pesticides can lead to soil mismanagement by (a) poisoning soil organisms; (b) taking minerals from the soil; (c) feeding plant roots; (d) forming holes in the soil.
10. Soils form over periods of (a) 20–25 years; (b) 10 years; (c) hundreds to thousands of years; (d) 50 years.

CHAPTER **18** REVIEW

TRUE/FALSE

Write true *if the statement is true. If the statement is false, change the underlined word to make it true.*

1. Hematite is an ore that is a source of <u>iron</u>.
2. Nonmetals are minerals that are <u>widely</u> used.
3. Gold can be called a mineral because it is <u>ductile and malleable</u>.
4. <u>Subsurface mining</u> uses open-pit mines to obtain minerals.
5. <u>Parent rock</u> is the rock from which soils form.
6. The <u>subsoil</u> in a mature soil profile is the most fertile layer of soil.
7. <u>Loam</u> is a type of soil with an even mixture of differently sized particles.
8. Grasslands have <u>thicker</u> soil profiles than deserts and tundras.

CONCEPT REVIEW

Write a complete response for each of the following.

1. Describe three ways in which minerals may be conserved.
2. Distinguish between chemical and mechanical weathering.
3. Name the three major types of soil, and describe the characteristics of each type.
4. How is climate related to soil formation?
5. How does agriculture contribute to soil abuse?

THINK CRITICALLY

1. Compare the fertility of soil in a grassland to that in a rain forest. Which soil is more fertile? Why?
2. How does political stability affect the trade of minerals?
3. If you were to build an environmentally sound house, what would you use as building material? Where would you get your building material? Would you damage anything to obtain this material?
4. What would happen to the agriculture on a river delta if the river upstream were dammed?
5. Can soil be considered a renewable or nonrenewable resource? Explain your answer.

WRITE CREATIVELY

You are traveling through the galaxy in your personal spacecraft when your sensors indicate the presence of life on a nearby planet. You land and discover a planet where all the humanlike inhabitants live underground. The conditions above the ground are unhealthy. The air is very dry and full of sand and dust. Imagine interviewing the inhabitants to find out what happened on this dusty planet. The humanlike inhabitants also have many questions to ask you. They wonder about the planet from which you come. After learning about your planet, these inhabitants request your aid in making their planet's surface livable again. If you were to assist the planet's inhabitants, consider the issues you would need to face. Write a story about this adventure.

PORTFOLIO

Collect magazine and newspaper articles on mining and soil issues. Organize these articles by date, into categories on changing methods in farming and mining, and environmental impacts. Try to determine trends in employment, productivity, and resource availability.

GRAPHIC ANALYSIS

Use Figure 18.5 to answer the following.

1. Where are the major natural resources of copper located?
2. What metals does North America import from South Africa?
3. How does Japan's economy depend on global political stability?
4. What minerals does the Commonwealth of Independent States (the former Soviet Union) supply to Japan and Europe?
5. Why do you think the United States imports additional copper from South America?
6. What pattern in the world mineral trade describes where minerals are most consumed?
7. What factors might influence government relations between South Africa and the United States?

ACTIVITY 18.2

PROBLEM
How do earthworms change soil?

MATERIALS (per group)
- 3 types of soil
- 1-L jar
- water
- partly decayed leaves (humus)
- apple peelings
- construction paper
- rubber band or tape
- shovel or trowel

HYPOTHESIS
Read the entire activity, then write a hypothesis that is related to the problem.

PROCEDURE

1. Add three different types of soil to the jar, one layer at a time. Each layer should fill about one-quarter of the jar. Sprinkle some water in the jar to make the soil moist but not wet.
2. Add partly decayed leaves and some apple peelings. Sprinkle a little more water inside.
3. Wrap a sheet of construction paper around the jar. Hold the paper in place with a rubber band or piece of tape.

4. Obtain a few shovelfuls of damp soil. Look in the soil for three earthworms. Return to class with the earthworms. Place the earthworms in the jar, and store it in a cool place. *Note: Handle the earthworms with care.*
5. The next day, take out the jar and remove the construction paper. Record your observations in a data table. If the soil is dry, add a little water. After making your observations, wrap the jar as before, and return it to its storage place.
6. Repeat step 5 every day for a week.

ANALYSIS
1. What happened to the partly decayed leaves and apple peelings?
2. What happened to the layers of soil?
3. What three types of soil did you use?
4. How might the soil type affect earthworm activity?
5. What would you predict would happen if no water was added to the jar?

CONCLUSION
What was the effect of earthworms on soil? Describe how specific earthworm behaviors caused this effect.

On March 22, 1987, the towed barge *Mobro* left from Long Island City, New York. On board were 2800 metric tons of garbage being carried to a landfill in Moorehead, North Carolina. When the barge arrived in North Carolina, its cargo was rejected. Similar rejections occurred in Florida, Alabama, Mississippi, Louisiana, Texas, Mexico, Belize, and the Bahamas. The repeated rejection became national news. For five months, the "garbage barge" searched for a port to accept its ripening cargo. Finally, an incinerator in Brooklyn, New York, accepted the garbage. The displaced garbage points to one of the many problems associated with industrialization: waste disposal.

19.1 SOLID WASTES

OBJECTIVES • *List* examples of solid wastes, and *identify* their sources. • *Describe* past and present methods used to dispose of solid wastes.

Garbage, trash, refuse, junk, scrap, and sewage are all examples of waste materials that need to be disposed of in a way that does not pollute the land. Collectively, these materials are called solid wastes. *In 1976, the U.S. Congress defined* **solid wastes** *as all garbage, refuse, and sludge products from agriculture, forestry, mining, and municipalities.*

Garbage Disposal in the Past

Early peoples were hunter-gatherers who followed game animals from place to place. Garbage disposal was not a problem in these societies. They simply left their garbage where it fell and moved on. Later, some hunter-gatherers began to develop agriculture and build small cities. As cities grew, refuse disposal became a problem.

As early as 500 B.C., the city of Athens, Greece, passed laws that resulted in the first garbage dump. Garbage could no longer be thrown into the streets. Instead, all garbage had to be placed in locations not closer than 1.6 km from the city walls. The rest of Europe, however, continued to deposit garbage into the streets for quite some time.

In 1892, outbreaks of typhoid and cholera forced New York City officials to establish better sanitary conditions. By 1900, garbage was collected from the streets, loaded onto barges, and dumped into the ocean. This method of garbage removal continued for some time, until swimmers in Atlantic City, New Jersey, observed mattresses and dead animals floating past them.

Think About It!

Every community is faced with the NIMBY syndrome. The letters stand for *Not In My Backyard*. The human population continues to grow, and garbage production continues to increase.

1. Where does the garbage from your community go?

2. Where can garbage be disposed of without placing it in somebody's "backyard"?

LINK

Social Studies

Benjamin Franklin established the first municipal street-cleaning service in 1757.

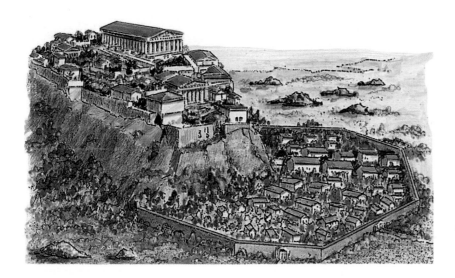

Figure 19.1 Perhaps the first garbage dump in Europe was developed in Greece in 500 B.C. City leaders in Athens declared that the dumping of refuse within city walls was illegal. Garbage had to be dumped at least 1.6 km outside the city walls.

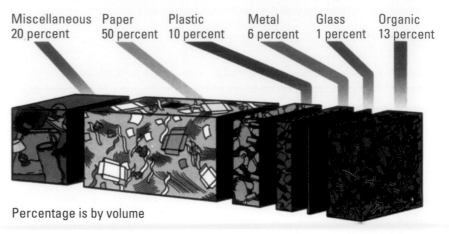

Figure 19.2 Wastes created by most communities consist largely of paper and paper products such as newspapers and packaging materials. Other solid wastes include food remains, plastics, glass, metals, textiles, yard wastes, leather, and rubber.

| Miscellaneous 20 percent | Paper 50 percent | Plastic 10 percent | Metal 6 percent | Glass 1 percent | Organic 13 percent |

Percentage is by volume

To solve the problem of the polluted waters, the first landfills were established. About 70 percent of today's garbage is dumped in landfills. *A* **landfill** *is a site where wastes are disposed of by burying them.*

The Landfill Problem

Today, hunter-gatherers have been replaced by people who work in industry and offices. Cities have grown larger. More food and goods are brought into the cities each day to meet the needs of the increasing population. In turn, larger and larger amounts of wastes are produced. The graph in Figure 19.2 shows the contents of city wastes in landfills.

As populations grow and more garbage is produced, a major problem arises: Where will all the garbage be placed? For many years, open dumping in landfills was the cheapest and most convenient way to dispose of garbage. A site was chosen, and truckloads of garbage were deposited there each day. But open dumping was stopped because it supported large populations of rats, insects, and other unwanted organisms. Foul odors given off by open landfills invaded areas close to the dumps.

Figure 19.3 Open landfills are no longer legal in most of the United States. They are breeding grounds for many harmful diseases. This open landfill in the Philippines, called Smoky Mountain, is home to more than 20 000 people. These people live and work here but suffer greatly from poverty and health problems.

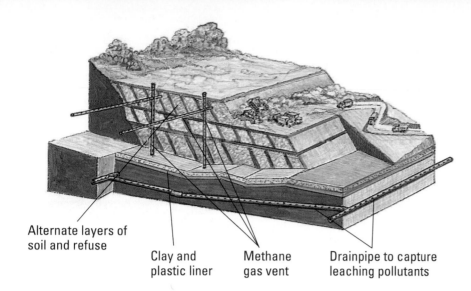

Figure 19.4 This sanitary landfill is designed to account for all possible problems associated with landfills. After the dump is completely filled, the land can be used as a recreation area, such as a golf course. It may even be used for a sports complex, such as the Meadowlands, where the New York Giants football team plays.

Alternate layers of soil and refuse

Clay and plastic liner

Methane gas vent

Drainpipe to capture leaching pollutants

In addition, rainfall over the open landfills carried pollutants from the garbage into the soil. Some of these pollutants were leached into groundwater systems. Because of these problems, this method of garbage disposal is now illegal in many states.

Many communities today use *sanitary landfills* for refuse disposal. In a sanitary landfill, wastes are spread in layers about 3 m deep and compacted by bulldozers. About 15 cm of soil is then spread on top of the refuse and compacted. The process is repeated daily until the mountain of garbage reaches a designated height. Covering the garbage with soil daily helps to control populations of rodents and insects. When the landfill is closed, a final layer of soil about 60 cm thick is placed over the entire area. Grass and trees are planted in the soil. The site may be reserved for use in the future.

Sanitary landfills are not as harmless as they may seem. Decomposition of some wastes produces methane gas. Methane is highly flammable and explodes easily. To keep methane gas from building up in the landfill, ventilation pipes are placed into the ground. These pipes enable methane to slowly escape from the landfill. At some landfills, the methane is collected and sold.

Another problem associated with sanitary landfills is the leaching of toxic substances. To avoid leaching, new landfills must place a double liner around the landfill area. However, liners sometimes tear from uneven land settling. To reduce liner tear, liners are constructed of layers of clay and a thick plastic sheet. This construction enables the liner to flex during uneven land settling.

SECTION REVIEW

1. What are solid wastes?
2. What are some ways that people have disposed of solid wastes?
3. **Infer** How might placing a landfill near an aquatic ecosystem be harmful to the organisms living in the water?

Figure 19.5 Farm workers are vulnerable to health risks because of their constant contact with dangerous pesticides.

Figure 19.6 The townspeople of Bhopal protested possible out-of-court agreements between their government and the company responsible for 3600 deaths in Bhopal.

19.2 HAZARDOUS WASTES

OBJECTIVES • *Identify* problems associated with hazardous wastes. • *Classify* hazardous wastes according to their characteristics.

The emergence of industrial and technological society has brought great advances in science and medicine, and a significant impact on global ecosystems. Technology makes bigger, better, and stronger materials for today's world. However, the production, use, storage, and disposal of these materials can have widespread effects.

Effects of Hazardous Materials

Solid, liquid, or gaseous wastes that are potentially harmful to humans and the environment, even in low concentrations, are called **hazardous wastes**. The problems of hazardous wastes are well illustrated by the example of the Love Canal community in New York. Homes in Love Canal were built next to an old chemical waste dump. An elementary school and playground were built on top of the dump.

Many cases of birth defects and cancer-related illnesses were reported by residents of the Love Canal community. However, it was not until after the steel containers that held the hazardous wastes rusted through, leaking chemicals to the surface, that the government was forced to take action. More than 1000 families were evacuated and relocated at the government's expense. The cleanup efforts and relocation policies cost more than $190 million. Now, the government has declared the area safe for the former residents to move back. Would you move back?

Similar situations have occurred in other parts of the world. In Bhopal, India, more than 3600 people died and another 200 000 were injured when a toxic gas escaped from a storage tank.

Figure 19.7 In the late 1970s, a serious problem arose in Love Canal. How could a community, school, and playground be built over a toxic chemical dump?

The accident left more than 2500 people with permanent disabilities to their eyes, lungs, and reproductive systems. The company responsible agreed to pay $470 million to the people of Bhopal as compensation.

There have been many dangerous incidents involving hazardous wastes. Table 19.1 lists only some of these incidents. The table does not show the impact of these incidents on other organisms.

Table 19.1   Accidents Involving Hazardous Wastes

Location	Year	Nature of Damage
Minamata, Japan	1959	By 1983, 300 people killed from mercury discharged into waterways
Detroit, Michigan	1966	Nuclear breeder core meltdown
Flixborough, UK	1974	22 dead in chemical plant explosion
Seveso, Italy	1976	190 injured in dioxin leak
Love Canal, New York	1970s	Toxic waste dump responsible for birth defects and illnesses
Elizabeth, New Jersey	1979	30 people injured when explosion produced toxic smoke over city
Three Mile Island, near Harrisburg, Pennsylvania	1979	Partial nuclear core meltdown and release of radioactive gas and water
Woburn, Massachusetts	1979	15 dead from leukemia associated with nearby toxic waste dump
Chernobyl, Ukraine	1986	Explosion and fire released huge amounts of radiation
Hagersville, Ontario	1990	Tire fire lasting 17 days produced toxic smoke over city

Classification of Hazardous Materials

Problems associated with hazardous wastes have become a global concern. In the United States, this concern has prompted the Environmental Protection Agency (EPA) to classify hazardous wastes. Categorizing hazardous wastes helps determine specific methods for disposal.

Reactive Wastes   Wastes that can explode are called *reactive wastes*. Certain chemicals are so unstable that they will explode when handled incorrectly or mixed with other substances. The metal sodium is an example of a reactive substance.

Corrosive Wastes   Wastes that can eat through steel and many other materials are called *corrosive wastes*. Such chemicals eat through clothing and burn the skin. Battery acid and the lye used in drain-cleaning solutions are examples of corrosive wastes.

Figure 19.8 Toxic wastes are a growing concern in today's society. The directions for proper use and disposal of such materials must be followed carefully.

Do It!

Field Activity

Many common household products contain hazardous chemicals.

1. Survey your home for examples of materials that are classified as hazardous wastes.

2. Organize your findings in a chart that identifies the material, the hazardous waste category to which it belongs, and the means of disposal recommended on the label. **Caution:** *Be sure to wear protective clothing.*

Because few containers can hold corrosive wastes for long periods of time, storing and transporting these substances is a problem. Materials engineers are constantly in search of suitable containers.

Ignitable Wastes   Substances that can burst into flames at relatively low temperatures are called ignitable. *Ignitable wastes* present an immediate danger from smoke and fire. They can also spread toxic fumes over a wide area. Paint thinners, oils, and some cleaning fluids are examples of ignitable wastes.

Toxic Wastes   Chemicals that are poisonous to people are called toxic, causing health problems such as birth defects or cancer. Wastes containing chemicals such as arsenic, cyanide, mercury, and some pesticides are classified as *toxic wastes.*

Radioactive Wastes   Radiation given off by *radioactive wastes* can harm people and other organisms. Radiation burns the skin and destroys body cells and tissues. While some radioactive materials take a relatively short time to decay, others may take hundreds of thousands of years to decay.

Radioactive wastes are produced in the mining of radioactive materials such as uranium. Protective clothing, tools, and equipment used in nuclear power plants, as well as mining and processing ores, can also give off radiation. Radioactive materials used in agricultural, medical, and scientific research give off radiation as well.

Medical Wastes   Old medicines, medicine containers, lab equipment, and lab specimens are referred to as *medical wastes.* Used syringes, blood vials, and tissue samples are also medical wastes. Some medical wastes may be considered toxic wastes.

Hazardous Home Wastes

Many households are warehouses of hazardous chemicals. Examples are ammonia, bleaches, toilet-bowl cleaners, drain cleaners, oven cleaners, disinfectants, furniture polish, medicines, paints, oils, and pesticides. Proper use and disposal of these substances should be practiced at all times. These materials have been regarded as necessities in households of industrial nations. However, natural and less hazardous products are beginning to replace these materials on supermarket shelves.

SECTION REVIEW

1. What are hazardous wastes?
2. **Classify** In what category of hazardous wastes are substances containing mercury or cyanide classified?
3. **Apply** Name five products in your home that contain hazardous materials and therefore require careful disposal.

19.3 TOPSOIL EROSION

OBJECTIVES • *Identify* ways in which soil is lost. • *Describe* the methods used in agriculture to prevent soil erosion.

Like water and a number of minerals, soil is cycled in the environment. While mechanical and chemical weathering form new soil, natural forces carry away soil in a process called erosion. The major causes of erosion are wind and running water.

Soil Loss and Desertification

If managed carelessly, soil may become unsuitable for planting crops and sustaining livestock. Activities such as overgrazing, deforestation, and poor irrigation and cultivation practices cause soil loss and desertification. These activities damage land by disturbing the balance between living organisms and soil.

The process of desertification is most visible in dry regions that border on deserts. It is estimated that about 30 percent of Earth's land has undergone desertification. Worldwide, about 6 million hectares are lost to desertification each year. In the United States, parts of Arizona, Colorado, California, and the High Plains region of Texas are at risk.

A report issued by the U.S. Department of Agriculture estimates that soil loss from erosion threatens one-third of all farmland in the United States. It is also estimated that about 2.5 billion metric tons of topsoil in the United States are washed away by water each year. The volume of topsoil lost as a result of wind erosion is estimated to be about 1.5 billion metric tons. Soil erosion is not limited to the United States. Table 19.2 shows the topsoil erosion rates for selected regions of the world.

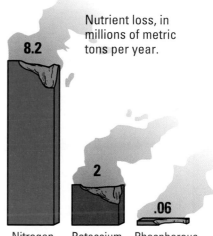

Nutrient loss, in millions of metric tons per year.

8.2 — Nitrogen
2 — Potassium
.06 — Phosphorous

Figure 19.9 Along with the 4 billion metric tons of topsoil lost annually from the United States, about 10 million metric tons of soil nutrients are also lost. Nitrogen, phosphorus, and potassium are the nutrients most needed by plant life. It is estimated that about $5 billion are spent annually to replace these valuable nutrients.

Table 19.2 Topsoil Erosion Rate in Selected Regions

Region	Erosion Rate, in Metric Tons/Hectare/Year	Causes
United States	18	Wind and water
China	43	Water
Belgium (central)	10–25	Water
Ethiopia (Gondor region)	20	Water
Salvador–Acelhuate Basin	19–190	Water
Guatemala (mountain region)	200–3600	Water
Thailand (Chao River Basin)	21	Water
Venezuela and Colombia (Orinoco River Basin)	18	Water

Figure 19.10 Some proper land management techniques, such as contour farming and strip-cropping (left) and terracing (right), are becoming more widespread in agriculture. The costs for such methods may be greater in the short term, but far less expensive in the long term.

Soil Conservation and Land Management

American farmers and ranchers, in cooperation with state and local governments, have developed many less destructive agricultural methods. But methods such as contour farming and terracing may be time-consuming. Also, efforts to use protective methods may be slowed because the cost of using them is higher than the cost of using traditional methods. Other soil protection methods include strip-cropping and shelter belts.

Strip-Cropping   Farmland is plowed so that plowed strips are separated by planted strips. Having at least part of the land covered by vegetation reduces soil loss. Different strips may be planted with crops that have overlapping growing seasons.

Contour Farming   Contour farming is a method of plowing along a slope instead of across it. The furrows between rows of crops collect water, preventing heavy soil erosion. Contour farming is often used together with strip–cropping where farmland is sloped.

Terracing   In terracing, a series of platforms called *terraces* are built into the slope of a hill. Each terrace is separated from the next by a vertical step. Terracing is effective on steep slopes and slows water flow, enabling water to soak into the soil.

Shelter Belts   Rows of trees may be planted along the outer edges of a field. These rows of trees are called windbreaks or *shelter belts*. Shelter belts help reduce erosion by slowing down the wind.

SECTION REVIEW

1. What is strip-cropping?
2. What types of practices lead to desertification?
3. **Predict** How might unusually heavy rains in the High Plains region of Texas affect local soil loss?

The Dust Bowl

During the 1800s, many people moved westward to farm the fertile land of the Great Plains. This vast grassland was believed to be large enough to support many farms and ranches.

Farmers plowed under the tough, drought-resistant native grasses and planted corn and wheat. Ranchers turned out herds of cattle and sheep to graze on the grassland. Over time, more and more acres of prairie were converted to farms and ranches.

The change in vegetation had unforeseen results. The native prairie grasses have extensive root systems, which hold the soil in place. As these plants were weakened by overgrazing or replaced by crops, the soil was poorly protected against the winds that blew across the land.

Settlement in the southern part of the Great Plains was especially active during the 30 years before 1915. In 1931, a drought began and lasted for several years. The corn, wheat, and other crops were not resistant to drought, so they died. The native vegetation, which was already weakened, died too. When the wind blew, there was nothing left to hold the soil in place, and it began to blow away.

During the 1930s, a drought in the southern part of the Great Plains led to the "dust bowl" disaster. During that period, scenes such as this were common.

Dust filled the air. It was like a dust blizzard, and people began to call the region the "dust bowl." Prevailing winds blew lighter particles as far as the Atlantic Ocean. Heavier particles were carried shorter distances, piling up on farm equipment, fences, and buildings. In many places, more than 8 cm of topsoil were lost.

Farms failed, and many families from Colorado, New Mexico, Kansas, and Oklahoma had no choice but to move away in search of work. Many people moved to California. Without money to buy new farms, they became migrant farm workers.

In 1935, the government began a program of soil conservation in the dust bowl region. Measures such as crop rotation, contour plowing, and terracing have helped to rehabilitate the region. In areas where there is enough rainfall to support the growth of trees, trees have been planted as windbreaks. Although many farmers are practicing soil conservation techniques, erosion and loss of nutrients continue to be problems, both in the United States and around the world. Wherever there is deforestation or overgrazing, there is the risk of soil loss.

Checkpoint

1. What factors contributed to the dust storms of the 1930s?

2. How can farmers prevent soil erosion?

19.4 CONTROLLING POLLUTION ON LAND

OBJECTIVES • *Identify* and *explain* four methods for reducing the volume of wastes. • *Discuss* the benefits and drawbacks of various forms of waste disposal.

The best way to eliminate wastes is not to produce them in the first place. Using materials in products and packaging that can be recycled or reused will reduce the amount of waste going into landfills. Reducing the use of hazardous materials in manufacturing will decrease the quantity of waste that needs treatment.

Disposal of the Disposable Society

Disposable items make up about one-quarter of all wastes placed in landfills. By substituting reusable or recyclable goods for disposable items, the volume of waste can be diminished. Cloth handkerchiefs, napkins, and towels can be used instead of paper ones. Reusable plastic or china plates can replace paper plates, and cloth diapers can be substituted for disposable ones. Repairing a broken appliance instead of discarding it will keep the appliance out of a landfill.

Recycling programs are another way of reducing refuse. Paper, metal, glass, and plastics are sorted from garbage and recycled. This recycled material is kept out of landfills, and it also serves as a source of revenue when used to make new products.

Some materials are naturally recycled. For example, plant cuttings, including grass clippings, leaves, and branches, are biodegradable. **Biodegradable** (BY-oh-dih-GRAY-duh-bul) *substances decompose easily and enrich the soil.* Plant wastes and food wastes may be collected to make a *compost pile.* The result is a sort of human-made humus. Many communities and industries are experimenting with producing and marketing compost material.

Figure 19.11 The world's largest compost producer is located in the Netherlands, in Wijister. On average, this facility collects about 1.1 million metric tons of refuse a year. After composting, about 110 000 metric tons of human-made humus are available for sale.

Figure 19.12 Controlled incinerators are used to destroy hazardous materials such as medical and toxic wastes. The method is considered the most efficient form of disposal for dangerous materials, but the ashes that are left behind pose another disposal problem.

Disposing of Hazardous Wastes

Is there a safe method for disposing of hazardous wastes? Many people think that no safe method of hazardous waste disposal exists. However, new technologies have been developed to combat the safety problem.

Waste Exchange   Many hazardous waste materials can be used in the production of other products or materials. When a company has waste material for disposal, it notifies a waste-exchange agency. The agency then notifies other companies that have some use for the waste. The first company avoids the cost of waste disposal and may make a profit by selling the waste. The second company may purchase the materials it needs, at a reduced price.

Deep-Well Injection   The petroleum industry uses deep-well injection to dispose of liquid hazardous wastes. In this process, liquid wastes are pumped into deep porous rocks through lined pipes. The rocks are located well below drinking-water aquifers.

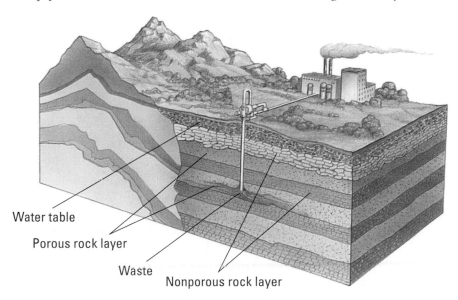

Water table

Porous rock layer

Waste

Nonporous rock layer

Figure 19.13 The disposal of hazardous wastes from petroleum refinement is done through the use of deep-well injection. As long as careful site inspection for the well is made, problems with disposal can be minimal.

Secure Chemical Landfill   A landfill constructed in an area of nonporous bedrock is considered to be secure. The nonporous bedrock prevents the leaching of pollutants into groundwater. Pipes are installed in the landfill containment area to monitor and collect any leached materials that may accumulate. Finally, the top of the landfill is covered with a layer of clay to keep out water.

Controlled Incineration   The burning of wastes at extremely high temperatures is called *controlled incineration*. At temperatures between 542 °C and 1662 °C, complete burning takes place, destroying most nonmetallic hazardous wastes. Some people consider controlled incineration to be the best method of hazardous waste disposal. However, it is also the most expensive.

Chemical and Biological Treatment Plants   Some hazardous wastes can be made harmless by treatment plants. Certain chemical or biological reactions can neutralize hazardous wastes. Once they are contained, they can be disposed of more safely.

Radioactive Waste Disposal   Radioactive wastes also need a proper method of disposal. At present, radioactive wastes are placed in water. The water, along with the waste, is sealed in stainless steel tanks. These tanks are then encased in concrete. The tanks are then placed into concrete vaults located deep underground.

Legislation

Environmental disasters have made the public more aware of potential dangers to global ecosystems. When the EPA was established in 1970, its job was to carry out federal laws designed to protect the environment. Some of the major laws passed to protect and restore the land environment are listed in Table 19.3.

To protect communities from the dangers of hazardous wastes, Congress passed a law, nicknamed Superfund. The official name of this law is the Comprehensive Environmental Response, Compensation, and Liability Act of 1980 (CERCLA). The obligations of CERCLA are listed below.

- Cleaning up hazardous waste dumps.
- Making polluters pay for cleanups.
- Developing a national priorities list (NPL), a list of sites presenting the most serious threat to health and the environment.
- Taking emergency actions in areas where there are spills or accidental releases of hazardous wastes.
- Encouraging research for the reduction, treatment, and disposal of hazardous wastes.

The EPA was authorized $1.6 billion for a 5-year period to fulfill the Superfund obligations. In 1986, an amendment to the original law allocated the spending of $9 billion. This amount of money is not enough. More money is needed to decrease the production of hazardous wastes.

Table 19.3 Federal Environmental Protection Legislation

Year	Legislation
1969	National Environmental Policy Act
1972	Ocean Dumping Act (Marine Protection, Research, and Sanctuaries Act)
1972	Environmental Pesticide Control Act
1973	Endangered Species Act
1976	Toxic Substances Control Act
1976	Resource Conservation and Recovery Act
1977	Surface Mining Control and Reclamation Act
1980	Comprehensive Environmental Response, Compensation, and Liability Act (Superfund)
1980	Low-Level Radioactive Waste Policy Act
1982	Nuclear Waste Policy Act
1984	Hazardous and Solid Waste Amendments
1985	Food Security Act
1986	Emergency Response and Community Right-to-Know Act
1986	Superfund Amendments and Reauthorization Act

The high cost of disposal and the lack of availability of convenient disposal sites have driven many American and European cities to ship their wastes to other nations, often developing nations. This practice is a sensitive political issue. Toxic wastes from the United States have ended up in West Africa and Zimbabwe. A treaty signed by 105 countries in 1989 regulates the international shipping of hazardous wastes.

Many governments and industries around the world are working to reduce hazardous waste. For example, the governments of France and Denmark are giving grants to industries to research and use cleaner technologies. Pollution prevention can eliminate many of the problems of treating or disposing of wastes. Processing methods can be redesigned to reduce the loss of hazardous materials to the environment. Nontoxic materials can replace toxic solvents. Waste exchange and recycling programs can reduce costs, reduce pollution, and eliminate costly cleanups.

SECTION REVIEW

1. How can making a compost pile reduce waste?
2. What is a secure chemical landfill?
3. **Infer** Why do you think hazardous wastes from the United States end up in developing nations?

Pollution and Plant Growth

PROBLEM
How is plant growth affected when the water source is polluted?

MATERIALS (per group)
- wax pencil
- 4 plastic Petri dishes with lids
- 40 radish seeds (approx.)
- 10 mL of 5% detergent solution
- 10 mL of 5% salt solution
- 10 mL of 5% oil solution
- tape
- water
- potting soil mix

HYPOTHESIZE
After reading through the entire activity, hypothesize how the different pollutants in each water sample will affect plant growth.

PROCEDURE

Preparations
1. Be sure the Petri dishes are clean. Using the wax pencil, label the Petri dishes as shown in the figure. Write your initials on the lids of the Petri dishes.
2. Lightly fill each Petri dish with potting soil. Pour 10 mL of tap water into the control dish. Then pour 10 mL of each of the solutions into the corresponding Petri dishes.
3. Place 10 radish seeds in each dish, lightly scattering the seeds over the soil.
4. Cover and tape the lid on each Petri dish. Store the dishes according to your teacher's instructions. *Note: Keep lids sealed so the water will not evaporate.*

Days 2,3, and 4
1. Make observations about what has occurred thus far in the Petri dishes. Copy the data table, and record the percentage of seeds that have germinated. If 3 out of 10 seeds

have germinated, the percentage is 30 percent. *Note: Do not throw the seeds away.*
2. Record your observations of the plant growth in your notebooks. Answer the following questions: Are the roots, stems, or leaves visible? Have the leaves unfolded? What color are the leaves? Are the root hairs visible?
3. Observe the seeds again for 2 more days. Record your observations.

Day/Hour	Percent Germinated in			
	Control	Oil	Detergent	Salt
2				
3				
4				

ANALYSIS
1. In which Petri dish did the seedlings seem to grow the best? Why do you think this is so?
2. Was your hypothesis correct? Describe how your data supports or disproves your hypothesis.

CONCLUSION
1. Write a paragraph describing the effects that polluted water has on crops.
2. Write another paragraph that describes how plants flourish with clean, pure water.

CHAPTER 19 REVIEW

KEY TERMS

solid waste 19.1
landfill 19.1

hazardous waste 19.2
biodegradable 19.4

CHAPTER SUMMARY

19.1 Wastes produced as a result of municipal, agricultural, forestry, and mining activities are considered solid wastes. Past and present methods of solid waste disposal include open dumping, landfills, sanitary landfills, and ocean dumping. Today, open dumping is limited in the United States, and ocean dumping is no longer used because of negative environmental impacts.

19.2 Hazardous wastes are solid, liquid, or gaseous wastes that are potentially harmful to humans and the environment, even in low concentrations. The EPA classifies hazardous wastes into several categories, including reactive wastes, corrosive wastes, ignitable wastes, toxic wastes, radioactive wastes, and medical wastes.

19.3 Cultivation, irrigation, deforestation, and overgrazing lead to soil loss and desertification in many parts of the world. Desertification is most visible in regions that border deserts. Strip-cropping and contour farming are examples of ways to control soil loss and desertification.

19.4 One method for controlling land pollution is reducing wastes by recycling, reusing, and reducing products. The safe disposal of hazardous wastes is a challenge. Disposal methods include controlled incineration, deep-well injection, and waste exchange. Several laws help protect the environment from solid and hazardous wastes.

MULTIPLE CHOICE

Choose the letter of the word or phrase that best completes each statement.

1. The type of waste in most landfills is (a) toxic waste; (b) radioactive waste; (c) solid waste; (d) compost.
2. Waste products that are easily broken down by nature are (a) hazardous wastes; (b) biodegradable; (c) toxic wastes; (d) pesticides.
3. Overgrazing and poor cultivation can lead to (a) deforestation; (b) incineration; (c) irrigation; (d) desertification.
4. Substances containing mercury would be classified as (a) radioactive wastes; (b) corrosive wastes; (c) toxic wastes; (d) medical wastes.
5. Legislation designed to help identify and clean up hazardous areas is the (a) Superfund; (b) NIMBY; (c) Love Canal Act; (d) Clean Land Act.
6. Substances that can eat through metals and other containers are classified as (a) ignitable wastes; (b) toxic wastes; (c) radioactive wastes; (d) corrosive wastes.
7. Ocean dumping is a source of pollution for (a) land environments only; (b) air environments only; (c) water environments only; (d) land and water environments.
8. Wastes that explode easily are classified as (a) ignitable wastes; (b) reactive wastes; (c) toxic wastes; (d) corrosive wastes.
9. Grass clippings and other plant material are returned to the environment for recycling by collecting them in a (a) deep well; (b) terrace; (c) compost pile; (d) concrete vault.
10. All of the following are methods for disposal of hazardous wastes except (a) deep-well injection; (b) controlled incineration; (c) waste exchange; (d) sanitary landfills.

CHAPTER **19** REVIEW

WORD COMPARISONS

Write the letter of the second word pair that best matches the first pair.

1. Cyanide: toxic waste as (a) compost: grass clippings; (b) radioactivity: radiation; (c) sodium: reactive waste; (d) trash: hazardous waste.
2. Overgrazing: desertification as (a) composting: recycling; (b) clear-cutting: deforestation; (c) open dumping: landfills; (d) deep-well injection: incineration.
3. Leaching: groundwater pollution as (a) acid rain: corrosion; (b) air: water; (c) flames: incineration; (d) heat: incineration.
4. Syringes: medical waste as (a) fuel rods: radioactive waste; (b) trees: deforestation; (c) disinfectants: home; (d) dumping: landfills.
5. Deep-well injection: petroleum wastes as (a) chemicals: landfills; (b) concrete vaults: radioactive wastes; (c) legislation: EPA; (d) chemical wastes: Love Canal.

CONCEPT REVIEW

Write a complete response for each of the following.

1. How are radioactive wastes disposed of?
2. How does a sanitary landfill differ from a secure chemical landfill?
3. How does composting help soil?
4. What methods can be used to reduce the amount of garbage produced by people?
5. Why is ocean dumping harmful to both aquatic and land ecosystems?

THINK CRITICALLY

1. What characteristics of radioactive wastes make their disposal especially difficult?
2. What are the benefits of incineration?
3. Would you live in an area that was once a disposal site for chemical wastes? Explain.
4. Why must care be used in the storage of substances such as kerosene and gasoline?

Computer Activity Use a graphing program to generate a line graph that compares topsoil loss for China and the United States over the next 20 years. Assume the erosion rates in Table 19.2 will remain constant. Also assume that there is an average of 5000 metric tons of topsoil per hectare in both China and the United States. The area of China is 960 million hectares. The area of the United States is 940 million hectares. How many metric tons of topsoil per hectare of land will be left in each nation?

WRITE FOR UNDERSTANDING

Identify the topic sentence for each paragraph in Section 19.2. Organize the sentences into a summary of the section. You may need to add sentences to make your summary clear.

PORTFOLIO

1. Interview someone from your local fire department about the proper methods of disposal for at least three types of hazardous wastes that are common in your home.
2. Begin a scrapbook of newspaper and magazine articles related to illegal dumping and land pollution. After a month, review the articles you have collected. Prepare a map summarizing the type of dumping or polluting involved, with locations and dates.

GRAPHIC ANALYSIS

Use Figure 19.13 to answer the following questions.

1. What type of waste disposal is shown in the diagram?
2. What would happen if the wastes were pumped above the top layer of nonporous rock?
3. What types of wastes are disposed of using this method?
4. How does nonporous rock differ from porous rock?
5. Why is it important to dispose of wastes well below the water table?
6. What geologic features do you think a site inspection would need to study?

ACTIVITY 19.2

PROBLEM
How does plant cover affect the erosion of soil by rainwater?

MATERIALS (per group)
- watering can
- 2 wide-mouthed jars with lids
- ice pick or nail
- large dish or roasting pan
- water
- topsoil
- fresh grass clippings

PREDICT
After reading through the activity, write a prediction about how ground cover affects the erosion of topsoil by rainwater.

PROCEDURE

1. Place the two jars at least 10 cm apart in the middle of the roasting pan.
2. Use the ice pick or nail to poke 10–15 holes in both jar lids. **Caution:** *Be careful when using the ice pick or nail.*
3. Fill both jar lids with lightly packed topsoil. Cover the soil in one jar lid with the grass clippings. Balance the soil-filled lids on the mouths of the jars.
4. Use the watering can to sprinkle the jars from a height of about one meter. Sprinkle about 2 L of water onto the jars. This water simulates rainwater.
5. As you sprinkle the water, observe the following and record your data in a data table. How much soil splashed from each lid? What color is the water that collects in the pan from each jar? How much water collected in each jar? What color is this water? How much time did it take for the water to soak through the soil?

ANALYSIS
1. From which lid was more soil removed by the water?
2. How did the color of the water in the two jars compare?
3. How long did it take for the water to soak through each soil sample?

CONCLUSION
1. Did the covering of grass clippings change the way the water affected the topsoil? Describe any differences that occurred.
2. How would the covering of grass clippings affect the sample over time? Which sample would last longer?
3. What do your findings suggest about the erosion of bare topsoil in a farm field or deforested area? What recommendations would you make to minimize erosion?

"Water, water, everywhere, nor any drop to drink." This famous line from Samuel Taylor Coleridge's poem, *The Rime of the Ancient Mariner*, describes a situation in which people on a boat, surrounded by water, have no water to drink. The problem is that the boat is sailing in the ocean—a body of salt water.

Many people throughout the world use water as if it were in endless supply. However, recall that only about 3 percent of Earth's water is fresh water. Only a very small part of this fresh water is available for use by all of Earth's organisms. An even smaller fraction of this fresh water is *potable*, or safe for drinking.

20.1 USES FOR WATER

OBJECTIVES • **Describe** the ways in which people use water.
• **Relate** how water use affects ecosystems.

Water should be used wisely. Sometimes, nature reminds people of just how important a resource fresh water is and how its availability is limited. For example, regions that normally receive sufficient precipitation to meet their needs may sometimes suffer periods of drought. Also, people who live in areas of deserts must rely on water from distant sources.

Natural disasters such as floods and earthquakes can leave entire communities without any fresh water for long periods of time. Earthquakes can destroy underground water pipes, leaving people without water for days or even weeks. Floods, such as the one that occurred along the Mississippi River in 1993, can mix sewage and sediments with drinking water, making the water unsafe to drink, or *unpotable*.

Residential Use

The average person in the United States uses about 300 L of water daily. Most of this water is used for personal hygiene and home cleaning. Only a very small amount of the 300 L is used for drinking and cooking. Table 20.1 lists estimates for the amounts of water used each day in the average U.S. household for various activities. Water uses outside the home, such as gardening, landscaping, car washing, and recreational activities, account for about half of residential water use. A lawn sprinkler uses as much as 40 L of water every minute. Depending on its size, a home swimming pool may require from hundreds to many thousands of liters of water to fill. More water must also be added to the pool throughout the season.

Figure 20.1 People stood in long lines at water trucks, their only supply of fresh water during the devastating Mississippi River flood of 1993 (top). The 1989 Loma Prieta earthquake, near San Francisco, disrupted the flow of fresh water to homes (bottom).

Table 20.1 Estimated U.S. Household Water Use

Activity	Daily Consumption
Brushing teeth	19–39 L (faucets running)
Shaving	39–58 L (faucets running)
Washing hands and face	4–8 L (faucets running)
Showering	75–80 L (faucets running)
Tub bathing	96–116 L (full tub)
Machine dishwashing	56–60 L (full cycle)
Dishwashing (in sink)	75–80 L (faucets running)
Clothes washing	140–170 L (full cycle)
Toilet flushing	16–21 L (per flush)

Industrial Use

Of the water used by people, about 44 percent of all fresh water is used by industry. Water is used to transport goods and dispose of wastes. Water is also used as a power source and as a coolant.

Industries use enormous amounts of water in the mining and refining of natural resources. Manufacturing the raw materials needed to make other products requires large quantities of water. For example, it takes more than 15 000 L of water to manufacture the steel needed to make one home washing machine. Producing synthetic materials, such as rayon fabric used in clothing, requires even larger amounts of water.

Access to water is a factor many businesses must consider as part of their short-term and long-term plans. The availability of water can affect where a company will locate. In turn, where a company locates can strongly affect the economy in the region. Also, the company's presence may generate other job opportunities in the area, because the community will need public services, such as health care.

Agricultural Use

The farming industry is the single largest user of water in the United States. As shown in Figure 20.2, almost half of all freshwater use is by agriculture. Most of this water, more than 200 billion L each day, is used for the irrigation of farmland. **Irrigation** *is the process of bringing water to an area for use in growing crops.*

Irrigation practices increase crop yield. However, increased crop yields are not without cost. Many people think the tax dollars spent on research and development related to irrigation systems could be more wisely spent. Others question the use of scarce water supplies to grow crops in an area that is not suitable for farmland.

Several types of irrigation systems are presently in use. The type of system depends on cost, the crop to be irrigated, the slope of the land, and the source of water being used. Four common methods of irrigation are flood irrigation, furrow irrigation, overhead irrigation, and subirrigation.

Social Studies

The importance of water to the economy is illustrated by the computer industry. When the computer industry emerged, many companies were located in the so-called Silicon Valley region of California. This region became one of the most prosperous areas in the nation. In the late 1980s, however, the region experienced hard times. Although many factors were involved, the 6-year drought that struck the region during that time played a role. The manufacturing of computer chips uses an enormous amount of water. Several companies chose to relocate to areas with more plentiful water supplies.

Water uses in the United States

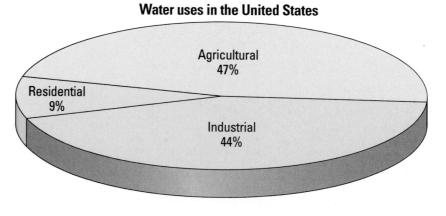

Agricultural 47%

Residential 9%

Industrial 44%

Figure 20.2 The United States drains over 1 trillion L of water a day from various water sources. About 75 percent is from surface waters such as lakes and streams. The other 25 percent is from groundwater in aquifers. About 500 billion L of the water drained is either consumed or lost to evaporation.

Figure 20.3 Flood irrigation (left) and furrow irrigation (right) are two of the most common methods used for irrigating crops in flat fields. These methods are inexpensive to use but may be costly in the long run because they both lose large amounts of water to evaporation.

Flood Irrigation   Flood irrigation is the flooding of an area of land that is flat. This method is commonly used because it is inexpensive. However, it is very wasteful because much of the water drains into soil not occupied by plants. Also, more than 50 percent of the water is lost to evaporation.

Furrow Irrigation   Furrow irrigation releases water into furrows, or ditches, dug between rows of crops. Furrow irrigation is also used in flat areas, but it is more efficient than flood irrigation because water is deposited closer to plants. However, the evaporation rate is high, and mineral salts accumulate quickly.

Overhead Irrigation   Sprinkler systems are the most common form of overhead irrigation. Sprinkler systems are useful on flat ground and uneven slopes. The efficiency of sprinkler systems decreases if strong winds blow the water away from its target.

Drip, or trickle, irrigation is an overhead irrigation method developed and commonly used in Israel. This system uses tubing to deliver small quantities of water directly to the root system of plants. Drip irrigation is expensive, but it is very efficient. This method may be used where slopes are irregular or where the water supply is low.

Figure 20.4 Drip, or trickle, irrigation (right) and sprinklers (left) are overhead irrigation methods used in areas with irregular slopes or low water supplies. Drip irrigation is very efficient but expensive. Sprinklers are also efficient, but they are not very useful when strong winds blow the water away from crops.

Figure 20.5 The runoff from melting snow and ice in the Sierra Nevada Mountains that naturally flows into Mono Lake is being diverted to Los Angeles, about 650 km away. The result has been the drying up of Mono Lake and an increase in the concentration of salt in the water. Excess salts form the towerlike structures you see here.

Subirrigation In a subirrigation system, water is introduced naturally or artificially beneath the soil. This system helps develop an artificial underground water source. Subirrigation is most effective in places where underground water sources are near the surface.

Effects of Water Use on Ecosystems

Often, human needs for water alter or destroy the habitats of other living things. The building of dams, draining of swamps, changing of stream courses, or removal of water from natural sources can all adversely affect wildlife. One example is illustrated by the case of Mono Lake in California.

Mono Lake is a saltwater lake fed by streams that carry meltwater rich in dissolved minerals from surrounding mountains. Mono Lake has no outlet. As water evaporates, salts are left behind. Algae, brine shrimps, and brine flies are the major organisms in the lake. They are food for California gulls and migratory birds such as grebes, phalaropes, and plovers.

In the 1940s, Los Angeles began diverting the meltwater that fed Mono Lake to other areas. The water-diversion project resulted in a major drop in the water level of the lake. The drop in water level has increased the salt concentration of the water. Some scientists predict that if this trend continues, the salt concentration in the lake will become so high that the lake will be unable to support the organisms now living in the water. How might this affect the gulls and migratory birds of the region?

SECTION REVIEW

1. Use Figure 20.2 to identify the three main consumers of water. Give two examples of how each of these consumers uses water.
2. What effects can human needs for water have on other living things?
3. **Infer** Review the ways that water is used in the home. Use the information in Table 20.1 to make five specific recommendations to reduce the amount of water use in the home.

20.2 WATER RESOURCES

OBJECTIVES • *Explain* ways in which fresh water is naturally stored as a resource. • *Predict* the effects of the depletion of an aquifer.

People store water by using dams and reservoirs. The water from rivers and rain runoff captured by dams may be used to meet water needs, to generate electricity, or both. The water in reservoirs comes from rain runoff, streams, and underground sources.

Surface Water

Surface water is water above the ground in streams, lakes, and ponds. Some sources of surface water are rainfall and the water from melting snow, glaciers, and ice sheets. The water resulting from rainfall and melting ice travels along the ground as *runoff*. Runoff is the water that does not seep into the ground, but instead flows down a slope over land. If the land is not covered with concrete or asphalt, the runoff carves shallow grooves in the ground called *rills*.

If the flow is continuous, the rills deepen and connect, forming streams. These streams flow and connect to form larger streams. The water in these larger streams is then deposited into lakes, ponds, or oceans.

A body of surface water may exist a great distance away from its source. For example, the Rio Grande originates from snow in the Rocky Mountains. Its mouth is located 3033 km away.

Surface water can also come from underground aquifers. If a stream channel intersects the aquifer, the water in the aquifer can flow into the stream channel. Water in aquifers that cross geological faults can flow to the surface as springs. Ponds, lakes, and bogs can form where depressions cross an aquifer.

Figure 20.6 The runoff from rainfall and melting snow in the Rocky Mountains is the source for the Colorado River, which brings water to California, Nevada, and Arizona. Runoff from the Rocky Mountains is also the source for the Rio Grande, which brings water to Texas and Mexico.

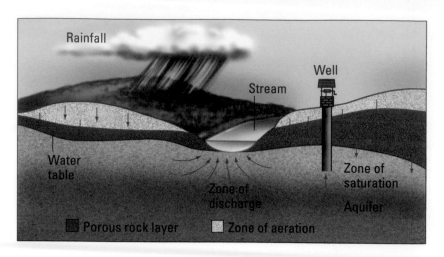

Figure 20.7 Slow-filling aquifers are fed by surface waters that seep into the ground through a zone of aeration. This groundwater may later leave the aquifer through a zone of discharge, or through wells that are used to pump water out of the aquifer for human use.

Rainfall

Well

Stream

Water
table

Zone of
saturation

Zone of
discharge

Aquifer

Porous rock layer

Zone of aeration

Aquifers

The water that does not flow as runoff seeps down through the spaces between soil particles. Water that fills the spaces between soil particles is called *soil water.* If the layer of bedrock beneath the soil is porous or full of cracks, called *joints,* the water is able to seep into the bedrock. Water within porous or jointed bedrock is called *groundwater.*

Over long periods of time, groundwater collects and saturates the layer of bedrock. *The top of the saturated layer of rocks is called the* **water table**. Look at Figure 20.7. Locate the *zone of saturation.* The zone of saturation is the saturated rock layer beneath the water table. An aquifer is another name for the zone of saturation.

Recall from Chapter 1 that an aquifer is a layer of porous rock that contains water. This layer is filled by the water seeping through overlying soil. The area where water enters an aquifer is called the *zone of aeration.* The place where groundwater leaves the aquifer and becomes surface water is called the *zone of discharge.*

The water in an aquifer does not move at a constant rate. It may move only a few centimeters a year or not at all. The rate at which water moves depends on the amount of precipitation or meltwater feeding the aquifer, the amount of open space, or porosity, of the rocks, and the slope of the aquifer.

Water Resource Problems

As the human population grows, there are increasing demands on freshwater resources. *When a body of water is drained faster than it is filled, the effect is called* **overdraft.** Overdraft can lead to some very serious problems.

In coastal areas the pressure from fresh water in an aquifer helps keep salt water from the ocean from intruding into the aquifer. If overdraft occurs, salt water can intrude into the freshwater aquifer, making the water unpotable.

Overdraft can also lead to subsidence. Two problems associated with overdraft are saltwater intrusion and subsidence, as shown in

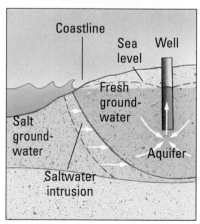

Coastline

Sea
level

Well

Fresh
ground-
water

Salt
ground-
water

Aquifer

Saltwater
intrusion

Figure 20.8 Subsidence (above) and saltwater intrusion (below) can result from overdraft of the groundwater in aquifers. The water within the aquifer can no longer support the weight of overlying structures or hold the salt water out of freshwater aquifers.

Figure 20.9 At one time, the Ogallala Aquifer is estimated to have held about 2000 km^3 of water. It is the largest known aquifer in the world. However, many scientists predict that the Ogallala Aquifer will run dry in about 40 years. The aquifer is being depleted very rapidly as a result of overdraft. The shaded area shows the underground extent of the Ogallala Aquifer relative to the surface.

Figure 20.8. The water within aquifers helps to solidify the bedrock and support the structures on top of the aquifers. When this water is removed, the bedrock may be weakened. The bedrock cannot support the overlying structures and it may sink, or subside. The San Joaquin Valley in California stretches nearly 400 km. The heavy agricultural activity in the valley has used huge amounts of water from local groundwater sources. Overdraft has caused a subsidence of up to 10 m in some areas.

Groundwater overdraft is also seen in the Ogallala Aquifer. As shown in Figure 20.9, the Ogallala Aquifer, the largest aquifer in the world, is located beneath parts of Texas, Colorado, Nebraska, Oklahoma, Kansas, Wyoming, South Dakota, and New Mexico. These High Plains states depend heavily on the Ogallala Aquifer for water, much of which is used for agriculture. However, because of the dry climate of the High Plains region, overdraft is occurring in the aquifer. Scientists estimate that the water remaining in the aquifer will last only about 40 more years.

The decrease of freshwater resources due to human activity is a serious concern for all organisms on Earth. Contamination of water supplies has led to the development of water-treatment projects. Also, the search for additional water resources has led to the development of ways to remove salt from water in the oceans and saline lakes.

SECTION REVIEW

1. Compare surface water and groundwater.
2. What causes overdraft?
3. **Infer** Water in the Ogallala Aquifer may be as old as a million years. This water is often called "fossil water." Why might people refer to this water as fossil water?

The Great Dam of China

The Yangtze River runs over 4000 mi from the mountains of Tibet, through China, to the Yellow Sea. Known in China as Chang Jiang, or "long river," the Yangtze is the third-longest river in the world. It cuts through steep mountains, forming spectacular gorges.

The Chinese government wants to harness the power of this great river with a giant dam. Construction of the dam, called Three Gorges Dam, began in 1994. It will be 670 ft high and 1.3 mi across and will create a reservoir 370 mi long. The government predicts that it will take approximately 25 years to build.

Is the Three Gorges Project necessary?

China Needs the Dam

The Three Gorges Dam will benefit China in several ways. Many people in China still live without running water or electricity. The dam will have a capacity of 18 200 MW, equal to the output of 18 nuclear power plants. The dam will make electricity available and affordable to more people.

The dam will also help prevent disastrous flooding from occurring along the Yangtze in the future. Devastating floods have claimed over 300 000 lives in the last century alone.

The Dam Will Be Destructive

Building Three Gorges Dam will have many serious repercussions. In addition to the 1.9 million people that will be required to leave their homes, thousands of ancient archaeological sites and artifacts will be lost under water. The Three Gorges area is also home to 47 rare and endangered species. These species may disappear as their habitat is altered.

About 80 percent of Chinese cities have no sewage-treatment facilities. Raw sewage is dumped directly into the river. It may collect behind the dam, causing serious health risks.

A channel is being built to divert the water and ships during the construction of the dam.

Consider the Issue

1. How will the Chinese people benefit from a large dam across the Yangtze River?

2. Do you think the Three Gorges Dam is necessary? Why or why not?

20.3 WATER TREATMENT

OBJECTIVES • *Explain* why fresh water in many parts of the world is not potable. • *Trace* the sequence of events involved in the purification of water.

In the United States and many other developed nations, water is treated in order to remove impurities. Safety checks monitor the quality of water to ensure it is safe to drink. This is not the case in many of the developing nations. For example, tap water is not considered safe to drink in much of South America, Mexico, China, and parts of Africa.

A large supply of fresh water is essential to a nation's development. Many areas of the world do not have a large supply of natural fresh water. These areas may not be able to support their human populations or the populations of other organisms.

Removing Salts

To increase their supply of fresh water, some nations seek alternative sources. They may look to the seas, salt lakes, or oceans for water. Few terrestrial organisms can meet their water needs with ocean water. Penguins can tolerate the high concentration of salt in ocean water because they have special glands that remove the salts. But most organisms do not have such adaptations.

The process by which salts are removed from water is called **desalination**. Desalination can be used to obtain fresh water for drinking, cooking, and irrigation. Desalination can also be used to remove salt from agricultural waste water. For example, high concentrations of salt in the waters of the Colorado River were killing crops in Mexico. The salts were leaching into the water as a result of the irrigation of farmland. To solve this problem, the United States built a desalination plant near Yuma, Arizona. The plant produces water with a lower salt content, which is returned to the river for use by Mexican farmers.

Three of the most common methods of desalination are distillation, reverse osmosis, and freezing. However, these methods may be very expensive. The cost of obtaining fresh water through these methods may be as much as four times greater than the cost of getting fresh water from traditional sources, such as lakes and streams.

Distillation In distillation, salt water is heated to boiling. Water is evaporated, but the salt remains. The water vapor is cooled, and liquid fresh water is collected.

Reverse Osmosis In reverse osmosis, salt water is forced through a strainer that traps the salt and lets the fresh water pass. The strainer is a thin membrane with tiny pores. The pores are large enough for water to pass through but too small for the salt.

Dateline 1993

In December of 1993, the Environmental Protection Agency issued a warning for residents of Washington, D.C., and nearby suburbs of Virginia and Maryland to avoid drinking water straight from the tap. The EPA told people to boil their water. It was feared that the tap water was contaminated with the parasite cryptosporidium. Cryptosporidium was responsible for thousands of illnesses in Milwaukee earlier that year. No illnesses were reported in the Washington, D.C., area. A week later, EPA tests showed water samples were healthy, and the warning was removed.

Figure 20.10 The salt removed from seawater also provides valuable nutrients and minerals for food and industrial uses.

Think About It!

People who drink bottled water while traveling in developing countries often use ice in their drinks. These people sometimes develop the same intestinal disorders associated with drinking contaminated water.

1. What is likely to be the cause of their illness?

2. How can this illness be avoided?

Figure 20.11 These steps are used in many typical water-treatment plants around the world. Treatment plants remove sediments and harmful microorganisms from the water, making it safe for human use.

Freezing In the freezing method, salt water is frozen. As it freezes, it separates, forming ice and a brine slush. The ice is free of almost all salt and can be melted to obtain fresh water. A desalination plant in Wrightsville Beach, North Carolina, obtains almost 1 million L of fresh water each day using the freezing process.

Water Purification

The treatment of fresh water for the removal of minerals may sometimes be combined with the treatment of water for purification. Water purification removes harmful chemicals and microorganisms that make the water unpotable. Water purification involves several processes: sedimentation, filtration, aeration, and sterilization. Similar processes are used in waste water treatment, which is discussed in Chapter 21. Refer to Figure 20.11 as you read about each process.

Sedimentation and Filtration In many water-treatment plants, screens are used to trap and remove debris that floats or is suspended in water. Once screened, the water is put into a settling tank, where it is allowed to stand undisturbed. As the water stands, particles suspended in the water settle to the bottom as sediment.

Some particles in the water are so fine they do not settle out but remain in the water. Often, chemicals called *coagulants* are added to the water to aid the settling process. The coagulant causes

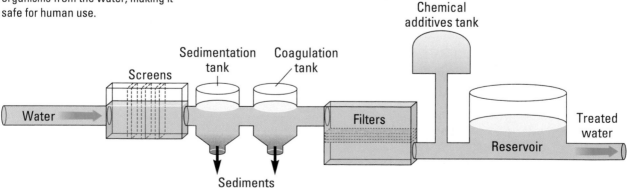

the fine particles to clump together. These heavier particle masses settle to the bottom of the tank. Together, sedimentation and coagulation remove most suspended particles, including bacteria, from the water. After the water is drained away, the sediment is removed from the settling tank.

Water drained from the settling tank is then ready for filtering. The water is passed through a 1-m-thick layer of fine sand. The sand filters out many of the particles that were not removed by sedimentation.

Aeration and Sterilization   Water that has been cleaned and filtered may still have undesirable qualities. For example, dissolved gases in water may give it an unpleasant taste or odor. In addition, harmful bacteria may still be present. Taste, odor, and bacteria are treated through aeration and sterilization.

The exposure of water to air is called **aeration**. Aeration is achieved by spraying the water into the air or by allowing it to flow as a waterfall. During aeration, bacteria that aid in purification enter the water. These bacteria break down organic matter still present in the water. At the same time, oxygen, a powerful purifying agent, mixes with the water.

Any harmful bacteria and microorganisms introduced by the previous processes are killed through sterilization. Sterilization can occur through the use of extreme heat or chemicals. The chemicals most often used in water sterilization are chlorine and ozone.

Chlorine is a very powerful purifier. It can be produced and stored easily. It destroys microorganisms and removes unwanted odors, colors, and tastes. Often, chlorine adds a distinctive smell to drinking water. The drinking water may smell like the water in most swimming pools.

Ozone is also a strong purifying agent and sterilizes water more rapidly than chlorine. The use of ozone, however, is limited because it is more expensive and more difficult to use than chlorine. Ozone must be refrigerated and can only be stored for a short amount of time.

At high concentrations, both chlorine and ozone are dangerous to most organisms. However, very little chlorine and ozone are needed to purify large volumes of water. Some studies show that the use of chlorine may produce other harmful chemicals.

Health

In many cities, fluoride is added to the water supply as part of the water-treatment process. Fluoride is added to water because it helps prevent tooth decay.

Field Activity

Obtain a water sample from a local pond or stream. Study the sample for color and clarity. Use the following steps to experiment with your water sample. Record and sketch your observations after each step.

1. First, examine a small amount of the water with a microscope.
2. Then pour another small amount of the sample through a piece of filter paper, and collect the water that passes through the paper. Examine a small amount of this new sample with a microscope.
3. Compare your observations of the water samples. Describe what effects, if any, filtering had on color and clarity. Also, what effect did filtering have on objects you may have seen under the microscope? **Caution:** *Wash hands after handling water that may contain microorganisms.*

SECTION REVIEW

1. Why is tap water not safe to drink in parts of China?
2. **Compare and Contrast** In what ways are the processes of screening, filtration, and sedimentation similar? How are these processes different?
3. **Infer** What types of methods may be needed to analyze water to make sure it is free of microorganisms?

Desalinating Seawater

PROBLEM
How can seawater be changed to fresh water?

MATERIALS (per group)
- 500-mL beaker
- metric measuring spoons
- 1000-mL flask
- glycerine
- glass tubing (fire polished) bent at right angle
- 1-hole rubber stopper
- rubber tubing
- pan of ice
- silver nitrate solution
- hot plate
- sodium chloride standards (prepared)
- cardboard
- coins
- salt
- 2 labelled test tubes with rack

PREDICTION
Write a prediction that is related to the problem.

PROCEDURE

1. To make salt water that has the salinity of seawater, pour 500 mL of tap water into the beaker. Add 18 g of salt with the metric measuring spoon and stir. Transfer about 15 mL of salt water from the beaker to a test tube labelled "seawater." Add silver nitrite solution to the test tube. Allow the test tube to stand for 2 to 3 minutes. Compare the amount of silver chloride precipitate in the test tube to the prepared sodium chloride standards. Record your observations in a data table. **Caution:** *Be sure all glassware used in this activity is clean.*

2. Transfer saltwater solution from beaker to flask. Rinse out the beaker. Set the flask on the hot plate, which should be turned off.

3. Rub some glycerine on both ends of the glass tubing, and construct the setup shown.

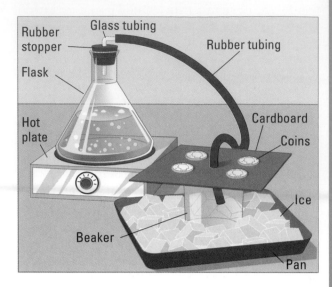

Caution: *Be careful when inserting the glass tubing into the rubber tubing and the glass tubing into the rubber stopper. If there is some difficulty in this step, please ask your instructor for help.*

4. Turn the hot plate on. Let the salt water boil until a small amount remains in the flask.

5. Turn the hot plate off, and let both the flask and the beaker cool before touching them.

6. Transfer 15 mL of water that has collected in the beaker to a second test tube, labelled "desalinated." Repeat silver nitrate procedure from step 1.

ANALYSIS
1. Why was it important to stopper the flask tightly?
2. How do the amounts of silver chloride precipitate in steps 1 and 6 compare?
3. What caused the change you described in question 2?

CONCLUSION
Imagine you are stranded on an island without fresh drinking water. You have only the following items in your possession: an army mess kit, a small mirror, a coffee cup, a roll of electric tape, and a pen. Describe in words and a sketch how you would obtain fresh drinking water from seawater.

KEY TERMS

irrigation 20.1   overdraft 20.2   aeration 20.3
water table 20.2   desalination 20.3

CHAPTER SUMMARY

20.1 Fresh water is used in great quantities by agriculture, industry, and households. The availability of fresh water in an area helps determine the type of agriculture and industry the region can support. Water availability is connected to the economy. Agriculture uses the greatest amount of water. Most of the water required for residential needs is used for hygiene. Human needs for water can often alter or destroy the ecology of an area.

20.2 Precipitation and meltwater are the sources of fresh water. Water from precipitation and runoff may flow as surface water, forming lakes, ponds, and streams. Water from precipitation and runoff may also flow beneath the ground in porous layers of bedrock. Water-bearing layers of

bedrock are called aquifers. Aquifers fill slowly and can be depleted. Results of aquifer depletion are reduced freshwater supplies and subsidence. In coastal areas, saltwater intrusion may result.

20.3 In the United States, most water used by people is monitored and treated to ensure its potability. Many developing nations do not have water-treatment plants, resulting in water that is not potable. In a water-treatment plant, screening, sedimentation, filtration, aeration, and sterilization are used to improve water quality. The ocean can serve as a source of fresh water after desalination. However, fresh water obtained from desalination methods, such as distillation and reverse osmosis, is very expensive.

MULTIPLE CHOICE

Choose the letter of the word or phrase that best completes each statement.

1. The process by which water is brought to an area for use on crops is called (a) desalination; (b) purification; (c) irrigation; (d) sedimentation.
2. The largest consumer of water in the United States is (a) agriculture; (b) industry; (c) urban centers; (d) residential areas.
3. In the home, most water is used for (a) cooking; (b) drinking; (c) personal hygiene; (d) washing dishes.
4. Water that is fit for use as drinking water is said to be (a) polluted; (b) runoff; (c) contaminated; (d) potable.
5. The type of irrigation that makes use of sprinkler systems is (a) flood irrigation; (b) drip, or trickle, irrigation; (c) furrow irrigation; (d) overhead irrigation.
6. The most wasteful and inefficient type of irrigation is (a) flood irrigation; (b) drip, or trickle, irrigation; (c) overhead irrigation; (d) subirrigation.
7. Many reservoirs are fed by underground water supplies flowing in (a) pipes; (b) aquifers; (c) streams; (d) runoff.
8. The water-treatment process in which water is forced into the air is called (a) purification; (b) aeration; (c) sedimentation; (d) filtration.
9. Particles in the water are able to settle out by (a) filtration; (b) aeration; (c) boiling; (d) sedimentation.
10. Two chemicals used to purify water are (a) bicarbonate and calcium; (b) sulfur and oxygen; (c) fluorine and sodium; (d) ozone and chlorine.

CHAPTER 20 REVIEW

TRUE/FALSE

Write true *if the statement is true. If the statement is false, change the underlined words to make it true.*

1. Most of the water used in households is for <u>drinking and cooking</u>.
2. Sprinklers are a method of <u>overhead irrigation</u>.
3. The most efficient method of irrigation is <u>furrow irrigation</u>.
4. <u>Distillation</u> is the process used by water-treatment plants to kill dangerous microorganisms.
5. Reverse osmosis is a method of <u>aeration</u>.
6. <u>Groundwater</u> can be a source of <u>surface water</u>.
7. <u>Subsidence</u> can result when overdraft occurs.
8. <u>Coagulants</u> are used to aid in sedimentation.

CONCEPT REVIEW

Write a complete response for each of the following.

1. Explain why water in some countries of the world is not fit for drinking.
2. Why is drip, or trickle, irrigation considered more efficient than flood or furrow irrigation?
3. Why must the zone of aeration for an aquifer be located at a point higher in elevation than the aquifer itself?
4. How are the zones of aeration and discharge similar to the source and mouth of a river?
5. How can human needs for water affect ecosystems?

THINK CRITICALLY

1. What can you infer about the properties of salt water based on the fact that freezing and boiling can be used as desalination processes?
2. Explain why icebergs could be used as sources of fresh water.
3. Why must wind be considered when using sprinkler systems but not when using flood or furrow irrigation techniques?
4. If you were the owner of a farm that had land with steep slopes, which irrigation method would you probably use? Why?
5. Why is the Ogallala Aquifer not able to replenish itself today?

WRITE CREATIVELY

Write a story telling of the attempts of a small island nation that is trying to get fresh water. Getting fresh water from the ocean is impossible because there are deadly microorganisms in the water. The small island is located in the southern hemisphere, and the island leaders are thinking of getting water from icebergs. However, the icebergs are located thousands of kilometers away, in Antarctica.

PORTFOLIO

1. Conduct library research to find out about Typhoid Mary. Report your findings in a written or oral presentation.
2. Interview a worker from the water-treatment plant that serves your community.

Find out what microorganisms are especially common in your area and what methods the facility uses to eliminate them from the water supply. If possible, arrange for the worker to speak to your class.

GRAPHIC ANALYSIS

Use the figure to answer the following.
1. In what part of a water-treatment plant does settling take place?
2. What happens to water when it first enters a water-treatment plant?

3. At what stage of the water-treatment process is fluorine likely to be added to the water?
4. What step of the water treatment process is left out of the figure?

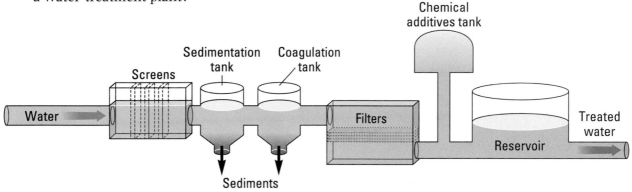

Water · Screens · Sedimentation tank · Coagulation tank · Sediments · Chemical additives tank · Filters · Reservoir · Treated water

ACTIVITY 20.2

PROBLEM
How does boiling make water potable?

MATERIALS (per group)
- pond water
- 500-mL beaker
- dropper
- 2 microscope slides and 2 coverslips
- microscope
- hot plate
- tongs

HYPOTHESIS
Write a hypothesis that is related to the problem.

PROCEDURE
1. Obtain 100 mL of pond water in a beaker. Using a dropper, transfer a drop of the pond water to a clean microscope slide. Apply a coverslip.
2. View the drop of pond water under a microscope set at low power. View all parts of the drop. Count the number of living organisms you see. Record this number.

Switch to high power, and record your observations in a data table. **Caution:** *Wash hands after handling pond water.*
3. Place the beaker of pond water on the hot plate. Turn the hot plate on, and bring the water to a full boil. Let the water boil for 10 minutes. **Caution:** *Wear safety goggles.*
4. After 10 minutes, turn the hot plate off. Carefully remove the beaker of water from the hot plate using tongs. Let the water cool to about room temperature.
5. Repeat steps 1 and 2 with the boiled water.

ANALYSIS
1. What did you see in the unboiled pond water with the microscope set at high power? In the boiled pond water?
2. Which sample of pond water had the most living organisms?

CONCLUSION
1. How does boiling water make it potable?
2. Describe three situations when you might have to boil water before drinking it.

Medical waste litters beaches in New York and New Jersey. In Delaware, health warnings are issued against eating shellfish because of bacteria in the water. Oil slicks near Texas and Alaska discolor beaches and damage ecosystems. Along the coast of California, fish, shorebirds, and sea mammals are threatened.

These are examples of why the ocean ecosystem is strained. Humans and other organisms are threatened by water pollution. The major cause of water pollution is ocean dumping. But water pollution is not limited to the ocean. Pollution is also a problem in lakes, ponds, rivers, and underground water systems.

21.1 THE WATER POLLUTION PROBLEM

OBJECTIVES • *Explain* the link between water pollution and human disease. • *Identify* the major types of water pollutants and their sources.

Water pollution is not a new problem. During the nineteenth century, people in England, France, Germany, and the United States often dumped their garbage into convenient waterways. The waterways became choked with wastes. Many rivers became unfit for drinking and bathing due to bacterial contamination. At the British Parliament building, located on the banks of the River Thames in London, England, the smell from the river became so bad on several occasions that Parliament was forced to close.

As waters all over the world became contaminated, infectious diseases such as cholera (KOL-er-uh), typhoid (TY-foyd) fever, and dysentery (DIS-uhn-TAIR-ee) became more common. For example, an outbreak of typhoid fever claimed the lives of 90 000 people in Chicago in 1885. In 1892, an outbreak of cholera killed many people in Hamburg, Germany.

Robert Koch, a German doctor, linked the cholera outbreak in Hamburg to contaminated water from the Elbe River. People began to realize that contaminated water was a major cause of human disease. As a result, the practice of direct dumping into waterways was banned in the United States and most European countries. Instead, barges were used to dump the garbage farther out to sea. As you can see in Figure 21.1, however, ocean dumping did not solve the problem. Contaminated water is still a major cause of disease in many parts of the world.

Ocean dumping is a common practice in the world today. Garbage that is dumped into the ocean does not simply disappear. It affects the ocean ecosystem and may drift back to shore, where it can become a health risk to humans. Many people are working hard to prevent the world's waterways from becoming a giant sewer

Sewage

Water that contains organic wastes from humans and industry is called **sewage**. Sewage comes from toilets, sinks, dishwashers, washing machines, and industrial equipment. In the United States, most sewage is treated before it is dumped. In many developing countries, however, the sewage is not treated. The United States government estimates that this country dumps about 8.9 trillion L of sewage into the ocean each year. Some of this waste is not

LINK
Biology

Robert Koch's work with diseases such as cholera, anthrax, and tuberculosis led him to develop a set of postulates that linked specific pathogens with diseases. Koch proved that anthrax and tuberculosis were caused by bacteria. Koch's postulates are still used today by scientists to link a disease with a pathogen.

Figure 21.1 Water pollution has been a problem for a long time. New York began dumping garbage into the Atlantic Ocean in 1900. The garbage often ended up on beaches in New Jersey, as shown in this cartoon.

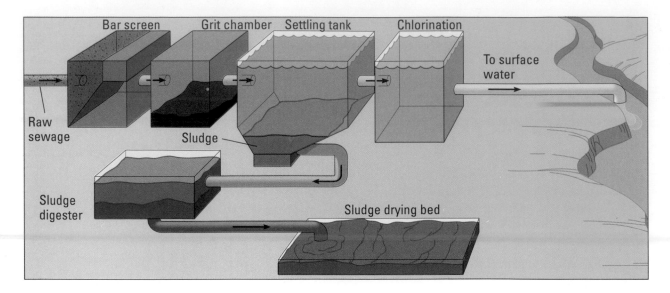

Figure 21.2 Sewage-treatment plants remove much of the pollution from sewage before it is dumped. Solids are separated out, and liquids are sterilized with chlorine. The dried solids are used as fertilizer or disposed of in landfills.

treated before it is dumped. Much of the waste is from factories and contains toxic chemicals and metals.

In urban areas, solid and liquid wastes enter an underground system of interconnected pipes called a *sewer system*. In many areas, rainwater from streets also enters the sewer system. Older sewer systems may dump untreated sewage directly into surface water. Modern sewer systems are connected to sewage-treatment plants. A **sewage-treatment plant** *is a facility that processes raw sewage before the sewage is returned to surface water systems.*

Figure 21.2 diagrams the path of sewage through a treatment plant. Sewage is first passed through screens that filter out plastics, fabrics, and metallic objects. Further processing includes the treatment of solid materials, called *sludge*, and the addition of bacteria and purifying chemicals. The bacteria break down organic pollutants. Chlorine and other chemicals are used to sanitize and deodorize the treated water. The chemical treatments remove microorganisms and harmful chemicals, but they do nothing to the organic matter in the sewage. This organic matter can lead to an excess of nutrients in the water system receiving the waste.

Sewage-treatment plants filter out most, but not all, of the pollutants in waste. Sometimes, untreated sewage is discharged into surface water systems if the treatment plant breaks down or is overloaded by surface runoff during heavy rains or floods. Water contamination occurred in 1993 in Des Moines, Iowa, after a treatment plant was flooded by the Mississippi River.

Many countries do not have effective sewage treatment. Sewage is a major health threat in these countries and a major source of pollution in rivers and oceans. Pollution from the Mexican city of Tijuana, for example, has forced beach closures in San Diego, California. The pollution also leads to outbreaks of diseases, such as cholera and dysentery. These diseases are treatable and preventable. However, the contaminated water makes disease a chronic problem.

Pathogens

Water pollution and disease are closely linked. Many disease-causing organisms spend part of their life cycle in water. *Parasites, bacteria, and viruses that cause diseases in living things are called* **pathogens** (PATH-uh-jens). Many pathogens enter water systems through infected raw sewage or animal wastes. The pathogens can then infect other organisms that come into contact with the contaminated water.

Pathogens carried by water result in more human illness and death than any other environmental factor. Typhoid fever and cholera, for example, are bacterial diseases spread by water contaminated by infected human wastes. With improved sewage and sanitation, these diseases have been controlled in most developed nations. However, people in many developing countries in Asia, the Middle East, Africa, and India still suffer from high rates of cholera and typhoid fever.

Schistosomiasis (SHIS-tuh-soh-MY-uh-sis) is a disease caused by microscopic worms. The worms enter through the skin of people who walk in water contaminated with infected human wastes. Once in the body, the worms attack the liver, urinary bladder, and intestines. Schistosomiasis is most common in Africa, the Middle East, and Egypt. This disease may affect as many as 100 million people in the tropics and causes more than 1 million deaths each year.

Malaria (muh-LAYR-ee-uh) is a disease caused by a *protozoan.* Protozoans are microscopic, animal-like protists. Malaria is usually transmitted to humans by the bite of an infected mosquito. Unlike typhoid fever, cholera, and schistosomiasis, malaria is not transmitted by contact with contaminated water. But water serves as the breeding ground for the mosquito that transmits the disease. Malaria is common in Africa, East Asia, and Latin America. Worldwide, more than 800 million people are infected with malaria. Of these, one million die each year.

Figure 21.3 These three organisms cause millions of human deaths every year. Water is an important part of the life cycle of the bacterium that causes cholera (left), the worm that causes schistosomiasis (center), and the protozoan that causes malaria (right).

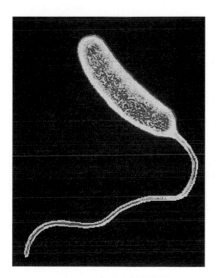

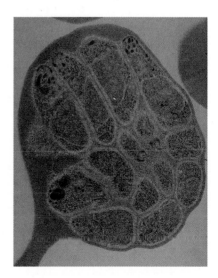

Types of Water Pollution

Sewage is the second-largest source of water pollution caused by humans. The largest source of water pollution is runoff from agriculture. Pesticides, fertilizers, and plant and animal wastes may end up in surface water systems as a result of poor agricultural practices. These pollutants can cause many environmental problems. Table 21.1 lists the most common water pollutants and their sources.

Table 21.1 Water Pollutants and Sources

Source	Pathogens	Nutrients	Sediments	Toxic Chemicals
Agriculture	•	•	•	•
Sewage-treatment plants	•	•		•
Industry		•		•
Urban runoff	•	•	•	
Mining runoff			•	•
Construction runoff		•	•	•

Field Activity

Conduct research on the use of pesticides by the growers who supply your supermarket with produce. There are references in libraries regarding pesticide use.

1. Make a list of pesticides used.

2. Research their related health risks.

Pathogens, nutrients, and sediments are the most common pollutants in sewage and agricultural wastes. Toxic chemicals are also dangerous pollutants. These range from crude oil and solvents to metallic elements, such as lead and mercury. Nontoxic substances can also pollute. Plastics, for example, are major pollutants. Because they do not break down easily in the environment, plastic items can trap or choke aquatic organisms.

Acids and radioactivity are pollutants that affect the land, water, and air. Acid from industrial air pollution can fall as rain, making lakes acidic and disrupting their ecosystems. You can read more about acid precipitation in Chapter 22. Radioactive substances are very dangerous and can last a long time. Even the waste heat from a power plant can be a pollutant. All these pollutants have one thing in common: they disrupt aquatic ecosystems. Many are also a threat to human health.

SECTION REVIEW

1. What is sewage?
2. **Organize Data** Make a list of the pollutants that appear in Table 21.1. Write a definition for each pollutant. Update your definitions as you read the rest of this chapter.
3. **Diagram** Create a flowchart or concept map that details the relationship among sewage, contaminated water, pathogens, and humans.

21.2 CHEMICAL POLLUTANTS

OBJECTIVES • *Examine* the sources and effects of inorganic and organic toxic chemicals. • *Describe* the process of eutrophication and its effects on lake ecosystems.

Elements and compounds that are directly harmful to living things are called **toxic chemicals**. Toxic chemicals are either inorganic or organic. *Inorganic* chemicals are elements or compounds that lack carbon. *Organic* chemicals are compounds that contain carbon. Many organic chemicals are derived from organisms.

Inorganic Chemicals

Inorganic chemicals include acids, salts, heavy metals, and plant nutrients. *A* **heavy metal** *is a metallic element with a high mass number.* Examples of dangerous heavy metals are mercury, lead, cadmium, nickel, and chromium. Plant nutrients are molecules that do not contain carbon yet are needed for plant growth. Phosphates and nitrates are important plant nutrients.

Acids and heavy metals enter groundwater and surface water systems as a result of seepage, runoff, and direct discharge into lakes, rivers, and streams. Recall that mine tailings often contain high levels of heavy metals, sulfur, or other toxic substances. Rain water may leach through tailings and carry wastes into groundwater and surface water. Heavy metals and acids enter water systems through leaching.

Heavy metal compounds are often by-products of industrial processes such as metal treatment and paint and plastics production. Factories sometimes discharge these materials directly into surface water systems. Metal drums filled with toxic factory wastes can corrode, allowing the waste to seep into groundwater or to

Literature

One reference to mercury poisoning occurs in Lewis Carroll's book *Alice's Adventures in Wonderland.* One character in the book is the Mad Hatter, an individual who suffers from Mad Hatter's disease. This disease was common among hat makers in seventeenth-century France. The material used to make hats was softened by soaking it in mercury compounds. Unprotected skin on a worker's hands and arms was in constant contact with the mercury. Mercury poisoning caused tremors, lack of coordination, nerve damage, and even insanity.

Figure 21.4 This toxic waste dump is on land, but it causes water pollution. Corroded drums release toxic waste, which can then be carried to streams and groundwater by rain.

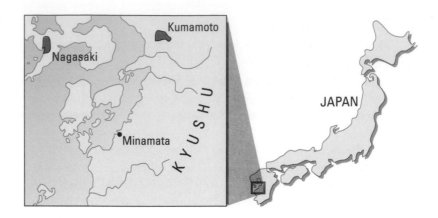

Figure 21.5 Minamata Bay was the site of mercury poisoning in the 1950s. Mercury from a plastics plant contaminated seafood that was eaten by the townspeople.

contaminate streams. These drums are also dumped into the ocean. Unfortunately, ocean water is very corrosive to most metals. The drums corrode quickly and release their contents.

Heavy metals are poisonous. Ingestion of these metals can cause brain, liver, and kidney damage, as well as coma and even death. A devastating case of mercury poisoning occurred in the 1950s in the coastal town of Minamata (min-uh-MAHT-uh) on the Japanese island of Kyushu (KYOO-shoo), shown in Figure 21.5.

The first sign of the problem was strange animal behavior. Birds began to fall out of trees and fly into buildings. Cats developed a strange walk, foamed at the mouth, meowed constantly, and sometimes ran in circles until they died. The problem became worse. Townspeople complained of headaches, dizziness, blurred vision, and numbness in their hands and feet.

Doctors soon discovered that the cause of the symptoms was mercury poisoning. The mercury came from a plastics factory that discharged mercury wastes into the waters of Minamata Bay. The mercury contaminated the fish and shellfish that were the main diet of the townspeople. Over a period of 20 years, 8000 people suffered paralysis or brain damage, and several hundred people died as a result of mercury poisoning.

Mercury poisoning in Minamata is one example of toxic chemical pollution. There are many others. Pesticides from agriculture are common inorganic pollutants. Acids from burning fossil fuels can accumulate in lakes, disrupting lake ecosystems. Inorganic pollutants can be very toxic, and they may be difficult to clean up once they contaminate an area.

Organic Chemicals

Organic chemicals can also be pollutants. Many of these chemicals come from living things, while others are made in the laboratory. Synthetic organic substances include gasoline, oils, plastics, some pesticides and fertilizers, solvents, and wood preservatives. Some organic chemicals can be poisonous to living things.

Organic chemicals enter surface and groundwater systems in

Most plastics are made from compounds taken from crude oil. The plastics themselves are usually not poisonous. In fact, most plastics do not decompose readily.

1. Why is this resistance to decomposition desirable in plastic products?

2. How could this resistance to decomposition lead to a pollution problem?

a number of ways. Wastes from petroleum refineries, chemical factories, and from canning, meat-packing, and food-processing plants are often discharged into sewer systems that empty into lakes or rivers. This discharge contains organic chemicals. Runoff from farmlands contains large amounts of organic insecticides, herbicides, and fertilizers. In time, these pollutants run into rivers and groundwater, and finally into the oceans.

Crude oil is one of the most common and dangerous organic pollutants. Because crude oil is transported along rivers and across oceans in huge amounts, its potential as a pollutant is a major concern. Crude oil often enters surface water systems as a result of spills at drilling sites, or from shipwrecked or damaged oil tankers. Oil may also be flushed into the sea when tanker crews use seawater to rinse out oil tanks.

A major oil spill occurred at an offshore drilling site in Mexico in 1979. An unsealed drill pipe allowed about 440 000 metric tons of crude oil to pour into the Gulf of Mexico. It took almost a year to control the flow of oil. In 1978, the oil tanker *Amoco Cadiz* tore open its hull when it ran aground off the coast of Brittany in France. Its entire cargo—220 000 metric tons of crude oil—was discharged into the Bay of Biscay. The largest oil spill in history occurred during the Persian Gulf War of 1991. Hundreds of thousands of metric tons of oil were spilled into the gulf, although no one knows the total amount.

The worst oil spill in U.S. history took place in 1989. The oil tanker *Exxon Valdez*, shown in Figure 21.6, ran aground on Bligh Reef in Prince William Sound off the coast of Alaska. About 42 000 metric tons of crude oil gushed into the water of the sound, polluting over 3000 miles of coastline. The ecosystem of the sound was devastated, and thousands of birds, mammals, and other organisms died. Marine biologists predict that the region's ecosystem will be affected for at least another 10 to 15 years.

Figure 21.6 The *Exxon Valdez* ran aground off the coast of Alaska in 1989. The bird in this photograph is one of thousands of animals affected by the resulting oil spill.

Using Microbes to Remove Pollutants

Oil spill. The words evoke images of a spreading iridescent layer on the surface of the ocean or globs of tarry stuff stuck to rocks, sand, and birds along the shoreline. Cleaning up an oil spill is a difficult task. In the past, efforts to clean up oil spills have included vacuuming the oil off the surface of the water and burning it off. Now scientists are using a new technique. They are using bacteria to digest the oil.

The process of using microorganisms to break down pollutants is called bioremediation. Recall that decomposer organisms are nature's recyclers, breaking down complex molecules into simpler substances. Some bacteria are able to do this with large hydrocarbons. When these bacteria are introduced into the spilled oil, they reproduce rapidly, consuming the oil. Sometimes the bacteria are already present, and all it takes is the addition of some nutrients, such as amino acids and vitamins, to stimulate the population growth.

Bioremediation has several advantages. The cost is about half the cost of traditional methods of dealing with spilled oil. With a variety of mixtures of bacteria, nutrients, and enzymes, the

Oil-eating bacteria (inset) are used to clean up water and beaches that have been polluted by oil spills.

material can be custom blended for each situation. The bacteria seem to have no side effects. Where bioremediation was used on a large oil spill in Japan, no harmful effects could be seen in local marine life.

Although bioremediation has been used most successfully on oil spills, it can also be used to break down other substances. Ethylene glycol, an ingredient in anitfreeze, is used at airports to deice planes. When this substance runs off the pavement into the ground, it can contaminate nearby bodies of water. Bacteria can be used to break down this chemical.

Not all substances can be cleaned up by bacteria. Heavy metals and radioac-

tive substances do not break down due to bacterial action. However, scientists are looking for bacteria that may concentrate these pollutants, making disposal of them simpler.

Checkpoint

1. What items are included in the bioremediation mixture added to an oil spill?

2. Bacteria are better at breaking down oil that is on water or in an aquifer than oil that has washed up on a beach. Suggest a reason for this.

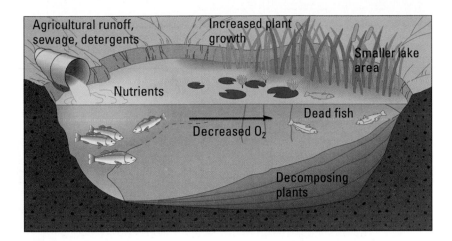

Figure 21.7 Eutrophication occurs in most ponds over time. Plant nutrient pollution can greatly accelerate this process. Large amounts of plant growth change the nature of the pond, leading to the disappearance of the original community.

Labels in figure:
Agricultural runoff, sewage, detergents
Increased plant growth
Smaller lake area
Nutrients
Dead fish
Decreased O₂
Decomposing plants

Eutrophication

Plant nutrients, nitrates, and phosphates are all used to fertilize crops. Solid and liquid animal wastes are also a rich source of plant nutrients. Some household detergents contain phosphates as well. These nutrients enter surface water systems as a result of runoff, industrial wastes, and sewage.

While these nutrients are generally not toxic and are good for plant growth, there are times when too many nutrients can cause environmental problems. Large amounts of nitrates and phosphates promote the runaway growth of algae and aquatic plants. In time, open-water areas become choked with plant growth. The plants die and decompose, resulting in a huge increase in the number of decomposer bacteria. This process lowers the amount of oxygen in the water, causing many animal communities to die out. *The process by which lakes and ponds are changed by excess plant nutrients is called* **eutrophication** (yoo-TRUHF-ih-KAY-shun)

Scientists estimate that more than 65 percent of the lakes in the United States are affected by eutrophication caused by human activity. One example of the effects of eutrophication is Chesapeake Bay, the largest estuary in the United States. Rivers carry farm fertilizers, mostly nitrates and phosphates, into Chesapeake Bay. Chemical factories also dump wastes. As a result, many fish, shellfish, and other important food organisms in the bay are in sharp decline.

Dateline 1955

Fishermen caught about 9 million kg of blue pike in Lake Erie. This was the largest catch ever. During the next few years, the blue pike fishery collapsed from pollution and overfishing. The blue pike is now extinct in Lake Erie. Fish such as the whitefish and cisco have been driven to extinction in a similar way. With the extinction of these species, fish such as carp and the freshwater drum, which are tolerant of pollution, experienced population increases.

SECTION REVIEW

1. What is eutrophication?
2. Describe the difference between an organic and an inorganic chemical. Give one example of water pollution by each.
3. **Analyze** The *Exxon Valdez* oil spill occurred because of human error. Can the possibility of human error ever be eliminated?

Nutrients and Algae Growth

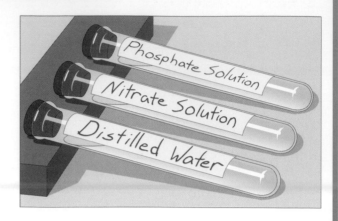

PROBLEM
How do phosphate and nitrate affect the growth of algae?

MATERIALS
- wax marking pencil
- 3 test tubes with screw caps
- distilled water
- 100-mL graduated cylinder
- 100 mL of 0.4% phosphate solution
- 100 mL of 0.4% nitrate solution
- *Chlorella* culture
- dropper
- light source
- pencil
- paper

PREDICTION
After reading through the entire activity, predict which of the solutions will contain the largest amount of the alga *Chlorella* after 6 days: phosphate solution, nitrate solution, or distilled water.

PROCEDURE

Day 1
1. Write your name on all three test tubes with the wax pencil.
2. Measure the volume of a test tube using the graduated cylinder. Then calculate 75 percent of this volume.
3. With the wax pencil, mark the first test tube *Distilled Water*, and fill it three-quarters full with distilled water.
4. Label the second test tube *Nitrate Solution*, and the third test tube *Phosphate Solution*. Fill both of these test tubes three-quarters full with the correct solutions.
5. Gently mix the *Chlorella* culture. Using the dropper, place 10 drops of the culture into each tube. Shake each tube gently to mix the contents.

6. Place the caps tightly on the test tubes, and lay them on their sides in a sunny, well-lighted area such as a windowsill.
Days 2–6
7. Check the test tubes every day for 5 days. Growth of *Chlorella* can be determined by an increase in the density of the algae, as well as an increase in the darkness of the green color in the tubes. Record any changes in density or color for each tube.

ANALYSIS
1. What were the changes, if any, in the *Distilled Water* test tube? Describe what you observed.
2. Were there any changes in the *Nitrate Solution* test tube? If so, describe them.
3. What occurred in the *Phosphate Solution* test tube? Describe what you observed.
4. Which test tube or tubes showed the most changes in color or density?

CONCLUSION
1. Which solution contained the most algal growth? Which contained the least?
2. Why did the algae grow in the pattern you observed?
3. Write a paragraph applying your findings. What effect would phosphate and nitrate run-off from farms have on a lake? How would organisms in the lake be affected? How could negative effects be prevented?

21.3 RADIOACTIVITY AND THERMAL POLLUTION

OBJECTIVE • *Explain* the problems of radioactive and thermal water pollution.

Nuclear power plants produce energy while releasing less air pollution. However, they do cause other kinds of pollution. Nuclear power plants have the same problem of waste heat disposal that other types of power plants have. Nuclear power plants also produce large amounts of radioactive water and other radioactive wastes. These radioactive pollutants are very dangerous.

Radioactivity

Recall from Chapter 16 that radioactive elements give off radiation when they decay. Radioactive elements such as uranium-235 and plutonium-239 are used as fuels in nuclear power plants. Other radioactive elements are used in medicine. Uranium mines and nuclear fuel refineries produce radioactive waste. Nuclear weapons detonations and power plant accidents produce the most radioactive waste of all.

Even under the safest operating conditions, tiny amounts of radiation are released into the air and water near a nuclear power plant. These emissions are not dangerous. The wastes produced by nuclear plants are dangerous. These wastes are very difficult to handle and pose a serious disposal problem.

The disposal of radioactive wastes, both solid and liquid, may also result in water pollution. Liquid wastes are placed in steel storage containers. These containers are encased in concrete and buried. Over time, these containers may corrode and break down allowing radioactive material to leak into the soil. The waste may eventually contaminate groundwater.

Figure 21.8 Tailings from uranium and copper mines are sources of metal pollutants. Uranium is mined to produce fuel for nuclear reactors and nuclear bombs.

Such events have occurred at many temporary disposal sites. In 1973, almost 1 million L of radioactive liquid waste leaked into the soil from the Hanford nuclear weapons site near Richland, Washington. Some of this contaminated material made its way into the Columbia River. A study released nearly 21 years after the leakage shows that the radiation contaminated fish and drinking water along the river. The study also states that about 2100 people were exposed to dangerous levels of radiation.

During the 1950s, the Savannah River Weapons Plant in South Carolina discharged radioactive waste into the Savannah River. This river is a source of drinking water for several southern states, including Georgia, Alabama, and parts of Florida and South Carolina. The Department of Energy is currently studying the possible health effects of this discharge.

Thermal Pollution

Power plants and other industrial facilities give off large amounts of heat, which can pollute water. *A large increase in water temperature due to human activity is called* **thermal pollution**. Thermal pollution usually occurs in lakes, rivers, or shallow bays located near power plants or industrial sites.

Power plants and industrial complexes often use water cooling systems to reduce excess heat. In such a system, cool water from lakes, rivers, or bays is pumped into pipes that lie alongside pipes containing hot water from the plant. Heat is transferred from the hot water to the cool water. Once cooled, the water is returned to the plant. The cool water, now heated, is returned to the water source.

Thermal pollution affects water ecosystems in several ways. The body temperature of fish is determined partially by the environment. Thus, as water temperature increases, so does their body temperature. Increased body temperature increases metabolism, which in turn increases respiration rate and the amount of oxygen the fish need. At the same time, an increase in water temperature decreases the amount of dissolved oxygen the water can hold. The fish suffocate because they cannot get enough oxygen. The increased water temperature is also destructive to developing eggs and young fish.

SECTION REVIEW

1. What is thermal pollution?
2. **Deduce** Nuclear power plants produce large amounts of radioactive water. Why? You may need to refer to Chapter 16.
3. **Predict** Many organic products give off heat as they decompose. Do you think this heat could serve as a source of thermal pollution? Explain.

21.4 CONTROLLING WATER POLLUTION

OBJECTIVES • *Identify* government attempts to control water pollution. • *Describe* the problems involved in enforcing laws regarding water pollution.

The first U.S. legislation to address water pollution was the Rivers and Harbors Act of 1899. Yet after a century of concern and laws designed to control pollution, the problem still exists. Why have many of the laws failed? The reasons are that the laws were often not strong enough, and strong laws were not obeyed or enforced.

Before 1948, individual states were responsible for enforcing laws governing water pollution. Scientific reports on kinds and amounts of pollution were not accurate. Several sources were often responsible for pollution at different sites along a given waterway, making it difficult to determine who was responsible and who should be punished. In addition, little was known about the effects of pollution on aquatic ecosystems.

The politics of industry was also an important factor in the failure of early water pollution laws. If a factory was charged with violating a law and fined, the factory might threaten to move to a state where laws were less strict. The removal of the factory would cause a large loss of jobs in the surrounding area, harming the economy. Some industries used the threat of moving to avoid fines and to get water pollution laws suspended.

In response to concerns about the environment and political pressure, Congress passed the Federal Water Pollution Control Act in 1972. That legislation, now called the Clean Water Act, was an attempt to set water-quality standards for all fifty states. The Clean Water Act provides a vision of water quality standards and a means of measuring improvement. The Clean Water Act is not, however, a set of laws for enforcement.

Although a number of states have shown some improvement in water quality, there are still many problems with sewage treatment, soil erosion, land-use control, and the removal of toxic chemicals and heavy metals. More recently, cancer-causing agents have been identified in the drinking water in several states. Local, state, and federal laws must be strengthened and enforced if water-quality standards are to be met.

Progress has been slow and the results mixed. Phosphates and other pollutants have been greatly reduced in Lake Erie. At the same time, however, the lower Mississippi River is dangerously polluted, and Chesapeake Bay is still threatened by an overload of nutrients and toxic chemicals. It is important to note that the quality of the U.S. water supply has not become worse at a time

Dateline 1969

The Cuyahoga River in Cleveland, Ohio, was so polluted that the river actually caught fire and burned for several days. This incident was a major factor behind the passage of the Clean Water Act of 1972.

Figure 21.9 Most plastics are not toxic, but they are still pollutants. Plastics break down very slowly in the environment. Discarded fishing nets and other plastic objects are a threat to sea animals. You can help solve this problem by disposing of plastics properly.

Water pollution is found almost every place where there are humans. Take a field trip to a river, stream, lake, or other water source near your school, and survey the site for pollution.

1. Make a table classifying the pollution you see. Try to identify the source of each pollutant.

2. After you leave the site, write a short essay describing your observations. What pollutants did you see? Where did the pollutants come from?

3. What can you do to help solve the problems you have identified?

when the population continues to grow. On the whole, the nation is moving toward better water quality. Table 21.2 summarizes water pollution legislation.

Table 21.2   Water Pollution Legislation

Year	Legislation
1899	**Rivers and Harbors Act:** U.S. Army is responsible for protecting navigable waters.
1934	**Fish and Wildlife Coordination Act:** Fish and Wildlife Service and other agencies to determine the impact of proposed projects on fish and wildlife.
1948	**Federal Water Pollution Control Act:** U.S. Army to apply environmental standards when approving water dumping.
1966	**Clean Water Restoration Act:** Authorizes federal assistance for sewage-treatment plant construction.
1970	**Water Quality Act:** Regulates oil pollution from vessels and offshore facilities.
1972	**Clean Water Act:** Establishes four broad national goals addressing the elimination of polluting wastes, better sewage treatment, and a cleanup program.
1972	**Ports and Waterways Safety Act:** Monitors pollution from ships; regulates ship design and safety.
1972	**Marine Protection and Sanctuaries Act:** Regulates ocean dumping and creates sanctuaries for endangered marine species.
1974	**Safe Drinking Water Act:** Establishes minimum safety standards for community water supplies.
1976	**Toxic Substance Control Act:** Regulates the use and disposal of toxic chemicals.
1985	**Clean Water Act Amendment:** Sets a national goal of making all surface waters "fishable and swimmable."
1990	**London Dumping Convention:** Calls for an end to all ocean dumping of industrial wastes, plastics, and tank washing wastes.

SECTION REVIEW

1. What is being done to control water pollution? Are these measures effective?

2. What can you do as an individual to reduce the effects of water pollution?

3. **Justify** You are on the town planning committee. A company that employs 75 percent of the people in your community has been cited for water pollution violations. The company says it will move if it is told to pay the fines. Will you vote to make the company pay? Explain your answer.

KEY TERMS

sewage 21.1
sewage-treatment plant 21.1
pathogen 21.1

toxic chemical 21.2
heavy metal 21.2

eutrophication 21.2
thermal pollution 21.3

....

CHAPTER SUMMARY

21.1 Contaminated water is closely linked to human diseases. In developed countries, sewage is treated to remove pollutants before it is discharged into waterways. Agricultural runoff is the largest source of water pollution; sewage and industry are other major sources.

21.2 Toxic chemicals are compounds or elements that are directly poisonous to living things. Toxic inorganic chemicals include acids, pesticides, and heavy metals such as lead and mercury. Toxic organic chemicals include some pesticides, oil, and oil products. Nutrient pollution can lead to eutrophication in lakes and estuaries.

21.3 Radioactive pollutants last for a long time and can be dangerous in small quantities. Thermal pollution is excess heat from power plants discharged into surface water systems. Thermal pollution can damage aquatic ecosystems.

21.4 The U.S. government has passed laws attempting to regulate water quality for about 100 years. State-controlled legislation failed because different states had different standards. The Clean Water Act was passed in 1972. Laws controlling water pollution have been difficult to enforce, and some laws have not been strong enough.

....

MULTIPLE CHOICE

Choose the letter of the word or phrase that best completes each statement.

1. Mercury is a pollutant classified as
   (a) an organic material; (b) a pathogen;
   (c) a radioactive waste; (d) a heavy metal.
2. The solid waste produced by a sewage-treatment plant is called (a) sludge;
   (b) slime; (c) discharge; (d) runoff.
3. The process by which excess nutrients enter an aquatic ecosystem is called (a) subsidence;
   (b) eutrophication; (c) thermal pollution;
   (d) pathogen pollution.
4. Thermal pollution is caused by excess
   (a) heat; (b) sewage; (c) inorganic materials;
   (d) radioactivity.
5. The pollutants associated with eutrophication are (a) pathogens and inorganic chemicals; (b) nitrates and pathogens; (c) nitrates and phosphates; (d) heavy metals.
6. Crude oil is a toxic chemical that is

(a) a pathogen; (b) inorganic; (c) organic;
(d) a heavy metal.
7. Microorganisms that cause disease are classified as (a) pathogens; (b) inorganic materials; (c) organic materials; (d) thermal pollutants.
8. The types of pollution that result from nuclear power plants are (a) radioactivity and pathogens; (b) thermal pollution and heavy metals; (c) radioactivity and thermal pollution; (d) thermal pollution and organic materials.
9. The first step in the sewage-treatment process is the (a) screening of large particles; (b) chlorination; (c) sedimentation;
   (d) grit chamber.
10. In 1972, the U.S. government passed an important act called the (a) Rivers and Harbors Act; (b) Clean Water Act; (c) Water Safety Act; (d) Strategic Water Initiative.

WORD COMPARISONS

Write the letter of the second word pair that best matches the first pair.

1. Cholera: sewage as (a) radioactivity: nuclear power plant; (b) nitrates: phosphates; (c) oil: plastics; (d) laws: enforcement.
2. Organic: inorganic as (a) nitrates: phosphates; (b) toxic: nontoxic; (c) oil: plastics; (d) lake: estuary.
3. Heat: thermal pollution as (a) lake: estuary; (b) inorganic: organic; (c) nitrates: eutrophication; (d) oil: plastics.
4. Mercury: heavy metals as (a) nitrates: phosphates; (b) cholera: pathogens; (c) agriculture: eutrophication; (d) agriculture: food.
5. Clean Water Act: water standards as (a) nitrates: phosphates; (b) oil production: pollution; (c) Ports and Waterways Safety Act: ship design; (d) nitrates: eutrophication.

CONCEPT REVIEW

Write a complete response for each of the following.

1. Name several sources of radioactivity that may result in water pollution.
2. Why is heat considered a form of pollution?
3. How do organic nutrients from human activity affect aquatic ecosystems?
4. Give examples of inorganic materials that are pollutants.
5. Where do the pathogens in water come from?

THINK CRITICALLY

1. Describe the process of sewage treatment. Are all pollutants removed during the process?
2. Suppose you observed a lake with a great deal of plant growth and large numbers of dead fish. Explain what may have caused this problem and what evidence you would look for to support your hypothesis.
3. Shellfish often collect and concentrate pollutants from their surroundings in their bodies. Could this fact have played a role in the mercury poisoning in Minamata Bay?
4. Suggest ways to make the transport of oil safer. Is there any way to transport oil without posing any environmental risk?
5. Explain how the differences in state water pollution standards for industry made state pollution laws difficult to enforce.

WRITE FOR UNDERSTANDING

Describe the mercury poisoning of Minamata Bay in your own words. Where did the pollution come from? Explain how the pollution got into the bodies of the people living near the bay. What were the effects of the mercury pollution?

PORTFOLIO

1. Identify and draw or photograph locations in your community where water pollution has occurred or is likely to occur. Create a visual display explaining why the area is at risk of pollution, including captions that explain how the situation could be corrected.
2. Begin a scrapbook of newspaper and magazine articles that cite examples of how people and other living things are being harmed by water pollutants. Group related articles together according to which means of legislation could be used to stop the pollution.

Use Figure 21.2 to answer the following.
1. What is shown in the diagram?
2. Where in the diagram are large solids separated from water by screening?
3. At what stage in the process shown are chemicals added to water to purify the water?
4. What is the material called that collects at the bottom of the tanks?
5. What happens to water that leaves this treatment facility?

ACTIVITY 21.2

PROBLEM
How does organic material break down and pollute water sources?

MATERIALS
- 3 different water samples (such as dishwater, well water, rainwater, tap water, or pond water)
- 3 test tubes and a rack
- masking tape
- graduated cylinder
- diluted methylene blue dye
- dropper

HYPOTHESIS
After reading through the activity, write a hypothesis about the relationship between the amount of organic matter in water sources and the resulting amount of water pollution.

PROCEDURE
Note: Bacteria act on methylene blue dye and cause it to change from blue to a colorless liquid. The more bacteria a water sample contains, the faster the color of the dye breaks down.
1. Mark three test tubes *A, B,* and *C.* Put 5 mL of a different water sample in each tube. *Note: Be sure and choose water samples that contain different amounts of organic material, such as tap water, rainwater, and pond water.*
2. Add 20 drops of diluted methylene blue dye to each of the water samples. Put the test tubes in the test-tube rack, and observe them at 10-minute intervals for 1 hour. Record your observations in the data table.

ANALYSIS
1. In which test tube did the color disappear first?
2. Which water sample contains the greatest amount of organic matter? Which contains the least?
3. Since bacteria use oxygen and do not carry out photosynthesis, which gases would be limited in water that is rich in organic material?

CONCLUSION
1. What are possible sources of organic matter in each positive sample?
2. Hypothesize about the reasons for a lack of organic material in each negative sample.

Appearance of Methylene Blue in Test Tube

Test Tube	Kind of Water	After 10 min	After 20 min	After 30 min	After 40 min	After 50 min	After 60 min
A							
B							
C							

22

AIR AND NOISE POLLUTION

Imagine you are hiking in the Adirondack Mountains in New York State. You walk through a forest and stop by the edge of a clear lake. No fish jump and break the glassy surface. You notice that there are no plants in the water at all. Suddenly you realize the lake doesn't hold a single living thing.

Scenes like this one are occurring more and more often across the Northern Hemisphere. The cause of the lake's death was acid precipitation. Acidic pollutants released into the atmosphere by coal-burning power plants fell into the lake as rain and snow. The organisms in the lake died when the lake water became too acidic to support life.

22.1 THE AIR POLLUTION PROBLEM

OBJECTIVES • **Describe** air pollution. • **Identify** common outdoor and indoor air pollutants.

Air is a mixture of gases, including nitrogen (78 percent), oxygen (21 percent), and small amounts of argon, carbon dioxide, and water vapor. As air moves across Earth's surface, it picks up materials formed by natural events and human activities. Some of these materials are harmful to both living and nonliving things. *Harmful materials that enter the environment are called* **pollutants** (poh-LOOT-unts).

Harmful substances released into the atmosphere are collectively called *air pollution*. Most pollutants entering Earth's atmosphere come from natural sources, such as sand and dust storms, volcanic eruptions, and forest fires. Ocean spray and gases produced by decaying organisms also add pollutants to the air. However, human activity has become a major source of air pollution.

Air pollution caused by human activity is not a new problem. Early Western philosophers complained of air pollution when they described the contaminated air of ancient Rome. Air pollution became a widespread problem during the Industrial Revolution of the 1700s. This period of rapid industrial growth depended on energy from the burning of huge amounts of coal and wood. The effects of polluted air on human life were devastating. For example, 1500 Londoners died from the effects of coal smoke in 1911. Table 22.1 lists other cases of illness and death caused by air pollution. These deaths were caused by everyday industrial pollution, not by chemical spills or other accidents.

Table 22.1 Air Pollution Disasters

Year	Location	Human Casualties
1880	London, England	1000 dead
1948	Donora, Pennsylvania	6000 ill, 20 dead
1950	Poza Rica, Mexico	322 ill, 22 dead
1952	London, England	3500–4000 dead
1953	New York, New York	250 dead
1956	London, England	900 dead
1957	London, England	700–800 dead
1962	London, England	700 dead
1963	New York, New York	200–400 dead
1965	New York, New York	400 dead
1966	New York, New York	165 dead

Figure 22.1 Air pollutants come from many sources. Coal-burning power plants, automobiles, and livestock are three main sources.

Outdoor Pollutants

Air pollutants are classified as either gases or particulates. *Tiny solids suspended in the atmosphere are called* **particulates** (par-TIK-yu-luts). The most common particulates are pieces of ash, dust, and soot from burning organic matter. Liquid droplets in smoke or smog are particulates. Traces of metals such as lead, iron, and copper are particulates as well. Pesticides, herbicides, and fertilizer dust are common pollutants in rural areas, as is plant pollen. Because of their size, particulates are dangerous to people. The tiny particles are easily inhaled with air and become trapped in the lungs.

Most gaseous pollutants come from a group of chemicals called oxides. **Oxides** (OK-syds) *are compounds of oxygen and another element.* The most common oxides are compounds of oxygen and carbon, sulfur, or nitrogen. These compounds are released when fossil fuels and organic matter are burned, especially in automobiles and coal-burning power plants.

Cities with heavy automobile traffic often develop a condition called photochemical smog. **Photochemical smog** *is a yellow-brown haze formed when sunlight reacts with pollutants produced by cars.* One of the chemicals in photochemical smog is ozone (O_3). Ozone is very corrosive and easily breaks down rubber and some synthetic fibers. In high concentrations ozone is also poisonous to plants and animals. Photochemical smog contains other pollutants as well. One of these pollutants is nitrogen dioxide (NO_2). Nitrogen dioxide is a brown gas that gives photochemical smog its distinctive brown color.

The hydrocarbons are another group of gaseous pollutants. Recall that hydrocarbons are compounds made up mostly of hydrogen and carbon. Methane is the most common hydrocarbon pollutant. It is produced by microorganisms in the digestive systems of livestock, certain bacteria, and by decaying organic matter. A related group of pollutants is called the chlorofluorocarbons. **Chlorofluorocarbons** (KLOR-oh-FLUR-oh-KAR-bunz), *or* **CFCs,** *are compounds of carbon, chlorine, and fluorine once used in refrigerators, air conditioners, aerosol cans, and in the production of polystyrene foam.*

Indoor Pollutants

With so many pollutants in the outside air, you may feel safer staying indoors. However, indoor air is not always cleaner than outdoor air. Air inside buildings often contains high levels of pollutants.

Several factors are responsible for the high levels of indoor air pollutants. Home products such as plastics, insulation, and cleaners give off harmful fumes. Air circulation in buildings is often poor, especially during winter, when buildings are closed up to save energy. The effects of fumes and decreased air circulation are multiplied because most people spend 16 to 18 hours a day indoors. This exposure to pollutants can cause serious health problems.

Table 22.2 Common Indoor Pollutants

Pollutant	Source
Carbon monoxide	Cigarette smoke, stoves and heaters, automobiles
Formaldehyde	Particle board, furniture, carpeting, foam insulation
Paradichlorobenzene	Mothballs
Methyl chloride	Paint thinner
Tetrachloroethylene	Dry-cleaning fluid
Ammonia	Cleaning agents
Hydrocarbons	Solvents, adhesives
Asbestos	Insulation, fireproofing materials
Particulates	Cigarette smoke, pollen, burning wood and coal
Bacteria, fungi	Heating and cooling ducts

The combination of particulates, gases, and other chemicals contained in cigarette smoke makes it the deadliest of all indoor pollutants. Cigarette smoke is hazardous not only to smokers but to nonsmokers as well. Nonsmokers breathe in secondhand, or sidestream, smoke. Secondhand smoke from filtered cigarettes contains higher levels of particulates from burning paper and tobacco than the smoke inhaled by the smoker.

Microorganisms are another kind of indoor air pollutant. Ventilation ducts and vents are often home to bacteria and fungi. Airtight buildings can fill quickly with potentially disease-causing organisms. Table 22.2 lists other common indoor pollutants.

In 1988, the National Council on Radiation Protection and Measurements alerted homeowners to another indoor pollutant, radon gas. **Radon** (RAY-don) *is a colorless, odorless, radioactive gas.* Scientists think that at least half of an average person's yearly radiation exposure comes from radon. Radon forms when radium, a radioactive element in soil, breaks down. Radon from soil is drawn into a home through the basement. Atoms of radon stick to particulates in the air and enter a person's lungs when they are inhaled. Long-term exposure to high levels of radon is one cause of lung cancer.

SECTION REVIEW

1. What is a pollutant?
2. **Organize Data** Make a table that lists common outdoor air pollutants and their sources.
3. **Analyze** Suggest ways that you could reduce the amount of air pollutants in your home.

22.2 AIR POLLUTION AND LIVING THINGS

OBJECTIVES • *Identify* the effects of air pollution on human health.
• *Describe* the effects of air pollution on plants and animals.

Air pollution has been linked to many health problems. Long-term exposure may cause diseases and chronic health problems. Pollutants may also worsen existing medical conditions, especially in children and the elderly.

Carbon monoxide is a dangerous air pollutant. It readily binds with hemoglobin, the substance in red blood cells that carries oxygen. Carbon monoxide actually binds to hemoglobin more easily than oxygen does. If carbon monoxide binds to a hemoglobin molecule, the hemoglobin can no longer carry oxygen. The amount of oxygen carried to all the cells of the body is reduced. Moderate levels of carbon monoxide stress the heart and can cause headaches and dizziness. High levels can be deadly.

Ozone and oxides of sulfur and nitrogen can also cause health problems. These gases irritate the eyes and respiratory tract. They cause discomfort and difficulty in breathing. They also may trigger asthma or allergy attacks. Long-term exposure to ozone and oxides can also cause more serious diseases such as bronchitis and emphysema. **Emphysema** (EM-fuh-ZEE-muh) *is a disease in which tiny air sacs in the lungs break down.* More than 1.5 million people suffer from emphysema in the United States. Emphysema is often caused by cigarette smoking.

Particulates in the air have been linked to cancer. **Cancer** *is a disease in which cells grow abnormally and without restraint.* Some forms of cancer are very difficult to treat and can be fatal. Lung cancer is responsible for more than 150 000 deaths each year in the United States. Most of these lung cancers are caused by cigarette smoking. Cigarette smoke is also a contributing factor to other diseases, such as heart disease.

Health

The number one cause of death in the United States is heart disease. Heart disease is responsible for about 750 000 deaths annually. Most scientists agree that the leading cause of heart disease is cigarette smoking.

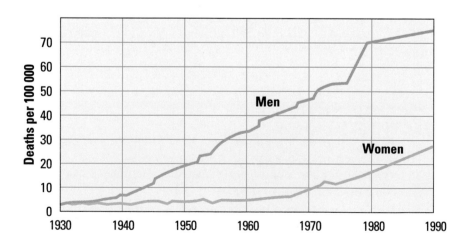

Figure 22.2 This graph shows the increase in the rate of lung cancer deaths since 1930. Cigarette smoking is almost the sole cause of this increase.

Figure 22.3 The trees in this forest were killed by air pollution. The pollution came from burning fossil fuels in power plants and automobiles.

Air pollution can affect organisms throughout an ecosystem. Ozone and the sulfur oxides are the pollutants most hazardous to plants. These chemicals damage plants directly, causing stems to become brittle and leaves to become spotted. Millions of ponderosa pines have been severely damaged by ozone pollution in the mountains around Los Angeles. Ozone and sulfur oxides damage agricultural crops as well. The United States loses up to $10 billion worth of crops each year because of air pollution.

Animals are also affected by air pollution. The loss of plants due to pollution in an ecosystem can disrupt the ecosystem's food chains and deprive animals of nourishment. Animals also suffer from many of the same pollution-related health problems as humans, including eye and lung irritation, bronchitis, and cancer.

Industrial air pollutants such as lead and zinc can contaminate rangeland. These poisons accumulate on grass and may enter the groundwater. Grazing animals such as cattle and sheep can take in large amounts of these pollutants as they feed and drink. The bones and teeth of these animals become weak. Lameness and weight loss often lead to death in severely poisoned animals.

SECTION REVIEW

1. What is emphysema? What causes this disease? How many people in the United States suffer from it?
2. **Organize Data** Make a table that lists air pollutants and the health problems each pollutant causes.
3. **Predict** List the diseases that cigarette smoking causes. How do you think industrial pollution would affect a person who smokes?

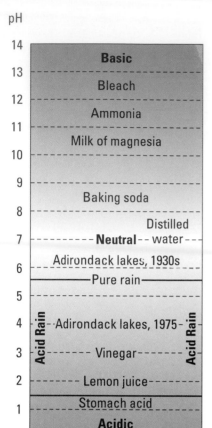

pH

14	**Basic**
13	Bleach
12	Ammonia
11	Milk of magnesia
10	
9	Baking soda
8	
7	Distilled **Neutral** water
6	Adirondack lakes, 1930s
	Pure rain
5	
4	Adirondack lakes, 1975
3	Vinegar
2	Lemon juice
1	Stomach acid
	Acidic
0	

Figure 22.4 This scale shows the pH of many common substances and of acid rain. Notice the large drop in the pH of Adirondack mountain lakes.

Field Activity

Rain is naturally slightly acidic, but polluted air can increase the acidity dramatically.

1. On a rainy day, uncover Petri dishes at various locations around your school or community. Let rain fall directly into the Petri dishes.

2. Record the location where each sample was taken.

3. In class, test the pH of the rain samples. How do your rain samples compare?

22.3 GLOBAL EFFECTS OF AIR POLLUTION

OBJECTIVES • *Identify the effects of acid precipitation and ozone depletion.* • *Explain the greenhouse effect and global warming.*

Pollutants harm living things directly. They can also cause far-reaching damage to the global environment. Some forms of pollution can threaten whole ecosystems. Pollution may even change the climate across the entire planet. Three major air pollution problems threatening the global environment are acid precipitation, ozone depletion, and global warming.

Acid Precipitation

Rain or snow that is more acidic than normal precipitation is called **acid precipitation**. Acidity is measured on a scale called the pH scale. A pH of 7 is neutral. A pH less than 7 is acidic, and a pH greater than 7 is basic. Figure 22.4 shows the pH of some common liquids, acid rain, and lakes affected by acid rain.

Normal rain and snow are slightly acidic and have a pH of about 5.6. Water in the atmosphere becomes acidic when it reacts with carbon dioxide, forming a weak acid called carbonic acid. However, water can also form much stronger acids when it reacts with other pollutants in the air. Recall that burning fossil fuels such as coal and gasoline produce oxides of sulfur and nitrogen. Sulfur and nitrogen oxides combine with water in the atmosphere, forming sulfuric acid and nitric acid. Both of these acids are strong, highly corrosive, and can be harmful to living things.

Sulfuric and nitric acids can fall to Earth with rain or snow. Much of the acid is carried downwind and falls into forests such as those in the Adirondack Mountains in New York. The acids accumulate in mountain lakes, lowering the lakes' pH. In Sweden, for example, 20 000 lakes are too acidic to allow fish to survive. Thousands of other lakes in Norway, Canada, and the northeastern United States are so acidic that they contain no fish or plant life. The absence of producers and other aquatic life disrupts food chains and causes the lake ecosystem to collapse. Some scientists predict that half of Quebec's 48 000 lakes will be destroyed by the year 2000.

Acid precipitation also damages trees. In former West Germany, more than 500 000 hectares of forest are dying from the caustic effects of acid rain. Forests are dying across Europe and in the United States and Canada. Acid rain also damages crops and buildings. Although it is impossible to put a dollar value on the destruction of entire lake and forest ecosystems, the economic cost of acid rain is estimated to be more than $5 billion a year in the United States alone.

Rain Forests on Fire

Imagine smog so dense that visibility is reduced to a few meters. People wear surgical masks when they go outside. Drivers have to keep their car lights on, even in the middle of the day. This is what happened during the most widespread ecological disaster ever to hit Southeast Asia.

In September 1997, a layer of dense smog covered much of Indonesia, Malaysia, Singapore, Brunei, Thailand, and the Philippines. The pollution was so bad that 35 000 people in Indonesia and 16 000 in Malaysia were treated for breathing problems. Five people in Indonesia died from smog-related respiratory ailments. Schools were closed and people stayed indoors, hoping it would soon be over. Officials in some cities considered evacuating people to an area where the air was cleaner, but there was nowhere to go. The entire region was covered with a thick, smoky haze.

The cause of the smog was in Indonesia, where large areas of rain forest were burning. The smoke from the fires was so thick it blanketed much of Southeast Asia. The usual city pollutants became trapped under the blanket of wood smoke. So in addition to wood smoke, people in urban areas were exposed to high levels of carbon monoxide, sulfur compounds, and particulates.

Thousands of firefighters tried to control the fires, which covered more than a half-million hectares. The president of Indonesia even sent soldiers to help fight the fire. The fires' severity was due to a drought, which scientists blamed on El Niño. And the monsoon rains, which were expected to put the fires out, were late that year, which was also an effect of El Niño.

But how did these terrible fires begin? They were set deliberately. In Indonesia, burning is routinely used as a way to clear forest areas. A common image is that of a small-scale farmer, burning the trees to clear new cropland. However, much of the land cleared by burning is actually used by large plantations, which grow crops for export

These citizens of Brunei wear surgical masks to prevent the inhalation of particulates from burning rain forests.

products such as palm oil. Although there are environmental regulations, they are not enforced. So year after year, the fires are set.

Checkpoint

1. What was the cause of the fires in Indonesia?
2. Why was the smog especially bad in urban areas?

Ozone Depletion

At the surface of Earth, ozone is a corrosive, poisonous gas. But a layer of ozone 20 to 50 km above Earth's surface is vital to life. Ozone in the stratosphere forms a protective layer around Earth. This ozone layer absorbs almost all of the ultraviolet (UV) radiation given off by the sun, preventing it from reaching Earth's surface. UV radiation is very damaging to living things.

Hole in the Sky   During the early 1980s, scientists discovered a thin area, or hole, in the ozone layer over the South Pole. Scientists have since found a small but growing hole over the North Pole. Some scientists claimed that holes in the ozone layer are normal and that more holes may exist. Other scientists thought that the ozone holes were early signs of a dangerous problem. Recent data, however, have quieted much of the debate. Most scientists now agree that the problem of ozone depletion is serious. The air over the South Pole now loses half its ozone every spring, and the global ozone layer has thinned by 2 to 3 percent in the last ten years.

Damage to the ozone layer could greatly increase the amount of UV radiation that reaches Earth. In humans, UV radiation can cause sunburn, blindness, and skin cancer. UV radiation can also cause severe crop damage. UV radiation could destroy the microorganisms that form the base of the aquatic food chain, disrupting the ocean ecosystem. Damage to land organisms would be equally severe.

Causes of Ozone Depletion   The main cause of ozone depletion is CFC pollution. Recall that CFCs are a kind of hydrocarbon in which atoms of chlorine and fluorine are attached to carbon atoms in place of hydrogen. CFCs, such as freons, have been used as coolants in refrigerators since the 1930s. CFCs were used as coolants in air-conditioning units and as propellants in aerosol sprays beginning in the 1950s. CFCs were also used in the manufacture of polystyrene and other plastic foams.

Figure 22.5 Air conditioners are a major source of CFCs.

Figure 22.6 These satellite data show the South Pole ozone hole since 1979. The hole is growing, and a similar hole has formed over the North Pole.

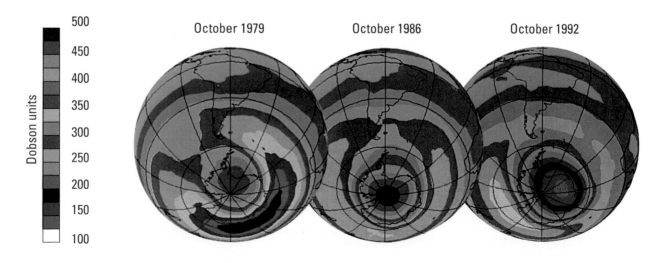

October 1979   October 1986   October 1992

Dobson units

500
450
400
350
300
250
200
150
100

In the lower atmosphere, CFCs do not react with other compounds; they are *inert*. Because they are inert, they do not break down readily. They circulate in the atmosphere and eventually rise into the stratosphere. In the stratosphere, CFCs are exposed to UV radiation. UV radiation causes the CFCs to break down, releasing chlorine and fluorine atoms. Both of these kinds of atoms destroy ozone. The chemical reactions in Figure 22.7 show how chlorine is produced and how it destroys ozone.

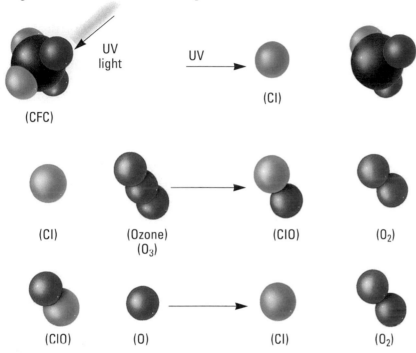

(CFC)   UV light   UV →   (Cl)

(Cl)   (Ozone) (O_3) →   (ClO)   (O_2)

(ClO)   (O) →   (Cl)   (O_2)

Think About It!

A catalyst is an atom or molecule that helps a chemical reaction take place. The catalyst is not consumed in the reaction.

1. Explain how chlorine causes the breakdown of ozone.
2. Why is chlorine considered a catalyst in this reaction?

Figure 22.7 These reactions show how chlorine is produced from a CFC by UV radiation, and how the chlorine destroys ozone. Notice that the chlorine atom is regenerated.

Dateline 1978

In 1978, the United States banned the use of CFCs in many products, such as aerosol spray cans. Denmark, Sweden, Norway, and Canada also banned the use of CFCs. In 1987, 24 nations agreed to reduce the use of CFCs by 50 percent by the end of this century. In 1990, this plan was changed in response to growing evidence that the ozone depletion problem was more serious than first thought. Nations belonging to the United Nations have agreed that CFCs will no longer be used by the year 2010.

Atoms of chlorine act as catalysts in the destruction of ozone. Chlorine is regenerated easily from chlorine oxide (ClO). The atoms are then free to destroy more ozone. Fluorine follows a similar pattern. Scientists think that every atom of chlorine or fluorine can destroy thousands of molecules of ozone.

Because CFCs are inert, they stay in the atmosphere for a long time, most of them for several thousand years. Some CFCs may last more than 50 000 years. These long lifetimes mean that most CFC pollution will eventually make it to the stratosphere—and ultimately destroy ozone.

Chlorine atoms are produced by many natural sources. Volcanoes emit large amounts of chlorine into the atmosphere, as do the oceans. Critics of the link between CFCs and ozone depletion have used this fact to argue that human-produced chlorine does not affect the ozone layer. But evidence from long-term experiments in the Swiss Alps has shown that natural sources contribute very little chlorine to the stratosphere. These experiments show that the major source of stratospheric chlorine and fluorine is CFCs produced by people.

Global Warming

Light energy from the sun enters the atmosphere and is absorbed by Earth's surface. Once absorbed, the light energy is changed to heat. Earth radiates this heat energy back into space in the form of infrared radiation.

The Greenhouse Effect   Earth's atmosphere acts much like a pane of glass. It allows light energy to enter, but traps some infrared radiation. The buildup of heat energy warms the air in the lower atmosphere. *The trapping of radiated heat by gases in the atmosphere is called the* **greenhouse effect.** Earth's greenhouse effect raises the average global temperature about 35 °C. Without the greenhouse effect, life on Earth would probably be impossible.

Some atmospheric gases trap infrared radiation. The atmospheric gases that trap heat are called *greenhouse gases*. The most abundant natural greenhouse gas is carbon dioxide. Methane, oxides of sulfur and nitrogen, ozone, CFCs, and water vapor are also greenhouse gases. Compared to carbon dioxide, these gases exist in the atmosphere in small amounts. However, they trap heat much better than carbon dioxide does. Methane traps heat 20 times better than CO_2, while nitrogen dioxide (NO_2) is 200 times more efficient. What do you think would happen if the amount of greenhouse gases in the atmosphere increased?

The amounts of carbon dioxide and other greenhouse gases in the atmosphere are rising because of the pollution caused by human activities. The main cause of this pollution is the burning of fossil fuels and other organic compounds. Look at the chemical

Figure 22.8 The greenhouse effect is a natural occurrence, although pollution caused by people can make the greenhouse effect stronger.

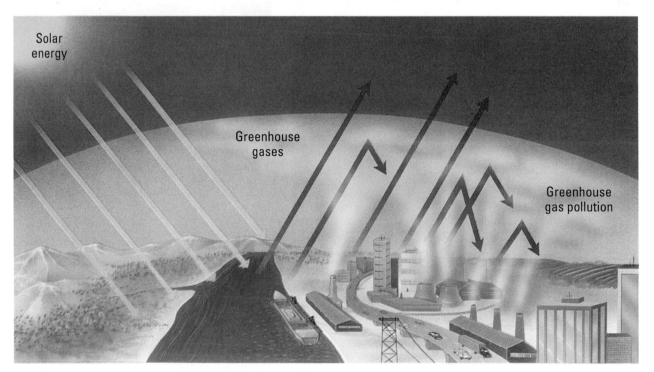

Solar energy

Greenhouse gases

Greenhouse gas pollution

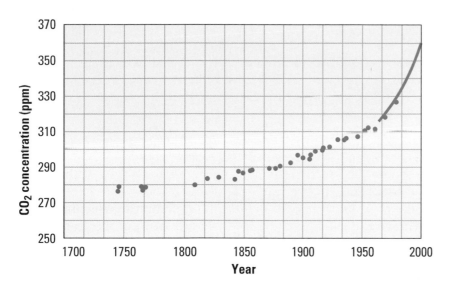

Figure 22.9 This graph shows the increase in CO_2 concentration in the atmosphere since 1750. The dots are ice core data. The solid line is a series of direct measurements.

reaction for the burning of a simple hydrocarbon called *octane*. Octane is a part of gasoline. Notice that CO_2 is produced:

$$2\ C_8H_{18} + 25\ O_2 \longrightarrow 16\ CO_2 + 18\ H_2O + Energy$$

Before 1750, the amount of carbon dioxide in the atmosphere was about 280 parts per million (ppm). Today, carbon dioxide levels are about 355 ppm and rising—an increase of over 21 percent. Figure 22.9 shows the increase in CO_2 levels during the last several hundred years.

The data for the graph in Figure 22.9 come from **ice cores**, *long cylinders of ice that are drilled and removed from deep within a sheet of polar ice*. The ice in these cores is filled with small bubbles, which are filled with air. The air has been locked in the bubbles for hundreds or even thousands of years. Scientists collect the air and test it for levels of greenhouse gases.

Figure 22.10 Ice cores like this one are used to study climate as it existed in the past.

Effects of Greenhouse Gas Pollution No one knows for certain what effect greenhouse gases will have on Earth's climate. But most scientists agree that they will have some impact. One thing *is* sure: The potential dangers of greenhouse gas pollution have made global warming a serious political issue. The powerful fossil fuel industry and environmentalists continue to debate the issue.

Greenhouse gas pollution may result in global warming. **Global warming** *is an increase in Earth's average surface temperature caused by an increase in greenhouse gases.* Recall that ice cores can be used to gather samples of the atmosphere as it existed in the past. Scientists now have reliable records of Earth's atmosphere for the last 200 000 years. These records show that another large increase (25 to 30 percent) in atmospheric CO_2 occurred at the end of the last ice age, about 14 000 years ago.

Scientists think that the large CO_2 increase at the end of the last ice age played an important part in changing Earth's climate. Earth's

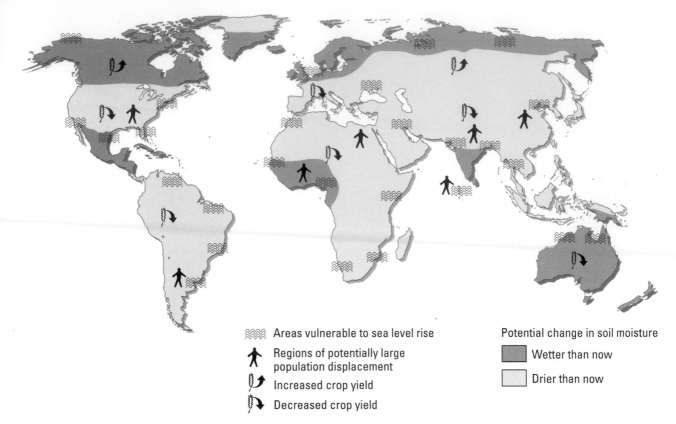

~~~~ Areas vulnerable to sea level rise

🧍 Regions of potentially large population displacement

🌾↑ Increased crop yield

🌾↓ Decreased crop yield

Potential change in soil moisture

⬛ Wetter than now

⬜ Drier than now

Figure 22.11 If global warming occurs, it will greatly affect the world's climate. This map shows many of the effects global warming may have.

temperature rose by several degrees. Glaciers that covered much of North America melted, and sea levels rose. These climate changes were caused, at least in part, by increased amounts of CO_2 in the atmosphere.

Computer models predict the same kind of climate change in the future. Because of greenhouse gas pollution, computer models project that Earth's temperature will rise by 2 °C to 4 °C by the year 2050. This increase may not seem large, but it could have disastrous results, as shown in Figure 22.11.

As Earth's temperature rises, the ice in the polar caps will begin to melt, and the ocean will expand. The water trapped in the ice will flow into the ocean, and sea level will rise more than 1 m, flooding lowlands, farmland, and coastal cities like New York and Los Angeles. In many areas, salt water from the oceans will enter the groundwater system. In addition, weather patterns will change. How might these changes affect housing, agriculture, transportation, and food production?

SECTION REVIEW

1. What are CFCs, and why are they harmful?
2. What is acid precipitation, and why is it harmful?
3. **Think Critically** Evaluate the evidence from ice cores and computer models. Do you think global warming will occur?

Greenhouse Model

PROBLEM
What causes the greenhouse effect?

MATERIALS (per group)
- 2 2-L plastic soft drink bottles
- scissors
- tape
- 2 thermometers
- 750 g dry potting soil
- clear plastic wrap
- rubber band
- 100-W lightbulb
- ring stand
- graph paper

HYPOTHESIS
After reading the entire activity, write a hypothesis that pertains to the problem.

PROCEDURE

1. Completely remove the labels from two 2-L plastic soft drink bottles. *Note: Use the figure to guide you through steps 2–7.*
2. Using scissors, cut off the top of the bottles where they begin to narrow.
3. Tape the thermometers to the inside of the bottles.
4. Tape small squares of paper directly over the thermometer bulbs.
5. Put about 375 g of dry potting soil into each bottle.
6. Cover one of the bottles with clear plastic wrap. Secure the plastic wrap with a rubber band.
7. Hang a 100-W lightbulb from a ring stand, and position the bottles at equal distances on each side of it. Face the thermometers away from the lightbulb. Do not turn the light on yet.
8. Read the thermometers, and record the temperatures. The thermometers should both show the same temperature. If they are different, you will have to add the dif-

ference to the thermometer showing the lower temperature.
9. Turn the light on for 25 minutes. Record the temperatures in the bottles every 5 minutes.

ANALYSIS
1. Make a graph of your data. Use a computer graphing program if one is available.
2. Compare how each bottle heated up over time. Explain your results.
3. What was the control of the experiment? The variable?
4. Identify four components of the experimental setup, and explain what parts of Earth each represents.

CONCLUSION
1. Did the results of the experiment support your hypothesis? Explain.
2. Would your results be affected if you used two pieces of plastic wrap instead of one? Test your answer by performing the experiment with two pieces of plastic wrap on one bottle.
3. In what other situations have you observed the greenhouse effect?

22.4 CONTROLLING AIR POLLUTION

OBJECTIVES • **Describe** natural processes that help control air pollution. • **Explain** human efforts to control air pollution. • **Identify** federal legislation for curbing air pollution.

Air pollution is a global problem. But government and industry in some nations are beginning to respond and work together to control and reduce air pollution. In addition, natural processes that are at work continue to remove some pollutants from the air.

Natural Air Pollution Controls

Precipitation, such as rain and snow, is the most effective natural method of removing particulates and aerosols from the air. As rain and snow fall, particles in the air stick to the precipitation and are carried to the ground. In addition, many aerosols dissolve in rain and snow. But removing a pollutant from the air often means putting it somewhere else.

Carbon dioxide is removed naturally from the atmosphere in two ways. One way is through biological activity. Plants and some microorganisms remove CO_2 from the air and use it to make sugars and shells. If this organic material is buried, the carbon in it cannot reenter the atmosphere. This carbon from buried organic deposits is the source of fossil fuels.

The water in the ocean can also remove CO_2 from the atmosphere. But the ability of ocean water to hold CO_2 depends on its temperature. The ocean already holds a large amount of CO_2. If seawater temperatures rise because of global warming, the ocean might release even more CO_2, making the problem worse.

Human Air Pollution Controls

Automobiles are a major source of air pollution. Many state governments have set strict emission-control standards for cars and other vehicles. Most cars are equipped with catalytic converters, which remove many pollutants from the exhaust. Today's cars get better gas mileage than in the past and burn unleaded gasoline. But burning gasoline will always produce large amounts of CO_2 and hydrocarbons.

The only way to end pollution from automobiles is to stop using gasoline as a fuel. California has taken a legislative step in this direction. A percentage of cars sold in California must produce zero emissions. This means that these cars must be fueled by electricity or clean fuels instead of gasoline. Burning a clean fuel, such as hydrogen, produces only water. Electric cars produce no emissions.

Figure 22.12 This electric car does not burn gasoline and therefore produces no gaseous pollutants.

Table 22.3   Air Pollution Legislation

Year	Legislation
1955	Air Pollution Control and Technical Assistance Act
1963	Clean Air Act
1965	Clean Air Act Amendments
1967	Air Quality Act
1976	Gasoline refineries required to reduce lead.
1977	Clean Air Act Amendments
1978	Use of CFCs banned in the United States.
1980	Acid Precipitation Act
1987	Montreal Protocol
1990	Amendment to Montreal Protocol

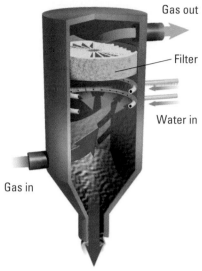

Gas out

Filter

Water in

Gas in

Pollutants and water out

Figure 22.13 This device is called a scrubber. It uses water to remove pollutants from coal smoke. The polluted water still must be disposed of safely.

The Federal Government has enacted legislation in response to growing concerns about the air pollution problem. Table 22.3 lists air pollution legislation since 1955.

Electric power plants that burn fossil fuels are another major source of air pollution. Coal plants use several different techniques to remove pollutants from the exhaust they produce. One device, called a scrubber, is shown in Figure 22.13. These techniques are fairly effective. The emission of most pollutants by coal plants has dropped during the last ten years. But the measures taken are expensive, and not all plants use them. There is also no way to stop the production of large amounts of carbon dioxide.

There is great debate surrounding legislation that requires factories to install and use pollution-control devices. Some people are against the use of such devices because they feel the economic costs are too high. The added costs of pollution control could cause businesses to fail, leading to job losses and financial hardship. Other people think that the importance of protecting and improving air quality outweighs the cost. They also argue that the jobs created by pollution control offset those that would be lost.

SECTION REVIEW

1. How have cars been changed to reduce the amount of pollution they produce?
2. Is there any way to produce energy without producing carbon dioxide? Make a list of carbon dioxide-free energy sources. You may wish to refer to Chapter 17, Alternative Energy Sources.
3. **Analyze** What things can you do as an individual to help reduce air pollution?

22.5 NOISE POLLUTION

OBJECTIVES • **Describe** the problem of noise pollution.
• **Explain** measures and legislation for controlling noise pollution.

Although noise is not a particle or a gas, it can be a form of pollution. Loud or high-pitched sounds can harm living things. Noise pollution can cause annoyance, stress, and even hearing damage. Noise pollution can come from airplanes, machines, and even loud concerts.

The unit used to measure sound intensity is the decibel (dB). The softest sounds you can hear are rated at 0 dB. Sounds rated at about 70 to 80 dB are annoying and can lead to hearing loss. Sounds louder than 120 to 130 dB can cause physical pain and serious hearing damage.

Figure 22.14 Rock concerts can be as loud as 120 dB. This sound level is equivalent to the sound of a jet airplane taking off about 65 m away from you.

Besides hearing loss, loud or persistent noise can cause other health problems. Over periods of time, noise can lead to stress and anxiety. Stress can produce harmful changes within the body. Chronic stress causes many health problems. Some of these are constricted blood vessels, vision problems, digestive disorders, and increased blood pressure and heart rate. Doctors have recently discovered that constant noise may also lead to emotional and psychological problems.

In 1972, Congress passed the Noise Control Act. This legislation directed the Environmental Protection Agency (EPA) to set standards for maximum noise levels. Industries have also attempted to reduce sources and levels of noise pollution in the workplace. Legislation at the state and local levels has also been enacted to reduce noise pollution.

In addition to legislation, individuals are now encouraged to protect themselves from the effects of noise. People should limit the amount of time they spend in noisy areas, and not listen to music too loudly. People who must work around loud noise should wear earplugs or specially designed earmuffs to reduce the amount of exposure. What other ways can you suggest to reduce or control noise pollution and its effects?

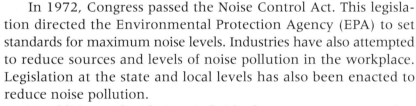

SECTION REVIEW

1. What is noise pollution?
2. What are some ways that long-term exposure to noise can affect people?
3. **Analyze** Why might signs prohibiting the honking of car horns be posted on roads surrounding hospitals?

KEY TERMS

pollutant 22.1
particulate 22.1
oxide 22.1

photochemical
  smog 22.1
chlorofluorocarbons
  (CFCs) 22.1

radon 22.1
emphysema 22.2
cancer 22.2
acid precipitation 22.3

greenhouse effect 22.3
ice core 22.3
global warming 22.3

CHAPTER SUMMARY

22.1 Pollutants are harmful substances that enter the environment. Air pollution may be made of particulates or gases, usually oxides. Air pollution can be present outdoors, such as photochemical smog, or indoors, such as cigarette smoke and radon.

22.2 Air pollution can affect human health and the health of plants and animals. Human health problems range from eye and respiratory tract irritations to emphysema and lung cancer. Air pollution can also damage crops and be passed from contaminated food and water to grazing animals.

22.3 Air pollution can have global as well as local effects. Acid precipitation is rain or snow with a very low pH, resulting from oxides combining with water in the air. Ozone depletion results from the breakdown of ozone molecules in the stratosphere by CFCs. The greenhouse effect, caused by gases such as carbon dioxide in the atmosphere, could lead to global warming.

22.4 Some air pollutants are removed by natural processes such as precipitation and biological activity. Air pollution can be reduced in part by controlling automobile emissions. Some types of legislation to reduce air pollution could cause economic hardship for certain industries.

22.5 Noise can be considered a type of pollution. Loud or persistent noise can cause stress, hearing loss, and other health problems. The federal government sets limits on allowable noise levels.

MULTIPLE CHOICE

Choose the letter of the word or phrase that best completes each statement.

1. The gas that is most abundant in the air is (a) oxygen; (b) nitrogen; (c) carbon dioxide; (d) argon.

2. Air pollution first became a widespread problem (a) 100 000 years ago; (b) during the thirteenth century; (c) during the 1700s; (d) about 100 years ago.

3. Photochemical smog results from automobile pollutants reacting with (a) ozone; (b) carbon dioxide; (c) acid rain; (d) sunlight.

4. The greatest source of indoor air pollution is (a) smog; (b) radon; (c) cigarette smoke; (d) insulation.

5. A pollutant that can reduce the amount of oxygen carried by blood is (a) carbon monoxide; (b) carbon dioxide; (c) ozone; (d) sulfur dioxide.

6. Normal rain has a pH of about (a) 4.0; (b) 5.6; (c) 7.0; (d) 8.4.

7. Acid rain is mostly a problem (a) in the eastern United States; (b) in Europe; (c) in Asia; (d) throughout the Northern Hemisphere.

8. The ozone layer absorbs (a) CFCs; (b) ultraviolet light; (c) photochemical smog; (d) chlorine molecules.

9. Greenhouse gases trap (a) UV radiation; (b) visible spectrum radiation; (c) infrared radiation; (d) carbon dioxide.

10. Sounds can cause physical pain if they are louder than (a) 10 dB; (b) 50 dB; (c) 80 dB; (d) 120 dB.

TRUE/FALSE

Write true *if the statement is true. If the statement is false, change the underlined word or phrase to make it true.*

1. Ash, dust, and liquid droplets in the air are <u>particulates</u>.
2. All oxides contain <u>carbon</u>.
3. A radioactive type of indoor air pollution is <u>ozone</u>.
4. Lung cancer is a <u>more</u> common cause of death in the United States than heart disease.
5. Industrial pollutants that contaminate rangeland include <u>heavy</u> metals.
6. Acid rain can result from the burning of <u>fossil fuels</u>.
7. Nations belonging to the United Nations have agreed to ban CFCs completely by the year 2010.
8. The softest sounds that you can hear are rated at <u>0 dB</u>.

CONCEPT REVIEW

Write a complete response for each of the following.

1. Explain why air pollution is a global problem.
2. How can ice cores be used to analyze changes in air quality?
3. How can the use of gasoline in automobiles cause a decrease in the number of fish in a lake hundreds of miles away?
4. Name two causes of emphysema. Which cause is more easily avoided?
5. Why can one molecule of CFC destroy many molecules of ozone?

THINK CRITICALLY

1. UV light causes the skin to become darker in most people. Why can sun-tanning be a dangerous activity?
2. Why do some people resist government limits on the release of air pollutants?
3. Ozone can be harmful to life, or it can be a protector of life, depending on its location in the atmosphere. Explain why this is true.
4. Compared to the United States, Canada is less industrialized. Why do you think acid precipitation is more serious in Quebec than in most of the United States?

Computer Activity Suppose that the ozone layer contains 1 million molecules of ozone, and that 50 atoms of chlorine are added to it. Each atom catalyzes the destruction of 1000 ozone molecules each day for five days. Use a computer to calculate the amount of ozone remaining after each day. Using a graphing program, display your results.

WRITE CREATIVELY

If the ozone layer was severely damaged, it would affect the way people live. Write a short story that takes place in a future time when the ozone layer has lost its ability to absorb UV radiation.

PORTFOLIO

1. Collect newspaper and magazine articles from the past ten years about the ozone layer, and compare the information in the older articles to more recent ones. What new information has come to light? How has public opinion changed?
2. How can electricity be used to fuel cars? Research the basic design of electric cars, and prepare a video or audio presentation comparing electric cars to gasoline-fueled cars.

GRAPHIC ANALYSIS

Use the Figure to answer the following.

1. According to the graph, what was the concentration of CO_2 in the atmosphere in 1850? In 1950?
2. What is the percent change of CO_2 concentration between the two years?
3. How was the data obtained?

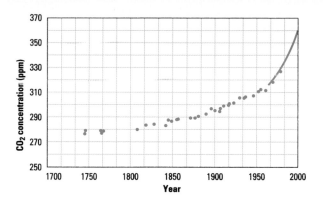

ACTIVITY 22.2

PROBLEM

How do the number and types of air particulates differ in areas around your school?

MATERIALS (per group)

- masking tape
- 5 microscope slides
- petroleum jelly
- 5 Petri dishes with lids
- binocular microscope or hand lens

HYPOTHESIS

Write a hypothesis that pertains to the problem.

PROCEDURE

1. Make five separate particulate collectors by writing your group name on masking tape labels, and sticking a label to an end of each slide. Identify one as the *Control*.
2. Smear the center of each slide with a thin layer of petroleum jelly.
3. Place each particulate collector in the bottom half of a Petri dish. Immediately place lids on the dishes.
4. Remove the particulate collectors from their Petri dishes, and leave them exposed to the air at four locations where particulate levels may differ.

5. Write the locations on the appropriate labels.
6. Keep the control in your classroom, and do not remove it from its covered Petri dish.
7. Retrieve the particulate collectors anywhere between 25 minutes and five days later. Put them in covered Petri dishes.
8. Examine the slides, including your control, with a microscope set at low power or a hand lens. Move the slides around and count the number of particulates that fell on each one. Record these numbers.

ANALYSIS

1. What was the purpose of the control?
2. Identify five particulates that landed in your particulate collectors. Which of these would you classify as pollutants? Explain.
3. Describe the locations you chose. Which location showed the greatest number of air particulates? The least?

CONCLUSION

1. Did the results of your experiment support your hypothesis? Explain.
2. List the possible sources of error in your experiment.

Lake Erie

During the 1960s, Lake Erie was not a place where you would want to swim. The lake's surface was covered by large mats of algae. Dead fish, rotting plants, and oil floated on top of the water and washed up on the beaches. The water was cloudy and full of sediments. Most of the beaches were closed because the water was unsafe.

In addition to the problem of unsafe lake water, some of the rivers draining into Lake Erie were so polluted that they were declared fire hazards. Several rivers actually caught fire.

Much of the pollution was caused by agricultural runoff and wastes from major industrial centers such as Detroit, Michigan; Buffalo, New York; and Erie, Pennsylvania. Because Lake Erie is the smallest of the Great Lakes, with an average depth of only 18.3 m, it could not dilute the wastes that poured into it daily. The lake was dying from chemical pollution and lack of oxygen.

As the sewage from cities, wastewater from factories, and fertilizers from farming accumulated in the lake, they released large amounts of phosphorus and nitrogen. These chemicals helped algae to flourish. The large algae blooms depleted the lake of oxygen, killing many fish and other organisms.

In the 1970s, the people and governments surrounding Lake Erie joined forces to clean up the lake. Laws were passed to stop any more dumping into the lake. As the pollutants entering the lake were reduced, the lake began to recover. The algae population decreased, and the fish populations grew.

Although some pollutants are still present in Lake Erie, most have settled to the bottom. If you were to visit Lake Erie today, you would probably never guess it had once been a giant pool of pollution.

1. How did Lake Erie become polluted? What kinds of pollutants were affecting the lake?
2. Why is Lake Erie considered a success story?

Lake Erie was once a polluted and unsafe eyesore. Today, the lake has much cleaner beaches and water.

Hydrologists ▶

These people monitor the quantity and quality of groundwater in an area. They develop computer models of groundwater flow and determine whether the groundwater supply has been contaminated. If it has been, they will find the source of the contamination. Hydrologists also study groundwater supplies, helping to determine if aquifers are overdrawn.

Information-Systems Specialists ▲

These individuals blend a science background with strong computer abilities. They input and analyze data, devise programs that estimate damage in a polluted area or project water quality in the future, and help find solutions for water sources that have been polluted.

◀ Water-Quality Technicians

Water-quality technicians work in private or public water-treatment facilities. They collect samples in the field and analyze data in the laboratory. Some water-quality technicians operate complicated equipment, whereas others are in managerial positions.

For More Information

American Water Resources Association
950 Herndon Parkway, Suite 300
Herndon, VA 20170
http://www.uwin.siu.edu/~awra/index.html

National Ground Water Association
601 Dempsey Road
Westerville, OH 43081
(614) 898-7791
(800) 551-7379
http://www.h2o-ngwa.org

The Center for the Great Lakes
35 East Wacker Drive, Suite 1870
Chicago, IL 60601

UNIT 7

MANAGING HUMAN IMPACT

If you have ever been at a crowded park or beach at the end of the day, you may have observed the impact that people can sometimes have on the environment. Fragile environments such as parks and beaches require great care and maintenance. This photograph of hikers at Vernal Falls in Yosemite National Park illustrates the need to find a balance so that people can enjoy, yet preserve, Earth's natural resources.

Discover It!

Recycling Resources

Every day you use products that are packaged for your convenience. These packages are made from, or require, natural resources. When they are disposed of in a landfill, these resources are lost.

1. Make a list of the containers (plastic, glass, boxes, and so on) that you use every day and record whether or not they have the recycling symbol on them.

2. If you were to recycle these containers instead of throwing them in the trash, how would you be helping to conserve natural resources? Explain.

PLANETDIARY.COM

You can find out more about humans and their impact on the environment by exploring the following Internet address:

http://www.planetdiary.com

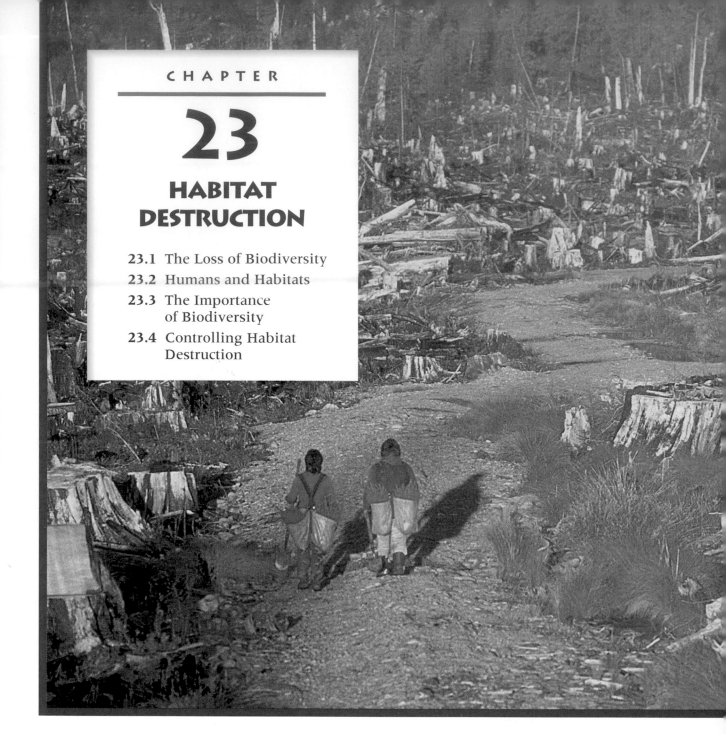

CHAPTER

23

HABITAT DESTRUCTION

D o the names *Stegosaurus*, *Triceratops*, and *Tyrannosaurus rex* sound familiar? These dinosaurs and many others roamed Earth millions of years ago. All that remains of these dinosaurs are fossils. The dinosaurs were well adapted to their environment. Yet 66 million years ago, the last dinosaurs died.

Today, the lowland gorillas, several species of whale, and countless plants and other organisms are threatened with extinction. Humans are causing the current extinctions. Human activity is destroying many of Earth's habitats. As habitats disappear, the organisms adapted to those habitats also disappear.

23.1 THE LOSS OF BIODIVERSITY

OBJECTIVES • *Discuss* extinction and how it occurs. • *Explain* habitat destruction and the loss of biodiversity, and how they are related.

Every organism is adapted to live in a certain habitat. If a habitat is altered or destroyed, the organisms adapted to that habitat must either find a new habitat or die. If a species is generalized, it may be able to occupy another niche. Specialized species almost always die with their habitats. *The disappearance of a species from all or part of the species' geographical range is called* **extinction.**

When the last population of a species dies, some diversity in the ecosystem is lost. *Recall from Chapter 3 that the variety of species in an ecosystem is known as* **biodiversity.** Because the extinction of a species affects factors such as the flow of energy and matter and the habitats of other organisms, a loss in biodiversity can upset the balance, health, and stability of an ecosystem.

Extinction

Extinctions are a natural part of ecosystem function. More than 99 percent of the species that have lived on Earth are extinct today. All ecosystems change, and niches appear and disappear with these changes. Species that lack adaptations for survival in a changing ecosystem become extinct. Other species may evolve to fill new niches or empty niches left by extinct species.

The rates of species extinction and species appearance are not constant. Figure 23.1 shows the rate of extinction and evolution of families of animals since the Cambrian period. Notice that the extinction rate is never zero. Relatively short periods of time in which many species die are called *mass extinctions.* Mass extinctions are typically followed by rapid evolution as the few organisms that survive evolve to fill vacant niches.

Biology

Look at the graph in Figure 23.1. You may notice that periods of mass extinction are followed by periods of rapid species evolution. These periods of fast evolution are called *adaptive radiations.* The largest adaptive radiation on the graph occurs at the start of the Cambrian period. In this radiation, almost all the major groups of animals evolved in just a few million years. This event is called the Cambrian explosion. You can read more about the Cambrian explosion in the book *Wonderful Life* by Stephen Jay Gould.

Figure 23.1 The rate of extinction and evolution of animal species has changed over time. Mass extinctions are followed by a high rate of species evolution. This graph covers about 600 million years.

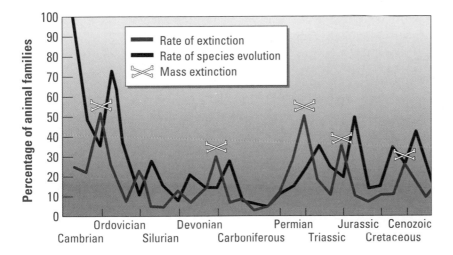

Earth may currently be experiencing another mass extinction. The activities of one species—humans—are causing many other species to become extinct each year. The number and kind of extinctions occurring today are comparable to the mass extinctions of the past. As is typical of mass extinctions, entire ecosystems are disappearing. There is no way to know if the human species will be able to survive such drastic changes in its environment.

Loss of Habitat

Extinctions and the resulting loss of biodiversity often occur when humans destroy the habitat of organisms. *Disturbing the part of an ecosystem that an organism needs to survive is called* **habitat destruction**. Cutting down all the trees in a forest is one form of habitat destruction.

Land development is another form of habitat destruction. Draining swamps for housing complexes, and altering wetlands for use as resorts, marinas, and farmlands, destroy fragile wetland habitats. Changing the course of rivers by using dams to control water flow can destroy aquatic habitats. Some mining and quarrying practices, overgrazing, and even recreation activities can drive native species away from a habitat.

Native species can also be threatened by other species that are introduced by humans. *Nonnative species introduced to an area by humans are called* **alien species.** The water hyacinth, for example, is an ornamental water plant that was brought into Louisiana from South America. The plant has invaded about 800 000 hectares of rivers and lakes stretching across the country to California. In many ecosystems, the water hyacinth has "outcompeted" other plants for the resources in the ecosystem. The result has been the disappearance of the native plants and a loss of biodiversity.

Human activity is destroying or altering habitats in all biomes. The rate of biodiversity loss increases every day. Many of the activities that destroy habitat result from people looking for places to live and food to eat. As the human population grows, Earth will continue to lose biodiversity as people alter more habitats. The biosphere has a limited amount of space. As the number of humans increases, the amount of space available to other organisms declines.

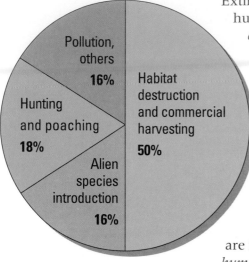

Figure 23.2
Many human activities contribute to the extinction of species. The most serious factor is deforestation and other types of habitat destruction.

SECTION REVIEW

1. What is extinction?
2. In what ways is the current pattern of extinctions different from those that have come before?
3. **Relate** Prepare a concept map showing the relationship between extinction, biodiversity, and habitat destruction.

23.2 HUMANS AND HABITATS

OBJECTIVES • *Explain* the causes of deforestation and its impact on biodiversity. • *Investigate* the disappearance of aquatic habitats.

About 150 years ago, rain forests worldwide covered an area larger than the United States. Today, rain forests cover an area half that size. The present rate of destruction is equal to the loss of an area the size of the state of Oregon each year. The rain forest is the most diverse and productive land biome on Earth, and the loss of even small areas may result in many extinctions. Deforestation in rain forests and other forests is the most important factor contributing to the loss of global biodiversity.

Causes of Deforestation

Several forces lead to deforestation in rain forests. All stem from the fact that most tropical rain forests are in developing countries. Developing countries are usually poor and have populations that are growing rapidly. The rain forest is often used in attempts to solve both of these problems, as shown in Figure 23.3.

Population Growth The growing populations in many developing countries need food and a place to live. Many rain forests are cleared or burned to make farmland. Recall from Chapter 9 that soil in rain forests is nutrient-poor because most of the nutrients are within the living plants. Removing the plants, therefore, also removes most of the nutrients. Because the soil is poor, conventional farming methods used on cleared land usually fail after several growing seasons. Within a few years, land that once was a habitat for many species becomes barren and unproductive. Habitat destruction of this kind is currently taking place in the Philippines, Southeast Asia, and in many South and Central American nations.

Figure 23.3 Most of the world's rain forests are being deforested rapidly. The planet may lose a large proportion of its total biodiversity if all of the rain forests are destroyed.

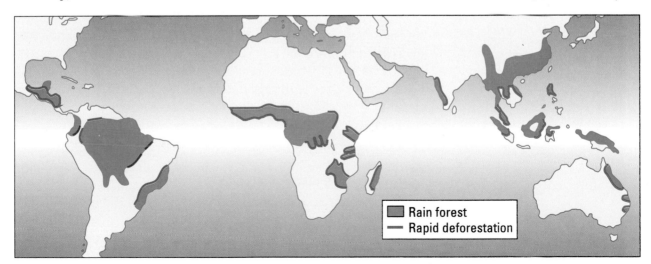

Rain forest
— Rapid deforestation

Figure 23.4 The rain forest that used to grow on this land was cleared to make grazing land for cattle. Almost all the beef grown in this way is exported to developed countries.

Demand for Resources Developing nations have resources that developed nations want. For example, Japan and other nations encourage the Philippines, Thailand, Borneo, and Indonesia to strip their forests of wood. The lumber is then sold to the developed nations. Similar deforestation is taking place in the old-growth forests in the United States. Almost all of the old-growth trees cut down in the United States are exported to other countries.

In Central and South America, the demand for grass-fed beef has led to the clearing of forests for cattle raising. The beef grown on the cleared rainforest land is often sold to industrialized countries, where the demand for beef is high. This large market encourages cash-poor governments to destroy rain forests and raise cattle for export. Beef from cattle raised on former rainforest land is often used to make hamburgers, luncheon meats, and other meat products.

No one knows how much time it will take for the rain forest to regenerate. Scientific estimates range from hundreds to many thousands of years. The rain forest will not regenerate at all if none of it is left; there will be no organisms adapted to rainforest life to fill empty niches. The destruction of all rain forests could result in the loss of up to 70 percent of the biodiversity on land.

Destruction of forest land is also a problem in the deciduous forests of developed nations. In the United States, deforestation has been ongoing since the first permanent settlements were founded. About half of all U.S. forest areas have been destroyed. The advanced deforestation in developed nations is one reason why these countries rely on developing nations for wood.

Aquatic Habitat Destruction

All land biomes are losing biodiversity through habitat destruction. Aquatic biomes are losing biodiversity as well. Recall from Chapter 11 that coral reefs and wetlands are productive and diverse ecosystems. Both of these ecosystems have been disturbed by human activity. Coral reefs are damaged by water pollution and overfishing. Wetlands are damaged by pollution and development.

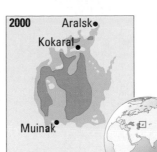

Figure 23.5 The Aral Sea has lost two-thirds of its volume and 40 percent of its surface area since 1960. (The map for the year 2000 is a prediction.) Towns such as Kokaral and Muinak were ports in 1960. Today, they are many kilometers away from the lakeshore. Ships have been stranded because of the water loss.

The Everglades The Everglades, a large group of marshes in southern Florida, is habitat for a variety of organisms, including grasses, fish, invertebrates, and migrating birds. Much of the Everglades is prime real estate property, which has been developed for recreation and commercial activities. Large areas in the Everglades and other wetlands have been drained to produce land for farming, housing, and industry. More than half of all the wetlands in the United States have been destroyed, and an estimated 175 000 hectares are being destroyed annually. Congress and the government of Florida have begun a project to return at least part of the Everglades to its natural state.

The Aral Sea The Aral Sea is actually a large, saltwater lake in the southern desert of the former Soviet Union, as shown in Figure 23.5. The Aral Sea used to be the fourth-largest lake in the world. But the diversion of the two rivers that feed the lake is making the Aral Sea disappear. The rivers were diverted to irrigate crops. In 1960, the lake held more than 1000 km³ of water. Today, it holds less than one-third of this amount, and it may disappear completely by the year 2010.

The amount of habitat loss caused by the disappearance of a 68 000-km² lake is very serious. The loss of biodiversity is serious, as well. The Aral Sea supported an aquatic ecosystem that no longer exists. Its disappearance has also caused problems for the people near the lake. A fishing industry that harvested 48 000 metric tons of fish in 1957 is now gone. Many people have lost jobs that depended on the lake. Salt carried by wind from the exposed lake bed also causes many health problems.

SECTION REVIEW

1. What two problems lead to deforestation in developing countries?
2. Explain the human activity that led to the disappearance of the Aral Sea?
3. **Deduce** What effect might deforestation have on global warming?

23.3 THE IMPORTANCE OF BIODIVERSITY

OBJECTIVES • *State* the ways that biodiversity benefits humans.
• *Describe* how the pattern of the current mass extinction differs from that of earlier extinctions.

If extinction is a natural part of all ecosystems, how can habitat destruction and the loss of biodiversity be undesirable? There are two answers. First, humans benefit directly from high biodiversity. Second, the loss of biodiversity threatens the health of the global ecosystem, and therefore indirectly threatens human health.

Crop Genetics

One direct benefit that biodiversity provides humans is new genetic material for farm plants. Today, about 30 species of plants are grown as crops. Selective crossing of these plants produces higher yields, but it also makes the crops more vulnerable to weather, disease, and insects. All the crops that humans grow for food were originally wild plants. The ancestors of these plants still grow wild in some areas.

The genetic material from wild plant strains can be used to improve the traits of food crops. This crossbreeding can develop crop strains that are more productive, more resistant to climate changes, and more resistant to disease and insects. In 1978, for example, a variety of wild corn was discovered in Mexico. Cross-breeding this corn with local varieties enabled farmers to avoid season-to-season plowing and sowing. Crossbreeding also offered resistance to several viruses that attacked the commercial corn.

Figure 23.6 Humans first grew wheat as a crop about 10 000 years ago. Today, there are about 22 000 varieties of domestic and wild wheat in two species. One species is used to make bread; the other, pasta.

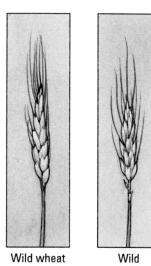

Wild wheat
ancestor

Wild
strains

Bread

Pasta

Crop plants

Genetic material is a vital resource because it makes the global food supply more flexible. As pathogens and insects evolve strains that resist pesticides, farmers will need new plant varieties that will resist pests. Pests are also less damaging to crops with high genetic variety. New strains of crop plants may also be useful if global warming changes the climate of Earth's agricultural regions.

Habitat destruction threatens many populations of wild crop ancestors. The loss of this genetic material might be a disaster because it could endanger the food supply of major parts of the human population. Several groups are currently working to collect and store the genetic material of crop ancestors before they disappear.

Medicines

Another direct benefit of biodiversity is the use of natural chemicals in medicine. Currently, about 40 percent of all medicines used in the United States comes from plants. Quinine, a malaria drug, comes from the cinchona plant. Digitalis, used in the treatment of heart disease, comes from foxglove. Researchers are also working with leaves of the periwinkle plant and the bark of the Pacific yew. These plants show promise in the treatment of certain types of cancer.

Think About It!

Crops with high genetic diversity are more resistant to disease and other pests than are crops with little genetic diversity.

1. Why is there so little genetic diversity among crop species?

2. Why does low genetic diversity put a crop at risk from diseases?

Figure 23.7 The cinchona plant (left) is the source of quinine, a drug that fights malaria. Foxglove (center) is the source of the heart medication digitalis. The Pacific yew (right) is the source of a potential anticancer drug called taxol.

No one knows how many more medicines are in the world's rain forests. Drug companies are spending millions of dollars trying to find out. But the species in the forest must escape destruction if they are to be evaluated for medicinal use.

If the rain forests and other habitats are destroyed, a cancer-curing drug may be lost before it can be discovered. The Pacific yew is a rare tree that grows only in old-growth forests on the west coast of North America. These forests are threatened by clearcutting and other types of habitat destruction. If the Pacific yew had become extinct before the discovery of the anticancer drug in its bark, the world would have lost an important medicine.

Figure 23.8 The beauty and solitude of wilderness areas are important to humans.

Wilderness Areas

Declining biodiversity will have other effects. One is the loss of wilderness areas for recreation. *A* **wilderness** *is an area where the ecosystem is relatively undisturbed by the activities of humans.* Wilderness areas are important to people. They are a haven from the pollution and hectic life of an industrial society. Many people feel that wilderness areas are vital to their emotional health.

Ecosystem Destruction

The most dangerous characteristic of the current mass extinction may be the pattern of the extinction. In the past, mass extinctions followed a general pattern. Some species died out, while others were affected a little or not at all. The dinosaur extinction, for example, did not affect most species of plants, birds, or mammals. With many elements of the ecosystem still in place, the surviving species were able to evolve and occupy empty niches.

The pattern of today's mass extinction is different. When people destroy a habitat, they do not remove just a few species. The whole ecosystem is often destroyed. After this kind of habitat destruction, there are few surviving species and few remaining niches. Biodiversity has already dropped sharply because of habitat destruction, and it continues to decline. No one knows how the loss of diversity will affect the global ecosystem. Ecologists have many more questions than answers.

SECTION REVIEW

1. Why are wild ancestors of crop plants important?
2. Name three plants that have yielded important drugs.
3. **Contrast** Write a paragraph comparing other mass extinctions and the one occurring today.

Superplants

C an people grow squash that resists disease? Can they grow tomatoes that last for weeks without spoiling? Scientists have been asking these and other questions about plants for years. Today, they are using genetic engineering to create a breed of "superplants" that will advance agricultural methods as well as help abate world food shortages.

One goal of genetic engineering is to improve the quantity and quality of food. Genetic engineers can improve crops in many ways. New genetic engineering techniques can make plants resistant to pests and weed killers, and produce fruits and vegetables that are better suited to shipping and storage.

Genetic engineering takes place in a laboratory. Scientists alter the genetic material (DNA) of a plant, changing its genetic makeup. In some cases, they insert a gene from another organism into the plant's DNA to give it a trait it does not normally have.

The DNA is inserted into only a few plant cells. The few engineered cells are grown in a nutrient-rich tissue culture to form genetically altered plants. These plants have a new trait produced by the inserted gene. A successful plant will pass the trait on to its offspring.

Scientists can also use genetic engineering to block the expression of a plant gene that produces undesirable effects. For example, scientists have produced genetically altered tomatoes that do not spoil as quickly as tomatoes picked off the vine. Tomatoes usually produce an enzyme that breaks down the chemical pectin, causing fruit to spoil. The gene for this enzyme has been shut off in the genetically altered tomatoes, giving the tomatoes a longer shelf life.

The ability to genetically engineer important world crops is especially beneficial to the world of biotechnology. Harvests of disease-resistant or herbicide-resistant crops, such as soybeans, rice or wheat, may help increase the world's food supply as the demand for these crops grows.

Scientists are now working to create cantaloupes and squashes that resist viral infections, strawberries

Genetic engineers make careful observations and take accurate records when gathering data from their experiments.

with a higher sugar content, rice with increased protein, and canola oil with fewer harmful fats. In the future, you may be able to find many of these products in the grocery store.

✔ Checkpoint

1. What is genetic engineering?

2. What kinds of traits could be added or removed from a crop to make it grow better?

23.4 CONTROLLING HABITAT DESTRUCTION

OBJECTIVES • *Describe* the social and economic factors that cause habitat destruction. • *Explain* the Endangered Species Act and how it is applied.

Recall that most rain forests are located in developing nations, and that many of these nations are poor and have rapidly growing populations. Their governments have urgent needs. When faced with overcrowding in cities and serious food shortages, expanding into rainforest land may seem like the only option. The governments can also make much-needed money by selling rainforest products to developed nations. As a result, the rain forests are being destroyed. Developed countries play a part in this destruction. These countries often exhaust their own resources and turn to other countries for raw materials. The demands of wealthy industrial societies cause deforestation by providing a market for rainforest products. Deforestation is a global problem that needs a global solution.

International Efforts

Some progress had been made in international efforts to stop deforestation and other types of habitat destruction. Several groups are working to discover and collect as many organisms as possible before they are destroyed. Seeds from wild crop plants are gathered and stored. *A secure place where seeds, plants, and genetic material are stored is called a* **gene bank**. Gene banks in many parts of the world are working quickly to preserve as much of Earth's biodiversity as possible. The best solution would be to end habitat destruction. But the continued growth of the human population makes this unlikely.

Figure 23.9 Habitat destruction is a problem in all nations. This clearcut is in Washington State.

The Endangered Species Act

The U.S. Congress passed the Endangered Species Act in 1973. This law requires the government to make a list of all species in the United States that are in danger of extinction. The government must also protect the habitat of these species. The Endangered Species Act has stopped many developments that threatened the habitats of endangered species.

The main provisions of the Endangered Species Act are:
- The United States Fish and Wildlife Service must keep a list of all threatened and endangered species.
- Threatened or endangered animals may not be caught or killed.
- Threatened or endangered plants may not be disturbed.
- Threatened or endangered species and products made from them may not be bought or sold.
- The federal government may not construct any project that jeopardizes endangered species.
- The Fish and Wildlife Service must prepare a species recovery plan for each threatened or endangered species.

The Endangered Species Act has flaws, however. In order to be protected, a species must be on the endangered species list. Getting a species on this list can be difficult. People get around the law by developing an area before it can be studied for endangered species. To get permission to build, a developer will promise to create a new habitat for the species. However, the task of reproducing a habitat is very difficult.

Many ecologists think the Endangered Species Act focuses too much on individual species. They feel the emphasis should be on whole habitats, not on individual species.

One example of the problem of focusing on an individual species is the case of a bird called the clapper rail in California. The clapper rail lives in wetland habitats that are prime real estate for development. In several areas, developers were allowed to build as long as they created new habitats for the birds. The new habitats did not work, however, because they did not replace the whole wetland ecosystem. The clapper rail disappeared from these areas.

Figure 23.10 The clapper rail is threatened by the development of wetlands in California. Efforts by developers to replace destroyed habitats have failed.

SECTION REVIEW

1. Explain how developing and developed countries are both responsible for deforestation.
2. What is a gene bank? Why are gene banks important?
3. **Analyze** Would it ever be possible for a developer to reproduce a whole ecosystem for the clapper rail or any other organism? Explain your answer.

Modeling a Bald Eagle Population

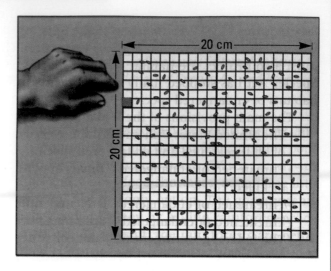

PROBLEM
How does the environment affect an eagle population?

MATERIALS (per pair of students)
- index card
- red marking pen
- #2 pencil
- 150 uncooked rice grains
- one 20-cm by 20-cm piece of paper
- metric ruler
- scissors
- graph paper
- several colored pencils
- notebook (one per student)

HYPOTHESIZE
After reading through the entire activity, hypothesize how a bald eagle population is affected by biotic factors.

PROCEDURE

1. Work in pairs. On the piece of paper, mark off a 20-cm by 20-cm grid in 1-cm increments. The grid represents a 4-km² lake where the eagles hunt (100 cm² = 1 km²).
2. Cut two 1-cm squares from the index card, then color both sides with the red marker. Use the #2 pencil and label one *F* for female and the other *M* for male.
3. Put the lake grid on a flat surface, and scatter the 150 rice grains over it.
4. Hold the *F* square about 30 cm over the grid and drop it. Remove all of the rice from under the square. Repeat the process with the *M* square. *Note: This step represents eagles catching fish.*
5. After each hunting expedition, rescatter the remaining rice, and repeat step 4. After each eagle has hunted four times, total the number of fish caught by each eagle on Day 1.

Make a data table in your notebook and record your data.

6. Repeat steps 4 and 5 nine times (representing the nine remaining days), recording the data in your notebook.
7. An eagle will share its food with its mate, but feeds itself first. If an eagle does not eat three fish per day, it becomes too weak to hunt and will die. Be sure to examine the data for each 3-day period. If one eagle dies, continue hunting with only one eagle.
8. Use different colored pencils for the male and the female eagles, and graph the data from your notebook, totaling the number of fish caught by each eagle per day. *Note: On the graph, record the days on the horizontal axis and the number of fish caught on the vertical axis.*

ANALYSIS
1. How might the fish population be affected by the eagles' hunting over time?
2. What effect might a small decrease in the fish population have on the eagle population?
3. What effect, if any, would an increase in the fish population have on the eagle population?

CONCLUSION
Write a paragraph describing the results of your experiment.

CHAPTER 23 REVIEW

KEY TERMS

extinction 23.1

biodiversity 23.1

habitat destruction 23.1

alien species 23.1

wilderness 23.3

gene bank 23.4

CHAPTER SUMMARY

23.1 Extinction is the disappearance of a species from some or all of its geographical range. Extinction is a natural part of the functioning of all ecosystems. Earth is currently experiencing a mass extinction due to habitat destruction. Habitat destruction is occurring in all biomes and is linked to the size of the human population.

23.2 The loss of Earth's rain forests could result in up to a 70 percent decline in biodiversity. The loss of rain forests is caused by factors linked to the rain forests' locations in developing countries. Developed countries contribute to deforestation by providing a market for rainforest products. Many aquatic ecosystems are experiencing habitat destruction. The Aral Sea has lost two-thirds of its volume since 1960.

23.3 Biodiversity is important to humans for several reasons. Wild strains of crop plants can be a valuable genetic resource. Plants and other organisms can provide new medicines to treat a variety of illnesses. The destruction of whole ecosystems may impair the biosphere's ability to regenerate.

23.4 Developed and developing countries are both responsible for deforestation. The pressing needs of people, economic forces, and a lack of international cooperation make controlling deforestation difficult. The Endangered Species Act protects species that are near extinction. Many ecologists think the focus of biodiversity legislation should be on whole habitats, not individual species.

MULTIPLE CHOICE

Choose the letter of the word or phrase that best completes each statement.

1. Most of the loss of biodiversity in ecosystems is caused by (a) pollution; (b) collectors; (c) habitat destruction; (d) poaching.
2. The medicines digitalis and quinine come from (a) animals; (b) plants; (c) fungi; (d) microorganisms.
3. Nonnative organisms introduced into an area by humans are called (a) helpful species; (b) alien species; (c) intruding species; (d) indigenous species.
4. Disturbing an area of an ecosystem where an organism lives is called (a) habitat destruction; (b) loss of biodiversity; (c) extinction; (d) evolution.
5. The disappearance of a species from all or some of its geographical range is called
(a) deforestation; (b) loss of biodiversity; (c) habitat destruction; (d) extinction.
6. An area that is undisturbed by human activity is a (a) wilderness; (b) state park; (c) national park; (d) forest.
7. The number of strains of domestic and wild wheat is about (a) 22; (b) 220; (c) 2200; (d) 22 000.
8. The volume that the Aral Sea has lost since 1960 is (a) one-quarter; (b) one-third; (c) two-thirds; (d) three-quarters.
9. The amount of biodiversity on land that will be lost if all rain forests are destroyed is (a) 10 to 30 percent; (b) 70 to 90 percent; (c) 30 to 50 percent; (d) 50 to 70 percent.
10. The Endangered Species Act has been criticized for its emphasis on protecting (a) species; (b) ecosystems; (c) habitats; (d) biomes.

WORD COMPARISONS

Write the letter of the second word pair that best matches the first pair.

1. Deforestation: trees as (a) irrigation: Aral Sea; (b) alien species: water hyacinth; (c) dams: salmon; (d) biodiversity: extinction.
2. Digitalis: plants as (a) parasites: animals; (b) genetic material: wild crop strains; (c) biodiversity: extinction; (d) water hyacinth: alien species.
3. Biodiversity: extinction as (a) water hyacinth: alien species; (b) dams: salmon; (c) pest resistance: inbreeding (d) genetic material: wild crop strains.
4. Biodiversity: healthy ecosystem as (a) alien species: water hyacinth; (b) extinction: unhealthy ecosystem; (c) habitat destruction: forests; (d) habitat destruction: biodiversity.
5. Gene banks: genetic diversity as (a) Endangered Species Act: species; (b) alien species: water hyacinth; (c) cinchona: digitalis; (d) Pacific yew: cancer.

CONCEPT REVIEW

Write a complete response for each of the following.

1. What is a mass extinction? When have mass extinctions occurred?
2. How do developing countries contribute to deforestation?
3. How do developed countries contribute to deforestation?
4. Why is the Aral Sea drying up?
5. What is a gene bank? What is stored there?

THINK CRITICALLY

1. Explain how the introduction of a species to an area might result in habitat destruction.
2. Why might the destruction of the rain forests deprive future generations of valuable medicine?
3. Describe the connection between habitat destruction and the loss of biodiversity.
4. Why are wild strains of crop plants important? Will they continue to be important in the future?
5. Why do many ecologists think it is better to protect whole habitats rather than individual species?

WRITE FOR UNDERSTANDING

Write a short essay summarizing the reasons that biodiversity is important. Which reason do you think is most important? Are there any reasons that are not in the text?

PORTFOLIO

1. Conduct library research on one organism that was once common in your area but is now extinct. Prepare an oral report that explains the conditions leading to the extinction of the organism.
2. Make a list of ten endangered organisms. Be sure to include plants and animals.

Survey 100 people to find out which organisms they would most like to save. Analyze your results. Which organisms would people most like to save? Why? Is public opinion a good way to make this decision?

GRAPHIC ANALYSIS

Use Figure 23.1 to answer the following.

1. How are mass extinctions shown on the graph? How many mass extinctions are there, not counting the present one?
2. When was the rate of evolution fastest?
3. Is there a pattern in the peaks in extinction and evolution rates? If so, describe the pattern.
4. Explain why the pattern in extinction and evolution rates exists. How are the two processes related?
5. Find the place on the graph where species' evolution is fastest. Why is evolution fastest at this time?

ACTIVITY 23.2

PROBLEM
What is the impact of various alternative energy sources on the environment?

MATERIALS (per group)
- newspapers
- scissors
- glue or tape
- paper
- pencil

INFERENCE
After reading through the activity, infer how alternative energy sources affect the environment.

PROCEDURE

1. Working in groups of three, scan the titles of the newspaper articles for an article that interests you about an alternative energy source and how it affects the environment.
2. One member of the group cuts out the article, attaches it to a sheet of paper, and goes through the reference materials provided by your teacher or the library. He or she then puts this information in outline form for the rest of the group. *Note: Discard any newspaper scraps in your recycle bin.*
3. A second member puts the collected information into a written report for the whole group. *Note: Be sure your report answers the questions in the Analysis and Conclusion sections.*
4. The third student prepares an oral report to be given to the entire class. After the oral presentation, other classmates may direct questions to any of the group members.

ANALYSIS

1. What energy source or technology does your article focus on? Is it a renewable or nonrenewable resource?
2. Does the author of the newspaper article seem to be for or against this energy source? Explain.
3. In your opinion, what are the benefits of your chosen energy source? What are the drawbacks?
4. What risks does this energy source present to the environment? Explain.

CONCLUSION

1. Summarize the potential benefits and hazards of your chosen energy source, and its environmental impact. Present your findings in the oral report.
2. After all groups have presented their oral reports, the whole class participates in a discussion of the following question: If the entire United States used nuclear energy as its only energy source, how do you think people would be affected 100 years from now? 1000 years from now?

The rapid growth of the human population has put a strain on the biosphere. Earth has limited resources. An increase in people means an increase in the demand on these resources. When the increasing population is combined with the frontier ethic, the damage to the biosphere can be severe.

Recall from Chapter 12 that the sustainable ethic is based on the idea that resources are limited. Building a sustainable society is a goal that many people share. A sustainable society minimizes waste and maximizes the benefit from each resource. The concepts behind a sustainable society have much in common with natural ecosystems.

24.1 CONSERVATION

OBJECTIVES • *Define* conservation, explaining how resources can be conserved. • *Describe* ways of conserving energy.

One basic concept in a sustainable society is conservation. **Conservation** *is a strategy to reduce the use of resources through decreased demand and increased efficiency.* If a resource is to be conserved, less of it must be used. What is used must be used completely, with waste kept to a minimum. Conservation also includes the protection and management of Earth's remaining ecosystems.

Waste Reduction

The frontier ethic has led to a disposable society. In a disposable society, products are used once and then thrown away. Newspapers, food and beverage containers, and the other items in Figure 24.1 are designed for only one use. The amount of waste generated by the use of disposable items is vast.

The amount of material and energy that humans waste is unique in the biosphere. No other species uses so many resources as inefficiently as humans. In a normal ecosystem, wastes left behind by one kind of organism will be used as a resource by another type of organism. A sustainable society models the other ecosystems on Earth. For example, just as a vulture will eat the remains of a lion's kill, one factory may use the waste products of another. Waste is minimized, and efficiency is increased.

Figure 24.1 Industrial societies produce many disposable items. These items are used once and then thrown away. Items like these increase the amount of garbage that needs disposal.

Field Activity

Survey your home, and try to assess how energy-efficient it is. Write a report summarizing your findings. Make some recommendations to make your dwelling more energy-efficient. As you survey your home, ask yourself the following questions:

1. Are your appliances energy-efficient?

2. Are your windows insulated?

3. Is there weather stripping around windows and doors? How much insulation does your home have?

Conservation can reduce waste in several ways. One way is through source reduction. **Source reduction** *is the lowering of the demand for a resource, resulting in a reduction in the amount of resource needed to satisfy that demand.* Source reduction decreases the amount of a resource taken from the environment in the first place. This type of conservation also reduces habitat destruction and pollution.

Another way waste can be reduced is by minimizing the amount of material that is thrown away. Glass, paper, aluminum, and plastics can all be recycled. Separating these items from trash and setting them aside for recycling reduces waste. You and other consumers play a crucial role in reducing garbage. If you buy products that are packaged in reusable or recyclable containers, you are helping reduce waste. Through the reduction of wastes and decreased demand for resources, a society can become more sustainable.

Conserving Energy

Minimizing the use of energy is another method of conservation. Energy can be conserved by using it more efficiently. For example, most of the energy used in the home is used for heat and hot water. Much of this heat escapes if a house is not well insulated. Checking for drafts and for the proper insulating materials is the first step in reducing such heat loss. Insulated windows also help conserve energy. Keeping the heat turned down when you are not at home conserves a great deal of energy, as does sleeping with heavy blankets and lowering the thermostat at night.

Hot water can be conserved by taking shorter showers and running washing machines and dishwashers only when full. Washing clothes at lower temperatures reduces the use of hot water and helps keep clothes in better condition for a longer time, reducing the need to replace them. Special devices provide energy savings of up to 60 percent by reducing the flow of water. These devices can also be used in areas that have chronic water shortages, such as California.

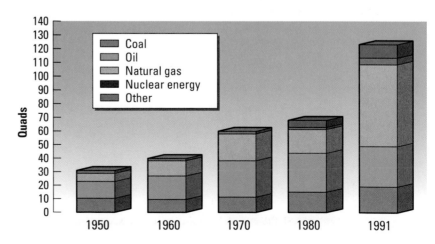

Figure 24.2 U.S. energy consumption has risen steadily since 1950. Most of the energy produced in the United States comes from fossil fuels. Nuclear energy and other types of energy, such as hydroelectric and geothermal, make up the balance. A quad is a measure of energy equal to 1×10^{15} BTU, or 2.93×10^{11} kilowatt hours of electricity.

The use of electricity can be limited in other ways. Turning off lights and other electric appliances when not in use saves energy. Fluorescent (floh-RES-unt) bulbs, such as the one in Figure 24.3, which use less energy than incandescent (in-kan-DES-unt) bulbs, are used in many homes and offices. Unlike incandescent bulbs, which give off much of their energy as heat, fluorescent bulbs produce little heat and generate light more efficiently. In addition, many office buildings, commercial centers, and homes are installing skylights. Skylights allow greater amounts of sunlight to enter a room during daylight hours. The increased sunlight reduces the need for overhead lighting powered by electricity.

Large appliances, such as air conditioners, refrigerators, washing machines, and dishwashers, are now constructed to operate in a more energy-efficient manner. Such appliances have an energy-rating number. When buying an appliance, it is important to know its energy rating. The consumer can use energy-rating numbers as a guide to energy-saving features when buying appliances. Look for the most efficient product when buying.

People are finding ways to conserve gasoline. More people are using mass transportation and carpooling. By traveling in groups, people use less fuel. They also help to decrease air pollution because fewer cars are on the road. In response, many states have established carpool lanes on highways. Properly tuned car engines also conserve fuel. Electric motors and more efficient gasoline-powered engines in cars conserve fossil fuels and reduce pollution. Most automobile manufacturers are developing more fuel-efficient engines. In the near future, electric cars and cars fueled by natural gas or hydrogen will very likely become available. Driving these cars will save gasoline and greatly reduce emissions.

Recall from Chapter 17 that solar, hydroelectric, wind, and geothermal energy are being used as alternative forms of energy in some parts of the world. Not only are these forms of energy renewable, they produce little pollution if operated correctly. They also help cut back on the use of fossil fuels and nuclear energy. The more often these forms of energy are used, the greater the long-term benefits from conservation.

Figure 24.3 A 15-W fluorescent bulb produces as much light as a 60-W incandescent bulb. The bulbs also last about ten times as long. Fluorescent bulbs conserve energy and reduce waste.

LINK
Technology

To help improve the efficiency of automobile engines and reduce pollution, the federal government has established standards for manufacturers to produce automobiles according to minimum efficiency requirements. The cars must emit only a low level of pollution. In the late 1980s, a major Japanese automobile manufacturer developed a car called the AXV, which averaged 98 miles to a gallon of gas (37.4 km/L). A high degree of efficiency is an important part of the sustainable ethic.

SECTION REVIEW

1. What is conservation?
2. Identify some methods currently in use that are designed to conserve energy or resources.
3. **Apply** List five specific things you can do in your home to cut back on the amount of garbage you produce and energy you use. Explain how each activity you list saves resources. Compare your list with the lists from other students.

Community Recycling

Recycling centers have become common sights all around the country, but they were rare a few decades ago. In the 1970s, the trash from Summit, New Jersey, a suburban city of about 21 000 people, was taken to a landfill in New Jersey. By the late 1970s, it was clear that the landfill was nearly full and would soon be closed. After the closure of the New Jersey landfill, trash would have to be hauled to a landfill in Pennsylvania. This would be very expensive.

Summit had a small recycling program in 1979 when eight concerned citizens decided that recycling more and throwing away less would help solve the city's trash disposal problems. These citizens formed the Summit Resource Recovery Corporation (SRRC). Their goal was to increase citizen participation in the newspaper, aluminum, and glass recycling already in place and to expand the recycling program to include other materials.

All materials to be recycled were collected at the transfer station, where the trash collected each day was loaded onto the large trucks that carried it to the landfill. City workers supervised the recycling center

on weekdays. On Saturday, the busiest day for recycling, volunteer groups such as scout troops and PTA groups sorted the recyclables. From the money that the SRRC was paid for the materials recycled, the volunteer groups were given $25 for each Saturday's work.

The SRRC continued to publicize the recycling program. The volunteer groups also helped to spread the word. As community interest and participation grew, the volunteer groups needed more members to staff the recycling on Saturdays, and the donation they received for their work quickly rose to $100.

The SRRC consulted frequently with the city council on ways to improve recycling. When the state

required communities to keep grass trimmings, leaves, and other yard waste out of the trash, the city expanded its composting area.

By 1991, after 12 years of the SRRC's leadership, the recycling program in Summit was collecting glass, newspaper, cardboard, white office paper, magazines, aluminum, mixed-metal ("tin") cans, plastic, motor oil, appliances, and lawn and yard wastes. During those 12 years, Summit went from recycling less than 5 percent of its trash to nearly 45 percent. In 1991, the city took over management of the recycling program. Since then, the recycling of the city's trash has remained at a level of about 45 percent.

Checkpoint

1. List four materials that were added to Summit's recycling program between 1979 and 1991.

2. It is not unusual for recycling programs to grow for many years and then level off. Why do you think the percent of trash recycled levels off?

24.2 RECYCLING

OBJECTIVES • *List* materials that are currently recycled.
• *Identify* the benefits of recycling.

Recycling is one of the most effective ways of conserving resources. **Recycling** *is reducing resource use by collecting usable waste materials and using them to produce new items*. In a natural ecosystem, all matter is recycled. Only energy is added to the system. In industrial societies, almost nothing is recycled. If all materials could be recycled without loss, humans would never need to cut down another tree or dig another iron mine. Many materials cannot be recycled, however, and even those that can are never recycled completely.

Recycling has several benefits, including a reduction in both the amount of waste produced and the resulting disposal problems. Recovered waste is also a good source of limited resources, such as steel and aluminum. Recovering waste materials is often less polluting, cheaper, and more energy-efficient than taking new materials from the environment. Recycling also prevents damage to the environment caused by the gathering of new resources. The fate of solid waste in the United States is shown in Figure 24.4.

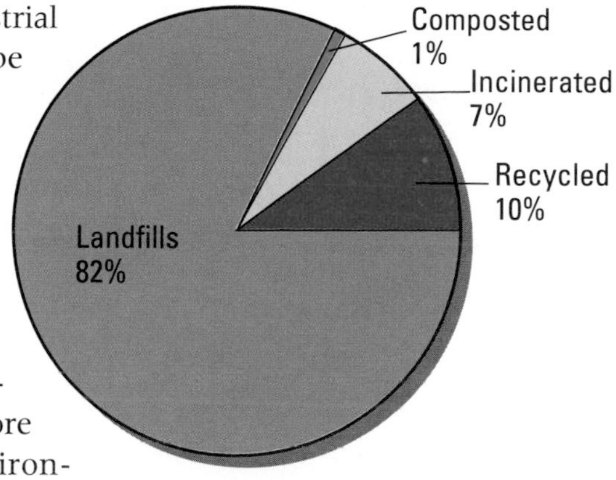

Just as in a natural ecosystem, recycling is a crucial part of a sustainable society. Japan currently recycles about half of its waste, the most of any country in the world. The United States does not do nearly as well. In 1994, the United States recycled 5 percent of its plastic, 23 percent of its glass, 35 percent of its paper and cardboard, and 38 percent of its aluminum. A large increase in the amount of recycled materials is an important part of the sustainable ethic.

Figure 24.4 Most solid waste from homes and industry is thrown away in the United States. Decreasing the amount of waste is a central part of the sustainable ethic.

Recycling Paper

Paper is one of the easiest materials to recycle. The recycling of a 1.2-m stack of newspaper saves one 12-m Douglas fir tree. Recycling paper requires 75 percent less energy and uses 50 percent less water than producing paper from trees. Making paper from recycled paper also produces less toxic waste because it uses fewer chemicals. Today, about one-third of the newspaper and one-half of the cardboard in the United States is recycled.

Unfortunately, paper cannot be recycled forever. Each time it is recycled, the cellulose fibers in the paper shorten and weaken, reducing the quality of the paper. These fiber particles are sometimes visible in lower-quality recycled papers. To improve the quality, more fresh wood must be added. Recycled paper is used for newsprint, and in cardboard boxes. Higher-quality recycled papers are becoming more common. They are used in books, packaging,

Figure 24.5 Paper is cheap and easy to recycle. Many items (including this book) are now printed on recycled paper.

Figure 24.6 Recycling glass uses half the energy of producing new glass. Recycling aluminum is 95 percent less polluting than producing it from ore.

and other paper products. You can support recycling by buying products made from recycled paper.

Recycling Minerals

Many minerals can be recycled. Glass and several different metals have been recycled for years. Aluminum is the most common metal on Earth, but it is never found in its elemental form. Aluminum must be separated from an ore called bauxite (BOKS-yt). Producing aluminum requires large amounts of energy and water. The use of 900 kg of recycled aluminum saves 3600 kg of bauxite and 700 kg of fossil fuels, which would have been used in the refining process. Eliminating the refining process also decreases water and air pollution. It is estimated that the use of recycled aluminum reduces air pollution, water pollution, and energy use by as much as 95 percent.

In the United States, about 90 percent of all junked cars are recycled. Much of the iron and steel of junked cars and appliances is used to make new appliances and automobiles. Many other metals are also recycled in large quantities. Silver, copper, lead, and zinc are some examples. Silver is recycled from photographic film used by hospitals and health clinics for X-rays. Copper is recycled from car radiators and telephone and utility cables. Almost all the lead in car batteries is recycled, and zinc is obtained from recycled plumbing materials.

One recent addition to the recycling effort is motor oil. The recycling of motor oil protects the environment in several ways. Used motor oil contains toxic elements such as lead, cadmium, arsenic, and benzene. Recycling the oil keeps these toxic substances from polluting both land and water. The EPA estimates that it takes only 1 L of used motor oil to contaminate 1 million L of fresh water. Used motor oil can be cleaned and reused again and again for the same purpose. It requires two-thirds less energy to clean oil than it does to refine it. Recycled motor oil can also be used as a fuel.

Dateline 1973

The OPEC (Organization of Petroleum Exporting Countries) nations caused a steep rise in the price of crude oil. The increased price of energy motivated people to find ways to conserve energy. One way is to add recycled glass to the raw ingredients of new glass. Glass melts at a lower temperature than its raw materials. Adding recycled glass reduces the temperature needed to make new glass, thus saving energy. Manufacturers had always used a small amount of recycled glass when making new glass. Today, manufacturers know they can use up to 80 percent recycled glass when making new glass without affecting its quality.

Figure 24.7 These plastic bags are waiting to be recycled. Almost all plastics carry marks used by recyclers to sort plastics into groups that can be recycled together.

Recycling Plastics

The United States produces about 9 million metric tons of plastic every year. Most plastics are made from petroleum, a limited resource. Recycling plastic is more difficult than recycling other materials. Most plastics are complex organic molecules that do not break down easily, and many give off toxic fumes if they are incinerated. In 1994, only about 5 percent of this plastic was recycled. There are many different kinds of plastics, most of which cannot be recycled together.

The amount of plastic being recycled is increasing. About 20 percent of all plastic soft-drink containers are recycled. Most plastics are now coded with a number that indicates the kind of plastic from which the product is made. These numbers can be used to separate plastics into groups that can be recycled together. Recovered plastic can be made into items such as bathtubs, containers, insulation, building materials, and synthetic fabrics.

Many communities now have recycling programs run by local governments. These programs provide containers for sorting discarded paper, aluminum, glass, and plastic. The materials are picked up like garbage and taken to recycling centers. Perhaps your school has a recycling program. If not, you can start one. Aluminum could be collected in the cafeteria, and paper could be collected in each classroom. Recycling is an important part of the sustainable ethic. Using materials more than once cuts down on waste, saves energy, and reduces the demand on the environment for new resources.

LINK
Health

The U.S. Food and Drug Administration (FDA) requires that all food containers be sterilized to guard against disease. Because the processing of recycled plastic does not expose the plastic to temperatures high enough for sterilization, recycled plastics are generally not used to produce new food containers.

SECTION REVIEW

1. What is recycling?
2. List five types of materials that are currently being recycled.
3. **Predict** Plastics are compounds made from carbon and other atoms. Where do you think most plastics come from?

Recycling Paper

PROBLEM
How is paper recycled?

MATERIALS
- sheet of newspaper
- large mixing bowl
- eggbeater
- water
- liquid laundry starch
- hand lens
- large square pan
- screen
- 4 sheets of blotting paper
- rolling pin
- pencil
- notebook

INFERENCE
After reading through the entire activity, make an inference about how recycling paper could improve the environment.

PROCEDURE
1. Tear a sheet of newspaper into small pieces.
2. In the bowl, mix the newspaper pieces with equal amounts of water and laundry starch (about $1\frac{1}{4}$ cups each).
3. With the eggbeater, beat the newspaper, water, and starch until it becomes cloudy and smooth.
4. *Note: A mixture of paper fibers and water is called a* slurry. Use the hand lens to observe the paper fibers in your slurry. Record your observations in your notebook.
5. Place the screen in the pan so that it rests evenly on the bottom.
6. Pour the slurry into the square pan, and add enough water so that the slurry is 8 or 9 cm deep. Be sure to mix well so the fibers are evenly distributed. Slosh the slurry back and forth over the screen.
7. Lift the screen out of the slurry slowly, but continue to hold it over the pan until much of the liquid has drained off.
8. Place the screen fiber-side-up on a sheet of blotting paper. Cover the top of the screen with another sheet of blotting paper to absorb the remaining water.
9. Repeat step 8 using two fresh sheets of blotting paper. Then use a rolling pin to squeeze out any excess water.
10. Let your sheet of recycled paper dry between the blotters. If necessary, peel off the blotters when your recycled paper is dry.

ANALYSIS
1. What made it necessary to beat the paper-water-starch mixture until it was cloudy and smooth?
2. Liquid laundry starch acts as a glue. Why is starch needed in this process?
3. Dense paper has many fibers arranged tightly together. Lighter-weight paper has fibers more loosely arranged and is, therefore, less dense. Was your recycled paper more or less dense than the newspaper?
4. How could you make your recycled paper more dense? Less dense?

CONCLUSION
1. Write a paragraph that describes how your recycled paper could be improved. Would you want to read a book that was printed on this type of recycled paper?
2. As a class, discuss the following: Do you think you could use this process to recycle plastics?

24.3 CONSERVING BIODIVERSITY

OBJECTIVES • *Identify* methods being used to preserve biodiversity, and assess their effectiveness. • *Relate* the loss of biodiversity to the growth of the human population.

As the human population increases, more and more people move into places where natural ecosystems once flourished. Forests are cut down, wetlands are drained, and land and water ecosystems are changed forever. The demand for resources leads to logging in old-growth forests and oil spills in protected areas. However, people are beginning to realize that something must be done to conserve Earth's biodiversity.

Until recently, scientists and the U.S. government focused their conservation efforts on individual species. If a species was endangered, it was protected and managed in an effort to keep it from becoming extinct. Complicated and expensive attempts were made to save individual species. Sometimes these efforts were successful, as in the case of the California condor. Habitat loss and the pesticide DDT led to a steep decline in the condor population. There were fewer than ten condors in the mid-1980s. All the remaining birds were captured, and a breeding program was started. Breeding was successful, and a few birds have now been introduced back into the wild.

Not all captive breeding programs are successful. In South America, captive herds of vicuña (vy-KOON-yuh), a member of the camel family, are doing better in wild preserves than in captivity. Even if captive breeding is successful, reintroducing a species back into the environment may be difficult or impossible because its habitat may no longer exist. Saving a species while allowing the destruction of its habitat is short-sighted. Ecologists now think that conservation efforts should be focused on preserving entire

Figure 24.8 These California condors were part of a breeding program in San Diego. Many ecologists think that conservation efforts should focus on saving whole ecosystems, not just species threatened by habitat destruction.

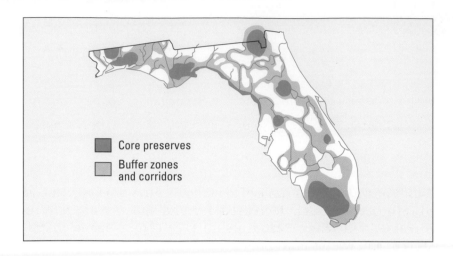

Figure 24.9 The controversial Wildlands Project recommends protecting and restoring large expanses of land in the United States. The project's plan for Florida is shown here. Many people feel the Wildlands Project is too radical. Most ecologists agree, however, that existing preserves are too small and fragmented.

Core preserves

Buffer zones and corridors

Think About It!

Areas that are set aside and protected from development and other human activities have several different names, such as *preserve*, *reserve*, and *refuge*.

1. Use a dictionary to find the meaning of each of these words.

2. Using the definitions, write a short essay describing how each of these terms is appropriate for the purpose it serves.

ecosystems instead of single species. Protecting an entire ecosystem will ensure that the natural habitats and interactions of many species will be preserved.

The United States has an extensive system of national parks and protected areas. *A* **preserve** *is an area of land or water set aside for the protection of the ecosystem in that area.* Only 19 percent of the continent's ecosystems are protected in preserves larger than 100 000 hectares (about 20 mi²). Ecologists are beginning to realize that even these preserves may not be large enough. Populations must be large enough to have the genetic variety needed to survive natural changes in size, and large populations need space. For example, 50 grizzly bears may require 5 million hectares of land. Conservation ecologists are working on plans to enlarge preserves and develop connecting corridors between them, resulting in a giant network of natural habitats. Expansion will conflict with the interests of people, however, so expanding the preserves may be difficult.

Unfortunately, the need to protect biodiversity is greatest in countries that are least able to protect it. The destruction of the rain forests is the greatest single threat to biodiversity. But most rain forests are in developing countries. Recall from Chapter 23 that these countries have social and economic problems that make it difficult to view biodiversity as a priority. Education in developing countries is often poor as well, meaning that people are not aware of the biodiversity problem.

SECTION REVIEW

1. Are most preserves in the United States large enough? How large must a preserve be to be effective?

2. What is the importance of using corridors to connect core preserves?

3. **Hypothesize** What problems do you think could result if an endangered species were introduced into a nonnative habitat?

CHAPTER 24 REVIEW

KEY TERMS

conservation 24.1   source reduction 24.1   recycling 24.2   preserve 24.3

CHAPTER SUMMARY

24.1 Conservation is a strategy to reduce the use of resources through decreased demand and increased efficiency. Resources must be conserved, and wastes must be reduced, if human societies are to become sustainable. Source reduction is lowering the demand for a resource, thereby reducing the amount taken from the environment. Energy can be conserved by using more efficient appliances, insulating homes, turning down the thermostat, and changing other behaviors that use a lot of energy.

24.2 Recycling is reducing resource dependence by collecting reusable waste materials and making them into new items. Recycling uses less energy and generates less pollution than starting with fresh resources. So recycling eases the demand on the environment for limited resources. Paper, glass, metals, and plastics can all be recycled. Many communities have curbside recycling programs.

24.3 Biodiversity must be conserved, just as other resources are. In the past, conservation efforts often focused on individual species. Ecologists now think conservation efforts should focus on preserving entire ecosystems. The United States has a large network of national parks and preserves. Most ecologists think the preserves are too small and fragmented.

MULTIPLE CHOICE

Choose the letter of the word or phrase that best completes each statement.

1. A strategy to reduce resource use through decreased demand and increased efficiency is (a) source reduction; (b) conservation; (c) recycling; (d) biodiversity.
2. The lowering of the overall demand for a resource is called (a) source reduction; (b) conservation; (c) recycling; (d) reducing.
3. Reducing resource use by collecting usable waste materials and using them to produce new items is (a) source reduction; (b) conservation; (c) recycling; (d) reducing.
4. A way that homes cannot be made more energy-efficient is by (a) raising the thermostat setting in cold weather; (b) reducing hot water use; (c) increasing insulation; (d) using fluorescent light bulbs.
5. The form of waste that is most difficult to recycle is (a) glass; (b) paper; (c) plastics; (d) aluminum.
6. Japan currently recycles about (a) 10 percent of its waste; (b) 25 percent of its waste; (c) 40 percent of its waste; (d) 50 percent of its waste.
7. Recycling a 1.2-m stack of newsprint saves (a) one 12-m fir tree; (b) three 12-m fir trees; (c) one 20-m fir tree; (d) three 20-m fir trees.
8. An area of land or water set aside for the protection of an ecosystem in the area is a (a) state; (b) county; (c) preserve; (d) national park.
9. In the mid-1980s the number of living California condors was (a) 560; (b) 110; (c) 20; (d) less than 10.

CHAPTER 24 REVIEW

TRUE/FALSE

Write true *if the statement is true. If the statement is false, change the underlined word or phrase to make it true.*

1. One concern of conservation is <u>increasing</u> the demand for resources.
2. In a disposable society, products are designed to be used <u>once</u> and then discarded.
3. Faucets that reduce hot water flow can result in energy savings of up to <u>60 percent</u>.
4. In a natural ecosystem, <u>all</u> matter is recycled.
5. Recycling paper uses <u>50 percent</u> less energy than producing paper from new trees.
6. <u>Iron</u> is the most common metal on Earth.
7. The breeding program for the California condor <u>was not successful</u>.
8. The Wildlands Project proposes a network of <u>core preserves</u> linked by corridors and buffer zones.

CONCEPT REVIEW

Write a complete response for each of the following.

1. What is source reduction?
2. Describe some ways that you can save energy.
3. Why are plastics more difficult to recycle than other materials?
4. Which metals are commonly recycled?
5. Describe the Wildlands Project in several sentences. Does everyone think that this project is a good idea?

THINK CRITICALLY

1. Describe some differences in the way an industrial society and a natural ecosystem function.
2. How can industrial societies be made to function more like natural ecosystems?
3. Why do you think it takes less energy and produces less pollution when materials are recycled instead of produced new?
4. Why do ecologists think the focus of conservation efforts should be ecosystems and not individual species?

Computer Activity Fifty grizzly bears require about 5 million hectares to live comfortably. How many hectares are needed to support a population of 1000 bears? Use a computer program to compute your answer and graph the relationship between grizzly bears and the land they need.

WRITE CREATIVELY

Write a short story describing life in a sustainable society of the future. Include details about how food and energy are produced, how people move around, and how wastes are disposed of. Include ideas such as source reduction and recycling.

PORTFOLIO

1. Use photographs from newspapers and magazines to build a collage of activities that can make society more sustainable.
2. Build a model of the sustainable city you wrote about in the Write Creatively section. Use whatever materials you need.

GRAPHIC ANALYSIS

Use Figure 24.9 to answer the following.

1. What are the basic areas of the Wildlands Project called? How many of these areas are there in Florida?
2. What is the purpose of the corridors and buffer zones? Why are they important?
3. About what percentage of Florida is covered by the Wildlands Project? Do you think that setting aside this much land is practical?

ACTIVITY 24.2

PROBLEM
How can you design a model city?

MATERIALS (per group)
- assorted colored marking pens
- large sheet of posterboard
- large assortment of magazines, suitable for cutting

HYPOTHESIS
After reading through the activity, hypothesize about what features should be included in the model city of the future.

PROCEDURE
1. Students work in groups of three. Each group designs a self-contained model city that will house 50 000 people. All basic services are provided, including housing, police, health care, shopping, waste disposal, water, power, and recreation. Include the criteria in the data table below when planning your model city.

Your Model City Must:	Method Used
Recycle all wastes	
Supply all power	
Be completely safe	
Have mass transportation	
Encompass 3 km² of land	
Be pollution-free	

2. Your model city must: Recycle all wastes; supply all power; be completely safe; have mass transportation; encompass 3 km² of land area; be pollution-free.
3. The first student in the group, the Researcher, collects research material about what features should be included in the model city of the future. *Note: You will know if you have enough information if you are able to fill in the data table.*
4. The second student, the Implementer, organizes the library material in a cohesive manner to make a poster, collage, or other visual image of the model city. Use your own drawings or pictures from magazines.
5. The third student, the Presenter, prepares an oral report and delivers it to the class. After the oral presentation, other class members may ask anyone in the group for more information about the group project.

ANALYSIS
1. What did your group choose for a power supply for your model city? Is your power supply pollution-free?
2. How did your model city recycle its wastes? Is this method pollution-free?

CONCLUSION
What do you think is the most important component of your model city of the future? *Note: For one possible answer, refer to the data table.*

CHAPTER

25

PROTECTING THE ENVIRONMENT

Earth is a complex collection of ecosystems, each with structured food webs and energy pyramids. Humans have created interactions among themselves and all the ecosystems of the world in their efforts to obtain food, shelter, and energy. Agriculture has carried grassland organisms into rain forests. Construction has placed homes on top of wetlands. Dams have been built across flowing freshwater ecosystems.

In order to create an economy based on sustainable development, interactions of humans and ecosystems must be regulated. Environmental policies at local, federal, and international levels provide guidance toward this goal.

25.1 THE GLOBAL ECOSYSTEM

OBJECTIVES • **Describe** *the relationship between the environment, human behavior, and human values.* • **Describe** *the steps involved in decision making and policy making.*

Chapter 24 discussed various approaches to applying a sustainable ethic to natural resources. Such concepts involve conservation, recycling, and source reduction. While it is essential to understand the theories behind recycling and conservation, it is equally important to understand how such plans can be applied effectively.

Economics and Values

Human behavior as it relates to resources can be modeled using economic concepts. Human values as they relate to resources, however, are not easily modeled. Our values regarding the environment reflect religious, cultural, and economic considerations.

Two main concepts in economics are the ideas of supply and demand. *Supply* is the amount of a resource available to consumers. *Demand* is the amount of a resource that people are willing to purchase. *A* **supply-demand curve**, *as shown in Figure 25.1, shows how price varies with respect to supply and demand.* If demand is high, people will be willing to pay a high price. High prices will encourage those who control resources to place more of them on the market. However, high prices may also inspire consumers to conserve resources or find other, alternative resources. Market prices are determined by the balance of supply and demand.

Supply and demand for a resource are controlled by different factors. Supply is not merely the availability of a resource. Business or political control can make a resource unavailable. Government policies may also subsidize development of a resource, increasing its availability. Demand is based on people's desire for a resource which is affected by their values.

Dateline 1977

President Jimmy Carter instructed the Council on Environmental Quality and the State Department to study changes in population, resource depletion, pollution, and land management through the year 2000. In 1980, the results of the Global 2000 Report concluded that "If present trends continue, the world in 2000 will be more crowded, more polluted, less stable ecologically, and more vulnerable to disruption than the world we live in now... unless the nations of the world act decisively to alter current trends."

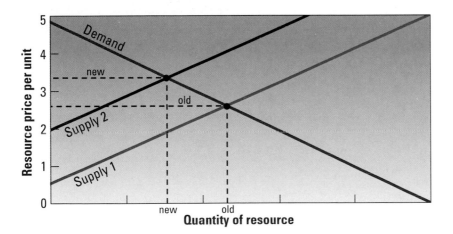

Figure 25.1 How people relate to the use of resources can be represented by a supply-demand curve. On a supply-demand curve, an entire "supply" or "demand" line is shifted to the left to represent a decrease, and to the right to represent an increase. The line labeled "Supply 2" represents a decrease from "Supply 1." Note how this decrease in supply is reflected by an increase in price.

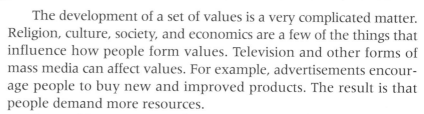

Figure 25.2 Different human values determine how people may view a resource such as gold. Gold may be valued for economic, scientific, or cultural reasons.

The development of a set of values is a very complicated matter. Religion, culture, society, and economics are a few of the things that influence how people form values. Television and other forms of mass media can affect values. For example, advertisements encourage people to buy new and improved products. The result is that people demand more resources.

Some things appear to have no direct economic value. Air, space, and warmth are basic requirements of all living organisms. The growing human population has demanded, and will continue to increase its demand for, these resources. People must consider the supply of these resources, because human activity not only depletes resources, it can damage them as well.

The market concept only applies to resources that can be owned and purchased. Many resources, such as air and water, are part of global cycles, and must be shared by all people. Water can be owned and sold on the market, but the global cycle that recharges aquifers cannot. Such resources are difficult to assess using the economic concepts of supply and demand. Scientists and economists are trying to determine the true value of such ecosystem functions.

Decisions for the Global Ecosystem

Each day, you make many decisions. To make decisions, you must determine priorities among the risks, costs, and benefits involved. Decisions may include which shoes to wear or when to shut the water off in the shower.

At this level, most people can easily come to a decision. However, when the decision must take into account risks, costs, and benefits concerning human health and the environment, matters become complicated. Who takes on the risks? Who benefits? Who pays the costs?

Group interests play an important role in environmental decision-making. For example, two groups may argue over the risks, costs, and benefits of controlling toxic waste discharge into streams. Industries that are forced to place controls in action may complain about their rising costs and the decrease in their profits. Groups not associated with these industries may argue that having less toxic waste in the stream will reduce health risks and health-care costs for the people who use or live near the stream. How are the risks, costs, and benefits evaluated so that a policy can be developed and put into effect?

Making Policies

There are questions involving time and money, and questions concerning whether changes need to be made. No one wants to change business or agricultural practices when there is no definite idea of the costs involved, or whether it is necessary, or if there will be any real benefits from the change.

To regulate practices and activities with respect to their impact on the global ecosystem, policies are developed. *A* **policy** *is an outline of actions, incentives, penalties, and rules that a company, group, or government follows concerning a particular issue.* Developing an environmental policy involves making decisions based on risk assessment and cost/benefit analysis. Risk assessment and cost/benefit analysis are based on educated estimates and predictions.

Determining how much risk is acceptable is called **risk assessment.** Scientists conduct laboratory studies, examine historical events, and develop models to determine the relationship between causes and effects. In many cases, assessing the risks involved in using a particular product, technology, or activity is quite difficult. Money for research may be insufficient, and real-life cause-and-effect models for new products and new technology are limited.

Risk assessment can become subjective. Independent researchers or research groups must provide definite research results in order to receive funding. Researchers who work with particular industries sometimes are encouraged to provide results that support the efforts of these industries.

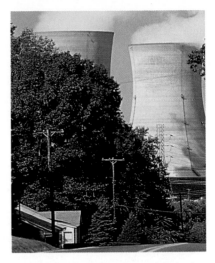

Figure 25.3 Today, and certainly in the future, close contact with a potential environmental disaster is almost certain. Here, a residential area stands next to the cooling tower of a nuclear power plant.

Much of the information concerning environmental protection is communicated through books, magazines, and scientific journals.

1. How might literacy be related to policy development and enforcement?

2. How important is an understanding of scientific concepts in policy development and enforcement?

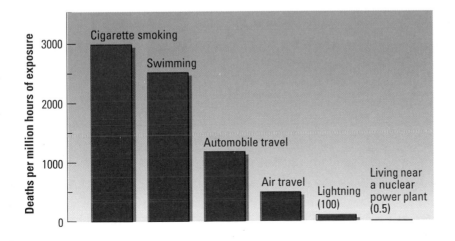

Figure 25.4 Historical research can help scientists and policymakers identify risks. However, where new technology and new activities are more frequent, historical models are rare. The only time to be certain of a potential risk is after problems occur.

Figure 25.5 This graph shows the costs of controlling pollution compared to environmental costs. A cost/benefit analysis shows that the most favorable level of pollution control is one that provides a balance between protection costs and health risks.

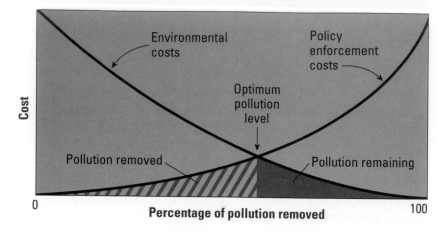

Environmental costs

Policy enforcement costs

Optimum pollution level

Pollution removed

Pollution remaining

Cost

0   Percentage of pollution removed   100

A **cost/benefit analysis** *is the analysis of social costs versus social benefits.* Cost/benefit analysis is a way of identifying the positive and negative impacts of environmental activities and determining the costs of these impacts. Next, the analysis reflects whether or not the benefits are greater than the costs. The goal is to determine how to increase benefits and reduce costs.

A cost/benefit analysis must be detailed and specific so that interest groups may assess the results of the analysis. Different interest groups may assign different values to items on the lists of costs and benefits, resulting in different decisions. For example, a developer who wants to build a mall can buy the land for it at market price. However, people living in the area may value the scenic nature of the undeveloped land, and feel that the advantages of a nearby mall do not outweigh the costs of losing the natural surroundings.

Many people argue that cost/benefit analysis is not effective for many issues. Critics of cost/benefit analysis maintain that not all things can be given a specific economic value, such as the beauty of a landscape or the cleanliness of air. Others argue that if an object is not given an economic value, its importance at the policy-making table will be reduced. Another drawback to cost/benefit analysis is that costs may be difficult to calculate if costs are shared by a large number of people, as is the case with air pollution.

SECTION REVIEW

1. List four factors that may influence value development, and give examples of how values may be communicated.
2. What processes are involved in policy development and decision-making? What are some problems related to these processes?
3. **Predict** What do you think the competition for basic resources such as food, water, and space will be like in 15 years in the United States?

Saving What's Left

Coral Springs, Florida, a city on the edge of the Everglades, was mainly developed during the 1970s and 1980s. By 1986, the city was growing rapidly. A group of high school students who were members of the ecology club called "Save What's Left" learned that a 70-acre stand of cypress trees near their school was about to be cut down to make way for a road and another housing development.

When the students learned that this was the last untouched portion of what had been an extensive stand of cypress trees, they decided to oppose the development. The students started by enlisting the public. They circulated petitions and made signs protesting the development. The students presented their petitions and spoke about the importance of saving this beautiful and natural area. Support grew, and many citizens joined the students' efforts. Meetings were held with commissioners, planners, developers, and students.

County naturalists and the city urban forester cataloged the species in the area and found that a rare fern was growing in the cypress forest. The county then designated the site as an envi-

Regions of the Everglades, and many of the species that live in them, are being replaced by roads and housing developments.

ronmentally sensitive area. One year later, Broward County voters passed a bond issue to buy environmentally sensitive sites, and the cypress area in Coral Springs was one of the first sites purchased. Now the site is a county park named Tall Cypress Nature Center. The students have access to the site to use it as a natural laboratory and for learning about a native ecosystem.

The city of Coral Springs has also passed its own bond issue for the purchase of additional environmentally sensitive sites in the city. The mayor established a Growth Management Committee to oversee the development of these sites and to advise on other environmental issues in the city. This committee includes citizens, builders, and students.

All of this happened because the students were interested, persistent, and vocal. They did their research thoroughly and they were prepared to speak to builders and city officials. They found a way to work within the system and accomplished more than they ever imagined.

✓ Checkpoint

1. What steps did students take to oppose the development of the cypress forest?

2. How do students continue to be active in environmental issues in Coral Springs?

25.2 LOCAL POLICIES

OBJECTIVES • *Identify* how environmental protection may be carried out at the local level. • *Explain* the reasons why policies may be more effective at the local level.

The words of a single voice must be informed and organized in order to be well heard. These words may be spoken through boycotts, letters, protests, court action, or voting. Personal concerns become community concerns when more people recognize the concern and understand that they all share it.

Many environmental problems are not spontaneous events. Instead, a potentially harmful condition persists, sometimes unnoticed, over an extended period of time during which a health hazard arises. The problem that occurred in Love Canal, New York, is a good example.

Problems related to the health hazard in Love Canal began in 1954. The company responsible for the dump maintains that local officials were aware of potential problems. However, it took until the late 1970s before local residents became aware of the toxic chemical dump under their feet.

Concerned citizens are often the first to vocalize the dangers of harmful environmental conditions. These people may sponsor discussions to enlighten the public about practices they feel affect their health and their environment. These people may choose to challenge existing policies.

In many communities, issues concerning environmental policies may be put on local ballots at election time. Such issues are

Figure 25.6 This map is an example of how local problems can be viewed as national concerns. Recall the crisis of the Ogallala Aquifer, and consider how the High Plains states are connected.

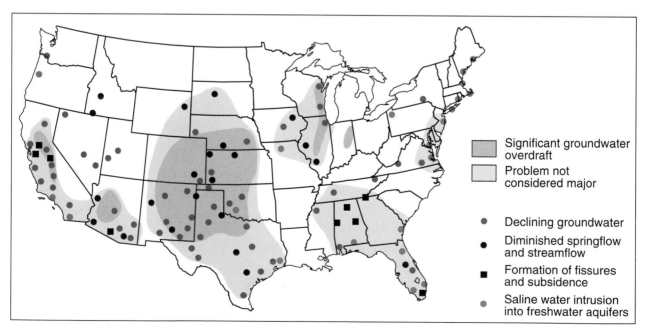

Significant groundwater overdraft

Problem not considered major

● Declining groundwater

● Diminished springflow and streamflow

■ Formation of fissures and subsidence

● Saline water intrusion into freshwater aquifers

often related to pollution, land management, and the quality of health. One example would be a vote on a bond issue to pay for improving a sewage-treatment system.

Land-management policies at the state and local levels address both land use and pollution. Land-use policies may require that, before land can be developed, environmental impact studies must be performed. Conducted by ecologists, other scientists, and engineers, these studies predict how a proposed project may affect the biotic and abiotic factors in the environment.

Recall that two goals of recycling are decreasing solid wastes and reducing the need to open new landfills. Most recycling efforts have been started at the state or local level. For example, in 1972, the Oregon state legislature passed the state's first bottle law. The law required a deposit on cans and bottles for beverages such as soft drinks and beer. The bottle law helps reduce litter and increases recycling. By 1992, ten other states had enacted similar laws: California, Connecticut, Delaware, Florida, Iowa, Maine, Massachusetts, Michigan, New York, and Vermont.

Recycling is only one of the ways that state and local governments are dealing with environmental issues. Prior to 1972, most environmental concerns were dealt with at the federal level. But since that time, the emphasis for environmental responsibility has been shifted back to state and local communities. This shift in focus is largely the result of individual states' preference to maintain control over their own environmental situations.

Many communities are implementing programs or practices designed to reduce energy consumption or provide alternatives to fossil-fuel use. Many utility companies now provide free home energy audits to show customers how to reduce their energy use. In addition, the utility companies provide homeowners with access to energy-saving bulbs. Some communities are meeting their electrical demands by using alternatives to fossil fuels. In some communities, trash is being burned to generate the steam needed to produce electricity. Several communities in California now require solar hot water systems in all new housing.

Awareness of issues in the global ecosystem is essential. Solving environmental problems at the state and local levels requires the education of citizens. Educated citizens are prepared to take responsible actions.

Figure 25.7 Residents sign petitions to protest the use of poisonous pesticides.

SECTION REVIEW

1. What is environmental responsibility?
2. List three ways in which local concerns may be communicated.
3. **Infer** Why might local policies be more easily developed and enforced than federal or international policies?

25.3 FEDERAL POLICIES

OBJECTIVES • *Explain* the necessity for federal intervention in local environmental issues. • *Identify* opposing values and how they complicate policy enforcement.

Federal policies involve a more complicated decision-making process than local policies. Whereas specific local issues are dealt with by local residents and local policies, federal policies must consider the local issues of many communities and states. Something that benefits one region of a nation may be a disadvantage to another region.

National Quality of Life

Although the responsibility for maintaining environmental quality lies largely with local and state governments, the federal government must intervene on behalf of the people when the actions of one state affect the quality of life in another state. Consider, for example, that a great deal of pollutants enter the Mississippi River at various points within the river's watershed. Because of the flowing nature of water, these pollutants have an impact on all the states located along the river. Resolution of such problems takes place most often in the form of environmental legislation.

The Environmental Protection Agency is responsible for managing and investigating environmental concerns so that effective federal legislation may be developed. Matters dealing with the environment, except those related to nuclear energy, fall under the EPA's control. Nuclear energy is regulated by the Nuclear Regulatory Commission (NRC). There are many divisions of the EPA, including the Office of Policy and Resources Management, Office of Compliance, Office of Environmental Justice, Office of Pollution Prevention and Toxics, Office of Water, and the Office of Atmospheric Programs.

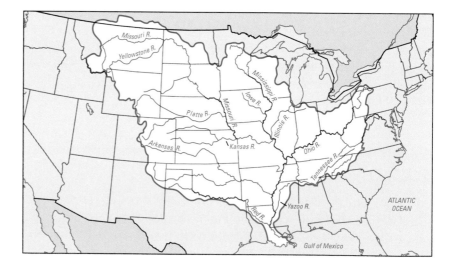

Field Activity

Keeping in mind that people view environmental risks differently, conduct a poll.

1. Develop a list of five environmental issues.

2. Ask twenty to twenty-five people how they rate the risks of these five environmental issues, from low to high. Try to poll as many people from different backgrounds as possible. Be sure to ask about occupation, educational background, and age.

3. Identify connections, if there are any, between these factors and environmental awareness.

4. Present your findings to your class.

Figure 25.8 Toxic chemicals entering any area of the Mississippi River watershed can have widespread effects that cross many state boundaries.

Figure 25.9 Fishing the waters of the Pacific Northwest and The Great Lakes is a way of life for many people in the United States. However, economic survival and concern for threatened fish populations has sparked many disputes among neighboring communities that fish these areas.

Native American Fishing Rights

Trout and salmon populations in the Pacific Northwest and the Great Lakes are seriously threatened. To reduce the threat to endangered fish populations, there are restrictions and bans on commercial fishing for the general public. However, treaties, or agreements, made between Native Americans and the U.S. government in the 1800s prohibit any changes from being made in Native American fishing rights.

The fishing-rights issue has gone to court many times. State and sport-fishing representatives argued that fishing methods had changed and that most fishing areas were stocked with fish from state hatcheries. In 1987, a federal judge ruled that because the treaty was a federal policy, the states had no right to regulate Native American fishing.

Native American nations involved in the fishing rights treaties are concerned with environmental issues and the livelihood of their communities. Attempts are being made between these nations and the federal government to develop policies that encourage a sustainable use for the fishing resources. For now, however, the controversies and conflicts continue—and probably will until new agreements are reached that settle these difficult issues.

SECTION REVIEW

1. What is a treaty?
2. Why is it important for the federal government to enforce environmental policies at the local level?
3. **Think Critically** What kinds of value issues may be involved in the fishing-rights dispute?

25.4 INTERNATIONAL POLICIES

OBJECTIVES • *Describe* the conflict between developed and developing nations over environmental policy issues. • *Identify* the importance of individuals in policy development at all levels.

Most scientists, environmentalists, and concerned citizens' groups agree that there is a need for international cooperation if a sustainable future is to be achieved. However, while cooperation is desirable, is it possible or even practical on a global scale?

Development and Environmental Protection

At present, there is a widening gap between the economic and political needs and interests of developed nations and those of developing nations. A common view among developing nations is that developed nations have already obtained wealth and consumed much of Earth's resources for their own needs. This comes at a time when developing countries, under pressure to obtain wealth through the sale of their resources, are cautioned by developed countries to conserve and better manage these resources. The argument is that developed nations dominate decision-making and policy-making to benefit themselves within international organizations such as the United Nations. Developing nations feel that such practices widen the economic gap between countries and encourage resentment and mistrust.

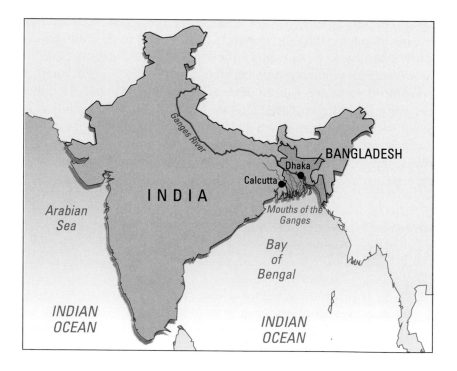

Figure 25.10 Half of India was once covered by forests. Today, in its race to meet economic needs, India has removed all but about 15 percent of its protective forests. Deforestation along the Ganges River has led to greater runoff and, consequently, to massive flooding in Bangladesh, located at the mouths of the Ganges.

Table 25.1 Outcomes of the Earth Summit

Agenda Item	Resolution
The Rio Declaration on Environment and Development	Statement of principle governing worldwide policy on the environment and development.
Agenda 21	Action plan for environmental protection and sustainable development.
Biodiversity Convention	Concerned with the extinction of species; requires signatory nations to inventory and protect endangered species.
Global Warming Convention	Commitment by nations to reduce greenhouse-gas emissions.
Statement on Forest Principles	A statement relating to the protection of the world's forests.

Figure 25.11 Here, on the Rio Grande between Mexico and the United States, Mexican citizens use water filled with runoff from nearby industrial activity for household needs. This is an example of why substantial international policies are needed.

A Global Agenda

In 1992, the United Nations had a meeting of all member nations in Rio de Janeiro. This meeting was called the Earth Summit. The countries attending this meeting addressed such issues as biodiversity, global warming, sustainable development, and relationships between developed and developing nations relating to environmental matters. Although these issues were addressed, many feel that more substantial action must be taken at this level. A summary of the major outcomes of the meeting is presented in Table 25.1.

Hearing a Single Voice

The policies made at local, federal, and international levels may involve scientists, powerful politicians, and business leaders, but those policies usually begin with a single voice. For example, a high school student in the United States became concerned about the number of dolphins captured and killed by fishing boats using tuna nets. This student began a writing campaign to heads of corporations that processed tuna products. As public pressure grew and boycotts threatened the tuna industry, several companies changed their fishing practices to reduce the threat to dolphins.

SECTION REVIEW

1. What was the Earth Summit?
2. In what ways are developed nations and developing nations divided over global environmental concerns?
3. **Infer** What is the relationship between environmental protection and economic development?

Government and the Environment

PROBLEM

How do you communicate your concerns about the environment to your elected government officials?

MATERIALS (per group)

- paper
- pen or pencil
- notebook (one per student)

PREDICTION

After reading through the activity, predict how a group of people polled will respond to a particular question regarding the environment.

PROCEDURE

1. Each group makes a list of four or more environmental issues. *Note: Topics might be local water quality, clear-cutting of timber stands, offshore oil drilling, use of public lands, and disposal of hazardous wastes.*
2. From the list, the group selects one issue that particularly interests all group members. Research the facts on this issue in the library, and put your data in your notebook.
3. Conduct your own opinion poll, with each group member asking ten people outside of the class their position on this issue. Use the data table to record the results of your poll.

Table 25.2

Issue Being Investigated:	
Number of people for:	
Number of people against:	
Number undecided:	

4. As a group, write a letter to send to several elected government officials in Washington, D.C., stating the results of your environmental poll. *Note: In your letter, be sure to include the facts about the issue that you compiled in your library research. Use a positive tone, and offer practical suggestions for a solution.*

5. Decide which officials will receive one of your letters. Make a photocopy of each of your letters, then put them in the mail.
6. If you receive any responses, describe the position of the person you contacted.
7. Have a class discussion summing up what you learned about communicating with people in the government about environmental issues.

ANALYSIS

1. Did your predictions about the results of your poll prove to be correct? Were you surprised by the data you collected?
2. What did you learn about conducting opinion polls? What would you do differently next time?

CONCLUSION

1. Considering all the data your group collected, are you happy with the response you received from government officials?
2. From all the data you collected and the people you polled, have you changed or modified your views on your particular environmental issue? Why or why not?

CHAPTER 25 REVIEW

KEY TERMS

supply-demand curve 25.1
policy 25.1

risk assessment 25.1
cost/benefit analysis 25.1

CHAPTER SUMMARY

25.1 While food supplies and living space are decreasing, the human population is increasing. Supply-demand curves show that competition for resources will intensify as more demands are placed on a scarce supply. Decisions and policies are made to regulate the ways supplies are used. They are based on risk assessment and cost/benefit analysis.

25.2 Voting, boycotts, and protests are a few ways in which the voice of the individual may be heard throughout the community. Attitudes need to change to include a complete picture of the global ecosystem. Education and action are the keys to dealing with environmental problems.

25.3 Federal policies must consider the costs and benefits for all members of the country. When states come into conflict over environmental issues, the federal government must intervene. Intervention can be complicated by issues of culture, morals, and economics.

25.4 There are disagreements on how to attain global cooperation. Developing and developed nations have different economic and political attitudes. Current attitudes need to change in order for people to act on ideas developed in international discussions, such as the Earth Summit. The voices and actions of individuals are the most important part of policy making.

MULTIPLE CHOICE

Choose the letter of the word or phrase that best completes each statement.

1. Earth can be considered a global ecosystem because its organisms (a) live on the same planet; (b) interact closely; (c) use oxygen; (d) gather food in special ways.
2. Competition for resources will intensify because (a) global temperatures are rising; (b) agriculture is improving; (c) supplies are becoming scarce; (d) technology is advancing.
3. Risk assessment depends on (a) scientific research; (b) climate; (c) political stability; (d) medicine.
4. Risk-assessment models are used to (a) control pollution; (b) maintain treaty agreements; (c) reduce population growth; (d) develop policies.
5. Definitions of risks are (a) objective; (b) persuasive; (c) subjective; (d) destructive.
6. An argument against cost/benefit analysis is that it requires (a) too much time; (b) placing a monetary value on everything; (c) risk-assessment models; (d) hidden costs.
7. Developing nations often suffer great environmental destruction because (a) they place little value on the environment; (b) they have so few environmental resources; (c) they are desperate for economic development; (d) they control environmental policy-making.
8. Boycotting is a way of (a) fishing for tuna; (b) voting; (c) protesting; (d) assessing risks.
9. In the United States, public perception and professional perception of risk are (a) similar; (b) different; (c) low; (d) high.
10. Native-American fishing rights are protected by (a) a state judge; (b) senators and congresspersons; (c) cultural practices; (d) federal treaties.

CHAPTER 25 REVIEW

WORD COMPARISONS

Write the letter of the second word pair that best matches the first pair.

1. Supply: demand as (a) basic resource: human population; (b) food: eating; (c) ice: water; (d) benefit: cost.
2. Value: demand as (a) food: human population; (b) voting: policy; (c) religion: culture; (d) television: popular media.
3. Individual: policy as (a) voting: democracy; (b) federal: international; (c) pollution: environment; (d) cars: pollution.
4. Environmental responsibility: sustainable resource as (a) frontier ethic: human population; (b) water use: depletion; (c) air travel: risk; (d) exercise: endurance.
5. Earth Summit: global agenda as (a) local policy: federal policy; (b) math class: math; (c) school: telecommunications; (d) federal policy: Earth Summit.

CONCEPT REVIEW

Write a complete response for each of the following.

1. What is meant by the terms *supply* and *demand*?
2. How is price related to demand?
3. What are the factors that can make risk assessment difficult?
4. List three drawbacks in identifying costs for a cost/benefit analysis.
5. Explain the connections that make Earth a global ecosystem.

THINK CRITICALLY

1. When two or more organisms compete for the same resource, such as food, what will happen?
2. What costs and benefits may be hidden or difficult to estimate in some agricultural or mining practices?
3. If you were in charge of the budgeting office of the EPA, what environmental issues would you make sure received federal funding? On what criteria would you base your funding?
4. What does the expression "Think globally, act locally" mean? How does it apply to the way you think and act?
5. At the personal level, what may be the largest obstacles to acting in the name of environmental protection?

WRITE FOR UNDERSTANDING

Use an outline to apply a step-by-step procedure for the use of insecticides in and around your home. Recall relevant concepts from previous chapters, such as ecosystem balance, hazardous wastes, and water pollution.

PORTFOLIO

Collect photographs, illustrations, and articles on environmental issues, such as water usage. Organize the materials into four categories: personal, local, federal, and international. Use your collection to highlight the issues that concern you most. Determine ways in which a resolution could be approached for each issue. Design a flowchart for each issue, showing the problem and your hypothetical solution. Include brief cost/benefit analyses.

GRAPHIC ANALYSIS

Use Figure 25.6 to answer the following.
1. Where are the regions of significant overdraft located?
2. Is the level of water use in these areas a local issue or a national issue? Explain.

3. How might the global ecosystem be affected by this intense water usage?
4. Predict changes that may occur in the light- and dark-shaded regions as agricultural methods allow more efficient water usage.

ACTIVITY 25.2

PROBLEM

How do you decide which community-owned lands should be developed and which ones should be left as open space?

MATERIALS

- colored pencils
- notebook

INFERENCE

After reading through the activity, make an inference about the value of open space in your community.

PROCEDURE

1. Walk around your neighborhood or community, noticing the open spaces, including gardens, lawns, parks, and playing fields.
2. In your notebook, make a scale map of your neighborhood, and shade in the areas that are open spaces. Write down the approximate percentage of land that is open space.
3. After you have finished shading in the open areas, choose one prime open space in a central location. Now consider constructing a much-needed community medical clinic on this site.
4. Do library research to find out which species, if any, would be affected by building in this open space. To help you sort your data, copy the following questions into your notebook, leaving spaces for the answers:
   - How many km² would the clinic occupy?
   - How many km² do you estimate would be used for parking?

- What is the total number of km² lost to this building site?
- How many animal species would be displaced by the building?
- Would any species be driven completely from its habitat?
- What is the total potential loss of wildlife?
5. Contact several local government officials, and ask them what the potential positive effects of building a clinic in your community would be. In your notebook, answer the questions in step 4. List the potential benefits to the community, such as increased revenues, as well as any negative effects you may be told about.

ANALYSIS

1. What would be the economic advantages to the community of building a clinic on this site? Would there be any economic disadvantages?
2. Consider the long-range effects on your neighborhood. How would the community ecosystem be affected by building a clinic?

CONCLUSION

1. Based on your research, what are the positive effects of building a clinic in the open space in your community?
2. Conduct a class discussion about the positive and negative environmental effects for the neighborhood. In the long run, which do you think is more important to the community: open spaces or increased revenues?

Better Landfills

Learning from the Past

For more than 20 years, towns have been finding ways to make use of closed landfills. Add a layer of dirt, roll out the sod, and what was once a trash pit becomes a useful recreational area, such as a playing field or a golf course. Often, this works out just fine. But in some places, strange things have happened on these reclaimed lands.

On one golf course, once-level fairways are tilted because the trash settled as it decayed. Fireballs erupt as methane gas, a product of decay, bubbles up through the soil and catches fire. There are bare patches where the grass won't grow, caused by heat given off by the decay process. A bowling ball popped out of the ground where the layer of soil covering the landfill was thin.

As a result of experiences such as these, the Environmental Protection Agency (EPA) has developed standards for landfill construction. Landfills must be lined to eliminate leaking, and each day's trash must be covered by at least 9 cm of dirt. When the landfill is closed, the top layer must be at least 60 cm thick.

Some of the larger waste-disposal companies are exceeding EPA standards. The Live Oak Landfill and Recycling Center near Atlanta, Georgia, is utilizing the newest methods for containing trash. As trash is dumped at Live Oak, it is pressed down by a 50-ton compacting machine that rolls across the landfill. This extreme compacting should prevent the surface from sinking in the future.

When the landfill is full, pipes will be installed to collect the methane that is produced within the trash, in order to reduce the risk of fire. There may be an additional benefit. Live Oak is so large that it may produce enough methane to fuel a small power plant, which would be built on the site.

These measures should help ensure that bowling balls and other objects stay buried where they belong.

Checkpoint

1. What are some problems that can occur when a landfill is turned into a recreational site?

2. How does the Live Oak Landfill design prevent the finished landfill from sinking?

Many former landfills have been converted into recreational areas such as parks and golf courses.

◀ Recycling Coordinators

With an increasing public awareness of the need to recycle, the demand for recycling coordinators has grown considerably. The formal education one obtains is not as important as a demonstrated ability to organize and manage diligently.

Recycling coordinators design and manage recycling programs, and educate the public about the need to decrease the amount of solid waste that goes into landfills.

Environmental Engineers ▶

Environmental engineers design systems and processes to reduce and recycle solid wastes, and also treat potentially hazardous waste water. Environmental engineers may design programs to reduce the amount of paper used in a large corporation, or they may devise methods to recycle and reuse Styrofoam packaging materials.

Solid-Waste Consultant ▲

These professionals design, build, and operate new landfill sites that are safe and effective, and also renovate older sites. Landfills have become highly technological systems, and consultants are needed who can work with collection, emission, and groundwater monitoring systems.

For More Information

Air and Waste Management Association
One Gateway Center, Third Floor
Pittsburgh, PA 15222
(412) 232-3444
http://www.awma.org/

National Recycling Coalition
1727 King Street, Suite 105
Alexandria, VA 22314
(703) 683-9025
http://www.recycle.net/recycle/Associations/rs000145.html

National Solid Waste Management Association
4301 Connecticut Avenue, NW, Suite 300
Washington, DC 20008
(202) 244-4700
http://www.envasns.org/nswma/

METRIC CONVERSIONS

Metric Units	Metric to English	English to Metric
Length		
meter (m) = 100 cm	1 m = 3.28 feet 1 m = 1.09 yards	1 foot = 0.305 m 1 yard = 0.914 m
kilometer (km) = 1000 m	1 km = 0.62 mile	1 mile = 1.609 km
centimeter (cm) = 0.01 m	1 cm = 0.39 inch	1 foot = 0.305 m 1 foot = 30.5 cm
millimeter (mm) = 1000 m	1 mm = .039 inch	1 inch = 2.54 cm
micron (μm) = 10^{-6} m		
nanometer (nm) = 10^{-9} m		
Area		
square meter (m^2) = 10 000 cm^2	1 m^2 = 1.1960 square yards	1 square yard = 0.8361 m^2 1 square foot = .0929 m^2
square kilometer (km^2) = 100 hectares	1 km^2 = 0.3861 square mile	1 square mile = 2.590 km^2
hectare (ha) = 10 000 square meters	1 ha = 2.471 acres	1 acre = 0.4047 ha
square centimeters (cm^2) = 100 mm^2	1 cm^2 = 0.155 square inch	1 square inch = 6.4516 cm^2
Mass		
gram (g) = 1000 mg	1 g = 0.0353 ounce	1 ounce = 28.35 g
kilogram (kg) = 1000 g	1 kg = 2.205 pounds	1 pound = 4536 kg
milligram (mg) = 0.001 g		
microgram (μg) = 10^{-6} g		
Volume (Solids)		
1 cubic meter (m^3) = 1 000 000 cm^3	1 m^3 = 1.3080 cubic yards 1 m^3 = 35.315 cubic feet	1 cubic yard = 0.7646 m^3 1 cubic foot = 0.0283 m^3
1 cubic centimeter (cm^3) = 1000 mm^3	1 cm^3 = 0.0610 cubic inch	1 cubic inch = 16.387 cm^3
Volume (Liquids)		
liter (L) = 1000 milliliters	1 L = 1.06 quarts	1 quart = 0.941 L
kiloliter (kL) = 1000 liters	1 kL = 264.17 gallons	1 gallon = 3.7851 L
milliliter (mL) = 0.001 liter	1 mL = 0.034 fluid ounce	1 pint = 0.471 L
microliter (μL) = 0.000001 liter		1 fluid ounce = 29.57 mL

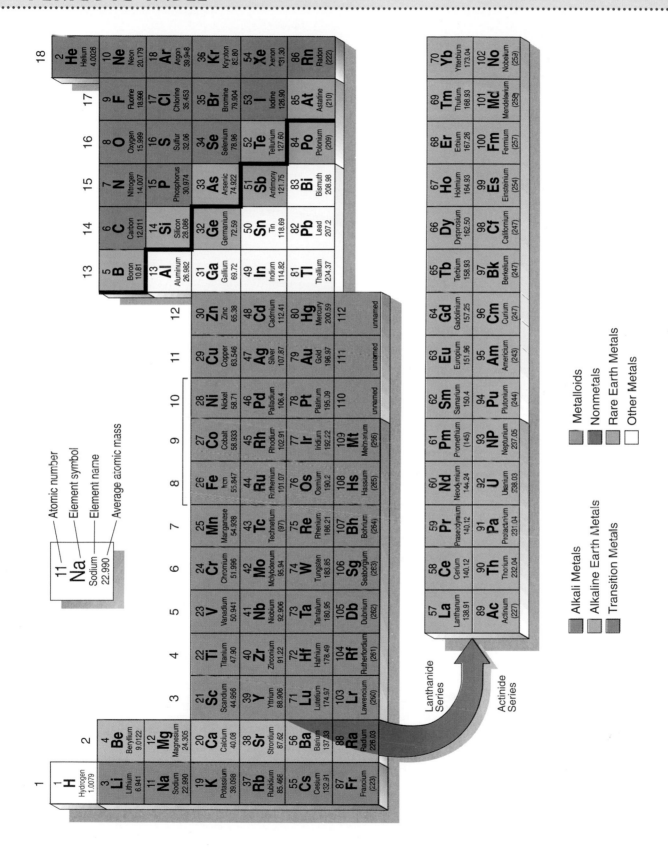

A science laboratory is a place where many exciting things can happen. It is also a place with many potential hazards and dangerous materials. Following sensible safety precautions will help to ensure that your experience in the lab is a positive one. Read the following guidelines before you begin working in the laboratory, and review them from time to time throughout your study of science.

Safety Guidelines

1. Read through the procedures of each laboratory activity before you come to class so that you are familiar with the activities.
2. Know how to use and be able to locate all safety equipment in the laboratory, including the fume hood, fire blanket, fire extinguisher, and eye washes. Also be sure to locate the nearest exit in case of an emergency.
3. Horseplay, running, or other unsuitable behavior can be dangerous in the laboratory.
4. Wear safety goggles when handling all hazardous chemicals, an open flame, or when otherwise instructed.
5. Wear an apron or a smock to protect your clothing in the laboratory.
6. Tie back long hair and secure any loose-fitting clothing.
7. Never eat or drink in the laboratory.
8. Wash your hands before and after each activity in the lab.
9. Keep the work area free of any unnecessary items.
10. Wash all utensils thoroughly before and after each use.
11. Never smell or taste any chemicals unless instructed to do so by your teacher and the experiment instructions.
12. Do not experiment or mix chemicals on your own. Many chemicals in the lab can be explosive or dangerous.
13. When using scissors or a scalpel, cut *away* from yourself and others.

14. When heating substances in a test tube, always point the mouth of the test tube *away* from yourself and others.
15. Clearly label all containers with the names of the materials you are using during the activity.
16. Report all accidents to the teacher immediately, including breakage of materials, chemical spills, and physical injury.
17. Don't pick up broken glass with your hands. Sweep it up with a broom, and dispose of it in a container labeled for glass disposal.
18. Never return unused chemicals to their original containers. Follow your teacher's instructions for the proper disposal and cleanup of all materials prior to the end of the lab period.
19. Make sure all your materials are washed and put away, and that your work area is clean before leaving the lab.
20. Be certain that all Bunsen burners, gas outlets, and water faucets are turned off before leaving the lab.
21. Look for the following symbols, which alert you to potential dangers of specific activities:

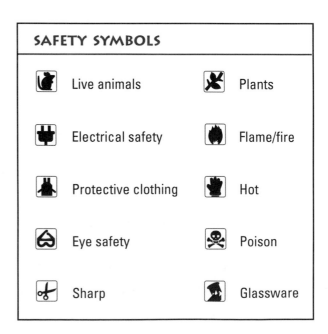

SAFETY SYMBOLS	
Live animals	Plants
Electrical safety	Flame/fire
Protective clothing	Hot
Eye safety	Poison
Sharp	Glassware

CONCEPT MAPPING

Throughout your study of environmental science, you will be presented with many new concepts and information. One way to organize the information so that you can understand and remember what you have learned is to make a concept map. A concept map is a graphic, visual representation of the information in a chapter or section. The process of making the concept map will help you to identify ideas that you do not understand, and to reinforce the ideas that you do understand. What makes a concept map most useful is the fact that you make it yourself.

Making a Concept Map

In a concept map, ideas are expressed as words or phrases enclosed in boxes. Boxes are connected by cross-links that state what the connection is between the ideas. The main idea is shown at the top of the map and is linked to several general concepts. Each general concept, in turn, is linked to more specific ideas and, finally, to examples. No ideas should appear more than once, and all ideas must be linked to others. Use the following steps to make a concept map:

- Identify the main idea and general concepts to be mapped. The name of the sections and subsections may help you identify the important ideas.
- Start making your map by placing the main idea at the top of your map and drawing a box around it. Draw lines to connect the main idea to the general concepts. Each concept should also be boxed.
- Choose linking words or phrases that explain the relationship between the boxed concepts.
- Continue to add more specific concepts and examples, boxing each one and linking it to other boxed words. Be sure to identify the relationships with linking words. Include as many links as you can.

Study Hint: Do not be discouraged if you find concept mapping difficult at first. You may find it helpful to start by writing the important words on slips of paper. The slips can be moved around on your desk easily until you decide which arrangement works best. Sharing your concept map with other students may help you to understand the concepts better.

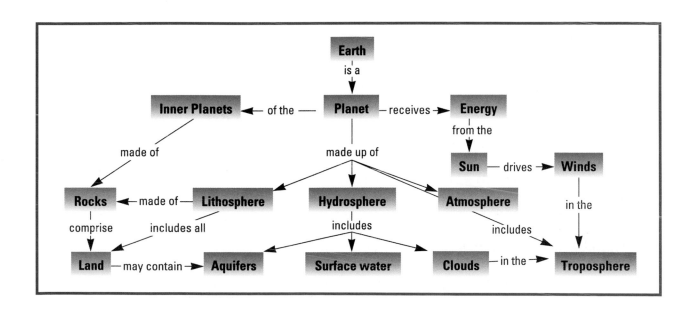

VOCABULARY BUILDER

Word Part	Meaning	Example
a-, an-	not, without	abiotic
aero-	air	aeration
agri-	field, farm	agriculture
aqua-	water	aquatic
bio-	life	biosphere
-cide	kill	pesticide
de-	from	detritus
decid-	fall down	deciduous
demo-	people	demography
eco-	house	ecosystem
gen-	produce, make	generator
geo-	Earth	geology
-graph	written	biography
hetero-	mixed, different	heterotroph
homo-, homeo-	same	homogeneous
hydro-	water	hydroelectric
hyper-	above, over	hyperactive
hypo-	under, beneath	hypothesis
iso-	equivalent	isotope
-logy	study	biology
mal-	bad, faulty	malnutrition
macro-	large	macronutrient
micro-	small	microscope
-meter	measure	kilometer
mono-	single	monoculture
para-	beside, along	parasite
patho-	suffering	pathogen
phos-, phot-	light	photic
phyto-	plant, plantlike	phytoplankton
poly-	many	polyunsaturated
sol-	sun	solar
syn-	put together	synthesis
sub-	under, beneath	subside
-troph	nourishment	autotroph
therm-	heat	thermosphere
-thesis	position, proposal	hypothesis
zoo-	animal	zooplankton

DIRECTORY

Environmental Organizations and Periodicals

American Farmland Trust
1920 N Street N.W., Suite 400
Washington, DC 20036
(202) 659-5170
http://www.farmland.org
email: *info@farmland.org*

Conservation and Renewable Energy Inquiry and Referral Service
P.O. Box 8900
Silver Springs, MD 20907
(800) 523-2929

Conservation International
2501 M Street N.W., Suite 200
Washington, DC 20037
(202) 429-5660
(800) 429-5660
http://www.conservation.org
Periodical: *Orion Nature Quarterly*

The Cousteau Society
870 Greenbrier Circle, Suite 402
Chesapeake, VA 23320
(804) 523-9335
(800) 441-4395
http://www.cousteau.org
Periodical: *Calypso Log*

Earth Island Institute
300 Broadway, Suite 28
San Francisco, CA 94133
(415) 788-3666
http://www.earthisland.org
email: *earthisland@earthisland.org*

League of Conservation Voters
1707 L Street, N.W., Suite 750
Washington, DC 20036
(202) 785-8683
http://www.lcv.org
email: *lcv@lcv.org*

National Audubon Society
700 Broadway
New York, NY 10003
(212) 979-3000
http://www.audubon.org
email: *jbianchi@audubon.org*
Periodical: *Audubon*

National Parks and Conservation Association
1776 Massachusetts Ave. N.W.
Washington, DC 20036
(202) 223-6722
(800) 628-7275
http://www.npca.org
email: *npca@npca.org*
Periodical: *National Parks and Conservation Magazine*

National Wildlife Federation
8925 Leesburg Pike
Vienna, VA 22184
(703) 790-4100
http://www.nwf.org
Periodicals: *National Wildlife,*
International Wildlife

Natural Resources Defense Council
40 West 20th Street
New York, NY 10011
(212) 727-2700
http://www.igc.apc.org/nrdc/
email: *nrdcinfo@nrdc.org*

Rainforest Action Network
221 Pine Street, Suite 500
San Francisco, CA 94104
(415) 398-4404
http://www.ran.org
email: *rainforest.ran.org*

Sierra Club
85 Second Street
Second Floor
San Francisco, CA 94105
(415) 776-2211
http://www.sierra.org
Periodical: *Sierra*

U.S. Public Interest Research Group
218 D Street S.E.
Washington, DC 20003
(202) 546-9707
email: *uspirg@pirg.org*

World Wildlife Fund
1250 24th Street N.W.
Washington, DC 20037
(202) 293-4800
http://www.wwf.org

WorldWatch Institute
1776 Massachusetts Avenue N.W.
Washington, DC 20036
(202) 452-1999
http://www.worldwatch.org
email: *worldwatch.worldwatch.org*
Periodicals: *WorldWatch,*
State of the World

World Terrain

20° E 40° E 60° E 80° E 100° E 120° E 140° E 160° E

ARCTIC OCEAN

Svalbard

Barents Sea

Severnaya Zemlya

Novaya Zemlya

New Siberian Islands

80° N

tic Circle

Baltic Sea

orth Sea

Northern European Plain

URAL MTS.

Ob'

Yenisey

Lena

60° N

Kamchatka Peninsula

EUROPE

Volga

Irtysh

SIBERIA

Sea of Okhotsk

Mt. Elbrus 5642 m (18,510 ft)

Aral Sea

ASIA

Lake Baykal

Amur

Kuril Is.

Blanc '1 ft)

Danube

ALPS

Caucasus Mts.

Black Sea

TIEN SHAN

GOBI DESERT

Hokkaido

Balkan Peninsula

Asia Minor

Caspian Sea

HINDU KUSH

Sea of Japan

Honshu

40° N

Mediterranean Sea

Tigris

Euphrates

Plateau of Tibet

HIMALAYAS

Huang

East China Sea

Shikoku
Kyushu

PACIFIC OCEAN

SAHARA

Nile

Persian Gulf

Indus

Ganges

Mt. Everest 8848 m (29,028 ft)

Chang

Taiwan

HEL

Red Sea

Arabian Peninsula

Thar Desert

Arabian Sea

Deccan Plateau

Bay of Bengal

20° N

Lake Chad

Niger

AFRICA

Ethiopian Highlands

Sri Lanka

Hainan

South China Sea

Philippine Islands

Micronesia

Congo

CONGO BASIN

Lake Victoria

Seychelles

Maldives

Sumatra

Malay Peninsula

Borneo

Celebes

0°

Lake Tanganyika

Kilimanjaro 5895 m (19,340 ft)

New Guinea

C

Lake Nyasa

INDIAN OCEAN

Java

Melanesia

Madagascar

Fiji

0° S

Kalahari Desert

AUSTRALIA

GREAT VICTORIA DESERT

GREAT DIVIDING RANGE

Cape of Good Hope

Cape Agulhas

Darling

Murray

Mt. Kosciusko 2230 m (7,316 ft)

Tasmania

0°

0 1000 2000 mi
0 1000 2000 km

Robinson Projection
© GeoSystems Global Corp.

60° S

ANTARCTICA

Ross Sea

80° S

20° E 40° E 60° E 80° E 100° E 120° E 140° E 160° E

North America

CITIES

⊛ National Capital
★ Territorial Capital
• Other City

ELEVATIONS

Feet	Meters
13,120	4000
6560	2000
1640	500
656	200
0	0
Below sea level	Below sea level

© GeoSystems Global Corp.

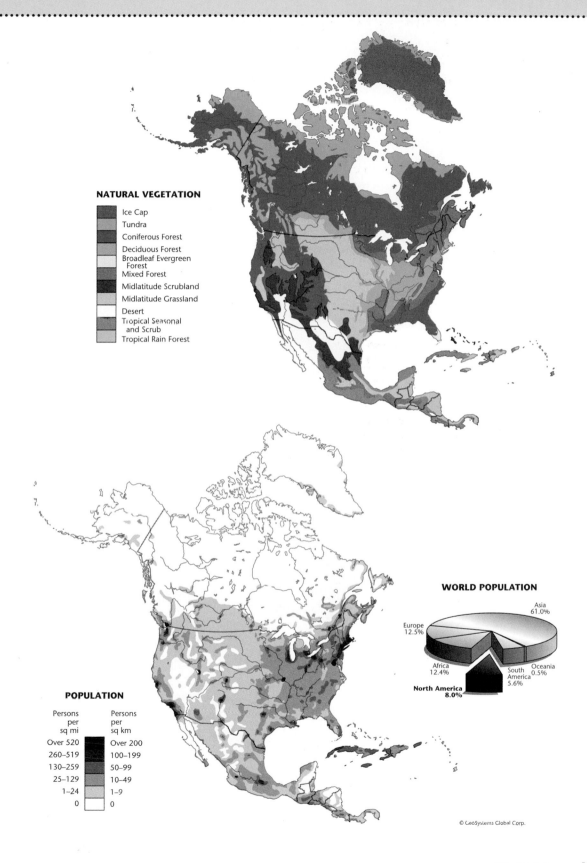

NATURAL VEGETATION

- Ice Cap
- Tundra
- Coniferous Forest
- Deciduous Forest
- Broadleaf Evergreen Forest
- Mixed Forest
- Midlatitude Scrubland
- Midlatitude Grassland
- Desert
- Tropical Seasonal and Scrub
- Tropical Rain Forest

POPULATION

Persons per sq mi	Persons per sq km
Over 520	Over 200
260–519	100–199
130–259	50–99
25–129	10–49
1–24	1–9
0	0

WORLD POPULATION

Asia 61.0%
Europe 12.5%
Africa 12.4%
South America 5.6%
Oceania 0.5%
North America 8.0%

© GeoSystems Global Corp.

South America

CARIBBEAN SEA

Barranquilla
Cartagena
Maracaibo
Barquisimeto
Valencia
Cúcuta
Maracay
Cumaná
Caracas
Maturín
Ciudad
Bolívar
Ciudad Guayana

San Cristóbal
Bucaramanga
Medellín
Manizales
Pereira
Ibagué

VENEZUELA
GUYANA
Georgetown
Paramaribo
Cayenne

Bogotá
COLOMBIA
GUIANA
HIGHLANDS
SURINAME
FRENCH
GUIANA
(FR.)

ATLANTIC
OCEAN

Cali
Pasto
Quito
ECUADOR
Guayaquil
Cuenca
Chimborazo
6267 m
(20,561 ft)
Iquitos
Piura

AMAZON

Negro
Manaus
Belém

Ilha
Marajó

Fortaleza

Chiclayo
Trujillo
Chimbote
PERU
SELVAS
BASIN
Juruá
Purus
Pucallpa
Pôrto Velho
Amazon
Tapajós
Teresina
Natal

BRAZIL

Recife
Maceió

Callao
Lima
Huancayo
Ica
Cuzco
Huascaran
6768 m
(22,205 ft)
Madeira

Guaporé

Xingu
Tocantins
São Francisco
Salvador

MATO GROSSO
PLATEAU
Cuiabá
Brasília

BRAZILIAN

Arequipa
La Paz
BOLIVIA
Cochabamba
Santa Cruz
Oruro
Sucre
Potosí
Goiânia
Uberlândia
HIGHLANDS

Arica
Iquique
Campo
Grande
Belo Horizonte
Vitória

PACIFIC
OCEAN

ATACAMA DESERT
GRAN CHACO
Paraguay
Campinas
São Paulo
Rio de Janeiro
Santos

Antofagasta
Salta
PARAGUAY
Asunción
Ciudad
del Este
Curitiba
Paraná

Isla San Ambrosio
(CHILE)
Isla San Félix
(CHILE)

San Miguel
de Tucumán
Ojos del Salado
6880 m
(22,572 ft)
Santiago
del Estero
Resistencia
Encarnación
Uruguay
Pôrto Alegre

CHILE
Aconcagua
6960 m
(22,834 ft)
Córdoba
San Juan
Mendoza
PAMPAS
Rosario
Santa
Fe
Salto
Paysandú
URUGUAY

ATLANTIC
OCEAN

Islas Juan Fernández
(CHILE)
Valparaíso
Santiago
Rancagua
Talca
Buenos
Aires
Montevideo
Río de la Plata

Concepción
Temuco
Neuquén
ARGENTINA
Bahía Blanca
Mar del Plata

N

Puerto Montt
Chiloé
Península
Valdés

PATAGONIA
ANDES
Archipiélago
de los Chonos
Península
Taitao
Comodoro Rivadavia

Falkland Is.
(Islas Malvinas)
(U.K.)
Stanley

Punta Arenas
Strait of
Magellan
Tierra del Fuego
Ushuaia
Cape Horn

CITIES
⊕ National Capital
★ Territorial Capital
• Other City

ELEVATIONS

Feet		Meters
13,120		4000
6560		2000
1640		500
656		200
0		0
Below sea level		Below sea level

0	250	500	750	1000 mi
0	250	500	750	1000	1250	1500 km

© GeoSystems Global Corp.

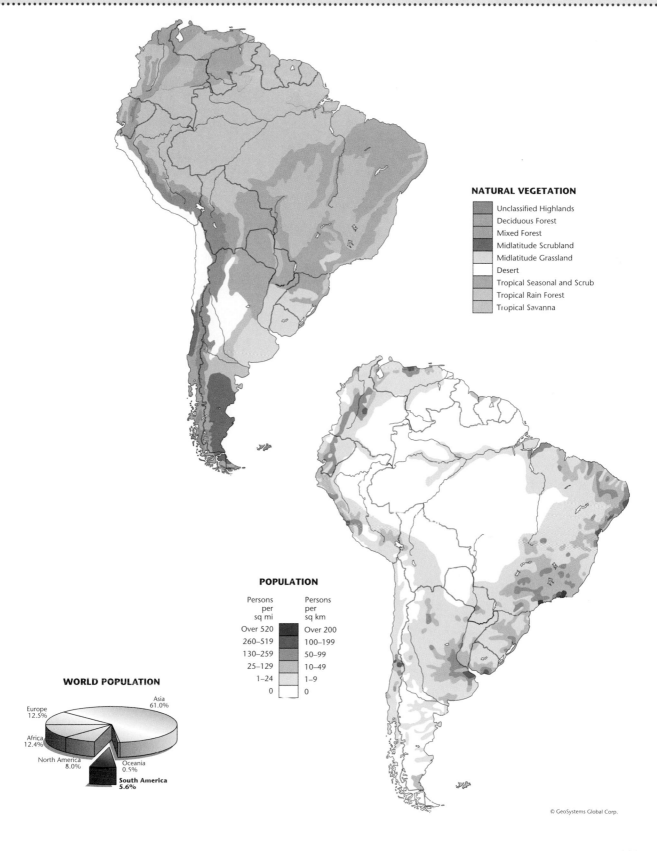

NATURAL VEGETATION

- Unclassified Highlands
- Deciduous Forest
- Mixed Forest
- Midlatitude Scrubland
- Midlatitude Grassland
- Desert
- Tropical Seasonal and Scrub
- Tropical Rain Forest
- Tropical Savanna

POPULATION

Persons per sq mi		Persons per sq km
Over 520		Over 200
260–519		100–199
130–259		50–99
25–129		10–49
1–24		1–9
0		0

WORLD POPULATION

- Asia 61.0%
- Europe 12.5%
- Africa 12.4%
- North America 8.0%
- Oceania 0.5%
- **South America 5.6%**

© GeoSystems Global Corp.

Europe

0   250   500   750 mi

0   250   500   750   1000 km

© GeoSystems Global Corp.

ATLANTIC OCEAN

Norwegian Sea

Barents Sea

North Cape

Hammerfest

Tromsø

Murmansk

LAPLAND

White Sea

Arkhangel'sk

Reykjavík Akureyri

ICELAND

Faeroe Is. (DEN.)

Trondheim

Oulu

FINLAND

Umeå

Tampere

Lahti

Turku

Helsinki

RUSSIA

Kirov

Perm'

Ufa

URAL MTS.

Shetland Is. (U.K.)

Bergen

Sundsvall

Oslo

NORWAY

SWEDEN

Uppsala

Stockholm

Tallinn

ESTONIA

Tartu

St. Petersburg

Yaroslavl'

Nizhny Novgorod

Moscow

Kazan

Samara

Orkney Is.

Aberdeen

North Sea

Göteborg

Linköping

Gotland (SWE.)

Öland

Riga

LATVIA

Daugavpils

Vitsyebsk

Smolensk

Saratov

Glasgow

Edinburgh

Belfast

Jutland

Århus

Helsingborg

Kaunas

Vilnius

LITHUANIA

Mahilyow

Volgograd

Voronezh

UNITED KINGDOM

Newcastle upon Tyne

Copenhagen

Malmö

DENMARK

Odense

Kaliningrad (RUSSIA)

Gdańsk

Hrodna

Minsk

BELARUS

Homyel'

Astrakhan'

Dublin

IRELAND

Liverpool

Leeds

Manchester

Sheffield

Hamburg

Szczecin

Poznań

Brest

Kiev

Kharkiv

Caspian Sea

Cork

Birmingham

Bremen

NORTHERN EUROPEAN

Warsaw

UKRAINE

Luhans'k

Rostov-na-Donu

Cardiff

Amsterdam

Hannover

Berlin

Łódź

Dnipropetrov'sk

Donets'k

Portsmouth

London

NETHERLANDS

Essen

Leipzig

Dresden

Wrocław

POLAND

L'viv

Kryvyy Rih

Zaporizhzhya

Mariupol'

Krasnodar

Antwerp

Rotterdam

GERMANY

Cologne

Bonn

Katowice

Kraków

Prague

Mykolayiv

PLAIN

English Channel

Brussels

Lille

BELGIUM

Liège

Frankfurt

CZECH REP.

Brno

CARPATHIAN

MOLDOVA

Chişinău

Odesa

Channel Is. (U.K.)

Le Havre

Rouen

LUXEMBOURG

Luxembourg

Mannheim

Ostrava

SLOVAKIA

Bratislava

Debrecen

Iaşi

Sea of Azov

Mt. Elbrus 5642 m (18,510 ft)

Brest

Paris

Strasbourg

Stuttgart

Linz

Vienna

Simferopol'

CAUCASUS

Baku

Nantes

Munich

AUSTRIA

Budapest

HUNGARY

Pécs

ROMANIA

Ploieşti

Sevastopol'

Tbilisi

GEORGIA

AZERBAIJAN

Bern

Graz

Bucharest

Black Sea

ARMENIA

Bay of Biscay

FRANCE

Geneva

SWITZERLAND

ALPS

Ljubljana

Zagreb

Novi Sad

Timişoara

Constanţa

Yerevan

AZER.

Bordeaux

Lyon

LIECHTENSTEIN

SLOVENIA

CROATIA

Belgrade

Varna

Mont Blanc 4807 m (15,771 ft)

Milan

Venice

BOSNIA AND HERZEGOVINA

Sarajevo

YUGOSLAVIA

BULGARIA

Sofia

Burgas

Toulouse

Nice

Turin

SAN MARINO

Split

Podgorica

Plovdiv

Istanbul

Vigo

Bilbao

PYRENEES

Marseille

Genoa

Bologna

Florence

Skopje

F.Y.R. MACEDONIA

TURKEY

Porto

Valladolid

Toulon

MONACO

CORSICA (FR.)

APENNINES

Dubrovnik

ALBANIA

Tirane

Thessaloníki

ANDORRA

Pico de Aneto 3404 m (11,169 ft)

Elba

VATICAN CITY

Bari

Lárisa

PORTUGAL

IBERIAN

Zaragoza

Barcelona

Majorca

Minorca

SARDINIA (IT.)

Rome

ITALY

Adriatic Sea

GREECE

Athens

Kérkira

Lisbon

Madrid

Valencia

Palma

BALEARIC IS. (SP.)

Naples

Salerno

Patrai

Cyclades

Rhodes

PENINSULA

SPAIN

Córdoba

Alicante

Palermo

Catania

SICILY (IT.)

Tyrrhenian Sea

Ionian Sea

PELOPONNESUS

Cabo São Vicente

Seville

Granada

Málaga

Mt. Etna 3369 m (11,053 ft)

Sea of Crete

Iráklion

Cádiz

MEDITERRANEAN SEA

GIBRALTAR (U.K.)

Strait of Gibraltar

MALTA

Valletta

CRETE (GR.)

N

CITIES
⊗ National Capital
★ Territorial Capital
● Other City

ELEVATIONS

Feet		Meters
13,120		4000
6560		2000
1640		500
656		200
0		0
Below sea level		Below sea level

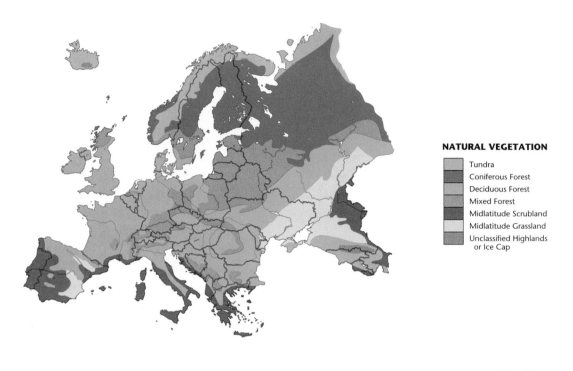

NATURAL VEGETATION

- Tundra
- Coniferous Forest
- Deciduous Forest
- Mixed Forest
- Midlatitude Scrubland
- Midlatitude Grassland
- Unclassified Highlands or Ice Cap

POPULATION

Persons per sq mi	Persons per sq km
Over 520	Over 200
260–519	100–199
130–259	50–99
25–129	10–49
1–24	1–9
0	0

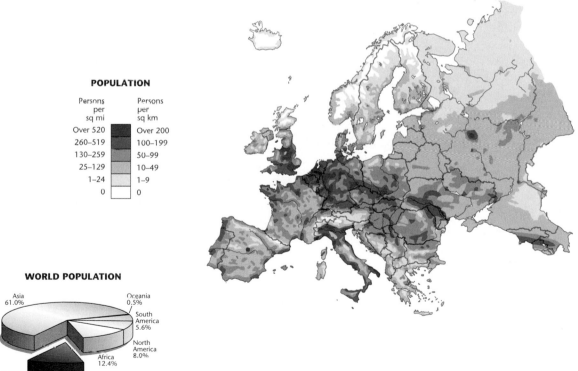

WORLD POPULATION

Asia 61.0%
Oceania 0.5%
South America 5.6%
North America 8.0%
Africa 12.4%
Europe 12.5%

Asia

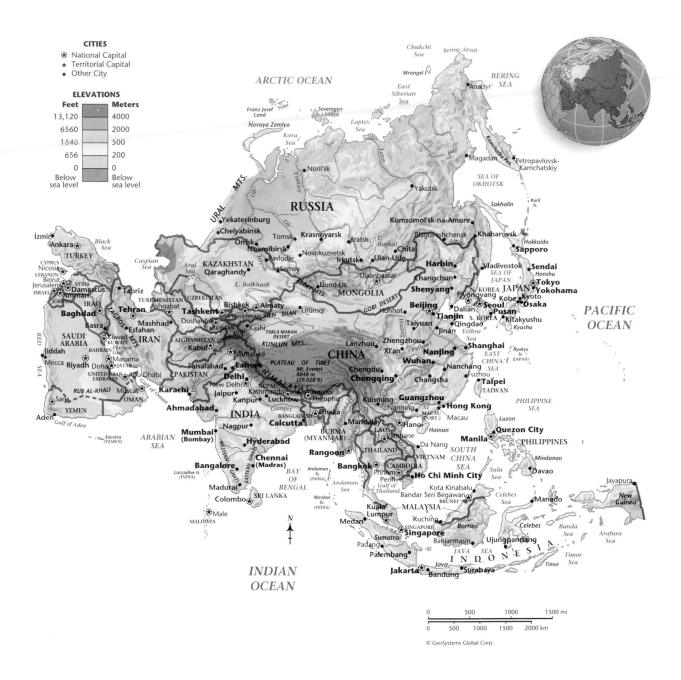

CITIES
⊛ National Capital
★ Territorial Capital
• Other City

ELEVATIONS
Feet		Meters
13,120		4000
6560		2000
1640		500
656		200
0		0
Below sea level		Below sea level

ARCTIC OCEAN

Chukchi Sea
Bering Strait
BERING SEA

Wrangel I.
East Siberian Sea
•Anadyr'

Franz Josef Land
Severnaya Zemlya
Novaya Zemlya
Kara Sea
Laptev Sea
Lena

•Magadan
•Petropavlovsk-Kamchatskiy
Kamchatka Pen.

SEA OF OKHOTSK
Sakhalin
Kuril Is.

RUSSIA

•Noril'sk
•Yakutsk

•Yekaterinburg
•Chelyabinsk
•Omsk •Tomsk •Krasnoyarsk •Bratsk
•Novosibirsk •Komsomol'sk-na-Amure
•Pavlodar •Novokuznetsk •Irkutsk •Blagoveshchensk •Khabarovsk
L. Baykal •Chita
•Semey •Ulan-Ude
Amur
Hokkaido

İzmir•
•Ankara
Black Sea
TURKEY
CYPRUS
Nicosia
LEBANON Beirut•
SYRIA •Damascus
Jerusalem•
ISRAEL JORDAN
IRAQ
Baghdad Basra•
•Tabriz
Caspian Sea
Aral Sea
KAZAKHSTAN
Qaraghandy•
L. Balkhash
MONGOLIA
Ulaanbaatar•
GOBI DESERT
Dund-Us•
•Harbin
•Changchun
•Shenyang
Hohhot•
ALTAI MTS.
Beijing⊛
•Vladivostok
SEA OF JAPAN
N. KOREA
Pyongyang⊛
S. KOREA
Seoul⊛ •Pusan
•Sapporo
•Sendai
Honshu
Tokyo
Yokohama
•Kobe •Kyoto
•Osaka
•Kitakyushu
Kyushu

TURKMENISTAN
Ashgabat⊛
UZBEKISTAN
Tashkent⊛
•Bishkek •Almaty
KYRGYZSTAN
TIEN SHAN
•Ürümqi
Tehran⊛
•Mashhad
Dushanbe⊛
TAJIKISTAN
•Kashi
TAKLA MAKAN DESERT
Esfahan•
IRAN
AFGHANISTAN
Kabul⊛
HINDU KUSH
KUNLUN MTS.
Lanzhou•
•Taiyuan
Shenyang
•Dalian
Tianjin
•Jinan
•Qingdao
Yellow Sea
Shanghai
EAST CHINA SEA
Ryukyu Is. (JAPAN)

SAUDI ARABIA
•Kuwait
KUWAIT
Riyadh⊛ •Doha•Manama
QATAR BAHRAIN
Persian Gulf
UNITED ARAB EMIRATES
Abu Dhabi⊛
Gulf of Oman
Muscat⊛
OMAN
RUB AL-KHALI
RED SEA
•Jiddah
•Mecca
•Sana
YEMEN
Aden•
Gulf of Aden
Socotra (YEMEN)

ZAGROS MTS.
Karachi•
PAKISTAN
Islamabad⊛
Faisalabad•
Lahore•
•Jaipur
New Delhi⊛
Delhi
•Kanpur
NEPAL
Kathmandu⊛
Thimphu⊛
BHUTAN
PLATEAU OF TIBET
Mt. Everest 8848 m (29,028 ft)
HIMALAYA
CHINA
•Chengdu
Chongqing
•Kunming
Nanning•
Huang (Yellow)
•Xi'an
Zhengzhou•
Wuhan
Nanjing
•Nanchang
Chang (Yangtze)
•Changsha
•Fuzhou
Taipei★
TAIWAN
Macau•
MACAU (PORT.)
Guangzhou
Hong Kong
PHILIPPINE SEA

Ahmadabad•
WESTERN GHATS
Mumbai (Bombay)
•Nagpur
INDIA
•Lucknow
Ganges
BANGLADESH
Dhaka⊛
•Mandalay
•Hanoi
Hainan
Hyderabad•
EASTERN GHATS
•Hyderabad
Calcutta•
BURMA (MYANMAR)
Rangoon⊛
LAOS
Vientiane⊛
Da Nang•
VIETNAM
Luzon
Manila⊛
Quezon City
PHILIPPINES
Mindanao

ARABIAN SEA
Laccadive Is. (INDIA)
Bangalore•
Chennai (Madras)
THAILAND
Bangkok⊛
Andaman Is. (INDIA)
SOUTH CHINA SEA
•Davao
•Madurai
Hyderabad
CAMBODIA
Phnom Penh⊛
Ho Chi Minh City
Gulf of Thailand
Andaman Sea
Nicobar Is. (INDIA)
•Kota Kinabalu
Bandar Seri Begawan⊛
BRUNEI
Sulu Sea
Celebes Sea
•Manado

•Colombo
SRI LANKA
BAY OF BENGAL
Male⊛
MALDIVES
MALAYSIA
•Kuching
Kuala Lumpur
•Medan
Singapore⊛
•Kuching
Borneo
Banjarmasin•
•Ujungpandang
Celebes
Banda Sea
Arafura Sea
New Guinea
•Jayapura

N

INDIAN OCEAN

•Padang
Sumatra
•Palembang
INDONESIA
Jakarta⊛ •Bandung
Java
•Surabaya
JAVA SEA
Timor
Timor Sea

PACIFIC OCEAN

0	500	1000	1500 mi
0	500	1000	1500 2000 km

© GeoSystems Global Corp.

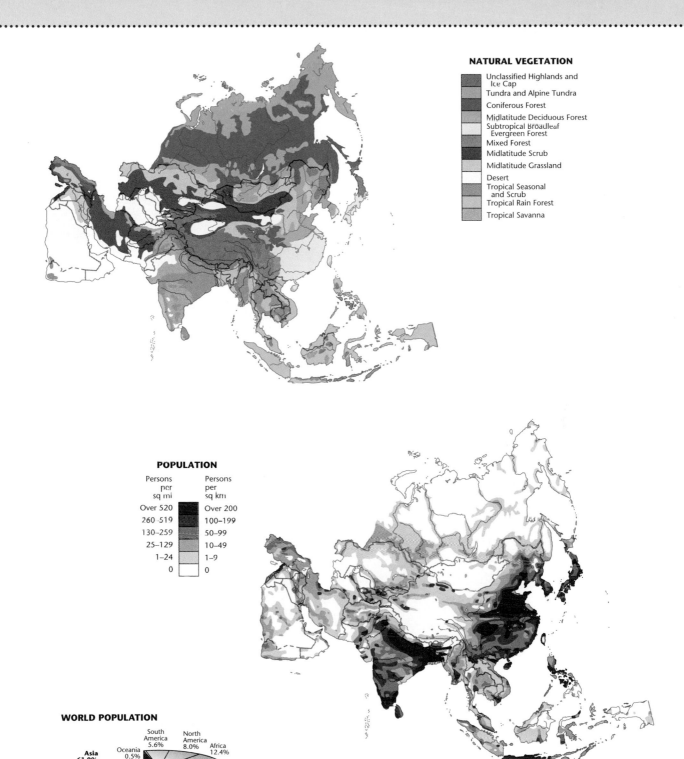

NATURAL VEGETATION

- Unclassified Highlands and Ice Cap
- Tundra and Alpine Tundra
- Coniferous Forest
- Midlatitude Deciduous Forest
- Subtropical Broadleaf Evergreen Forest
- Mixed Forest
- Midlatitude Scrub
- Midlatitude Grassland
- Desert
- Tropical Seasonal and Scrub
- Tropical Rain Forest
- Tropical Savanna

POPULATION

Persons per sq mi	Persons per sq km
Over 520	Over 200
260–519	100–199
130–259	50–99
25–129	10–49
1–24	1–9
0	0

WORLD POPULATION

Asia 61.0%
Oceania 0.5%
South America 5.6%
North America 8.0%
Africa 12.4%
Europe 12.5%

© GeoSystems Global Corp.

Africa

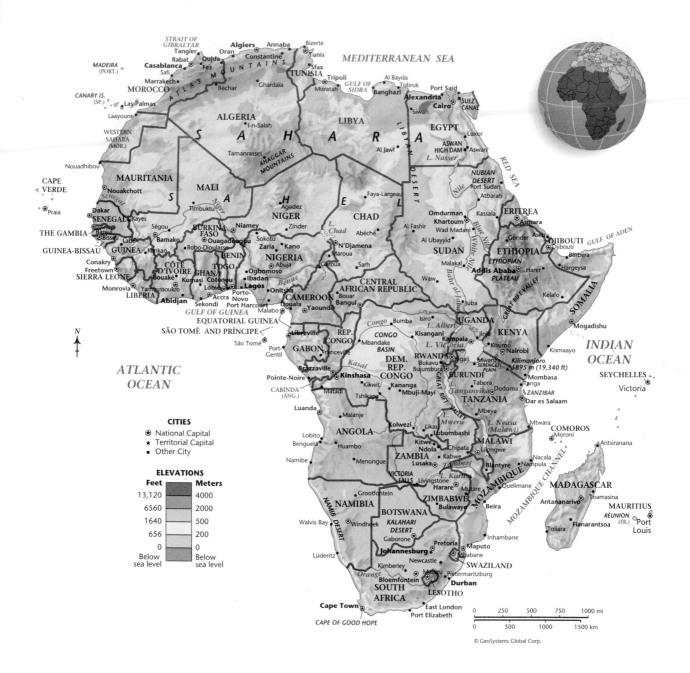

STRAIT OF GIBRALTAR

MEDITERRANEAN SEA

MADEIRA (PORT.)

Tangier
Algiers · Annaba · Bizerte
Oran · Tunis
Rabat · Constantine
Oujda · Sfax
Casablanca · Fez
Safi
Marrakech · Ghardaïa · TUNISIA · Tripoli · GULF OF SIDRA · Al Bayda
Béchar · Misratah · Tobruk · Port Said
MOROCCO · Banghazi · Alexandria · SUEZ CANAL
CANARY IS. (SP.) · Las Palmas · ATLAS MOUNTAINS · Siwah · Cairo
Laayoune · ALGERIA · LIBYA · EGYPT
WESTERN SAHARA (MOR.) · I-n-Salah · Al Jawf · Luxor · ASWAN HIGH DAM · Aswan
Nouadhibou · SAHARA · Tamanrasset · AHAGGAR MOUNTAINS · L. Nasser · NUBIAN DESERT · Port Sudan · RED SEA
CAPE VERDE · MAURITANIA · MALI · SAHEL · Faya-Largeau · Atbarah
Nouakchott · Niger · Agadez · L. Chad · CHAD · Omdurman · Kassala · ERITREA
Praia · Dakar · Timbuktu · NIGER · Zinder · Al Fashir · Khartoum · Asmara
SENEGAL · Kayes · Ségou · Niamey · Sokoto · Abéché · Wad Madani · Gonder · Aseb · DJIBOUTI · GULF OF ADEN
THE GAMBIA · Banjul · Bamako · BURKINA FASO · Zaria · Kano · N'Djamena · Al Ubayyid · SUDAN · Djibouti · Berbera
Bissau · Labé · Ouagadougou · Maroua · Sarh · Waw · ETHIOPIA · Harer · Hargeysa
GUINEA-BISSAU · GUINEA · Kankan · Bobo-Dioulasso · NIGERIA · Caroua · ETHIOPIAN · Addis Ababa · PLATEAU
Conakry · CÔTE · BENIN · Abuja · CENTRAL AFRICAN REPUBLIC · Juba · Kelafo · SOMALIA
Freetown · D'IVOIRE · GHANA · TOGO · Ogbomoso · Bouar · Bangui · GREAT RIFT VALLEY
SIERRA LEONE · Bouaké · Kumasi · Ibadan · Benue · Mogadishu
Monrovia · Yamoussoukro · Cotonou · Lagos · Onitsha · CAMEROON · Bumba · Isiro · UGANDA · KENYA · INDIAN OCEAN
LIBERIA · Abidjan · Accra · Porto-Novo · Douala · Yaoundé · Congo · Kisangani · L. Albert · Kampala · Jinja
Sekondi · Port Harcourt · Malabo · EQUATORIAL GUINEA · CONGO BASIN · Kisumu · Nairobi · Kismaayo
GULF OF GUINEA · Libreville · REP. CONGO · Mbandaka · L. Victoria · Mwanza · Kilimanjaro · SEYCHELLES
SÃO TOMÉ AND PRÍNCIPE · Port-Gentil · GABON · Franceville · DEM. REP. CONGO · RWANDA · Bukavu · Kigali · SERENGETI PLAIN · 5895 m (19,340 ft) · Victoria
São Tomé · Brazzaville · Kasai · BURUNDI · Bujumbura · Mombasa
ATLANTIC OCEAN · Pointe-Noire · Kinshasa · Kikwit · Kananga · Tabora · Tanga
CABINDA (ANG.) · Matadi · Tshikapa · Mbuji-Mayi · L. Tanganyika · Dodoma · ZANZIBAR
Luanda · TANZANIA · Dar es Salaam
Malanje · Kolwezi · L. Mweru · Mbeya · L. Nyasa (Malawi) · Mtwara · COMOROS
ANGOLA · Likasi · Moroni
Lobito · Huambo · Lubumbashi · Chipata · MALAWI · Nampula · Antsiranana
Benguela · Kitwe · Ndola · Lilongwe · Nacala
Namibe · Menongue · ZAMBIA · Kabwe · Blantyre · MADAGASCAR
Lusaka · Zambezi · MOZAMBIQUE · Quelimane · MAURITIUS
VICTORIA FALLS · L. Kariba · Harare · Mutare · Beira · Antananarivo · Toamasina
Grootfontein · Livingstone · ZIMBABWE · RÉUNION (FR.) · Port Louis
NAMIBIA · Bulawayo · MOZAMBIQUE CHANNEL · Toliara · Fianarantsoa
Walvis Bay · BOTSWANA · Inhambane
Windhoek · KALAHARI DESERT · NAMIB DESERT
Gaborone · Pretoria · Maputo
Lüderitz · Johannesburg · Mbabane
Kimberley · Newcastle · SWAZILAND
Orange · Maseru · Pietermaritzburg
Bloemfontein · Durban
SOUTH AFRICA · LESOTHO
Cape Town · East London
CAPE OF GOOD HOPE · Port Elizabeth

CITIES
⊛ National Capital
★ Territorial Capital
• Other City

ELEVATIONS

Feet	Meters
13,120	4000
6560	2000
1640	500
656	200
0	0
Below sea level	Below sea level

0 · 250 · 500 · 750 · 1000 mi
0 · 500 · 1000 · 1500 km

© GeoSystems Global Corp.

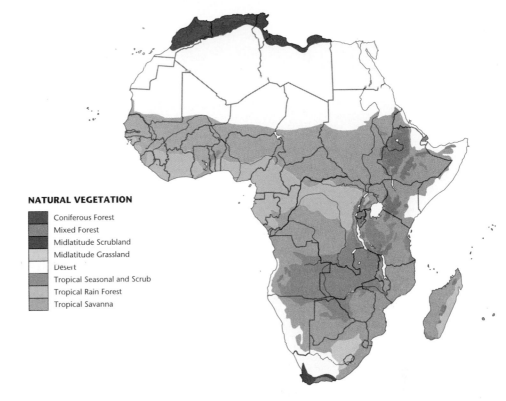

NATURAL VEGETATION

- Coniferous Forest
- Mixed Forest
- Midlatitude Scrubland
- Midlatitude Grassland
- Desert
- Tropical Seasonal and Scrub
- Tropical Rain Forest
- Tropical Savanna

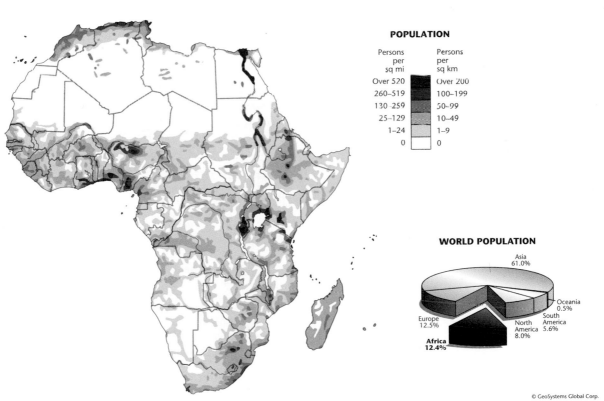

POPULATION

Persons per sq mi	Persons per sq km
Over 520	Over 200
260–519	100–199
130–259	50–99
25–129	10–49
1–24	1–9
0	0

WORLD POPULATION

Asia 61.0%
Oceania 0.5%
South America 5.6%
North America 8.0%
Africa 12.4%
Europe 12.5%

Australia

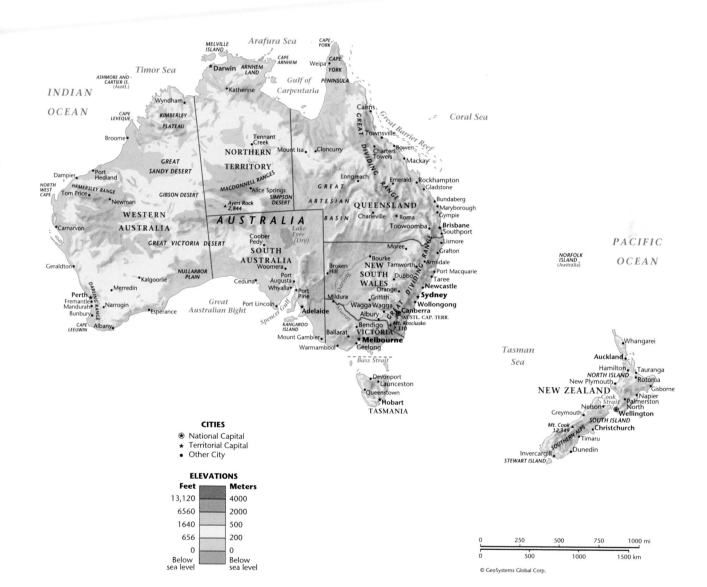

INDIAN OCEAN

Timor Sea

Arafura Sea

MELVILLE ISLAND

CAPE ARNHEM

ASHMORE AND CARTIER IS. (Austl.)

CAPE YORK

CAPE YORK PENINSULA

★ Darwin

ARNHEM LAND

Weipa

Gulf of Carpentaria

• Katherine

Coral Sea

CAPE LEVEQUE

• Wyndham

KIMBERLEY PLATEAU

Cairns

Great Barrier Reef

• Broome

• Tennant Creek

Townsville •

GREAT DIVIDING RANGE

NORTHERN TERRITORY

Mount Isa •

• Cloncurry

Bowen •
Charters Towers •
Mackay •

NORTH WEST CAPE

• Dampier
Port Hedland •

HAMERSLEY RANGE

• Tom Price
• Newman

GREAT SANDY DESERT

MACDONNELL RANGES

GIBSON DESERT

Alice Springs •

SIMPSON DESERT

GREAT ARTESIAN BASIN

Longreach •

Emerald •

Rockhampton •
Gladstone •

QUEENSLAND

Bundaberg •
Maryborough •
Gympie •

Charleville •
Roma •

• Carnarvon

WESTERN AUSTRALIA

AUSTRALIA

▲ Ayers Rock 2,844

Coober Pedy •

Lake Eyre (Dry)

Toowoomba •

★ Brisbane
Southport •

GREAT VICTORIA DESERT

SOUTH AUSTRALIA

Lismore •

• Geraldton

Moree •

Grafton •

NULLARBOR PLAIN

Woomera •

Bourke •

Tamworth •

Armidale •
Port Macquarie •

• Kalgoorlie

Ceduna •

Broken Hill •

NEW SOUTH WALES

Dubbo •

Taree •

★ Newcastle

Port Augusta •

Perth ★

• Merredin

Whyalla •

Orange •

Sydney

Fremantle •
Mandurah •
Bunbury •

• Narrogin

Port Pirie •

Mildura •

Griffith •

Wollongong •

DARLING RANGE

• Esperance

Great Australian Bight

Port Lincoln •

Spencer Gulf

KANGAROO ISLAND

Wagga Wagga •

Albury •

Canberra
AUSTL. CAP. TERR.

CAPE LEEUWIN

• Albany

★ Adelaide

Ballarat •

Bendigo •

VICTORIA

Mt. Kosciusko 7,310

Mount Gambier •

Geelong •

★ Melbourne

Warrnambool •

Bass Strait

Devonport •
Launceston •

Queenstown •

TASMANIA

★ Hobart

PACIFIC OCEAN

NORFOLK ISLAND (Australia)

Tasman Sea

Whangarei •

★ Auckland

Hamilton •
Tauranga •

NORTH ISLAND

New Plymouth •

Rotorua •

Gisborne •

NEW ZEALAND

Cook Strait

Napier •
Palmerston North •

Greymouth •

Nelson •

Wellington ★

Mt. Cook 12,349

SOUTH ISLAND

Christchurch •

SOUTHERN ALPS

Timaru •

Invercargill •

Dunedin •

STEWART ISLAND

CITIES
⊛ National Capital
★ Territorial Capital
• Other City

ELEVATIONS

Feet		Meters
13,120		4000
6560		2000
1640		500
656		200
0		0
Below sea level		Below sea level

0	250	500	750	1000 mi
0		500	1000	1500 km

© GeoSystems Global Corp.

Vegetation

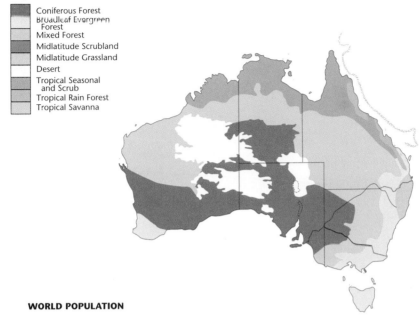

- Coniferous Forest
- Broadleaf Evergreen Forest
- Mixed Forest
- Midlatitude Scrubland
- Midlatitude Grassland
- Desert
- Tropical Seasonal and Scrub
- Tropical Rain Forest
- Tropical Savanna

WORLD POPULATION

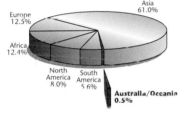

- Asia 61.0%
- Europe 12.5%
- Africa 12.4%
- North America 8.0%
- South America 5.6%
- Australia/Oceania 0.5%

POPULATION

Persons per sq mi	Persons per sq km
Over 520	Over 200
260–519	100–199
130–259	50–99
25–129	10–49
1–24	1–9
0	0

© GeoSystems Global Corp.

GLOSSARY

Key Terms and other important terms from the text are defined in the glossary to clarify their meaning. The numbers following the definitions correspond to sections in the text.

In the text some terms and names have been respelled as an aid to pronunciation. A key to pronouncing the respelled words appears here.

Pronounciation Key

Like other words in this book, the term *aquifer* has been respelled to indicate its pronunciation: AK-wih-fer. A hyphen is used between syllables. Capital letters mean that a syllable should be spoken with stress.

Pronounce "a" as in hat

ah	father
ar	tar
ay	say
ayr	air
e, eh	hen
ee	bee
eer	deer
er	her
g	go
i, ih	him
j	jet
k	car
ng	ring
o	frog
oh	no
oo	soon
or	for
ow	plow
oy	boy
sh	she
th	think
u, uh	sun
y	kite
z	zebra
zh	measure

abiotic factor a nonliving part of the environment *2.3*

acid precipitation rain or snow that is more acidic than normal precipitation *22.3*

active solar heating a process that uses devices to collect, store, and circulate heat produced from solar energy *17.1*

aeration a water treatment method in which cleaned and filtered water is exposed to air *20.3*

aerogenerator a windmill used to generate electricity; also called a wind turbine generator *17.3*

agribusiness a business concern engaged in industrialized agriculture, which requires large inputs of resources and is very productive. These businesses may be involved in several stages of food production. *14.3*

agricultural revolution occurred around 8000 B.C. when hunters and gatherers began to develop farming techniques, and learned to domesticate animals *13.1*

agricultural society a society in which crops are grown and people have specialized roles *12.2*

air pollution harmful substances released into the air *22.1*

alien species a non-native species introduced to an area by humans *23.1*

alpha particle a large particle made up of two protons and two neutrons, given off by radioactive atoms *16.1*

anthracite coal metamorphic rock that has been changed from sedimentary bituminous coal into hard coal that contains up to 95 percent carbon *15.2*

aphotic zone in a body of water, the layer of water below the photic zone that receives no sunlight *10.1*

aquaculture the commercial production of fish in a controlled, maintained environment *14.2*

aquatic describes a habitat in which the organisms live in or on water *10.1*

aquifer an underground layer of porous rock that contains water *1.2, 20.2*

artesian well a well in which water flows to the surface due to high pressure underground *1.2*

atmosphere the layer of gases that surrounds Earth *1.1*

atomic number the number of protons in the atoms of a given element *16.1*

autotroph   a producer that makes its own food; the first trophic level in an ecosystem *4.1*

bedrock   the combination of the igneous, metamorphic, and sedimentary rock of the lithosphere that exists as mountains, cliffs, or low-lying plains *18.3*

benthic zone   the floor of a body of water *10.1*

beta particle   a high-speed electron given off by radioactive atoms *16.1*

bioconversion   the conversion of organic materials into fuels *15.4*

biodegradable   describes substances that decompose easily and enrich the soil *19.4*

biodiversity   the variety of species in an ecosystem *3.3, 23.1*

biological magnification   the increasing concentration of a pollutant in organisms at higher trophic levels in a food web *4.2*

biomass   the total amount of organic matter present in a trophic level *4.3*

biomass fuel   a fuel, such as wood, formed from the products of living organisms *15.4*

biome   a major type of ecosystem with distinctive temperature, rainfall, and organisms *6.4*

biomedical revolution   an occurrence of the twentieth century that has resulted in population growth because the death rate has decreased as many life-threatening diseases have been controlled by antibiotics, vaccines, and modern hygiene techniques *13.1*

biosphere   he combined parts of the lithosphere, hydrosphere, and atmosphere in which life exists *1.4*

biotic factor   a living part of the environment *2.3*

bituminous coal   a coal composed of up to 85 percent carbon, found deep in Earth's crust *15.2*

brackish   describes water that is more saline than fresh water, but less saline than ocean water *10.1*

breeder reactor   a reactor that generates fuel as it works *16.2*

bubonic plague   a plague that struck much of Europe and Asia in the mid-fourteenth century, resulting in the deaths of about 25 percent of the adult populations of these areas; also known as the Black Death *13.1*

bunchgrass   a short, fine-bladed grass that grows in a clump *8.2*

buttress   a ridge of wood on the trunk of a rainforest tree that provides support for the tree *9.3*

cancer   a disease in which cells grow abnormally and out of control *22.2*

canopy   the highest layer of a deciduous forest *9.2*

carbohydrate   a compound of carbon, hydrogen, and oxygen in a 1:2:1 ratio *14.1*

carnivore   an organism that captures and eats herbivores or other carnivores *4.1*

carrying capacity   the number of individuals of a species that can be supported by an ecosystem *5.3*

cash crop   a crop grown for the purpose of sale *14.2*

chain reaction   the continuous action of neutrons splitting atomic nuclei *16.2*

chaos theory   a type of mathematics that suggests that ecosystems may be sensitive to even very small changes, and that the beginning state of an ecosystem is crucial to its later development *6.3*

chemical and biological treatment plants   treatment plants where some hazardous wastes are treated and made harmless (neutralized), then safely disposed of *19.4*

chlorofluorocarbon (CFC)   a compound of carbon, chlorine, and fluorine once used in refrigerators, air conditioners, aerosol cans, and in the production of polystyrene foam *22.1*

clay soil   soil that contains grains smaller than 0.002 mm in diameter *18.3*

climax community   a diverse community that does not undergo further succession *6.2*

coagulant   a chemical that is added to water to aid in the settling process *20.3*

coevolution   the process by which species interact so closely with one another that they adapt to one another *5.2*

commensalism   a symbiotic relationship that benefits one of the organisms and neither helps nor harms the other organism *6.1*

community   all the populations that live and interact in the same environment *3.3*

compaction   a process in which the space between the particles of soil decreases, preventing the flow of air and water, which makes the soil very hard and less able to absorb moisture *18.4*

competitive exclusion   the extinction of a population due to direct competition with another species for a particular resource in a niche *5.1*

compost pile   a combination of plant waste and food waste collected together to form a type of humus *19.4*

conductor   any material through which heat and electricity flow relatively freely *18.1*

conifer   a tree that produces seed cones *6.4, 9.1*

conservation a strategy to reduce the use of resources through decreased demand and increased efficiency *24.1*

consumer an organism that cannot make its own food *4.1*

continental shelf the shallow border that surrounds the continents *11.2*

contour farming a soil conservation method of plowing along the slope instead of across the slope *19.3*

control an experimental situation in which the variable being tested is missing *2.2*

controlled incineration the burning of wastes at extremely high temperatures *19.4*

control rod rod of neutron-absorbing material used to regulate the chain reaction in a nuclear reactor *16.2*

convergent evolution the independent development of similar adaptations in two species with similar niches *5.2*

corrosive wastes hazardous wastes that can eat through steel and many other types of materials *19.2*

cost/benefit analysis the analysis of the social costs versus the social benefits of an activity or policy *25.1*

crop rotation a farming method in which the type of crop grown in a particular area is changed on a regular cycle *14.4*

deciduous describes a tree that sheds its leaves during a particular season each year *6.4, 9.2*

decomposer a bacterium or fungus that consumes the bodies of dead organisms and other organic wastes *4.1*

deep-well injection a disposal method in which liquid hazardous wastes are pumped deep into porous rocks below drinking-water aquifers *19.4*

deforestation the destruction of forestlands as a result of human activity *9.3*

demand the amount of a resource that people desire and are willing to purchase *25.1*

demography the science of the changing vital statistics in a human population *13.2*

density-dependent limiting factor a limiting factor that is dependent on population size *5.3*

density-independent limiting factor a limiting factor that affects the same percentage of a population regardless of its size *5.3*

desalination a water treatment method in which salts are removed from water *20.3*

desert a biome occurring throughout the world characterized by low humidity, high summer temperatures, and low annual rainfall *6.4, 7.1*

desert-grassland boundary an area between a desert and a grassland where increased rainfall enables some grasses to grow *8.1*

desertification the processs of changing semiarid land into desert as a result of human activity *7.2, 19.3*

detritus tiny pieces of dead organic material that are food for organisms at the base of an aquatic food web *11.1*

distillation a water treatment method in which salt water is heated to boiling and salts separate out from the water vapor *20.3*

dormant a condition of an organism when the life processes within the body slow down *3.2*

doubling time of a population how long it will take, at the present rate of growth, for a particular population to double its size *13.2*

dredging a mining method that involves the scraping or vacuuming of desirable minerals from ocean floors, lakes, or streambeds *18.2*

drip (or trickle) irrigation an overhead irrigation method that uses tubing to deliver small quantities of water directly to the root system of plants *20.1*

drought a long period of abnormally low rainfall in a given area *8.1*

ductile describes any material that can be pulled and stretched into wires *18.1*

ecological pyramid a diagram that shows the relative amounts of energy in different trophic levels in an ecosystem *4.3*

ecology the study of interactions among living and nonliving things *1.1*

ecosystem all the communities that live in an area together with the abiotic factors in the environment *3.3*

El Niño a disturbance of ocean winds and currents when a warm-water current lasts for several months along the western coast of South America *3.1*

emphysema a disease in which the tiny air sacs in the lungs break down *22.2*

environment everything that surrounds a particular organism *2.3*

equilibrium a state of balance between opposing forces *6.3*

erosion the wearing away of land by weather and water; a natural process where soil is lost, transported, and reformed *3.1, 14.4, 19.3*

essential amino acid   one of eight amino acids that humans must obtain from food to remain healthy *14.1*

estuary   a region of water where a freshwater source meets salt water from the ocean *11.2*

ethic   a guideline or rule for determining what is right and what is wrong *12.3*

eutrophication   the process in which lakes and ponds receive runoff rich in life-supporting plant nutrients *21.2*

evaporation   the movement of water into the atmosphere as it changes from a liquid to a gas *4.4*

evergreen   a tree that does not lose its leaves at a given time every year *9.1*

evolution   a gradual change in a population of organisms over time *5.2*

experimental variable   the variable being tested in an experiment *2.2*

exponential growth   population growth in which the rate of growth in each generation is a multiple of the previous generation *5.3*

extinction   the disappearance of a species from all or part of its geographical range *23.1*

famine   a severe food shortage that causes starvation and death to the inhabitants in a specific area *13.1*

filtration   a water treatment method in which water is passed through screens to trap particles *20.3*

flood irrigation   a type of irrigation in which flat expanses of land are flooded *20.1*

flowing-water ecosystem   a freshwater environment on land such as a river, stream, creek, or brook *10.3*

fluorescent light   a type of lighting that uses less energy than incandescent light and produces little heat *24.1*

food chain   a series of organisms that transfer food between the trophic levels in an ecosystem *4.2*

food web   a network of food chains representing the feeding relationships among the organisms in an ecosystem *4.2*

fossil fuel   fuel derived from the remains of organisms that lived long ago *15.1*

freezing   a water treatment method in which salt water is frozen so that it separates into ice and brine slush; the ice is then melted and used as fresh water *20.3*

frontier ethic   the system of ethics in the modern industrial world, based on the view that humans are apart from nature *12.3*

fuel   any substance from which energy can be obtained *15.1*

fundamental niche   the theoretical niche that an organism can occupy *5.1*

furrow irrigation   a type of irrigation in which water is released into ditches that have been dug between crop rows *20.1*

Gaia hypothesis   states that Earth is a single, living organism that regulates itself to maintain life *12.1*

gamma ray   a form of elecromagnetic radiation given off by the decay of unstable atomic nuclei *16.1*

gene bank   a secure place where seeds, plants, and genetic material are stored *23.4*

generalized species   a species that occupies a wide niche *5.2*

geographical range   the total area in which a species can live *3.3*

geothermal energy   heat energy that is generated deep within Earth *17.4*

germ theory of disease   developed about 300 years ago, this theory identified bacteria and other microorganisms as the agents responsible for many diseases *13.1*

global warming   an increase in Earth's average surface temperature caused by an increase in greenhouse gases *22.3*

grassland   an ecosystem in which there is too much water to form a desert, but not enough water to support a forest *8.1*

greenhouse effect   the trapping of radiated heat by gases in the atmosphere *3.1, 22.3*

greenhouse gas   an atmospheric gas that traps heat *22.3*

Green Revolution   the development of new, disease-resistant strains of rice and wheat, plus the use of expensive modern farming methods, machinery, and technology that has brought about huge crops and lowered the overall price of the world's main food crops *14.2*

groundwater   water contained in porous or jointed bedrock *20.2*

growth rate of a population   arrived at by subtracting the death rate of a population from the birth rate *13.2*

habitat   the environment in which a particular species lives *3.3*

habitat destruction   disturbing the part of an ecosystem that an organism needs to survive *23.1*

half-life the amount of time it takes half the atoms in a sample of a radioactive element to decay *16.1*

hazardous wastes solid, liquid, or gaseous wastes that are potentially harmful to humans and the environment, even in low concentrations *19.2*

heavy metal a poisonous metallic element with a high mass number *21.2*

herbivore an organism that eats only plants *4.1*

heterotroph a consumer that forms the second or higher levels in a trophic system *4.1*

hibernation dormancy in some animals when the heart rate and breathing slow down, the body temperature drops, and the animal enters a sleeplike state *3.2*

high-level wastes radioactive wastes that emit large amounts of radiation *16.3*

horizon a layer of topsoil or subsoil *18.3*

host the organism on which a parasite feeds *6.1*

humus a layer of organic matter formed from decaying plant matter *8.2*

hunter–gatherer society a society in which people gather natural food, hunt, and are nomadic *12.2*

hydrocarbon a compound made only of carbon and hydrogen *15.1*

hydroelectric power electricity that is produced from the energy of moving water *17.2*

hydrogenate the process of adding more hydrogen to liquid vegetable oils to give the oils more texture *14.1*

hydrosphere the parts of Earth that are made of water *1.1*

hypersaline describes lakes that are more saline than the ocean *10.1*

hypothesis a possible explanation for a set of observations *2.1*

ice age a long period of cooling when glaciers move from the poles and cover much of Earth's surface *3.1*

ice core a long cylinder of ice that is drilled and removed from deep within a sheet of polar ice *22.3*

igneous rock rock that is formed when liquid rock solidifies and cools *1.2*

ignitable wastes hazardous waste substances that can burst into flames at relatively low temperatures *19.2*

incandescent light the traditional type of lighting that gives off much of its energy as heat and is less efficient than fluorescent light *24.1*

industrial society a society in which the production of food and other products is performed by machines, requiring large amounts of energy and resources *12.2*

integrated pest management (IPM) a farming method that makes use of natural predators to control harmful pests, reducing the use of pesticides *14.4*

intertidal zone the region of ocean shoreline that alternates between periods of exposure and periods of submersion at least twice each day *11.3*

ionosphere a layer of the thermosphere where gas molecules lose electrons and become ions *1.3*

irrigation the process of bringing water to an area for use in growing crops *20.1*

isotopes atoms of the same element that have different mass numbers *16.1*

keystone predator a predator that causes a large increase in the diversity of its habitat *5.1*

kilocalorie (kcal) the amount of energy needed to raise the temperature of 1 kg of water 1° C *14.1*

landfill a site where wastes are disposed of by burial *19.1*

leaching a process in which rainwater moving through soil carries minerals deeper into the soil *7.1*

legume a plant that has colonies of nitrogen-fixing bacteria on its roots *4.4*

lichen a plantlike organism that is a mutualistic relationship involving a fungus and an alga *6.2, 7.3*

lignite a soft, brown coal composed of 40 percent carbon *15.2*

limiting factor a factor that slows growth in a population *5.3*

lipid an organic compound that contains three long chains of fatty acids and is a main component of all cell membranes *14.1*

lithosphere the layer of land that forms Earth's surface *1.1*

loam a soil type containing roughly equal amounts of clay, sand, and silt particles *18.3*

macronutrient a nutrient that provides the body with energy *14.1*

magma molten rock deep within Earth that becomes lava when it reaches the surface *17.4*

malleable any material that can be hammered and shaped without breaking *18.1*

malnutrition the lack of a specific type of nutrient in the diet *14.1*

mangrove swamp a coastal wetland that occurs in warm climates, characterized by mangrove trees or shrubs and water with little dissolved oxygen *11.3*

marine describes the ocean *11.1*

mass extinction a relatively short period of time during which many species die *23.1*

medical wastes hazardous wastes such as old medicines, lab containers, and specimens, some of which are considered toxic wastes *19.2*

medium-level and low-level wastes radioactive wastes that are not as dangerous as high-level wastes, although a much larger volume of these wastes is generated *16.3*

meltdown the process in which a nuclear chain reaction goes out of control and melts the reactor core *16.3*

mesosphere the layer of the atmosphere beyond the stratosphere, extending about 85 km above Earth's surface *1.3*

metamorphic rock rock that has been transformed by heat, pressure, or both *1.2*

micronutrient a nutrient that provides the body with small amounts of chemicals needed in biochemical reactions *14.1*

migration long-distance seasonal travel by animal populations *7.3*

mineral a naturally occurring, inorganic solid material that has a definite chemical composition, with atoms arranged in a specific pattern *18.1*

monoculture a farming technique in which only the highest dollar-yield crops are grown *14.3*

mutualism a symbiotic relationship in which both species benefit *6.1*

natural gas fossil fuel in the gaseous state *15.3*

neritic zone the region between the edge of the continental shelf and the low-tide mark *11.2*

niche the role of an organism in an ecosystem *5.1*

nocturnal describes animals that sleep during the day and are active at night *7.1*

noise pollution loud, continuous, or high-pitched sounds that are harmful to living things *22.5*

nonrenewable resource a resource that does not regenerate quickly *12.3*

nuclear fission a reaction in which the nucleus of a large atom is split into smaller nuclei, emitting large amounts of energy *16.2*

nuclear fusion the source of the energy given off by the sun, this process occurs when two atomic nuclei fuse to become one larger nucleus *17.4*

nuclear reactor vessel the structure where the fission of U-235 takes place *16.2*

nucleus the cluster of protons and neutrons in the center of an atom *16.1*

nutrient a substance needed by the body for energy, growth, repair, or maintenance *3.2*

ocean current water flow in the ocean in a characteristic pattern *11.1*

oceanic zone the open ocean; the largest zone in the marine biome and more than 90 percent of the surface area of the world ocean *11.1*

octane (iso-octane) an important component of gasoline that rates the amount of energy contained in a particular gasoline *15.1*

omnivore an organism that eats both producers and consumers *4.1*

open-pit mining a surface mining method in which large machinery is used to dig huge pits from which minerals are removed *18.2*

ore a rock or mineral that contains economically desirable metals or nonmetals *18.1*

organism any living thing *1.1*

overdraft the process in which a body of water is drained faster than it is filled *20.2*

overhead irrigation a type of irrigation method in which a sprinkler system waters crops from above the ground *20.1*

oxide a type of gaseous pollutant that is a compound of oxygen and another element *22.1*

ozone an oxygen gas containing three oxygen atoms per molecule *1.3*

ozone depletion a 2 to 3 percent thinning of the global ozone layer that has occurred over the last ten years *22.3*

parasitism a relationship in which one organism feeds on the tissues or body fluids of another organism *6.1*

parent rock bedrock that is the source of an area of soil *18.3*

particulate a type of air pollutant made of tiny solids suspended in the atmosphere *22.1*

passive solar heating the process by which the sun's energy is collected, stored, and distributed in an enclosed dwelling. *17.1*

pathogen a parasite, bacterium, or virus that causes diseases in living things *21.1*

pavement the desert floor, made up of hard-baked sand, bare rock particles, or both *7.1*

peat a brittle, brown plant material used as a fuel that contains a great deal of water and a low percentage of carbon *15.2*

permafrost the frozen soil below the active zone in tundra regions *7.3*

petroleum a liquid fossil fuel; also known as crude oil *15.3*

phosphate a nutrient containing phosphoric acid that can be a pollutant in large amounts *21.2*

photic zone in a body of water, the top layer of water that receives enough sunlight for photosynthesis to occur *10.1*

photochemical smog a yellow-brown haze that is formed when sunlight reacts with pollutants produced by cars *22.1*

photovoltaic cell (PV cell) a device that uses thin wafers of semiconductor material to produce electricity directly from solar energy *17.1*

phytoplankton plankton that carry out photosynthesis and are the main producers in aquatic biomes *10.2*

pioneer community the first community to colonize a new habitat *6.2*

plankton a general term for microorganisms that float near the surface of water *10.2*

policy an outline of actions, incentives, penalties, and rules that a company, group, or government follows concerning a particular issue *25.1*

pollutant a harmful material that enters the environment *22.1*

population all members of a particular species that live in the same area *3.3*

prairie a grassland area characterized by rolling hills, plains, and sod-forming grasses *6.4, 8.2*

predator an organism that actively hunts other organisms *5.1, 6.1*

preserve an area of land or water set aside for the protection of the ecosystem in that area *24.3*

prey an organism upon which a predator feeds *5.1, 6.1*

primary succession the sequence of communities that forms in an originally lifeless habitat *6.2*

producer an organism that makes its own food from inorganic molecules and energy *4.1*

protein a large compound of amino acids used by the body to make blood, muscle, and other tissues *14.1*

radiation alpha and beta particles and gamma rays that are given off in the decaying of unstable nuclei *16.1*

radioactive describes atoms that emit particles and energy from their nuclei when they decay *16.1*

radioactive decay the process that occurs when an atom emits radiation and becomes a different element or isotope *16.1*

radioactive wastes hazardous wastes that give off radiation that is harmful to people and other organisms *19.2, 21.3*

radon a colorless, odorless, radioactive gas formed by the decay of radium *22.1*

rain forest a biome with a dense canopy of evergreen, broadleaf trees that receives at least 200 cm of rain each year *6.4, 9.3*

rainshadow effect occurs when warm, moist air cools and loses most of its moisture as precipitation over the western side of mountainous regions, and the resulting cool, dry air picks up moisture from soil on the eastern side of the mountains *7.2*

rainy season in a grassland area, part of the cycle of heavy rains that is followed by long periods of little or no rain *8.1*

range of tolerance the range of temperatures at which an organism can survive *3.2*

reactive waste an explosive type of hazardous waste *19.2*

realized niche the actual niche that an organism occupies *5.1*

recycling reducing resource use by collecting usable waste materials and using them to produce new items *24.2*

reef a natural structure built on a continental shelf from the shells of small sea animals *11.2*

renewable resource a resource that regenerates quickly *12.3*

reverse osmosis a water treatment method in which salt water is forced through a strainer to remove the salts *20.3*

rill a shallow groove carved in the ground by runoff *20.2*

risk assessment determining how much risk is acceptable in a given situation *25.1*

runner the long, horizontal stem of many plants that runs below the ground, making the plant resistant to drought, fire, and grazing animals *8.3*

runoff water from rainfall and melting ice that runs along the ground *20.2*

S-shaped curve a growth curve with an initial rapid growth rate followed by a slower growth rate *5.3*

salinity a measure of the dissolved salts in a sample of water *10.1*

salt marsh a flat, muddy wetland that surrounds estuaries, bays, and lagoons *11.3*

sandy soil soil in which most of the mineral grains vary in diameter from 0.5 mm to 2.0 mm *18.3*

sanitary landfill a landfill where wastes are spread in layers and compacted by bulldozers *19.1*

saturated fat a fat that contains the maximum number of hydrogen atoms on the fatty acid chains *14.1*

savanna a tropical grassland ranging from dry scrubland to wet, open woodland *6.4, 8.3*

scavenger an animal that feeds on the bodies of dead organisms *4.1*

secondary succession a type of succession that occurs when a community has been cleared by a disturbance that has not destroyed the soil *6.2*

secure chemical landfill a secure landfill constructed in an area of nonporous bedrock *19.4*

sedimentary rock rock that is formed when layers of sediments accumulate, compress, and cement together *1.2*

sedimentation a treatment method in which water that has gone through screens is allowed to settle in tanks, with the remaining particles falling to the bottom *20.3*

sediments small particles that settle to the bottom of a body of water *10.3*

semiarid region a dry area that borders a desert and supports communities of grasses and shrubs *7.2*

sewage water that contains organic wastes from humans and industry *21.1*

sewage treatment plant a facility that processes raw sewage before it is returned to surface water systems *21.1*

shelter belt (windbreak) a row of trees planted along the outer edges of a field as an aid to reducing erosion *19.3*

silt a soil type with mineral grains between 0.002 mm and 0.05 mm in diameter *18.3*

smelting the process of heating and refining an ore to separate out the valuable minerals *18.1*

sod-forming grass a grass that forms a mat of soil and roots *8.2*

soil a mixture of mineral particles and organic particles from living and decaying organisms *18.3*

soil profile a vertical cross section of soil from the ground surface down to bedrock *18.3*

soil water water that seeps into the ground and fills the spaces between soil particles *20.2*

solar collector a device used to gather and absorb the sun's energy in a solar heating system *17.1*

solar energy energy from the sun that is absorbed by plants and used as fuel by virtually all organisms *17.1*

solid wastes all garbage, refuse, and sludge products from agriculture, forestry, mining, and municipalities *19.1*

source reduction the lowering of demand for a resource, reducing the amount used and wasted *24.1*

specialized species an organism that occupies a small niche *5.2*

species a group of organisms so similar that they breed and produce fertile offspring *3.3*

spoil pile a mound of mineral wastes deposited outside a mine *18.2*

standing-water ecosystem a type of freshwater biome such as a lake, pond, or marsh *10.2*

steppe a grassland area that gets less than 50 cm of rain per year, characterized by short bunchgrasses *6.4, 8.2*

sterilization a water treatment method in which any residual harmful bacteria and microorganisms are destroyed with extreme heat or chemicals *20.3*

stratosphere the layer of Earth's atmosphere beyond the troposhere, reaching a height of 50 km above Earth *1.3*

strip-cropping a soil conservation method in which farmland is plowed so that the plowed strips are separated by planted strips, reducing soil loss *19.3*

subirrigation an irrigation system where water is introduced naturally or artificially beneath the soil surface *20.1*

subsidence a process in which land sinks, due either to the weight of sediments or the extraction of subsurface water *11.3, 20.2*

substitution a conservation method in which a more plentiful material is used for a product instead of a less plentiful material *18.2*

subsurface mining a method used to extract mineral deposits from below the surface of

Earth *18.2*

succulent a plant such as a cactus that has thick, water-filled tissues *7.1*

supply the availability of a resource to be purchased *25.1*

supply-demand curve represents the relationship between supply, demand, and the purchase price for a particular resource *25.1*

surface water the water that is above ground in streams, lakes, rivers, and ponds *20.2*

sustainable agriculture a type of farming based on crop rotation, reduced soil erosion, pest management, and minimum use of soil additives; also called regenerative farming *14.4*

sustainable development ethic a development plan that meets the current needs of society without limiting the ability of future generations to meet their needs *12.3*

sustainable lifestyle a way of life that focuses on reducing energy and material consumption *24.1*

symbiosis a relationship in which two species live closely together *6.1*

tailings low grade ore and other mineral wastes generated by mining *18.2*

tectonic plate one of several large, movable plates that make up the lithosphere *3.1*

terracing a soil conservation method in which crops are planted on a series of terraced platforms built into the slope of a hill *19.3*

territorial animal an animal that maintains a territory with specific boundaries *3.2*

territory an area claimed as a living space by an individual animal *3.2*

thermal pollution a large increase in water temperature due to human activity *21.3*

thermonuclear fusion the process in which the high temperatures in the sun's core cause hydrogen nuclei to fuse, forming helium nuclei; as each helium nucleus forms, a loss of mass occurs. This lost mass is converted to the heat and light energy of the sun. *17.1*

thermosphere the outer layer of the atmosphere *1.3*

toxic chemical an element or molecule that is directly harmful to living things *21.2*

toxic wastes hazardous wastes made of chemicals that are poisonous to humans *19.2*

transpiration the evaporation of water from the leaves of plants *4.4*

trophic level a layer in the structure of feeding relationships in an ecosystem *4.1*

tropical zone an area located at latitudes near the equator that receives direct rays from the sun during most of the year *9.3*

troposphere the layer of the atmosphere that touches the surface of Earth *1.3*

tuft a large clump of tall, coarse grass *8.3*

tundra a cold, windy, dry area just south of the polar ice caps in Alaska, Canada, Greenland, Iceland, Norway, and Asia *6.4, 7.3*

understory in a forest, trees that are younger and smaller than those of the canopy *9.2*

unpotable describes water that is polluted and unfit to drink *20.1*

unsaturated fat a fat with some hydrogen atoms missing from the fatty acid chains *14.1*

variable any factor that affects the outcome of an experiment *2.2*

vertical feeding pattern the pattern in which different species eat vegetation at different heights *8.3*

waste exchange a process where a waste product from one company or industry is used by another company in the production of its products or materials *19.4*

water purification a treatment method that removes the harmful chemicals and microorganisms that make water unpotable *20.3*

water table the top of the saturated layer where groundwater collects and saturates the bedrock *20.2*

weathering the breaking down of rocks by weather and water *3.1*

wetland an ecosystem in which the roots of plants are submerged under water at least part of the year *10.2*

wilderness an area where the ecosystem is relatively undisturbed by the activites of humans *23.3*

zone of aeration the area where water enters an aquifer *20.2*

zone of discharge the place where water leaves an aquifer and becomes surface water *20.2*

zone of saturation the saturated rock layer beneath the water table; also called aquifer *1.2, 20.2*

zooplankton plankton that do not carry out photosynthesis, including microscopic organisms and protozoans *10.2*

INDEX

Page numbers in **boldface** indicate definitions of terms in the text.
Page numbers in *italics* indicate figures or illustrations in the text.

Hydrogenation, **217**
Hydrologists, *27*
Hydrosphere, **3**, 6–7, 36
Hypothesis, **19**–20, **23**
   choosing, 23
   testing, 24. *See also*
    Experiments

I

Ice ages, **36**
Ice cores, 367
   analysis of, *37*
Identification, of species, 96
Igneous rock, **5**, *5*
Ignitable wastes, **309**–310
Incineration, controlled, **315**
Indoor air pollution, 358–359
Industrial societies, 66, **191**, *192*
   nonrenewable resources as
    basis of, 195
   population growth, 202, 206
Industries
   in developing nations, 193
   environmental impact of,
    192, 357
   fuel needs and, 235–236
   minerals in, 289
   soil abuse by, 300
   thermal pollution by, 350
   toxic wastes from, *343*, 343, 344
   water use by, 324
Infrared radiation, 366
Insect control. *See* Pesticides
Insects, number of species, 148
Interactions, in ecosystems, 28,
   72–83
International policies, environmental, 420–421
Intertidal zones, *169*, 169,
   175–176
Ionosphere. *See* Thermosphere
Irrigation, *225*, **324**–326, *325*
Isotopes, **251**–252

J

Journals, scientific, 25

K

Kelp forests, 63
Keystone predators, 75
Koch, Robert, 339
Kwashiorkor, **218**

L

Lake Erie, 376
Lakes, *157*
   and acid precipitation, 362
Land, study of, 27
Landfills, **306**–307
   sanitary, **307**
   for secure hazardous-waste
    disposal, **315**
Land formations
   erosion and, 35
   tectonic movement and, 35
Land-management policies, 416
Land-management techniques, 313
Land pollution, 304–317
   controlling, 314–317
Land-use policies, 416
Lava, 5
Leaching, **111**, 307, 343, 349
Legislation
   on air pollution, 370–371
   on noise pollution, 372
   to protect environment,
    316–317
   water pollution control
    through, 351–**352**
Legumes, **67**
Lichen, **92**
Lichens, **118**
   caribou and, 118
Lifestyle, sustainable, 400
Light energy, 4, 366
Lignite, **238**, *238*
Limestone, *5*, 5
Limiting factors, of population
   growth, 82–83
   density-dependent, **82**, 83
   density-independent, **82**–83
Line graphs, *25*
Lipids, **216**
Lithosphere, **3**, 5–6, 35, 287
Living space. *See* Territory
Loam soils, *296*, 296
Local policies and programs,
   416–417
Locke, John, 186
Love Canal, 308, *417*
Lovelock, James, 97, 189
Low-level wastes, **256**, 257
Lumber industry, 30
Lung cancer, 359, **360**, *360*

M

Maathai, Wangari, 182
Macronutrients, 215
Magma, **276**
Malleability, **288**
Malnutrition, **218**
Malthus, Thomas, 80, 201
Mangrove swamps, 176
Mangroves, *176*, 176
Marble, 6
Marine biome, 168–177
Marshes, *157*
Mass extinctions, **381**–382, 388
Matter, **26**
   recycling of, in ecosystems, 52
Medical wastes, 310, 338
Medicines, and biodiversity, 387
Medium-level wastes, **256**, 257
Meltdown, **260**
Meltwater, 326, 327
Meningitis, 207
Mercury pollution, 343, 344
Mesosphere, 9, **11**
Metals
   heavy, **343**, 344
   properties of, 288
Metamorphic rock, **5**–6, *5*
Meteorologists, 27
Methane, 159, **237**, *237*, 245,
   307, 358, 366
Methanogens, 159
Micronutrients, 215, 217
Microscopes, transmission
   electron, *20*
Microwaves, *4*
Migration, **117**
Migratory animals, 117–118, 119,
   130–131, 163
Mineral extraction and
   processing, effects of,
   on environment, *292*
Minerals, 38, 217, **287**–293
   characteristics of, 287
   common uses of, *288*
   conservation of, 293
   extraction and processing of,
    292, 292
   in international trade, 289
   methods of extracting,
    290–293
   as nonrenewable resources, 195
   recycling of, *402*, 402

biological, 316
chemical, 316
Trees. *See also* Forests
  and acid precipitation, 362
  coniferous, **139**
  deciduous, **142**
  of rain forests, 146
Tribal people, and modern
    technology, 190, 193
Trickle irrigation, 325
Trophic levels, **54**–55, 56
  of biomass pyramid, 62
  of energy pyramid, *61*, 61
  interactions between, 56
  of numbers pyramid, 62
Tropical rain forests. *See* Rain
    forests
Tropical zone, **146**
Tropic of Cancer, 114
Tropic of Capricorn, 114
Troposphere, 9, **10**
Tufts, **132**
Tundra, 99, 116–119
  animals of, 117–118, 119
  climate of, 116–118
  lack of biodiversity in, 116
  oil exploration in, 119
  plants of, 117
  soil profile, 297
Turbines, 271–272

U

Ultraviolet radiation, *4*, 11,
    364, 365
Understory, **143**
Uranium, 251, *252*
  U-235, 253–254, 349
  U-238, *255*, 255

V

Validity, 22, 24
Value development, 412
Variable(s), **24**
Vertical feeding patterns,
    133, 133
Visible spectrum, 4
Vitamins, 38, 217
Volcanoes, 35, 36, 365

W

War, effect of, on human
    populations, 203
Warm-blooded organisms, 40

Warming, global, 366–368, *368*
Waste materials. *See* Solid wastes
Water, 3, 322–333. *See also* Fresh
    water; Salt water; *and other
    Water headings*
  movement of, over Earth, 60
  scientists studying, 27
Water cycle, *65*
Water hyacinth, 79
Water pollution, 338–352
  aquatic habitat destruction
    and, 384
  controlling, through
    legislation, *351–352*
  coral reef damage and, 173
  health problems posed by,
    339–342
  sources of, *342*, 342
  by toxic chemicals, 343–345
  undoing of, 346, 376
Water purification, 332–333
Water quality, factors affecting,
    38
Water resources, 327–329
  contamination of, 329
  problems, 328–329
  surface water, 327–329
Water table, **328**
Water treatment, 329, 331–333
  steps used in, *332*
Water use, 323–326
  effects of, on ecosystems, 326
  industrial, 324
  residential, *323*, 323
Weather. *See also* Climate;
    Precipitation;
    Temperature(s)
  in stratosphere layer, 10
  in troposphere layer, 10
Weathering, of rock, **35**,
    295–296, 297
Wetlands, **158**–159. *See also*
    Mangrove swamps;
    Salt marshes
  wilderness areas, **387**, 387
Wilson, E. O., 148
Wind(s), 10
  direction of, *10*
  dispersal of seeds by, 130
  ocean currents and, 171
Wind energy, 274–275
Wind erosion, 312, 313
Wind farms, *275*, 275
Windmills, 274–275

Wood, 138
  deforestation for, 149
  as fuel, 244
World ocean, **169**

Y

Yangtze River hydroelectric
    project, 330
Yucca Mountain, 260

Z

Zone of aeration, **328**
Zone of discharge, **328**
Zone of saturation, **328**
Zooplankton, **158**, 170
Zoos, *39*

ACKNOWLEDGMENTS

PHOTO ACKNOWLEDGMENTS

Contents
iiiT Bill Wassman/The Stock Market
iiiB Oddo & Sinibaldi/The Stock Market
ivT Tom Bean/DRK Photo
ivB Steve Kraseman/Peter Arnold, Inc.
vT Kevin Schafer/Tom Stack & Associates
vB Ronald L. Sefton/Bruce Coleman Inc.
vi William Campbell/Peter Arnold, Inc.
viiT Thomas Braise/The Stock Market
viiB Bruce Hands/Tony Stone Images
viiiT Keith H. Murakami/Tom Stack & Associates
viiiB J. Lotter/Tom Stack & Associates
x Lawrence Migdale/Stock, Boston
xiT Stan Wayman/Photo Researchers
xiBL Pat & Tom Leeson/Photo Researchers
xiBR Jeffrey Aaronson/Network Aspen

Unit 1
xii–1 William Campbell/DRK Photo

Chapter 1
2 NASA
5T Alastair Black/Tony Stone Images
5B Geoffrey Nilsen Photography*
7 Albert Copley/Visuals Unlimited
11 Johnny Johnson/DRK Photo
12L Erwin & Peggy Bauer/Bruce Coleman Inc.
12C Peter Ryan/Scripps/SPL/Photo Researchers
12R Darrell Gulin/Tony Stone Images
14 NASA

Chapter 2
18 Krafft/Explorer/Photo Researchers
20 Dr. Brian Eyden/SPL/Photo Researchers
21 Stan Wayman/Photo Researchers
23 David Austen/Stock, Boston
26L Lawrence Migdale/Tony Stone Images
26C Lori Adamski Peek/Tony Stone Images
26R Guy Marche/Tony Stone Images
27 Giraudon/Art Resource, NY
28L William Grenfell/Visuals Unlimited
28C Larry Ulrich/Tony Stone Images
28R Stephen G. Maka/DRK Photo
30T Michael Ventura/Bruce Coleman Inc.
30B Kim Heacox/DRK Photo

Chapter 3
34 T. A. Wiewandt/DRK Photo
37T Tom Bean/DRK Photo
37B Alberto Garcia/SABA
39 John Nees/Animals, Animals
40T Dr. Eckart Pott/Bruce Coleman Inc.
40B J. C. Stevenson/Animals, Animals
41 Allan Tannenbaum/Sygma
48 Mark C. Burnett/Stock, Boston
49T Tomas del Amo/West Stock
49C Brownie Harris/The Stock Market
49B Bob Daemmrich/Uniphoto Picture Agency

Unit 2
50–51 Mike Bacon/Tom Stack & Associates

Chapter 4
52 Gary S. Withey/Bruce Coleman Inc.
53T Doug Wechsler/Earth Scenes
53B Manfred Kage/Peter Arnold, Inc.
54L Steven Fuller/Peter Arnold, Inc.
54C Renee Lynn/Tony Stone Images
54R Steve Kraseman/Peter Arnold, Inc.
55 Peter Davey/Bruce Coleman Inc.
63 Kennan Ward/The Stock Market

Chapter 5
72 C. K. Lorenz/Photo Researchers
73T Joe McDonald/DRK Photo
73B Alan Blank/Bruce Coleman Inc.
74 Anne Wertheim/Animals, Animals
75 Patti Murray/Animals, Animals
77 Mike Bacon/Tom Stack & Associates
78 Patti Murray/Animals, Animals
79 Bob McKeever/Tom Stack & Associates

Chapter 6
88 Dwight R. Kuhn/DRK Photo
90 Tom & Pat Leeson/DRK Photo
91T Jonathan T. Wright/Bruce Coleman Inc.
91BL M. P. L. Fogden/Bruce Coleman Inc.
91BR Rich Buzzelli/Tom Stack & Associates
92 Jeff Foott/Tom Stack & Associates
94T Sharon Gerig/Tom Stack & Associates
94B John Shaw/Tom Stack & Associates
96 Spencer Swanger/Tom Stack & Associates
98 Steve Dunwell/The Image Bank
106 Stephen J. Krasemann/DRK Photo
107T Joe McDonald/Animals, Animals
107C Lawrence Migdale/Stock, Boston
107B Mark C. Burnett/Photo Researchers

Unit 3
108–109 Tim Davis/Davis-Lynn Images

Chapter 7
110 David Hughes/Bruce Coleman Inc.
111L Carr Clifton/Tony Stone Images
111R Tom Bean/DRK Photo
112L K. G. Preston-Mafham/Earth Scenes
112R James R. Simon/Bruce Coleman Inc.
113 J. Cancalosi/Tom Stack & Associates
115 Wendy Watriss/Woodfin Camp & Associates
117L Tom Walker/Stock, Boston
117R Stephen J. Krasemann/DRK Photo
118L G. C. Kelley/Photo Researchers
118R Jeff Lepore/Photo Researchers
119 Thomas Kitchin/Tom Stack & Associates

Chapter 8
124 Joe McDonald/Tom Stack & Associates
125T Spencer Swanger/Tom Stack & Associates
125B Fred Whitehead/Earth Scenes
126BL David Muench/Tony Stone Images
126BR Dave Millert/Tom Stack & Associates
126T Grant Heilman/Grant Heilman Photography
127C Phil Schermeister/Tony Stone Images
127L R. Van Nostrand/Photo Researchers
127R Stephen J. Krasemann/DRK Photo
128 C. K. Lorenz/Photo Researchers
129 Greg L. Ryan & Sally A. Beyer/Tony Stone Images
130T Runk-Schoenberger/Grant Heilman Photography
130B Tom Walker/Tony Stone Images
131 Corbis-Bettmann
132 R. F. Head/Earth Scenes

Chapter 9
138 Phil Degginger/Bruce Coleman Inc.
139L S. Nielsen/DRK Photo
139C Doug Sokell/Tom Stack & Associates
139R Spencer Swanger/Tom Stack & Associates
140TL Leonard Lee Rue III/Tony Stone Images
140TR Leonard Lee Rue III/Bruce Coleman Inc.
140B W. E. Ruth/Tony Stone Images
141 Pat & Tom Leeson/Photo Researchers
142 Michael P. Gadomski/Photo Researchers
143 John Shaw/Bruce Coleman Inc.
144L Brian Parker/Tom Stack & Associates
144C Leonard Lee Rue III/Animals, Animals
144R Randy Ury/The Stock Market
145 J. H. Robinson/Earth Scenes
146 Geoff Tompkinson/Aspect Picture Library/ The Stock Market
148TL Michael Fogden/DRK Photo
148TC Kevin Schafer/Tom Stack & Associates
148TR Michael Fogden/DRK Photo

148C   Kevin Schafer/Tom Stack & Associates
148B   Kevin Schafer/Tony Stone Images
149   Sam Bryan/Photo Researchers

Chapter 10
154   David Muench/Tony Stone Images
158   Harold Taylor Abipp/Oxford Scientific Films/
         Animals, Animals
160T   Vic Beunza/Bruce Coleman Inc.
160B   Marty Cordano/DRK Photo
161   Kennan Ward/The Stock Market
163   Robert Fried/Tom Stack & Associates

Chapter 11
168   James Randklev/Tony Stone Images
170L   Norbert Wu/The Stock Market
170R   Francois Gohier/Photo Researchers
172   Brian Parker/Tom Stack & Associates
173   Ronald L. Sefton/Bruce Coleman Inc.
174   Nicholas Devore III/Bruce Coleman Inc.
175   Pat & Tom Leeson/Photo Researchers
176   John Shaw/Bruce Coleman Inc.
177   Stephen Krasemann/DRK Photo
182   William Campbell/Peter Arnold, Inc.
183T   Cameramann/The Image Works
183C   D. Cavagnaro/DRK Photo
183B   Liane Enkelis/Stock, Boston

Unit 4
184–185   Renee Lynn/Davis-Lynn Photography

Chapter 12
186   M. P. Kahl/DRK Photo
187   Jet Propulsion Lab/Newell Color Lab
189   Richard Pasley/The Viesti Collection
190   Jason Laure/Woodfin Camp & Associates
193   Jeffrey Aaronson/Network Aspen
195   Ben Gibson/Woodfin Camp & Associates

Chapter 13
200   David Pollack/The Stock Market
203   Corbis-Bettmann
207   Carolyn Watson/UNICEF
208   Bill Wassman/The Stock Market
209   Alon Reininger/Contact Press/Woodfin Camp
         & Associates

Chapter 14
214   Hilarie Kavanagh/Tony Stone Images
218L   Ken Greer/Visuals Unlimited
218R   Betty Press/Woodfin Camp & Associates
220   Grant Heilman/Grant Heilman Photography
221T   Clyde H. Smith/Peter Arnold, Inc.
221B   Greg Vaughn/Tom Stack & Associates
222   Jeffrey Aaronson/Network Aspen
223   Thomas Hovland/Grant Heilman Photography
224   Jack Fields/Photo Researchers
226   Anthony Mercieca Photo/Photo Researchers
230   Ken Cobb, Beanz Studio/Friends of the National Zoo
231T   Arthur Grace/Stock, Boston
231C   Paul Conklin/Uniphoto Picture Agency
231B   Ken Graham/Tony Stone Images

Unit 5
232–233   Otto Rogge/The Stock Market

Chapter 15
234   Vince Streano/Tony Stone Images
235T   Corbis-Bettmann
235B   Larry Lefever/Grant Heilman Photography
238T   John Colwell/Grant Heilman Photography
238C   E. R. Degginger/Bruce Coleman Inc.
238B   Barry L. Runk/Grant Heilman Photography
241   Michele Burgess/The Stock Market
242   Rafael Macia/Photo Researchers
243   Epipress/Sygma
245   Gary E. Holscher/Tony Stone Images

Chapter 16
250   Pete Saloutos/The Stock Market
252   Paul Silverman/Fundamental Photographs

257   Doug Wilson/Black Star
258   Sander/Gamma-Liaison
260L   Igor Kostin/Imago/Sygma
260R   Sovfoto/Eastfoto

Chapter 17
264   T. J. Florian/Rainbow
267T   T. J. Florian/Rainbow
267B   Brian Parker/Tom Stack & Associates
269   Courtesy General Motors
271T   Manfred Gottschalk/Tom Stack & Associates
271B   Brian Parker/Tom Stack & Associates
274T   Culver Pictures, Inc.
274BL   John Mead/SPL/Photo Researchers
274BR   Ken W. Davis/Tom Stack & Associates
275   Thomas Braise/The Stock Market
276   David Ball/The Stock Market
282   Andy Sacks/Tony Stone Images
283T   Jeff Zaruba/The Stock Market
283C   Dawson Jones, Inc./Uniphoto Picture Agency
283B   Joe Sohm/Chromosohm/Uniphoto Picture Agency

Unit 6
284–285   D. Cavagnaro/DRK Photo

Chapter 18
286   J. Kyle Keener/Philadelphia Inquirer Matrix
287T   Charles Gupton/Stock, Boston
287B   Geoffrey Nilsen Photography*
288   Jon Feingersh/Tom Stack & Associates
290T   Barry L. Runk/Grant Heilman Photography
290B   Rod Allin/Tom Stack & Associates
291   Grant Heilman/Grant Heilman Photography
292   Steve Kaufman/DRK Photo
293   Dan Budnik/Woodfin Camp & Associates
294   Joe Bensen/Stock, Boston
297   Tom Bean/DRK Photo
300   Walt Anderson/Tom Stack & Associates

Chapter 19
304   Oliver Strewe/Tony Stone Images
306   Susan Meiselas/Magnum Photos, Inc.
308T   L. L. T. Rhodes/Tony Stone Images
308C   Dilip Mehta/Contact Press Images
308B   Eugene Richards/Magnum Photos, Inc.
309   W. Hodges/Westlight
312L   Bruce Hands/Tony Stone Images
312R   Bob Davis/Woodfin Camp & Associates
313   Library of Congress Photo by Arthur Rothstein.
314   Louis Psihoyos/Contact Press Images
315   Gabe Palmer/The Stock Market

Chapter 20
322   Tom Bean/Tony Stone Images
323T   Allan Tannenbaum/Sygma
323B   Mark Downey/The Gamma Liaison Network
325TL   Grant Heilman/Grant Heilman Photography
325TR   Joe Bator/The Stock Market
325BL   Shelly Katz/Black Star
325BR   Grant Heilman/Grant Heilman Photography
325BR (inset)   Lowell Georgia/Photo Researchers
326   Oddo & Sinibaldi/The Stock Market
327   Grant Heilman/Grant Heilman Photography
328   Leif Skoogfors/Woodfin Camp & Associates
330   Jeffrey Aaronson/Network Aspen
332   David Madison/Bruce Coleman Inc.

Chapter 21
338   P. Schutte/SuperStock, Inc.
339   Corbis-Bettmann
341L   Moredun Animal Health Ltd./SPL/Photo Researchers
341C   Sinclair Stammers/SPL/Photo Researchers
341R   Moredun Animal Health Ltd./SPL/Photo Researchers
343   Victoria Hurst/Tom Stack & Associates
345L   Sygma
345R   Natalie Fobes/Tony Stone Images
346   Thomas R. Fletcher/Stock, Boston
346 (inset)   Manfred Kage/Peter Arnold, Inc.
349   Grant Heilman/Grant Heilman Photography
351   Frans Lanting/Photo Researchers

Chapter 22
356   D. Logan/Tony Stone Images

358T   Don Spiro/Tony Stone Images
358C   Norman Owen Tomalin/Bruce Coleman Inc.
358B   William Johnson/Stock, Boston
361   Richard Packwood/Oxford Scientific Films/Earth Scenes
363   Thierry Falise/Gamma Liaison
364T   D. P. Hershkowitz/Bruce Coleman Inc.
364BL   NASA
364BC   NASA
364BR   NASA
367   Tad Ackman/University of New Hampshire
370   Courtesy General Motors
372   Gabe Palmer/The Stock Market
376   Mark C. Burnett/Stock, Boston
377T   Pedrick/The Image Works
377C   Mark Burnett/Photo Researchers
377B   Rob Crandall/Stock, Boston

Unit 7
378–379   Lewis Kemper/DRK Photo

Chapter 23
380   Jim Richardson
384   Mireille Vautier/Woodfin Camp & Associates
385   Novosti/Lehtikuva/Woodfin Camp & Associates
387L   Michael J. Balick/Peter Arnold, Inc.
387C   John Gerlach/Tom Stack & Associates
387R   Greg Vaughn/Tom Stack & Associates
388   J. Lotter/Tom Stack & Associates
389   Lawrence Migdale/Photo Researchers
390   Calvin Larsen/Photo Researchers
391   Keith H. Murakami/Tom Stack & Associates

Chapter 24
396   C. Bradley Simmons/Bruce Coleman Inc.
397   Richard Megna/Fundamental Photographs
399   Richard Megna/Fundamental Photographs
400   Peter Beck/The Stock Market
401   Alex Bartel/SPL/Photo Researchers
402L   Mark Sherman/Bruce Coleman Inc.
402R   Will McIntyre/Photo Researchers
403L   H. R. Bramaz/Peter Arnold, Inc.
403R   Norman O. Tomalin/Bruce Coleman Inc.
404   Paula Lerner/Woodfin Camp & Associates
405L   Roy Toft/Tom Stack & Associates
405R   Roy Toft/Tom Stack & Associates

Chapter 25
410   H. Sutton/Tony Stone Images
412L   IFA/Bruce Coleman Inc.
412R   D. Brewster/Bruce Coleman Inc.
413   Byron Augustin/Tom Stack & Associates
415   Brian Parker/Tom Stack & Associates
417   Robert E. Daemmrich/Tony Stone Images
419   Natalie B. Fobes/Tony Stone Images
421   Jim Richardson
422   Brian Parker/Tom Stack & Associates
426   David Madison
427T   Will & Deni McIntyre/Photo Researchers
427C   Bill Denison/Uniphoto Picture Agency
427B   Tom Tracy/Tony Stone Images

*Photographed expressly for Addison Wesley Longman, Inc.

ILLUSTRATION CREDITS

Warren Budd & Associates 3, 9, 13, 77, 147, 169, 240, 266, 273, 277, 328

Dave Danz All unit openers symbols and full-page activity leaf pattern art

Mark Foerster 61, 62, 68, 102, 150, 210, 215, 219, 298, 318, 334, 340, 347, 348, 392

Terry Guyer 114, 187, 328

Bill Hollowell 268, margin feature art

Marlene May-Howerton 93, 97

Carlyn Iverson 291, 295, 296, 365, 366, 369

Lois Lovejoy 76, 95, 311, 386

Trevin Lowrey 202, 256, 263, 288

Mapping Specialists Ltd. 10, 35, 43, 100–101, 119, 123, 160, 171, 191, 193, 239, 289, 297, 329, 344, 368, 383, 385, 406, 416, 418, 420

Michael Maydak 56, 57, 58

Roberto Osti 169

Precision Graphics 4, 6, 25, 33, 43, 58, 59, 61T, 89, 120, 153, 167, 174, 181, 324, 332, 360, 362, 367

Rolin Graphics 42, 44, 128, 132, 133, 134, 305, 307, 315

Margo Stahl-Pronk 114, 156, 162, 164, 292, 299

Beowulf Thorne 8, 24, 74, 80, 81, 82, 83, 84, 205, 206, 216, 217, 229, 236, 237, 249, 254, 258, 272, 281, 306, 312, 371, 381, 382, 398, 401, 411, 413, 414, margin feature art

Sarah Woodward 65, 66, 67, 93, 188, 189, 251, 252, 253, 255, 268T, 278

Qin-Zhong Yu margin feature art

Biology Atlas Maps © 1998 GeoSystems Global Corporation. This product contains proprietary property of Geosystems Global Corporation. Unauthorized use, including copying, of this product is expressly prohibited.